LEARN, TEACH...

SUCCEED...

With **REA's TExES™ Core Subjects 4–8 (211)**
test prep, you'll be in a class all your own.

TExES™ CORE SUBJECTS 4-8 (211)

TEXAS EXAMINATIONS OF EDUCATOR STANDARDS™

Ann Cavallo, Ph.D.
Assistant Vice Provost and
Director, Center for Research on
Teaching and Learning Excellence
University of Texas at Arlington

Karen Allmond, Ed.D.
Program Coordinator
Accelerated Online Program
University of Texas at Arlington

Mary Curtis, Ph.D.
Assistant Professor, Curriculum and Instruction
University of Texas at Arlington

Christina Gawlik, Ph.D.
Former Assistant Professor, Mathematics and
Mathematics Education
Texas Woman's University

Melissa Hulings, Ph.D.
Clinical Assistant Professor, Science Education
University of Texas at Arlington

Peggy Semingson, Ph.D.
Associate Professor, Curriculum and Instruction
University of Texas at Arlington

Mathematics Consultant
Stu Schwartz

 Research & Education Association

Research & Education Association
258 Prospect Plains Road
Cranbury, New Jersey 08854
Email: info@rea.com

**TExES™ Core Subjects 4-8 (211)
with Online Practice Tests**

Printed in the United States of America

Library of Congress Control Number 2018956360

ISBN-13: 978-0-7386-1197-6
ISBN-10: 0-7386-1197-2

Cover image: © iStockphoto.com/Wavebreakmedia

Contents

About Our TExES Exam Experts ix

About REA xii

Chapter 1
Getting Started   1

How to Use This Book + Online Prep. 1

An Overview of the Test 2

TExES Core Subjects 4–8 Study Schedule 8

Chapter 2
Proven Test-Taking Strategies for TExES Core Subjects   11

Chapter 3
Subject Test I: English Language Arts and
Reading (806)   15

ELAR Diagnostic Test . . . .*available online at www.rea.com/studycenter*

Overview of Subject Test I: ELA and Reading 15

Competency 001: Oral Language 16

Competency 002: Early Literacy Development 27

Competency 003: Word Identification Skills and Reading Fluency 42

Competency 004: Reading Comprehension and Assessment 52

Competency 005: Reading Applications 62

Competency 006: Written Language—Writing Conventions 74

Competency 007: Written Language—Composition 80

Competency 008: Viewing and Representing 93

Competency 009: Study and Inquiry Skills 97

Chapter 4
Subject Test II: Mathematics (807)   107

Mathematics Diagnostic Test . . . .*available online at www.rea.com/studycenter*

Overview of Subject Test II: Mathematics 107

Competency 001: Number Systems 108

Competency 002: Number Operations and Computational Algorithms 111

Competency 003: Number Theory. 121

Competency 004: Using Mathematical Reasoning to Identify, Extend, and Analyze
Patterns. 128

Competency 005: Linear Functions. 130

Competency 006: Nonlinear Functions 135

Competency 007: Conceptual Foundations of Calculus 142

Competency 008: Measurement. 148

Competency 009: Geometric Relationships and Euclidian Geometry 154

Competency 010: Two- and Three-Dimensional Figures. 162

Competency 011: Algebra and Geometry through the Cartesian Coordinate
System 168

Competency 012: Graphical and Numerical Techniques to Explore Data and
Patterns. 170

Competency 013: The Theory of Probability. 182

Competency 014: The Relationship Among Probability Theory, Sampling, and
Statistical Inference 189

Competency 015: Mathematical Reasoning and Problem Solving 193

Competency 016: Mathematical Connections Within and Outside of Mathematics . . . 195

Competency 017: How Children Learn and Develop Mathematical Skills, Procedures,
and Concepts. 197

Competency 018: Planning, Organizing, and Implementing Instruction. 207

Competency 019: Using Assessment Techniques to Monitor and Guide Instruction
and Mark Progress 208

References. 210

Chapter 5
Subject Test III: Social Studies (808)   213

Mathematics Diagnostic Test. . . . . *available online at www.rea.com/studycenter*

Overview of Subject Test III: Social Studies 213

Competency 001: History 215

Competency 002: Geography 268

Competency 003: Economics. 288

Competency 004: Government and Citizenship 302

Competency 005: Culture, Science, Technology, and Society. 318

Competency 006: Social Studies Foundations and Skills 324

Competency 007: Social Studies Instruction and Assessment 329

References. 345

CONTENTS

Chapter 6
Subject Test IV: Science (809)   349

Science Diagnostic Test . . . . *available online at www.rea.com/studycenter*

Overview of Subject Test IV: Science. 349

Competency 001: Safety 352

Competency 002: Tools, Materials, Equipment, and Technologies 355

Competency 003: The Process of Scientific Inquiry and the History and Nature
of Science 357

Competency 004: The Impact of Science on Daily Life and Its Influence on Personal
and Societal Decisions 364

Competency 005: Unifying Concepts and Processes 367

Competency 006: Forces and Motion 368

Competency 007: Physical Properties of and Changes in Matter. 370

Competency 008: Chemical Properties of and Changes in Matter 371

Competency 009: Energy and Interactions Between Matter and Energy 374

Competency 010: Energy Transformations and the Conservation of Matter and
Energy 377

Competency 011: The Structure and Function of Living Things 379

Competency 012: Reproduction and the Mechanisms of Heredity. 387

Competency 013: Adaptations of Organisms and the Theory of Evolution 391

Competency 014: Regulatory Mechanisms and Behavior 393

Competency 015: The Relationships Between Organisms and the Environment 396

Competency 016: The Structure and Function of Earth Systems 398

Competency 017: Cycles in Earth Systems 404

Competency 018: The Role of Energy in Weather and Climate 407

Competency 019: The Solar System and the Universe 409

Competency 020: The History of the Earth System 411

Competency 021: Teaching Science and How Students Learn It 413

Competency 022: Scientific Inquiry and Its Role in Science Instruction 418

Competency 023: Assessments and Assessment Practices 429

References 431

TExES Core Subjects 4–8 Practice Test Battery 1

Also available online at: www.rea.com/studycenter

Practice Subject Test 1: English Language Arts and Reading   433

Answer Sheet 434
Answer Key 449
Detailed Answers 450

Practice Subject Test 1: Mathematics   461

Answer Sheet 462
Answer Key 470
Detailed Answers 471

Practice Subject Test 1: Social Studies   477

Answer Sheet 478
Answer Key 487
Detailed Answers 488

Practice Subject Test 1: Science   497

Answer Sheet 498
Answer Key 508
Detailed Answers 509

TExES Core Subjects 4–8 Practice Test Battery 2

Available online at: www.rea.com/studycenter

Practice Subject Test 2: English Language Arts and Reading
Practice Subject Test 2: Mathematics
Practice Subject Test 2: Social Studies
Practice Subject Test 2: Science

Appendix   519

TExES Mathematics 4–8 Definitions and Formulas Sheet 520
Periodic Table 522

Index   523

About Our TExES Exam Experts

Lead Author

Ann Cavallo, Ph.D., is Assistant Vice Provost and Director of the Center for Research on Teaching and Learning Excellence, Co-director of UTeach Arlington, and Distinguished University Professor of Science Education at the University of Texas at Arlington (UTA). Dr. Cavallo earned her B.S. from Niagara University, and her M.S. in Science Education/Biology, M.S. in General Science, and Ph.D. in Science Education from Syracuse University. She holds secondary teacher certification in Biology, Chemistry, Earth Science, and General Science, and taught middle and high school science prior to earning her graduate degrees. At the university level, she has developed programs and instructed courses on campus and online in science methods, educational psychology, research methodology, biology, and earth science.

Dr. Cavallo is currently Principal Investigator of two National Science Foundation Robert Noyce grants totaling over $2 million. Her research investigates high school and college students' learning approaches and strategies, scientific reasoning, self-efficacy, and their acquisition of conceptual understandings of science, particularly through inquiry-based teaching models. She also studies teacher learning, induction, and retention in the profession.

In 2015, Dr. Cavallo received the Distinguished Record of Research Award from UTA, and in 2016 was inducted into the Academy of Distinguished Scholars, UTA's most prestigious research and scholarship award. Dr. Cavallo has to her credit over 40 publications in internationally and nationally refereed journals and proceedings, as well as several books and book chapters. In total, she has secured more than $10 million in grants and gifts from various funding agencies to support her work. She serves on the Advisory Board for the National Science Foundation and the American Association for the Advancement of Science for STEM Teacher Preparation. She has made more than 70 presentations at professional conferences, and has held significant leadership positions in professional education organizations.

Contributing Authors

Dr. Karen Allmond is the Program Coordinator for the University of Texas at Arlington's Accelerated Online program for teachers working toward their Master in Education with an emphasis in Mathematics and Science. She works with pre-service teachers in the College of Education and UTeach program, a science and mathematics teacher preparation program at UT Arlington.

Dr. Allmond has been in the field of education for over 24 years. She taught in the Texas public school system for 18 years, working with the Arlington, Mansfield, and North East Independent school districts. Although her teaching experience has encompassed all subject areas, her main emphasis is mathematics education. She has been a Teacher Trainer, Consultant, Math Enrichment Specialist, and Math Team manager with special cases in the area of math for schools and districts.

Throughout her 18 years in public schools Dr. Allmond worked in Title I schools meeting the needs of diverse students and learners. This has included students in Special Education, General Education, English Language Learners, and Gifted and Talented students. Her Certifications include Special Education, ESL, and Principal.

Professional activities include facilitating math workshops for teachers, including topics of vertical alignment, manipulative-based instruction, and using literature in the math classroom. Dr. Allmond has also created and conducted Math & Science Family Nights and school-wide mathematic programs that integrate math concepts throughout grade levels. She has presented at national and state mathematic conferences. Her research interests include diverse learners, mathematical struggles for students, numeracy and problem-solving/creative thinking concerns. She co-authored a book, *Pencil Points*, that synthesizes her experiences with Title I schools and shares insight on working with administrators, teachers, parents, and students.

Dr. Mary D. Curtis, Assistant Professor of Curriculum and Instruction at the University of Texas at Arlington, specializes in geography education and social studies curriculum and instruction. For nearly 20 years she has provided K–12 professional development for educators. She has conducted research on the awareness and use of geospatial technologies in high school geography education and the implementation of GIS-based GeoInquiry instructional activities in elementary social studies. She teaches courses in social studies pedagogy, diversity in today's schools, adolescent development, and research methodology. Her current research focuses on K–12 social science and geospatial pedagogy, teaching with geospatial technologies, social science teacher preparation—which includes critical thinking methods of instruction (i.e., inquiry)—and the development of teacher technological pedagogical content knowledge (TPCK). Dr. Curtis has made over 50 presentations at professional conferences, and has held leadership positions in local and national professional organizations.

Dr. Christina Gawlik is a former assistant professor of Mathematics and Mathematics Education at Texas Woman's University in Denton and Saint Xavier University in Chicago. She earned her B.S.Ed. and M.S.Ed. degrees from the University of Kansas and a Ph.D. from Kansas State University. Prior to earning her doctorate, she taught high school mathematics and served as adjunct faculty at several two- and four-year institutions across Kansas. Dr. Gawlik is a leader in professional development for teaching mathematics who has presented extensively at national and international conferences. She has facilitated workshops for K–12 mathematics teachers across the United States, Canada, and Dubai. Dr. Gawlik has published student workbooks, learning guides, and videos for K–12 and higher education, and is actively developing resources for developmental mathematics and courses in mathematics for non-math majors.

Melissa Hulings, Ph.D., is a Clinical Assistant Professor of Science Education at the University of Texas at Arlington (UTA). She earned her B.S. in Secondary Science from Oklahoma State University, her M.Ed. from Northeastern State University, and her Ph.D. in Professional Education Studies from Oklahoma State University. She holds secondary teacher certification in Chemistry, Earth Science, Biological Sciences, and Mid-level Science for grades 5–8, and has taught middle and high school science prior to teaching at the university level. At the university level, she has revised programs and courses, as well as taught courses on campus and online in science methods and physical science. In 2017 she received the College of Education Award for Excellence in Teaching by a Clinical Faculty Member. Dr. Hulings is currently the Program Coordinator for the Middle-Level Certification Program. Her research investigates how pre-service teachers' prior experiences influence their self-efficacy as science teachers. Dr. Hulings has presented at both the state and national level for various professional education organizations.

Dr. Peggy Semingson is an Associate Professor of Curriculum and Instruction at the University of Texas at Arlington (UTA) where she teaches courses in Literacy Studies. She has been at UTA since 2008, when she began teaching in the online literacy Master's of Education program and in the pre-service teacher educator preparation program. She has taught entirely online since 2013. She received her M.Ed. in Reading Education from Texas State University, San Marcos in 2004 and her Ph.D. in Curriculum and Instruction with a specialization in Language and Literacy Studies from the University of Texas at Austin in 2008. Her research interests include digital pedagogies, media-based learning, online learning, and literacy teacher education. Current research studies examine the ways that we can use digital pedagogies to engage pre-service and in-service teachers to most effectively help them to teach literacy in their current and future classroom contexts. She has won two awards related to distance learning including the 2013 United States Distance Learning Association Best Practices Platinum Award for Excellence in Distance Learning Teaching. In 2013 Dr. Semingson was the recipient of the prestigious University of Texas System Regents' Outstanding Teaching Award.

Mathematics Consultant

Stu Schwartz taught high school mathematics for 35 years and continues to offer mathematics resources for students and teachers alike at his website, *MasterMathMentor.com*. Mr. Schwartz is a recipient of the Presidential Award for Excellence in Mathematics and Science Teaching, the United States' highest honor for teachers of science, technology, engineering, and mathematics.

About REA

Founded in 1959, Research & Education Association (REA) is dedicated to publishing the finest and most effective educational materials—including study guides and test preps—for students of all ages. Today, REA's wide-ranging catalog is a leading resource for students, teachers, and other professionals. Visit *www.rea.com* to see a complete listing of all our titles.

Acknowledgments

Publisher: Pam Weston

Editorial Director: Larry B. Kling

Technology Director: John Paul Cording

Graphic Design and File Prep: Jennifer Calhoun

Copy Editors: John Kupetz and Karen Lamoreux

Mathematics Accuracy Checker: Ryann Shelton

Indexer: Casey Indexing and Information Service

Typesetter: Caragraphics

Proofreaders: Diane Goldschmidt and Alice Leonard

Getting Started

Congratulations! By taking the TExES Core Subjects 4–8 (211) test, you're on your way to a rewarding career as a teacher of young students in Texas. Our book, and the online tools that come with it, give you everything you need to succeed on this important exam, bringing you one step closer to being certified to teach in Texas.

This TExES Core Subjects 4–8 test prep package includes:

- A **complete overview** of the TExES Core Subjects 4–8 (211) test

- A **comprehensive review** for all four subject tests in the TExES Core Subjects 4–8 test battery

- An **online diagnostic test** to pinpoint your strengths and weaknesses and focus your study

- **Two full-length practice test batteries:** one in the book and online, plus an additional test online that comes with powerful diagnostic tools to help you personalize your prep

HOW TO USE THIS BOOK + ONLINE PREP

About Our Review

The review chapters in this book are designed to help you sharpen your command of all the skills you'll need to pass the Core Subjects 4–8 test. Each of the skills required for all four domains is discussed at length to optimize your understanding of what the test covers. Keep in mind that your schooling has taught you most of what you need to know to answer the questions on the test. Our content review is designed to reinforce what you have learned and show you how to relate the information you have acquired to the specific competencies on the test. Studying your class notes and textbooks together with our review will give you an excellent foundation for passing the test.

About the REA Study Center

We know your time is valuable and you want an efficient study experience. At the REA Study Center (*www.rea.com/studycenter*), you will get feedback right from the start on what you know and what you don't to help make the most of your study time. Here is what you will find at the REA Study Center:

- **Diagnostic Test**—Before you review with the book, take our online diagnostic test. Your score report will pinpoint topics for which you need the most review, to help focus your study.

- **2 Full-Length Practice Test Batteries**—Our practice tests give you the most complete picture of your strengths and weaknesses. After you've studied with the book, test what you've learned by taking the first of two practice exams (online or in the book) for each of the four subjects. Review your score reports, then go back and study any topics you missed. Take the second practice test online to ensure you've mastered the material.

Our online exams simulate the computer-based format of the actual TExES test and come with these features:

- **Automatic scoring**—Find out how you did on your test, instantly.

- **Diagnostic score reports**—Get a specific score tied to each competency, so you can focus on the areas that challenge you the most.

- **On-screen detailed answer explanations**—See why the correct response option is right, and learn why the other answer choices are incorrect.

- **Timed testing**—Learn to manage your time as you practice, so you'll feel confident on test day.

AN OVERVIEW OF THE TEST

What is assessed on the Core Subjects 4–8 test?

The Core Subjects exam is actually a battery of four subject tests, with four unique test codes:

- English Language Arts and Reading (806)

- Mathematics (807)

- Social Studies (808)

- Science (809)

The TExES Core Subjects 4–8 test is a criterion-referenced examination constructed to measure the knowledge and skills that an entry-level educator in Texas public schools must have. The test is a requirement for candidates seeking a Core Subjects 4–8 certificate. Because it's a computer-administered test, the exam is available throughout the year at numerous locations across the state and at select locations nationally. To find the test center near you, visit *www.tx.nesinc.com*.

Candidates are limited to five attempts to take any of Texas's teacher certification tests, but in the event you don't pass the Core Subjects 4–8 test, you need to retake only the individual subtest(s) where your score falls short. Below are the four domains covered on the Core Subjects exam. The table covers the percentage and number of questions in each domain, as well as the time allocated for each subject test. These domains and the competencies rooted in them represent the knowledge that teams of teachers, subject area specialists, and district-level educators have determined to be important for beginning teachers.

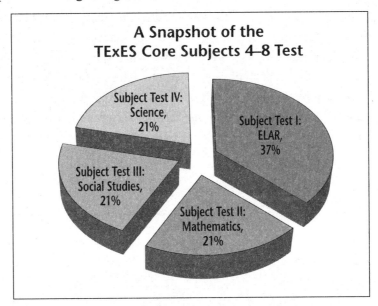

A Snapshot of the
TExES Core Subjects 4–8 Test

Subject Test	Competencies	Total Items	Percentage of Total Test	Time
English Language Arts and Reading (ELAR)	9	74	37%	1 hour and 55 minutes
Mathematics	19	42	21%	1 hour and 5 minutes
Social Studies	7	42	21%	50 minutes
Science	20	42	21%	50 minutes
Total	55	200		4 hours and 40 minutes

What is the format of the TExES Core Subjects 4–8 test?

The test includes a total of 200 multiple-choice items. You may encounter non-scorable questions but you won't know which is which, so they surely aren't worth worrying about. Your final scaled score will be based only on the scorable items. The test is organized into four subject tests.

Multiple-Choice Questions

Though all the questions on the test are multiple-choice, they may not all be the type of multiple-choice question with which you're familiar. The majority of questions on the Core Subjects test are standard multiple-choice items. The questions are not intended merely to test your command of facts but also your critical-thinking skills. For example, you may be asked to analyze information and compare it with knowledge you have, or make a judgment about it. To acquaint yourself with all the standards and competencies covered on the test, be sure to download Pearson Education's test framework at *www.tx.nesinc.com*.

Some multiple-choice questions are self-contained while others are clustered, branching off a common stimulus. Each question will generally have four choices: A, B, C, and D. (Some questions may have more.) In most cases, the correct answer will require you to identify the single best response. Some questions, however, will require you to select *all* the responses that answer the question correctly. In such instances, you will click check boxes instead of ovals. Also be aware that this test occasionally presents non-traditional formats for multiple-choice items, both to present the information and to allow you to select the best answer. A rundown of these new formats follows.

Unfamiliar Question Types

There are several unfamiliar question types that may show up on the Core Subjects test. First, let's look at the kind of question that asks test-takers to identify more than one correct response option to a question.

Example

1. Which of the following led to the American Revolution? Select *all* that apply.

    A.   the French and Indian War

    B.   the Intolerable Acts

    C.   the French Revolution

    D.   the Articles of Confederation

Answer and Explanation

Options (A) and (B) are correct. The French and Indian War (A), fought from 1754 to 1763, served as a powerful vehicle by which the British Empire extended its reach in North America. The British sought to impose taxation on the colonists to finance the defense of the newly acquired territory, which aggravated growing discontent with British governance. The Intolerable Acts (B) embraced measures enacted by the British Parliament in 1774 to strike back at the colonists' defiance (e.g., the Boston Tea Party in 1773) of British rule. The move backfired, spawning the First Continental Congress later that year. Simple chronology helps you root out the French Revolution (C) as an incorrect option. The French Revolution, fought from 1787 to 1799, is an anachronistic response that could not have led to the American Revolution, which ended in 1783. Finally, the Articles of Confederation instead of leading to the American Revolution actually *resulted from* it. The Articles were drafted in 1776–77 and adopted by Congress on Nov. 15, 1777, as the first U.S. constitution.

According to the Texas Education Agency, the Core Subjects 4–8 test may use interactive questions that may include audio or video clips instead of, say, a static map or reading passage.

Item formats may ask you to select the correct answer(s) by any of these means:

1. Click on a sentence or sentences, or on parts of a graphic representation, such as a map, chart, or figure—sometimes termed a "hot spot."

2. Drag and drop answer options into "target" areas in a table, piece of text, or graphic.

3. Use a drop-down menu.

More than anything, these innovative item types require that you read the instructions carefully to be sure you are fully responsive to the question.

The TExES Core Subjects test is scored based on the number of questions you answer correctly. With no penalty for guessing, you won't want to leave any item unanswered.

When should the test be taken?

Traditionally, teacher preparation programs determine when their candidates take the required tests for teacher certification. These programs will also clear you to take the examinations and make final recommendations for certification to the Texas State Board for Educator Certification (SBEC).

A candidate seeking 4–8 certification may take the appropriate Core Subjects test at such time as his or her Educator Preparation Program (EPP) determines the candidate's readiness to take the test, or upon successful completion of the EPP, whichever comes first. The EPP will determine readiness through benchmarks and structured assessments of the candidates' progress throughout the preparation program.

The test is generally taken just before graduation. Taking all appropriate TExES examinations is a requirement to teach in Texas, so if you are planning on being an educator, you must take and pass these tests.

How do I register for the test?

To register for the test, you must create an account in the Pearson online registration system. Registration will then be available to you online, 24/7, during the regular, late, and emergency registration periods. Visit Pearson's TExES website at *www.tx.nesinc.com* and follow the instructions.

The TExES Registration Bulletin provides information about test dates and locations, as well as information on registration and testing accommodations for those with special needs. The registration bulletin is available at *www.tx.nesinc.com*.

Registration bulletins are also available at the education departments of Texas colleges and universities. To address issues that cannot be solved at the teacher preparation program level, you can contact the offices of SBEC at (888) 863-5880 or (512) 469-8400.

You must pay a registration fee to take the TExES tests, and you will also incur additional late fees if registering after the scheduled date.

What's the passing score?

Your score on each of the TExES 211's four subject tests (test codes 806 to 809) will be reported on a 100–300 scale. A scaled score of 240 is set as the minimum passing score. To put this in context, you want to be confident you can answer between 70% and 80% of the questions correctly. To achieve the 70% level, you must get 140 questions correct; to reach the 80% level, you need to get 160 questions correct. As you work your way through our practice tests, scores in this range will suggest that you are sufficiently absorbing the test content. On the actual test, however, some (unknown number) of the questions will be field-tested and thus will not be scored. There is no holistic score for the full Core Subjects 4–8 battery; overall results are reported as "pass" or "not pass" because, as the Texas Education Agency puts it, "there is no total scaled score for the overall exam."

If you do not get a passing score on our online diagnostic test or the practice tests, review your online score report and study the detailed explanations for the questions you answered incorrectly. Note which types of questions you answered wrong, and re-examine the corresponding review content. After further review, you may want to retake the practice tests online.

When will I receive my score report?

As part of the registration process to take TExES examinations, test candidates set up an account with Pearson in which they are assigned a username and password. Use this account to access your score report information on Pearson's TExES website. Score reports will be posted by 5 p.m. CT on the score reporting date and will be available for 90 days.

What if I don't pass each subject test?

You must pass all parts of the Core Subjects 4–8 test in order to meet the examination requirement for Texas's Core Subjects 4–8 certificate. If you don't do well on every part of the Core Subjects test, don't panic. You can retake the entire test or any individual subject area subtests up to four times. Both options require a 45-day waiting period after the first and subsequent attempts. You are given four attempts to retake all portions of the Core Subjects exams. After your first attempt, each testing session counts as another try, regardless of whether the session includes the entire exam battery or one of the subject tests.

How should I prepare for the test?

It is never too early to start studying for the TExES. The earlier you begin, the more time you will have to sharpen your skills. Do not procrastinate. Cramming is not an effective way to study, since it does not allow you the time needed to learn the test material. It is important for you to choose the time and place for studying that works best for you. Be consistent and use your time wisely. Work out a study routine and stick to it.

When you take our diagnostic test and practice tests, simulate the conditions of the actual test as closely as possible. Go to a quiet place free from distraction. Read each question carefully, consider all answer choices, and pace yourself.

As you complete each test, review your score reports, study the diagnostic feedback, and thoroughly review the explanations to the questions you answered incorrectly. But don't overdo it. Take one problem area at a time; review it until you are confident that you have mastered the material. Give extra attention to the areas giving you the most difficulty, as this will help build your score. Because the test covers content areas in grades 4–8, you should review the state curricula for these grades (Texas Essential Knowledge and Skills) available at *http://www.tea.state.tx.us*.

TEXES CORE SUBJECTS 4–8 STUDY SCHEDULE

Week	Activity
1	Take the online Diagnostic Test Battery at the REA Study Center. Your detailed score report will identify the topics where you need the most review.
2–3	Study the review chapters. Use your Diagnostic Test score report to focus your study. Useful study techniques include highlighting key terms and information and taking notes as you read the review. Learn all the competencies by making flashcards and targeting questions you missed on the diagnostic test.
4	Take Practice Test Battery 1 either in the book or online at the REA Study Center. Review your score report and identify topics where you need more review.
5	Reread all your notes, refresh your understanding of the test's competencies and skills, review your college textbooks, and read class notes you've taken. This is also the time to consider any other supplementary materials that your advisor or the Texas Education Agency suggests. Visit the agency's website at *http://www.tea.state.tx.us/*.
6	Take Practice Test Battery 2 online at the REA Study Center. Review your score report and restudy the appropriate review section(s) until you are confident you understand the material.

Are there any breaks during the test?

Although there is no designated break during the Core Subjects test, you do have a little time to use for the restroom or snacking or stretching outside the testing room. The total time allotted for all the subtests is 4 hours and 40 minutes. But the grand total for the entire testing period is 5 hours. That leaves you 20 minutes to make your own break.

Bear in mind the following:

- You need to get permission to leave the testing room.

- You cannot take a break during any of the subtests—only between tests.

- The overall test clock never stops.

- The timer for individual subtests starts only when you begin a test.

- Consult your test admission materials for further details, including updates from Pearson and the Texas Education Agency.

What else do I need to know about test day?

The day before your test, check for any updates in your Pearson testing account. This is where you'll learn of any changes to your reporting schedule or if there's a change in the test site.

On the day of the test, you should wake up early after a good night's rest. Have a good breakfast and dress in layers that can be removed or added as the conditions in the test center require. Arrive at the test center early. This will allow you to relax and collect your thoughts before the test, and will also spare you the anguish that comes with being late. As an added incentive to make sure that you arrive early, keep in mind that no one will be admitted into the test center after the test has begun.

Before you leave for the testing site, carefully review your registration materials. Make sure you bring your admission ticket and two unexpired forms of identification. Primary forms of ID include:

- Passport

- Government-issued driver's license

- State or Province ID card

- National ID card

- Military ID card

You may need to produce a supplemental ID document if any questions arise with your primary ID or if your primary ID is otherwise valid but lacks your full name, photo, and signature. Without proper identification, you will not be admitted to the test center.

Strict rules limit what you can bring into the test center. We recommend that you consult the Texas Education Agency's "Texas Educator Certification Registration Bulletin" for a complete rundown. You may not bring watches of any kind, cellphones, smartphones, or any other electronic communication devices or weapons of any kind. Scrap paper, written notes, books, and any printed material is prohibited.

No smoking, eating, or drinking is allowed in the testing room. Consider bringing a small snack and a bottle of water to partake of beforehand to keep you sharp during the test.

Good luck on the TExES Core Subjects 4–8 test!

Proven Test-Taking Strategies for TExES Core Subjects

All test-taking strategies have the same practical goal: to show you the best way to answer questions so you can improve your score.

The strategies and tips that follow come straight from teacher education students who have passed the TExES Core Subjects tests. We have worked directly with students just like you to see what works best.

Remember: There is no one right way to study. Savvy test-takers sharpen their skills while minimizing obstacles such as poor time management and test anxiety. As you assess these strategies, identify those you already use in your daily life and adapt the approaches that best address your problem areas—that is, the ones for which you'll need to invest more study time.

To make the most of whatever strategies you use, it's best to have an overall plan in mind. Our strategy list can be adjusted according to your needs, which no one knows better than you. Do what best fits your style of learning and method of study.

1. Guess Away

One of the most frequently asked questions about the TExES Core Subjects test is: Can I guess? The answer: absolutely! There is no penalty for guessing on the test. That means if you refrain from guessing, you may lose points. To guess smartly, use the process of elimination (see Strategy No. 2). Your score is based strictly on the number of correct answers. So answer all questions and take your best guess when you don't know the answer.

2. Process of Elimination

Process of elimination is one of the most important test-taking strategies at your disposal. Process of elimination means looking at the choices and eliminating the ones you know are wrong, including answers that are partially wrong. Your odds of getting the right answer increase from the moment you're able to get rid of a wrong choice.

3. All in

Review all the response options. Just because you believe you've found the correct answer—or, in some cases, answers—look at each choice so you don't mistakenly jump to any conclusions. If you are asked to choose the *best* answer, be sure your first answer is really the best one.

4. Choice of the Day

What if you are truly stumped and can't use the process of elimination? It's time to pick a fallback answer. On the day of the test, choose the position of the answer (e.g., the third of the four choices) that you will pick for any question you cannot smartly guess. According to the laws of probability, you have a higher chance of getting an answer right if you stick to one chosen position for the answer choice when you have to guess an answer instead of randomly picking one.

5. Use Choices to Confirm Your Answer

The great thing about multiple-choice questions is that the answer has to be staring back at you. Have an answer in mind and use the choices to *confirm* it. For the Math test, in the cases in which you're given a problem to solve, try to find the match among the choices. Or try the opposite: *backsolving*—that is, working backwards—from the choices given.

6. Watch the Clock

Among the most vital point-saving skills is active time management. The breakdown and time limits of each section are provided as you begin each test. Keep an eye on the timer on your computer screen. Make sure you stay on top of how much time you have left for each section and never spend too much time on any one question. Remember: Most multiple-choice questions are worth one raw point. Treat each one as if it's the one that will put you over the top. You never know, it just might. The last thing you want on test day is to lose easy points because you ran out of time and focused too much on difficult questions.

7. Read, Read, Read

It's important to read through all the multiple-choice options. Even if you believe answer choice A is correct, you can misread a question or response option if you're rushing to get through the test. While it is important not to linger on a question, it is also crucial to avoid giving a question short shrift. Slow down, calm down, read all the choices. Verify that your choice is the best one, and click on it.

8. Take Notes

Use the scratch paper provided to you to make notes to work toward the answer(s). If you use all the scratch paper you're initially given, you can get more.

9. Isolate Limiters

Pay attention to any limiters in a multiple-choice question stem. These are words such as *initial, best, most* (as in *most appropriate* or *most likely*), *not, least, except, required,* or *necessary.* Especially watch for negative words, such as "Choose the answer that is *not* true." When you select your answer, double-check yourself by asking how the response fits the limitations established by the stem. Think of the stem as a puzzle piece that perfectly fits only the response option(s) that contain the correct answer. Let it guide you.

10. It's Not a Race

Ignore other test-takers. Don't compare yourself to anyone else in the room. Focus on the items in front of you and the time you have left. If someone finishes the test 30 minutes early, it does not necessarily mean that person answered more questions correctly than you did. Stay calm and focus on *your* test. It's the only one that matters.

11. Confirm Your Click

In the digital age, many of us are used to rapid-clicking, be it in the course of emailing or gaming. Look at the screen to be sure to see that your mouse-click is acknowledged. If your answer doesn't register, you won't get credit. However, if you want to mark it for review so you can return later, that's your call. Before you click "Submit," use the test's review screen to see whether you inadvertently skipped any questions.

12. Creature of Habit? No Worries.

We are all creatures of habit. It's therefore best to follow a familiar pattern of study. Do what's comfortable for you. Set a time and place each day to study for this test. Whether it is 30 minutes at the library or an hour in a secluded corner of your local coffee shop, commit yourself as best you can to this schedule every day. Find quiet places where it is less crowded, as constant background noise can distract you. Don't study one subject for too long, either. Take an occasional breather and treat yourself to a healthy snack or some quick exercise. After your short break—5 or 10 minutes can do the trick—return to what you were studying or start a new section.

13. Knowledge is Power

Purchasing this book gave you an edge on passing the TExES Core Subjects test. Make the most of this edge. Review the sections on how the test is structured, what the directions look like, what types of questions will be asked, and so on. Take our practice tests to familiarize yourself with what the test looks and feels like. Most test anxiety occurs because people feel unprepared when they are taking the test, and they psych themselves out. You can whittle away at anxiety by learning the format of the test and by knowing what to expect. Fully simulating the test even once will boost your chances of getting the score you need. Meanwhile, the knowledge you've gained will also save you the valuable time that would have been eaten up puzzling through what the directions are asking As an added benefit, previewing the test will free up your brain's resources so you can focus on racking up as many points as you can.

14. B-r-e-a-t-h-e

Anxiety is neither unusual nor necessarily unwelcome on a test. Just don't let it stifle you. Take a moment to breathe. This won't merely make you feel good. The brain uses roughly three times as much oxygen as muscles in the body do: Give it what it needs. Now consider this: What's the worst that can happen when you take a test? You may have an off day, and despite your best efforts, you may not pass. Well, the good news is that this test can be retaken. Fortunately, the TExES Core Subjects test is something you can study and prepare for, and in some ways to a greater extent than other tests you've taken throughout your academic career. In fact, study after study has validated the value of test preparation. Yes, there will be questions you won't know, but neither your teacher education program nor state licensing board (which sets its own cut scores) expects you to know everything. When unfamiliar vocabulary appears or difficult math problems loom, don't despair: Use context clues, process of elimination, or your response option of the day (i.e., choose either A, B, C, or D routinely when you need to resort to a guess) to make your choice, and then press ahead. If you have time left, you can always come back to the question later. If not, relax. It is only one question on a test filled with many. Take a deep breath and then exhale. You know this information. Now you're going to show it.

Subject Test I: English Language Arts and Reading (806)

OVERVIEW OF SUBJECT TEST I: ELA AND READING (806)

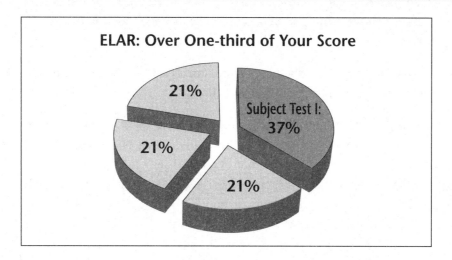

ELAR: Over One-third of Your Score

English Language Arts and Reading, or ELAR, accounts for approximately 37% of the questions you will see on the TExES Core Subjects 4–8 test. That makes this by far the largest subject test in the test battery. This is the section where you are expected to spend most of your time and where you will encounter the most questions. You'll be allotted 1 hour and 55 minutes to answer 74 test items. That gives you just over 1.5 minutes for each question. (Each of the four subject tests that make up the Core Subjects 4–8 test is individually timed.)

The ELAR subject test assesses eight Texas educator standards in connection with the statewide curriculum, known as Texas Essential Knowledge and Skills (TEKS). These standards frame what it takes to teach middle school English Language Arts and Reading, including that the teacher:

1. Understands the importance of oral language, knows the developmental processes of oral language and provides a variety of instructional opportunities for students to develop listening and speaking skills.

2. Understands the foundations of reading and early literacy development.

3. Understands the importance of word analysis skills (including decoding, blending, structural analysis, sight word vocabulary) and reading fluency and provides many opportunities for students to practice and improve their word analysis skills and reading fluency.

4. Understands the importance of reading for understanding, knows the components of comprehension and teaches students strategies for improving their comprehension.

5. Understands that writing is a developmental process and provides instruction that helps students develop competence in written communication.

6. Understands the importance of study and inquiry skills as tools for learning and promotes students' development in applying study and inquiry skills.

7. Understands how to interpret, analyze, evaluate and produce visual images and messages in various media and to provide students with opportunities to develop skills in this area.

8. Understands the basic principles of assessment and use a variety of literacy assessment practices to plan and implement instruction.

This subject test embraces nine competencies, which are based on the above standards and broadly define "what an entry-level educator in this field in Texas public schools should know and be able to do," according to the Texas Education Agency. These competencies are covered in turn in this chapter, which synthesizes the content you're most likely to encounter on the ELAR subject test.

COMPETENCY 001: ORAL LANGUAGE

The teacher understands the importance of oral language, knows the developmental processes of oral language, and provides a variety of instructional opportunities for students to develop listening and speaking skills.

The beginning teacher:

A. Knows basic linguistic concepts (e.g., phonemes, segmentation) and developmental stages in acquiring oral language, including stages in phonology, semantics, syntax and pragmatics, and recognizes that individual variations occur.

B. Knows characteristics and uses of informal and formal oral language assessments and uses multiple, ongoing assessments to monitor and evaluate students' oral language skills.

C. Provides language instruction that acknowledges students' current oral language skills and that builds on these skills to increase students' oral language proficiency.

D. Plans, implements and adapts instruction that is based on informal and formal assessment of students' progress in oral language development and that addresses the needs, strengths and interests of individual students, including English-language learners (ELLs), in accordance with the English Language Proficiency Standards (ELPS).

E. Recognizes when oral language delays or differences warrant in-depth evaluation and additional help or intervention.

F. Knows how to provide explicit, systematic oral language instruction and supports students' learning and use of oral language through meaningful and purposeful activities implemented one-to-one and in a group.

G. Selects and uses instructional materials and strategies that promote students' oral language development; that respond to students' individual strengths, needs and interests; that reflect cultural diversity; and that build on students' cultural, linguistic and home backgrounds to enhance their oral language development.

H. Understands relationships between the development of oral language and the development of reading and provides instruction that interrelates oral and written language to promote students' reading proficiency and learning (e.g., preview-review, discussion, questioning).

I. Knows similarities and differences between oral and written language and how to promote students' awareness of these similarities and differences.

J. Selects and uses instructional strategies, materials, activities and models to strengthen students' oral vocabulary and narrative skills in spoken language and teaches students to connect spoken and printed language.

K. Selects and uses instructional strategies, materials, activities and models to teach students skills for speaking to different audiences for various purposes and for adapting spoken language for various audiences, purposes and occasions.

L. Selects and uses instructional strategies, materials, activities and models to teach students listening skills for various purposes (e.g., critical listening to evaluate a speaker's message, listening to enjoy and appreciate spoken language) and provides students with opportunities to engage in active, purposeful listening in a variety of contexts.

M. Selects and uses instructional strategies, materials, activities and models to teach students to evaluate the content and effectiveness of their own spoken messages and the messages of others.

N. Knows how to promote students' development of oral communication skills through the use of technology and applications found in smartphones, tablets and e-readers.

Let's turn first to a conceptual overview of the key ideas that fall under Competency 001: Oral Language. It is essential to understand that the ideas relating to instruction and assessment strictly align with Texas's state standards for what your students need to know and be able to do. These standards are known as the **Texas Essential Knowledge and Skills**, or TEKS. When teaching English Language Learners, practice should also be in accordance with the English Language Proficiency Standards. We encourage you to take the time to review both of these sets of standards as they relate to the mid-level grades (4–8) that falls within the scope of this Core Subjects exam.

Language acquisition results from the combination of innate ability, imitation of what is said and heard, and multiple environmental influences.

Innate ability. Most children are born with innate abilities and mechanisms to develop language. Noam Chomsky called this mechanism a Language Acquisition Device (LAD). According to Chomsky, humans possess an "internal grammar" or set of linguistic principles that are activated for all languages. Interestingly, the LAD is considered universal, as it adapts depending on the language being learned. However, it should be noted that linguists have argued that language only emerges if this internal mechanism is triggered by stimuli from people in the child's environment.

Imitation is a learning strategy that young children frequently use to replicate someone's behaviors, actions, phrases, etc. In language acquisition, imitation provides young learners with the opportunity to begin producing language by observing and replicating their caregivers' phrases and words. Imitation decreases in effectiveness, however, as language learning becomes more complex.

Multiple environmental influences. After age two, imitation alone cannot meet the communication needs of children. It is at this point when they become creative rule makers. Toddlers begin testing language rules on their own as a way of trying to figure out how language operates. For example, imitation alone cannot explain idiosyncratic statements such as "I goed out yesterday." These nonstandard utterances show that the child is field-testing language rules. In this case, the child is testing the rule for the formation of the regular past tense and has applied it to an irregular verb. This type of overgeneralization characterizes the process of first-language acquisition during most of the early childhood years. Direct language correction will not generally help in this case. Instead, parents and those around the child will present the standard version of the word, and the child will seem to ignore it until he or she is ready to internalize it. Parents and teachers should always be encouraged to address the communication needs of the child while modeling the standard version of the language. Moreover, appropriate modeling of the target language is a necessary task for teachers, especially when working with students for whom English is not their native language.

Language Is Learned in Social Settings

Participation in conversation provides children with the vocabulary and the format of conversations they need to begin developing oral language (Stewig and Jett-Simpson, 1995). Interestingly, parents do not always engage in direct language teaching; instead, parents assist in their children's language acquisition by communicating with the child and using the adult version of the language. As a result of this linguistic support, most children come to school with a strong vocabulary and language background. Conversely, some ethnic and linguistic groups might not follow the same pattern of linguistic interaction with their children.

Children quickly understand that the main purpose of language is communication. Children begin to understand that language is used to generally have their needs met.

Language Components

All teacher candidates need to have a clear understanding of the basic components of any given language. The six components, which are interlocking pieces in a puzzle, are phonology, morphology, syntax, lexicon, semantics, and pragmatics. **Phonology** is the study of the sound system of a language. The basic units of sound are called **phonemes.** Graphemes or individual letters represent phonemes. For example, the word *through* has seven graphemes (i.e., letters) that represent only three sounds /th/ /r/ /u/. Teacher candidates should be able not only to differentiate these two terms, but they should also make their students aware of the difference between letters in a word and the sounds that the letters represent. **Morphology** is the study of the structure of words and word formations. **Morphemes** are the smallest representation of meaning. For example, the word *cars* is made up of two morphemes: the basic word or root word *car* and the plural morpheme *s*. Having an understanding of the morphology of a language will help students when they are required to decode printed information. **Syntax** entails the ways in which words are organized and arranged in a language. English has specific basic sentence structures that are referred to as *kernel sentences*. Examples of the four most common sentence structures in English can be found in Table 3.1.

Table 3.1
Types of Kernel Sentences

Noun	Intransitive Verb	Predicate Nominative
Katrina	was	a hurricane.
Katrina	was	destructive.
"Bear Mountain"	won	an Academy Award.
Mark Cuban	gave	the Mavericks incentive.

Lexicon refers to the vocabulary of a language. Because the meanings of words change based on context and historical framework, vocabulary is said to be one of the most variable and rich components of a language. For example, the word *hot* can have several meanings. These include high temperature, sexy, fashionable, and lucky (e.g., a "hot streak"). In a few years, any of the meanings might change or become obsolete.

Pragmatics describes how context can affect the interpretation of communication. Pragmatics describes the hidden rules of communication understood by native speakers of the same language. Native speakers often call these rules "common sense rules." However, these rules might be only common to native speakers. These rules are not immediately evident to ELLs. Thus, teachers should again introduce these rules within context.

Take, for example, a greeting exchange. In English, one person greets another with such routine statements as "How are you?" Pragmatically, the receiver is expected to answer with such generic statements as "Not bad," "I'm OK," or "Fine." Once such an exchange of words is completed, that line of conversation is expected to end. However, ELLs and people new to the culture might misinterpret the routine question as a literal inquiry and try to answer it directly. They will often provide more information than the greeter expected.

Semantics refers to how meaning is conveyed in a language through the use of its vocabulary. The meaning of words is also based on culture as well as the context of the conversation taking place. Connotation and denotation are used in a language to convey meaning.

On the one hand, **connotation** refers to the implied meaning of words and ideas, requiring that speakers have knowledge of the culture to understand an expression's implied meaning. Idiomatic expressions are an example of how usage implies meaning as a communication tool. Having this prior knowledge often presents a challenge to ELLs because they lack the familiarity with American culture that native speakers generally have. For instance, the idiom "it's raining cats and dogs" may confuse ELLs who do not have the cultural knowledge to be familiar with this. Thus, teachers should teach idioms in context so that students can understand them and learn to use them. Teachers also must describe the idiom, especially its intended meaning, so that students fully understand its use.

Denotation refers to the literal meaning of words and ideas. For instance, a sign that reads "Dog contained by invisible fence" might be confusing for those not aware of this new technology. Curious passersby might try to see if they can find the "invisible fence." However, pragmatically, this phrase requires people to go beyond the literal meaning of the phrase and understand that whoever posted the sign meant that the dog is contained with an electronic device, not necessarily with a literal fence.

The *Amelia Bedelia* series written by Peggy Parish is about a character who understands everything only literally (i.e., denotation). Her limited understanding creates many communication problems and comedic situations.

Stages of Language Development

The process of first-language acquisition is characterized by stages of development and maturation. Also, these stages are highly influenced by the learner's level and quality of exposure to the native language. Therefore, assigning a definite age for each of the language development stages is not possible. Linguistic milestones, however, can provide pointers to identify these stages and develop a working framework for readers. A description of these stages follows.

Ages 6 and 7

Six- to 7-year-olds have a speaking vocabulary of about 2,100 words and a comprehension vocabulary of more than 20,000 words. Children use well-constructed sentences using all parts of speech. They still might have problems with certain words and structures, but their speech is fluent and clear. However, speakers at this age might still struggle with words containing sounds like /v/, /th/, /ch/, and /sh/. Some children will use the sound of the /w/ in place of the required /r/ and /l/ sounds. They are able to separate words into syllables and begin decoding written language. They are beginning to understand and address questions that call for reasons for an action. For example, they can explain their actions and answer questions such as "Why did you pick number five as the answer?" After age 6, children continue to polish their language skills and add new and more sophisticated vocabulary.

Ages 8 to 12

The speaking repertoire of children ages 8 to 12 continues to grow and improve, as their communication needs change from using language to have their needs met, to becoming language makers in academic settings. Eight-year-olds begin using relative pronoun clauses (i.e., The boy *that* you met yesterday is my friend). They also begin to use subordinated clauses that begin with *when, if,* and *because* (i.e., *If* you bother me, I am going to tell the teacher). At age 9, the use of the gerund (a noun formed from a verb by adding *-ing*) has become common for speakers of this age (i.e., *Cheating* is bad). Children begin using more complex sentences, vocabulary, and verb construction. Their speech is more coherent through the use of connectors like *first, during, after,* and *finally*. At ages 10 through 12, students are able to make use of roots, prefixes, and suffixes to understand new words in the language. Also, their sentence structure is more complex.

Assessing Speaking Ability

Intelligibility

A child's speaking ability is generally assessed informally in class as part of daily activities and conversations. First, teachers have to determine whether the speech of the child is **intelligible** and can be understood by native speakers with minimum effort. Developmental issues, the use of dialectical variations, and speech disorders can cause communication or intelligibility problems in native speakers. To assess the speech of the child, teachers need an understanding of the developmental patterns in the process of language mastery, in order to use these patterns as a foundation for assessing a child's performance. Teachers should also develop an understanding of features from dialects spoken in the community to avoid confusion with features that contrast with Standard English. For example, speakers of **Ebonics**, a language variant used by some African-American children, and speakers of the **Boston dialect** drop the /r/ after a vowel. One example of this is in the statement ". . . park the ca**r** in Ha**r**va**r**d yard" [Pa**h**k the ka**h** in Ha**h**vud ya**h**d]. In this case, the omission of postvocalic /r/ cannot be identified as a pronunciation problem. Because of this, teachers need a working knowledge of the dialects used in the community in order to make accurate assessments of the children's speech.

Speaking Checklist

Students' speaking abilities can also be assessed in the classroom with a structured checklist identifying specific features that teachers want to observe. Lapp et al. (2001) developed an instrument to assess speaking ability called the Speaking Checklist. A summary of key elements is presented below.

The Speaking Checklist

1. Sticks to the topic
2. Builds support for the subject
3. Speaks clearly
4. Takes turns and waits to talk
5. Talks so others in the group can hear
6. Speaks smoothly
7. Uses courteous language
8. Presents in an organized and interesting way
9. Supports the topical thesis
10. Answers questions effectively
11. Is comfortable speaking publicly
12. Maintains listeners' interest
13. Volunteers to answer in class

The Texas Education Agency (TEA) has developed an instrument in compliance with the federal Every Student Succeeds Act's state accountability system called the Texas Observation Protocol (TOP) to assess language proficiency of ELLs in Texas. This instrument is administered by teachers in the bilingual or ESL classroom and contains a speaking component that assesses speaking ability, using a holistic scoring system, based on four levels of proficiency: beginning, intermediate, advanced, and advanced-high (TEA, 2011).

Listening and Speaking

In any given language, meaning is created through socially shared conventions. During the first months of life, babies are active listeners. Long before they can respond orally, however, they communicate nonverbally by waving their arms, smiling, or wiggling. They are also capable of communicating their needs and wants through nonverbal communication, including body language and crying. Through listening, they develop the receptive language needed to begin communicating orally. Although listening is used extensively in communication, it does not receive much attention at school.

Listening and reading both require the use of skills in phonology, syntax, semantics, and knowledge of the structure of text, and both language skills seem to be controlled by the same set of cognitive processes. Teachers can guide students' listening activities by setting a purpose for listening, providing questions before and after the listening activity, and encouraging children to forge links between the new information that was just heard and the knowledge already in place. In addition, children need to be coached in the use of appropriate volume and speed when they speak, and in the rules to participate in discussions. Students also need to follow the culturally defined rules for maintaining a polite conversation. In the American culture, such rules include staying on a topic and taking turns without interrupting speakers.

A communication disorder occurs when a person's speech interferes with his/her ability to convey messages during interactions with community members. The four classifications of language disorders include disorders in voice, fluency, articulation, and language processing (Piper, 2006).

Voice Disorders

Voice disorders are considered any type of distortion of the pitch, timbre, or volume of spoken communication. There are two types of voice disorders: phonation and resonance. **Phonation** disorder describes any kind of abnormality in the vibration of the vocal fold. For example, *hoarseness* or extreme breathiness can interfere with comprehension. **Resonance** disorder describes abnormalities created when sound passes through the vocal tract. The most typical example of resonance disorder occurs when the sound passing through the nasal cavity changes oral sounds to nasal. This is called *hypernasality*. This type of disorder should not be confused with the nasal quality of Southern dialects like the Texas twang.

Fluency Disorders

Fluency disorders refer to any kind of condition that affects the child's ability to produce coherent and fluent communication. *Stuttering* and *cluttering* cause the most common types of fluency disorders. **Stuttering** is characterized by multiple false starts or the inability to produce the intended sounds. **Cluttering** occurs when children try to communicate in an excessively fast mode that makes comprehension difficult. Teachers should be cautious when assessing ELLs who might experience temporary fluency dysfunction, such as hesitations, false starts, and repetition, which can be attributed to anxiety or confusion with the two languages. For instance, ELLs may stutter because they cannot find or might not know the appropriate word in English. Temporary remedies to stuttering that can be used include (a) allowing students to code-switch from English to their first language and (b) providing them more wait time. Additionally, children new to the language often use the intonation pattern and the speed of delivery of their native language. Thus, the delivery might become incomprehensible and may be mistaken for a cluttering disorder.

Articulation Problems

The most common articulation disorder is *lisping*. **Lisping** is a term used when children (or adults) produce the sound /s/, /sh/, /z/, and /ch/ with their tongue between the upper and lower teeth. Some other sounds that can present challenges to children are the /w/, /l/, and /r/ sounds. Children may have problems with specific sounds that can cause unintelligibility and the production of aesthetically displeasing sounds. Some of these problems might be developmental and will eventually be eliminated, while others might require speech therapy.

Activities to Promote Oral Communication

The best way to promote oral communication is to guide students into using language in meaningful situations. In classroom situations, teachers can organize activities to resemble real-life situations in order to promote communication among students. Some of these activities are described below.

Role-Play

Role-play or dramatic enactment allows students to recreate a variety of scenarios across the curriculum. Using scripts or Readers' Theatre is an ideal activity to develop communication. In role-play, students are given open opportunities to act out real-life situations. Students may be given either a specific role to play, or they can improvise roles. For instance, fifth grade students in a history class could reenact the Boston Tea Party. Students can also play the role of a talk show host and "interview" classmates who can pretend to be characters from a novel or famous historical figures from a specific time era.

Language Play

Language play involves the use of language in rhyme, alliteration, songs, and repeating patterns to amuse children. Tongue twisters are commonly used to practice pronunciation and language patterns. Through these activities, children acquire language knowledge in a relaxed and fun environment. Teachers can also use content related songs, poems, and stories that contain rhyme to introduce these language features.

Sharing

In sharing, children bring artifacts and personal items to class. Children show the object and are expected to describe its features to the class. In addition to the obvious benefit of oral communication, this kind of activity can be used to promote both home and cultural pride as well as multicultural awareness in one's classroom. Older students can prepare presentations that describe and detail information for a specific audience.

Pair Interview

Pair interview is an additional strategy that can be used to promote oral communication. In this strategy, children are paired to learn information from each other and then report their findings to the larger group. Depending on the children's age, the responses gathered during the pair interview can also be recorded in writing to be used later in the children's presentation. This strategy can be used throughout the year and for different classroom activities. The pair interview is also a recommended instructional strategy that can be used for the first day of class when students need to get to know each other.

Presentations

Preparing children to communicate what they think and know is common practice in classrooms. Elementary and middle school students are expected not only to use correct language when speaking, but also to have accurate information when creating a presentation. To this end, students are also expected to also find reliable information and sources when investigating a topic of interest or one assigned.

Elementary and middle school students also learn that a topic of a presentation can be delivered to multiple and different audiences. In other words, students will need to be given opportunities to understand how one presentation can be modified to meet the needs of their audience. For example, children can be led to prepare a short presentation to inform other children at their school why recycling is important to the environment. This could then set the stage for starting a recycling project in their classrooms. Later, these same students could be asked to revise their presentation to deliver it to community leaders so that they could receive the resources needed to start recycling projects in their communities. Regardless of the audience, however, students should be expected to create and deliver presentations in groups and individually.

Explicit, Systematic Oral Language Instruction

Key principles of oral language development can help both native speakers and English Language Learners in their oral language development. Some key ideas, based on work by Gersten et al., (2007), include the following:

- Increase academic vocabulary and ensure multiple encounters with words.

- Provide lots of opportunities to engage in dialogue.

- Vocabulary can be enhanced by combining oral language with visual supports (e.g., increase visual aids).

- Focus on comprehension through strategic reading and think-aloud practice.

Connecting Oral Language to Reading Instruction

Students can be encouraged to connect oral language to reading instruction through the use of discussions and questioning. Both small-group and large-group discussions can facilitate comprehension by encouraging students to integrate reading, listening, and speaking. Teachers should ask all levels of questions of students including literal questions, inferential (higher-level), and application (real-world) questions. Additionally, teachers should consider whether the questions posed orally genuinely invite dialogue and response from all students. To foster discussion, the questions should not be retrieval or yes/no questions. Teachers should also allow sufficient wait time for student response. Asking follow-up questions such as, "Why do you think so?" or "What evidence in the text told you that?" can help to foster both critical thinking and a deeper level of dialogue.

Furthermore, through read-aloud and shared reading, the teacher can increase exposure to higher-level academic vocabulary of both narrative and expository text. Students can participate in dialogue with support and modeling from the teacher and their peers. Other benefits of shared reading to enhance oral language development include the following (Herrell & Jordan, 2007):

- Shared reading supports fluency as well as vocabulary and comprehension development. English is an *intonation* language; meaning and understanding are created through expression, pitch, and tone in reading.

- Understanding of text can be aided through hearing the story as the teacher models expressive reading and active reading of the text.

Spoken and Written English

The productive skills of language—speaking and writing—are interconnected. A strong oral development can facilitate the development of written communication. However, because spoken language is generally more informal than written language, teachers need to be sure that students use formal language when writing.

English favors the use of active voice as opposed to passive voice in both oral and written communication. For example, the sentence *Katrina devastated the city of New Orleans* is stronger and more effective than a sentence using the passive voice such as *The city of New Orleans was devastated by Katrina*. To provide support in this area, guide students to work with a partner in converting passive sentences to active sentences; then guide them to discuss how these changes affect the tone and meaning of the sentences. If a student is having problems connecting sounds to written text, teachers can provide phonics instruction. Guiding students to "sound out" or "stretch out" words as a foundation for spelling can improve written performance.

Using Technology to Develop Oral Language

There are many technological resources available to develop students' oral language. For listening skills, students can view multimedia presentations to hear stories, news events, and other types of formal, academic language. Students can listen to or view podcasts, video clips, and CDs on a variety of topics. To increase speaking opportunities, students can design and create their own podcasts, videos, and other multimedia presentations to share with other students and families. Increasingly, students are expected to be skilled in using digital media to create their assignments.

With the increasing presence of mobile devices (e.g., smartphones, tablets, and e-readers), teachers can make use of digital tools. The following are ways that oral language can be supported by integrating mobile devices:

- **Singing and rhyming apps.** Make use of apps that focus on singing, songs, and rhyming.

- **Videos.** Have children view and discuss videos that focus on nursery rhymes, stories, and other early language experiences.

- **Storytelling apps.** Have students retell stories presented in storytelling apps.

- **E-books.** Use e-books for storybook reading to foster interactivity by having the children discuss the story and engage in dialogue.

COMPETENCY 002: EARLY LITERACY DEVELOPMENT

The teacher understands the foundations of early literacy development.

The beginning teacher:

A. Understands the significance of phonological and phonemic awareness for reading and typical patterns in the development of phonological and phonemic awareness and recognizes that individual variations occur.

B. Understands elements of the alphabetic principle (e.g., letter names, graphophonemic knowledge, the relationship of the letters in printed words to spoken language) and typical patterns of students' alphabetic skills development, and recognizes that individual variations occur.

C. Understands that comprehension is an integral part of early literacy.

D. Understands that not all written languages are alphabetic and that many alphabetic languages are more phonetically regular than English and knows the significance of this for students' literacy development in English.

E. Understands that literacy acquisition generally develops in a predictable pattern from prereading (emergent literacy) to conventional literacy and recognizes that individual variations occur.

F. Understands that literacy development occurs in multiple contexts through reading, writing, speaking and using various media.

G. Knows characteristics of informal and formal literacy assessments (e.g., screening devices, criterion-referenced state tests, curriculum-based reading assessments, informal reading inventories, norm-referenced tests).

H. Knows how to select, administer and use results from informal and formal assessments of literacy acquisition.

I. Knows how to use ongoing assessment to determine when a student needs additional help or intervention to bring the student's performance to grade level, based on state content and performance standards for reading in the Texas Essential Knowledge and Skills (TEKS).

J. Analyzes students' errors in reading and responds to individual students' needs by providing focused instruction to promote literacy acquisition.

K. Selects and uses instructional materials that build on the current language skills of individual students, including English-language learners (in accordance with the ELPS), to promote development from emergent literacy to conventional literacy.

L. Knows how to promote students' early literacy development skills through the use of technology and applications found in smartphones, tablets and e-readers.

Balanced Reading Program

Today, many classrooms are places where young children enjoy learning to read and write in a balanced reading instructional program. Research into best practices strongly suggests that the teaching of reading requires solid skill instruction, including several techniques for decoding unknown words. These techniques include, but are not limited to, phonics instruction embedded in interesting and engaging reading and writing experiences with whole and **authentic literature-based texts** to facilitate the construction of meaning. In other words, this approach to instruction combines the best skill instruction and the whole-language approach in order to teach both skills and meaning as well as to meet the reading needs of individual children. Some of the reading strategies used in a balanced literacy program include:

- Teacher-directed reading to students (read-aloud)

- Shared reading, guided reading, and reading workshops

- Student-directed reading and independent reading

- Teacher-directed writing, writing to/for students as part of the classroom routines, and process writing

- Shared writing as in language experience, interactive writing, and writing workshops

- Student-directed writing and independent writing activities

It should be noted that with changes to the definition of literacy and broader experiences of literacy beyond print (e.g., digital reading and writing), literacy development occurs in an increasing numbers of contexts, media, and platforms including not just reading, writing, and speaking, but also various uses of media. Examples of media include: videos, movies, audio, social media, email, and text on a wide array of devices including computers, laptops, smartphones, tablets, and television.

Importance of Phonological and Phonemic Awareness for Reading and Writing

Phonological and phonemic awareness constitute the foundation for the development of the metalinguistic awareness that children need to become successful language learners and effective readers. **Phonemic awareness** refers to a child's ability to understand that words have smaller components called sounds, and that these sounds together create syllables and words. Phonemic awareness is the basic linguistic principle required to develop an understanding of oral and written communication. Once children understand this principle, they begin discovering more sophisticated linguistic principles like phonological awareness. Children who have developed phonemic awareness are able to dissect a word into each phoneme, and put it back together to recreate the word. The ability to manipulate spoken words has been linked to successful reading development.

Phonological Awareness

Phonological awareness is the ability to recognize and manipulate components of the sound system of a language. It includes the ability to segment words into smaller units like syllables and phonemes (sounds). Phonological awareness also encompasses the ability to identify and separate words within a sentence, identify stress in individual words, and identify the intonation pattern used in sentences.

Syllabication

Syllabication is an important component of phonological awareness. It refers to the ability to conceptualize and segment words into their basic pronunciation components, which are syllables. Syllables can be as simple as one vowel, or can be a combination of vowels and consonants. For example, the word *elegant* contains three syllables (el/e/gant), one of which is a vowel alone. Phonemes are the basic unit of a syllable, and syllables constitute the basic units for the pronunciation of the English language. Consequently, syllables influence the rhythm of the language, poetic meter, and word stress. Syllabication can be taught using the appropriate voice intonation in order to indicate the beginning and ending of a syllable. Teachers often use clapping to indicate syllable boundaries.

Phonemic Stress

Phonemic stress can be taught through the use of nursery rhymes, short poems, or stories like the traditional Humpty Dumpty character of Mother Goose nursery rhymes. The use of these rhythmic patterns in an enjoyable and relaxed environment introduces children to the sounds and music of language. Eventually, children will notice the ending of the words and how specific sounds relate to each other. Moreover, rhymes are particularly beneficial to ELLs as they begin to develop phonemic awareness and phonemic stress. They can also learn chunks of language that they can use to participate in classroom conversations and communicate with peers and their teacher in the classroom.

Alliteration

Alliteration is a technique used to emphasize phonemes by using successive words that begin with the same consonant sound or letter. Tongue twisters are the best-known form of alliteration. Children can repeat tongue twisters for fun, and, at the same time, develop an awareness of the sound–symbol correspondence. In the following example, the /p/ sound is emphasized:

Peter **P**iper **p**icked a **p**eck of **p**ickled **p**eppers.

Word Stress

English has at least four levels of word stress, but for practical purposes, we only need to be concerned with the first two: **main stress** and **secondary stress**. Word stress can affect the ability to understand words and can also alter meaning. For example, the word *present* can have two meanings depending on how it is pronounced. With the stress on the first syllable (*present*), it becomes a noun; but if the stress is placed on the last syllable (*present*), it becomes a verb.

Intonation Patterns

The **intonation pattern** describes the pitch contour of a phrase or a sentence that is used to change the meaning of the sentence. In English, there are utterances that might appear to be identical but convey a different meaning. In the question below, the rising point at the verb *are* makes the utterance a question, while a slight change of intonation to the pronoun *you* changes the utterance to a reply to the question.

Question: How **are** you? Reply: How are **you**?

Teaching Phonemic and Phonological Awareness

Teachers can promote phonemic and phonological knowledge through a variety of strategies. A list of these strategies follows:

- Teach the child to isolate phonemes. To follow a pattern from the simplest to the most difficult, begin with initial and final sounds first, and then add phonemes in the middle. Ask questions such as, "What is the first sound of the word *boy*?"

- Guide children to blend sounds and come up with rhymes. Ask the child, "What word can you create when you blend the sounds *l* and *ake,* or *t* and *ake*?"

- Introduce blending by guiding children to identify the word created when the following sounds are blended: /b/, /a/, and /t/.

- Guide children to identify a word like *tape* and then remove the onset and ask the child: "What word is left when we remove the first sound, *t*?" (Answer: *ape.*) Then ask students, "Is this a word?"

- Teach word segmentation by saying a word, and then guiding children to identify the sounds that they hear. Teachers can begin with simple monosyllabic words like *cat* and then expand to more sophisticated words.

- Use onsets and rimes to teach the sound symbol–relationship. Guide children to create new words by substituting the first letter of monosyllabic words. For example, using the word *ring*, the child can replace the initial sounds to create additional words like *sing*, *king*, and *spring*. An activity like this can emphasize phonemic awareness and also teach how word families can support vocabulary development.

- Teachers should lead children to segment or separate the sounds in words. Begin with words with consistent sound–symbol correspondence, like *bag* and *lag*, and later expand to words that contain clusters/blends as in the word *splash* and digraphs as in the word *church*.

- Introduce minimal pairs, which are sets of words that differ in only one phoneme like *pail* and *bail*, to guide students to notice the difference. Teachers should pronounce both words and ask students if the words are the same or different. Initially, contrast words with initial consonant sounds as in *pat* and *bat*, and later expand to include more sophisticated contrasting pairs as in *bit* and *beet*.

- Say words and guide children to identify the number of sounds that they hear. Initially, avoid "stop" sounds because children might have difficulties perceiving the brief sound represented by these sounds.

The **alphabetic principle** has been described as the ability to connect letters with sounds, and to create words based on these associations. Children learning to read also must develop an understanding that letters and letter patterns represent the sounds of spoken English (TEA, 2002). Understanding the ways in which these sound–symbol relationships are created allows them to conceptualize that there are predictable connections between phonemes and graphemes.

How Is the Alphabetic Principle Learned?

Traditionally, children go through specific stages in the process of learning new words and mastering the alphabetic principle (Ehri, 1998). Preschoolers are exposed to components of the alphabetic principle through their environment. They can identify the logo of stores like Walmart or Burger King by their design instead of by the specific letters contained in the logo. But because they are not connecting the letters and the sounds of the logo, this stage is generally considered a **pre-alphabetic phase.**

At home, children might also get exposed to the alphabet song, which most of them learn in a subconscious manner. Eventually, children engage in a **partial alphabetic phase** as they get exposed to alphabet block playing and concrete letter objects that are typical in early childhood programs. They begin connecting the shape of the letters with the sound that they represent. Children are also often exposed to children's literature and books in which the sound–symbol correspondence is carefully controlled. Children also begin connecting initial letters with the sound of the names of peers, like the **N** in Nancy or the **A** In Alex.

A third phase of learning new words is identified as the **full alphabetic stage**. At this stage, children begin making connections between the letters, the sounds that they represent, and the actual meaning of the word. Children get very excited during this stage because they are beginning to "crack" the written code of the language. In the fourth and last stage of development, called the **consolidated alphabetic stage**, children begin conceptualizing that they can use components of words that they know to decode new words. They begin discovering how they can create new words with the use of onsets, rhymes, and other letter sequences. One of the main purposes of phonics instruction at this stage is to guide children into understanding the connection between the grapheme and phoneme and the sequence that they create to form words and sentences. This knowledge allows students the opportunity to expand the number of words that they recognize instantly (sight words), which prepares them for literacy.

Teaching the Grapheme–Phoneme Correspondence

The introduction of the grapheme–phoneme correspondence can be presented through games, songs, and other engaging activities; but eventually, the correspondence should be presented explicitly. Teachers have to bring the skills to the surface level and make students aware of the concepts and skills that they need to learn in order to become effective readers. Teachers should take into account the complexity of the language and the maturity level of the children when introducing children to the alphabetic principle. A list of considerations and strategies for teaching the grapheme–phoneme connection follows.

- The introduction of the letter–sound correspondence should be guided by the potential support of the children's efforts to become readers. That is, introduce the spelling of the letters that the child is most likely to encounter in text. For example, the letters *m*, *a*, *t*, *s*, *p*, and *h* are used more frequently in writing than letters like *x* or *q*, or consonant digraphs like *ght* or *gn*.

- It is also important to begin instruction in the graphophonemic relationship using sounds that present the least possible distortion or confusion with other sounds. Some of the sounds that are easier to perceive are the nasals /m/ and /n/, the fricatives /f/, the sibilant /s/, and the English retroflex /r/.

- Teachers should postpone the introduction of less clear phonemes like the nasal /ng/, the distinction between the sibilants /s/ and /z/, the troublesome sounds in English like the voiced *th* in the word *them*, and the voiceless counterpart in words like *think*.

- Introduce words with one or two consonants and one short vowel sound such as in the words *on* and *sit*. Later, long vowel sounds can be introduced.

- Next, add consonant blends like *try*, followed by digraphs like *th*, *sh*, and *ch* in words like *thanks*, *show*, and *chop*. Digraphs can lead students to recognize common words such as *this*, *she*, and *chair*. Introduce single consonants and consonant blends or clusters in separate lessons to avoid confusion.

- Avoid voiceless stop sounds (/t/, /p/, /k/) at the beginning or middle of words because the short duration of these phonemes makes them difficult to perceive. Teachers should postpone the introduction of conflicting letter–sound correspondence of phonemes like the /b/ and /v/ or /i/ and /e/, or visually confusing graphemes like the *b* and *d* or *p* and *g*.

Types of Writing Systems

Several classifications exist for writing systems. Three of the most commonly known writing systems are pictographic, syllabic, and alphabetic writing. In a **pictographic writing system**, words, ideas, and concepts are represented with a visual or image. Pictographic writing was the first type of written language developed in the history of civilizations. In **syllabic writing systems**, syllables are depicted through the use of unique symbols. The **alphabetic writing system** uses the sounds of the language as a basic unit for writing. English uses an alphabetic writing system that is based upon phonetic signs. Theoretically, each symbol represents one unit of sound in this system. However, this principle works better with languages with consistent sound–symbol relationships. Many alphabetic languages such as Spanish are more phonetically consistent than English. An analysis of the grapheme–phoneme correspondence of English follows.

The Grapheme–Phoneme Correspondence of English

The connection between graphemes and phonemes in English is not always consistent. English has 26 graphemes to represent 44 phonemes. The consonant system is more consistent than the vowel system. English has five letters to represent 12 vowel sounds, which makes decoding and pronunciation more challenging. This inconsistency is partially caused by the evolution of the English language and the influence of multiple languages in the development of modern English. Teachers need to be proactive by identifying these troublesome areas and organizing instruction accordingly. Let's look at some of the potential areas of concern. Graphemes can represent multiple phonemes. For example, the grapheme *s* can represent multiple phonemes: car**s/z/**, call**s/z/**, sugar/**sh/**, mission/**sh/**, and walk**s/s/**. This grapheme–phoneme inconsistency represents a challenge when attempting to use a phonic approach to teach reading.

English has graphemes that represent a sound in some words and remain silent in other words. For example, the graphemes *s* and *l* become silent in the following examples without giving readers a reliable cue for this change: *island*, *calm*, and *palm*. (Some speakers will make an attempt to pronounce the /s/ and /l/ in these words.)

English has multiple consonant digraphs, which are two or more letters representing one sound. These consonant digraphs are voiceless. This inconsistency presents a challenge to native English speakers as well as ELLs.

Table 3.2
Consonant Digraphs

Digraphs	Examples
ch	chair
gh	ghost
gn	gnat
kn	know
ght	thought
pn	pneumonia
ps	psychology

Table 3.2 (cont'd)

Digraphs	Examples
rh	rhythm
wr	write
sc	scene

English speakers use multiple contractions in daily communication. Contractions can create listening comprehension problems for students and especially for ELLs. To avoid confusion, teachers should introduce contractions together with the long version of the words. Table 3.3 presents a few examples of the type of confusion that contractions can cause.

Table 3.3
Contractions in English

Contractions	Regular Form	Possible Confusion
they're	they are	there and their
he's	he is	his
he'll	he will	hill, heel, heal
you're	you are	your

English has multiple initial consonant clusters, which require students to be able to blend the sounds and at the same time recognize the sounds of individual phonemes. These sounds also represent a challenge for native Spanish speakers because Spanish does not have words that begin with particular letter sequences that exist in English. These types of clusters occur in medial positions and are always preceded by the vowel *e*, such as in the words *espero*, *escapar*, and *estar*. Based on this feature, Latino children will have a tendency to place an *e* in front of English words containing the following clusters: *sp* (as in *speak*), *sc* (*school*), *st* (*street*), *spr* (*spring*), *scr* (*scream*), *str* (*stream*), *sm* (*small*), *sn* (*snow*), and *sl* (*slate*).

Several words in English end in consonant clusters (e.g., *rant*, *cord*, *first*, and *card*). Both young native English-speaking children and ELLs may have difficulties blending clusters at the end of the words. For native Spanish speakers, these clusters represent a unique challenge because Spanish does not have words that end in consonant clusters. Based on this feature, Spanish-speaking children, and possibly most children in early childhood, may tend to simplify a final consonant cluster in English. For example, the word *board* might become *boar*.

Stages of Reading Development

A vast amount of research has been conducted on the stages of reading development. There are three widely used labels for these stages: emergent readers, early readers, and fluent readers. It is important to note that researchers have concluded that these stages are considered to be cumulative (Chall, 1983); that is, children need to develop the skills and knowledge in each of these stages to be used in subsequent ones.

Emergent Readers

Emergent readers understand that print contains meaningful information. They imitate the reading process and display basic reading readiness skills like directionality movement (i.e., eye movement from top to bottom and from left to right). Emergent readers can participate in shared reading activities and are able to follow and match words with their pronunciation when teachers point to the words as they are read. Additionally, children at this stage:

- Use illustrations embedded in the texts to support comprehension.

- Listen and follow a story attentively and can easily develop an awareness of the story structure.

- Represent the main idea of a story through drawings and can retell major events in the story with or without illustrations.

- Use illustrations and prior experiences to make predictions and to support comprehension.

- Possess some degree of phonemic awareness.

- Are able to connect the initial letter of a word with its representing phoneme.

Early Readers

Early readers have mastered reading readiness skills and are beginning to read simple text with some degree of success. They are also developing an internal list of high-frequency words in print. Their reliance on picture clues has decreased now that they can get more information from print. Children at this stage also:

- Begin using the cuing system to confirm information in the text.

- Rely on graphophonemic information to sound out words as a decoding strategy.

- Show preference for certain stories.

- Begin noticing features from language and text such as punctuation and capitalization, as well as the use of bold print and variation in format.

- Retell with detail and accuracy stories that they have read.

- Engage in discussion of stories read and identify the main idea and story characters.

- Engage in self-correction when text does not make sense to them.

Newly Fluent Readers

Newly fluent readers can read with relative fluency and comprehension. They are able to use several cuing systems to obtain meaning from print (i.e., semantic, structural, visual, and graphophonemic cuing systems). They self-monitor their reading, and can identify and correct simple errors with minimum external support. They ask clarification questions to develop an understanding of the content. Newly fluent readers can also:

- Summarize the part of the story that they have read, and make inferences about the content.

- Handle more challenging vocabulary through the use of context clues.

- Begin using literary terms and grammar concepts.

- Enjoy reading from a variety of genres for information and for pleasure.

Children at this stage are not totally independent readers, but with practice and support from teachers, they soon become fluent and independent readers.

Using Technology to Foster Early Literacy

The classroom teacher should be able to promote students' early literacy development skills through the use of technology and applications, e.g., by making use of smartphones, tablets, and e-readers. The following suggestions are ways that this might be effectively accomplished in the early literacy classroom:

- Reading e-books repeatedly.

- Listening to digital audio books to practice listening to fluent reading. Students can also read along with the audiobook.

- Using apps such as *Starfall* that focus on alphabetic knowledge, phonics and other letter–sound focused digital learning tools.

Knowledge and Use of Literacy Assessment

There are two main types of assessment: formal and informal. Both have a place in the classroom, particularly in the literacy classroom. The effective teacher understands the importance of ongoing assessment as an instructional tool and uses both informal and formal assessment measures to understand students' learning in his or her classroom. Children should never be grouped permanently on the basis of one assessment, either formal or informal. Rather, any grouping of students should come about after the consideration of several assessments, and the grouping should be flexible enough to consider individual differences among the students in each group.

Additionally, technology now allows assessments to be done via computer, eliminating the need for paper and pencil. This can potentially provide quicker feedback for both student and instructor, while facilitating the learning process for both informal and formal assessments. Increasingly, there is a shift toward electronic assessments, including e-portfolios and digital tools such as analytics.

Informal Assessments

Teachers can learn valuable information by simply observing their students at work. Many school districts use a type of inventory/report card to inform adults at home about the progress their children are making. Experienced teachers usually develop, through trial and error, their own means of assessing the skills of students in their classes. Almost every book on teaching reading and writing contains its own informal tests. Teachers can also develop their own informal reading assessment. The purpose of these assessments is to collect meaningful information about what students can and cannot do. A **running record** (Clay, 2002) is a way to assess students' word identification skills, accuracy, and fluency in oral reading. In a running record, the teacher uses a copy of the page to mark each word the child mispronounces as the teacher listens to a student read a text. The teacher writes the incorrect word over the printed word, draws a line through each word the child skips, and draws an arrow under repeated words. Through informal observations and through the use of inventories (formal and informal), teachers should be able to determine the **learning styles** of their students. Student learning styles play an important role in determining classroom structure.

Formal Assessments

Formal measures may include teacher-made tests, district exams, and standardized tests. Both formative and summative evaluations are part of effective instruction. **Formative evaluation** occurs during the process of learning when the teacher or the students monitor progress while it is still possible to modify instruction. **Summative evaluation** occurs at the end of a specific time span or course of study. Usually, a summative evaluation applies a single grade or score to represent a student's performance.

The effective teacher uses a variety of formal assessment techniques. Teacher-made instruments are ideally developed at the same time as the planning of goals and outcomes, rather than at the last minute after the completion of the lessons. Carefully planned objectives and assessment instruments serve as lesson development guides for the teacher. Paper-and-pencil tests are the most common method for evaluating student progress.

Criterion-Referenced Tests

In **criterion-referenced tests (CRTs)**, the teacher attempts to measure each student against uniform objectives or criteria. CRTs allow for the possibility that all students can score 100 percent on the test if they understand the concepts being tested. Teacher-made tests should be criterion-referenced because the teacher should develop them to measure the achievement of predetermined outcomes for the course. If teachers have properly prepared lessons based on the outcomes and, if students have mastered the outcomes, then scores on CRTs should be high. In this type of test, students are not in competition with each other for a high score, and there is no limit to the number of students who can score well. Some commercially developed tests are criterion-referenced; however, most are norm-referenced.

Norm-Referenced Tests

The purpose of a **norm-referenced test (NRT)** is to compare the performance of groups of students. This type of test is competitive because a limited number of students can score well. A plot of NRT scores resembles a bell-shaped curve, with most scores clustering around the center, and a few scores at each end. The midpoint is the average of test data; and, therefore, half of the population will score above average and half will score below average. The bell-shaped curve is a mathematical description of the results of tossing coins. As such, it represents the chance or normal distribution of skills, knowledge, or events across the general population. A percentile score (not to be confused with a percentage) is a way of reporting a student's NRT score. The percentile score indicates the percentage of the population whose scores fall at or below the student's score. For example, a group score at the 80th percentile means that the group scored as well as or better than 80 percent of the students who took the test. A student with a score at the 50th percentile has an average score. Percentile scores rank students from highest to lowest. By themselves, percentile scores do not indicate how well the student has mastered the content objectives. Raw scores indicate how many questions the student answered correctly and are, therefore, useful in computing a percentage score. The Texas Education Agency has a comprehensive list of approved norm-referenced tests that districts can choose from to assess achievement of students in the state.

Performance-Based Assessment

Some states and districts are moving toward **performance-based tests**, which assess students on how well they perform certain tasks. Students must use higher-level thinking skills to apply, analyze, synthesize, and evaluate ideas and data. For example, a performance-based assessment might require students to read a problem, design and carry out a laboratory experiment, and then write summaries of their findings. The performance-based assessment would evaluate both the processes students used and the output they produced. An English performance-based test might ask students to first read a selection of literature and then write a critical analysis. Performance-based assessments allow students to be creative in solutions to problems or questions, and it requires them to use higher-level skills. During these assessments, students work on content-related problems and use skills that are useful in various contexts. There are weaknesses in this approach, however. This type of assessment can be time-consuming. Performance-based assessments often require multiple resources, which can be expensive. Teachers must receive training in applying the findings of the test. Nonetheless, many schools consider performance-based testing to be a more authentic measure of student achievement than traditional tests.

Classroom Tests

Teachers must consider fundamental professional and technical factors when constructing effective classroom tests. One of the first factors to recognize is that test construction is as creative, challenging, and important as any aspect of teaching. The planning and background that contribute to effective teaching are incomplete unless evaluation of student performance provides accurate feedback to the teacher and the student about the learning process.

Good tests are the product of careful planning, creative thinking, hard work, and technical knowledge about the various methods of measuring student knowledge and performance. Classroom tests that accomplish their purpose are the result of the development of a pool of items and refinement of those items based on feedback and constant revision. It is through this process that evaluation of students becomes valid and reliable. Tests serve as a valuable instructional aid because they help determine student progress and also provide feedback to teachers regarding their own effectiveness. Student misunderstandings and problems that the tests reveal can help the teacher understand areas of special concern in providing instruction. This information also becomes the basis for the remediation of students and the revision of teaching procedures. Consequently, the construction, administration, and proper scoring of classroom tests are among the most important activities in teaching.

Authentic Assessments

These days, paper-and-pencil tests and essay tests are hardly the only methods of assessment. Other assessments include projects, observations, checklists, anecdotal records, portfolios, self-assessments, and peer assessments. Although these types of assessments often take more time and effort to plan and administer, they can often provide a more authentic measurement of student progress.

Essay Tests

There are advantages and disadvantages to essay tests. Advantages of essay questions include the potential for students to be creative in their answers and explain their responses. Essay questions also allow for testing of higher-level thinking skills. Disadvantages of essay questions include the time students need to formulate meaningful responses, and the time teachers need to evaluate the essays. In addition, language difficulties can make essay tests extremely difficult for some students, including ELLs. Consistency in evaluating essays can also be a problem for some teachers, but an outline of the acceptable answers—a scoring rubric—can help teachers avoid grading inconsistency. Teachers who write specific questions and know what they are looking for are more likely to be consistent in grading. Also, if there are several essay questions, the effective teacher grades all student responses to the first question, then moves on to all responses to the second, and so on.

Using Rubrics for Assessment

A **rubric** is a checklist with assigned point values. To construct a rubric, teachers use the lesson objectives. Students should receive an explanation of the rubric *before* starting to work on their writing assignment, and they can use the rubric as a guideline while they are preparing their writing assignment. Teachers can use the rubric to evaluate the completed assignment. Then teachers can provide clear, well-planned instructions and guidelines for activities; these can significantly decrease student frustration. Rubrics can provide this valuable guidance. When teachers model what they expect and state clear objectives or goals for each assignment, students perform better. Accordingly, there should be a clear and obvious link between the assignment's goals and the students' achievement.

Ongoing Assessment

Ongoing assessment provides teachers with updated information about the progress and challenges that children are facing in writing. This information can then be easily incorporated in daily instruction.

Monitoring Reading Comprehension with Retellings

Story retelling is a strategy used with children to assess listening and reading comprehension. This strategy can also assess sentence structure knowledge, vocabulary, speaking ability, and knowledge about the structure of stories. An informal or more structured checklist can be used to assess a student's comprehension, sentence structure knowledge, and vocabulary development as they retell a story. Any checklist for listening comprehension should assess the ability of the child to (Lapp et al., 2001):

1. Retell the story with details.

2. Show evidence of comprehension of the story line and plot, including the characters, setting, author's intention, and literal and implied meaning.

3. Show evidence that the child understood major ideas and the ideas that support it.

4. Bring background information to the selection.

5. Analyze and make judgments based on facts.

6. Retell the selection in sentences that make grammatical sense.

7. Retell the story using sentences that include standard usage of verbs, adjectives, conjunctions, and compound sentences.

8. Use a rich and meaningful vocabulary with minimal use of slang and colloquial expressions.

9. Adapt spoken language for various audiences, purposes, and occasions.

10. Listen for various purposes including critical listening to evaluate a speaker's message, and listening to enjoy and appreciate spoken language.

COMPETENCY 003: WORD IDENTIFICATION SKILLS AND READING FLUENCY

The teacher understands the importance of word identification skills (including decoding, blending, structural analysis and sight word vocabulary) and reading fluency and provides many opportunities for students to practice and improve word identification skills and reading fluency.

The beginning teacher:

A. Understands that many students develop word analysis skills and reading fluency in a predictable sequence and recognizes that individual variations occur.

B. Understands differences in students' development of word identification skills and reading fluency and knows instructional practices for meeting students' individual needs in these areas.

C. Understands the connection of word identification skills and reading fluency to reading comprehension.

D. Knows the continuum of word analysis skills in the statewide curriculum and grade-level expectations for attainment of these skills.

E. Knows how students develop fluency in oral and silent reading.

F. Understands that fluency involves rate, accuracy and intonation and knows the norms for reading fluency that have been established in the Texas Essential Knowledge and Skills (TEKS) for various age and grade levels.

G. Knows factors affecting students' word identification skills and reading fluency (e.g., home language, vocabulary development, learning disability).

H. Understands important phonetic elements and conventions of the English language.

I. Knows a variety of informal and formal procedures for assessing students' word identification skills and reading fluency on an ongoing basis and uses appropriate assessments to monitor students' performance in these areas and to plan instruction for individual students, including English-language learners (in accordance with the ELPS).

J. Analyzes students' errors in word analysis and uses the results of this analysis to develop and adjust future instruction.

K. Applies norms and expectations for word identification skills and reading fluency, as specified in the Texas Essential Knowledge and Skills (TEKS), to evaluate students' reading performance.

L. Knows how to use ongoing assessment of word identification skills and reading fluency to determine when a student needs additional help or intervention to bring the student's performance to grade level, based on state content and performance standards for reading in the Texas Essential Knowledge and Skills (TEKS).

M. Knows strategies for decoding increasingly complex words, including using the alphabetic principle, structural cues (e.g., prefixes, suffixes, roots) and syllables, and for using syntax and semantics to support word identification and confirm word meaning.

N. Selects and uses instructional strategies, materials, activities and models to teach students to recognize high-frequency irregular words (e.g., by completing analogies, identifying meanings of foreign words commonly used in written English, identifying and explaining idioms and multiple-meaning words) to promote students' ability to decode increasingly complex words and to enhance word identification skills for students reading at different levels.

O. Selects and uses appropriate instructional strategies, materials, activities and models to improve reading fluency for students reading at different levels (e.g., having students read independent-level texts, engage in repeated reading activities, use self-correction).

Word analysis refers to the way children approach a written word in order to decode and obtain meaning from it. Vocabulary building is a skill that needs to be practiced daily in the classroom. One of the goals of this is to assist children in becoming skillful in rapid word recognition. Research suggests that fluent word identification needs to be accomplished before a child can readily comprehend text. If a child needs to painstakingly analyze many words in a text, the memory and attention needed for comprehension are absorbed by word analysis, and the pleasure in a good story is lost. Typically, children who are beginning readers decode each word as they read it. Through repeated exposure to the same words, instant-recognition vocabulary grows. It is particularly important that developing readers learn to recognize words that occur very frequently in print. These words are called sight words.

Vocabulary is an especially important area for English language learners (Kieffer & Lesaux, 2007). Instruction and assessment that focuses on fluency and word identification that is designed with ELLs in mind should be in accordance with the English Language Proficiency Standards.

Sequence of Word Analysis Instruction

Phonics is a method of teaching beginners to read and pronounce words by teaching them the phonetic value of letters, letter groups, and syllables. Because English has an alphabetic writing system, an understanding of the letter–sound relationship may prove helpful to the beginning reader. However, this view of reading instruction is that these relationships should be taught in isolation, in a highly sequenced manner, followed by reading words that represent the regularities of English in print. The children are asked to read decodable texts by sounding out words. Typically, this approach uses reading programs that offer stories with controlled vocabulary that are made up of letter–sound relationships and words with which children are already familiar.

Teaching children to use phonics is different from teaching them about phonics. In summary, the skills-based approach begins reading instruction with a study of single letters, letter sounds, blends and digraphs, blends and digraph sounds, and vowels and vowel sounds in isolation, all in a highly sequenced manner. The children read and write decodable words, with a great emphasis on reading each word accurately, as opposed to reading to comprehend the text as a whole. More information about the TEKS standards as they relate to word study and spelling can be found at the Texas Education Agency website: *www.tea.state.tx.us*.

Dolch Words

In 1948 Edward W. Dolch identified 220 of the most frequently used words in the English language. He believed that if children were exposed to these words and learned to recognize them as sight words, they would become fluent readers. Some examples of Dolch words are *a*, *an*, *am*, *at*, *can*, *had*, *has*, *ran*, *the*, *after*, *but*, *got*, and *away*. The introduction of these sight words can expedite the decoding process and develop fluency among early readers.

Decoding Clues

In addition to working on placing sight words into readily available memory, there is sound research suggesting that students can use **context clues** to help identify unknown words. This body of research further suggests that instruction can help improve students' use of context clues. There are three main kinds of context clues: **semantic, syntactic, and structural**.

Semantic Clues

Semantic clues require a child to think about the meanings of words and what they already know about the topic being read. For example, when reading a story about hawks, teachers can help children to activate prior knowledge about the bird, and to develop an expectation that the selection may contain words associated with hawks, such as *predator*, *carnivorous*, *food chain*, and *wingspan*. This discussion might help a child gain a sense of what might be reasonable in a sentence. For ELLs who might not be familiar with the hawk, teachers need to identify equivalent species from their geographical area.

Syntactic Clues

The word order in a sentence might also provide clues to readers. For example, in the sentence opening with, "Hawks are," the order of the words in the sentence indicates that the missing word must be an adjective. This open-ended sentence can lead students to words such as *carnivorous*, *predators,* or other descriptors for the bird. Furthermore, illustrations in the book can often help with the identification of a word. A picture of a hawk eating prey can lead students to the words *predator* or *carnivorous.* Still, context clues are often not specific enough to allow students to predict the exact word. However, when context clues are combined with other clues such as phonics and structural clues, accurate word identification is usually possible.

Structural Clues

Another strategy to provide clues to readers is to pay attention to morphemes, which are many groups of letters that frequently occur within words. These specific clusters of letters can be taught. Common **derivational morphemes** in the form of prefixes, suffixes, and **inflectional endings** should be pointed out to students. An analysis of derivational and inflectional endings follows.

Most of the **derivational morphemes** come from foreign languages like Greek and Latin, and they represent relatively consistent meanings. For example, the meaning of the prefixes *pre-, anti-,* and *sub-* is very consistent in English and in other languages; namely *pre-* = before, *anti-* = against, and *sub-* = under. A large number of English prefixes are common to multiple Western languages such as Spanish, French, and German. See Table 3.4 below for examples in English and Spanish. Derivational morphemes can change the syntactic classification of the word. That is, by adding a morpheme to a word, it can be changed from a verb to a noun or from an adjective to an adverb. Children who are guided to recognize derivational morphemes will have a definite advantage when decoding words.

Table 3.4
Examples of Common Prefixes in English and Spanish

Roots	Meaning	Words in English	Words in Spanish
bio	life	symbiosis	simbiosis
phobia (fobia)	fear of	xenophobia	xenofobia
phono (fono)	sound	phonetics	fonética
photo (foto)	light	photography	fotografía
geo	land, earth	geology	geología

Inflectional morphemes do not change the syntactic classification and typically follow derivational morphemes in a word. These are native to English and always function as suffixes. English has eight inflectional endings.

1. Short plural **-s,** e.g., two *cars,* three *pens*

2. Long plural **-s.** Use long plurals after *ch, sh, s, z,* and *x,* e.g., *churches, washes, cases,* and *boxes*

3. Third person singular **s**, e.g., Mary *walks* quickly.

4. Possessive **-'s**, e.g., *Martha's* boy

5. Progressive **-ing**, e.g., She is *walking*. The gerund is not included in this group, i.e., **Walking** is good for your health.

6. Regular past tense **-ed**, e.g., He *worked* very hard.

7. Past participle **-en** or **-ed**, e.g., She has *beaten* the system, or It has been *ruined*.

Comparative and superlative adjectives are used to compare two or more things or people. Such adjectives are usually created by adding **-er (better)** and **-est (best)**, e.g., "Alex Rodríguez is **better** than Derek Jeter," or "He is the rich**est** player in the major leagues." Understanding the meaning of these morphemes can enhance students' decoding and comprehension skills. The ability to rapidly and accurately associate sounds with a cluster of letters leads to more rapid and efficient word identification. As young readers build an increasing repertoire of words they can recognize with little effort, they can use the words they know to help them recognize other, possibly related words that are unfamiliar. The best way to help students gain skill in word recognition is to have them read and write.

As children read and reread texts of their own choice, they have many opportunities to successfully decode a word, and realize that each time a letter combination such as *c-a-t* is found in the selection, it's read as *cat*. With each exposure to that word, the child reads it more easily. A child who writes a sentence with that word is developing a greater sensitivity to meaning or context clues. The child attempting to spell that word is reviewing and applying what he knows about letter–sound associations.

Words That Can Create Comprehension Problems

There are words that children can decode but whose meaning may elude them. Such words presenting this difficulty include homonyms and homophones. **Homonyms** have the same sound and the same spelling but differ in meaning. They are common in the content areas and can create comprehension problems. Context determines the meaning of such words. Examples of homonyms are presented in Table 3.5.

**Table 3.5
Examples of Homonyms**

Word	Meaning 1	Meaning 2
Club	A place to socialize	A wooden stick
Fine	To imply good or okay	A penalty
Bank	A place where money is stored	Margins of a river
Rock	A stone	Type of music

Homophones are words that sound the same but are spelled differently and have different meanings. Examples of homophones are *blew* and *blue*, *cents* and *sense*, *heir* and *air*, *wait* and *weight*, *hear* and *here*, *eight* and *ate*, *to*, *two*, and *too*, *there* and *their*, *deer* and *dear*, and *hair* and *hare*. **Homographs** are yet another source of difficulty, because they're spelled the same but have more than one pronunciation as well as different meanings. For example, the word *bow* has two pronunciations—the first referring to the front part of a ship or the way that people bend to salute, the second referring to a decorative knot used in clothing or as part of gift wrapping. Consider the use of the word in the following sentence: The Japanese ambassador wore a red **bow**, stood on the **bow** of the ship and graciously **bowed** to the audience.

Compound words are created when two independent words are joined to create a new word. Often, knowing the meaning of the two words will guide students to understand the meaning of the compound word. For example, the compound word *birdhouse* is composed of the words *bird* and *house*. Armed with this information, children can understand that the new word refers to a refuge or literally a house for birds. However, there are some examples of compound words in which the two words can create confusion for children. Examples of these deceptive compound words are *butterfly*, *nightmare*, and *brainstorm*.

Teaching Word Identification by Completing Analogies: Students can be taught to use words they already know as clues in discerning how to pronounce new words. Patricia Cunningham, in the book *Phonics They Use* (Pearson, 2012), names the practice of reading by rimes as decoding by analogy. For instance, if the teacher were to focus on the rime pattern of words that end in "-at" by teaching the words in the "-at" family, students can learn to decode, and even spell, by analogy. If students can read "-at", they can be taught to read and write "sat," "fat," "mat," "cat," "hat," etc.

Identifying Meanings of Foreign Words Commonly Used In Written English: Students can learn the etymology or origin of common English words of foreign origin. English words can draw from French, Spanish, Sanskrit, Chinese, and other languages.

Identifying and Explaining Idioms: Idiomatic phrase or expressions are not literally true. These can be especially difficult for English language learners to fully comprehend when learning English. Examples include:

- Can't judge a book by its cover.

- Don't cry over spilt milk.

- Off the record

Multiple-meaning Words: Some words carry multiple meanings depending on their context and purpose.

Assessing Word Identification

Miscue Analysis

Miscue analysis is an assessment procedure to assess oral reading (Clay, 2002). Miscues refer to any deviation from text made during oral reading. Here is the procedure for its implementation:

- Select reading material slightly above the current reading level of the child. The complete story should be about 500 words in length.

- Provide a copy of the selection to the child.

- Get a copy of the selection that is triple-spaced to allow room to write comments.

- Record the reading.

- Provide instructions to the child, and tell the student that you cannot help him or her during the reading.

- Ask questions about the story.

- Let the reader listen to the recording and then analyze it.

- Look for consistent miscues and pay special attention to initial and final clusters/blends and digraphs.

Correcting a Student's Miscues During Oral Reading

Teachers can provide feedback and assistance to students as they read aloud. If you hear a meaning-changing error, wait to see whether he/she self-corrects it. If he/she finishes the sentence or paragraph without self-correcting, try one of these **scaffolding tools:**

- Ask, "Does that make sense?"

- Help the student to recognize visual and phonetic cues. Ask, "Do you see any word parts/ chunks that you recognize?"

- Give nonverbal cues. For example, scaffold with gestures by pointing to the word or its first letter.

- Suggest starting the sentence again. Say, "Try that again."

- Quickly supply the word to keep the flow going, if needed.

Other Factors that Affect Word Analysis and Spelling

Various factors affect students' ability to identify words. Home factors can affect oral language vocabulary, receptive vocabulary, and other issues related to word identification.

The classic study by Hart and Risley (1995) suggests there are discrepancies in vocabulary across different socioeconomic classes. To compound this gap in language and vocabulary, the phenomenon of the Matthew Effect impacts students' reading achievement (Stanovich, 1986). According to Stanovich, good readers, already fluent and skilled at reading text, become better readers, while poor readers become worse. According to Chall and colleagues (1990), this slump in achievement in reading after 4th grade can be largely attributed to this gap in vocabulary and limited skill in fluently reading text. The school therefore becomes a crucial site of learning for academic vocabulary; this is especially the case for students in poverty (Chall et al., 1990).

Reading Fluency

Reading fluency is the ability to decode words quickly and accurately in order to read text with the appropriate word stress, pitch, and intonation pattern (or prosody). Reading fluency requires automaticity of word recognition and reading with prosody to facilitate comprehension. **Automaticity** is the quick and accurate recognition of letters, words, and language conventions. Automaticity is achieved through continuous practice using texts written at the child's reading level..

Fluency and Comprehension

Fluency is a prerequisite for language comprehension. Children struggling with fluency devote their time to mastering their language skills, which is an effort that takes away from the concentration they should be placing on reading comprehension. When students read aloud in class, the main purpose of the activity is to develop fluency. If after reading aloud, teachers ask the child comprehension questions, the child will most likely have to read the same passage silently to be able to respond to the questions. Thus, teachers should separate these two activities—read silently for comprehension and read aloud to promote fluency.

What Is the Expectation?

The typical child in first grade should be able to read about 60 words correct per minute (wcpm) and the rate should increase by 10 words in each successive grade, i.e., second grade (70 wcpm), third grade (80 wcpm), and fourth grade (90 wcpm). To determine the number of words that are read correctly per minute, a simple formula is used—namely, words read in one minute minus errors equals words per minute. The expectation is that children in the first to fourth grades will be able to read independently with minimum difficulty, i.e., finding no more than one in 20 words difficult. Students in middle school should be reading at about 120–150 wcpm (Denton et al., 2007).

How Do We Teach Fluency?

Teachers can use several strategies to promote reading fluency. Descriptions of these strategies follow.

Guided Oral Repeated Reading

Teachers can promote opportunities for **guided oral repeated reading** using text at the child's reading level. Teachers, parents, and peers can provide support and feedback for these students. Allow the child to read the same story repeatedly to develop fluency.

Choral Reading

Reading "in group" is another activity used to promote reading fluency. This activity is ideal for ELLs and struggling readers because pronunciation and fluency problems will not be publicly noticed and these readers can use the model provided by more fluent readers.

Pairing Students

Pairing proficient readers with ELLs or struggling readers can benefit both groups— the proficient child receives additional practice reading, and the ELLs and struggling readers are able to listen to fluent readers. ELLs and struggling readers can also read to their partners and receive input.

Interactive Computer Programs

Using interactive reading programs can provide individualized reading support for children. These computer programs often contain colorful pictures and interesting stories. The child should have the option of clicking on the words or pictures in order to have the selected word read aloud or to get animation illustrating the word's meaning. The program can also read a story at normal speed while the child follows the highlighted words in a printed text.

Silent Sustained Reading (SSR)

While the primary goal of Silent Sustained Reading (SSR) is to boost reading comprehension, guiding the child to read silently and continuously for about 20 minutes a day can definitely improve reading fluency. Students might need assistance in learning how to select a book that is appropriate for them and that they will find interesting. Books should be appropriately challenging.

Readers' Theatre

Readers' Theatre has been used successfully to emphasize reading fluency. In this activity, a story is modified so that students are reading a scripted play. Students rehearse their reading part and then create a theatre format to present the reading. Children enjoy this new approach and it improves reading fluency.

Developing Reading Fluency

Pointing to words while reading helps students see the letter–sound correspondence; however, this practice can also affect the development of reading fluency. Second graders should be guided to discontinue this practice. Continuous monitoring of reading fluency is required to ensure children develop and maintain reading fluency when they are exposed to more challenging text. To be sure that students maintain reading fluency, teachers can conduct individual assessment using teacher-developed checklists or timed readings.

Assessing Reading Fluency

A running record is an assessment strategy designed by Marie Clay (2002) to assess students' word identification skills and fluency in oral reading. As the teacher listens to a student read a page, the teacher uses a copy of the page or a blank page to mark each word the child miscues on while reading. The teacher writes the incorrect word over the printed word, draws a line through each word the child skips, and draws an arrow under repeated words. In this activity teachers can identify the type of miscues made and can then provide additional support to individual learners.

Timed Readings

Because there are three key components of fluency instruction: rate, accuracy, and expression (prosody), each aspect can be evaluated. Typically, students are assessed for fluency through timed one-minute readings. Students should generally be reading at or above grade-level norms for wcpm (words correct per minute). Any words read incorrectly are subtracted from the number of words read aloud accurately in one minute. Students can graph their fluency rates as a visual sign of progress. To assess expression in reading, teachers can informally observe and monitor student's use of expression or prosody in their oral reading.

Two other ways to support oral reading include **echo reading** and **choral reading**. In echo reading, the teacher models the page or sentence of text at the student's instructional reading level and then asks the student(s) to echo or repeat the reading of the same text. These continue until the students can build fluency and are able to read the text independently (Rasinksi, 2003). In choral reading, students read together at the same time in unison. This is best done in small groups. Other research-based ways to **build fluency** include independent reading and assisted reading (having students listen to an audio book).

Independent reading is a crucial component of a balanced literacy program. Students can read alone or with partners for extra support.

To review, the key components of balanced reading include:

- Read Aloud

- Shared Reading

- Guided Reading

- Independent Reading

This means teachers are reading **TO children** to model the reading process, **WITH children** to provide support in the reading process, and children are reading **BY themselves** to practice and develop fluency and automaticity (Mooney, 1990). Matching students to the right text is essential for independent reading.

COMPETENCY 004: READING COMPREHENSION AND ASSESSMENT

The teacher understands the importance of reading for understanding, knows components and processes of reading comprehension and teaches students strategies for improving their comprehension.

The beginning teacher:

A. Understands reading comprehension as an active process of constructing meaning.

B. Understands the continuum of reading comprehension skills in the statewide curriculum and grade-level expectations for these skills.

C. Understands factors affecting students' reading comprehension (e.g., oral language development, word analysis skills, prior knowledge, language background, previous reading experiences, fluency, vocabulary development, ability to monitor understanding, characteristics of specific texts).

D. Knows characteristics of informal and formal reading comprehension assessments (e.g., criterion-referenced state tests, curriculum-based reading assessments, informal reading inventories, norm-referenced tests).

E. Selects and uses appropriate informal and formal assessments to monitor and evaluate students' reading comprehension.

F. Analyzes student errors and provides focused instruction in reading comprehension based on the strengths and needs of individual students, including English-language learners (in accordance with the ELPS).

G. Knows how to use ongoing assessment to determine when a student needs additional help or intervention to bring the student's performance to grade level, based on state content and performance standards for reading in the Texas Essential Knowledge and Skills (TEKS).

H. Understands metacognitive skills, including self-evaluation and self-monitoring skills, and teaches students to use these skills to enhance their own reading comprehension.

I. Knows how to determine students' independent, instructional and frustration reading levels and uses this information to select and adapt reading materials for individual students and to guide their selection of independent reading materials.

J. Uses various instructional strategies to enhance students' reading comprehension (e.g., linking text content to students' lives and prior knowledge, connecting related ideas across different texts, engaging students in guided and independent reading, guiding students to generate questions and apply knowledge of text topics).

K. Knows how to provide students with direct, explicit instruction in the use of strategies to improve their reading comprehension (e.g., previewing, self-monitoring, visualizing, retelling, summarizing, paraphrasing, inferring, identifying text structure).

L. Uses various communication modes (e.g., written, oral) to promote students' reading comprehension.

M. Understands levels of reading comprehension and how to model and teach literal, inferential and evaluative comprehension skills.

N. Knows how to provide instruction to help students increase their reading vocabulary.

O. Understands reading comprehension issues for students with different needs and knows effective reading strategies for those students.

P. Knows the difference between guided and independent practice in reading and provides students with frequent opportunities for both.

Q. Knows how to promote students' development of an extensive reading and writing vocabulary by providing them with many opportunities to read and write.

Helping students read for understanding is the central goal of reading instruction. Comprehension is a complex process involving the text, the reader, the situation, and the purpose for reading. There are a number of factors that come into play as a child attempts to comprehend a passage. First, students cannot understand texts if they cannot read the words. Thus, a teacher who is interested in improving students' comprehension skills needs to teach them to decode well. In addition, children need time during the school day to read texts that are easy for them to read, and also have time to discuss what has been read. Children need to read and reread easy texts often enough that decoding becomes rapid, easy, and accurate. It has been noted frequently in the literature that children who comprehend well have bigger vocabularies than children who struggle with reading. In part, this is true because their knowledge of vocabulary develops through contact with new words as they read text that is rich in new words. However, it has also been suggested that simply teaching vocabulary in isolation does not automatically enhance comprehension.

As instruction is designed with English Language Learners in mind, it is essential that it is planned in accordance with the English Language Proficiency Standards (ELPS). Keep in mind that vocabulary is a crucial component of comprehension for English Language Leaners (Kieffer & Lesaux, 2007). The more vocabulary words children learn, the better they can read and understand what they've read. (Strickland & Snow, 2002, p. 62)

Continuum of Reading Comprehension Skills

You will need to browse the actual TEKS documents (English Language Arts and Reading) to look for comprehension TEKS for each of the grade levels covered in this test domain (grade levels 4–8). Specific grade-level TEKS that relate to comprehension can be found in the TEKS documents. The English Language Arts and Reading TEKS for all levels can be reviewed at the Texas Education Agency website at *www.tea.state.tx.us*. Many TEKS continue across grade levels while others introduced in later grades are at a more sophisticated level. You are responsible for learning the TEKS covered by your grade levels.

Background Knowledge

Reading comprehension can be affected by **prior knowledge**, and readers who possess rich prior knowledge about the topic of a reading often understand the reading better than classmates with less prior knowledge. A discrepancy between the schema intended by the author and the schema that the reader brings to the reading process can create confusion and comprehension problems. When students lack the background knowledge related to the topic(s) in a text, the teacher will need to build background knowledge and schema prior to reading the text.

Guided Practice and Independent Practice

Through a gradual release of responsibility (Pearson & Gallagher, 1983) and careful and strategic scaffolding, teachers can guide students to practice and apply specific reading strategies in their independent reading. In guided practice, teachers provide various types of support and resources. Scaffolding learners with guided support means working within their zone of proximal development, or what the students can do with the assistance of a peer or adult (Vygotsky, 1978). In independent practice, students have opportunities to practice and apply the skills and strategies they learned during modeling and guided practice. Students, through independent practice, practice reading skills with text that is at their instructional and independent reading level. Teachers should reinforce reading strategies and skills on an ongoing basis through both guided and independent practice.

Pre-Reading Activities

Prior knowledge affects students' interest in what they read and what they want to read about. Generally, students like to read about topics that are familiar to them. This is an area in which the skill of the teacher can play a significant role. Teachers should identify interests in children and find appropriate stories to match their interests. A teacher can also make a previously unfamiliar topic seem familiar through **pre-reading activities** during which prior knowledge is activated, new prior knowledge is formed, and interest is stirred up. Teachers of ELLs often have to spend more time in pre-reading activities than the actual time devoted to reading the stories as they need to review unknown vocabulary, assess students' understanding of terminology and then build on this newly formed knowledge to increase students' interest in what is about to be read.

Setting the Purpose for Reading

Effective teachers clearly set up a purpose for reading and ask the students to predict what the purpose of the text being read is. By doing so, both the teacher and the students can obtain and draw on students' prior knowledge about the topic. Making predictions about the upcoming text and then reading based on their predictions allows them to identify key points they need to pay attention to while reading. Children should be encouraged to generate questions about ideas in the text while reading. Successful teachers encourage children to also construct mental images representing ideas in the text, or to construct actual images from texts that lend themselves to this kind of activity.

Linking Prior Knowledge to New Knowledge

A successful teacher will help readers to process text containing new factual information through reading strategies, and to relate the new information to their prior knowledge. Questioning techniques is a simple but powerful mechanism to guide children to link current knowledge to new knowledge. Through questioning, teachers guide children to question the facts and the intent of the author, and also to check the answers through text verification. It is through conversation that children are able to compare their predictions and expectations about the content. It is also through these conversations that children see the need to revise their prior knowledge when encountering compelling new ideas are encountered that conflict with their prior knowledge. As part of these ongoing conversations, teachers will become alert to students who are applying the incorrect schema as they read, and will be able to encourage use of more appropriate knowledge. These conversations help children figure out the meanings of unfamiliar vocabulary words based on context clues, the opinions of others, and sometimes through the use of appropriate source materials such as glossaries, dictionaries, or an appropriate selection in another text. After reading activities, teachers should encourage children to revisit the text—to reread and make notes and paraphrase—in order to remember important points, interpret the text, evaluate its quality, and review important points. Children should also be encouraged to think about how ideas encountered in the text might be used in the future. As children gain competence, they enjoy showing what they know.

Integrating Reading, Writing, Listening, and Speaking

Conversation is a crucial component of integrating reading, writing, listening, and speaking towards the goal of developing comprehension. One research-based method to facilitate this with students in grades 4–8 is by implementing **reciprocal teaching** (Palincsar & Brown, 1984).

Reciprocal Teaching

Reciprocal teaching is a research-based method that develops comprehension (Palincsar & Brown, 1984). In small groups of four, students take on roles and practice four key comprehension strategies. The four strategies are:

1. summarizing

2. questioning

3. clarifying

4. predicting

The procedure is as follows:

- Students should be taught the four key roles prior to implementation in a small-group setting.

- With a shared text, and in small groups, students read to a pre-designated stopping point (usually a few paragraphs or a few sentences, depending on the grade and reading level of the students).

Students take turns doing the following activities, according to their designated role. Roles vary each time the students engage in reciprocal teaching. Reciprocal teaching can be used across the content areas anytime there is a shared text to be read.

- The summarizer highlights and synthesizes a few key ideas from the selected text.

- The questioner poses a higher-level or literal question or set of questions the group.

- The clarifier tries to clarify any confusing or unusual ideas in the text.

- The predictor makes a hypothesis about what will happen next. If it's non-fiction text, the predictor can guess what the author will write about next in the selection.

Comprehension Strategy Instruction

Comprehension and metacognitive strategy instruction is a crucial component of the reading process. The Texas Education Agency outlines for the middle grades a series of strategies that can be taught not only in English Language Arts, but in content areas as well, when students are reading and interacting with content-focused text.

Some of the strategies that should be directly and explicitly modeled and taught to students, modeled, and practiced include the following:

- **Previewing:** Students can be taught to browse the text to make predictions and connect to background knowledge, prior to reading.

- **Self-monitoring:** Students can be taught to stop periodically while reading and self-assess whether they are truly understanding what they are reading.

- **Summarizing:** Students can be taught to "chunk" the text and provide a concise summary of what was read. This can be done at the end of a paragraph, section, or chapter of text. Students can also annotate the text to take notes while reading and then write a summary from these notes.

- **Paraphrasing:** Students can be taught to put what they are reading into their own words.

- **Visualizing:** Students can be taught to create mental images of what they are reading.

- **Inferring:** Students can be taught to use clues from the text combined with what they know (prior knowledge) to form new ideas while reading. This is also known as drawing conclusions.

- **Identifying Text Structure:** Students can analyze and determine the type of text structure (e.g., sequential, compare and contrast, problem/solution, descriptive) to help them better understand the text. This is more typically used with non-fiction (expository) text.

Monitoring Comprehension

Children need to be taught to monitor their own comprehension and to decide when they need to exert more effort, or to apply a strategy to make sense of a text. The goal of comprehension instruction is for the child to reach a level at which the application of strategies becomes automatic. In summary, comprehension is maximized when readers are fluent in all the processes of skilled reading—from the decoding of words to the articulation and easy application of the comprehension strategies used by good readers. Therefore, teachers need to teach predicting, questioning, seeking clarification, relating to background knowledge, constructing mental images, and summarizing. The teaching of comprehension strategies has to be conceived as a long-term developmental process, and the teaching of all reading strategies is more successful if they are taught and used by all of the teachers on a staff. In addition, teachers need to allow time for in-school reading, and recognize that good texts are comprehended on a deep level only through rereading and meaningful discussions.

Assessing Comprehension

A frequent device for assessing comprehension is the use of oral or written questions. A question may be **convergent**, which indicates that only one answer is correct, or **divergent**, which indicates that more than one answer is correct. Most tests, however, include a combination of question types. Questioning, whether done formally, or informally, can be done to check for students' understanding of reading and listening comprehension.

Levels of Questioning

Generally, there are three levels of questions: literal, inferential, and applied. The state standardized test will cover the first two areas: literal and inferential types of questions. These three types of questions can be described as follows:

Literal questions: Questions that are easily answered and can be easily located within the text.

Inferential questions: Students must draw conclusions, e.g., about a feeling, a new idea; "reading between the lines."

Applied questions: These are creative questions that extend beyond the text, e.g., "So what does this mean for us?" or "What would you have done if you were _____?" Additionally, teachers can use *Bloom's Revised Taxonomy* (Bloom, 1956; Anderson and Krathwohl, 2001) to make sure they are asking questions from across the taxonomy.

Another device for checking on comprehension is a **cloze test**, or a passage with omitted words the test-taker must supply. The test-maker must decide whether to require the test-taker to supply the exact word or to accept synonyms. Passing scores reflect which type of answer is acceptable. If assessing an understanding of meaning is the intent of the exercise, the teacher might accept synonyms and not demand the surface-level constructs, or the exact word.

The **speed** at which a student reads helps in determining the level of comprehension, up to a point. The faster that a student reads, the better that student comprehends, with some limitations. In general, the slow reader who must analyze each word does not comprehend as well as the fast reader. It is possible, however, to read too fast. Most students have had the experience of having to reread materials. For example, a student reading a chapter in preparation for a test might read more slowly than when reading a short story for pleasure or reading to get the main idea of a story.

Semantic mapping (Nagy, 1988) can also be used as a strategy to make direct connections between the vocabulary or words they are learning in the classroom and those that they may have seen, heard or learned. The strategy generally works as follows:

1. The teacher puts a word or phrase representing the story in the middle of the board/ paper/transparency. The teacher can have preselected categories related to the central word (3–5 categories).

2. The teacher asks students to brainstorm related words in each category. The teacher also introduces words related to the text.

3. Students can also look through the text to locate more words that may fit with the key word or phrase. Related words that may appear in future readings can be included also.

4. In discussing the words, students can also talk about their personal connections with the book.

5. Have some categories ready to add to the organizer. Preselect key words from the text and/or related to the concept to introduce to the semantic map.

Teachers must find creative ways to enhance students' awareness of words. Teaching a word a day is not enough. Instead of relying on worksheets or textbooks, teachers can help expand students' vocabularies by:

- Reading aloud from a variety of texts.

- Planning thematic instruction in which students will encounter the same conceptually-related vocabulary in a variety of contexts and subject areas.

- Actively engaging students in a range of experiences such as field trips, projects, and/or science experiments, and providing new words associated with these experiences.

- Providing opportunities for students to role play or visually illustrate the meanings of new words.

Reading Levels

Reading specialists have identified three reading proficiency levels—independent, instructional, and frustration. If the student reads 95% of the words correctly, the book is at the child's **independent level**. If the student reads 90% to 94% of the words correctly, the book is at the child's **instructional level**, which means the child can perform satisfactorily with help from the teacher. If the student reads 89% or fewer words correctly, the book is probably at the child's **frustration level**. These reading levels are determined based on the ability of children to answer comprehension questions after reading passages, typically done with an informal reading inventory. Reading levels help the teacher to know whether the student is appropriately matched with the level of text he or she is reading. The ongoing assessments a teacher can conduct in the classroom such as comprehension questions, teacher-designed quizzes, informal reading inventories, and other informal assessments can help the teacher to determine whether a student is meeting the objectives of the state content and performance standards. If students are not meeting the objectives, materials can be retaught more explicitly.

Informal Reading Inventories

Informal reading inventories are informal assessment instruments designed to identify the reading levels of children. Most basal reader books contain some type of informal reading inventory. These are graded (by reading levels) passages that include **comprehension questions**. Teachers begin with a passage at the reading level of the child and continue increasing the complexity until the child is not able to respond to the comprehension questions.

Asking a child to **retell a story** is another type of informal assessment. The ability to retell a story is an informal type of assessment that is useful to the teacher, parent, and eventually, the child. Informal assessment measures can also include observations, journals, written drafts, and conversations. The teacher can then use this information to determine individual student's strengths and challenges in the area of comprehension. This data can be used in forming guided reading groups or in forming additional intervention groups beyond the regular classroom instruction.

The teacher may also make **observations** during individual or group work. Usually, the teacher makes a **checklist** of competencies, skills, or requirements, and then uses the list to check off the ones a student or group displays. A teacher wishing to emphasize interviewing skills could devise a checklist that includes personal appearance, mannerisms, confidence, and addressing the questions asked. A teacher who wants to emphasize careful listening might observe a discussion with a checklist that includes paying attention, not interrupting, summarizing the ideas of other members of the group, and asking questions about others.

Checklists give teachers the potential for capturing behaviors that cannot be accurately measured with a paper-and-pencil test, such as following the correct sequence of steps in a science experiment, or including all-important elements of a speech in class. One characteristic of a checklist that is both an advantage and a disadvantage is its structure, which provides consistency but inflexibility. However, an open-ended comment section at the end of a checklist can help overcome this disadvantage.

Anecdotal records are helpful in some instances, such as capturing the process a group of students' uses to solve a problem. These anecdotal records can be useful when giving feedback to the group. Students can also be taught to write explanations of the procedures they use for their projects or science experiments. One advantage of an anecdotal record is that it can include all relevant information. Disadvantages include the amount of time necessary to complete the record and the difficulty in assigning a grade. If the anecdotal record is used solely for feedback, no grade is necessary.

Developing Comprehension with Writing Journals

Teachers should provide students with many opportunities to read, write, and discuss what they have read. Drawing on ideas from reader-response theory (Rosenblatt, 1993), students can respond to literature in open-ended and interpretive ways by recording their thinking about the text in written response journals. Students can write in response to the text heard (through read-aloud) or a text the student reads in guided reading or independent reading. The teacher can use the student's journal writing as an informal assessment to gain insight into the student's understanding of the text. Students can do the following with written response journals that align with the Texas state standards:

- Write about their understanding

- Make inferences

- Predict

- Give reasons for the inferences they make

- Write about the author's use of craft and style

- Make connections to self, other text(s), and the world

Criterion-Referenced Tests: STAAR

The **State of Texas Assessments of Academic Readiness** (STAAR) is a basic skills testing program for children in grades 3 to 12. This criterion-referenced test series assesses the implementation and the mastery of the TEKS—the Texas state K-12 standards. The STAAR contains both literary and informational types of texts, so teachers should expose students to a broad array of text genres in the classroom. More information about the STAAR reading test can be found at the Texas Education Agency website at *www.tea.state.tx.us* under *"Testing/Accountability."*

Assessing English Language Learners

The Texas English Language Proficiency Assessment System (TELPAS) was designed to comply with the accountability system required in the No Child Left Behind (NCLB) Act (TEA, 2011) and continued in NCLB's successor, the Every Student Succeeds Act of 2015. The legislation requires that ELLs are assessed yearly in all language skills—listening, speaking, reading, and writing. The multiple-choice online reading test is an assessment that measures reading skills of ELLs.

The TELPAS is broken down into four levels: beginning, intermediate, advanced, and advanced high. To assess the writing component for ELLs in grades 2 through 12, writing samples are collected and assessed holistically at each of the four language levels. More information on the TELPAS assessment can be found at the Texas Education Agency website at *www.tea.state.tx.us* under *"Testing/Accountability"* and *"TELPAS."*

Interventions for Students Who Face Challenges

Students who face challenges in reading need more intensive support and intervention. Based on the data from the comprehension section of informal reading inventories and other formative and ongoing classroom assessment data, the teacher can develop targeted interventions in the area of comprehension for students below grade level for work with the reading specialist or other educational support person to develop these interventions. The following techniques can be helpful to students who need additional support in this area. Many of these techniques are beneficial for all students:

- Teachers can identify crucial concepts to be covered in the reading and activate prior knowledge about the topic (Caldwell & Leslie, 2005).

- Build background knowledge through visual scaffolds (video clips, internet, pictures, real objects). (Caldwell & Leslie, 2005).

- Implement vocabulary instruction throughout the reading process. (Caldwell & Leslie, 2005)

- Engage students in oral retellings. Model this technique to students using graphic organizers, checklists, or other aids to support retellings. (Caldwell & Leslie, 2005)

Students can learn successful strategies for developing comprehension by using these techniques, in addition to participating in smaller intervention groups that meet regularly with the teacher and/or reading specialist for more intensive intervention.

COMPETENCY 005: READING APPLICATIONS

The teacher understands reading skills and strategies appropriate for various types of texts and contexts and teaches students to apply these skills and strategies to enhance their reading proficiency.

The beginning teacher:

A. Understands skills and strategies for understanding, interpreting and evaluating different types of written materials, including narratives, expository texts, persuasive texts, technical writing and content-area textbooks.

B. Understands different purposes for reading and related reading strategies.

C. Knows and teaches strategies to facilitate comprehension of different types of text before, during and after reading (e.g., previewing, making predictions, questioning, self-monitoring, rereading, mapping, using reading journals, discussing texts).

D. Provides instruction in comprehension skills that support students' transition from "learning to read" to "reading to learn" (e.g., matching comprehension strategies to different types of text and different purposes for reading).

E. Understands the importance of reading as a skill in all content areas.

F. Understands the value of using dictionaries, glossaries and other sources to determine the meanings, pronunciations and derivations of unfamiliar words and teaches students to use these sources.

G. Knows how to teach students to interpret information presented in various formats (e.g., maps, tables, graphs) and how to locate, retrieve, and retain information from a range of texts and technologies.

H. Knows how to help students comprehend abstract content and ideas in written materials (e.g., by using manipulatives, examples, diagrams) and formulate, express and support responses to various types of texts.

I. Knows literary genres (e.g., historical fiction, poetry, myths, fables, drama) and their characteristics.

J. Knows literary nonfiction genres (e.g., biographies, memoirs) and their characteristics.

K. Recognizes a wide range of literature and other texts appropriate for students.

L. Provides multiple opportunities for students to listen and respond to a wide variety of children's and young people's literature, both fiction and nonfiction, and to recognize characteristics of various types of narrative and expository texts.

M. Understands and promotes students' development of literary response and analysis (e.g., formulating, expressing, and supporting responses to various types of literary texts) including teaching students elements of literary analysis (e.g., story elements, literary devices, figurative language, characterization, features of different literary genres, influences of historical and cultural contexts, themes and settings) and providing students with opportunities to apply comprehension skills to literature.

N. Selects and uses a variety of materials to teach students about authors, including the cultural, historical and contemporary contexts, and about different purposes for writing.

O. Provides students with opportunities to engage in silent reading and extended reading of a wide range of materials, including expository texts and various literary genres.

P. Engages students in varied reading experiences and encourages students to interact with others about their reading.

Q. Uses strategies to encourage reading for pleasure and lifelong learning.

R. Knows how to teach students strategies for selecting their own books for independent reading.

S. Uses technology to promote students' literacy and teaches students to use technology to access a wide range of appropriate narrative and expository texts.

Transition from "Learning to Read" to "Reading to Learn"

Children from pre-K to second grade spend much of the language arts portion of their day trying to decode and make sense of written language. The main purpose of this stage is to read for pleasure. Traditionally, short stories with pictures that have a specific structure and predictable story line are used to guide the child in the process of "learning to read." However, in the upper elementary grades, the needs of the children go beyond decoding and reading for pleasure, and "reading to learn" becomes the main task. The "reading to learn" stage requires students to decode written language, understand the content, and obtain vital information from the content. One important component of the process of "reading to learn" is to understand how text is organized in the content areas. Children need to identify key components of the organizational format and identify the type of information offered. Teachers have to guide children to notice and study the structure of text, including the table of contents, titles, subtitles, and headings.

Structure of Text

Students need to look closely at the structure of the text in order to comprehend it and understand the different purposes for reading. For instance, when reading narrative text, readers need to understand the components of narrative text and how they differ from the components and structures of expository text. To accomplish this task, skillful teachers guide the students through a picture, table, and graphic walk-through of the text while asking questions and pointing out useful text features to the students. Most texts have titles, subtitles, headings, glossaries, and bolded words. What techniques were used to make them stand out? Figuring out the structure of a text helps readers to read more efficiently. Children can anticipate what information will be revealed in a selection when they understand textual structure. Understanding the pattern of the text helps students organize ideas. Authors have a fairly short list of organizational patterns to choose from. The following are the most common patterns:

- **Chronological order** relates events in a temporal sequence from beginning to end.

- **Cause-and-effect relationships** between described events, with the causal factors identified or implied.

- **Problem description**, followed by solutions.

- **Comparisons and/or contrasts** to describe ideas to readers.

- **Sequential materials**, presented as a series of directions to be followed in a prescribed order.

Once children understand how information in the content areas is organized, they can become more efficient readers.

Content Area Literacy

Students in grades 4 to 8 are "reading to learn" (Chall, 1983). Even if the teacher specializes in a content area, they need to continue teaching students literacy skills so that students can be successful in reading expository text. Additionally, students should know how to use resources such as dictionaries, glossaries, and other tools to help them as they encounter unknown or lesser-known words. In addition, the Internet provides resources such as visual dictionaries and other multi-modal representations of words that can help students' develop conceptual understandings of technical content area vocabulary (e.g., in science, social studies, math, health, and other areas). The teaching and practice of academic vocabulary is especially important for ELLs.

The teacher should also help students to understand how to comprehend information that is in a representational format (e.g., maps, tables, graphs). Teachers can model and have students practice locating these types of resources in both text and digital resources. With increased use of digital literacies and technologies, many examples of these types of informational representations should be demonstrated to students. One way to point out these items of information in text to students is by doing shared reading where the teacher is reading the text aloud and pointing out text features, text structure, and format along the way.

Fluent Readers

Students in upper-primary and middle-school grades are reading across the content areas and encounter technical vocabulary in the types of texts they encounter in school. In this stage, students are:

- Developing an academic vocabulary.

- Reading broadly across both expository and narrative texts.

- Making inferences about more abstract concepts.

Becoming More Efficient Readers

Students with strong comprehension skills and decoding ability are now ready to become more efficient readers by practicing the techniques of scanning and skimming to get content information. In **scanning**, children are guided to look for specific information in text. Children are taught to use headings, indices, boldface and italics to guide them.

Reading Strategies

Identifying strategies used by proficient readers can help teachers make skillful choices of activities that will maximize student learning. Anne Goudvis and Stephanie Harvey (2000) offer suggestions for useful activities under the headings that follow.

Activating Prior Knowledge

Readers pay more attention when they can relate to the text. Readers naturally bring their prior knowledge and experience to reading, but they comprehend better when they think about the connections they make between the text, their lives, and the larger world. This strategy is especially important when teaching children from diverse cultural and linguistic backgrounds. Teachers need to explore the schemata necessary for children to understand the story and the background knowledge that children bring to the reading process. One of the strategies used to explore a child's background is the **KWL chart**. This is a chart that asks students to describe what they **K**now, **W**ant to know, **L**earned and still want to learn, or areas that the students did not understand that well. Because this is a class activity, children can benefit from what others already know, what others want to learn, and what areas were difficult for others.

Predicting or Asking Questions

Questioning is the strategy that keeps readers engaged. When readers ask questions, even before they read, they clarify understanding and forge ahead to make meaning. Asking questions is also at the heart of active reading. A variation of this strategy is to give students true-or-false questions about the content to be read. Once the students complete the questions, they then read to corroborate the answers.

Visualizing

Active readers create visual images based on the words they read in the text. These created pictures, in turn, enhance readers' understanding.

Drawing Inferences

Inferring is when the readers take what they know, garner clues from the text, and think ahead to make a judgment, discern a theme, or speculate about what is to come.

Determining Important Ideas

Thoughtful readers grasp essential ideas and important information when reading. Readers must differentiate between less important ideas and the key ideas that are central to the meaning of the text.

Synthesizing Information

Synthesizing information involves combining new information with existing knowledge to form an original idea or interpretation. Reviewing, sorting, and sifting important information can lead to new insights that change the way readers think.

Repairing Understanding

If confusion disrupts meaning, readers need to stop and clarify their understanding. Readers may use a variety of strategies to "fix" comprehension when meaning goes awry.

Confirming Predictions

As students read and after they have finished reading, they should confirm the predictions they originally made. One can confirm negatively or positively. Determining if a prediction is correct is a goal. A good strategy to practice this is to make a two-column "T-chart" where students can list predictions about the text prior to reading. Then, during reading, students can check off in the second column whether their confirmations were correct or incorrect.

Using Parts of a Book

Students should use the various parts of a book such as the charts, diagrams, indexes, and table of contents to sharpen their understanding of the reading content.

Reflecting

An important strategy is for students to think about, or reflect on, what they have just read. Reflection can be just thinking, or it can be more formal, such as a discussion or writing in a journal.

Skimming and Scanning

In skimming and scanning, students read major headings, the table of contents, bold letters, graphic materials, and summary paragraphs to get the main idea of the content. This helps keep the overview in focus for nonfiction reading.

Children's Literature

Genre is the type of literature of a particular work. Genres are classified according to multiple categoreis. Some of the most common genres used in elementary schools are science fiction, biography, and traditional literature, which encompasses folktales, fables, myths, epics, and legends. Classifications of genre are largely arbitrary and are based on conventions that apply a basic category to an author's writing. Classifications give the reader a general expectation of what sort of book is being chosen. Teachers today are expected to share a wide range of texts with children. The most common type of books for younger children is picture books. **Picture books** are books in which the illustrations and the text work together to communicate the story. It is a very good idea to share picture books with children in several different formats. Sometimes, teachers simply read the book to the children without showing any of the pictures. The story is then discussed, and the children are asked if they would like the book to be reread, this time with the pictures being shared. Typically, this technique sparks a lively conversation about why the book with its illustrations is better than hearing the words alone. Picture books can also be used with upper-grade and even middle-school students for specific teaching purposes.

Traditional literature comprises stories that have their roots in the oral tradition of storytelling and have been handed down from generation to generation. This genre also includes the modern versions of these old stories. Teachers can read and share multiple versions of old stories, and then compare and contrast each version. It is also interesting to read a number of folktales and keep track of the elements that these old stories have in common. Children can be guided toward noticing where elements of these old stories show up in their day-to-day lives. Children enjoy sharing what they notice. Some examples of folk literature are:

- **Animal tales** in which the characters are animals exhibiting human characteristics, e.g., *Anansi the Spider*.

- **Fables** in which the main characters are also animals and these present a moral, e.g., *The Tortoise and the Hare*.

- *The Pourquois Tales* comprise stories from around the world that explain how things were created. Every culture may have a different version of the way things were created, e.g., *How the Sea Was Created* and *The Legend of the Bluebonnet*.

- **Wonder tales** describe stories of enchantment in faraway lands. Traditionally, it presents the themes of good versus evil, e.g., *Snow White*.

- **Noodlehead tales** are stories of lovable fools. These stories include individuals that are not very bright, but manage to survive and often succeed, e.g., *Puss in Boots*.

- **Cumulative tales** represent stories in which the information is presented in a sequence and all the events in the sequence are repeated, e.g., *The Gingerbread Man* and *The Three Little Pigs*.

- **Tall tales** describe the story of legendary people or fictitious characters who manage to accomplish great things in life, e.g., *Paul Bunyan*, *John Henry*, and *Pecos Bill*.

- **Ghost stories** have traditionally been used to regulate the behavior of children. For example, the "Boogie Man" has been used in multiple cultures to scare children and encourage them to behave properly. In the Mexican culture, the "Boogie Man" is called "El Cucuy"; in the Puerto Rican culture, "El Cuco" or "El Coco."

Multicultural literature is a term used to describe literature other than traditional European stories. Traditionally, these are stories from countries throughout the world that are written by people from those countries. Original works of people from other countries are regularly used in American public schools. The term **authentic multicultural** has been used to describe literature written by members of a particular cultural group to represent their own historical development and culture. Some examples of literature that reflect the Latino experience are *The Gold Coin* by Alma Flor Ada, *Chato's Kitchen* by Gary Soto, *Hairs-Pelitos* by Sandra Cisneros, *Friends from the Other Side* by Gloria Anzaldua, *When I Was Puerto Rican* by Esmeralda Santiago, and *Tomas and the Library Lady* by Pat Mora.

Modern fantasy is a genre that presents make-believe stories that are the product of the author's imagination. Often, they are so beyond the realm of everyday life that the stories can't possibly be true. Extraordinary events take place within the covers of these books. Fantasy allows a child to move beyond the normal life in the classroom and speculate about a life that never was, and may never be. Fantasy is a genre that typically sparks intense discussions and provides ample opportunities to illuminate the author's craft for the child. The popular *Harry Potter* series by J. K. Rowling is a perfect example of both the genre and the resulting debate generated by this type of fiction.

Historical fiction is fiction set in the past. This type of fiction allows children to live vicariously in times and places they cannot experience in any other way. This type of fiction often depicts real people and real events, with fiction laced around them. Historical fiction informs the study of social studies. Examples include *Don't You Know There's a War On?* by James Stevenson (WWII), *Klara's New World* by Jeanette Winter (Swedish immigrant family), *A Horse Called Starfire* by Betty Boegehold (Native Americans' first encounter with the horse), and *Wagon Wheels* by Barbara Brenner (an African-American boy and family in 1870 Kansas).

Nonfiction books have the real world as their point of origin. These books help to expand the knowledge of children when they are studying a topic; however, these books need to be evaluated for accuracy, authenticity, and inclusion of the salient facts. Nonfiction books can be used to support the teaching of content and to promote higher-level comprehension skills. Nonfiction can also be a type of literary nonfiction, which goes beyond mere recitation of facts to try to persuade the audience. Literary nonfiction includes speeches, biographies, travel writing, memoirs, and nature writing.

Biography is a genre that deals with the lives of real people. Autobiography is a genre that deals with the life of the author. These books invigorate the study of social studies because, through careful research, they often include information that transforms a name in a textbook into a person that one may like to get to know better. **Memoir** similarly focuses on the author's reflections across the lifespan.

Drama is written to be performed and encompasses a wide variety of themes, characters, tone, and style. While it typically tells a narrative story, the focus is on the dialogue and performance of the actors.

Poetry is a genre that is difficult to define for children, except as "not prose." Poetry is the use of words to capture something: a sight, a feeling, or perhaps a sound. Poetry needs to be chosen carefully for a child, as poetry ought to elicit a response from the child—one that connects with the experience of the poem. All children need poetry in their lives. Poetry should be celebrated and enjoyed as part of the classroom experience, and a literacy-rich classroom will always include a collection of poetry to read, reread, savor, and enjoy. *The Owl and the Pussycat* by Edward Lear, Mother Goose rhymes, limericks, and haiku are all poems or types of poems that appeal to young children.

In summary, today there is an overwhelming variety of children's literature from which to choose. When selecting books for use in a classroom, a teacher has a number of issues to consider: Are the facts presented in the book accurate? Is the book aesthetically pleasing? Is the book engaging? Bear in mind that all children deserve to see positive images of children like themselves in the books they read, as illustrations can have a powerful influence on their perceptions of the world. Children also need to see positive images of children who are not like themselves, as who is or is not depicted in books can have a powerful influence on children's perception of the world. Teachers ought to provide children with literature that depicts an affirming, multicultural view, and the selection of books available should show many different kinds of protagonists. Both boys and girls, for example, should be depicted as able and strong.

Introducing Terminology

Teachers can introduce most of the terminology to study literature by using words to which students can relate. Once students understand the concept, teachers can introduce standard terminology to describe literature. Some of the concepts and terminology to describe literature follow:

- *Information* about the story including the author and illustrators, the publishing company, and even the International Standard Book Number (ISBN)

- Terminology to describe the characters of the story (the protagonist, the antagonist or villain, animals, humans)

- For older students, introduce the *point of view* of the author. A story's point of view can be first person (the author is one of the characters of the story and the narrator), the omniscient point of view (the narrator is an outsider who knows what the characters are thinking or feeling), or the *limited point of view*, or subjective consciousness (the narrator is not a character in the story). In the limited point of view, the narrator guides readers to see the story from a point of view of one of the characters.

- The *narrator* also conveys information that might seem unnatural coming from a character in the story.

- The *setting* refers to the geographical location and the general environment and historical circumstances of the story.

- The **plot** tells us what happens and the theme tells us why it happens.

Some examples of **themes** in children's literature include problems of growing up and maturing, linguistic and cultural adjustment, love and friendship, family issues, and achieving one's identity.

Literary style includes writing components such as the following:

Exposition: Usually used to introduce the background information and to understand or introduce characters

Dialogue: Communication among the characters

Vocabulary: Word choice, use of concrete versus abstract terminology (i.e., Is the vocabulary appropriate for the intended audience?)

Imagery: The use of words to create sensory impressions. It conveys sights, sounds, textures, smells, and tastes. Imagery includes the collection of images used to create an emotional response in the reader.

Tone: The author's mood and manner of expression. It might be humorous, serious, satirical, passionate, sensitive, childlike, zealous, indifferent, poignant, or warm.

Literary Analysis: Might be multicultural or traditional, or include possible stereotypes, sexism, religious issues, or controversial elements, words, or ideas.

Story Grammar

Children should be encouraged to analyze stories using the story-grammar components of setting, characters, problems encountered by characters, attempts at a solution to the problem, successful solution, and ending. Teachers can use graphic organizers to present a visual clue to these components. Story frames can be modified to introduce various components of literature, as well as an assessment tool to check for comprehension.

As children's comprehension grows more sophisticated, they move from merely attempting to comprehend what is in the text to reading more critically. This means that they grow in an understanding that comprehension can go beyond the denotative components of the facts portrayed in text. With skillful instruction, children come to read not only what a text says, but also how the text portrays the subject matter. Students recognize the various ways in which every text is the unique creation of a unique author, and they also learn to compare and contrast the treatment of the same subject matter in a number of texts. For example, teachers can introduce the multiple versions of stories like *Cinderella* in order to discuss how stories can represent similar themes using unique settings and situations. To see different versions of the Cinderella story, visit *The Children's Literature Web Guide* (Brown, 1997). Examples of variations on Cinderella are *Mufaro's Beautiful Daughters: An African Tale*, by John Steptoe; *Yeh-Shen, a Cinderella Tale from China*, by Ai-Ling Louie; and *The Egyptian Cinderella*, by Shirley Climo. Teachers can help students grow in comprehension through stages. In the beginning, teachers are usually happy if children are able to demonstrate their comprehension of what a text says in some authentic way.

The next stage is to have the children ponder what a text does—to describe an author's purpose, to recognize the elements of the text, and how the text was assembled. Finally, some children can attain the skill set needed to successfully engage in text interpretation, to be able to detect and articulate tone and persuasive elements, discuss point of view, and recognize bias. Over time, and with good instruction, children learn to infer unstated meanings based on social conventions, shared knowledge, shared experience, or shared values. They make sense of text by recognizing implications and drawing conclusions, and they move past the point of believing the content of a selection simply because it is in print.

Literary analysis is another important tool. The following are key concepts for teaching and implementing literary analysis as a way for students to interact with literature:

Literary devices: These include devices used by the writer in literature such as literary allusion (referring to another event), foreshadowing (giving a hint of something to come later in the narrative or text), symbolism (an object standing for another),

Figurative language: This is language used by the author(s) to enhance the text. Examples include metaphor (comparing two unlike things), simile (comparing using "like" or "as"), personification, and hyperbole.

Characterization: This component involves descriptions of characters and their development in a narrative text. Characterization can be seen in what the character says, does, and thinks in the text.

Influences of historical and cultural contexts: Analysis of literature can include the discussion and investigation of the time the story is set and how this might impact the style of writing, the ways the characters interact, and the type of dialect or language used by the writer. A noted literary example is *Huckleberry Finn* by Mark Twain, where learning about the historical and cultural setting of the story are crucial to understanding the broader narrative.

Theme(s): These include broad overarching ideas that are the focus of the story or text. Themes in literature might include such ideas as: change, friendship, struggle, friendship, and more.

Settings: This is the location and time period of the story or text.

Reflecting Reading—Bias in Traditional Stories

Certain traditional children's stories are filled with episodes of violence, sexism, and stereotypes. Fairy tales like *Cinderella* and *Snow White* portray women as weak creatures in need of support and rescuing. They also present old people as ugly and often evil, e.g., the evil witch. Killing is also rampant in stories such as *Hansel and Gretel*, in which the main characters are left to die in the woods, and then are imprisoned by an "ugly and old witch" whom they eventually kill. Thievery and killing are also promoted in the story of *Jack and the Beanstalk*. In the original story the main character, Jack, steals from the "ugly" giant and kills him. Teachers should not ignore violence and bias in literature, and they should use these stories as a foundation to guide children to discuss and challenge bias and stereotypes.

Teachers can use traditional stories to examine controversial events in the stories. Teachers can lead children to discuss the actions of characters like Jack in *Jack and the Beanstalk* who steals the golden goose from the giant. Teachers can also introduce new stories and modern versions of traditional stories in which stereotypes and violence are challenged. In *Paper Bag Princess*, the protagonist presents the idea that women do not always need to be saved by men or to marry a man who will protect them. In this story, the princess saves the prince from the dragon and eventually decides not to marry him. Guiding children to examine themes and bias in literature can make them better readers and, more importantly, they can become reflective learners.

Reading Application: Authors as Mentors

A well-stocked and well-chosen classroom library should be full of books by exemplary authors who can become mentors and exemplars for students' writing. Students can choose an author or genre they are familiar with from books that they have read or that have been read aloud in class. They can look for other books by this author and then read all they can by and about that author. Additionally, through read-aloud and thinking-aloud, the teacher can feature and highlight aspects of craft, style, and structure about the author's writing to students in order to encourage them to model their own writing after the author's sense of craft and style. In addition to teaching students about a wide variety of authors, students can be taught about the cultural and historical context in which the author wrote.

Reading Workshop to Foster Independent Reading

Not all students and districts in Texas use guided reading groups. The reading workshop model uses a different design and rationale for reading instruction. In reading workshop, students read on their own while applying reading strategies that were modeled by the teacher during a mini-lesson. The reading workshop model fosters skills in independent reading while building fluency and vocabulary.

Independent and oral reading builds reading fluency (Worthy et al., 2001). Additionally, it is important to have a well-stocked classroom library so that students can select texts they will be motivated to read during independent reading (Worthy et al., 1999).

Through independent reading, students can be exposed to a wide variety of texts and genre. Students should be encouraged to interact with their classmates to discuss their reading. These methods can encourage students to become lifelong learners and readers. Students can also be taught to select their own independent reading texts, based on both their personal preferences in reading as well as their independent and instructional reading levels. However, in helping students select independent reading materials, the teacher should also be aware of the student's background knowledge as this will impact understanding of the text.

Technology: Reading Applications

A wide range of technologies can be used to enhance reading applications in the classroom. Often, students are reading and writing using computers and mobile technologies. Storybooks and textbooks are increasingly available in digital formats. Many public libraries have books available as digital downloads for students to access. With the teacher's guidance, students can read books online and also discuss books online (e.g., on blogs or other types of moderated forums). Care should be taken to ensure online "netiquette," student privacy, as well as that appropriate content filters are in place. Additionally, students should be taught to think critically and evaluate the credibility of online information.

Reader Response: Fostering Student Expression about Text

According to reader response theorists like Louise Rosenblatt (1978), readers may take one of two stances while reading. An **efferent** stance, or purpose for reading, involves reading to locate and remember information. An **aesthetic** stance, or purpose for reading, involves reading purely for pleasure or enjoyment. Often, readers use a combination of these two stances when they read, but the stance a reader takes is very frequently determined by the reading instruction he or she receives in school. Three key points differentiate a transactional theory of reading:

1. Readers create meaning as they read.

2. Meaning is based upon a transaction between the reader, the text, and the context for reading.

3. Readers vary how they read depending upon whether they are reading for efferent or aesthetic purposes.

With instruction aligned with a reader-response theory of reading, students would also be asked to respond to literature they read in a variety of ways such as through writing, discussion, art, music, or drama. Such a type of instruction might involve having students do any of the following:

- Write in journals.

- Participate in literature circles (book discussion groups).

- Act out a story.

COMPETENCY 006: WRITTEN LANGUAGE—WRITING CONVENTIONS

The teacher understands the conventions of writing in English and provides instruction that helps students develop proficiency in applying writing conventions.

The beginning teacher:

A. Knows predictable stages in the development of writing conventions (including the physical and cognitive processes involved in letter formation, word writing, sentence construction, spelling, punctuation and grammatical expression) and recognizes that individual variations occur.

B. Knows and applies appropriate instructional strategies and sequences to teach writing conventions and their applications to all students, including English-language learners (in accordance with the ELPS).

C. Knows informal and formal procedures for assessing students' use of writing conventions and uses multiple ongoing assessments to monitor and evaluate students' development in this area.

D. Uses ongoing assessment of writing conventions to determine when a student needs additional help or intervention to bring the student's performance to grade level, based on state content and performance standards for writing in the Texas Essential Knowledge and Skills (TEKS).

E. Analyzes students' errors in applying writing conventions and uses the results of this analysis to develop and adjust future instruction.

F. Knows writing conventions and appropriate grammar and usage and provides students with direct instruction and guided practice in these areas.

G. Understands the use of conventional spelling and its importance for success in reading and writing.

H. Understands stages of spelling development (prephonetic, phonetic, transitional and conventional) and how and when to support students' development from one stage to the next.

I. Provides systematic spelling instruction and gives students opportunities to use and develop spelling skills in the context of meaningful written expression.

Competency 006 focuses on written language. We encourage you to also review the TEKS standards for grades 4–8 that focus on written language and writing conventions. Keep in mind that instruction and assessment for English language learners should be in accordance with the English Language Proficiency Standards (ELPS).

The transition from oral language development to written communication requires students to develop an awareness of the following concepts (Peregoy et al., 2008):

1. Print carries meaning and it conveys a message.

2. Spoken words can be written and preserved.

3. English reading and writing follows a specific direction; that is, from left to right, and top to bottom.

4. Spoken language is composed of phonemes, and these sounds can be represented by specific letters of the alphabet (alphabetic principle).

5. As an alphabetic language, English has a sound–symbol correspondence but often is inconsistent.

6. Spoken language can be used as a foundation for spelling (phonics).

Spelling Stages

As children begin to name letters and read print, they also begin to write letters and words. Writing development seems to occur at about the same time as reading development—not afterward, as traditional reading readiness assumed. Holistic approaches seek to integrate the language arts rather than sequencing them. Just as change has marked educators' beliefs about reading instruction and the way that reading develops, change has also marked the methods and philosophies behind the teaching of writing in schools.

Drawing is the beginning of children's attempt to convey a message in written form. Teachers can use this interest to introduce writing skills by guiding them to add words to drawings to supplement the information. Initially, the children can dictate the story to teachers until they feel comfortable enough to write it on their own. The development of written communication generally follows a predictable sequence beginning with scribbling, then developing pseudo-letters and invented words until conventional spelling is achieved. An analysis of the stages of spelling follows.

Scribbling

In this phase, children pretend that they are writing. Eventually, they develop letter-like symbols. This stage represents an awareness of the difference between writing and drawing to communicate. Scribbling is different from drawing because in scribbling, the child purposely scribbles from left to right and often also follows the top-to-bottom progression.

Pseudo-letters

In this phase, children attempt to create forms that resemble letters, but these forms cannot always be identified as such. Children become aware that the alphabet contains characters of different shapes and attempt to reproduce these in a random way, resulting in some form of invented spelling.

Random Letters

In this phase, children create individual letters from the alphabet in an attempt to create words. The letters are randomly selected with no clear connection with the phonemes that they are to represent. That is, children are not producing phonetic spelling at this stage. They write letter strings and often leave a space between strings, which suggests that they are beginning to understand word boundaries.

Invented Spelling

At this stage, children try to connect the sounds (phonemes) and the letters (graphemes) to create words, resulting in nonstandard writing. A single letter or a series of letters, which represent the phonemes contained in the intended word, often represent this phonetic spelling. A child can write an *m* to represent the word *mother* and often they can point to the word. They can also use strings of letters, mostly consonants, to represent a word. For example, a kindergartner may write the word *park* as *prk*, producing the three consonants but omitting the vowel. Because the phoneme–grapheme correspondence of vowels is not consistent, children generally have problems writing them.

Transitional Spelling

Eventually, children discontinue overreliance on phonetic spelling and begin noticing visual clues and developing a knowledge of word structure. Sight word training becomes critical at this stage. Students begin producing more standard spelling and attempt self-correction. Writing samples may become difficult to read because students erase continuously in an attempt to self-correct. Some inflectional endings (e.g., plurals, comparative, superlative, past tense, and present progressive) may appear in writing samples. Students may continue having problems with words with double vowels, like *book* and *feed*, and words containing consonant digraphs like ***through*** or *eight*.

Conventional Spelling

At the conventional-spelling stage, children spell most words using conventional spelling. They still may have problems with consonant digraphs, homonyms, contractions, compound words, as well as prefixes, suffixes, and some of the more difficult letter combinations.

Writing Expectations

Children in grades 4 to 8 are expected to progress through the stages of writing and develop conventional spelling and coherent compositions. The fourth-grade and seventh-grade STAAR exams require students to develop a coherent piece of writing free of major errors. It is also expected that children produce and refine compositions for general and specific audiences. Children are required to edit their work as well as the work of others based on clarity of ideas, coherence, and the conventions of writing.

Strategies for Using Writing Conventions

The main objective of writing is to put ideas in writing in a logical pattern. Once this is accomplished, students have to check for writing conventions—grammar, punctuation, and capitalization. Let's look at some of the strategies to introduce writing conventions.

Modeling

Modeling is one of the best tools to introduce effective writing. To model effective writing, teachers can introduce writing samples in which conventions are used appropriately. A variant of this activity is to present a writing sample to the whole class that contains typical errors in English conventions and to ask them to provide corrective feedback.

Sentence Builders

One of the typical problems found in the writing samples produced by children is the use of sentence fragments. To guide children to produce complete sentences, teachers can use a technique called "sentence builders." With this technique, the teacher provides students with a list of words by syntactic categories (articles, adjectives, nouns, verbs, and conjunctions) and guides children to produce sentences using each component. As a follow-up activity, children are asked to identify the subject and the predicate, and specifically the verb. They are also asked to read the sentence to see if it contains a complete idea.

Punctuation Exercises

To teach the importance of punctuation, teachers can use sentences in which commas or periods are necessary to deliver the intended ideas and guide students to use punctuation to clarify the intended message. For example, let's look at the following sentence:

Mary, a student from Italy, requested bread, coffee and olive oil for breakfast.

Notice that it is not clear whether Mary wants coffee mixed with olive oil or just coffee and also olive oil. In this case a serial comma (placed after *coffee,* the penultimate item in the list) is needed after the word *oil* for clarification.

Identifying Common Grammar Problems

Assess students' writing to identify common problems across the group, and design lessons to address the identified problems. For example, if students are producing words like *bred* and *sale boat* in place of *bread* and *sailboat*, provide training in vowel digraph and compound words. A vowel digraph occurs when two vowels produce one sound, e.g., *ea* in *beach*. A consonant digraph is more than one consonant that produces only one sound, e.g., *th* in *thought*.

Connecting Discourse

Connecting discourse can be a challenge to some students. Children can produce choppy sentences without transition words or phrases to connect ideas or paragraphs. Most of these connectors are not used in daily speech unless students have had some speech training or academic preparation in the area; thus, teachers need to teach connectors directly. When writing a composition, teachers can provide a list of possible sentence connectors to guide students to use them. Some of these include phrases such as "on the one hand," "moreover," and "furthermore," among others.

Dependent and Independent Clauses

Another way to minimize the use of choppy sentences in compositions is by guiding children to combine sentences in one of the following ways:

1. Use conjunctions such as *and, but, or, nor,* and *yet*. For example:

    My car is beautiful, but it is getting old.

    Notice that in this sentence, there are two independent clauses joined by a coordinate conjunction, *but*. A comma is required before the conjunction.

2. Join two complete sentences with a semicolon. For example:

    Maricela is a highly intelligent student; she was the valedictorian of the class of 2018.

    Notice that lowercase is used after the semicolon.

3. Use dependent and independent clauses. For example:

    Although Dora is my friend, she did not vote for me.

    Notice that in this case, the use of the dependent linking word *although* at the beginning of the first clause makes the second clause necessary to complete the whole idea. Though the last statement makes sense by itself, and could in theory stand alone, the two clauses working together provide critical context.

Assessing Writing Conventions

Teachers can provide ongoing assessment of writing conventions using multiple measures. Some of these measures include editing checklists, revision checklists, student self-assessment, peer editing, and use of technology (such as spelling and grammar check) to help support correct use of conventions in writing. These tools can be used on a daily and weekly basis as students work through the writing process. Typically, editing is done after students have composed, drafted, and revised their original work.

Teachers can also provide daily or weekly "quizzes" in which students make corrections to sentences or paragraphs that contain multiple types of convention errors. These activities should be discussed in class so students understand the rules and rationale for the conventions. Teachers can also design their own rubrics for students to use during the composing process. Students in grades 4–8 should be encouraged to do self-editing of their own written work, in addition to seeking editing help from the teacher, peers, or trustworthy resources. Editing rubrics can be created with the help of websites such as RubiStar: *http://rubistar.4teachers.org*.

Interventions for Students Below Grade Level

Through ongoing assessment, the teacher can determine which students need additional support in the classroom. Students can work with the teacher in small groups and also be paired with other students to get additional help. Editing checklists can help students to monitor their own work. Other resources and tools that will help students in the area of writing conventions include these:

- Word bank lists with sight words and other high-frequency words to help with spelling
- Spelling tools (spell-check, electronic spelling tools, etc.)
- Editing checklists
- Examples of model papers
- Direct instruction in conventions (spelling, punctuation, grammar, etc.)
- Modeling and demonstration of the editing process
- Mini-lessons (as described below)

Mini-Lessons on Conventions

Another way to use informal, ongoing assessment in the classroom to teach conventions is for the teacher to periodically (e.g., weekly) read through students' writing to look for patterns of errors with conventions. The teacher can then design a mini-lesson (from 5 to 20 minutes) surrounding one or more writing conventions. The rule and examples of the rule can be discussed and demonstrated for the class, followed by student practice with the convention. Teachers can also use classroom data on individual students to tailor instruction towards helping students who are working below grade level in the area of writing instruction. It is important that mini-lessons are followed with time for students to spend time writing, for instance, during a writing workshop, which is a dedicated time and space to practice authentic composition.

COMPETENCY 007: WRITTEN LANGUAGE—COMPOSITION

The teacher understands that writing to communicate is a developmental process and provides instruction that promotes students' competence in written communication.

The beginning teacher:

A. Knows predictable stages in the development of written language and recognizes that individual variations occur.

B. Promotes student recognition of the practical uses of writing, creates an environment in which students are motivated to express ideas in writing and models writing as an enjoyable activity and a tool for lifelong learning.

C. Knows and applies appropriate instructional strategies and sequences to develop students' writing skills (e.g., effective introduction, clearly stated purpose, controlling ideas).

D. Knows characteristics and uses of informal and formal written language assessments and uses multiple, ongoing assessments to monitor and evaluate students' writing development.

E. Uses assessment results to plan focused instruction to address the writing strengths, needs and interests of all individuals and groups, including English-language learners (in accordance with the ELPS).

F. Uses ongoing assessment of written language to determine when a student needs additional help or intervention to bring the student's performance to grade level, based on state content and performance standards for writing in the Texas Essential Knowledge and Skills (TEKS).

G. Understands the use of self-assessment in writing and provides opportunities for students to self-assess their writings (e.g., for clarity, interest to audience, comprehensiveness) and their development as writers.

H. Understands differences between first-draft writing and writing for publication, and provides instruction in various stages of writing, including prewriting, drafting, editing and revising.

I. Understands and teaches writing as a tool for inquiry, research and learning.

J. Provides instruction about plagiarism, academic honesty and integrity as applied to students' written work and their presentation of information from different sources, including electronic sources.

K. Teaches students to critically evaluate the sources they use for their writing.

L. Understands the development of writing in relation to the other language arts and uses instructional strategies that connect these various aspects of language.

M. Understands similarities and differences between the language (e.g., syntax, vocabulary) used in spoken and written English and helps students use knowledge of these similarities and differences to enhance their own writing.

N. Understands writing for a variety of audiences, purposes and settings and provides students with opportunities to write for various audiences, purposes and settings.

O. Knows how to write using voices and styles appropriate for different audiences and purposes, and provides students with opportunities to write using various voices and styles.

P. Understands the benefits of technology for teaching writing and writing for publication and provides instruction in the use of technology to facilitate written communication.

Writing is a developmental process that requires students to go through a series of steps to complete a written product. Some of these steps include brainstorming, semantic mapping, outlining, reading, and researching. Students must also know that they need to write for various audiences and purposes (e.g., expressive, informative, persuasive), and that they will be required to use their knowledge of text genres, structures (e.g., letter, poem, story, play), and strategies (e.g., peer conferences) for completing a written piece. Some of the steps that students must go through include drafting, editing, revising, proofreading, and publishing. Students should be aware, however, that writing is a recursive and iterative process; that is, there are always opportunities to continue to improve what they are writing.

Children also need knowledge of English grammar and mechanics to revise their writing. It includes revising given texts in terms of sentence construction like revising run-on sentences and misplaced modifiers; revising subject-verb and pronoun-antecedent agreement; revising verb forms, pronouns, adverbs, adjectives, and plural and possessive nouns; and revising capitalization, punctuation, and spelling. Students also need to analyze and revise written work in relation to style, clarity, organization, intended audience, and purpose. This includes revising text prepared for a given audience or purpose, and improving organization and unity. Adding transition words and phrases, reordering sentences or paragraphs, deleting unnecessary information, and adding a topic sentence are other ways students can revise their work. Another strategy is to increase text clarity, precision, and effectiveness through word choices.

Many students struggle with writing instruction in grades 4–8. Graham and Perin (2007) report on the strong need for professional development for teachers based on data that suggest that students in K–12 settings in the United States are generally performing poorly on standardized tests in writing. The National Writing Commission highlights the significance of effective writing instruction and calls it the "neglected 'R'" (National Commission on Writing, 2003).

Dr. Donald Graves, a professor of education at the University of New Hampshire, developed an approach to writing instruction called **process writing** (2003). His notion was simple: Teach children to write the way practiced writers write. What do writers do? They tend to write about what they want to write about. They may read about the subject, talk about the subject, take notes, or generally play with the topic before they compose. Then they may write a draft, knowing upfront that they are not done at this point. Writers may share the draft with others, who end up making comments all over it. They may also go over every sentence, thinking about word choice and looking for vague spots, or places where the piece wanders off-topic. Writers may then revise the draft again, share it again, revise it again, and so on, until they are satisfied with the product. Then they publish it. Often, writers receive feedback before and after the piece is published, which may lead to a new writing effort. Some writers save scraps of writing in a journal. They may save a turn of phrase, a comment overheard on the train or at a coffee shop, a new word, good quotes, or an interesting topic.

Another aspect of process writing is celebration. Children are invited to share their work with the class. After young authors read their piece, classmates can offer affirmations and suggestions. Teachers should have children save each piece of paper generated in the writing process, and store them in a personal portfolio for review.

Writing Stages

In addition to the traditional spelling stages, students also go through specific stages of writing. Lapp divided the process into three stages: emerging writers, early writers, and newly fluent writers. A summary of these stages follows (Lapp et al., 2001).

Characteristics of Emerging Writers

Students at the emerging stage of writing development are generally able to:

- Dictate an idea or a complete story
- Use initial sounds in their writing
- Use pictures, scribbles, symbols, letters, and/or known words to communicate a message
- Understand that writing symbolizes speech

Educational Implications

Read stories to children and ask them to retell the story while you record it. Then, read the story back to the child to emphasize the connection between speech and print. When children begin writing words or pseudo-words, ask them to read it to you; if necessary, provide conventional spelling as an alternative to what the child has written. Use the *Language Experience Approach* to guide children to connect spoken words with their written representations. That is, guide children to dictate words and sentences while you record them on the board. Read the words while pointing to them. Then, ask students to copy the sentences. The next day, review the sentences written and use them for additional language development. Introduce writing for functional tasks like labeling objects and places in the classroom, writing the plan of the day, taking notes, and listing names or things to remember.

Characteristics of Early Writers

Typically, children at the early stage of writing exhibit the following behaviors:

- Understand that a written message remains the same each time it is read

- Utilize their knowledge of sounds and letters as they progress through the stages of spelling development

- With modeling and assistance, incorporate feedback in revising and editing their own writing

- Begin to use conventional grammar, spelling, capitalization, and punctuation

Educational Implications

Guide children to read and reread the same information to establish a connection between letters and sounds. Identify specific words and divide them into syllables to establish a connection between the sounds within a syllable. Take expressions that are commonly used in children's literature and oral communication and guide them to hear word boundaries. For example, children at this stage might write the statement "Once upon a time" as one solid word, "Oncesoponditim," which represents the way the expression is produced orally without appropriate word boundaries. Model the writing process using an LCD projection system or a traditional chalkboard. Think aloud while you are writing and ask for guidance from students (e.g., Do we need a comma here or a final period? Do we need a capital *A* in the word "American"?). In children's writing samples, use peer input for editing and guide students to do self-corrections. Instead of making direct error corrections, ask questions leading children to examine the grammaticality of the sentences and to make their own corrections.

Characteristics of Newly Fluent Writers

Newly fluent writers are generally able to:

- Use prewriting strategies to achieve their purposes

- Address a topic or write to a prompt creatively and independently

- Organize writing to include a beginning, a middle, and an end

- Consistently use conventional grammar, spelling, capitalization, and punctuation

- Revise and edit written work independently and/or collectively

- Produce many genres of writing

Educational Implications

Use prewriting activities to plan for writing using an outline that indicates the sequence of ideas. This activity is especially important for children whose native language does not require the use of the linear progression required in English writing. The outline will guide children to comply with this linear rhetorical pattern. Provide interesting writing prompts to children to guide their writing. You may use the prompt given on the STAAR released tests available online. Traditionally, the Texas Education Agency releases the tests used in its yearly examinations. For information on released STAAR tests, visit the TEA online at *www.tea.state.tx.us* and search under "Student Assessment/STAAR."

Continue to use peer editing and to encourage self-corrections. Guide students to produce different kinds of writing such as response to literature, journal writing, and persuasive writing (writing to convince someone or to argue a point).

Characteristics of Fluent Writers

Students in the upper-elementary and middle-school grades generally

- have an improved sense of audience

- write from different points of view

- have more skills in revising and editing their own and other's work

- show a wide range of skill in writing

- like to experiment with voice and new forms of writing

Educational Implications

Teachers can expose students to a wide variety of genre and format. Students should be able to write for a sense of audience and teachers can model this through "mentor text" lessons by focusing on the author's use of style to write for a certain audience. Students should be encouraged to write with increasing complexity in sentence length and fluency. They should also be encouraged to use a writing notebook in which to experiment with different forms and styles of writing. Pieces from the writing notebook can be drafted, revised and edited to become complete pieces that students take through different iterations of the writing process. Students should be expected to peer edit one another's work, with modeling and guidance from the teacher.

New Trends in Writing

In addition to process writing, there is a new trend emphasizing specific elements of the writing process. The best-known system is called the 6+1 Trait Writing. This system, which was developed by the Northwest Regional Educational Laboratory (NREL), emphasizes seven elements of the writing process (2012). These elements are described below.

1. **Organization**—the internal structure of the sample

2. **Ideas**—how ideas are presented in the sample

3. **Voice**—the uniqueness of the author and how ideas are projected

4. **Word Choice**—the vocabulary used to convey meaning

5. **Sentence Fluency**—the flow of ideas and the use of connectors

6. **Conventions**—the use of capitalization, punctuation, and spelling

7. **Presentation**—how the final product looks in print

The Texas Education Agency developed a similar writing program emphasizing similar components for scoring student writing. Expository and narrative writing rubrics for both the Grade 4 and Grade 7 STAAR writing tests focus on the following on their scoring rubrics:

- Organization/Progression

- Development of Ideas

- Use of Language/Conventions

Both the 6+1 Trait Writing and the STAAR writing program guide children to demonstrate knowledge of writing traits. To assess their performance, both programs develop a four-point rubric for each of the writing traits.

Identifying the Characteristics of Modes of Writing

Writing serves many different functions. The main functions are to narrate, to describe, to explain, and to persuade. Students need to be aware of each of these functions. In any event, these four categories are neither exhaustive nor mutually exclusive. The **narrative** is a story or an account. It may recount an incident or a series of incidents. The account may be autobiographical to make a point. The narrative may be fiction or nonfiction.

The purpose of **descriptive** writing is to provide information about a person, place, or thing. Descriptive writing can be fiction or nonfiction. Description is a powerful tool in advertisement. Advertisements describe items using factual information, but the way the information is presented can become a persuasive type of writing for prospective buyers.

The purpose of **expository** writing is to explain and clarify ideas. Students are probably most familiar with this type of writing. While the expository essay may have narrative elements, the storytelling or recounting aspect is minor and subservient to the explanation element. Expository writing is typically found in many textbooks; for instance, a textbook on the history of Texas would likely be expository in nature.

The purpose of **persuasive** writing is to convince the reader of something. Persuasive writing fills current magazines and newspapers, and permeates the Internet. The writer may be trying to push a political candidate, convince someone to vote for a zoning ordinance, or even promote a diet plan. Persuasive writing usually presents a point, provides evidence, which may be factual or anecdotal, and supports the point. The structure may be very formal, with counter positions and counterarguments. Whatever the organizational pattern, the writer's intent is to persuade readers of the validity of some claim. Nearly all essays have some element of persuasion. Authors choose their form of writing not necessarily just to tell a story, but also to present an idea. Whether writers choose the narrative, descriptive, expository, or persuasive format, they have something on their minds that they want to convey to their readers.

Writing for a Variety of Audiences, Occasions, and Purposes

The writer must consider the audience, the occasion, and the purpose when choosing the writing mode. The writer's responsibility is to write clearly, honestly, and cleanly for the reader's sake and so the **audience** is very important. The teacher can designate an audience for students' writing. Knowing who will read their work, students can modify their writing to suit the intended readers. For instance, a fourth-grade teacher might suggest that the class take their compositions about a favorite animal to second-graders and allow the younger children to read it. The writers soon will realize that they need to use manuscript and not cursive writing, employ simple vocabulary, and omit complex sentences when they write for their young audience.

The **occasion** also helps to determine the elements of writing. The language should fit the occasion. Students should keep in mind that particular words may have certain effects, such as evoking sympathy or raising questions about an opposing point of view. The students and teacher might try to determine the likely effect on an audience of a writer's choice of a particular word or words.

The **purpose** helps to determine the format (narrative, expository, descriptive, or persuasive) and the language of the writer. The students, for instance, might consider the appropriateness of written material for a specific purpose such as a business letter, a communication with residents of a retirement center, or a thank-you note to parents. The teacher and students might try to identify persuasive techniques used by a writer in a passage.

In selecting the mode of writing and the content, the writer might ask the following:

1. What would the audience need to know to believe you or to accept your position? Imagine someone you know (visualize her or him) listening to you declare your position or opinion and then saying, "Oh yeah? Prove it!" What evidence do you need to prove your idea to this skeptic?

2. With what might the audience disagree?

3. What common knowledge does the audience share with you?

4. What information do you need to share with the audience?

The teacher might wish to have the students practice selecting the mode and the language by adapting forms, organizational strategies, and styles for different audiences and purposes. Students should also be taught to write an effective introduction and organized controlling ideas in writing. These can be modeled and practiced with students.

Types of Writing

Teachers should encourage children to write for meaningful purposes. Such writing can be easily incorporated as part of daily classroom activities and can enhance not only writing skills, but also content-area mastery. Some of the types of writing that lend themselves to this are functional writing and journal writing.

Functional Writing

Functional writing describes activities in which writing is used to achieve a specific purpose. For example, labeling areas and objects in the classroom is a meaningful and useful activity for all students, especially ELLs. Note-taking or developing a grocery list or list of holiday gifts becomes a meaningful activity and will motivate children to write.

Journal Writing

Various types of journals can be used in elementary grades. Some of these include:

- **Personal journals** are used to record personal information and to encourage self-analysis of their experiences. This is a personal document and it is up to the child to make it available to others.

- **Dialogue journals** promote written communication among students and between the teacher and students. The main purpose is to communicate, not to teach writing skills. Teachers can model writing when they reply to children.

- **Reflective journals** are used to respond in writing about specific situations or problems. It is often shared with the teacher for input.

- **Learning logs** are commonly used in the content areas to record elements discussed in class. In these logs, students describe what they have learned and elements in which they have difficulties. Teachers read the document and act on the request for assistance.

Writing as a Tool for Inquiry, Research, and Learning

Writing helps students to organize their thinking, and can be used for note-taking, organizing, synthesizing, and presenting information. Writing as a tool for inquiry can be done across subject areas such as research. Digital tools can be used to annotate digital text. Students can also use traditional hard copy note-taking and information organization. Graphic organizers can be used as students gather information. Digital concept maps are available as a tool to help students organize and engage in prewriting. Students can also collaborate to write reports to synthesize what they have read.

Teachers should be sure to critically evaluate the sources that students use for their writing. In a digital age, it is especially crucial that students are taught to evaluate who wrote the text, for what purpose, and for what audience. Modeling of this process can provide insight into evaluating the claims made on any source that students could potentially use for writing. Checklists for evaluating sources are a good tool for helping students to think about the sources they are using for references and research in their own writing.

Strategies to Promote Written Communication

Reading to students can provide multiple benefits to children. It develops print awareness and understanding of the intonation pattern of the language. A discussion of the content of a story allows students opportunities to enhance comprehension and practice speaking. It also provides a model of fluent reading together with the appropriate intonation pattern of the language. Reading together can be enjoyable. Students laugh and talk about the story and the characters. Children can also be exposed to different genres and different kinds of writing such as fiction, biography, and short stories. Finally, they are exposed to the story framework, which is the setting, characters, plot, climax, and resolution.

Interactive Journals

As discussed earlier in the chapter, writing in journals provides students with opportunities to use language authentically in literary contexts. Teachers and students can have a designated time for journal writing to communicate on a daily basis. This gives students the freedom to use their own mechanics and invented spellings. Because the purpose of written journals is to communicate, teachers should not correct children's journal writing, but rather should write comments on content and provide encouragement and reassurance. Some of the key advantages of interactive journals for children and teachers are located in Table 3.6.

Table 3.6
Advantages of Interactive Journal Writing for Students and Teachers

Advantages for Students	Advantages for Teachers
• Students learn that written language communicates. • Students experience making choices about topics and develop a sense of ownership of the written product. • Students develop their writing within meaningful context. • Students develop a personal interaction with the teacher and with peers. • Students can use this safe environment to experiment with language.	• Teachers learn about each child's interest, ideas, and everyday concerns. • Teachers interact and communicate on an individual basis with each child. • Teachers model standard convention or writing in the context of authentic communication.

Technology and Writing Instruction

A wide variety of technology can be incorporated into writing instruction and the writing process for students in grades 4–8. In addition to word processing and publishing, students can participate in more interactive types of writing such as creating and participating in a blog (weblog). In this way, students can write for a real audience of peers or even students in other classes. Additional types of technology-based writing include:

- PowerPoint Presentations
- Brochures
- Newsletters
- Websites

Mentor Texts: Connecting Reading and Writing

There are many ways teachers can combine reading, writing, listening, and speaking in the writing composition experience. One way is to incorporate mentor text lessons (e.g., see Dorfman & Cappelli, 2007) into writing composition instruction for students in grades 4–8.

Connecting Reading and Writing with Mentor Texts

With mentor texts, teachers model good writing by a certain author or genre by sharing exemplar texts that are representative of that author or genre with students. An example of a mentor text writing lesson to teach the writing of historical fiction is *Minty: A Story of Young Harriet Tubman* by Alan Schroeder and Jerry Pinkney. An overarching goal of this mentor text writing lesson might be the following: Through listening to a touchstone text during a teacher read-aloud, the students will begin to develop their understanding of the characteristics of the genre of historical fiction. By the end of the unit, they will be able to articulate and explain what historical fiction is. Through a read-aloud experience, the teacher can think aloud about how the author uses dialogue and details to portray a realistic and authentic account of what a glimpse into the life of a historical figure, Harriet Tubman, might have been like. The teacher can say something like, "As I read, I want you to keep noticing what kind of person Harriet Tubman is. What words and details does the author use to let us know she was a strong person?" Mentor texts can be used for both fiction and nonfiction writing.

Assessing Writing Composition

Informal assessment can be very useful in giving students feedback on their writing. It can be based on observations, conferring (conversations with students), and collection of student work in a systematic way (portfolios). Each is described below.

Informal, Ongoing Assessment: Conferring with Students

Conferring (Graves, 2003) with students offers teachers a chance to discuss student's written work informally. Teachers can meet with students individually on a weekly basis to check in and ask informal questions about what each student is composing and offer assistance. Teachers can record observations in the form of anecdotal notes and records to keep track of a student's strengths, needs, and overall progress.

Informal, Ongoing Assessment: Revising Checklists and Self-Assessment

Teachers can provide revision checklists to students so that they can self-monitor their own compositions. These checklists can help students to consider their audience as they write. Students can also focus on clarity, coherence, and other traits of quality writing. Teachers can design their own revision checklists or find ready-made ones online. Students need to be taught the purpose of these checklists and how to use them. The best way for a teacher to model the use of a revision checklist is by demonstrating how to use it with her or his own writing.

Informal, Ongoing Assessment: Portfolios

Portfolios are collections of a student's best work. They can be used in any subject area in which the teacher wants students to take more responsibility for planning, carrying out, and organizing their own learning. Like a portfolio created by an artist, model, or performer, a student portfolio provides a succinct picture of the child's achievements over a certain period. Portfolios may contain essays or articles written on paper, videos, multimedia presentations on CDs, or a combination of these. Language arts teachers often use portfolios as a means of collecting the best samples of student writing over an entire year. Teachers should provide guidelines for what materials should go in their portfolios, or assist students in developing their own since it would be unrealistic to include every piece of work in one portfolio. Using portfolios requires that students devise a means of evaluating their own work. A portfolio should not be a scrapbook for collecting handouts or work done by other individuals, but it can certainly include work by a group in which the student was a participant.

Some advantages that portfolios have over testing are that they provide a clear picture of a student's progress, they are not affected by one inferior test grade, and they help develop students' self-assessment skills. One disadvantage of portfolios is the amount of time required to teach students how to develop meaningful portfolios. However, the time is well spent if students learn valuable skills. Another concern is the amount of time teachers must spend to assess portfolios. However, as students become more proficient at self-assessment, the teacher can spend more time coaching and advising students throughout the development of their portfolios. Another concern is that parents may not understand how the teacher will grade the portfolios. The effective teacher devises a system that students and parents understand before work on the portfolios begins.

Scoring Compositions

Holistic scoring is used to evaluate the composition and writing performance of students in Texas. The whole writing sample is scored based on a pre-established criterion contained in a rubric.

Criterion-Referenced Writing Assessment

As of this writing, the state of Texas has implemented the STAAR assessments. For the purposes of this test guide, you will need to know how writing is assessed on the STAAR test for students in grades 4 and 7. Browse and try part or all of a STAAR writing test for fourth or seventh grade found on the TEA website under "Student Assessment/STAAR" under "Writing."

Especially note the writing prompts. Students are now expected to write *two* essays for the STAAR writing test in fourth and also in eighth grade. Rubrics for this test can be found at the Texas Education Agency website. Also, if instruction is planned for English language learners, it should be done in accordance with the English Language Proficiency Standards.

Plagiarism, academic honesty, and integrity

Students need to be taught the difference between summarizing, paraphrasing, and quoting source materials in order to avoid plagiarism. Citing sources correctly is also something that can be directly taught and practiced when students are writing, creating, and/or producing content. They must also be taught to properly source images and other multimedia, in addition to text-based content. This includes teaching students about educational **fair use** principles, and when fair use applies in educational contexts. It is important that students understand that academic honesty and integrity are components of digital citizenship and need to be at the forefront of digital communications.

Additional skills for teaching about plagiarism, academic honesty, and integrity might also include:

- Respecting intellectual property and seeking permission to use other's works.

- Understanding the difference between paraphrasing and directly quoting work and how to cite sources for both.

- Preventing plagiarism by directly teaching skills for citing sources of a wide variety of sources.

COMPETENCY 008: VIEWING AND REPRESENTING

The teacher understands skills for interpreting, analyzing, evaluating and producing visual images and messages in various media and provides students with opportunities to develop skills in this area.

The beginning teacher:

A. Knows grade-level expectations in the Texas Essential Knowledge and Skills (TEKS) and procedures for assessing students' skills in interpreting, analyzing, evaluating and producing visual images, messages and meanings.

B. Uses ongoing assessment and knowledge of grade-level expectations in the Texas Essential Knowledge and Skills (TEKS) to identify students' needs regarding the interpretation, analysis, evaluation and production of visual images, messages and meanings and to plan instruction.

C. Understands characteristics and functions of different types of media (e.g., film, print) and knows how different types of media influence and inform.

D. Compares and contrasts print, visual and electronic media (e.g., films and written stories).

E. Evaluates how visual image makers (e.g., illustrators, documentary filmmakers, political cartoonists, news photographers) represent messages and meanings and provides students with varied opportunities to interpret and evaluate visual images in various media.

F. Knows how to teach students to analyze visual image makers' choices (e.g., style, elements, media) and evaluate how these choices help to represent or extend meaning.

G. Provides students with opportunities to interpret events and ideas based on information from maps, charts, graphics, video segments and technology presentations and to use media to compare ideas and points of view.

H. Knows steps and procedures for producing visual images, messages and meanings to communicate with others.

I. Teaches students how to select, organize and produce visuals to complement and extend meanings.

J. Provides students with opportunities to use technology to produce various types of communications (e.g., digital media, class news-papers, multimedia reports, video reports, movies) and helps students analyze how language, medium and presentation contribute to the message.

According to the TEKS, students in grades 4–8 need to develop the necessary skills to create and understand images and messages in a variety of media. The skills required by the students increase in complexity as they move from lower elementary grades to upper elementary. For instance, students in grades 1–3 are required to produce visual representations of the information they are learning in school or the tasks they are involved in (e.g., creating an image summarizing a story that was read). Students are also required to know how to discuss the visual representations they have created. In grades 4–8, students need to be able to understand, interpret, analyze, critique, and produce these visual representations as well as discuss their meaning or significance through the use of multiple media, including newsletters, charts, and electronic presentations, among others. Students are also required to understand the author's purpose and choice of various elements that were used by him/her to get a message across through the use of multiple media. The characteristics and functions of the various different types of media are explained below. More information on the TEKS that relate to viewing and representing for students in grades 4–8 can be located in the TEKS documents on the Texas Education Agency website at *https://tea.texas.gov*.

Types and Characteristics of Media

Media is considered to be any means used to convey information to others. There are at least three main types of media available. These include print, visual, and electronic media. **Print media** is information disseminated in print form, such as that found in newspapers, magazines, and direct mail. Print media is static; that is, once it is published, the information cannot be changed. **Visual media** incorporates the use of visual imagery to either complement or supplement the message being carried. Visual media can also stand by itself. For example, photographs and paintings can convey meaning without including text. Moreover, visual media is also an integral part of print media to illustrate messages. As such, visual media can take many forms, including photography, film, and even cartoons. Visual media can be either static (e.g., still photograph) or dynamic, as seen in movies or videos. In addition to incorporating print and visual imagery, **electronic media** requires the use of an external device such as a television, computer, or personal assistant device to display the information and images being presented. Electronic media is used in many different fields including journalism, fine arts, commerce, education, and communications. A primary type of electronic media that encompasses different electronic tools is the Internet, where one can find blogs, email, websites, etc.

Technology changes at a rapid pace, and teachers must keep this in mind when working with students. In fact, many of the tools used for presenting information are improved and refined every day. For instance, the process for creating photographs has evolved from creating images on plates, then film, to the current digital form.

In this information era, beginning teachers should understand that there is a vast array of possibilities to create and display information by making use of existing types of media. As the need for using and sharing massive amounts of information with others becomes necessary, some of these types of media will take precedence over others. Take, for instance, the use of electronic media such as online sources. For example, the use of online information has become so pervasive in today's society that static types of media, such as print, are now being channeled electronically, as in the case of newspapers whose content is presented via websites and digital apps. Also, the use of online resources and websites has become commonplace. Most students are familiar with emerging digital tools, and they want opportunities to produce different types of products by using various types of media.

Digital media and movies are increasingly prevalent. Teachers can use videos to analyze how the language, medium, and presentation contribute to the message. Students have widespread access to digital media and movies via mobile devices. Tablet devices can also be used to access and analyze media.

Representing Messages and Meanings through Media

Charts, tables, graphs, and pictures in print and digital media are examples of materials used to present or summarize information and/or to complement the message being conveyed. For instance, a chart can be used to summarize large amounts of information without the need for extensive written explanations. Students should understand that visual representations are important and that their purpose is to present information and facilitate the communication of the message. Visual images also make information more understandable. A graphic can expand a concept, serve as an illustration, support points, summarize data, organize facts, add a dimension to the content (such as a cartoon adding humor), compare information, demonstrate change over time, or furnish additional information. Through graphics, the reader can interpret, predict, and even apply information with careful observation. Actively questioning students as they create visual images is important (e.g., asking them what they are trying to convey or how they think someone will interpret their image). Also, providing ongoing feedback will help students learn to focus on and clarify the information that can be derived from graphic formats.

Understanding How Students May Interpret and Evaluate Visual Images

It is important for teachers to realize that even a graphic that appears uncomplicated may challenge a reader's interpretive skills. Many inferences may be necessary for even the simplest visual aid or graphic. Many students may initially skip over graphics, or may just notice their presence without interpreting them. Alternatively, students may *only* focus on the graphics present-ed in visual media but not focus on the complementary or written explanations. Even students who have some training in the use of graphic information may not be able to transfer that knowledge to other content areas. Also, they may have trouble going from print to graphic presentations and then back to print again. In either case, students may not have been taught how to absorb multiple representations of information. Teachers can help students make use of multiple representations of information by using open-book and guided reading. A teacher can also demonstrate how to use a chart or graph by using electronic tools including overhead projectors and interactive whiteboards. Examples of presentations and steps toward creating an effective presentation can be shared with the students. Resources and software that would be useful as "mentor texts" (Dorfman & Cappelli, 2007) can give students representative examples of how to best select images to use in parallel with the text (e.g., consideration of how the image parallels or complements the text).

Visual design can be thought of as containing its own grammar (Kress & van Leeuwen, 2001). Teachers can help students to understand and apply the elements of such visual grammar by teach-ing its component parts (Wysocki et al., 2004):

- **Visual impact:** the ways in which the overall visual design appeals to the reader (e.g., through detail, layout, use of color).

- **Visual coherence:** the ways in which the design of the piece creates a sense of unity and wholeness (e.g., by use of shapes, line, imagery).

- **Visual salience:** using design features to generate a certain effect (e.g., through varying size, colors, clip art, etc.).

- **Organization:** the layout of the page to create a unique pattern, especially one that is under-standable to the reader (e.g., through consideration of how the different aspects of the layout might be arranged).

Of course, these features of visual literacy overlap and can be used flexibly to guide students toward creating an awareness of the visual literacy that parallel and differ from the features of print literacy.

Teachers should model how to read, complement, and interpret visual images whenever stu-dents are required to create visual images as part of their work in the classroom. Pictures and other graphics can arouse interest and stimulate thinking. Additionally, graphics can add clarity; prevent misunderstandings; show step-by-step developments; exhibit the status of things, events, and pro-cesses; and demonstrate comparisons and contrasts (Vacca & Vacca, 1989).

Integrating Technology for Producing Communications

Teachers should provide students with opportunities to use current technology and tools to not only motivate children to read, write, and monitor their writing, but to create various kinds of communications products with a variety of media. For instance, one could assume that the goal for using **word-processor** software is to simply record written information. Interestingly, with the advances in technology, such software has improved its features to offer writers assistance with the editing of their documents. Other uses for this type of software include creating semantic maps, tables, charts, and graphs. Writing-related elements like spell-check, definitions of terms, thesaurus, and even suggestions for sentence constructions are commonly available in programs like Microsoft Word. The real function of a spell-checker is not only to identify misspelled words, but also to free students from the pressure of getting spelling right, at least at the drafting stage. Students should be encouraged to put their ideas in writing without stopping to check for spelling. Once they finish the content of the writing, they can take care of other important elements like spelling. Students should, however, be aware that there may be cases in which the spell-checker may be ineffective. Therefore, children should be guided to pay attention to corrections and to learn from them.

Teachers have to teach children how to use and take advantage of programs available for communicating and creating electronic products in their classrooms. Some of these products include creating a classroom newsletter, a multimedia presentation, and a video response to a group project. Students should be aware that they must keep both their audience and their purpose for creating such products in mind while creating their pieces. Students should also make sure that the language they use is appropriate and understandable for their audience.

COMPETENCY 009: STUDY AND INQUIRY SKILLS

The teacher understands the importance of study and inquiry skills as tools for learning in the content areas and promotes students' development in applying study and inquiry skills.

The beginning teacher:

A. Understands study and inquiry skills (e.g., using text organizers; taking notes; outlining; drawing conclusions; applying test-taking strategies; previewing; setting purposes for reading; locating, organizing, evaluating, synthesizing and communicating information; summarizing information; using multiple sources of information; correctly recording bibliographic information for notes and sources; interpreting and using graphic sources of information) and knows the significance of these skills for student learning and achievement.

B. Knows grade-level expectations for study and inquiry skills in the Texas Essential Knowledge and Skills (TEKS) and procedures for assessing students' development and use of these skills.

C. Knows and applies instructional practices that promote the acquisition and use of study and inquiry skills across the curriculum by all students, including English-language learners (in accordance with the ELPS).

D. Knows how to provide students with varied and meaningful opportunities to learn and apply study and inquiry skills to enhance their achievement across the curriculum.

E. Uses ongoing assessment and knowledge of grade-level expectations in the Texas Essential Knowledge and Skills (TEKS) to identify students' needs regarding study and inquiry skills, to determine when a student requires additional help or intervention and to plan instruction.

F. Responds to students' needs by providing direct, explicit instruction to promote the acquisition and use of study and inquiry skills.

Study and Inquiry Skills

The types of skills and tools discussed in this section with respect to Competency 009 focus on both print and digital tools for students to develop their study and inquiry skills. For ELLs, instruction and assessment should be in accordance with the English Language Proficiency Standards (ELPS).

Students need to know how to study the information that has been presented to them in texts and other media. Graphic organizers help students review material, and see the relationships between bits of information. For example, a Venn diagram helps students identify how things are alike and different. A Venn diagram can also be used to help students recognize how a single topic is treated in two readings, or how two books, animals, or ecosystems are alike and different. The student labels the two overlapping circles and lists items that are unique to each one in each respective circle. In the area in the center where there is an overlap, the student records the elements that the two items have in common.

Another skill students need to master is **note-taking.** Unless a teacher wants to read passages directly out of an encyclopedia or other source material, he or she should take the time to actively teach note-taking techniques. Teachers should also think of an authentic task that requires students to accomplish higher-level manipulation of the given information. First, help the children to formulate a researchable question. Second, have them highlight the words that might be used as key words in searching for information. Third, have students brainstorm in groups of other words to be used as key words. Next, ask then to list appropriate sources. Finally, as they skim articles, they can fill in the chart with little chunks of information.

Other examples of using study and inquiry skills in the classroom include having students take notes, incorporate test-taking strategies using metacognitive strategies such as organizing information, creating summaries of information, and reading graphic information. Teachers can incorporate demonstration and practice of these skills across the content areas. Additionally, teachers need to be able to use formative assessment and knowledge of the state standards (TEKS) to support students in their acquisition of study skills. At times, intervention will be needed to support students who would benefit from additional instruction in the area of study skills.

Graphic Organizers

Graphic organizers help students improve organizational skills and provide a visual representation of facts and concepts and their relationships within an organized framework. The ability to organize information and ideas is fundamental to effective thinking. To increase reading comprehension among ELLs, allow students to share information about the story or passage. Through this activity, students can help each other using peer scaffolding and oral language interaction. Semantic mapping can be used before and after readings to organize materials in new ways by highlighting connections among ideas.

Think-Aloud

Think-alouds allow the teacher and students to problem solve together. The teacher poses a question to students and then, the teacher, group of students, or entire class respond(s) at the same time. This strategy can be easily used to increase reading comprehension in the content areas. In modeling a think-aloud, the following steps are used (Wilhelm, 2001).

1. The teacher explains *what* the strategy is and what it is used for.

2. The teacher explains *why* the strategy is important for improving reading comprehension.

3. The teacher explains in what context to use the strategy: *when* to use the strategy.

4. The teacher models *how* to use the strategy using an authentic text. Modeling continues until the students begin to use prompts and strategies aloud.

5. The teacher guides student practice using *authentic* text. The teacher gradually releases responsibility for doing the think-aloud to students.

6. Students practice the *strategy* in pairs or independently. The teacher asks that students do a think-aloud in which they explain and articulate their thought processes for using the strategy.

Summarizing and Organizing Content

When children are guided to summarize and organize content, they are using basic reading comprehension and taking this content to a higher level of thinking including evaluation, analysis, and synthesis. By guiding children to go beyond the literal meaning and to reorganize content requires students to develop a deeper understanding of content. Guide students to reorganize content (study skills) by creating their own tables, charts, and graphs. For example, students can develop a chart containing the longest rivers of the world organized by regions and countries. When children are required to process and present information using a new structure, comprehension and knowledge of the content area increases and memory retention is enhanced.

Bibliographies: Organizing and Creating

Students can also record bibliographic information as they are reading and conducting inquiry. They can track their sources through pen and paper note-taking and/or through electronic curation of sources using digital bibliographic tools. Increasingly, there are digital tools that can help facilitate the bibliographic recording process. By keeping track of citations and sources, students are better equipped to report on information, curate content, and to organize information for presentations.

Study Plans

To increase content comprehension, teachers might acquaint students with several study plans to help them read content materials. Many of these plans are well known and easily accessed, and the teacher and the students can simply select the plan(s) that works best for them within various subjects. Students may use **mnemonic devices**, or memory-related devices, to help them remember the steps in reading a chapter effectively.

SQ4R

Students often use plans like **SQ4R** when reading text in content areas. The acronym stands for **survey, question, read, reflect, recite, and review** (Tomas & Robinson, 1972). An explanation of the different components of the SQ4R follows:

- **Survey:** During the **survey (S)** part, readers examine the headings, illustrations, bold letters, and major components of the text in order to develop predictions and generate **questions (Q)** about the topic.

- **Question:** The student may wish to devise some questions that the chapter will probably answer. Through these questions, students establish the purpose for reading and the questions serve as a reading guide. If the chapter has questions at the end, the student can also study these before reading the chapter.

- **Read (1R):** During the next stage, students read while looking for answers to the questions previously generated and/or those questions written by the publishers, which are usually located at the end of the section.

- **Write (2R):** Students monitor their comprehension as they write a summary of the story or text. Creating a summary allows students opportunities to internalize and make their own interpretation of the content.

- **Recite (3R):** The student attempts to answer orally, or in writing, the student-developed questions or the questions at the end of the chapter.

- **Review (4R):** Finally, students review the text to evaluate the accuracy of their answers and to show how much they learned about the content.

Reciprocal teaching is an instructional activity designed for struggling readers in which the teacher engages students in a dialogue about specific portions of a text (Palinscar & Brown, 1984). The main purpose of this activity is to guide children to construct meaning and to monitor reading comprehension. The dialogue is structured to elicit four components:

1. Summarizing the content of a passage

2. Asking a question about the main idea

3. Clarifying difficult parts of the content

4. Predicting what will come next

DRTA

The acronym **DRTA** stands for Directed Reading/Thinking Activity. This teacher-directed strategy helps students to establish a purpose for reading a story or reading expository writing from a content book (Reutzel & Cooter, 1992). The teacher models the process of creating and correcting predictions as the story progresses to strengthen comprehension. DRTA has three main steps:

1. **Sample the text to develop background:** Children are guided to read the title, look at pictures or any kind of visual representations, and read some sample lines from the text to develop hypothesis about the content of the text.

2. **Make predictions:** Students make predictions based on a sample of the text.

3. **Confirm or correct predictions:** Children read the text and engage in follow-up activities to corroborate if the predictions were correct.

Reading Comprehension in the Content Areas

To assist children, and especially ELLs, in approaching reading material that may be beyond their reading level, teachers can incorporate the following strategies.

- Record selected passages that students can listen to while reading along with the text. Teachers can use adult volunteers and fluent readers in the group to read to children unable to read it for themselves.

- Pair children off into a tutor/tutee arrangement or in a small group reading format. Teachers should pair children of different linguistic levels and degree of achievement to create a peer-support system.

- Introduce the technical vocabulary of the content areas prior to reading. Introduce elements such as connotation (implied meaning), denotation (literal meaning), and idioms in the way they are used in text. For example, the word *right* can have multiple meanings depending on the content area or the activity. In mathematics, *right* is used to describe an angle of 90 degrees, but in social studies, *right* can be used to provide directions or to declare correctness.

- Teach content vocabulary through direct, concrete experiences as opposed to definitions. Definitions can lead to misinterpretations since additional words are required to define the term. Teaching vocabulary in a contextualized situation is particularly important for ELLs because they often rely on translations that do not always represent the intended concept. For example, in English the word *bayou* is used extensively in Texas and Louisiana. However, *bayou* is very difficult to define for someone who has never seen one. What is the difference between a bayou, a creek, a swamp, or a marshland? How big is a bayou? If an adult has difficulty answering these questions, imagine how young children may struggle!

- Introduce instructional strategies for self-monitoring reading comprehension. In this kind of strategy, students read aloud a passage and then pause to question themselves about the meaning of the passage.

Strategies for Developing Critical-Thinking Skills

Critical-thinking skills include analysis, synthesis, and evaluation. Benjamin Bloom (1956) created taxonomy for categorizing levels of thinking processes typical in schoolchildren. The taxonomy presents a structure to categorize the levels of thinking required in order to ask and answer questions. These questions have traditionally been used to guide children from the basic recalling of information (**knowledge**) and understanding information (**comprehension**) to using higher order thinking skills such as analysis, synthesis, and evaluation. Recalling and understanding are important parts of reading comprehension; however, it is a teacher's responsibility to help children move from literal comprehension and explicit ideas to a more figurative comprehension and implicit ideas. Teachers have to guide children to analyze the ideas presented in text and then to make inferences (**analysis**), to assess their inferences (**evaluation**), to draw conclusions about the ideas (**synthesis**), and perhaps to apply the ideas to new situations (**application**). Children who are able to go beyond the literal and explicit information in text develop a deeper understand of the content areas and are able to manipulate the content at higher levels of thinking.

Linguistic Accommodation Testing for ELLs and Special Education Students

The state of Texas allows for linguistic accommodation for ELLs and special education children taking the content portion of the STAAR examination in grades 3–8 and 10 in order to ensure that reading comprehension does not interfere in assessing content mastery. Based on specific recommendations from the Admission, Review, and Dismissal (ARD) and/or the Language Proficiency Assessment Committee (LPAC), districts can allow linguistic accommodations for special education and ELL students when taking the basic skills test (i.e., the STAAR).

References

Anderson, L.W., and Krathwohl, D.R. (Eds.). (2001). A taxonomy for learning, teaching and assessing: A revision of Bloom's Taxonomy of educational objectives: Complete edition, New York: Longman.

Bloom, B.S., Englehart, M., Hill, W., Furst, E., & Krathwohl, D. (1956). Taxonomy of educational objectives: The classification of educational goals: Handbook I, cognitive domain. New York: Toronto: Longman, Green & Co.

Caldwell, J.S. and L. Leslie. (2005). Intervention strategies to follow, informal reading inventory assessment: So what do I do now? Boston: Pearson Education, Inc.

Chall, J.S. (1983). Stages of reading development, New York: McGraw-Hill.

Chall, J.S., Jacobs, V.A., & Baldwin, L.E. (1990). The reading crisis: Why poor children fall behind. Cambridge, Mass.: Harvard University Press.

Clay, M.M. (2002). An observation survey of early literacy achievement. 2nd ed. Portsmouth, NH: Heinemann.

Cunningham, P. (2012). Phonics They Use: Words for Reading and Writing (5th ed.). New York: Pearson.

Denton, C., Bryan, D., Wexler, J., Reed, D., & S. Vaughn. (2007). Effective instruction for middle school students with reading difficulties: The reading teacher's sourcebook. Austin, TX: Vaughn Gross Center for Reading and Language Arts at The University of Texas at Austin.

Dorfman, L.R., and R. Cappelli. (2007). Mentor texts: Teaching writing through children's literature, K–6. Portland, ME: Stenhouse Publishers.

Ehri, L. (1998). Grapheme-phoneme knowledge is essential for learning to read words in English. In J. Metsala and L. Ehri Word Recognition in Beginning Literacy, (Eds.), 3–40. Mahwah, NJ: Erlbaum.

Gersten, R., Baker, S.K., Shanahan, T., Linan-Thompson, S., Collins, P., and R. Scarcella. (2007). Effective literacy and English language instruction for English Learners in the elementary grades: A practice guide. Washington, DC: National Center for Education Evaluation and Regional Assistance, Institute of Education Sciences, U.S. Department of Education.

Goudvis, A. and S. Harvey. (2000). Strategies that work. Portland, ME: Stenhouse Publishers.

Graham, S., and D. Perin. (2007). Writing next: Effective strategies to improve writing of adolescents in middle and high schools – A report to Carnegie Corporation of New York. Washington, DC: Alliance for Excellent Education.

Graves, D. (2003). Writing: Teachers and children at work, 20th Anniversary Ed. Portsmouth, NH: Heinemann.

Hart, B., and R.T. Risley. (1995). Meaningful differences in the everyday experience of young American children. Baltimore: Paul H. Brookes.

Herrell, A. and M. Jordan. (2007). Fifty strategies for teaching English language learners. (2nd ed.) New York: Pearson.

Kieffer, M.J. & Lesaux, N.K. (2007). Breaking down words to build meaning: Morphology, vocabulary, and reading comprehension in the urban classroom. *The Reading Teacher, 61*, 134–144, (2007)

Kress, G. & T.J. Van Leeuwen. (2001). Multimodal discourse: The modes and media of contemporary communication. London, England: Oxford University Press.

Lapp, D., D. Fisher, J. Flood, and A. Cabello. (2001). An integrated approach to the teaching and assessment of language arts. In Literacy assessment of second language learners. S. Rollins Hurley & J. Villamil Tinajero (Eds.). 1–24. Boston: Allyn and Bacon.

Mooney, M. (1990). Reading to, with and by Children. Katonah, NY: Richard C. Owen.

Nagy, W.E. (1988). Teaching vocabulary to improve reading comprehension. Newark, DE: International Reading Association.

The National Commission on Writing in America's Schools and Colleges. (2003). The neglected "R:" The need for a writing revolution. Washington, DC: College Entrance Examination Board.

Northwest Regional Education Laboratory. 2012. 6+1 Trait Writing.

Palinscar, A.S. & Brown, A.L. (1984). Reciprocal teaching of comprehension-fostering and comprehension-monitoring activities. Cognition and Instruction (1): 117–175.

Pearson, P.D., & M.C. Gallagher. (1983). The instruction of reading comprehension. Contemporary Educational Psychology, 8, 317–344.

Peregoy, S.F., O.F. Boyle, and K. Cadiero-Kapplan. (2008). Reading, writing and learning in ESL: A resource book for K-12 teachers. 5th. ed. New York: Pearson.

Piper, T. (2006). Language and learning: The home school year. 4th ed. Columbus, OH: Merrill Prentice Hall.

Rasinski, T.V. (2003). The fluent reader: Oral reading strategies for building word recognition, fluency, and comprehension. New York: Scholastic.

Reutzel, R.D., and R. Cooter. (1992). Teaching children to read: From basals to books. New York: Macmillan Publishing Co.

Rosenblatt, L. (1993). Literature as exploration. New York: Modern Language Association of America

Stanovich, K.E. (1986). Matthew Effects in Reading: Some consequences of individual differences in the acquisition of literacy. Reading Research Quarterly. 21(4), 360–407.

Stewig, J.W. and Jett-Simpson. (1995). Language arts in the early childhood classroom. Belmont, CA: Wadsworth.

Strickland, D., & Snow, C. (2002). Preparing our teachers: Opportunities for better reading instruction. Washington, DC: Joseph Henry Press.

TEKS. 2009a. Chapter 110. English Language arts and reading. Subchapter A. Elementary. Texas Education Code, §28.002.

TEKS. 2009b. Chapter 110. English Language arts and reading. Subchapter B. Elementary. Texas Education Code, §28.002.

TEA. 2011. Texas English Language Proficiency Assessment System (TELPAS).

Tomas, E., and H. Robinson. (1972). Improving reading in every class: A source book for teachers. Boston: Allyn and Bacon.

Vacca, R.T., and J.A. Vacca. (1989). Content area reading. Glenview, IL: Scott Foresman.

Vygotsky L. (1978) Mind in society Cambridge Mass: Harvard University Press.

Worthy, J., Broaddus, K., and G. Ivey. (2001). Pathways to independence: Reading, writing, and learning in grades 3–8. New York: Guilford.

Worthy, J., Moorman, M., and M. Turner. (1999). What Johnny likes to read is hard to find in school. Reading Research Quarterly, 34(1), 12–27.

Wysocki, A.F., J. Johnson-Eilola, C. L. Selfe, & G. Sirc. (2004). Writing new media: Theory and applications for expanding the teaching of composition. Logan, UT: Utah State University Press.

Subject Test II: Mathematics (807)

OVERVIEW OF SUBJECT TEST II: MATHEMATICS

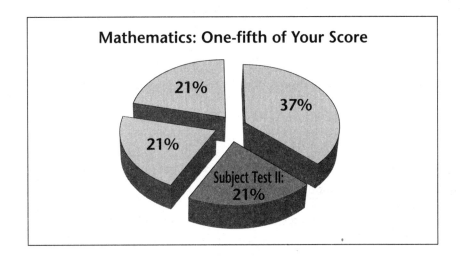

Subject Test II: Mathematics, like the Social Studies and Science subtests, makes up approximately one-fifth of the questions you will see on the TExES Core Subjects 4–8 test. You'll have 1 hour and 5 minutes to answer 42 test items. That gives you about a minute and a half for each question.

The Mathematics subject test assesses eight Texas educator standards, in connection with the statewide curriculum, known as Texas Essential Knowledge and Skills (TEKS). These standards are presented as part of Competency 017, covered later in this chapter.

This subject test embraces 19 competencies, which broadly define "what an entry-level educator in this field in Texas public schools should know and be able to do," according to the Texas Education Agency. These competencies are covered in turn in this chapter. As part of your preparation, we encourage you to drill down in the official test framework to the descriptive statements, which describe the finer points of the knowledge and skills for which you are accountable. With the proviso that the Core Subjects 4–8 test by its nature is notably wide-ranging, this REA guide hits the content you're most likely to see on the exam.

COMPETENCY 001

The teacher understands the structure of number systems, the development of a sense of quantity and the relationship between quantity and symbolic representations.

The beginning teacher:

A. Analyzes the structure of numeration systems and the roles of place value and zero in the base ten system.

B. Understands the relative magnitude of whole numbers, integers, rational numbers, irrational numbers and real numbers.

C. Demonstrates an understanding of a variety of models for representing numbers (e.g., fraction strips, diagrams, patterns, shaded regions, number lines).

D. Demonstrates an understanding of equivalency among different representations of rational numbers.

E. Selects appropriate representations of real numbers (e.g., fractions, decimals, percents, roots, exponents, scientific notation) for particular situations.

F. Understands the characteristics of the set of whole numbers, integers, rational numbers, real numbers and complex numbers (e.g., commutativity, order, closure, identity elements, inverse elements, density).

G. Demonstrates an understanding of how some situations that have no solution in one number system (e.g., whole numbers, integers and rational numbers) have solutions in another number system (e.g., real numbers, complex numbers and irrational numbers).

H. Approximates (mentally and with calculators) the value of numbers.

I. Represents fractions and decimals to the tenths or hundredths as distances from zero on a number line.

Place Value

Place value is based on powers of 10. It assigns a value to a digit depending on its placement in a numeral.

Millions	Hundred thousands	Ten thousands	Thousands	Hundreds	Tens	Ones		Tenths	Hundredths	Thousandths	Ten thousandths	Hundred thousandths
			7	3	2	5	.	4				

Expanded Form

Any number can be written in expanded form, which shows place value by multiplying each digit in a number by the appropriate power of 10.

Example $7{,}325.4 = 7 \times 10^3 + 3 \times 10^2 + 2 \times 10^1 + 5 \times 10^0 + 4 \times 10^{-1}$

or

$7{,}325.4 = 7 \times 1{,}000 + 3 \times 100 + 2 \times 10 + 5 \times 1 + 4 \times \dfrac{1}{10}$

Natural Numbers

Natural numbers, which are also called counting numbers, include $\{1, 2, 3, 4, \ldots, \infty\}$.

Whole Numbers

Whole numbers are the set of natural numbers including zero.

Integers

The set of integers includes positive and negative whole numbers. The set of integers includes: $\{-\infty, \ldots, -4, -3, -2, -1, 0, 1, 2, 3, 4, \ldots, \infty\}$. Integers are often represented on a number line that extends in both directions from zero.

Rational Numbers

A rational number can be expressed as a ratio or quotient of two integers, where the denominator is not zero. Rational numbers are commonly expressed as fractions or decimals, such as $\frac{3}{10} = 0.3$, or $\frac{2}{3} = 0.\overline{666}$. Rational numbers, when represented in decimal form, either terminate or repeat. Nonrepeating decimals cannot be expressed in this way and are called irrational numbers.

Irrational Numbers

Irrational numbers are not rational, meaning they cannot be represented as fractions, and when in decimal form, they do not terminate or repeat. Common examples of irrational numbers are π, e, or $\sqrt{2}$.

Real Numbers

Real numbers consist of rational and irrational numbers. The figure below is an illustration of the real numbers.

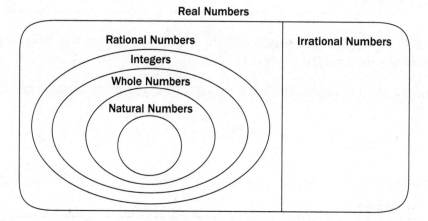

Scientific Notation

Scientific notation is a form of writing a number as the product of a power of 10 and a decimal number between 1 and 10.

Example 1 $4,040,700,000 = 4.0407 \times 10^9$

Example 2 $0.005806 = 5.806 \times 10^{-3}$

Absolute Value

The absolute value of a number is the distance of that number from zero on a number line.

The absolute value of any number is positive or zero.

Example $|-3| = 3$ since the position of -3 on a number line is 3 units away from zero.

COMPETENCY 002

The teacher understands number operations and computational algorithms.

The beginning teacher:

A. Works proficiently with real and complex numbers and their operations.

B. Analyzes and describes relationships between number properties, operations and algorithms for the four basic operations involving integers, rational numbers and real numbers.

C. Uses a variety of concrete and visual representations to demonstrate the connections between operations and algorithms.

D. Justifies procedures used in algorithms for the four basic operations with integers, rational numbers and real numbers and analyzes error patterns that may occur in their application.

E. Relates operations and algorithms involving numbers to algebraic procedures (e.g., adding fractions to adding rational expressions, division of integers to division of polynomials).

F. Extends and generalizes the operations on rationals and integers to include exponents, their properties and their applications to the real numbers.

G. Compares and orders real numbers with and without a calculator.

H. Uses models, such as concrete objects, pictorial models and number lines, to add, subtract, multiply and divide integers and connect the real-world problems to algorithms, including equivalent ratios and rates.

I. Divides whole numbers by unit fractions and unit fractions by whole numbers.

Operations and Algorithms

Several of the rules of properties of numbers will be helpful as you develop an understanding of this competency.

Properties of Numbers

Closure Property of Addition or Subtraction

If a and b are real numbers, then $a + b$ is a real number.

If a and b are real numbers, then $a - b$ is a real number.

Commutative Property of Addition

The order of the addends does not change the sum.

$$a + b = b + a$$

Associative Property of Addition

Grouping the addends differently does not change the sum.

$$(a + b) + c = a + (b + c)$$

Identity Property of Addition and Subtraction

The sum or difference of a number and zero is the number itself.

$$a + 0 = a - 0 = a$$

Closure Property of Multiplication

If a and b are real numbers, $a \times b$ is also a real number.

Commutative Property of Multiplication

The order of the factors does not change the product.

$$a \times b = b \times a$$

Associative Property of Multiplication

Grouping the factors differently does not change the product.

$$(a \times b) \times c = a \times (b \times c)$$

Identity Property of Multiplication

The product of a number and 1 is the number itself.

$$a \times 1 = 1 \times a = a$$

Zero Multiplication Property

The product of a number and zero is zero.

$$0 \times a = a \times 0 = 0$$

Distributive Property

To multiply a number by a sum or difference, multiply the number by each addend and then add or subtract, respectively.

$$\text{For all numbers } a, b, \text{ and } c, a(b + c) = ab + ac$$

$$\text{and } a(b - c) = ab - ac$$

Order of Operations

Often students learn the distributive property when they investigate problems requiring the order of operations. When presented with the task of evaluating $2(7 + 3)$, two possible approaches will produce the same correct result. One approach is to add first, then multiply: $2(10) = 20$, whereas another approach is to multiply first, then add: $14 + 6 = 20$. Obtaining the same answer using two different strategies may be cumbersome for some students.

Providing more examples of a different nature is needed for students to understand that the order of calculating mathematical problems will impact the outcome. Consider the problems $3 + 4 \times 8$ and $4 \times 8 + 3$. Work both problems from left to right and notice two different results.

Example 1 $3 + 4 \times 8 = 7 \times 8 = 56$ **INCORRECT**

Example 2 $4 \times 8 + 3 = 32 + 3 = 35$ **CORRECT**

Notice that the numbers in both expressions are the same but the order of the mathematical operations is different. In the first example, the addition sign comes before the multiplication, and the second example is the reverse. The second example actually shows the process that should be completed for the first example. Although the addition symbol is the first symbol one encounters in the problem when reading from left to right, addition is one of the last operations when evaluating expressions.

Please Excuse My Dear Aunt Sally or **PEMDAS** is the common phrase and acronym students learn to remember the order of operations. The words in the phrase or the letters of PEMDAS stand for *Parentheses*, *Exponents*, *Multiplication*, *Division*, *Addition*, and *Subtraction*. More important is the understanding of what each word means in regard to evaluating problems. Presenting the order of operations vertically can be helpful to explain the order of the calculations.

Parentheses: First, compute within any grouping symbols, which may include parentheses ( ), brackets [ ], absolute value $|\ \ |$, or square root $\sqrt{\ \ }$ symbols.

Exponents: Next, calculate any exponential terms, including powers and square roots.

Multiplication/Division: Read the problem from left to right and top to bottom. If a division symbol comes before a multiplication symbol, perform the division first. If a multiplication symbol occurs before a division symbol, perform the multiplication first.

Addition/Subtraction: The process is similar to the rule for multiplication and division. Subtraction will occur before addition if the subtraction symbol comes before the addition symbol, whereas addition will precede subtraction if an addition symbol occurs before a subtraction symbol.

Computations with Fractions

A fraction is a number that represents part of a set, part of a whole, or a quotient in the form $\frac{a}{b}$, which can be read as a divided by b. Computations with fractions include finding equivalent fractions and simplifying; converting improper fractions to mixed numbers; and addition, subtraction, multiplication, and division.

Equivalent Fractions and Simplifying

Although the fractions $\frac{1}{4}$ and $\frac{2}{8}$ do not look alike, they represent the same value and are called equivalent or equal fractions; hence $\frac{1}{4} = \frac{2}{8}$.

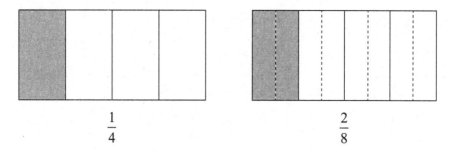

$$\frac{1}{4} \qquad\qquad\qquad \frac{2}{8}$$

Simplifying fractions requires identifying common factors among the numerator and denominator of a fraction. For example, to simplify we can recognize that both 60 and 140 are divisible by 10.

$$\frac{60}{140} = \frac{6 \bullet 10}{14 \bullet 10} = \frac{6}{14}$$

Also,

$$\frac{6}{14} = \frac{3 \bullet 2}{7 \bullet 2} = \frac{3}{7}$$

It was shown that $\frac{60}{140}$ was simplified to $\frac{6}{14}$ by factoring out the common factor of 10; then $\frac{6}{14}$ was simplified to $\frac{3}{7}$ by factoring out a common factor of 2. This means that $\frac{60}{140} = \frac{3}{7}$. Since the simplification process identified two common factors of 10 and 2, the **greatest common factor** (GCF) or **divisor** (GCD) of 60 and 140 is 20. This means the simplification process could have been completed in one step instead of two by factoring out the greatest common factor of both numbers.

$$\frac{60}{140} = \frac{3 \bullet 20}{7 \bullet 20} = \frac{3}{7}$$

The greatest common factor of a and b is the greatest number that divides both a and b evenly.

Converting Improper Fractions to Mixed Numbers

To convert an improper fraction like $\frac{7}{2}$, divide the numerator by the denominator. Many problems like this can be computed mentally by asking yourself, "How many times does 2 go into 7 evenly?" The answer is 3 times. "How much is left over?" One. The remainder is the numerator of the fractional portion of the mixed number and the denominator stays the same. So, $\frac{7}{2} = 3\frac{1}{2}$.

Addition and Subtraction of Fractions

There are two different cases to consider when adding or subtracting fractions: fractions with like denominators (homogeneous fractions) and fractions with unlike denominators. To add or subtract fractions with like, or the same, denominators, combine numerators and the denominator stays the same. For example, $\frac{2}{7} + \frac{4}{7} = \frac{6}{7}$ and $\frac{3}{5} - \frac{1}{5} = \frac{2}{5}$.

When denominators are unlike, first determine a common denominator, create equivalent fractions with that common denominator, and then combine numerators as above. For example, find the sum of $\frac{2}{7} + \frac{1}{3}$. To determine a common denominator, find the **least common multiple** of 7 and 3, which is 21. Next, change both fractions into equivalent fractions with 21 as the denominator. Finally, combine numerators.

$$\frac{2}{7} + \frac{1}{3} = \frac{2 \cdot 3}{7 \cdot 3} + \frac{1 \cdot 7}{3 \cdot 7} = \frac{6}{21} + \frac{7}{21} = \frac{13}{21}$$

Depending on the resulting fraction, you may need to simplify it.

Multiplication of Fractions

If $\frac{a}{b}$ and $\frac{c}{d}$ are any rational numbers, then $\frac{a}{b} \cdot \frac{c}{d} = \frac{a \cdot c}{b \cdot d}$. In short, find the product of the numerators and the product of the denominators, and simplify if possible.

$$\frac{5}{6} \times \frac{3}{4} = \frac{15}{24}$$

$$\frac{15}{24} = \frac{5 \cdot 3}{8 \cdot 3} = \frac{5}{8}$$

Division of Fractions

If $\frac{a}{b}$ and $\frac{c}{d}$ are any rational numbers and $\frac{c}{d} \neq 0$, then $\frac{a}{b} \div \frac{c}{d} = \frac{a}{b} \cdot \frac{d}{c} = \frac{a \cdot d}{b \cdot c}$. To divide fractions, multiply the first fraction by the reciprocal of the second fraction, and simplify if possible. A common phrase to recall is *invert and multiply*.

$$\frac{1}{6} \div \frac{2}{3} = \frac{1}{6} \cdot \frac{3}{2} = \frac{3}{12}$$

$$\frac{3}{12} = \frac{1 \cdot 3}{4 \cdot 3} = \frac{1}{4}$$

Computations with Decimals

Rational numbers can be expressed in the form of decimals, which are fractional numbers written using base 10. A mixed decimal number has a whole number part, too. For example, 2.8 is a mixed decimal number, and 0.75 is a mixed decimal number. The whole number part of .75 is zero.

Addition and Subtraction of Decimals

Decimal numbers can be written as fractions whose denominators are powers of 10 (i.e., 10, 100, 1,000, etc.). For example, 0.125 written in word form is one hundred twenty-five thousandths and is equivalent to the fraction $\frac{125}{1000}$. When adding or subtracting fractions, we created equivalent fractions that had common denominators, then combined numerators. Similarly, with decimal addition or subtraction, we will combine digits of the same place value. Using the standard algorithm to add or subtract two decimal numbers, arrange the decimal numbers vertically, aligning the decimal points, and then combine the digits in the same place values.

> **Example** Find the sum of 25.07 and 14.326.
>
> $$\begin{array}{r} 25.07 \\ + \ 14.326 \\ \hline 39.396 \end{array}$$

Multiplication of Decimals

Multiplication of decimals does not require aligning decimal points. Like addition/subtraction, the numbers can be arranged vertically but with right justification. The numbers can be multiplied as if they were whole numbers and the number of digits to the right of the decimal point in the product should be equal to the total number of decimal places within the two factors.

> **Example** Find the product of 3.25 and 0.3.
>
> $$\begin{array}{r} 3.25 \\ \times \ 0.3 \\ \hline 0.975 \end{array}$$

Division of Decimals

Division of decimals can be calculated in the same way as division of traditional whole numbers. When the divisor is a whole number, the division can be handled as with whole numbers and the decimal point placed directly over the decimal point in the dividend. When the divisor is not a whole number, as in $1.44 \div 0.2$, we can obtain a whole-number divisor by treating the quotient as a fraction and multiplying both numerator and denominator by a power of 10. Thus, 1.44 becomes 14.4, and 0.2 becomes 2.

$$
\begin{array}{r}
7.2 \\
2\overline{\smash)14.4} \\
\underline{-14} \\
0\ 4 \\
\underline{-4} \\
0
\end{array}
$$

Laws of Exponents

First Law of Exponents

$$a^n \bullet a^m = a^{n+m}$$

$$5^2 \bullet 5^1 = 5^{2+1} = 5^3 = 125$$

Second Law of Exponents

$$(ab)^n = a^n \bullet b^n$$

$$(4 \bullet 3)^2 = 4^2 \bullet 3^2 = 16 \bullet 9 = 144$$

Power of a Power

$$\left(a^n\right)^m = a^{nm}$$

$$\left(4^3\right)^2 = 4^{3 \bullet 2} = 4^6 = 4{,}096$$

Power of a Quotient

$$\left(\frac{a}{b}\right)^n = \frac{a^n}{b^n}$$

$$\left(\frac{1}{3}\right)^4 = \frac{1^4}{3^4} = \frac{1}{81}$$

Fractional Exponents

$$a^{1/n} = \sqrt[n]{a}$$

$$27^{1/3} = \sqrt[3]{27} = 3$$

Negative Exponents

$$a^{-n} = \frac{1}{a^n}, a \neq 0$$

$$6^{-2} = \frac{1}{6^2} = \frac{1}{36}$$

Complex Numbers

Complex numbers, which combine real numbers and imaginary numbers, are not a part of the real number system, but they exist in their own number system. Similar rules or properties for computation exist in the complex number system. Standard form for complex numbers is $a + bi$, where a and b are real numbers. The imaginary number i is defined as

$$i = \sqrt{-1}$$

Also,

$$i^2 = \left(\sqrt{-1}\right)^2 = -1$$

A pattern can be developed for investigating the powers of i.

$$i = i$$
$$i^2 = -1$$
$$i^3 = -i$$
$$i^4 = 1$$
$$i^5 = i$$
$$i^6 = i^2 = -1$$
$$i^7 = i^3 = -i$$
$$i^8 = i^4 = 1$$

Computations with Complex Numbers

Computations with complex numbers are similar to those of variable expressions — combining like terms. However, if an i^2 appears in the problem, we can substitute the value –1.

Example 1 Evaluate $5 + 7i - 3i + 9$.

Combine the constants and the imaginary terms.

$14 + 4i$

Example 2 Evaluate $3i(-2 + 5i)$.

Begin by distributing the $3i$ through the parentheses.

$-6i + 15i^2$

Next, substitute $i^2 = -1$ and multiply 15 by –1.

$-6i + 15(-1) = -6i - 15$

Then write the expression in standard form, $a + bi$.

$-15 - 6i$

Example 3   Evaluate $(7 + 2i)(3 - 4i)$.

FOIL is a common mathematical process used to multiply two binomials. It is similar to the distributive property. Take the first term in the first set of parentheses and distribute through the second set of parentheses. Continue the process with the second term in the first set of parentheses. FOIL stands for

First: multiply the first terms in the parentheses $7(3) = 21$

Outer: multiply the outside terms of the problem $7(-4i) = -28i$

Inner: multiply the inside two terms of the problem $2i(3) = 6i$

Last: multiply the last two terms in the parentheses $2i(-4i) = -8i^2$

After calculating each product, combine like terms, substitute -1 for i^2, and write the expression in standard form, $a + bi$.

$(7 + 2i)(3 - 4i)$

$21 + (-28i) + 6i + (-8i^2)$

$21 - 22i + (-8)(-1)$

$21 - 22i + 8$

$29 - 22i$

Rationalize the Denominator

To rationalize a quantity literally means to make the quantity rational. A rational number is one that can be expressed as the ratio or quotient of two non-zero integers. Rational numbers are commonly expressed as fractions or decimals, such as $\frac{3}{10} = 0.3$, or $\frac{2}{3} = 0.\overline{666}$. So, to rationalize the denominator of a fraction, we will create an equivalent fraction with a rational denominator.

Consider the example $\frac{6 + i}{3i}$. The denominator, $3i$, is imaginary and not a rational number. However, we will use the fact that $i^2 = -1$ to rationalize the denominator. Multiply $\frac{6 + i}{3i}$ by a factor of one, which can be written as $\frac{i}{i}$.

$$\frac{6 + i}{3i} \cdot \frac{i}{i} = \frac{6i + i^2}{3i^2}$$

Next, substitute –1 for i^2, and simplify.

$$\frac{6i + (-1)}{3(-1)} = \frac{-1 + 6i}{-3} = \frac{1 - 6i}{3}$$

The new denominator, 3, is a rational number; therefore, the denominator is now rational. In addition, we can say $\frac{6 + i}{3i}$ is equivalent to $\frac{1 - 6i}{3}$, or $\frac{6 + i}{3i} = \frac{1 - 6i}{3}$.

If the denominator to be rationalized is a binomial, multiply by a factor of 1, changing the sign within the binomial. For example, consider $\frac{5i}{3 - 2i}$. To rationalize this denominator, we multiply by $\frac{3 + 2i}{3 + 2i}$. This is called a conjugate.

$$\frac{5i}{3 - 2i} \cdot \frac{3 + 2i}{3 + 2i} = \frac{15i + 10i^2}{9 + 6i - 6i - 4i^2}$$

Substitute –1 for i^2, and simplify.

$$\frac{15i + 10(-1)}{9 - 4(-1)} = \frac{-10 + 15i}{9 + 4} = \frac{-10 + 15i}{13}$$

COMPETENCY 003

The teacher understands ideas of number theory and uses numbers to model and solve problems within and outside of mathematics.

The beginning teacher:

A. Demonstrates an understanding of ideas from number theory (e.g., prime factorization, greatest common divisor) as they apply to whole numbers, integers and rational numbers and uses these ideas in problem situations.

B. Uses integers, rational numbers and real numbers to describe and quantify phenomena such as money, length, area, volume and density.

C. Applies knowledge of place value and other number properties to develop techniques of mental mathematics and computational estimation.

D. Applies knowledge of counting techniques such as permutations and combinations to quantify situations and solve problems.

E.   Applies properties of real numbers to solve a variety of theoretical and applied problems.

F.   Makes connections among various representations of a numerical relationship and generates a different representation of data given another representation of data (such as a table, graph, equation or verbal description).

Composite Number

A composite number is a number that is divisible by at least one other number besides 1 and itself. For example: 12 is a composite number because it has more than two factors: 1, 2, 3, 4, 6, 12.

Prime Numbers

A prime number is a number that is divisible by only 1 and itself, meaning it has only two factors. For example, 11 is a prime number since its only factors are 1 and 11.

Prime Factorization

Exponents can be used to write the prime factorization of a number; that is, every number can be written as a product of prime numbers. When a factor is repeated in a prime factorization, express the repeated factor in exponential form. Most often, students use a factor tree to find the prime factorization of a composite number. To begin factorizing, choose two factors of the number and continue factoring each number until you have all prime numbers.

Example   What is the prime factorization of 36?

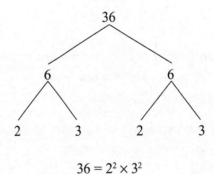

$$36 = 2^2 \times 3^2$$

Divisibility Rules

Sometimes it is handy to know if one number is divisible by another just by looking at a number or by performing a simple test.

Divisibility Rule for . . .	Rule
2	Any integer is divisible by 2 if it is an even number.
3	Any integer is divisible by 3 if the sum of its digits is divisible by 3.
4	Any integer is divisible by 4 if the last two digits of the integer represent a number divisible by 4.
5	Any integer is divisible by 5 if it ends in 0 or 5.
6	Any integer is divisible by 6 if it is divisible by both 2 and 3.
8	Any integer is divisible by 8 if the last three digits of the integer represent a number divisible by 8.
9	Any integer is divisible by 9 if the sum of the digits is divisible by 9.
10	Any integer is divisible by 10 if it ends in 0.

Common Multiple

A common multiple is a whole number that is a multiple of two or more given numbers. For example, the common multiples of 2, 3, and 4 are 12, 24, 36, 48, ...

Some students might claim 6 and/or 8 are common multiples of 2, 3, and 4, but this is incorrect. Six is a common multiple only among the numbers 2 and 3, but not 4. Likewise, 8 is a common multiple among the numbers 2 and 4, but not 3.

Greatest Common Divisor

The greatest common divisor (GCD) of two or more non-zero integers is the largest positive integer that divides into the numbers without producing a remainder. The GCD is useful for simplifying fractions into lowest terms, which was explored earlier in this chapter. The term *greatest common factor* (GCF) is often used when simplifying fractions.

Example: Find the greatest common divisor of 40 and 56. To identify the GCD, make a list of all the factors of each number. Then, identify the largest common factor between the two sets of numbers.

$$\begin{cases} 40 : 1, 2, 4, 5, 8, 10, 20, 40 \\ 56 : 1, 2, 4, 7, 8, 14, 28, 56 \end{cases}$$

The largest or greatest common factor of each list is 8. Therefore, the GCD of 40 and 56 is 8.

Using Dollars, Dimes, and Pennies

Money is familiar to students and an apt manipulative for classroom use. Since 10 dimes are worth a dollar and 100 pennies are also worth a dollar, fractional concepts and decimal computations can easily be taught. Since a dollar is worth 1 or one whole, a dime represents $\frac{1}{10}$ and a penny represents $\frac{1}{100}$. A natural progression of this is to represent decimal numbers in the form of money. For example, the number 24.78 can be modeled with two $10 bills, four $1 bills, seven dimes, and eight pennies. Expanded notation easily follows as

$$24.78 = 2 \bullet 10 + 4 \bullet 1 + 7 \bullet \frac{1}{10} + 8 \bullet \frac{1}{100}.$$

Decimal Representations with Base-10 Blocks

Base-10 blocks are handy manipulatives for fractional and decimal representations and computations. Graph paper or 10-by-10 grids can be used to transform the concrete use of base-10 blocks into pictorial form. The number 1.45 is represented in the figure below.

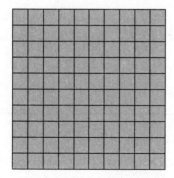 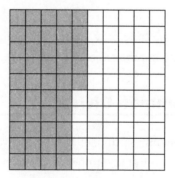

The first shaded 10-by-10 grid shows $\frac{100}{100} = 1$, and the second grid has 45 of the 100 cells shaded; therefore, it models $\frac{45}{100} = 0.45$. The pictorial representation is also an area model, meaning the visual representation shows the amount of space taken up by the shaded region. By modeling multiple decimal numbers in this form, students can more easily order a set of numbers from least to greatest.

Mental Mathematics and Estimation

The ability to make accurate estimates is important in today's society. Always look for **easy combinations** or **compatible numbers** when doing mental calculations. Consider the two examples below:

Example 1   Evaluate 25×8.

Compute $25 \times 4 = 100$ and then $100 \times 2 = 200$. Ultimately, the number 8 was broken down to its factors of 4×2 to rearrange the problem to be $25 \times 4 \times 2$.

Example 2   Evaluate $25 + 17 + 15$.

First combine $25 + 15 = 40$, and then find $40 + 17 = 57$. The numbers 25 and 15 are good compatible numbers since they both have 5 in the ones place-value; 40 is a nice round even number to add any other value to, hence we add 17 last.

Rounding is often a common task in mathematics. The **5-up rule** is the standard method used when rounding numbers to a certain place value. First, determine which position you are rounding. If the digit to the right of this position is 5 or more, add 1 to the digit in the position to which you are rounding and replace zeros for all of the digits to the right of the position to which you are rounding. If the digit to the right of the position to be rounded is less than 5, leave the digit unchanged and drop all of the digits to the right of the position. For example, round 37,250 to the nearest (a) hundred and (b) thousand.

(a) The digit 2 is in the hundreds position with the digit 5 to its right. Since the digit to the right is 5, round 2 to 3. Rounding the given number to the nearest hundred produces 37,300.

(b) The digit 7 is in the thousands place, and 2 is the digit to the right. Since 2 is less than 5, we will leave the 7 as is and replace all numbers to its right with zeros. Rounding the given number to the nearest thousand produces 37,000.

Permutations

The **counting principle** allows you to determine the number of possibilities of a real-life event or activity.

When dealing with the occurrence of more than one event or activity, it is important to be able to quickly determine how many outcomes exist, rather than actually listing them. If there are "*m* ways" for one activity to occur and "*n* ways" for a second activity to occur, the counting principle states that there are "*m* × *n* ways" for both to occur.

Example: A vending machine sells snacks and soft drinks. If there are 8 different snacks and 5 different soft drinks, there are 8 • 5 = 40 different ways to choose a snack and a soft drink.

Example: A popular car comes in 10 different colors, 4 different interiors, 3 engine sizes, and with or without a navigation system. There are 10 • 4 • 3 • 2 = 240 configurations of the car that are possible.

A permutation is a set of objects in which position (or order) is important. An example is a password to a bank account. If the password is HJ2M6, the order is important. MH62J will not gain access to the account.

Permutations with replacement: An object can be repeated. In the example, it is possible for a password to be HJ22M or HH22H. If we have *n* things to choose from each time we choose, the counting principle says that there will be *n* • *n* • *n* • ... permutations.

Example: In the password example containing 5 characters, there are 36 possibilities for each character (26 letters and 10 digits) and we want 5 of them. There are $36 \times 36 \times 36 \times 36 \times 36 = 36^5 = 60,466,176$ permutations. Note that this assumes that it is possible for a number to repeat.

Permutations without replacement: An object *cannot* be repeated. Once we choose it, it can no longer be chosen.

Example: In the password example, suppose that you cannot use a character over again. Once you use it, you cannot reuse it. The first character has a choice of 36. Once you use it, you now have only 35 choices for the second character. Once you use it, you only have 34 choices for the third character. So, there are $36 \times 35 \times 34 \times 33 \times 32 = 45,239,040$ permutations.

Example: An ice cream shop has 25 flavors. If a person orders a triple-decker cone, how many different cones are possible if (a) it is allowed to repeat a flavor and (b) no replacement of flavors is allowed? Note that a cone of vanilla on top, chocolate in the middle, and strawberry on the bottom is different than a cone of chocolate on top, strawberry in the middle, and vanilla on the bottom because usually the scoop on the bottom is larger than the scoop on top.

Solution:

a) 25(25)(25) = 15,625

b) 25(24)(23) = 13,800

Permutations with Like Objects

In the above examples, each object was distinct. Suppose we wanted to arrange the letters in the words *ALMOST* and *BANANA*. *ALMOST* is easy as there are 6 distinct letters and the answer is 6! = 720. But *BANANA* has the letter A appearing 3 times and the letter N appearing twice. So the number of arrangements in the word *BANANA* is 6! divided by the factorial of the number of objects that are identical. So for *BANANA*, we get $\frac{6!}{3!2!} = \frac{6 \cdot 5 \cdot 4 \cdot 3 \cdot 2 \cdot 1}{3 \cdot 2 \cdot 1 \cdot 2 \cdot 1} = 60$.

Combinations

A set of objects in which position (or order) is *not* important. An example is a dish of ice cream including scoops of vanilla, chocolate, and strawberry. Unlike a cone, we don't care about the order of the ice cream. A dish of vanilla, chocolate, and strawberry is the same as a dish of strawberry, vanilla, and chocolate.

The way to determine the number of combinations possible is to use a formula. The number of combinations of *n* objects taken *r* at a time has several notations and is computed as follows: $_nC_r = \frac{n!}{r!(n-r)!}$. When calculating combinations using this formula, we can usually use cancellation, or simplifying, to make the calculations easier.

Example: A basketball team has 9 members and 5 players are on the floor. The number of combinations of teams on the floor that are possible is given by:

$$_9C_5 = \frac{9!}{5!(9-5)!} = \frac{9!}{5! \cdot 4!} = \frac{9 \cdot 8 \cdot 7 \cdot 6 \cdot 5 \cdot 4 \cdot 3 \cdot 2 \cdot 1}{5 \cdot 4 \cdot 3 \cdot 2 \cdot 1 \cdot 4 \cdot 3 \cdot 2 \cdot 1}$$

$$= \frac{9 \cdot 8 \cdot 7 \cdot 6 \cdot 5 \cdot 4 \cdot 3 \cdot 2 \cdot 1}{5 \cdot 4 \cdot 3 \cdot 2 \cdot 1 \cdot 4 \cdot 3 \cdot 2 \cdot 1} = 126$$

It is important to be able to determine whether a problem defines a permutation or a combination.

Permutation	Combination
Picking a player to pitch, catch, and play shortstop from a group of players.	Picking three team members from a group of players.
In a dog show, choosing 1st place, 2nd place, and 3rd place from a group of dogs.	In a dog show, choosing 3 dogs that will go to the finals from a group of dogs.
From a color paint brochure, choosing a color for the walls and a color for the trim.	From a color paint brochure, choosing two colors to paint the room.

An alternate notation for combinations is sometimes used: $\binom{n}{r} = {}_nC_r$. So ${}_9C_5$ can be written as $\binom{9}{5}$.

Example: An essay exam has 10 questions and students are instructed to answer exactly 4 of them. How many ways can this be done?

Solution: ${}_{10}C_4$ or $\binom{10}{4} = \dfrac{10!}{4! \cdot 6!} = \dfrac{10 \cdot 9 \cdot 8 \cdot 7 \cdot 6 \cdot 5 \cdot 4 \cdot 3 \cdot 2 \cdot 1}{4 \cdot 3 \cdot 2 \cdot 1 \cdot 6 \cdot 5 \cdot 4 \cdot 3 \cdot 2 \cdot 1} = 210$

COMPETENCY 004

The teacher understands and uses mathematical reasoning to identify, extend and analyze patterns and understands the relationships among variables, expressions, equations, inequalities, relations and functions.

The beginning teacher:

A. Uses inductive reasoning to identify, extend and create patterns using concrete models, figures, numbers, and algebraic expressions.

B. Formulates implicit and explicit rules to describe and construct sequences verbally, numerically, graphically and symbolically.

C. Makes, tests, validates and uses conjectures about patterns and relationships in data presented in tables, sequences or graphs.

D. Gives appropriate justification of the manipulation of algebraic expressions.

E. Illustrates the concept of a function using concrete models, tables, graphs and symbolic and verbal representations.

F. Uses transformations to illustrate properties of functions and relations and to solve problems.

G. Uses graphs, tables and algebraic representations to make predictions and solve problems.

H. Uses letters to represent an unknown in an equation.

I. Formulates problem situations when given a simple equation and formulates an equation when given a problem situation.

Patterns

There are two types of patterns explored in grades 4 through 8: repeating patterns and growing patterns. An important concept in working with repeating patterns is identifying the core of the pattern, or the string of elements that repeats. Consider the musical pattern created by clapping and stomping: *stomp, stomp, clap, stomp, stomp, clap, stomp, stomp, clap, ...* The core of the pattern is *stomp, stomp, clap* and can be written in the form of *AAB*. Number patterns can be used to predict numbers down the line. For example, consider 3, 5, 7, ... The number pattern is odd numbers beginning with 3. Add 2 each time. The next three numbers in the pattern would be 9, 11, and 13.

Growing patterns involve a progression from step to step. Students should not only extend these patterns but also look for a generalization or an algebraic relationship to create a function that represents the pattern. Investigate the three steps below and generalize the growing pattern.

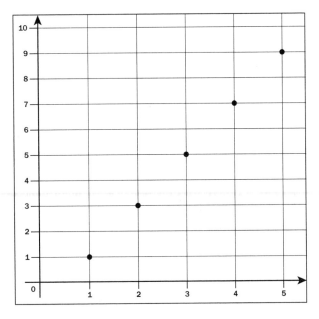

A table can be constructed to record the number of objects per step and identify the pattern.

Step	1	2	3	4	. . .	n
Number of Objects	1	3	5		. . .	

The pattern is increasing by 2 on each step, so on the fourth step there will be 7 objects, and on the nth step there will be $2n - 1$ objects. Moreover, we can graph this relationship or function:

$$f(n) = 2n - 1$$

The function $f(n) = 2n - 1$ represents the number of objects is one less than twice the step. This problem illustrates the concept of a function using models, tables, graphs, and symbolic and verbal representations, which are important concepts within mathematics.

Variables

Variables can express relationships. Consider the following statement and question: Jose was born on his three-year-old sister Kendra's birthday. How are their ages related? Three different relationships can be represented:

- Jose is three years younger than Kendra. $J = K - 3$

- Kendra is three years older than Jose. $K = J + 3$

- The difference in age between Kendra and her
  younger brother Jose is three years. $K - J = 3$

COMPETENCY 005

The teacher understands and uses linear functions to model and solve problems.

The beginning teacher:

A. Demonstrates an understanding of the concept of linear function using concrete models, tables, graphs and symbolic and verbal representations.

B. Demonstrates an understanding of the connections among linear functions, proportions and direct variation.

C. Determines the linear function that best models a set of data.

D. Analyzes the relationship between a linear equation and its graph.

E. Uses linear functions, inequalities and systems to model problems.

F. Uses a variety of representations and methods (e.g., numerical methods, tables, graphs, algebraic techniques) to solve systems of linear equations and inequalities.

G. Demonstrates an understanding of the characteristics of linear models and the advantages and disadvantages of using a linear model in a given situation.

H. Uses multiplication by a given constant factor (including unit rate) to represent and solve problems involving proportional relationships, including conversions between measurement systems, (e.g., ratio, speed, density, price, recipes, student teacher ratio).

I. Identifies proportional or nonproportional linear relationships in problem situations and solves problems.

Linear Functions and Slope

Linear functions are commonly written in the form of $y = mx + b$, where m is the slope of the function and b is the y-intercept, $(0, b)$, or the point at which the line crosses the y-axis. When the slope of a line is positive, $m > 0$, the line goes up from left to right (increases); if the slope is negative, $m < 0$, the line goes down from left to right (decreases).

Example 1 The function $y = x$ has a positive slope of $m = 1$ and a y-intercept of $(0, 0)$.

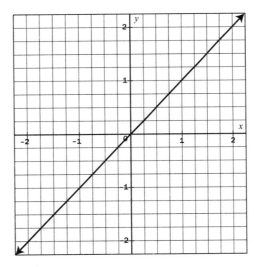

This particular function is called the linear parent function.

Example 2 The function $y = -x$ has a negative slope of $m = -1$ and a y-intercept of $(0, 0)$.

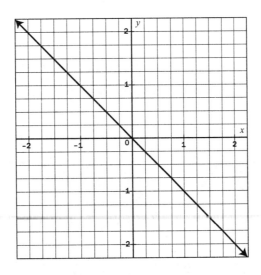

A line is defined by two points or coordinates. To find the equation of a line passing through two points, (x_1, y_1) and (x_2, y_2), we will calculate the **slope** and use the **point-slope formula**.

$$\text{slope} = m = \frac{y_2 - y_1}{x_2 - x_1} \qquad \text{point-slope formula: } y - y_1 = m(x - x_1)$$

Example 3   Find the equation of a line passing through the points $(-1, -3)$ and $(2, 2)$.

Begin by calculating the slope between the two points.

$$m = \frac{2 - (-3)}{2 - (-1)} = \frac{2 + 3}{2 + 1} = \frac{5}{3}$$

Next, choose one point and the slope to evaluate the point-slope formula.

$$y - (-3) = \frac{5}{3}[x - (-1)]$$

$$y + 3 = \frac{5}{3}(x + 1)$$

$$y + 3 = \frac{5}{3}x + \frac{5}{3}$$

$$y + 3 - 3 = \frac{5}{3}x + \frac{5}{3} - 3$$

$$y = \frac{5}{3}x - \frac{4}{3}$$

The equation of the line passing through points $(-1, -3)$ and $(2, 2)$ is $y = \frac{5}{3}x - \frac{4}{3}$, where $m = \frac{5}{3}$ and the y-intercept is $(0, -\frac{4}{3})$. The graph of the line is shown below.

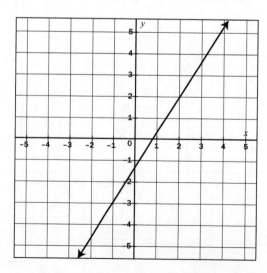

Linear equations can also be written in **standard form**, $Ax + By = C$, where A, B, and C are integers and $A \neq 0$ and $B \neq 0$. Let's take the equation from above, $y = \dfrac{5}{3}x - \dfrac{4}{3}$, and write it in standard form. First, all coefficients need to be integers. Since the slope is in fractional form, we can multiply both sides of the equation by 3 (the denominator) to clear the fractional portion of the equation, making all coefficients integers:

$$3(y) = 3\left(\frac{5}{3}x - \frac{4}{3}\right)$$
$$3y = 5x - 4$$

Then, subtract $5x$ from both sides to isolate the constant from the variable terms.

$$-5x + 3y = -4$$

By multiplying both sides of the equation by -1, it can also be written as $5x - 3y = 4$.

Modeling Linear Functions to Solve Problems

Applications, or word problems, are frequently used to help students understand linear functions and modeling problems. They can prepare students for situations they might encounter later in life. The following scenario requires students to perform multiple mathematical tasks such as creating a table, drawing a graph, and evaluating problems within the posed scenario.

Scenario:

A survey of car owners shows that the monthly cost (in dollars) to own and drive a car is given by the function $f(x) = 0.41x + 225$. Here, x represents the number of miles driven throughout the month and 225 represents the monthly expenses that come with ownership of a vehicle, such as insurance, vehicle license fees, and so on, which are independent of the miles driven.

(a) Make a table that shows the cost of having a car that is driven 0, 100, 200, . . . , 500 miles per month.

(b) Use the table to draw a graph that shows the cost of driving a car for up to 500 miles in a month.

(c) Use your graph to estimate the corresponding limit on the number of miles driven in a month if your monthly budget is limited to $400.

(d) What is the approximate number of miles driven throughout the month if the expenditures are $350?

Solution:

(a) To create a table we must first identify the variables: x is the miles driven, and y is the cost (in dollars) of owning and driving the car. We will evaluate the function $f(x) = 0.41x + 225$ when x is 0, 100, 200, 300, 400, and 500. The outputs represent the cost of owning and driving the car based on those numbers of miles driven in the month.

Miles, *x*	0	100	200	300	400	500
Cost, *y*	225	266	307	348	389	430

(b) To use the table to create a graph, plot the coordinates from the table. For example, (0, 225) is the y-intercept of the graph.

Cost of Owning and Operating a Car

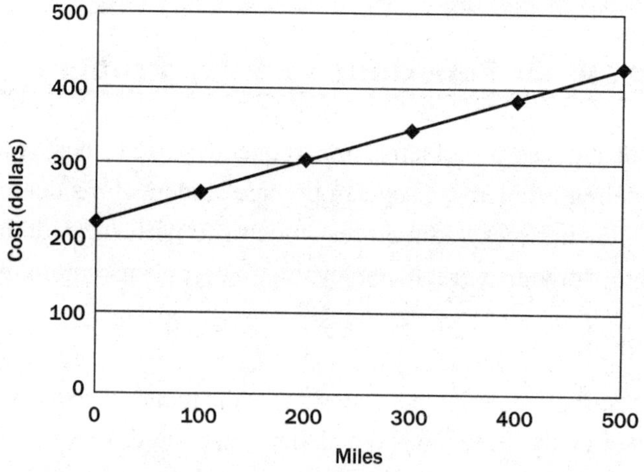

(c) To use the graph to determine how many miles can be driven if there is a budget of \$400, place your finger where 400 is on the y-axis and then slide your finger to the right until it meets the function. The x-value below this intersection tells how many miles can be driven if the budget is \$400. Based on the graph above, one could drive about 425 miles for the cost of \$400.

(d) To determine the approximate amount of miles driven if the expenditures are $350, we will evaluate the function when $f(x) = 350$. Therefore, our equation to solve is

$$
\begin{aligned}
350 &= 0.41x + 225 \\
-225 & -225 \\
\hline
\frac{125}{0.41} &= x
\end{aligned}
$$

$$x \approx 304.88 \text{ miles driven}$$

COMPETENCY 006

The teacher understands and uses nonlinear functions and relations to model and solve problems.

The beginning teacher:

A. Uses a variety of methods to investigate the roots (real and complex), vertex and symmetry of a quadratic function or relation.

B. Demonstrates an understanding of the connections among geometric, graphic, numeric and symbolic representations of quadratic functions.

C. Demonstrates an understanding of the connections among proportions, inverse variation and rational functions.

D. Understands the effects of transformations such as on the graph of a nonlinear function $f(x)$.

E. Applies properties, graphs and applications of nonlinear functions to analyze, model and solve problems.

F. Uses a variety of representations and methods (e.g., numerical methods, tables, graphs, algebraic techniques) to solve systems of quadratic equations and inequalities.

G. Understands how to use properties, graphs and applications of nonlinear relations including polynomial, rational, radical, absolute value, exponential, logarithmic, trigonometric and piecewise functions and relations to analyze, model and solve problems.

Quadratic Functions

A function defined by $f(x) = ax^2 + bx + c$, where a, b, and c are constants with $a \neq 0$, is called a quadratic function. The most elementary quadratic function is $f(x) = x^2$, often referred to as the quadratic parent function. The graph of a quadratic function is called a **parabola** (see figure below).

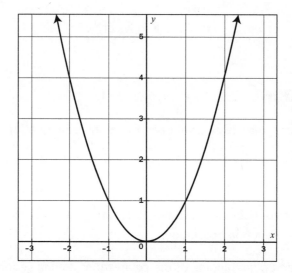

The parabola is a symmetrical function, meaning it has a **line of symmetry** through the **vertex**. In the figure above, the vertex is at (0, 0), or the bottom point on the graph, also called the **minimum**. This graph of $f(x) = x^2$ opens upward, but a similar quadratic function of $f(x) = -x^2$ opens downward (see graph below). The vertex on a parabola that opens downward is the topmost point of the function, called the **maximum**.

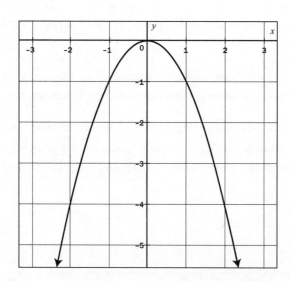

The value of the leading coefficient a determines if the graph of a quadratic function will open up or down. If $a > 0$, the parabola opens up, as in the function $f(x) = x^2$, where $a = 1$. If $a < 0$, the parabola opens down, as in the similar function $f(x) = -x^2$, where $a = -1$.

Transformations

We often call the function $f(x) = x^2$ the parent function for quadratics, and any manipulation to this function performs a transformation of the graph. As shown above, the graph of $f(x) = -x^2$ opens downward, whereas the parent function opens upward. The graph of the function when $a = -1$ was reflected across the x-axis. To reflect the graph across the x-axis, examine the function $g(x) = -f(x)$ or in our case $g(x) = -x^2$. Below is a table of transformations that may occur on any type of function.

Transformations of Functions

Examining the function $g(x)$	Result	Example $\left[f(x) = x^2\right]$
$g(x) = -f(x)$	Reflects $f(x)$ across the x-axis.	$g(x) = -x^2$
$g(x) = f(-x)$	Reflects $f(x)$ across the y-axis.	$g(x) = (-x)^2$
$g(x) = f(x) + c$	Translates $f(x)$ c units up.	$g(x) = x^2 + 2$
$g(x) = f(x) - c$	Translates $f(x)$ c units down.	$g(x) = x^2 - 2$
$g(x) = f(x + c)$	Translates $f(x)$ c units left.	$g(x) = (x + 2)^2$
$g(x) = f(x - c)$	Translates $f(x)$ c units right.	$g(x) = (x - 2)^2$
$g(x) = af(x)$	Dilates the graph vertically. If $a > 1$, graph is stretched. If $0 < a < 1$, graph is compressed.	$g(x) = 2x^2$ $g(x) = \frac{1}{2}x^2$
$f(ax)$	Dilates the graph horizontally. If $a > 1$, graph is stretched. If $0 < a < 1$, graph is compressed.	$g(x) = (2x)^2$ $g(x) = \left(\frac{1}{2}x\right)^2$

Vertex and Line of Symmetry

The vertex of a parabola occurs at the point $\left(\frac{-b}{2a}, f\left(\frac{-b}{2a}\right)\right)$, where the values for a and b are found in the function $f(x) = ax^2 + bx + c$. As mentioned before, parabolas are symmetrical about a line of symmetry. Such a line is $x = \frac{-b}{2a}$, a vertical line through the vertex. This may also be called the axis of symmetry.

Identify the vertex and line of symmetry in the function $f(x) = -16x^2 + 32x - 10$. To find the x-coordinate of the vertex, we compute $\frac{-b}{2a} = \frac{-32}{2(-16)} = \frac{-32}{-32} = 1$. Next find the y-coordinate by computing $f(1) = -16(1)^2 + 32(1) - 10 = 6$. Therefore, the vertex or maximum is located at $(1, 6)$ and the line of symmetry is at $x = 1$. Below is the graph of $f(x) = -16x^2 + 32x - 10$.

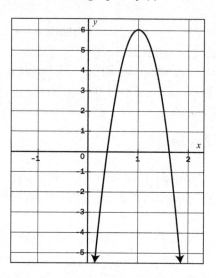

Solving Quadratic Equations

The solutions to a quadratic equation are called *zeros* or *roots*. Graphically, the solutions are x-intercepts, or where the graph crosses or touches the x-axis. We determine the value(s) when $y = 0$, which are the x-intercepts.

If the graph crosses the x-axis in two places, there are two solutions to the equation when $f(x) = 0$. The function above, $f(x) = -16x^2 + 32x - 10$, crosses the x-axis at two places when x is positive. Therefore, the two answers for x are both positive.

The function $f(x) = x^2$ does not cross the x-axis, but it touches it at the point $(0, 0)$. Quadratic functions that touch but do not cross the x-axis have only one solution when $f(x) = 0$: the x-value of the coordinate at which it touches the axis. The one solution to $f(x) = 0 = x^2$ is $x = 0$.

Some quadratic equations do not touch or cross the x-axis. Instead, they are suspended above or below the x-axis, and their solutions are complex or imaginary. The function $f(x) = x^2 + 2$ lies above the x-axis and has two complex solutions when $f(x) = 0$ (see graph that follows).

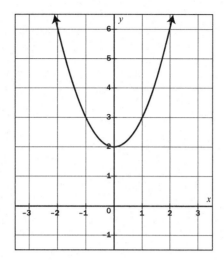

The solutions for $f(x) = 0$ can be found by evaluating the **quadratic formula**: $x = \dfrac{-b \pm \sqrt{b^2 - 4ac}}{2a}$, where a, b, and c are the coefficients in the function $ax^2 + bx + c = 0$. Determine the values for a, b, and c, and then substitute them into the quadratic formula. For the function $f(x) = x^2 + 2$, the x-intercepts can be calculated as:

$$a = 1,\ b = 0,\ c = 2$$

$$x = \frac{0 \pm \sqrt{0^2 - 4(1)(2)}}{2(1)} = \frac{\pm\sqrt{-8}}{2} = \frac{\pm\sqrt{-4(2)}}{2} = \frac{\pm 2i\sqrt{2}}{2} = \pm\sqrt{2}\,i$$

The $\pm$ symbol means there are two answers for x: $\sqrt{2}\,i$ and $-\sqrt{2}\,i$. The fact that the two solutions are imaginary is an indication that the graph does not cross the x-axis and thus has no x-intercepts.

To determine the type (real or complex) and number of solutions (one or two), calculate the **discriminant**, $b^2 - 4ac$, and follow these rules:

If $b^2 - 4ac > 0$, there are two real solutions.

If $b^2 - 4ac = 0$, there is one real solution.

If $b^2 - 4ac < 0$, there are two complex solutions.

Example   Determine the type and number of solutions to the function $f(x) = 0 = x^2 - 7x + 12$, then find the solutions. First, determine the values for a, b, and c and use them to find the discriminant.

$$a = 1, b = -7, c = 12$$

$$(-7)^2 - 4(1)(12) = 49 - 48 = 1$$

Since $1 > 0$, there are two real solutions. Next, compute the quadratic formula to find these two real solutions.

$$x = \frac{-(-7) \pm \sqrt{(-7)^2 - 4(1)(12)}}{2(1)} = \frac{7 \pm \sqrt{49 - 48}}{2} = \frac{7 \pm 1}{2}$$

$$x = \frac{7 + 1}{2} = \frac{8}{2} = 4 \text{ and } x = \frac{7 - 1}{2} = \frac{6}{2} = 3$$

Therefore, $x = 3$ and 4, or the x-intercepts are (3, 0) and (4, 0).

Factoring can be a helpful and quick method for solving some quadratic equations. Consider the example we just solved using the quadratic formula: $x^2 - 7x + 12 = 0$. When the leading coefficient, a, equals 1, as is the case here, the first step is to determine the factors of c that when added together equal b. In this example, the factors of 12 whose sum is -7 are -3 and -4. Next, use these factors to factor the quadratic into $(x - 3)(x - 4) = 0$. To solve the factored quadratic, set each binomial equal to zero and solve for x.

$$x - 3 = 0 \quad \text{and} \quad x - 4 = 0$$
$$x = 3 \qquad\qquad x = 4$$

As seen on the graph below, the x-intercepts are (3, 0) and (4, 0).

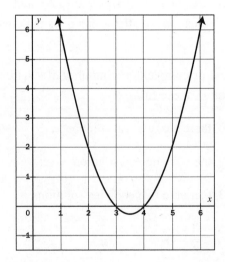

Additional Nonlinear Functions

Function	Equation	Graph
Cubic	$y = x^3$	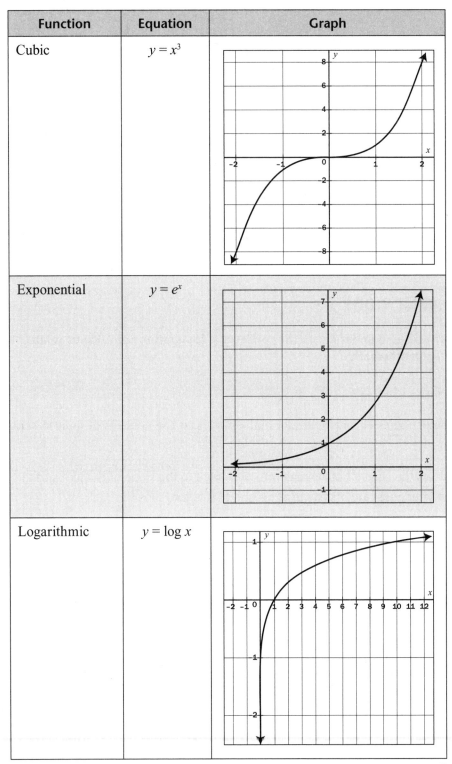
Exponential	$y = e^x$	
Logarithmic	$y = \log x$	

(continued)

Function	Equation	Graph
Absolute value	$y = \lvert x \rvert$	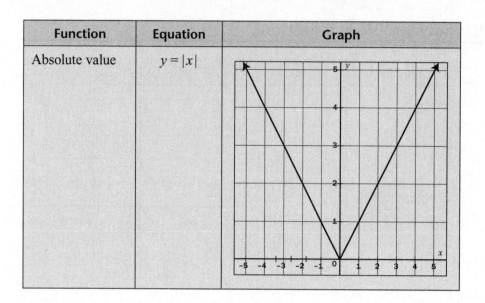

COMPETENCY 007

The teacher uses and understands the conceptual foundations of calculus related to topics in middle school mathematics.

The beginning teacher:

A. Relates topics in middle school mathematics to the concept of limit in sequences and series.

B. Relates the concept of average rate of change to the slope of the line and the concept of instantaneous rate of change as a slope of the line.

C. Demonstrates an understanding of the use of calculus concepts to answer questions about rates of change, areas, volumes and properties of functions and their graphs.

In terms of the Core Subjects 4–8 Mathematics subject test, you are required to understand only the most rudimentary aspects of calculus. Calculus is the study of how things change. Since change is all around us, it is obviously applicable to the real world. Many real-life examples of calculus occur in the world of physics, economics, engineering, and medicine.

Calculus studies three basic problems, all concerning themselves with the concept of infinity.

Slopes of Secant Lines and Tangent Lines

Given a curve $y = f(x)$, we define the secant line between two points P and Q as the line connecting the two points (diagram 1).

We define the tangent line at point P as the line that touches $y = f(x)$ only at point P (diagram 2).

We draw the secant line through PQ. Point Q moves along $y = f(x)$ towards point P. The closer that Q gets to P, the more the secant line resembles the tangent line at P (diagram 3). So, the closer that Q gets to P, the closer the slope of the secant line gets to the slope of the tangent line at P.

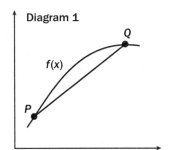

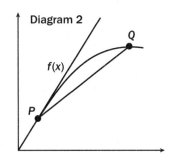

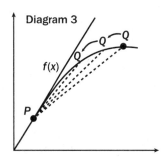

The formula for the slope of the secant line between the points $(a, f(a))$ and $(b, f(b))$ = $\dfrac{f(b) - f(a)}{b - a}$. It looks confusing but is merely the formula for the slope of a line. The slope of the tangent line at $(a, f(a))$ is beyond what is asked in the TExES Core Subjects exam, but if you choose another point close to $x = a$, you can approximate the slope of the tangent line at $x = a$ with great accuracy.

Example: If $f(x) = x^2 + x - 2$, find a) the slope of the secant line between $x = -1$ and $x = 2$. Then b) approximate the slope of the tangent line at $x = 1$.

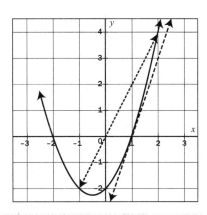

Solution: a) $f(2) = 4 + 2 - 2 = 4$

$f(-1) = 1 - 1 - 2 = -2$

slope of secant line $= \dfrac{f(2) - f(-1)}{2 - (-1)} = \dfrac{4 - (-2)}{2 + 1} = \dfrac{6}{3} = 2$

b) To approximate the slope of the tangent line at $x = 1$, we will use $x = 1$ and $x = 1.1$

$f(1) = 1 + 1 - 2 = 0$

$f(1.1) = 1.21 + 1.1 - 2 = 0.31$

slope of tangent line is approximately $\dfrac{f(1.1) - f(1)}{1.1 - 1} = \dfrac{0.31 - 0}{0.1} = 3.1$

The closer you choose your second point to $x = 1$, the more accurate the slope of the tangent line. If you get infinitely close, it turns out that the slope of the tangent line is exactly 3.

The reason that the slopes of secant lines and tangent lines are so important is that we can use them to make an analogy to the concept of motion. When we have motion in a straight line, we can find the average velocity between two times as well as the instantaneous velocity at a certain time.

If $s(t)$ describes the position of a particle moving along a straight line, the average velocity between t_1 and t_2 is given by $\dfrac{s(t_2) - s(t_1)}{t_2 - t_1}$. This formula is similar to the one used for the slope of a secant line.

If a train is traveling along a straight track and is 50 miles from a station at $t = 2$ hours and 70 miles from the station at $t = 2.5$ hours, its average velocity is $\dfrac{s(2.5) - s(2)}{2.5 - 2} = \dfrac{70 - 50}{0.5} = \dfrac{20}{0.5} = 40$ mph. However, just because the train averages 40 mph between $t = 2.5$ hours and $t = 2$ hours doesn't mean we know how fast the train is traveling at $t = 2.25$ hours. It could be traveling at 60 mph. It could even be stopped. This is called the instantaneous velocity, and the way it is found is similar to the way we found the slope of the tangent line.

Area Under a Curve

The second problem that calculus studies is finding the area between a curve and the x-axis. For instance, given the function $y = 1 - x^2$, we wish to find the area under the curve between $x = -1$ and $x = 1$ as shown in the following graph. The problem is that the parabola is curved and that means that it is difficult to find the exact area. Similar to finding the slope of the tangent line, we approximate the area using rectangles. Since the curve is symmetric to the y-axis, we will start building rectangles at $x = 0$.

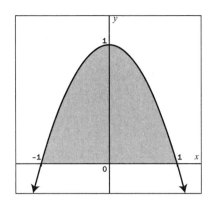

We choose to have the width of each rectangle equal to $\frac{1}{4}$. We start at $x = 0$ and draw a rectangle whose height is the value of the function at $x = 0$ and whose width is $\frac{1}{4}$. We build a second rectangle whose height is the value of the function at $x = \frac{1}{4}$ and whose width is $\frac{1}{4}$. We build a third rectangle whose height is the value of the function at $x = \frac{1}{2}$ and whose width is $\frac{1}{4}$. We continue the pattern until we get to the x-intercept. The following graph illustrates what we are describing.

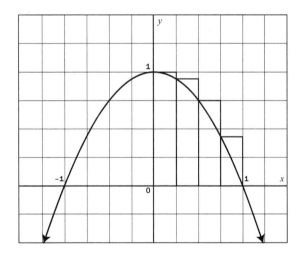

Since all the bases of the rectangles are $\frac{1}{4}$, we need to find the height of each rectangle. This involves finding the value of the function at $x = 0$, $x = \frac{1}{4}$, $x = \frac{1}{2}$, and $x = \frac{3}{4}$.

Rectangle	x	Height = $f(x)$	Base	Area = Base • Height
1	0	$1 - 0 = 1$	$\dfrac{1}{4}$	$\dfrac{1}{4}(1) = \dfrac{1}{4}$
2	$\dfrac{1}{4}$	$1 - \dfrac{1}{16} = \dfrac{15}{16}$	$\dfrac{1}{4}$	$\dfrac{1}{4}\left(\dfrac{15}{16}\right) = \dfrac{15}{64}$
3	$\dfrac{1}{2}$	$1 - \dfrac{1}{4} = \dfrac{3}{4}$	$\dfrac{1}{4}$	$\dfrac{1}{4}\left(\dfrac{3}{4}\right) = \dfrac{3}{16}$
4	$\dfrac{3}{4}$	$1 - \dfrac{9}{16} = \dfrac{7}{16}$	$\dfrac{1}{4}$	$\dfrac{1}{4}\left(\dfrac{7}{16}\right) = \dfrac{7}{64}$

Adding these areas $\dfrac{1}{4} + \dfrac{15}{64} + \dfrac{3}{16} + \dfrac{7}{64}$ and changing to a decimal, we get 0.78125. Since this is half of the area under the curve, we double it to find the total area under the curve is approximately 1.5625.

Between $x = 0$ and $x = 1$, we used "outer rectangles" and the sum of the areas of these rectangles will be greater than the actual area. It is possible to use "inner rectangles" as well and the sum of the areas of these rectangles will be less than the actual area. The picture looks like this:

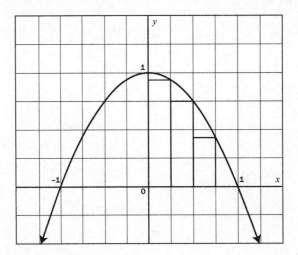

Note that there are only 3 rectangles as the height of the 4th rectangle has height zero.

Another way to solve this is to use "midpoint rectangles." These rectangles both overestimate and underestimate the true area at the same time making it a very accurate technique. However, the calculations are more cumbersome.

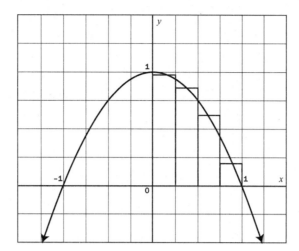

The more rectangles that are chosen, the more work is necessary but the more precise the answer. As the number of rectangles gets infinitely large, the area under the curve becomes infinitely close to $1.\overline{33}$.

Infinite Series

The third problem calculus studies is more theoretical and has to do with whether a sequence of numbers gets infinitely large or small or approaches a specific number.

We define a **sequence** $\{a_n\}$ as a set of numbers following some algebraic rule for $n = 1, 2, 3, 4,$ ... going to infinity. For instance, if $\{a_n\} = n^2 + n + 1$, the terms of the sequence are 3, 7, 13, 21, ...

We say a sequence **diverges** or is **divergent** if the terms of the sequence get infinitely large or small. $\{a_n\} = n^2 + n + 1$ is divergent because as n gets larger and larger, the terms get larger and larger without bound. No matter how large the number you can think of, $\{a_n\} = n^2 + n + 1$ will eventually become larger than it.

But if the terms of the sequence never get larger than a number L, then we say that the sequence is **convergent** or **converges to L**.

For instance, if the sequence is given by $\{a_n\} = \dfrac{1}{n}$, its terms are $1, \dfrac{1}{2}, \dfrac{1}{3}, \dfrac{1}{4}, ...$ These terms get smaller and smaller and get infinitely closer to zero. We say that the sequence converges to zero. It doesn't actually reach zero, but then again, the terms are generated infinitely.

If the sequence is given by $\{a_n\} = \dfrac{n}{n+1}$, its terms are $\dfrac{1}{2}, \dfrac{2}{3}, \dfrac{3}{4}, \dfrac{4}{5}, ... \dfrac{99}{100}, ... \dfrac{99999}{100000}, ...$ These terms get larger and larger and because the numerator is one smaller than the denominator, the sequence gets closer and closer to 1. We say that the sequence converges to 1.

A **series** is the sum of the terms of a sequence. For instance, if we add the terms of the sequence $\{a_n\} = n^2 + n + 1$, we get $3 + 7 + 13 + 21 + \dots$, it is clear that the sum of these terms gets infinitely large, and we say that the series is divergent as well as the sequence being divergent.

If we add the terms of the convergent sequence $\{a_n\} = \dfrac{n}{n+1}$, we get $\dfrac{1}{2} + \dfrac{2}{3} + \dfrac{3}{4} + \dfrac{4}{5} + \dots + \dfrac{99}{100} + \dots + \dfrac{99999}{100000} + \dots$, our terms are getting closer to one so eventually we will be adding numbers similar to $1 + 1 + 1 + \dots$ This gets infinitely large and the series is divergent although the sequence is convergent.

If we add the terms of the convergent sequence $\{a_n\} = \dfrac{1}{2^n}$, we get $1 + \dfrac{1}{2} + \dfrac{1}{4} + \dfrac{1}{8} + \dfrac{1}{16} + \dots$. This sum will never get larger than 2, and we say that the series converges to 2.

On the other hand, if we add the terms of the convergent sequence $\{a_n\} = \dfrac{1}{n}$, we get $1 + \dfrac{1}{2} + \dfrac{1}{3} + \dfrac{1}{4} + \dots$, and even though the terms are getting smaller and smaller, it turns out that contrary to logic, the series is divergent, meaning its sum will eventually get larger than any number you can think of.

On the TExES Core Subjects 4–8 exam, any questions about the convergence and divergence of a sequence or series will be easily answerable if you generate just a few terms of the sequence.

COMPETENCY 008

The teacher understands measurement as a process.

The beginning teacher:

A. Selects and uses appropriate units of measurement (e.g., temperature, money, mass, weight, area, capacity, density, percents, speed, acceleration) to quantify, compare and communicate information.

B. Develops, justifies and uses conversions within measurement systems.

C. Applies dimensional analysis to derive units and formulas in a variety of situations (e.g., rates of change of one variable with respect to another) and to find and evaluate solutions to problems.

D. Describes the precision of measurement and the effects of error on measurement.

E. Applies the Pythagorean Theorem, proportional reasoning and right triangle trigonometry to solve measurement problems.

Measurement is an area of mathematics used by many on a daily basis, whether it be calculating the area of a garden, estimating time to complete a project, or calculating distance of travel from point *A* to *B*. Often we are asked to convert units of measure. Below are charts of the U.S. and metric units of measure. Note that U.S. units are sometimes called U.S. customary units, standard units, or English units.

Units of Measure

U.S.	
12 inches	1 foot
3 feet	1 yard
5,280 feet	1 mile
Metric	
10 millimeters	1 centimeter
1,000 millimeters	1 meter
100 centimeters	1 meter
10 centimeters	1 decimeter
10 decimeters	1 meter
10 meters	1 decameter
1,000 meters	1 kilometer

Example Sasha walked $\frac{1}{4}$ mile from home to her friend Nick's house. Together they walked 30 yards to the public pool. How many feet did Sasha walk altogether?

We use the fact that 1 mile = 5,280 feet and 1 yard = 3 feet to answer this question. First, we need to convert $\frac{1}{4}$ of a mile into feet: $\frac{1}{4}$(1 mile) = $\frac{1}{4}$(5,280 feet) = 1,320 feet. Next, we convert 30 yards into feet: 30(3 feet) = 90 feet. Finally, find the sum of the two distances: 1,320 + 90 = 1,410 feet. Sasha walked a total of 1,410 feet.

Units of Mass

U.S.	
16 ounces	1 pound
2,000 pounds	1 ton
Metric	
1,000 grams	1 kilogram
1,000 kilograms	1 metric ton

Example   Jesse sells heavy furniture. For shipping purposes, he must inform the movers of the weight of each shipment in metric tons. Jesse will be shipping an order of furniture that weighs 750 kilograms. How many metric tons will he be shipping?

Creating a proportion can be handy when converting units.

$$\frac{1 \text{ metric ton}}{1,000 \text{ kilograms}} = \frac{x \text{ metric tons}}{750 \text{ kilograms}}$$

$$750 = 1,000x$$

$$x = \frac{750}{1,000} = 0.75 \text{ metric tons}$$

Jesse will be shipping 0.75 metric tons of furniture.

Units of Capacity

U.S.	
3 teaspoons	1 tablespoon
2 tablespoons	1 fluid ounce
8 fluid ounces	1 cup
16 fluid ounces	1 pint
2 cups	1 pint
2 pints	1 quart
4 quarts	1 gallon
Metric	
10 milliliters	1 centiliter
10 centiliters	1 deciliter
1,000 milliliters	1 liter
10 deciliters	1 liter
1,000 liters	1 kiloliter

Example A recipe for lemonade spritzer requires 1 pint of fresh lemon juice, 1 cup of sugar, 2 quarts of club soda, and 2 limes sliced very thin for garnishing. How much liquid, in cups, is needed for this recipe?

First, we need to know which ingredients are liquid: 1 pint of lemon juice and 2 quarts of club soda. Next, we need to convert pints and quarts into cups. We know 1 pint = 2 cups. We know 1 quart = 2 pints, so 2 quarts = 4 pints. Since 1 pint = 2 cups, then 4 pints = 8 cups. Altogether, we need 2 cups of lemon juice and 8 cups of club soda for a total of 10 cups of liquid for the recipe.

Units of Time

60 seconds	1 minute
60 minutes	1 hour
24 hours	1 day
7 days	1 week
52 weeks	1 year
12 months	1 year

Example Mercedes determined she worked on her science project for a total of 1 day, 7 hours, and 24 minutes. How many total hours did she spend on her project?

First, let's start by converting the 24 minutes into a portion of an hour. We know 60 minutes = 1 hour, so 24 minutes = $\frac{24}{60}$ = 0.4 hours. Also, 1 day = 24 hours. Mercedes spent 24 + 7 + 0.4 = 31.4 hours working on her science project.

Temperature

A thermometer measures temperature in **Fahrenheit** and/or **Celsius**. Conversion formulas can be used to convert temperatures from Fahrenheit to Celsius and vice versa.

$$F = C \cdot \frac{9}{5} + 32$$

$$C = \frac{5}{9}(F - 32)$$

Error of Measurement

Often, measuring physical objects with tools such as rulers and protractors can result in a slight error of measurement. For example, most textbooks are rectangular in shape and have four right angles. If using a protractor to measure the angle of a book corner results in finding the angle to be 88.5 degrees instead of 90 degrees, there is a 1.5 degree error of measure. To determine the percent of error, divide the amount of error by the original amount that should be present. For example, $\frac{1.5}{90} = 0.01\overline{66}$ or $1.\overline{66}\%$ error.

Right Triangle Trigonometry

The study of right triangles and their measures of sides and angles is right triangle trigonometry.

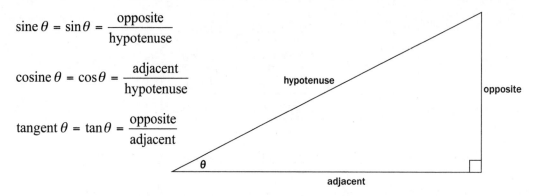

$$\text{sine } \theta = \sin \theta = \frac{\text{opposite}}{\text{hypotenuse}}$$

$$\text{cosine } \theta = \cos \theta = \frac{\text{adjacent}}{\text{hypotenuse}}$$

$$\text{tangent } \theta = \tan \theta = \frac{\text{opposite}}{\text{adjacent}}$$

A good way to remember this is the mnemonic *SOHCAHTOA* (Sine Opposite Hypotenuse, Cosine Adjacent Hypotenuse, Tangent Opposite Adjacent).

Example   Using the figure below, find the sine, cosine, and tangent of θ.

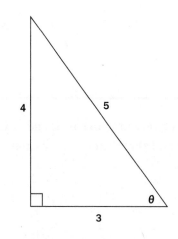

$$\sin \theta = \frac{\text{opposite}}{\text{hypotenuse}} = \frac{4}{5}$$

$$\cos \theta = \frac{\text{adjacent}}{\text{hypotenuse}} = \frac{3}{5}$$

$$\tan \theta = \frac{\text{opposite}}{\text{adjacent}} = \frac{4}{3}$$

Similar Triangles

Triangles are said to be similar if they have congruent corresponding angles (equal measure) and their corresponding sides are proportional. Consider the figure below of similar triangles $\triangle ABC$ and $\triangle ADE$. Find the measure of x using proportional reasoning.

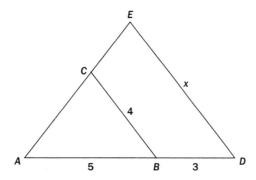

In the figure, we can see $\overline{AB} = 5$, $\overline{AD} = 8$, and $\overline{CB} = 4$. Using this information, we can create a proportion to solve for $\overline{ED} = x$.

$$\frac{AB}{CB} = \frac{AD}{ED}$$

$$\frac{5}{4} = \frac{8}{x}$$

Using cross products or cross multiplication, we find

$$5x = 32$$

$$x = \frac{32}{5} = 6.4$$

Pythagorean Theorem

The Pythagorean Theorem is a relation among the three sides of a right triangle, $a^2 + b^2 = c^2$, where a and b are the **legs** of the right triangle and c is the **hypotenuse**, or side across from the right angle. We use the equation $a^2 + b^2 = c^2$ when given two of the side lengths of a right triangle and we need to find the third.

Example   Diane is going to mount a new 40-inch LCD TV on the wall. The base of the TV is 35 inches. What is the height? Round your answer to the nearest inch.

Before beginning this problem, some background knowledge on televisions is needed. When buying a 40-inch television, the 40 inches refers to the diagonal (see picture following). A television is also a rectangle, not a triangle. However, the diagonal of the rectangle creates two right triangles, allowing the Pythagorean Theorem to be a solution strategy.

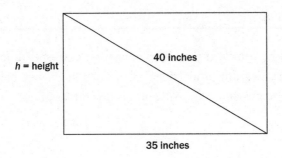

Next, substitute the values into the Pythagorean Theorem and solve for h.

$$35^2 + h^2 = 40^2$$

$$1,225 + h^2 = 1,600$$

$$h^2 = 375$$

$$\sqrt{h^2} = \sqrt{375} \approx 19.36 \approx 19 \text{ inches}$$

The LCD TV is about 19 inches high and 35 inches wide, with a 40-inch diagonal.

COMPETENCY 009

The teacher understands the geometric relationships and axiomatic structure of Euclidian geometry.

The beginning teacher:

A. Understands concepts and properties of points, lines, planes, angles, lengths and distances.

B. Analyzes and applies the properties of parallel and perpendicular lines.

C. Uses the properties of congruent triangles to explore geometric relationships and prove theorems.

D. Describes and justifies geometric constructions.

E. Applies knowledge of right angles to identify acute, right and obtuse triangles.

F. Measures angles correctly using a protractor.

The fundamental building blocks of geometry are **points**, **lines**, and **planes**. These terms are called undefined terms, but an intuitive notion of these terms is illustrated in the table that follows.

Term and Symbol	Illustration
Point A Point A is a vertex of the triangle. Point A is located at $(-3, 0)$.	
Line ℓ Line ℓ is similar to the center line of a road. The outer lines and the center line are ***parallel*** lines. The x-axis and y-axis are ***perpendicular*** lines. Two points are needed to create a line, as they determine the direction or slope of the line. Line m passes through $(-5, 0)$ and $(0, 5)$.	
Ray A portion of a line which starts at a point and extends infinitely in a particular direction to infinity	
Line segment A portion of a line which links two points without extending beyond them	

Term and Symbol	Illustration
Plane γ Plane γ is like a tabletop or a flat surface; however, it would extend infinitely and have zero thickness. Plane *ABC* or plane γ	

Angles and Their Measures

When two rays or lines meet at a point, they form an **angle**, measured in **degrees**. Congruent angles are two or more angles that have the same size or measure, regardless of their orientation or how they are drawn. If angles *A* and *B* are congruent, we write $\angle A \cong \angle B$. Descriptions of types of angles are given below.

- **Right angles** measure exactly 90 degrees.

- **Acute angles** measure between 0 and 90 degrees.

- **Obtuse angles** measure greater than 90 degrees but less than 180 degrees.

- **Straight angles** measure 180 degrees and are also called lines.

- **Reflex angles** measure greater than 180 and less than 360 degrees.

- **Supplementary angles** are any two angles whose sum is 180 degrees.

- **Complementary angles** are any two angles whose sum is 90 degrees.

- **Vertical angles** are opposite angles formed by two intersecting lines, where vertical angles are congruent.

Angles Formed by Parallel Lines Cut by a Transversal

Let parallel lines *m* and *n* be cut by another line, called a transversal *t*. The following congruent angles are formed by these lines (see figure below):

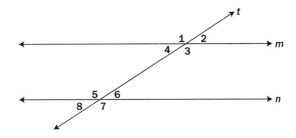

- There are four pairs of congruent **vertical** or **opposite angles:** $\angle 1 \cong \angle 3$, $\angle 2 \cong \angle 4$, $\angle 5 \cong \angle 7$, $\angle 6 \cong \angle 8$.

- There are four pairs of **congruent corresponding angles:** $\angle 1 \cong \angle 5$, $\angle 4 \cong \angle 8$, $\angle 2 \cong \angle 6$, $\angle 3 \cong \angle 7$.

- There are two pairs of congruent **alternate interior angles:** $\angle 4 \cong \angle 6$, $\angle 3 \cong \angle 5$.

- There are two pairs of congruent **alternate exterior angles:** $\angle 1 \cong \angle 7$, $\angle 2 \cong \angle 8$.

- There are two pairs of **same side interior angles** that are supplementary: $\angle 4 + \angle 5 = 180°$, $\angle 3 + \angle 6 = 180°$.

Constructions with a Compass and Straight Edge

Constructing Parallel Lines

Parallel lines never intersect as they have the same slope or incline.

Example   Given line ℓ and point *P*, we will construct a parallel line to line ℓ.

To construct a line parallel to a given line follow these four steps:

Step 1: Choose a point *A* anywhere on line ℓ, and draw the line passing through it and point *P*.

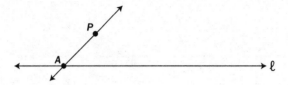

Step 2: Set the compass to the width of $\overline{AP}$, with the point on point *A* and the pencil on point *P*. With the pointer still on point *A*, draw an arc that intersects line ℓ. Where the arc intersects line ℓ, label this point *X*.

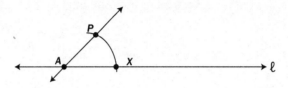

Step 3: With the same opening of the compass, draw intersecting arcs, first with the pointer at *P* and then with the pointer at *X* to create a point *Y*. Point *Y* is the fourth vertex of the rhombus.

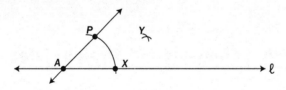

Step 4: Draw $\overleftrightarrow{PY}$. Line $\overleftrightarrow{PY} \parallel$ line ℓ.

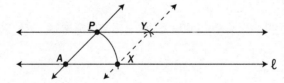

Constructing an Angle Bisector

An angle bisector is a ray that divides an angle into two congruent parts. To construct an angle bisector, follow these three steps:

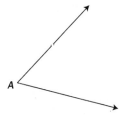

Step 1: With the compass pointer on *A*, the vertex of the angle to be bisected, draw an arc intersecting the angle at points *B* and *C*.

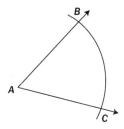

Step 2: Keep the compass set at the same distance as in Step 1. Place the pointer on point *B* and create a small arc near the center of the angle, then place the pointer on point *C* and make an intersecting arc near the center of the angle. Where the two small arcs intersect, label this point *D*.

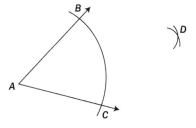

Step 3: Draw $\overline{AD}$, which is the angle bisector of ∠*A*. Therefore, ∠*BAD* ≅ ∠*CAD*.

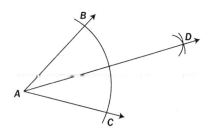

Constructing Perpendicular Lines

Lines that are perpendicular form right angles. To construct a line perpendicular to line ℓ going through point P, follow these three steps:

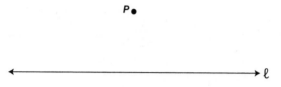

Step 1: Place the compass pointer on P and draw an arc that intersects line ℓ at points A and B.

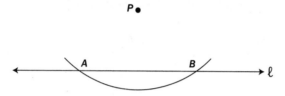

Step 2: With the same compass opening, place the pointer on A and make an arc below line ℓ, and then place the pointer on B and make an intersecting arc. Call the intersection point C.

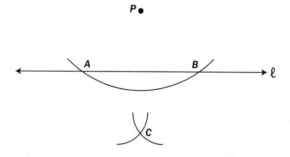

Step 3: Draw a line from point P through C, creating a perpendicular line. Line $\overleftrightarrow{PC} \perp$ line ℓ.

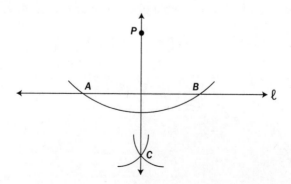

Constructing a Perpendicular Bisector

A perpendicular bisector is a line that is perpendicular to a given line segment and bisects the line segment into two congruent parts. To construct a perpendicular bisector of segment $\overline{AB}$, follow these two steps:

Step 1: Set the compass pointer on A and the pencil between points A and B, but more than halfway between the points. Then, create an arc through the line. Keeping the same compass setting, place the pointer on B and create an arc intersecting the first. Label the points of intersection C and D.

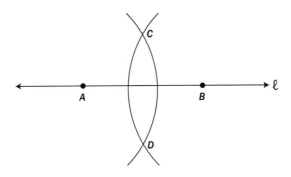

Step 2: Draw a line through points C and D. Label point M the point of intersection of $\overleftrightarrow{CD}$ and $\overleftrightarrow{AB}$. Point M is the midpoint of $\overline{AB}$.

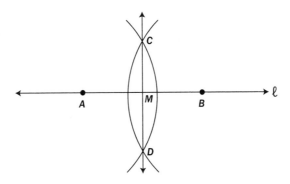

We now know $\overleftrightarrow{CD} \perp \overleftrightarrow{AB}$, $\overleftrightarrow{CD}$ bisects $\overline{AB}$, and $\overline{AM} \cong \overline{MB}$.

COMPETENCY 010

The teacher analyzes the properties of two- and three-dimensional figures.

The beginning teacher:

A. Uses and understands the development of formulas to find lengths, perimeters, areas and volumes of basic geometric figures.

B. Applies relationships among similar figures, scale and proportion and analyzes how changes in scale affect area and volume measurements.

C. Uses a variety of representations (e.g., numeric, verbal, graphic, symbolic) to analyze and solve problems involving two- and three-dimensional figures such as circles, triangles, polygons, cylinders, prisms and spheres.

D. Analyzes the relationship among three-dimensional figures and related two-dimensional representations (e.g., projections, cross-sections, nets) and uses these representations to solve problems.

E. Generates formulas involving perimeter, area, circumference, volume and scaling.

Area (A) and Perimeter (P) Formulas

		Area	Perimeter
Square		$A = s^2$	$P = 4s$
Rectangle		$A = l \times w$	$P = 2(l + w)$ or $2l + 2w$
Parallelogram		$A = b \times h$	$P = 2(a + b)$ or $2a + 2b$
Trapezoid		$A = \frac{1}{2}(b_1 + b_2)h$	$P = b_1 + b_2 + a + c$

		Area	Perimeter
Triangle		$A = \frac{1}{2}(h \times b)$	$P = a + b + c$
Right triangle		$A = \frac{1}{2}(a \times b)$	$P = a + b + c$ $P = a + b + \sqrt{a^2 + b^2}$
Equilateral triangle		$A = \frac{\sqrt{3}}{4}s^2$	$P = 3s$
Circle		$A = \pi r^2$	$C = 2\pi r = \pi d$ (C = circumference d = diameter = $2r$)

Volume (*V*) and Surface Area (*SA*) Formulas

B = area of the base shape
P = perimeter of the base shape

		Volume	Surface Area
Rectangular solid		$V = l \times w \times h$	$SA = 2lw + 2wh + 2lh$
Triangular prism		$V = B \times h$ or (area of triangle) $\times h$	$SA = 2B + Ph$

(continued)

		Volume	Surface Area
Pyramid	*The base shape can change	$V = \frac{1}{3} \times B \times h$	$SA = B +$ (area of each triangle)
Cylinder		$V = \pi r^2 h$	$SA = 2\pi rh + 2\pi r^2$
Cone	$SA = \pi r\left(r + \sqrt{r^2 + h^2}\right)$	$V = \frac{1}{3}\pi r^2 h$	$SA = \pi r^2 + \pi rs$
Sphere		$V = \frac{4}{3}\pi r^3$	$SA = 4\pi r^2$

Nets

A **net** of a three-dimensional solid is what it would look like if it were opened out flat.

Three-dimensional Solid	Net
Cube	

Three-dimensional Solid	Net
Rectangular prism	
Triangular prism	
Square-based pyramid	
Tetrahedron	

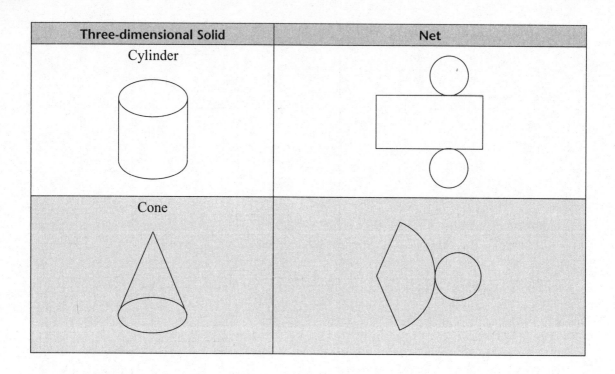

Three-dimensional Solid	Net
Cylinder	
Cone	

Euler's Formula

A **polyhedron** is a solid object whose surface is made up of polygons. The **vertices** are the points at which the polygons meet. Each polygon is called a **face** of the polyhedron, and an **edge** is the side of the polygon. For any convex polyhedron, the sum of the **vertices** and **faces** is two more than the number of **edges**: $V + F = E + 2$.

Solid	Vertices	Faces	Edges
Cube	8	6	12
Rectangular prism	8	6	12
Triangular prism	6	5	9
Square-based pyramid	5	5	8
Tetrahedron	4	4	6

Dimensions and Relationships

Example 1   A certain cylinder has height 5 units and radius 3 units. If the height triples, how is the volume affected?

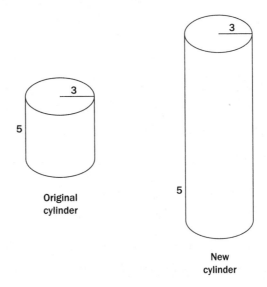

The volume of the original cylinder is $V = \pi r^2 h = \pi(3^2)(5) = 45\pi$.

The volume of the new cylinder with the height tripled is $V = \pi r^2 h = \pi(3^2)(15) = 135\pi$.

The new volume is three times that of the original cylinder.

Example 2   A certain cylinder has height 5 units and radius 3 units. If the radius triples, how is the volume affected?

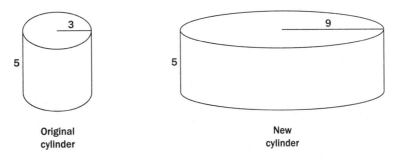

The volume of the original cylinder is $V = \pi r^2 h = \pi(3^2)(5) = 45\pi$.

The volume of the new cylinder with the radius tripled is $V = \pi r^2 h = \pi(9^2)(5) = 405\pi$.

The new volume is nine times that of the original cylinder.

COMPETENCY 011

The teacher understands algebra and geometry through the Cartesian coordinate system and demonstrates knowledge of transformational geometry.

The beginning teacher:

A. Describes and justifies geometric constructions made using a reflection device and other appropriate technologies.

B. Uses translations, reflections, glide-reflections and rotations to demonstrate congruence and to explore the symmetries of figures.

C. Uses dilations (expansions and contractions) to illustrate similar figures and proportionality.

D. Uses symmetry to describe tessellations and shows how they can be used to illustrate geometric concepts, properties and relationships.

E. Applies concepts and properties of slope, midpoint, parallelism and distance in the coordinate plane to explore properties of geometric figures and solve problems.

F. Applies transformations in the coordinate plane.

G. Uses geometry to model and describe the physical world.

H. Identifies, locates and names points on a coordinate plane using ordered pairs of real numbers in all quadrants.

I. Graphs in the first quadrant of the coordinate plane ordered pairs of numbers arising from mathematical and real-world problems, including those generated by number patterns or found in an input-output table.

J. Graphs reflections across the horizontal or vertical axis and graphs translations on a coordinate plane.

Transformations

Transformations for algebraic functions were discussed in Competency 006. The same concepts apply to shapes defined in the Cartesian coordinate system with several more included.

Translations

A translation is a motion or transformation of a plane that moves every point of the plane a specified distance in a specified direction along a straight line. A **translation in a coordinate plane** is a function that slides a point (x, y) to the corresponding point $(x + a, y + b)$, where a and b are real numbers.

Reflections

A reflection about a line ℓ is a transformation of the plane that pairs each point P of the plane with a point P' in such a way that line ℓ is the perpendicular bisector of $\overline{PP'}$, as long as P is not on line ℓ. If P is on line ℓ, then $P = P'$.

The coordinates of a **reflection in a coordinate plane** about the x- or y-axis can be quite easy to find, given the coordinates of the original point. A reflection across the x-axis takes a point (x, y) to the corresponding point $(x, -y)$. A reflection across the y-axis takes a point (x, y) to the corresponding point $(-x, y)$. A reflection about the line $y = x$ interchanges the coordinates of the point. For example, if we reflect the point $(1, 3)$ across the line $y = x$, the new point is $(3, 1)$.

Rotations

A rotation is a transformation of the plane determined by holding one point, the center, fixed, and rotating the plane about this point by a certain amount (degrees) in a certain direction (clockwise or counterclockwise).

Glide Reflections

Another basic transformation is called a glide reflection. A glide reflection is a transformation consisting of a translation followed by a reflection in a line parallel to the slide direction.

Dilation

A dilation is also referred to as a **size transformation** that assigns some point A to a collinear point A'. To dilate a point or figure we use a scale factor r and multiply both the x- and y-coordinates by r. When dilating a figure, if $r > 0$, the figure is enlarged by a factor of r; if $0 < r < 1$, the figure is contracted or made smaller by a factor of r.

For example, suppose we have a triangle with vertices at A $(1, 2)$, B $(3, 5)$, and C $(5, 3)$ and we want to dilate the figure by a scale factor of 3. The transformed points are A' $(3, 6)$, B' $(9, 15)$, and C' $(15, 9)$. The triangles are similar and the side lengths are proportional by a scale factor of 3.

Lines of Symmetry

Figures may have lines of symmetry, which can be thought of as imaginary folding lines that produce two congruent mirror-image figures. In the figures below, we can see a square has four lines of symmetry and a circle has an infinite number of lines of symmetry.

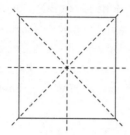 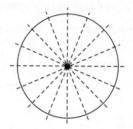

Tessellations

A tessellation is a pattern formed by repeating a single unit or shape that when repeated fills the plane with no gaps and no overlaps. Brick patterns or a cross section of a beehive are common tessellations found in the real world.

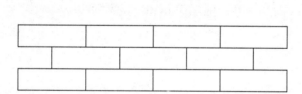 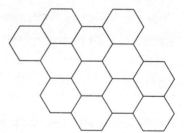

COMPETENCY 012

The teacher understands how to use graphical and numerical techniques to explore data, characterize patterns and describe departures from patterns.

The beginning teacher:

A. Organizes and displays data in a variety of formats (e.g., tables, frequency distributions, stem-and-leaf plots, box-and-whisker plots, histograms, pie charts).

B. Applies concepts of center, spread, shape and skewness to describe a data distribution.

C. Supports arguments, makes predictions and draws conclusions using summary statistics and graphs to analyze and interpret one-variable data.

D. Demonstrates an understanding of measures of central tendency (e.g., mean, median, mode) and spread (e.g., range, interquartile range, variance, standard deviation).

E. Analyzes connections among concepts of center and spread, data clusters and gaps, data outliers and measures of central tendency and dispersion.

F. Calculates and interprets percentiles and quartiles.

We describe data analysis as a process of inspecting, describing, and summarizing data with the goal of discovering useful information, suggesting conclusions, and making decisions. We use statistical methods to analyze what occurred in the past in order to predict what will happen in the future with a fair degree of probability. So while probability concerns itself with the future, statistics and data analysis concerns itself with the past.

A number of graphs can be used to organize and describe data. Categorical data represent characteristics of objects of individuals in groups or categories. Numerical data are collected on numerical variables (distance, time, scores, etc.).

Pictographs

A picture graph, or *pictograph*, represents tallies or frequencies of categories. A picture, or symbol, represents a quantity of items and is denoted in a legend. In the following example, a class of students was surveyed about the types of animals they have at home. The frequencies are displayed in the table below, followed by a pictograph representing the data. For instance, 7 students have a dog, 4 students have a cat, etc.

Type of Animal	Frequency
Dog	7
Cat	4
Snake	2
Fish	10

Type of Animal	☺ = 2 Animals
Dog	☺ ☺ ☺ ☖
Cat	☺ ☺
Snake	☺
Fish	☺ ☺ ☺ ☺ ☺

Bar Graphs

A bar graph is used to depict frequencies of categorical data. The following bar graph represents the same data as the pictograph just shown.

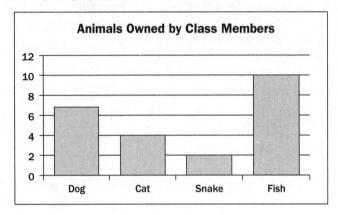

Circle Graphs or Pie Charts

A circle graph, also called a pie chart, is used to depict frequencies of categorical data. The data from the pictograph and bar graph produces the circle graph below. The reason that the percentages do not add to 100% is because of round-off error.

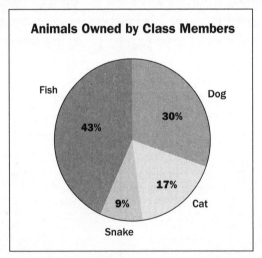

Line or Dot Plots

A line or dot plot provides a quick way of organizing numerical data when the number of values is not excessively large. Suppose there is a set of test scores: 70, 72, 83, 75, 88, 81, 94, 94, 80, 85, 93. A line plot for the set of test scores consists of a horizontal number line on which each score is denoted by an X or a dot.

Stem and Leaf Plots

The stem and leaf plot is akin to the line plot, but the number line is typically vertical and digits are used to represent data rather than dots or X's. The numbers on the left side of the vertical segment are called the **stem**. The **leaves** are the numbers on the right side.

The high temperatures for Jack's recent trip to Dallas, Texas, were as follows: 65, 72, 69, 81, 74, 78, 73, 78, 70, 82, 71, 77, 80, 67, 78, 73. The stemplot for this data is as follows:

Temperatures in Dallas, Texas, in October

8	0, 1, 2
7	0, 1, 2, 3, 3, 4, 7, 8, 8, 8
6	5, 7, 9

Legend: 6|5 = 65

Histograms

Histograms look similar to bar graphs, but they display grouped numerical data and have adjoining bars. Below is a stem and leaf plot showing ages of presidents at death with its accompanying histogram.

The histogram is similar to the stemplot in that it gives the number of data entries in each bin, but loses the actual data.

4	6, 9
5	3, 6, 7, 7, 8
6	0, 0, 3, 3, 4, 5, 6, 7, 7, 7, 8
7	0, 1, 1, 2, 3, 4, 7, 8, 8, 9
8	0, 1, 1, 2, 3, 5, 8
9	0, 0, 3, 3

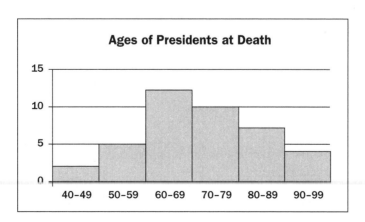

Bivariate Data

Bivariate data examines the relationship between two variables. The two variables are called the response variable and the explanatory variable. The data is given as points (explanatory, response).

The response variable measures the outcome of a study. The explanatory variable attempts to explain the response variable.

> **Example:** How does studying affect the score in a final exam? The explanatory variable is hours of study which explains the response variable, the score. Someone who studies 8 hours and received a score of 75 would have the point (8, 75).

A **scatter plot** shows the relationship between two quantitative variables measured on the same individuals.

The values of one variable appear on the horizontal (*x*) axis and the values of the other variable appear on the vertical (*y)* axis. Each piece of bivariate data appears as a point in the plot. The explanatory variable is placed on the *x*-axis and the response variable is placed on the *y*-axis.

Interpreting scatter plots

- Form—does the data appear linear or curved?

- Direction of association

- Positive association—data goes up to the right

- Negative association—data goes down to the right

- Strength of an association—how closely the points follow a clear form. Both of the associations above are strongly linear.

- Line of best fit (sometimes called the regression line)—The line of best fit is a straight line that describes how a response variable *y* changes as an explanatory variable *x* changes. Lines of best fit are used to predict the value of *y* for a given value of *x*. These lines require an explanatory variable and a response variable.

The closer that the line of best fit comes to the data points, the stronger the association is:

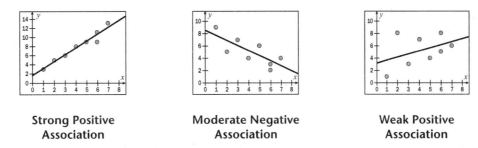

**Strong Positive
Association**

**Moderate Negative
Association**

**Weak Positive
Association**

- Meaning — an association between x and y means that as x changes, y changes. An association between x and y does not mean necessarily that x causes y.

Example: There is a strong positive association between the number of firefighters sent to a fire and the amount of damage the fire does. However, sending firefighters to a fire surely does not cause damage.

We can measure the strength of the association. The **correlation coefficient**, denoted by r, measures the strength and direction of a linear relationship between variables. The value of r will be between -1 and 1 inclusive. Positive values of r mean a positive association (as x increases, y increases) while negative values of r mean a negative association (as x increases, y decreases). The closer r is to 1 or -1, the stronger the association is.

For the hours-studied-versus-final-exam example, below is a scatter plot of the data and the line of best fit. We would interpret this as a fairly strong positive association between the duration of study and the final grade. Computer analysis confirms what we see by eye: r is equal to 0.9. But we must fall short of saying that studying causes grades to be higher. There are other issues that determine the grade such as how smart the student is and how much sleep he or she got the night before.

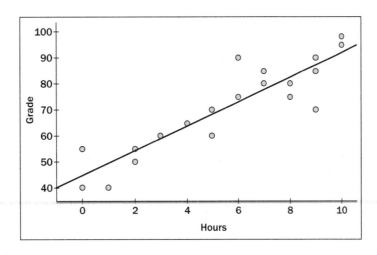

Measures of Central Tendency

When we have a great deal of data in numerical form such as the heights of every student in the school, your grades in all the math tests you took this year, every purchase that was made in a store today, or the yearly salary of every worker in a building, there is usually too much data to grasp at one time. Usually we prefer to have a single number that can represent that data. We call this a measure of central tendency.

- **Mean or average:** The mean of a set of data is the average and is usually denoted $\bar{x}$. To find it, you add up all the data and divide by the number of pieces of data.

  Example: 8 people went out to dinner. Following are the amounts they spent. Find the average cost.

  $18.55, $21.35, $17.45, $20.50, $24.25, $14.75, $19.65 and $22.90.

  $$\bar{x} = \frac{18.55 + 21.35 + 17.45 + 20.50 + 24.25 + 14.75 + 19.65 + 22.90}{8}$$

  $$= \frac{159.40}{8} = \$19.93$$

- **Median:** The median of a set of data is the middle score. To find the median, first put the data in increasing or decreasing order. Let n represent the number of pieces of data. If n is odd, the median is the data value: $\frac{n+1}{2}$. If n is even, take the average of data $\frac{n}{2}$ and the piece of data directly after it. When one of the data is much larger or smaller than the rest of the data, the mean can be strongly affected while the median is not.

  Example: A small class is made up of the students with first names: Susie, Joe, Michael, Shawn, Caroline, Steve, Kurt, Jennifer, Matthew, and Jonathan. Find the median name length.

  The lengths of the names are 5, 3, 7, 5, 8, 5, 4, 8, 7, and 8. When put in order we get: 3, 4, 5, 5, **5, 7**, 7, 8, 8, 8. Since there are 10 pieces of data, the median is the average of the 5th and 6th pieces of data, which are 5 and 7. The median is 6.

- **Mode:** The mode of a set of data is the data that occurs the most often.

  Example: In the class mentioned above, since a name with 8 letters occurs more often than any other number of letters, 8 is the mode.

Example: When leaving a movie, people rated it 1 to 5 with 5 the strongest positive rating and 1 the strongest negative. As the moviegoers voted, their ratings were tallied. At right are the results. Find the average score, the median score, and the mode.

5	ᚷᚷᚷᚷᚷᚷ III
4	ᚷᚷᚷᚷᚷᚷ IIII
3	ᚷᚷᚷᚷ II
2	ᚷᚷ II
1	IIII

Solution:

Score	Frequency
5	18
4	19
3	12
2	7
1	3

$$\bar{x} = \frac{18(5) + 19(4) + 12(3) + 7(2) + 3(1)}{59}$$

$$= \frac{219}{59} = 3.71$$

Median is the 30th score, which is 4.

Mode is the most common score, which is 4.

It is sometimes useful to make comparisons about the relative values of the mean and median. We can do that sometimes without knowing the actual data.

The most common shape of a smoothed-out histogram is one of the following three. In a symmetric distribution the mean and median are very close to each other. If the data is right-skewed with the bulge of the data to the left and the tail of the data to the right, the mean will be to the right of the median as some larger values tend to make the mean greater while the median is not affected by size. Similarly, if the data is left-skewed with the bulge of the data to the right and the tail of the data to the left, the mean will be to the left of the median as some smaller values tend to make the mean smaller while the median is not affected by size. Knowing the mode is impossible unless we actually see the data.

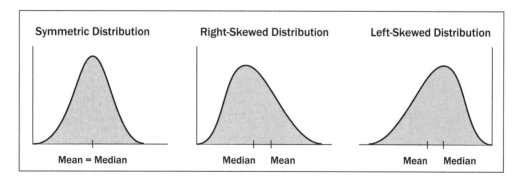

Box-and-Whisker Plots

A box-and-whisker plot, or box plot, is a way to represent the **five-number summary** of the data. The five numbers are the minimum, first quartile, median (or second quartile), third quartile, and maximum (or fourth quartile). A box plot can be either horizontal or vertical. We draw lines at the first, second, and third quartiles, which will form the box, and place dots or short lines at the minimum and maximum values; draw segments from each end of the box to these extreme values to create the whiskers.

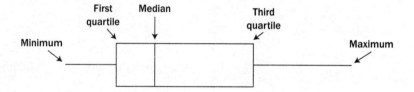

The quartiles of a data set divide the data into four regions with the same number of data values in each. The first quartile has 25% of the data values below it, the second quartile has 50% of the data values below it, the third quartile has 75% of the data values below it, and the fourth quartile has 100% of the data values below it. If there are 12 data points in the set, the third quartile includes the first 9 data values when in order from least to greatest.

Notice, the lengths of the whiskers and portions within the box are not the same. Many students confuse this to mean there are more data values represented between the median to the third quartile, but this is untrue. Box-and-whisker plots divide the data set into four regions with the same amount of data values in each region. The lengths differ based on the ranges of each area. The data described by the box plot above is skewed to the right as 50% of the data lies below the median while there is a much greater spread of data above the median. The **interquartile range** is the range between the values at the third and first quartiles.

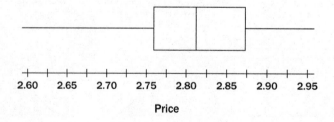

Price

The box-and-whisker plot above describes the price of a gallon of gas at filling stations along the main street of a town. Although the actual data is not given, we see that the median price is about $2.81, with 50% of the prices within the interquartile range of 12 cents (approximately $2.88 – $2.76). Since the data tails off to the left, the prices are skewed left and the mean price will be less than the median of $2.81.

Measures of Variability

While mean, median, and mode measure the center of a data set, they say nothing about how spread out the data is. We call this spread a measure of **variability**. A manufacturer of light bulbs would like small variability in the number of hours the bulbs will likely burn. A track coach who needs to decide which athletes go on to the finals may want larger variability in heat times because it will be easier to decide who are truly the fastest runners. There are two measures of variability that you are responsible for: range and standard deviation.

- **Range:** The range is the difference between the highest and lowest data values. If we are given all of the data, the range is easy to find. The larger the range, the greater the spread of the data.

    Example: If the heaviest person in a room is 205 pounds and the lightest person is 130 pounds, the range is 205 − 130 = 75 pounds.

- **Standard Deviation:** The standard deviation is a measure of how spread out the data is from the mean and is quite useful for data that is fairly symmetric. The greater the standard deviation, the greater the spread of the data from the mean. On the exam, you are not responsible for the actual calculations of standard deviation and variance, which is the square of the standard deviation.

    Example: 6 people are standing on a subway platform. If the average position on the platform is measured, arrange the following choices in order from smallest to largest standard deviation.

    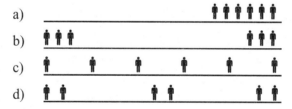

    Solution: In a) all the people are standing at the end of the platform so the standard deviation should be close to zero. In b), c), and d), the mean position is in the center of the platform. Choice b) has the people furthest from the center so it will have the largest standard deviation.

- **Outliers:** An outlier is a score that is dramatically different from the other scores in a group of data. Outliers can have a huge effect on the mean and standard deviation and it is important to know whether the outlier is a true score and not a typographical error, or occurring because of special circumstances.

At this stage of statistics, the standard deviation by itself tells us little about how the data is distributed. However, when two or more data sets are compared, the standard deviations of each allow us to compare the data sets.

Example: This shows exam scores of 4 classes of 5 students each. Each class has a mean of 80 but the data is quite different. Students should be able to compute the mean, median, and range of each The standard deviation was also calculated. Interpret the variability of the classes.

Solution:

Class 1	Class 2	Class 3	Class 4
80	90	100	100
80	85	90	100
80	80	80	100
80	75	70	100
80	70	60	0
$\bar{x} = 80$	$\bar{x} = 80$	$\bar{x} = 80$	$\bar{x} = 80$
Median = 80	Median = 80	Median = 80	Median = 100
Range = 0	Range = 20	Range = 40	Range = 100
St. Dev = 0	St. Dev = 7.07	St. Dev = 14.14	St. Dev = 40

Class 1 has a standard deviation of 0 because there is no spread about the mean of 80. Classes 2, 3, and 4 have larger standard deviations, meaning that there is a bigger spread about the mean. 0 is an outlier in class 4, which dramatically changes the mean and standard deviation.

Normal Distributions

One of the most important distributions in statistics is called the **normal distribution.** If a histogram is "smoothed out," many times its curve will appear symmetric, single-peaked, and bell-shaped. These are called *normal curves* or sometimes called the *bell-curve*. At right is a picture of a normal curve. Note how most of the data is in the center and it tails off symmetrically to the sides with little amount of data at the far left and right.

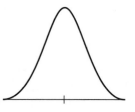

The reason these curves are so important in statistics is that so much of real-life statistics appears "normal." Here are some common examples:

- **Most data about the human body:** Examples include height, weight, fingernail length, hair length, how long people live, and so on.

- **Consumer prices:** Go to many markets and price a 2-liter bottle of soda. The data will appear normal with most prices about average, and fewer much cheaper and fewer much more expensive.

- **Wages:** Most people make an average amount of money while fewer make little money and fewer make a lot of money.

- **Time it takes to get to work:** Most days it might take 30 minutes to drive to work while fewer days it might take 20 minutes and fewer days it might take 40.

- **Grades:** Collect GPAs for a class of students and many students will have an average GPA, with fewer with low GPAs or with high GPAs.

The normal distribution follows an important rule called the **68-95-99.7% rule**. It states that in any normal distribution,

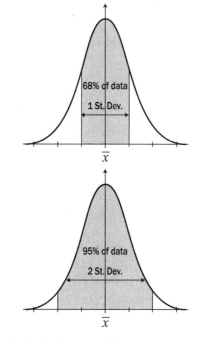

- 68% of the data lies within one standard deviation of the mean. In the figure provided, we have a normal distribution with the mean $\bar{x}$ in the center. Going out one standard deviation to the left and right of $\bar{x}$ will encompass 68% of the data.

- 95% of the data lies within two standard deviations of the mean. In the figure at right, we have a normal distribution with the mean $\bar{x}$ in the center. Going out two standard deviations to the left and right of $\bar{x}$ will encompass 95% of the data.

- 99.7% (or just about all) of the data lies within three standard deviations of the mean.

The more "normal" a distribution is, these relationships become closer to being perfectly true. No distribution is perfectly normal and therefore, these relationships are approximations in most real-life settings.

Example: The distribution of heights of adult American men is approximately normal with mean 69 inches and standard deviation 2.5 inches. On the normal curve at right, we mark the values for the mean and 1, 2, and 3 standard deviations above and below the mean.

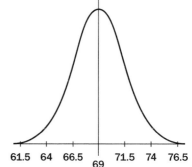

Although many distributions are normal, there are some that are not. For instance, although the time relative to the start of a class in which students arrive might be normal, the time that students leave relative to the end of class is not normal as everyone usually leaves at the same time.

We can make the following observations:

- 68% of adult American men are between 66.5 and 71.5 inches (5'6.5" and 5'11.5") tall.

- 95% of adult American men are between 64 and 74 inches (5'4" and 6'2") tall.

- 99.7% of adult American men are between 61.5 and 76.5 inches (5'1.5" and 6'4.5") tall.

COMPETENCY 013

The teacher understands the theory of probability.

The beginning teacher:

A. Explores concepts of experimental and theoretical probability through data collection, experiments and simulations.

B. Uses the concepts and principles of probability to describe the outcome of simple and compound events, including independent and dependent events.

C. Generates, simulates and uses probability models to represent a situation.

D. Determines probabilities by constructing sample spaces to model situations.

E. Solves a variety of probability problems using combinations, permutations and geometric probability (i.e., probability as the ratio of two areas).

F. Uses the binomial, geometric and normal distributions to solve problems.

Sample Spaces and Counting

In an event or activity that has a few or many possible outcomes, a sample space lists all of those possible outcomes.

Example: A piggy bank contains a good number of nickels, dimes, and quarters. Two coins are chosen at random. Write the sample space of possible sums.

Solution: $\{.10, .15, .30, .20, .35, .50\}$

In probability, we are usually concerned with how many ways an event can occur. You should review the section on permutations and combinations under Competency 003—Number Theory.

Probability

Probability refers to how likely an event is to occur. The probability of an event is a number between 0 and 1 inclusive. A probability of 0 means the event cannot occur, a probability of 1 means the event must occur, and a probability of 0.5 means that the event is as likely to occur than not. Probability can be expressed as a fraction, decimal, or percent. If a fair coin is tossed, the probability of heads is 0.5, and the probability of tails is 0.5.

In general: the probability of an event happening $= \dfrac{\text{number of ways the event can happen}}{\text{total number of outcomes}}$.

Example: A class has 20 students with 14 boys and 6 girls. The teacher calls on a student at random. The probability that she chooses a boy is $\dfrac{14}{20} = \dfrac{7}{10} = 0.7 = 70\%$.

Example: 5 people line up at random. If Jack and Jill are boyfriend and girlfriend, what is the probability that they will be next to each other?

Probability that Jack and Jill are together =

$\dfrac{\text{Number of ways Jack and Jill can be together}}{\text{Number of ways 5 people can line up}}$

Number of ways 5 people can line up $= 5! = 5 \bullet 4 \bullet 3 \bullet 2 \bullet 1 = 120$.

It is easy to simply generate the sample space of the possibilities with Jack and Jill together:

1	2	3	4	5
Jack	Jill			
	Jack	Jill		
		Jack	Jill	
			Jack	Jill

1	2	3	4	5
Jill	Jack			
	Jill	Jack		
		Jill	Jack	
			Jill	Jack

For each row where Jack and Jill are together there are $3! = 3 \bullet 2 \bullet 1 = 6$ different ways of lining up the three other people. So, there are 6 ways Jack can be in the 1st position and Jill in the 2nd position. There are 6 ways that Jack can be in the 2nd position and Jill in the 3rd position, and so forth. So

Probability that Jack and Jill are together $= \dfrac{8(6)}{120} = \dfrac{48}{120} = 40\%$

Example: There are 5 ice cream flavors and I choose a dish at random with 3 different flavors. What is the probability that I have both chocolate and vanilla?

Probability of having chocolate & vanilla =

$$\frac{\text{Number of dishes with chocolate, vanilla, and 1 other flavor}}{\text{Number of dishes with 3 flavors}}$$

Number of dishes with 3 flavors $= {_5}C_3 = \dfrac{5!}{3!\,2!} = \dfrac{5 \bullet 4 \bullet 3 \bullet 2 \bullet 1}{3 \bullet 2 \bullet 1 \bullet 2 \bullet 1} = 10$

Number of dishes with chocolate, vanilla and 1 other flavor = 3

Probability of having chocolate and vanilla $= \dfrac{3}{10} = 0.3 = 30\%$.

Mutually Exclusive and Complementary Events

Events that are **mutually exclusive** (also called disjoint) are events that cannot happen at the same time. Examples of choosing mutually exclusive events are:

- Choose a whole number. It is either even or odd.

- When you get to a traffic light, you can go either straight, turn left, or turn right.

Two events are described as **complementary** if they are the only two possible outcomes. The two examples above are complementary events. For any event A, the probability of A complement is given by $P(A)^C = 1 - P(A)$.

Examples:
- If the probability of choosing a boy is 62%, the probability of choosing a girl is $1 - 0.62 = 0.38$, which is 38%.

- If the probability that a lamp turns on is 98%, the probability that it does not turn on is $1 - 0.98 = 0.02$, which is 2%.

- If two events A and B are mutually exclusive, the probability of A or B = Prob(A) + Prob(B).

Example: If a cooler contains 5 Cokes, 8 Pepsis, 10 Sprites, and 7 Waters, the probability of choosing a Coke or a Pepsi $= \dfrac{5}{30} + \dfrac{8}{30} = \dfrac{13}{30}$. The probability of not choosing a Water is $1 - \dfrac{7}{30} = \dfrac{23}{30}$. That is because choosing a Water and not choosing a water are complementary events.

Probability questions can be answered by examining a Venn diagram. In a school, students can only be in one fall sport. This Venn diagram shows how many students participate in soccer or football or neither. The probability that a student is chosen who plays soccer or football $= \frac{59}{337} + \frac{75}{337} = \frac{134}{337}$. The probability of choosing a student who does not play soccer is $\frac{337 - 59}{337} = \frac{278}{337}$.

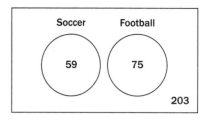

Non-Mutually Exclusive Events

If two events A and B are *not* mutually exclusive (meaning that they *can* occur at the same time), we cannot add the respective probabilities, as we have to concern ourselves with the overlap.

- A poll was taken in an office building as to how people got to work. The result is shown in the Venn diagram. There are 120 people taking the car exclusively, 55 people taking the train exclusively, 15 people taking both, and 10 people taking neither. To find the probability that someone takes a car *or* a train (which are *not* mutually exclusive events), compute $\frac{120 + 15 + 55}{120 + 15 + 55 + 10} = \frac{190}{200} = 95\%$.

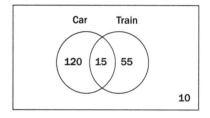

  Note: In probability theory, computing the probability that A or B occurs is interpreted as A occurring, B occurring or both.

- In a class of 30 students, their status is shown by this table. The probability of choosing a student who is a boy *and* passing is $\frac{15}{30} = \frac{1}{2} = 50\%$. The probability of choosing a student who is a boy *or* passing is found by either $\frac{15 + 7 + 3}{30} = \frac{25}{30} = \frac{5}{6} = 83.3\%$.

	Passing	Failing	Total
Boy	15	3	18
Girl	7	5	12
Total	22	8	30

Conditional Probability

In Florida, it is more likely to have rain if it is summer, rather than winter. So, the probability of rain in Florida is dependent on the month of the year. This is called conditional probability. Conditional probability is the probability event A occurs, given that event B occurs. For instance, the probability of a rainy day in South Florida is only 2% but, given that the month is June, the probability is over 50%.

Example: Suppose we have a class with this makeup: A student is chosen at random.

	Senior	Junior	Total
Boy	8	4	12
Girl	3	5	8
Total	11	9	20

The probability of choosing a boy is $\frac{12}{20} = \frac{3}{5} = 60\%$.

The probability of choosing a senior is $\frac{11}{20} = 55\%$.

The probability of choosing a boy and a senior is $\frac{8}{20} = \frac{2}{5} = 40\%$.

Suppose we wish the probability of choosing a senior *given* that we have chosen a boy. This is an example of conditional probability. The condition is choosing a boy. Since there are 12 boys and 8 of them are seniors, the denominator is no longer 20 but 12. So, the probability of choosing a senior given that we have chosen a boy is $\frac{8}{12} = \frac{2}{3} = 66.\overline{6}\%$. Since, as we saw, the probability of choosing a senior is 55%, it is more likely to choose a senior, given that we choose a boy.

If we want the probability of choosing a boy *given* that we have chosen a senior, we see that there are 11 seniors and 8 of them are boys, so $\frac{8}{11} = 72.7\%$.

One special type of probability question that occurs quite regularly in the real world has to do with binomial experiments.

Binomial experiments have all four of the following conditions:

1. Each observation falls into one of two categories—we call them "success" or "failure."

2. There is a fixed number of n observations.

3. The n observations are independent. Knowing the result of one observation tells you nothing about the other observations.

4. The probability of success p is the same for each observation.

Examples: We pick 5 cards from a standard deck and count the number of hearts. We replace the card each time and reshuffle. This is a binomial experiment as success is a heart and failure is a non-heart. There are 5 observations and since we replace the card each time, the chances of drawing a heart on any pick has nothing to do with previous draws. The probability of choosing a heart is always 25%.

If we pick 5 cards from a standard deck and count the number of hearts but do not replace the cards, we do not have a binomial experiment as the chance of drawing a heart on any pick is dependent on whether we chose a heart on the previous pick. If we did, then there are fewer hearts in the deck and thus the probabilities are not the same.

Example: Suppose a teacher gives a short quiz with 3 multiple-choice questions with choices A, B, C, and D. A student didn't study and randomly guesses. What is the probability that he gets at least 2 of the 3 questions correct?

First, we determine that this is a binomial experiment. Success means getting a problem right and failure means getting it wrong. There are 3 observations and getting a problem correct has nothing to do with getting another problem correct. The chance of getting a problem correct by guessing is 25% and the chance of getting a problem wrong is 75%.

There are two ways to solve this. First, we can create the sample space for getting 3 questions either right (R) or wrong (W). We then multiply the probabilities.

Sample Space	Probability
RRR	$(0.25)(0.25)(0.25) = 0.1015625$
RRW	$(0.25)(0.25)(0.75) = 0.046875$
RWR	$(0.25)(0.75)(0.25) = 0.046875$
RWW	$(0.25)(0.75)(0.75) = 0.140625$
WRR	$(0.75)(0.25)(0.25) = 0.046875$
WRW	$(0.75)(0.25)(0.75) = 0.140625$
WWR	$(0.75)(0.75)(0.25) = 0.140625$
WWW	$(0.75)(0.75)(0.75) = 0.42187$

Getting at least 2 questions right means getting either 2 questions right or all 3 questions right. So, we add the probabilities of the boxed items: $0.15625 + 3(0.46875) = 0.15625$. So, there is less than a 16% chance of getting 2 or more questions correct by mere guessing.

We can also do this by using the binomial formula. This formula uses combinations as reviewed in Competency 002. Recall that $_nC_r = \dfrac{n!}{r! \bullet (n-r)!}$ with 0! defined as 1.

In a binomial experiment, the chances of r successes from n trials with the probability of success equal to p is given by the formula: $_nC_r \bullet p^r \bullet (1-p)^{r-n}$.

The probability of all 3 questions correct is:

$$_3C_3 \bullet (0.25)^3 \bullet (1-0.25)^{3-3} = \frac{3!}{3! \bullet 0!}(0.25)^3 \bullet (0.75)^0 = 0.015625 \,.$$

The probability of 2 questions correct is:

$$_3C_2 \bullet (0.25)^2 \bullet (1-0.25)^{3-2} = \frac{3!}{2! \bullet 1!}(0.25)^2 \bullet (0.75)^1 = 0.140625 \,.$$

The probability of 1 question correct is:

$$_3C_1 \bullet (0.25)^1 \bullet (1-0.25)^{3-1} = \frac{3!}{1! \bullet 2!}(0.25)^1 \bullet (0.75)^2 = 0.421875 \,.$$

The probability of no questions correct is:

$$_3C_0 \bullet (0.25)^0 \bullet (1-0.25)^{3-0} = \frac{3!}{0! \bullet 3!}(0.25)^0 \bullet (0.75)^3 = 0.421875 \,.$$

So, the probability of at least 2 questions correct is:
0.015625 + 0.140625 = 0.15625.

Geometric Probability

Geometric probability typically refers to finding a ratio of two areas. For example, if a player throws a dart blindfolded that lands in the square with side length s, find the probability that it lands in the shaded region. For example, find the probability of throwing a dart at the shaded region in a square with side length s.

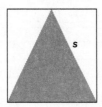

The probability of throwing a dart at the shaded region is the area of the shaded region divided by the area of the total region or square. We know the area of a square with side length s is s^2. The shaded region is exactly half of the square. One might draw a line through the middle of the triangle to see that there are four congruent triangles that make up the whole square (see figure below). Of course, this makes the assumption that the vertex of the triangle is at the midpoint of the top side of the square. But it doesn't matter. No matter where the vertex hits the top side of the square, its base is s and its height is s and the area is $\frac{1}{2}s^2$.

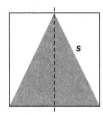

The area of half of the square is $\frac{1}{2}s^2$. Therefore, the probability of throwing a dart in the shaded region is $\dfrac{\frac{1}{2}s^2}{s^2} = \dfrac{1}{2}$.

COMPETENCY 014

The teacher understands the relationship among probability theory, sampling and statistical inference and how statistical inference is used in making and evaluating predictions.

The beginning teacher:

    A. Applies knowledge of designing, conducting, analyzing and interpreting statistical experiments to investigate real-world problems.

    B. Demonstrates an understanding of random samples, sample statistics and the relationship between sample size and confidence intervals.

    C. Applies knowledge of the use of probability to make observations and draw conclusions from single variable data and to describe the level of confidence in the conclusion.

    D. Makes inferences about a population using binomial, normal and geometric distributions.

    E. Demonstrates an understanding of the use of techniques such as scatter plots, regression lines, correlation coefficients and residual analysis to explore bivariate data and to make and evaluate predictions.

We saw that Competency 012 for the most part deals with descriptive statistics. **Descriptive statistics** uses the data to provide descriptions of the population, either through numerical calculations or graphs or tables. In contrast, **inferential statistics**, the focus of Competency 014, which we'll look at now, makes inferences and predictions about a population based on a sample of data taken from the population in question.

For example, suppose we were interested in the average monthly price of renting an apartment in Miami, Florida. We will call all apartments that are currently rented in Miami as the **population.** One way we could accomplish our goal is by taking a **census**: finding the cost of every apartment that is currently being rented in Miami and averaging them. By doing so, there would be no question of accuracy. But although theoretically possible, in practice it is not doable. There are too many apartments. Unless you had a large number of people to help, a census makes absolutely no sense.

Another strategy is to **sample**. We examine the rental cost of a smaller number of apartments, perhaps 100 of them. Because we expect the distribution of their cost to be normal (following the bell-shaped curve), with a few of them very expensive and a few of them very cheap, we then believe that the average of this sample to be very close to the average of our population: all apartments currently rented in Miami.

The key to this process is how the sample is taken. The best way to accomplish this is by taking a **simple random sample (SRS)**. Although there are technical ways to do this, an SRS is taken by essentially placing the name of every apartment in the city in a hat and choosing 100. From there, necessary work is done to find the rental price to the point of knocking on doors. An SRS makes every apartment and every combination of apartments equally likely to be chosen.

If the sample is not done correctly, **bias** can enter the process and any conclusion of the study may be flawed. Here are some types of sampling involving bias.

- A **convenience sample** might be taken by just sampling the rental prices on a major tourist street. It is less work for the sampler. But, by doing that, the average rental cost of the sample may be higher than that of the population.

- We could use the Internet to help choose the apartments, but our sample would possibly suffer from **undercoverage** as it wouldn't include some of the lower-rent apartments that may not be advertised on the Internet.

- Sometimes **systematic sampling** is used where all the apartments are placed in some kind of order, maybe alphabetical. Then maybe the first apartment on the list is taken, the 100th, the 200th, and so on. This may appear to be fair, but if the first apartment is the Acme and the second is the Adelphia, once Acme is chosen, then Adelphia cannot be taken and that introduces bias.

- **Stratified sampling** could involve taking exactly one apartment from every street in Miami. Again, this appears fair but if a street only has one apartment, then that apartment must be taken as opposed to streets that have multiple apartments.

Bias can be quite subtle and when it is introduced, it is called **hidden bias**. For instance, in a taste test between two brands of soda, if one is served at 35° and the other served at 40°, then people's judgment might be clouded by the temperature and not the taste.

Once the sample has been chosen and the data averaged, we are ready to create a **confidence interval**. This is in the form of:

sample average ± margin of error for *n*% confidence.

For example, we might find that the average cost of an apartment in Miami is $1,700 ± $150 for 95% confidence. The interpretation for this statement is:

> We are 95% sure that the average cost of renting
> an apartment in Miami is between $1,550 and $1,850.

Using a confidence interval, we hedge our bets in two ways:

- We say that we believe the average rental cost is $1,700. But the margin of error says that our average could be off as much as $150 in either direction.

- We say that we are 95% sure of our estimate, acknowledging that perhaps we could be wrong. This means that if we were to repeat this process doing it a total of 100 times, in 5 out of 100 times, our confidence interval wouldn't contain the true average rental price.

If the true average price of an apartment in Miami is $1,825, our 95% confidence interval is correct as $1,825 lies between $1,550 and $1,850.

If the true average price of an apartment in Miami is $1,600, our 95% confidence interval is correct as $1,600 lies between $1,550 and $1,850.

But if the true average price of an apartment in Miami is $1,930, our 95% confidence interval is incorrect as $1,930 does not lie between $1,550 and $1,850.

But whether our calculated confidence interval is right or wrong, we never know it. The only true way to know the average cost of a Miami apartment is to do a census, and again that is impractical.

Think of it as a court trial. A jury makes a judgment on whether a defendant has committed a crime. Their conclusion is based on a degree of confidence. If it is a murder trial, the degree of confidence must be 99.9% (it is never 100%). If the jury votes guilty, the defendant goes to jail. If the jury votes not guilty, the defendant goes free. But ultimately only the defendant truly knows whether he or she committed the crime. So, in our case, we estimate the average rental cost to the best of our ability and make decisions based on that. But we never really truly know if our estimate is correct.

This type of estimation is done all the time during elections. A poll might proclaim that a candidate is expected to win 52% of the vote in an election with a margin of error of 3% for 95% confidence. That is saying that the pollsters are 95% certain that the candidate will win between 49% and 55% of the vote. This means that it is possible that he could lose because 49% is within the confidence interval. And they are only 95% sure of this. Is it any wonder that we are told not to believe polls! Still, typically when polls are proved wrong by the actual election (which is a census), it was because there was bias in the selection of the data.

Confidence intervals can have smaller margins of error or have greater confidence (like 99%) by increasing the sample size. The greater the sample size, the smaller the margin of error. But increasing the sample size creates more work and if the sample size gets too large, it becomes similar to actually taking a census which gives the exact information rather than an estimation. The goal of statistical inference is to estimate an unknown average using a relatively small sample compared to the size of the population.

In the TExES exam, you are not responsible for calculating a confidence interval. Rather, you simply need to be able to interpret what a given confidence interval means as well as to examine a sampling technique to see if there is any bias.

Example: A farmer has just cleared a cornfield that can be divided into 64 smaller plots. The farmer isn't sure whether harvesting the entire field is worth the expense. So, he decides to harvest 8 plots and use this information to estimate the total yield for the entire field. Based on this information, he will decide whether to harvest the remaining plots.

Match the samples with the most likely sampling technique.

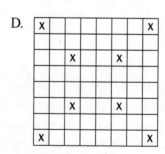

I. Stratified
II. Simple Random

III. Systematic
IV. Convenience

Solution:

I. B. It appears one plot of land was taken from each column.

II. C. There appears to be no pattern to the plots taken, which is a clear sign of an SRS.

III. D. There appears to be a specific and systematic pattern to the plots taken.

IV. A. All the plots taken are in one corner making it convenient to obtain the data.

Example: The farmer finds that after sampling his chosen plots, the average yield from each plot was 10.2 bushels of corn with a margin of error of 1.8 plots for 95% confidence. Interpret this.

Solution: The farmer is 95% confident that the average yield of his field will be between 8.4 and 12.0 bushels of corn per plot. Since he has 64 plots, this also means that he is 95% confident that his total field will yield between 537.6 and 768 bushels of corn.

COMPETENCY 015

The teacher understands mathematical reasoning and problem solving.

The beginning teacher:

A. Demonstrates an understanding of proof, including indirect proof, in mathematics.

B. Applies correct mathematical reasoning to derive valid conclusions from a set of premises.

C. Demonstrates an understanding of the use of inductive reasoning to make conjectures and deductive methods to evaluate the validity of conjectures.

D. Applies knowledge of the use of formal and informal reasoning to explore, investigate and justify mathematical ideas.

E. Recognizes that a mathematical problem can be solved in a variety of ways and selects an appropriate strategy for a given problem.

F. Evaluates the reasonableness of a solution to a given problem.

G. Applies content knowledge to develop a mathematical model of a real-world situation and analyzes and evaluates how well the model represents the situation.

H. Demonstrates an understanding of estimation and evaluates its appropriate uses.

Teachers need to create opportunities to motivate children to develop logical thinking skills through exploratory mathematics and problem solving. Such exploration can be done with partners or in learning centers, which are designed to expose students to manipulatives, which are used to teach mathematical concepts in an indirect fashion through student-selected activities.

Problem solving requires frequent opportunities to formulate, grapple with, and solve complex problems. Students are able to acquire ways of thinking, habits of persistence, and curiosity in unfamiliar situations (NCTM, 2000). Solving problems requires more than numerical computations. There are a number of problem-solving strategies. These can include drawing a picture, making a list, acting out a problem, creating a graph, using logical reasoning, looking for a pattern, developing a systematic list, working backward, writing an equation, and using guess-and-check methods.

George Polya wrote a classic book, *How to Solve It* (1994), which outlined four steps for doing mathematics. These steps are widely adopted in textbooks and resource books to help students develop problem-solving skills. The four steps are described briefly in the following list:

1. *Understanding the problem.* In this phase students determine what the problem is about and identify what question or problem is being posed.

2. *Devising a plan.* Students think about how they intend to solve the problem and select a problem-solving strategy.

3. *Carrying out the plan.* Students implement the plan they just devised. If they get stumped, students can reevaluate their plan and try a different approach if needed.

4. *Looking back.* This phase can be the most important as well as the most skipped by students. Once they've arrived at an answer after the first three steps, students should determine whether their answers make sense and check their work if possible.

Logical reasoning is thinking about something in a way that makes sense to the student. Thinking about mathematics problems involves logical reasoning. Logical reasoning can be used to find patterns in a set of data, then those patterns can be used to draw conclusions about the data, which can then be used to solve problems. Finding patterns involves identifying characteristics that numbers or objects have in common. A sequence of geometric objects may have some property in common. For example, they may all be quadrilaterals or all have right angles.

Through mathematical reasoning skills, students should investigate mathematical conjectures and develop, as well as evaluate, mathematical arguments and proofs (NCTM, 2000). Strong reasoning skills are needed for building skill sets in all five content standards: Number and Operations, Algebra, Geometry, Measurement, and Data Analysis and Probability.

Deductive reasoning requires moving from the assumptions to the conclusion, or from the general to the specific. Deductive reasoning is often used in students' daily lives. For example, if a student sees it is raining outside before leaving home to head to school, she might conclude she needs an umbrella. The student's conclusion is reached through deductive reasoning.

Inductive reasoning involves examining particular instances to come to some general assumptions, and should be intuitive. When thinking inductively, students will make hypotheses, extend patterns of thought, use analogies, and make reasonable conclusions from examining what appears to be a body of evidence.

COMPETENCY 016

The teacher understands mathematical connections within and outside of mathematics and how to communicate mathematical ideas and concepts.

The beginning teacher:

A. Recognizes and uses multiple representations of a mathematical concept (e.g., a point and its coordinates, the area of circle as a quadratic function in r, probability as the ratio of two areas).

B. Uses mathematics to model and solve problems in other disciplines, such as art, music, science, social science and business.

C. Expresses mathematical statements using developmentally appropriate language, Standard English, mathematical language and symbolic mathematics.

D. Communicates mathematical ideas using a variety of representations (e.g., numeric, verbal, graphic, pictorial, symbolic, concrete).

E. Demonstrates an understanding of the use of visual media such as graphs, tables, diagrams and animations to communicate mathematical information.

F. Uses the language of mathematics as a precise means of expressing mathematical ideas.

G. Understands the structural properties common to the mathematical disciplines.

H. Explores and applies concepts of financial literacy as it relates to teaching students (e.g., describes the basic purpose of financial institutions, distinguishes the difference between gross income and net income, identifies various savings options, defines different types of taxes, identifies the advantages and disadvantages of different methods of payments).

I. Applies mathematics to model and solve problems to manage financial resources effectively for lifetime financial security as it relates to teaching students (e.g., distinguish between fixed and variable expenses, calculate profit in a given situation, develop a system for keeping and using financial records, describe actions that might be taken to balance a budget when expenses exceed income and balance a simple budget).

Mathematics is an integrated field of study. When students connect mathematical ideas, their understanding is deeper and more lasting. Students can come to view mathematics as a coherent whole (NCTM, 2000). One of the challenges teachers face in promoting interest in mathematics is to convince students that mathematics plays an important role in their lives. Based on this assumption, teachers need to introduce mathematics concepts in a problem-solving format using situations that are real to the students' lives. Some examples to connect mathematics to students' lives are explained below.

Planning Projects

- Have students plan a field trip for the class. As a class or in small groups, students might have to decide where the field trip will take place and estimate the cost of the trip. They will need to determine a means of transportation, number of adult volunteer chaperones, the duration of the field trip including travel time, cost per student, and total cost of the trip. Students can also develop a plan to pay for the field trip, including fund-raising opportunities, and create a field trip permission slip form for parents/guardians to sign. Once all information is collected, they can write a proposal for the field trip and present it to the principal and potentially get approval to take the trip.

- Have students plan a road trip to a vacation spot they would like to visit one day. Using an online mapping website, students can obtain the appropriate information to determine distance from one place to the other, and use this distance to calculate travel time and gas expenses based on mileage of driving their family car. Students can also investigate traveling by bus, train, or plane, and then they can compare costs to determine the most cost-effective trip.

- Organize cooking activities using recipes requiring specific units of measurement. These activities should include some that can be completed in school and at home. The recipes should require students to convert units and use proportional reasoning to double recipes or make portions of a recipe.

- Develop a "class store" to help students with concepts of fractions, decimals, and percents, as well as basic computational skills. Using a token or sticker system, students can earn forms of money as tokens or stickers, and use them to purchase items in the class store. Often teachers reward students for good behavior for following directions or having good listening skills. However, students could earn their tokens/stickers by helping students in class mathematically, presenting a problem to the class, posing questions, leading class discussions, or explaining where they used mathematics outside of school and/or bringing proof of such experience.

COMPETENCY 017

The teacher understands how children learn and develop mathematical skills, procedures and concepts.

The beginning teacher:

A.   Applies theories and principles of learning mathematics to plan appropriate instructional activities for all students.

B.   Understands how students differ in their approaches to learning mathematics with regards to diversity.

C.   Uses students' prior mathematical knowledge to build conceptual links to new knowledge and plans instruction that builds on students' strengths and addresses students' needs.

D.   Understands how learning may be assisted through the use of mathematics manipulatives and technological tools.

E.   Understands how to motivate students and actively engage them in the learning process by using a variety of interesting, challenging and worthwhile mathematical tasks in individual, small-group and large-group settings.

F.   Understands how to provide instruction along a continuum from concrete to abstract.

G.   Recognizes the implications of current trends and research in mathematics and mathematics education.

Contextual factors are important elements that help teachers plan and meet the needs of all students. Understanding students' backgrounds, prior knowledge, and personal experiences can influence what content is taught and how to teach it. Understanding how students differ in their problem-solving approaches can create an effective learning environment.

Students should experience mathematics through the use of manipulatives and technological tools that allow learning to occur at a concrete level. Manipulatives and tools allow students to touch, move, rearrange, and explore mathematics. From these experiences, students can then transfer their knowledge to the pictorial level, where they use pictures to problem solve. They can create and design their own pictorial representations for the given task. Once students master the concrete and pictorial phases, they can then apply the mathematical content in a more abstract form.

The teacher is responsible for motivating and engaging students in challenging and worthwhile mathematics, through individual, small-group, and large-group settings. The five Process Standards defined by the National Council of Teachers of Mathematics (NCTM) are essential for students to successfully learn mathematics. They are problem solving, reasoning and proof, representations, communication, and connections (NCTM, 2000). Rarely are these standards experienced in isolation. Rather, students fluctuate among and within the standards regularly during their mathematical learning experiences.

The NCTM, established in 1920, is one of the most well-known organizations in mathematics education to date. NCTM's goals include the development and improvement of mathematics education through six principles and ten standards that children in kindergarten through grade 12 should master. In 2000, NCTM published the *Principles and Standards for School Mathematics*, a resource intended for all who make decisions that affect mathematics education for K–12 students. This document has influenced states and district curricula development, and specifies the mathematics content students should learn.

Principles of Mathematics

The NCTM (2000) identified six principles that should guide mathematics instruction. These include equity, curriculum, teaching, learning, assessment, and technology.

- **Equity:** Excellence in mathematics education requires equity: high expectations and strong support for all students.

- **Curriculum:** A curriculum must be coherent, focusing on important mathematics and clearly articulating concepts across grades. Curriculum is more than a collection of activities.

- **Teaching:** Effective mathematics teaching requires understanding what students know and need to learn and then challenging and supporting students to learn it well.

- **Learning:** Students must learn mathematics with understanding, actively building new knowledge from experience and former knowledge.

- **Assessment:** Assessment should support the learning of important mathematics, and furnish useful information to both teachers and students.

- **Technology:** Technology is essential in teaching and learning mathematics; it influences the teaching of mathematics and enhances students' learning.

Standards of Mathematics

NCTM (2000) has identified five Content Standards and five Process Standards. The Content Standards explicitly describe the mathematical content students should learn, whereas the Process Standards highlight ways of attaining and using content knowledge.

Texas Mathematics Standards

The State Board of Educator Certification (SBEC) and the State Board of Education (SBOE) approved Texas educator standards that outline what the beginning educator should know and be able to do. These standards are based on the required state curriculum for students, the Texas Essential Knowledge and Skills (TEKS). The Texas Education Agency (TEA, 2009) has defined eight mathematical standards as follows:

Standard I — Number Concepts

The mathematics teacher understands and uses numbers, number systems and their structure, operations and algorithms, quantitative reasoning, and technology appropriate to teach the state-wide curriculum (Texas Essential Knowledge and Skills [TEKS]) in order to prepare students to use mathematics.

Standard II — Patterns and Algebra

The mathematics teacher understands and uses patterns, relations, functions, algebraic reasoning, analysis, and technology appropriate to teach the statewide curriculum (Texas Essential Knowledge and Skills [TEKS]) in order to prepare students to use mathematics.

Standard III — Geometry and Measurement

The mathematics teacher understands and uses geometry, spatial reasoning, measurement concepts and principles, and technology appropriate to teach the statewide curriculum (Texas Essential Knowledge and Skills [TEKS]) in order to prepare students to use mathematics.

Standard IV — Probability and Statistics

The mathematics teacher understands and uses probability and statistics, their applications, and technology appropriate to teach the statewide curriculum (Texas Essential Knowledge and Skills [TEKS]) in order to prepare students to use mathematics.

Standard V — Mathematical Processes

The mathematics teacher understands and uses mathematical processes to reason mathematically, to solve mathematical problems, to make mathematical connections within and outside of mathematics, and to communicate mathematically.

Standard VI — Mathematical Perspectives

The mathematics teacher understands the historical development of mathematical ideas, the interrelationship between society and mathematics, the structure of mathematics, and the evolving nature of mathematics and mathematical knowledge.

Standard VII — Mathematical Learning and Instruction

The mathematics teacher understands how children learn and develop mathematical skills, procedures, and concepts; knows typical errors students make; and uses this knowledge to plan, organize, and implement instruction; to meet curriculum goals; and to teach all students to understand and use mathematics.

Standard VIII — Mathematical Assessment

The mathematics teacher understands assessment and uses a variety of formal and informal assessment techniques appropriate to the learner on an ongoing basis to monitor and guide instruction and to evaluate and report student progress.

Mathematics and Cognitive Development

Learning mathematics requires students to create mathematical relationships and develop meanings for abstract ideas. Students need concrete interactions with mathematical ideas that may not be accessible from abstractions and symbols. Jean Piaget, a developmental psychologist, observed and recorded the intellectual abilities of infants, children, and adolescents. Piaget developed stages of intellectual development related to brain growth that led him to conclude that thinking and reasoning skills of children were dominated by preoperational thought, a pattern of thinking that is egocentric, centered, irreversible, and nontransformational (Piaget and Inhelder, 1969). His theory included the growth of intelligence and emergence and acquisition of schemata—schemes of a child using "developmental stages" to explain how children acquire new information. The four main stages are the Sensorimotor stage (birth–2 years), Preoperational stage (years 2–7), Concrete Operational stage (years 7–11), and Formal Operational stage (years 11–adult).

Piaget describes the Preoperational stage of development to include the processes of symbolic functioning, centration, intuitive thought, egocentrism, and inability to conserve. Students in the Concrete Operational stage exhibit the developmental processes of decentering, reversibility, conservation, serialization, classification, and elimination of egocentrism. The Formal Operation stage of Piaget's cognitive development focuses on the ability to use symbols and to think abstractly (Piaget and Inhelder, 1969).

Students in the Preoperational stage experience problems with at least two perceptual concepts: conservation and centration, according to Susan Sperry Smith (2008). Conservation is the understanding that the quantity, length, or number of items is unrelated to the arrangement or appearance of the object or items. Students encountering problems with conservation may have difficulty measuring volume or understanding the value of money. For example, students may think a dime is worth less than a nickel since it is thinner and smaller in diameter. Centration is characterized by a child's focus on one aspect of a situation or problem. For example, take two 8.5-inch-by-11-inch sheets of paper and roll each into a tube, one a long skinny tube, and the other a short wider tube. A young student might judge the capacity of the shorter tube to be less than that of the taller tube based on his perception of short and tall.

Children ages 7 to 11 years old (about second through seventh grades) experience rapid growth during the Concrete Operational stage of cognitive development. At this time students are developing the ability to think logically about concrete objects or relationships. Some of the characteristics of students at this stage are:

- **Classification:** The student can identify and name sets of objects according to appearance, size, color, or other characteristics. The student can arrange objects based on characteristics.

- **Conservation:** The student understands that the quantity, length, or number of items is unrelated to the arrangement or appearance of the object. The student can discern that if water is transferred from a glass to a pitcher, the quantity of water will be conserved; that is, the quantity of water in the pitcher will be equal to the quantity that had been in the glass.

- **Decentering:** The student can take into account multiple aspects of a problem to solve it. The student can form conclusions based on reason rather than perception.

- **Elimination of egocentrism:** The student is able to view things from another student's perspective. The student can retell or summarize a story from another child's perspective.

- **Reversibility:** The student understands that objects can be changed and then returned to their original state. The student can determine that four rows of two crayons is the same original quantity as two rows of four crayons.

Piaget's stages of cognitive development were foundational during his time. Contemporary researchers have found Piaget underestimated the abilities of children in preschool and early elementary years. Some students can develop more sophisticated thinking and reasoning skills by as early as second or third grade, especially if they have adequate instruction and support from teachers and peers (Vygotsky, 1986). Students' cognitive development is influenced by their culture and instruction and is related to cognitively guided instruction (CGI) (Carpenter et al., 1999; Kamii, 2000; Santrock, 2003).

Mathematical Literacy

Literacy skills are essential for students to be successful learners. More than reading and writing, literacy includes purposeful social and cognitive processes that help students discover ideas and create meaning; it requires analysis, synthesis, organization, and evaluation of reading tasks (Jacobs, 2008; Moss, 2005; Tovani, 2000). Mathematical literacy involves the capacity to identify, understand, and engage in mathematics; it includes the ability to make sound judgments about the role mathematics plays in one's present and future life as a constructive, concerned, and reflective citizen (Kramarski and Mizrachi, 2006). NCTM (1989) describes mathematically literate students as having an appreciation of the value and beauty of mathematics and being able, as well as being inclined, to value and use quantitative information.

Successful readers determine what is important. They synthesize information to create new thinking, construct sensory images, and self-monitor their own comprehension. Students struggle when reading if they lack the comprehension strategies needed to unlock meaning, sufficient background knowledge, and the ability to recognize organizational patterns (Tovani, 2000). Gardner (1983, 1993) would describe students with mathematical literacy to have logical-mathematical intelligence, which is the ability to understand and use logical structures including patterns, relationships, statements, and propositions through experimentation, quantification, conceptualization, and classification.

Students may face a number of challenges with the technical vocabulary and literacy skills of mathematics. The mathematics classroom tends to abound in assumptions concerning students' prior knowledge of specialized academic terms such as *numerator, denominator, product, quotient, minuend, divisor, subtrahend,* and other technical concepts and vocabulary. The terms that have one meaning in one subject domain can have an entirely different meaning in the vocabulary of mathematics. These terms include *quarter, column, product, rational, even,* and *table.* Also, mathematics vocabulary tends to encompass a variety of homophones (words pronounced in the same way but having different meanings). Table 4-1 depicts various mathematics terms and their structures that may be confusing for all students. Table 4-2 lists homophones that may pose challenges for students.

Table 4-1 Mathematical Terminology and Meanings

Terminology	Common Meaning	Mathematical Meaning
Even	Equal amount, same level	Numbers divisible by 2
Face	Front of a human head	Surface of a geometric solid
Plane	Aircraft	A two-dimensional surface
Mean	Not nice, or to express a particular message	Arithmetic average of a set of data values
Right	Correct, proper; or a direction	A 90-degree angle
Volume	Loudness of sounds	Capacity or quantity of liquid

Table 4-2 Homophones

Mathematical Term	Everyday Term
Sum	Some
One	Won
Two	To, too
Whole	Hole
Plane	Plain
Hour	Our
Chord	Cord
Eight	Ate
Weigh	Way
Real	Reel

Contextual Mathematics

Mathematical concepts are integral aspects of daily life. Students should encounter mathematics in real-world contexts that are associated with activities found in their daily lives. For instance, children may often be involved in recreational activities such as baseball or softball. Common mathematics associated with these sports includes players' batting averages, calculated by the number of hits divided by the number of times at bat. Providing students with a mathematical context allows students to develop a deeper meaning to the mathematics, assisting in conceptual versus procedural understanding.

Consider the following examples:

Example 1   During the second week of July 2011, the temperatures for Monday through Friday were 98, 102, 99, 99, and 105 degrees. What was the average temperature during this week?

Example 2   Find the average of 98, 102, 99, 99, and 105.

Both examples ask for the same mathematical task: compute the average of the data set by calculating the sum of the numbers and dividing by the number of data values—five. However, Example 1 poses the mathematical problem in a context or real-world scenario that students can relate to: temperature. Knowledge of the daily temperature is helpful to determine what a student might wear to school one day. In warm temperatures, as depicted in the problem, students might wear shorts to school, but if the temperatures were in the 30s and 40s, they'd probably choose to wear jeans and a jacket. Example 2 has less connotation or meaning to students, as the problem is not posed in a specific context. Although having the ability to calculate the mean or average of a set of values is important, students should have a balance of problems presented and not presented in real-world contexts.

Manipulatives in the Mathematics Classroom

Manipulatives are powerful tools to help students explore mathematics in a concrete and hands-on approach. Manipulatives provide a visual representation of a concept that assists in developing deeper understanding, which will help explain and improve the abstract meaning of mathematics. Students need opportunities to work collaboratively, applying numeric and algebraic reasoning; generating and analyzing data; and developing an understanding of ratios, proportions, and rate, as well as of critical thinking and making sound predictions and estimates. The importance of using manipulatives to teach these skills and mathematical concepts is reinforced by Piaget's theories on the cognitive development in children (Dienes and Sriraman, 2008).

Two-Color Counters

Two-color counters are circles, often with one side red and the other white. Sometimes the product is sold in sets of yellow and red. In primary grades, two-color counters are used for building number concepts from 0 to 20 using five-frames and ten-frames. In grades 4 through 8, two-color counters can depict multiplication problems in the form of rectangular arrays. They are great tools for teaching operations with integers, specifically zero pairs and why the product of two negative numbers is positive.

Fraction Bars

Fraction bars can be constructed from paper using paper-folding techniques, or the product can be purchased. As their name implies, fraction bars are length models of fractions. They model relationships and equivalencies. For example, by the diagram below, we can see two $\frac{1}{4}$ bars is equivalent to one bar the length of $\frac{1}{2}$. So, $\frac{2}{4} = \frac{1}{2}$. Although students learn how to simplify fractions by finding a GCF and removing a factor of 1, the fraction bars approach equivalent fractions by using length to model the equivalencies. In addition to exploring fraction equivalencies, students can use fraction bars to display mixed numbers and to solve addition and subtraction problems.

1															
$\frac{1}{2}$								$\frac{1}{2}$							
$\frac{1}{4}$				$\frac{1}{4}$				$\frac{1}{4}$				$\frac{1}{4}$			
$\frac{1}{8}$		$\frac{1}{8}$		$\frac{1}{8}$		$\frac{1}{8}$		$\frac{1}{8}$		$\frac{1}{8}$		$\frac{1}{8}$		$\frac{1}{8}$	
$\frac{1}{16}$	$\frac{1}{16}$	$\frac{1}{16}$	$\frac{1}{16}$	$\frac{1}{16}$	$\frac{1}{16}$	$\frac{1}{16}$	$\frac{1}{16}$	$\frac{1}{16}$	$\frac{1}{16}$	$\frac{1}{16}$	$\frac{1}{16}$	$\frac{1}{16}$	$\frac{1}{16}$	$\frac{1}{16}$	$\frac{1}{16}$

Fraction Circles

Fraction circles are similar to fraction bars. However, this manipulative models fractions in an *area* model. Students can explore equivalent fractions, mixed numbers, and computations with fraction circles.

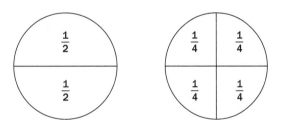

Pattern Blocks

Pattern blocks consist of six different polygons that are identified by color and shape: orange square, green equilateral triangle, yellow regular hexagon, red isosceles trapezoid, blue rhombus, and brown parallelogram. Pattern blocks can be used to teach number and operation skills of basic fractional concepts and relationships, as well as addition, subtraction, multiplication, and division of fractions. In geometry, they are used for modeling transformations, tessellations, and geometric probability.

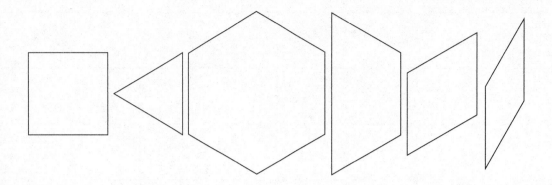

Cuisenaire Rods

Cuisenaire rods are similar to fraction bars as they depict length models. There are 10 different rods denoted by color and length. The rods are used in primary grades to discuss whole number addition and subtraction. In grades 4 through 8, they are frequently used to explore fractional concepts, equivalencies, and computations.

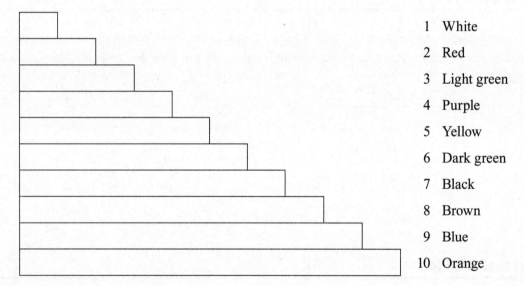

1	White
2	Red
3	Light green
4	Purple
5	Yellow
6	Dark green
7	Black
8	Brown
9	Blue
10	Orange

Algebra Tiles

Algebra tiles comprise three different shapes, each with two different-colored sides. They represent variables and constants and are used to solve equations, factor polynomials, expand or multiply polynomials, and investigate zero pairs. A strong foundation of integer operations should be formed prior to using algebra tiles. Specifically, students should understand why the product of two negative numbers is a positive number, most often taught using two-color counters. Then, when students apply their knowledge of integer operations to algebra tiles, the approach is less procedural and more conceptual.

Often, the constant has one side red and the other beige or yellow. The x bar has one side red and the other green. The square has one side red and the other blue. The red side is to represent negative values. The beige, green, and blue sides are to represent positive values.

Double-Sided Geoboard

Double-sided geoboards include a five-by-five pin array on one side and a circular array on the other side. They come with rubber bands to create various shapes used to explore properties, area, and perimeter. The side with the circular array can be used to investigate chords, angle measures and their relationships, sectors, and so on. The circle can represent a clock, too, so students can represent a time and then discuss angle measures and fractions or portions of a circle. Of course, with more and more students only being exposed to digital clocks, the use of analog clocks in math problems is on the wane.

COMPETENCY 018

The teacher understands how to plan, organize and implement instruction using knowledge of students, subject matter and statewide curriculum (Texas Essential Knowledge and Skills [TEKS]) to teach all students to use mathematics.

The beginning teacher:

A. Demonstrates an understanding of a variety of instructional methods, tools and tasks that promote students' ability to do mathematics described in the TEKS.

B. Understands planning strategies for developing mathematical instruction as a discipline of interconnected concepts and procedures.

C. Develops clear learning goals to plan, deliver, assess and reevaluate instruction based on the TEKS.

D. Understands procedures for developing instruction that establishes transitions between concrete, symbolic and abstract representations of mathematical knowledge.

E. Applies knowledge of a variety of instructional delivery methods, such as individual, structured small-group and large-group formats.

F. Understands how to create a learning environment that provides all students, including English-language learners, with opportunities to develop and improve mathematical skills and procedures.

G. Demonstrates an understanding of a variety of questioning strategies to encourage mathematical discourse and to help students analyze and evaluate their mathematical thinking.

H. Understands how technological tools and manipulatives can be used appropriately to assist students in developing, comprehending and applying mathematical concepts.

Substantial thought to lesson planning is crucial for all teachers regardless of experience. Every class of students is different, so choices of which tasks to use and how they are presented to students must be made daily. Addressing all students' needs for a diverse classroom and including the state and local curriculum objectives are essential components of the lesson-plan process. The following are key components to consider when planning a lesson:

- Determine the mathematics and learning objectives.

- Consider the students' needs.

- Select, design, or adapt a task or activity.

- Identify essential questions.

- Design lesson assessments.

Differentiated instruction is a teaching method in which the teacher's plan includes strategies to support the range of different academic backgrounds. Students' interests and their prior knowledge impact instruction. Three elements to consider when differentiating instruction are content (what you want each student to be able to do), process (how you will engage students in that learning), and product (what students will show for what they have learned at the end of the lesson) (Tomlinson, 2001).

The state curriculum, Texas Essential Knowledge and Skills (TEKS), should guide the mathematical content taught in the classroom. How the specific content is taught is up to the classroom teacher but can often be guided by curriculum specialists within school districts.

COMPETENCY 019

The teacher understands assessment and uses a variety of formal and informal assessment techniques to monitor and guide mathematics instruction and to evaluate student progress.

The beginning teacher:

A. Demonstrates an understanding of the purpose, characteristics and uses of various assessments in mathematics, including formative and summative assessments.

B. Understands how to select and develop assessments that are consistent with what is taught and how it is taught.

C. Demonstrates an understanding of how to develop a variety of assessments and scoring procedures consisting of worthwhile tasks that assess mathematical understanding, common misconceptions and error patterns.

D. Understands how to evaluate a variety of assessment methods and materials for reliability, validity, absence of bias, clarity of language and appropriateness of mathematical level.

E. Understands the relationship between assessment and instruction and knows how to evaluate assessment results to design, monitor and modify instruction to improve mathematical learning for all students, including English-language learners.

One of NCTM's (2000) six principles for school mathematics is assessment, which should support the learning of important mathematics and furnish useful information to both teachers and students. In traditional testing, the focus is on what students do not know, but a shift toward assessing students has led to an emphasis on determining what students do know. This shift resulted in the *Assessment Standards for School Mathematics* published by NCTM in 1995. This document outlines four specific purposes of assessment: (1) monitoring student progress, (2) making instructional design, (3) evaluating student achievement, and (4) evaluating programs. Additional considerations about what should be assessed were identified as concepts and procedures, mathematical processes, and productive dispositions (NCTM, 1995).

Assessments can be formative or summative. **Formative assessments** are regularly planned checkups of students' progress. When implemented well, formative assessments can increase the speed of learning by providing feedback that promotes learning. Formative assessments should also guide instruction, impacting decision making for future steps in the learning progression (NCTM, 1995; Van de Walle et al., 2010). Some formative approaches include performance-based tasks, journals, observations of problem solving, and diagnostic interviews.

Summative assessments are cumulative evaluations that often generate a single score, such as a unit exam or standardized test. This type of assessment shows what students know at that particular point in time, whereas formative assessments depict active student thinking and reasoning over time.

REFERENCES

Billstein, Rick, Shlomo Libeskind, and Johnny Lott. 2010. *A Problem Solving Approach to Mathematics for Elementary School Teachers*, 10th ed. Boston: Pearson Education, Inc.

Carpenter, T.M., E. Fennema, M.L. Franke, L. Levi, and S.B. Empson. 1999. *Children's Mathematics: Cognitively Guided Instruction*. Portsmouth, NH: Heinemann.

Dienes, Z.P., and B. Sriraman, eds. 2008. *Mathematics Education and the Legacy of Zoltan Paul Dienes*. Charlotte, NC: Information Age Publishing.

Gardner, Howard. 1983. *Frames of Mind*. New York: HarperCollins Publishers, Inc.

Gardner, Howard. 1993. *Multiple Intelligences: The Theory in Practice*. New York: HarperCollins Publishers, Inc.

Jacobs, V. A. 2008. "Adolescent Literacy: Putting the Crisis in Context." *Harvard Educational Review* 78: 7–39.

Kamii, C. 2000. *Young Children Reinvent Arithmetic: Implications of Piaget's Theory*. New York: Teachers College Press.

Kramarski B., and N. Mizrachi. 2006. "Online Discussion and Self-regulated Learning: Effects of Instructional Methods on Mathematical Literacy." *Journal of Educational Research* 99: 218–230.

Long, Calvin T., Duane W. DeTemple, and Richard S. Millman. 2012. *Mathematical Reasoning for Elementary Teachers*, 6th ed. Boston: Pearson, Inc.

Moss, B. 2005. "Making a Case and a Place for Effective Content Area Literacy Instruction in Elementary Grades. *The Reading Teacher* 59: 46–55.

National Council of Teachers of Mathematics (NCTM). 1989. *Curriculum and Evaluation Standards for School Mathematics*. Reston, VA: NCTM.

National Council of Teachers of Mathematics (NCTM). 1995. Assessment Standards for School Mathematics. Reston, VA: NCTM.

National Council of Teachers of Mathematics (NCTM). 2000. *Principles and Standards for School Mathematics*. Reston, VA: NCTM.

Piaget, J., and B. Inhelder. 1969. *The Psychology of the Child*. New York: Basic Books.

Polya, George. 1994. *How to Solve It*. Princeton, NJ: Princeton University Books.

Santrock, J.W. 2003. *Children*, 7th ed. Boston: McGraw-Hill.

Smith, Karl J. 2007. *The Nature of Mathematics*, 11th ed. Belmont, CA: Brooks/Cole.

Sperry Smith, S. 2008. *Early Childhood Mathematics*, 4th ed. Boston: Allyn and Bacon.

Tan, S.T. 1999. *Applied Calculus*, 4th ed. Pacific Grove, CA: Brooks/Cole.

Texas Education Agency (TEA). 2009. Texas Essential Knowledge and Skills. Texas Administrative Code (TAC), Title 19, Part II, Chapter 111. Texas Essential Knowledge and Skills for Mathematics. Austin: Texas Education Agency.

Tomlinson, C. 2001. *How to Differentiate Instruction in Mixed-Ability Differentiated Classrooms*, 2nd ed. Alexandria, VA: Association for Supervision and Curriculum Development.

Tovani, C. 2000. *I Read It, but I Don't Get It: Comprehension Strategies for Adolescent Readers*. Portland, ME: Stenhouse Publishers.

Van de Wall, John A., Karen S. Karp, and Jennifer M. Bay-Williams. 2010. *Elementary and Middle School Mathematics: Teaching Developmentally*, 7th ed. Boston: Allyn and Bacon.

Vancil, C. 1966. *College Algebra: A Graphing Approach*, preliminary ed. Fort Worth, TX: Saunders College Publishing.

Vygotsky, Lev Semyonovich. 1986. *Thought and Language*, new rev. ed. Cambridge, MA: MIT Press.

Subject Test III: Social Studies (808)

OVERVIEW OF SUBJECT TEST III: SOCIAL STUDIES

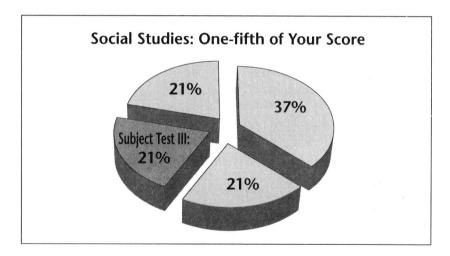

Social Studies: One-fifth of Your Score

Subject Test III: Social Studies, like the Mathematics and Science subject tests, makes up approximately one-fifth of the questions you will see on the TExES Core Subjects 4–8 test. You'll have 50 minutes to get through 42 test items. That gives you just over one minute for each question. Each of the four subject tests that make up the Core Subjects 4–8 test is individually timed.

The Social Studies subject test assesses 10 Texas educator standards for teaching middle school social studies, including that the teacher:

1. Has a comprehensive foundational knowledge of social sciences, understands and applies the many social studies skills, and recognizes the value of the social sciences.

2. Effectively integrates the social science disciplines into the curriculum;

3. Commands the social studies subject matter, as framed by the Texas Essential Knowledge and Skills (TEKS), to plan and carry out effective curriculum, instruction, assessment and evaluation;

4. Applies knowledge of significant historical events and developments, as well as of multiple historical interpretations and ideas, in order to foster student understanding of relationships across historical periods and eras as well as implications for the future;

5. Applies knowledge of people, places, and environments to foster students' understanding of geographic relationships in Texas, the United States, and the world.

6. Demonstrates ability to apply knowledge of how economic systems are organized to produce, distribute and consume goods and services, and deploys this knowledge to enable students to understand economic systems and make informed economic decisions;

7. Demonstrates ability to apply knowledge of how governments and structures of power function, provide order, and allocate resources, as well as using this knowledge to foster student understanding of how individuals and groups achieve their goals through political systems, particularly in the United States and Texas;

8. Demonstrates ability to apply knowledge of the United States, Texas, and other societies and deploys this knowledge to prepare students to participate in our society through an understanding and application of citizenship and democratic principles;

9. Demonstrates ability to apply knowledge of cultures and how they develop and adapt and deploys this knowledge to foster students' appreciation for and respect of cultural diversity in Texas, the United States and the world; and

10. Demonstrates the ability to apply knowledge of the dynamic relationship of science, technology, and society as well as the diversity, adaptation, and cultural development in modern and historical societies in the United States, Texas, and the world.

This subject test embraces seven competencies, which broadly define, as the Texas Education Agency puts it, "what an entry-level educator in this field in Texas public schools should know and be able to do." These competencies are covered in turn in this chapter, which synthesizes the material you're most likely to encounter on the Social Studies subject test.

COMPETENCY 001: HISTORY

The teacher understands and applies knowledge of significant historical events and developments, multiple historical interpretations and ideas and relationships between the past, the present and the future as defined by the Texas Essential Knowledge and Skills (TEKS).

The beginning teacher:

A. Understands traditional historical points of reference in the history of Texas, the United States and the world.

B. Analyzes how individuals, events and issues shaped the history of Texas, the United States and the world.

C. Analyzes the influence of various factors (e.g., geographic contexts, processes of spatial exchange, science and technology) on the development of societies.

D. Demonstrates knowledge of common characteristics of communities, past and present.

E. Applies knowledge of the concept of chronology and its use in understanding history and historical events.

F. Applies different methods of interpreting the past to understand, evaluate and support multiple points of view, frames of reference and the historical context of events and issues.

G. Understands similarities and differences among Native-American groups in Texas, the United States and the Western Hemisphere before European colonization.

H. Understands the causes and effects of European exploration and colonization of the United States and the Western Hemisphere.

I. Understands the impact of individuals, events, and issues on the exploration of Texas (e.g., Cabeza de Vaca, Alonso Álvarez de Pineda, Francisco Coronado, La Salle, the search for gold, conflicting territorial claims between France and Spain).

J. Identify important events, issues and individuals related to European colonization of Texas; Mexico becoming an independent nation, including the establishment of Catholic missions, towns and ranches (e.g., Fray Damián Massanet, José de Escandón, Antonio Margil de Jesús, Francisco Hidalgo, the Mexican Federal Constitution of 1824, and the State Colonization Law of 1825).

K. Understands the foundations of representative government in the United States; significant individuals, events and issues of the revolutionary era; and challenges confronting the U.S. government in the early years of the republic (e.g., Mayflower Compact, Virginia Houses of Burgesses, John Adams, Abigail Adams, George Washington, Crispus Attucks,

Battle of Saratoga, winter at Valley Forge, Battle of Yorktown, the arguments of the Federalists and Anti-Federalists, Articles of Confederation, United States Constitution, War of 1812).

L. Demonstrates knowledge of the individuals, events and issues related to the independence of Texas, the founding of the Republic of Texas, and Texas statehood (e.g., Moses Austin, Samuel Houston, Erasmo Seguín, Antonio López de Santa Anna, the Fredonian Rebellion, the Battle of the Alamo, the Battle of San Jacinto, the annexation of Texas, the U.S.-Mexican War).

M. Understands westward expansion and analyzes its effects on the political, economic and social development of the United States and Texas — including its effects on American Indian life (e.g., Louisiana Purchase, Monroe Doctrine, building of U.S. forts, the destruction of the buffalo, Indian Removal Act, Trail of Tears, Red River Indian War).

N. Analyzes ways in which political, economic and social factors led to the growth of sectionalism and the Civil War (e.g., nullification crisis, Compromise of 1850, the roles of John Quincy Adams, John C. Calhoun, Henry Clay and Daniel Webster).

O. Demonstrates knowledge of individuals, issues and events of the Civil War and analyzes the effects of Reconstruction on the political, economic and social life of the nation and Texas (e.g., Abraham Lincoln, Jefferson Davis, John Bell Hood, Vicksburg Campaign, Battle of Gettysburg, Emancipation Proclamation, Battle of Galveston, Battle of Palmito Ranch).

P. Demonstrates knowledge of major U.S. and Texas reform movements of the nineteenth and twentieth centuries (e.g., abolition movement, women suffrage movement, temperance movement, Civil Rights movement, agrarian groups, labor unions, James L. Farmer Jr., Jane Addams, Hector Pérez García, Oveta Culp Hobby, the League of United Latin American Citizens (LULAC), the evangelical movement).

Q. Understands important issues, events and individuals of the twentieth and twenty-first centuries that shaped the role of Texas in the United States and the world (e.g., Great Depression, First and Second World Wars, Civil Rights movement, Lyndon B. Johnson, emergence of a two-party system, political and economic controversies, immigration, migration).

R. Understands and traces the impact of boom-and-bust cycles of leading Texas industries (e.g., railroads, cattle, oil and gas, cotton, real estate, banking, computer technology).

S. Understands the contributions of people of various racial, ethnic and religious groups in Texas, the United States and the world.

T. Analyzes ways in which particular contemporary societies reflect historical events (e.g., invasions, conquests, colonizations, immigrations).

World History

The World History Encyclopedia divides the history of the world into five periods: the Ancient World, the Middle Ages, the Age of Discovery, Revolution and Industry, and the Modern World (Ganeri, Martell, and Williams, 1999). A summary and timeline of key events in each period is presented here.

The Ancient World (4 Million Years Ago to 500 CE*)

Study of the ancient world focuses on the development of the first humans, the first farmers, and the first civilizations. It documents the critical change in human behavior from hunter-gatherer to agrarian societies, which occurred after man learned to domesticate plants and animals. This time period emphasizes the history of the ancient civilizations of Mesopotamia, Sumer, Assyria, Babylon, Egypt, the Indus Valley, megalith Europe, ancient China, Phoenicia, ancient America, ancient Greece, the Celts, the Romans, and empires in Africa and India.

Timeline of the Ancient World

4000 BCE	Homo sapiens appear in various regions in the world
3500 BCE	The Sumerians of Mesopotamia invent writing and the wheel
3100 BCE	Egypt becomes unified
2800 BCE	Building begins in Stonehenge, England
2500 BCE	Indus civilization flourishes in India
1600–1100 BCE	Mycenaean control of Greece
1200–400 BCE	Olmecs civilization flourishes in western Mexico
1000–612 BCE	New Assyrian Empire flourishes
753 BCE	Foundation of Rome
605–562 BCE	King Nebuchadnezzar rebuilds the city Babylon
476–431 BCE	Golden age of Athens
336–323 BCE	Alexander the Great rules the world
27 BCE to 14 CE	Augustus rules as the first Roman emperor
1 CE	Birth of Christ (Est.)
476 CE	Western Roman Empire falls

---

* The terms "Before the Common Era (BCE)" and "Common Era (CE)" are used here in place of the traditional "Before Christ (BC)" and "Anno Domini (AD)." These designations cover the same historical periods.

The Middle Ages (500–1400 CE)

This period includes the Byzantine civilization, the rise of Islam, civilizations of the Americas, the Vikings, the feudal system, the Crusades, Genghis Khan and China, the African kingdoms, and the Hundred Years' War.

Timeline for the Middle Ages (CE)

500	Eastern Roman (Byzantine Empire) at its peak.
600	Teotihuacán civilization flourishes in Mexico.
600	Rise of Islam.
700	Mayan civilization at its height in Central America.
700	Feudal system begins in Europe; peasants serve a lord in exchange for protection.
711	Moors invade Spain.
750	Abbasid dynasty is founded; Arab Empire at its peak.
800	Charlemagne crowned emperor of the Holy Roman Empire.
900	Rise of Toltec civilization in Mexico.
1000	Vikings land in North America.
1095	Muslim Turks take Jerusalem and ban Christian pilgrims from the city.
1096–1270	Crusades try to rescue Jerusalem from the Muslims.
1215	Genghis Khan and the Mongols invade China.
1271	Marco Polo travels to China from Italy.
1300	Renaissance begins in Europe.
1325	Aztecs established Tenochtitlán near modern day Mexico City.
1368	Foundation of the Ming dynasty in China.
1453	Fall of the eastern Roman Empire (Constantinople).
1454	Gutenberg invents the printing press.
1500	Inca Empire at its peak in Peru.

Age of Discovery (1400–1700)

The Age of Discovery was a period in history starting in the early 15th century and continuing into the early 17th century during which Europeans engaged in intensive exploration and mapping of the world, and establishing contact with Africa, the Americas, and Asia. This period in history bridges the distance between the Middle Ages, which was characterized by a rise in Islam, the feudal system, the Crusades, the Hundred Years' war, and the Modern Era. Accounts from exploring distant lands and maps spread with the help of the new printing press, which increased curiosity about the world and ushered in a new age of scientific and intellectual inquiry. European colonization led to the rise of colonial empires; increased and diversified trade routes; a wide transfer of plants, animals, foods, and human populations (including slaves); the spread of communicable diseases; and the sharing of culture between the Eastern and Western hemispheres. The Age of Discovery includes the Renaissance, the development of the Aztec and Inca civilizations, voyages of discovery from Spain and Portugal, African empires, the Reformation, and the Ottoman Empire. This period also marks when European citizenry became more educated and questioned the power of the church and the monarchy. The Age of Discovery resulted in a new world-view as distant civilizations came into contact with one another.

Timeline for the Age of Discovery

1441	Portuguese begin slave trade from Africa to Europe
1448	Portuguese explorers reach the southern part of Africa
1453	Fall of the eastern Roman Empire (Constantinople)
1454	Gutenberg invents the printing press
1492	Columbus sails from Spain to America
1492	Spain becomes unified and expels the Moors
	Colonization of the Americas begins with Christopher Columbus in the Dominican Republic
1497	Portuguese reach India
1500	Inca Empire at its peak in Peru
1508	Begin the colonization of Puerto Rico
1511	Begin the colonization of Cuba
1517	Martin Luther begins the religious Reformation in Europe
1520	Suleiman rules the Ottoman Empire
1522	Magellan travels around the world
1535	Spain completes the conquest of the Aztecs in Mexico and the Incas in Peru
1543	Copernicus suggests that the sun is the center of the universe, not the Earth
1571	Europeans defeat the Muslim Ottomans in the battle of Lepanto
1588	England defeats the Spanish Armada and becomes the greatest naval power in the world
1607	England begins the colonization of North America
1609	Galileo uses a new invention, the telescope, to study the universe

1618   Thirty Years' War begins (The key participants in the war included: The Holy Roman Empire, Great Britain, the Dutch Republic, Denmark, Germany, Sweden, France, Spain, and Austria)

Revolution and Industry (1700–1900)

This period includes the Russian Empire, the Manchu dynasty in China, the period of Enlightenment in Europe, the growth of Austria and Prussia, the birth of the United States, the French Revolution, the Napoleonic Era, the Industrial Revolution, the British Empire, the American Civil War, and the unification of both Italy and Germany.

Timeline for the Age of Revolution and Industry

1644   The Manchu overthrow the Ming dynasty of China.

1682–1725   Peter the Great rules Russia; expanded territory, strong military.

1740   Frederick the Great becomes king of Prussia—Domination of Europe.

1756–1763   Seven Years' War ensues, with France, Austria, and Russia clashing against Prussia and England.

1768   James Cook visits regions in the Pacific.

1776   America declares independence from England.

1789   French Revolution begins with the fall of the Bastille in Paris.

1791   As part of the Enlightenment period, Thomas Paine publishes *The Rights of Man*, his best-seller.

1804   Napoleon declares himself emperor of France, beginning the Napoleonic Era.

1808   Wars for independence begin in Spanish America.

1837–1901   British Empire at its peak under Queen Victoria.

1848   Year of revolution in all of Europe.

1861–1865   American Civil War.

1869   Union Pacific Railroad links the East and West coasts of the United States.

The Modern World (1900–Present)

This period includes the struggle for equal rights for women, World War I, the Russian Revolution, the Great Depression, the rise of fascism, revolution in China, World War II, Israel versus Palestine, the Cold War, the space race, the Korean and Vietnam wars, and globalization. The early 1900s also saw some revolutions, the seeds for which were sown in the previous period.

Timeline for the Modern World

1910	Mexican revolution begins. Large numbers of Mexicans immigrate to the United States
1914	World War I begins when Austria declares war on Serbia and Germany on Russia
1917	Woodrow Wilson signs Jones-Shafroth Act into law, granting American citizenship to Puerto Ricans
	The United States declares war against Germany and the Central Powers
	Russian Revolution starts when the Bolsheviks, led by Lenin, seize power from Czar Nicholas II and kill his family; this is also called the Bolshevik Revolution
1918	World War I ends; Europe is in ruins, and Germany is heavily punished
1929	Great Depression begins in the United States
1933	Adolf Hitler achieves power in Germany
1936–1939	Spanish Civil War brings Francisco Franco to power
1939	World War II begins when Germany invades Poland and Czechoslovakia
1941	United States enters World War II
1945	Germany surrenders to the Allied Forces, and Japan surrenders after the United States detonates two atomic bombs over Hiroshima and Nagasaki
1947	Pakistan and India obtain independence from Great Britain
1948–1949	State of Israel is founded in Palestine, and the Arabs declare war
1949	Communist Mao Zedong (Tse-tung) gains control of China
1959	Cuban Revolution
1960	Many countries in Africa gain independence
1965–1972	America participates in the Vietnam War
1969	Neil Armstrong becomes the first person to set foot on the moon
1986	Space Shuttle *Challenger* explodes over Texas
1990	Germany is reunited
1991	Soviet Union collapses, and the Cold War ends
1994	Free elections in South Africa and the end of apartheid
2001	9/11 terrorist attacks in New York City and near Washington, D.C.
2001	War in Afghanistan against the Taliban
2003	U.S. Space Shuttle *Columbia* disintegrates during re-entry on Feb. 1
	War in Iraq
2009	Barack Obama sworn in as the 44th president of the United States, becoming the first African American to hold the office

2010	The final two main pieces of the International Space Station are installed
	American, British, and Afghan military launch largest offensive in Afghanistan since 2001
	President Obama signs landmark $938 billion health-care reform bill
	One of the largest oil spills in history results from the explosion of the Gulf of Mexico oil platform *Deepwater Horizon*
2011	Arab Spring movement, a series of protests against chronic unemployment and brutality, begins in Tunisia and continues throughout North Africa and southwest Asia (i.e., Egypt, Bahrain, Syria)
	Japan experiences one of the largest recorded earthquakes at a magnitude of 9.0, causing a 23-foot tsunami to hit Japan. Four of the country's nuclear power plants were affected. Official death toll: 18,500.
	Osama bin Laden, founder and leader of al-Qaeda, is killed during an American military operation in Pakistan
	NASA space shuttle program canceled
	United States formally declares end to Iraq War
2012	Vladimir Putin wins Russian presidential election
	Diplomatic missions of Germany, Switzerland, the United Kingdom, and the United States suffer a series of attacks worldwide. The U.S. ambassador to Libya, J. Christopher Stevens, is killed.
2013	Pope Benedict XVI voluntarily resigns. He is the first pope to resign since 1415, and the first to voluntarily resign since Celestine V in 1294
	Cyprus receives a 10 billion euro bailout from the European Union
	Two bombs explode at the Boston Marathon that were planted by two Islamist Chechen brothers, killing three people and wounding 264 others
	Saudi Arabia becomes first country to refuse a seat on the United Nations Security Council
	Iran agrees to limit nuclear development program for sanction relief
2014	Russia formally and forcibly annexes Crimea using military action, a controversial action opposed by many in Europe
	The Islamic State (ISIS) begins offensive in northern Iraq
	Malaysia Airlines Flight 17 crashes in eastern Ukraine, shot down by undetermined source
	President Obama formally resumes diplomatic relations between the United States and Cuba
2015	Chinese and Taiwanese presidents formally meet for the first time

Paris suffers multiple attacks, responsibility for which is claimed by the Islamic State (ISIS).

Egypt and Turkey, separately, take action against ISIS.

Turkey shoots down Russian fighter jet; first NATA member to destroy Russian aircraft since 1950s.

U.S. resumes export of crude oil, which had stopped in 1973.

2016   The United Kingdom holds referendum in which voters choose 51.9% to 48.1% to leave the European Union; the shorthand for this vote is "Brexit."

Increased anti-immigration tensions play a role in elections in the United States and Europe.

Many countries in the West experience attacks claimed by the Islamic State, including Belgium, France, Germany, and the United States.

The Islamic State claims attacks in Afghanistan, Algeria, Bangladesh, Egypt, Indonesia, Libya, Nigeria, Pakistan, Philippines, Saudi Arabia, Somalia, Tunisia, Turkey, and Yemen.

The United States and China join the Paris Climate Accord.

North Korea conducts fifth nuclear test, condemned by South Korea, Japan, China, and the United States.

U.S. intelligence agencies conclude that Russia interfered with the 2016 U.S. presidential election.

Donald Trump elected 45th president of the United States.

For details about these historical periods, go to these websites: History Channel (*https://www.history.com/*) and Encyclopedia Britannica *(https://www.britannica.com)*, as well as *www.bbc.com/news/world-europe-38569254; http://www.bbc.com/news/world-europe-34814203; http://www.bbc.com/news/world-europe-36800730; http://www.bbc.com/news/uk-england-manchester-40254594; http://www.bbc.com/news/uk-40258989; https:///www.theatlantic.com/international/archive/2016/12/ten-most-significant-world-events-in-2016/511079/.* For more information regarding the Space Shuttle tragedies, visit *https://www.history.com* and *http://www.space.com*.

The Enlightenment—The Age of Reason

The Enlightenment refers to a period during the 17th and 18th centuries when people questioned religious dogmas and emphasized scientific reasoning and knowledge. This quest for knowledge resulted in the development of modern chemistry and biology. People questioned governments and demanded more individual freedoms. The search for freedom led countries to seek independence and fight tyranny. For example, the quest for freedom led to the American War of Independence and the French Revolution. The American Revolution motivated the Spanish colonies to seek independence. Some of the leading thinkers of this period were Jean-Jacques Rousseau, John Locke,

Charles Montesquieu, Voltaire, and Francis Bacon. Enlightenment ideas quickly reached the British colonies. Many leaders responsible for the writing of the Constitution were familiar with the leading Enlightenment thinkers, and framed the Constitution to protect the natural rights of the individual and limit the power of the government.

The Industrial Revolution and Modern Technology

The Industrial Revolution began in England in the mid-18th century. Inventions that made mining of fossil fuel (coal) easier provided the energy needed to expand and promote industrial development. Improvement on the steam engine and industrial machines led to the mass production of goods and a better distribution system. The economic growth motivated people to leave the rural areas and move to the cities. The following timeline highlights inventions that supported the industrial revolution and modern life:

Timeline for Industrial and Technological Development

1769   Richard Arkwright patents the spinning machine powered by a waterwheel, which marks the beginning of industrial mass production of textiles

1814   German Printer Friedrich Koenig's improved printing press is used by *The Times* of London

1831   An American, Cyrus H. McCormick, invents the mechanical reaper, which revolutionizes farming so that more crops can be harvested by machines. This allowed for greater food production, marking a move toward commercial farming. Mass food production supported urbanization by providing a food source for cities.

1836   Samuel Colt invents the first revolver in the U.S. to be used as a practical weapon. Colt's manufacturing firm would later produce the pistols most widely used in the U.S. Civil War.

1832–1838   Samuel Morse develops the telegraph and Morse Code

1846   Ascanio Sobrero, an Italian chemist, invents nitroglycerin

1856   French chemist and microbiologist Louis Pasteur invents the process of pasteurization

1858   Belgian Étienne Lenoir invents the first commercially successful internal-combustion engine

1867   Alfred Nobel invents dynamite

1876   Alexander Graham Bell patents the telephone

1885   Gottlieb Daimler invents the first gas engine motorcycle

1900   Ferdinand von Zeppelin invents a rigid dirigible airship

1903   The Wright brothers invent the first gas-powered airplane (but their historic first flight on Dec. 17 is mentioned in only three newspapers)

1905	Albert Einstein publishes the theory of relativity: $E = mc^2$
1914	Henry Ford introduces the assembly line to mass-produce automobiles
1928	Biologist Alexander Fleming discovers penicillin
1930	Vannevar Bush at the Massachusetts Institute of Technology invents the first modern analog computer
1940	Peter Goldmark inventsthe first commercial color-television system (eight years later, in 1948, he would unveil the long-playing phonograph record)
1945	The atomic bomb is tested in Alamogordo, New Mexico
1955	The antibiotic tetracycline is invented
1959	Jack Kilby and Robert Noyce invent the microchip
1969	The predecessor of the Internet, called the ARPAnet, is invented
1971	Ray Tomlinson invents Internet-based e-mail
	Engineer Ted Hoff develops the first microprocessor
1973	First mobile cellular phone call placed
1974	Micro Instrumentation and Telemetry Systems (MITS) makes the Altair available, a mail-order personal computer building kit
1975	Paul G. Allen and Bill Gates form Microsoft
1985	Microsoft invents the Windows program
1988	Digital cell phones are invented
1990	Tim Berners-Lee creates the Internet protocol HTTP and the World Wide Web language HTML

Settlements, Building Communities, and Understanding Culture

Historically, communities have formed to fulfill a number of needs. They include security, religious freedom, and material well-being, as well as the protection provided by laws. For example, farmers and townspeople under feudalism during the Middle Ages would offer their allegiance to a noble who promised to protect them. As another example, immigrants throughout history have come to the United States to practice the religion of their choice as well as to have their rights and freedom protected under the law. As communities develop, they seek to meet their needs by educating their members, creating a system to govern and to protect the people, establishing communication and transportation systems, and providing recreation. Throughout history, certain members rise to meet or advocate for the needs and well-being of others within a community or for the community as a whole. These leaders are often recognized as patriots and become historical figures. They help shape societies and can even impact the development of a state or nation. Good members of the community include such people as political and military leaders (e.g., mayors, governors, presidents, generals), police officers, firefighters, educators (e.g., principals, teachers), doctors, inventors, scientists, athletes, doctors, artists, writers, activists, etc.). In the United States many individuals have shaped communities as well as the nation. They include George Washington, Benjamin Franklin, Harriet Tubman, Abraham Lincoln, Upton Sinclair, Susan B. Anthony, Ida Tarbell, Henry Ford, Steve Jobs, Franklin D. Roosevelt, Dwight Eisenhower, Harry Truman, Jonas Salk, Thomas Dewey, Mark Twain, Edward Hopper, Georgia O'Keeffe, Charlie Chaplin, Louis Armstrong, Billie Holiday, Booker T. Washington, W.E.B. Du Bois, Martin Luther King, Jr., Daniel K. Inouye, Cesar Chavez, Jackie Robinson, and Lyndon Johnson (from Gillespie County, Texas) to name but a few. In Texas, many patriots and historical figures shaped our communities such as Sam Houston, Davy Crockett, Stephen F. Austin, Sarah Driscoll, José de Escandón, Capt. Anthony F. Lucas, James Stephen Hogg, Molly Ivins, and Ann Richards.

Culture is "the sum total of knowledge, attitudes, and habitual behavior patterns shared and transmitted by the members of a society" (De Blij & Murphy, 1999). Cultures change and adapt for a number of reasons. For example, cultural attire can be a simple adaptation to account for cold or hot weather, mild or harsh climates. For example, during the winter, a parka may be worn in Alaska while light jackets are worn in Texas. Native Americans exemplified adaptation when some groups used grease from animal fat to ward off mosquitoes. Cultures may also change through modifications. For example, the extreme heat and humidity in the South are better withstood through the invention of air conditioning. Modifications, such as roads and railroads, as well as steel frames for buildings, allowed cultures to develop and expand their population and their geographic area over time. Moving to a new location and interacting with communities can also impact groups of people. For example, in Texas, many cultural groups (e.g., Hispanic, Germans, Polish, Czech, African-American, etc.) have learned from each other through cultural diffusion. **Cultural diffusion** is "the process of dissemination, the spread of an idea or innovation from its source area to other cultures" (De Blij, Murphy, Alexander, 1999). This can be seen in Texas through many foods (e.g., tacos, burritos, pork rinds, cornbread, sauerkraut, and sausage) and cultural traditions (e.g., Oktoberfest, Cinco de Mayo, festivals and state fairs, Kwanzaa, Christmas, Hanukkah, etc.). These are also examples of a **cultural exchange**, whereby groups of people take on some of the traits of other cultural groups.

Ancient Civilizations of the Americas

Native Americans lived throughout what we now call the Americas for centuries prior to European colonization. These ancient civilizations each had a unique and rich cultural heritage. They made major contributions to the development of the Americas in all aspects of social, political, and cultural life. Their legacies continue to influence modern day history. Unfortunately, many of the ancient civilizations were destroyed as a result of European colonization. Among the most developed ancient civilizations in the Americas were the Olmecs, Mayas, Toltecs, Aztecs, and Incas.

Mayans (1800 BCE to 900 CE)

One of the earliest civilizations of Mesoamerica was the Mayan, from regions of Mexico's Yucatán Peninsula, Guatemala, and Honduras. The Mayas developed a highly integrated society with elaborate religious observances for which they built stone and mortar pyramids. The center of the Maya civilization was the city of Chichén Itzá and its religious centers, where human victims were sacrificed. The Mayas developed an elaborate calendar, a system of writing, and the mathematical concept of zero. They also had highly advanced knowledge of astronomy, engineering, and art. By the time the Spanish conquerors arrived, most of the Mayan religious centers had been abandoned and the civilization was in decline.

Zapotecs, Olmecs, and Toltecs

Further north in Mexico, three highly sophisticated civilizations emerged: the Olmecs, Zapotecs, and Toltecs. Beginning with the Olmecs, who flourished around 1200 BCE and followed by the Toltecs and Zapotecs, these groups developed highly sophisticated civilizations. They had already begun to use a ceremonial calendar and had built stone pyramids on which they performed religious observances. Teotihuacán is the best-known example of religious ceremonial sites built by these civilizations. They developed a partly alphabetic writing system and left codices describing their history, religion, and daily events. They also built pyramids starting in about 1000 BCE, which predates the pyramids in Egypt. Two of the most famous are the Pyramid of the Sun and the Pyramid of the Moon in Teotihuacán, Mexico, built between 1 and 250 CE.

Aztecs (6th century to 1525 CE)

The Aztec civilization achieved the highest degree of development in Mexico. They had a centralized government headed by a king and supported by a large army. The Aztecs were also skilled builders and engineers, accomplished astronomers, and mathematicians. They built the famous city of Tenochtitlán, with many pyramids, palaces, plazas, and canals. At the peak of their civilization, the Aztecs had a population of about five million. According to the Native Languages of America, Classical Nahuatl, the administrative language of the Aztec empire, is practically extinct. However, modern Nahuatl varieties are still being used in Mexico, and used in their bilingual education programs (Rosado, Hellawell & Zamora, 2011). For more information on native languages go to *http://www.native-languages.org*.

Incas—Children of the Sun

The Inca civilization covered the modern countries of Ecuador, Peru, and central Chile. Although they were not as advanced in mathematics and the sciences as the Mayans and Aztecs, the Incas had a well-developed political system. They also built a monumental road system to unify the empire. Their civilization was at its peak when the Spanish conquerors arrived in Cuzco, the capital of the empire. The Quechua are descendants of the Incas and still live in large numbers in South America, mainly in the Andes Mountains.

Mound Builders in North America

In North America, two major groups, known as the Woodland and Mississippian peoples, lived in the Great Lakes and Mississippi area. These people built burial mounds dated as early as 500 CE. The Mississippian people built flat-topped mounds as foundations for wooden temples. The chiefs and the priests of these groups lived in residences built on the top of the mounds, while the rest of the population lived in houses below. These mound-building civilizations declined gradually and disappeared by the 14th century.

Inhabitants of the South and Southwest

In the southwestern United States and northern Mexico, two ancient cultures developed: the Anasazi and the Hohokam. The Anasazi developed adobe architecture consisting of individual apartments, storage areas, and a central plaza. They worked the land, developed a system of irrigation, and made cloth and baskets. The Hohokam built separate stone and timber houses around a central plaza. Neither group developed a written language. Drought and attacks from rival tribes contributed to the decline of these civilizations. Historians believe that the Anasazi built the cliff dwellings at Mesa Verde, Colorado, during the 14th and 15th centuries to protect against these attacks.

Algonquians

The Algonquians are perhaps the most famous Native American tribe because they were the first to interact with the English settlers at Plymouth. They were skilled hunters, gathers, and trappers who were adept at farming. They wore clothing made from animal skins and lived in wigwams. The Algonquians shared their extensive knowledge of agriculture with the English settlers, a practice that most likely saved the colonists' lives.

Iroquois

The Iroquois inhabited the area of Ontario, Canada, and upstate New York for at least 4,500 years before the arrival of Europeans. They hunted and fished, but farming became the main economic activity for the group. The Iroquois had a matrilineal line of descent, with women doing most of the farming to support the community. They developed the Iroquois Confederation to discourage war among the groups and to provide for a common defense.

Seminoles and Muscogee Creeks

The Seminoles and Muscogee Creeks lived in the Southeastern United States in open bark-covered houses called *chickees*. They were excellent hunters and planters. They are best known for their struggle against Spanish and English settlers in the mid-1800s.

Cherokee

The Cherokee also lived in the Southeast, and were one of the most advanced tribes, with their domed houses and deerskin and rabbit-fur clothing. Accomplished hunters, farmers, and fisherman, they were known on the continent for their basketry and pottery.

Pueblo

Evidence suggests that the Anasazi settled along the Rio Grande and intermarried with the local population, leading to the emergence of the Pueblo people. The Pueblo culture improved on the architectural tradition and farming techniques of their predecessors. The Pueblo people lived in dwellings called pueblos and wore clothes made of wool and woven cotton. They were able to produce drought-resistant corn and squash, which became the foundation of their diet. The Pueblo Indians managed to survive the Spanish conquest and colonization period.

Apache

The Apache and their famous leader Geronimo lived in wickiups, simple dome-shaped shelters made of bark, grass, and branches. They wore cotton clothing and were skilled hunters and gatherers. The Apache lived in the Southwestern portion of the United States.

Navajo

The Navajo people lived in the Southwest as well, and were excellent weapon makers, weavers, and silversmiths. They lived in Hogans, round homes built of forked sticks, and wore rabbit-skin clothes.

American History

Colonization

In the early 15th century, Portugal, under the leadership of Prince Henry the Navigator, began sea exploration. Over the next few decades, the Portuguese explored further south along the African coast. In 1498, Vasco da Gama successfully navigated the Cape of Good Hope at the southern tip of Africa, opening a new route to India.

Columbus's voyage to the New World in 1492 had tremendous impact on both Europe and the New World. By opening the Western Hemisphere to political and economic development by Europeans, Columbus changed the face of the world. Native populations that had existed prior to Columbus were decimated by disease and warfare. As Spanish, French, and English settlers began claiming territories in the Americas as their own, they displaced and killed millions of Native Americans.

In 1565, the Spaniards established the first successful European settlement in North America in St. Augustine, Florida, near what is now Jacksonville, Florida. Following the Spaniards, the English attempted to establish a permanent colony on Roanoke, an island off the coast of North Carolina. This colony eventually disappeared. Nearly 20 years later, the first permanent English settlement in North America was established on May 14, 1607, near present-day Williamsburg, Virginia. Further north, the Dutch settled colonies in the region of present-day New York and New Jersey. Following the Dutch, numerous private companies received royal charters, or patents, permitting them to begin the colonization process in North America. Three of the first and most successful companies were the Plymouth Company, the Massachusetts Bay Company, and the London Company. The London Company was the first to exercise this patent.

The English Colonies

Thirteen colonies were established on the Atlantic coastline. English settlers left England to establish colonies for several reasons. Three types of colonies developed based on three types of charters: corporate colonies, royal colonies, and proprietary colonies. These were divided into three geographical regions: the New England Colonies, the Middle Colonies, and the Southern Colonies. The New England Colonies consisted of Massachusetts, Connecticut, Rhode Island, and New Hampshire. The economy of the New England colonies was based on farming and very small industries such as fishing, lumber, and crafts. The Middle Colonies consisted of New York, New Jersey, Delaware, Maryland, and Pennsylvania. The economy of the Middle Colonies was based on farming, shipping, fishing, and trading. The Southern Colonies were Virginia, North Carolina, South Carolina, and Georgia. The economy of the Southern Colonies was based on the crops of tobacco, rice, indigo, and cotton. Plantations produced agricultural crops in large scale and exploited workers as well as the environment. Each colonial region had unique cultures, communities, and geographical settings that affected their political and economic development.

Virginia (1607)

The London Company established the first English colony in Jamestown, Virginia. The leader of the colony was Captain John Smith. Natives of the area captured Smith and sentenced him to death. Pocahontas, daughter of the tribe's chief, intervened and saved his life. Contrary to popular belief, John Smith did not marry Pocahontas; instead, Pocahontas married John Rolfe, a tobacco farmer from the same colony. In 1619, the colony of Virginia established the first European-style form of government in North America, the **House of Burgesses**.

Massachusetts (1620)

Puritanism grew out of the English Reformation. **Puritans** were people who wanted to reform or "purify" the Church of England. In the early 1600s, some Puritans separated themselves from the main congregation of the local church, others went a step further by declaring themselves to be separate from the national church. One such group, the **Pilgrims**, fled England to avoid religious persecution. First they moved to Holland in 1608 and then, in 1620, they sailed to what is today Massachusetts. The Pilgrims obtained a patent from the London Virginia Company to finance their pilgrimage to America; hence the name *Pilgrim*. The ship used for the journey was called the ***Mayflower.*** The Pilgrims were separatists, a faction of Puritans who wanted to separate from the Church of England rather than merely purify it. Before arriving, they wrote the **Mayflower Compact**, a document containing rules to guide life in the community. This compact, signed November 11, 1620, established one of the first types of government in North America. Initially landing on the shores of what is today Cape Cod, Massachusetts, in December 1620, they founded the **Plymouth Colony**, which is the first permanent European settlement in New England. With the help of local Native Americans, the colonists learned how to survive by farming and hunting for food. For more information go to *http://www.history.com/topics/ puritanism* and *http://www.history.com/topics/pilgrims*. Other information can be found at *https:// www.britannica.com/place/Massachusetts-Bay-Colony, http://www.history.com/topics/us-states/ massachusetts,* and *http://www.history.com/topics/thirteen-colonies.*

New Hampshire (1623)

Two groups founded the colony of New Hampshire. The first group was led by Captain John Mason, who established a fishing village in 1623. In 1638, a group led by John Wheelwright founded a second settlement called *Exeter*. That colony began as a proprietorship but eventually became a royal colony.

New Jersey (1623)

The Dutch founded the New Jersey colony in 1623. After taking over the Dutch territory between Virginia and New England in 1664, King George II of England gave these possessions to his brother, the Duke of York. The duke then gave the territory as a proprietary grant to Sir George Carteret and Lord Berkeley. In 1702, New Jersey became an English colony.

New York (1624)

The area of New York was part of New Amsterdam, a possession of the Dutch government. In 1674, the British took control of the territory, and in 1685 New York officially became a royal colony.

Maryland (1633)

In 1632, King Charles I granted a Maryland Charter to Lord Baltimore (George Calvert). In 1633, the colony was established as a refuge for freemen, especially Catholics.

Rhode Island (1636)

Roger Williams founded the Rhode Island colony in 1636, and in 1638 Anne Hutchinson settled an additional part of the colony. Both Williams and Hutchinson had been banned from Massachusetts for their religious and political views and were looking for sanctuary. The colony was initially a corporation and eventually became a royal colony.

Connecticut (1636)

As early as 1633, Dutch traders had established a permanent settlement near Hartford. After the decline of the Dutch influence in the area, Thomas Hooker established the colony of Connecticut. Hooker and his followers were also seeking religious freedom after being expelled from Massachusetts. In 1662, Connecticut obtained a Royal Charter under the leadership of John Winthrop Jr.

Delaware (1638)

The Dutch and Swedish initially settled this colony. With the decline of the Dutch influence in the area, the English took control. In 1682, Delaware was awarded to William Penn.

North Carolina (1653)

By 1653, Virginia colonists began moving south and settling in the North Carolina region. In 1691, the region was officially recognized as a colony, and Charles I granted a royal charter in 1729.

South Carolina (1663)

In 1663, King Charles II created the colony of Carolina by granting the territory, of what is now the region of present-day North Carolina, South Carolina, and Georgia, to loyal supporters. It began as a proprietary colony and became a royal colony in 1719. Sir John Yeamans, a plantation owner from Barbados, founded the city of Charleston in 1670.

Pennsylvania (1683)

As early as 1647, Swedish, Dutch, and English settlers tried to establish permanent settlements in Delaware. In 1681, a large territory, which included Pennsylvania, was granted to William Penn. Penn was a member of a religious group persecuted in England, the Quakers. He made Pennsylvania a safe haven for Quakers, and a large number of German Quakers settled in the colony. In 1683, the first group of settlers arrived in Pennsylvania and formed Germantown near Philadelphia.

Georgia (1732)

The colony of Georgia was founded with two main purposes: establish a buffer zone from the Spanish settlement south of the colony; and provide a safe haven for poor people. The British government had put many people in jail for being unable to pay their debts. These debtors were removed from jail and placed in this colony with the thinking that if the Spanish were to attack, it would give the other colonies time to prepare.

Table 5-1 summarizes the key historical figures and events of the colonies.

Table 5-1
The Thirteen American Colonies

Colony	Year Established	Colonizer	Historical Features/ Characters
Virginia	1607	London Company	Capt. John Smith, John Rolfe, and Pocahontas
Massachusetts	1620	Puritans with a patent from the London Virginia Company	Puritans, Mayflower, Mayflower Compact, William Bradford
New Hampshire	1623	Proprietary colony	Capt. John Mason, John Wheelwright
New Jersey	1623	Dutch possession, then a proprietorship	Duke of York
New York	1624	Dutch possession, then a proprietorship	Purchase of Manhattan Island, Duke of York
Maryland	1633	Proprietorship	George Calvert (Lord Baltimore). The colony was to be a refuge for persecuted Catholics.
Rhode Island	1636	Corporate colony	Roger Williams and Anne Hutchinson
Connecticut	1636	Corporate colony	Thomas Hooker and John Winthrop
Delaware	1638	Corporate colony	First, under the Dutch, Swedish, and finally under British control. William Penn
North Carolina	1653	Proprietorship	King Charles II
South Carolina	1663	Proprietorship, then a charter colony	King Charles II, Sir John Yeamans
Pennsylvania	1681	Proprietorship	William Penn and Quakers
Georgia	1732	Charter colony	James Edward Oglethorpe

Representative Government in Colonial America

The United States was settled by pioneers who wanted to experience freedom and have a voice in how they were governed. These settlers were influenced by such enlightened individuals as John Locke, Montesquieu, Thomas Hobbes, and Thomas Paine, as well as by their experiences in establishing and governing their settlements. Colonists thus developed greater expectations for representation in their government. Actions and documents such as the Magna Carta (English Bill of Rights), the Mayflower Compact, the Virginia House of Burgesses, and the Fundamental Orders of Connecticut exemplify this belief.

The colonies were founded with the idea that people would have a substantial autonomy and liberty in regards to political and religious life. The colonists were unique because they were English citizens who chose to move to the New World. They were not natives who were conquered and forced to become a colony. They brought with them their tradition of hard work, individual freedom, and representative government that reflected English values and the influence of Locke and the Age of Reason. When the colonists first arrived in America they were still under British rule. Believing in the right to elect the people who would represent them on issues such as taxation, the colonists felt that they should have representation in the British Parliament. Unfortunately, the colonists (those in America and in other British colonies) were not given a seat in parliament or given the right to vote for any member of parliament. As such the colonists did not have any form of representation in the British political system. This reality would later be a major cause of the American Revolution and formation of a new nation.

The idea of representative government, or the idea that people can vote for their own lawmakers, would become fundamental to the formation of the United States. Along with the ability to elect lawmakers, representative government also includes the notion that concepts and ideas can be deliberated and discussed by both legislators and the people who elected them. This principle would later be reflected in the design of United States Congress.

The Virginia House of Burgesses was the first colonial assembly of elected representatives from the Virginia settlement. It was established in Jamestown to represent the colonists in the state of Virginia in the lawmaking process and met for the first time in July 1619.

The Mayflower Compact was drawn and signed in 1620 by the Pilgrims aboard the Mayflower. They pledged to consult one another to make decisions and to act by the will of the majority. It is one of the earliest agreements to establish a political body and to give that political body the power to act for the good of the colony. Eventually, the lack of representation for colonists led to rebellions, like the Boston Tea Party, and to such meetings as the Continental Congress and the Second Continental Congress, which led to the Declaration of Independence July 4, 1776. After the colonists won the War for Independence, also called the Revolutionary War, their desire for representational government led to the development of the Articles of Confederation and then to the Constitution of the United States.

Indentured Servants

The indentured servant system was used to bring workers to the New World. In practice, the indentured servant would sell him or herself to an agent or ship captain before leaving England. In turn, the contract would be sold to a buyer in the colonies to recover the cost of passage. Criminals and people in debt could also be sold for life or until they paid their debts. In some cases, at the end of the service, servants remained as salaried workers, or in the best situations, the servants were given a piece of land for their services. This system of provisional servitude was not applied to Africans; instead, permanent slavery was instituted.

The Enlightenment—The Age of Reason

The Enlightenment refers to a period during the 17th and 18th centuries when people began questioning religious dogmas and emphasizing scientific reasoning and knowledge. As a result of this quest for knowledge, modern chemistry and biology were developed. Additionally, people also began to think critically about the rights, freedoms, and powers of man in relation to political systems. The Enlightenment stirred people to action in fighting the tyranny of religious and political oppression. For example, the quest for freedom led to the American and the French Revolutions. Some of the leading thinkers of this period were Jean-Jacques Rousseau, John Locke, Montesquieu, Voltaire, and Francis Bacon. The ideas of the Enlightenment quickly reached the British colonies. Many of the leaders responsible for the writing of the Constitution were familiar with and influenced by the leading thinkers of the movement. They framed the Constitution around the powerful ideas of these thinkers, including the protection of the natural rights of the individual and limiting the power of the government.

The French and Indian War

The French and Indian War, the North American part of the Seven Years' War, began in 1754 as part of a larger imperial war in Europe between France and Britain. Both countries sought to expand their control in the Americas. Their poorly defined borders and attempts to militarily strengthen their claims caused increased tensions that led to war. The war officially ended with the Treaty of Paris in 1763 and a solid British victory. However, the conflict was expensive. Therefore, the British government levied heavy taxes on the American colonists to help pay for the war, adding to the rising tensions in the colonies. Coupled with limitations on colonists' westward expansion and increased war with the Indians, the colonists would soon rebel and fight for their independence.

American Revolution

The main reasons why the British colonists revolted against British control were economic. England, as well as other European nations, had established **mercantilism** to exploit the colonies. This system had three main principles:

1. The wealth of the nation is measured in terms of commodities accrued, especially gold and silver.

2. Economic activities can increase the power and control of the national government.

3. The colonies existed for the benefit of the mother country.

England used the system of mercantilism quite effectively in the 13 colonies, but after more than a century of British rule, the colonists resented England's economic and political control. Outraged and spurred on by Enlightenment ideas, the colonists were primed for independence, and war with England became inevitable.

Another reason for the rebellion was the cost of the French and Indian War. This war emptied the British coffers and the British Crown needed a quick way to recover financially. The taxation system that followed the French and Indian War was unbearable for the colonies. The colonies responded with civil disobedience and by boycotting the government of King George. In response to civil disobedience, the British sent troops to Boston, where the groups clashed and several colonists were killed. The event was called the **Boston Massacre**. One of the best-known boycotts was the **Boston Tea Party**, in which the colonists dumped tea in the Boston Harbor to protest against taxation. "No taxation without representation" became a rallying cry for the colonists. All these events and the repression that followed led to the **American Revolution**, which is also known as the **American War of Independence** or **American Revolutionary War**.

Continental Congress

Following the events in Boston, representatives of the colonies met in Philadelphia to discuss the political and economic situation in the colonies. No clear solutions were reached at this congress. Once the hostilities started, the Second Continental Congress met to discuss preparations for war. George Washington was elected commander of the American forces, and war was declared against the British. The congress named a committee, led by Thomas Jefferson, to prepare the *Declaration of Independence*, which was officially signed on July 4, 1776.

The Declaration of Independence

The **Declaration of Independence** pronounced the colonies free and independent states (hence the celebration of "Independence Day"). It consists of a preamble, or introduction, followed by three main parts. The first part stresses natural unalienable rights and liberties that belong to all people from birth. The second part consists of a list of specific grievances and injustices committed by Britain. The third part announces the colonies as the United States of America. This document provided the foundation to establish equal rights for all people. By signing this document, the colonists formally declared they were independent from English rule, thus officially beginning the American Revolution. Because it was signed on July 4, 1776, we celebrate "Independence Day," also known as "The 4th of July." **Note:** Students will remember "The 4th of July", but do not always understand that it is America's Independence Day and the reason for this celebration.

Revolution (April 19, 1775–September 3, 1783)

The **American Revolution** began in Massachusetts on the outskirts of the towns of Concord and Lexington. In 1775, while the colonists were preparing for war, hundreds of British soldiers marched against them. Paul Revere warned the colonists of British troop movements, and minutemen took up arms to face the enemy. At Concord, the British were repelled and forced back to Boston. On their way back, American sharpshooters ambushed and killed hundreds of British soldiers. Following this initial victory for the colonists, the battle of Bunker Hill was fought near Boston. In this battle, the British lost large numbers of soldiers but managed to defeat the colonial troops. Later, in Long Island, the British won another decisive victory over the Americans. The French joined the war in support of the Americans, in retaliation for the French defeat at the hands of the British in the Seven Years' War. Eventually, with the support of the French, the American troops defeated the British forces in Yorktown, Virginia, in 1781. The **Treaty of Paris**, officially signed in 1783, ended the war and gave independence to the new nation. For additional details about the American Revolution, go to *http://www.historycentral.com*.

Articles of Confederation

During the Revolutionary War, the Second Continental Congress ran the government. After independence, the Articles of Confederation defined a new form of government. The **Articles of Confederation** was an agreement among the 13 founding states that legally established the United States of America as a confederation of sovereign states and served as its first constitution. It was drafted by the Continental Congress in 1776–77, went into use in 1777, and was formally ratified by all 13 states in 1781. The Articles gave legitimacy to the Continental Congress to direct the American Revolutionary War, conduct diplomacy with Europe, and deal with territorial issues and Indian relations. The Articles of Confederation established a new government, with limited power, that was composed of representatives from 13 independent states. The Congress could not declare war or raise an army. It could, however, ask the states for money or for soldiers, but it was up to the states to agree to provide them. Under this type of government, each state printed its own money and imposed taxes on imports from the other states.

On the positive side, the new government provided for a common citizenship—citizens of the United States. It organized a uniform system of weights and measurements and a postal service. It also became responsible for issues related to Native Americans living within the borders of the new nation. The confederation served as the official government of the young republic until 1789, when the states ratified the **Constitution**.

United States Constitution

After six years under the Articles of Confederation, the leaders of the nation realized that the American government needed revision to bolster its strength. To accomplish this goal, a constitutional convention was held in Philadelphia in 1787. The leaders of this initiative were George Washington, James Madison, Benjamin Franklin, and Alexander Hamilton. From this convention, a new form of government emerged. The **Constitution** was officially ratified in 1788, and in 1789 George Washington was selected to be the first president of the United States. The U.S. Constitution allowed for a much stronger national government, with a president, courts, and taxing powers. The republic defined by the Constitution was composed of three branches—the executive, judicial, and legislative—with a system of checks and balances to regulate each branch. To learn more about historical American documents, go to "A Chronology of U.S. Historical Documents," a website created and maintained by the University of Oklahoma Law Center, at *www.law.ou.edu/hist*.

War of 1812

Twenty-nine years after the end of the American Revolution, conflict between Great Britain and the young United States flared up again. The **War of 1812** broke out for a variety of reasons, including Britain's seizure of American ships, impressment of American sailors into the British navy, and restriction of trade between the United States and France. In June 1812, James Madison became the first U.S. president to ask Congress to declare war. In 1814, Francis Scott Key had boarded a British ship in hopes of persuading officials to release a prisoner. Due to an impeding battle, he was forced to remain on the ship during a relentless effort by the British to take Fort McHenry in Baltimore Harbor. While watching the bombardment of the fort, he wrote a poem describing what he saw and felt. It was originally published by the name "Defence of Fort M'Henry." It is now called "**The Star-Spangled Banner**." In 1916, President Woodrow Wilson announced that it should be played at all official events and was designated as the National Anthem of the United States with the stroke of President Herbert Hoover's pen on March 3, 1931. Fought in three theaters, the War of 1812 ended with the Treaty of Ghent in 1815. Learn more about the War of 1812 visit *http://www.history.com* and *http://www.smithsonianmag.com/history/the-story-behind-the-star-spangled-banner-149220970/*

Monroe Doctrine

In 1823, President Monroe made clear to European countries that the United States was not going to permit the establishment of colonies in the Western Hemisphere. Monroe also banned European countries from attacking the new American republics that were just becoming established in the early 19th century. The U.S. was not to become involved in European affairs. This concept of "America for Americans" is known as the **Monroe Doctrine**.

Westward Expansion (1807–1912)

After the War of 1812, much of America's attention turned to exploration and settlement of its territory to the West, which had been greatly enlarged by the Louisiana Purchase. Pioneer families moved westward and founded new communities throughout what is now the Midwest. Between

1816 and 1821, six new states were admitted to the Union. This westward expansion occurred for a number of reasons, primarily economic.

First, cotton had become an important resource in the southern states. As the effects of the industrial revolution—which began in England—reached the United States, new inventions, for example Eli Whitney's cotton gin, encouraged faster and more efficient production of goods. With the invention of the cotton gin, the demand for cotton grew, and more and more farmers became involved in the production of cotton. Innovations in long-distance transportation, most notably the railroad, allowed cotton and other goods to be shipped cross-country with more ease. As demand for cotton and prices increased, southern farmers began expanding their farms toward the West where there was fertile soil. As farm sizes increased, so did the demand for a large supply of cheap labor. As a result, the system of slavery expanded both in numbers and in regional movement to the West.

Secondly, expansion westward continued as people moved west to seek their economic fortunes. Miners, trappers, ranchers, merchants, and others went west to find new resources and economic riches. The Lewis and Clark Expedition played a prominent role in promoting westward expansion and in mapping the West. Fur companies recruited "mountain men" to search for fur-bearing animals that would increase the supply of such goods and meet the needs of the East and of Europe. Finally, the California Gold Rush attracted easterners to push westward in hopes of finding riches.

Thirdly, increased settlement in the West encouraged missionaries to travel west with the fur traders to seek converts among the native peoples. Missionaries sent word back to the East encouraging more settlers to come to the West. This encouragement by missionaries helped produce a tremendous influx of westward settlers.

Finally, **Manifest Destiny**, or the belief that the United States was destined to expand across the country encouraged westward expansion. In 1844, President James K. Polk declared to the world that the United States would eventually become a world power and expand to its natural borders. Some of the borders mentioned were the Pacific to the west and Mexico to the south. Manifest Destiny would ultimately cause huge issues between the U.S. Government and Native Americans, England, Spain, and Mexico. Eventually, Polk's expectations became a reality as a result of the war between Mexico and the United States that lasted from 1846 to 1848.

Many Americans believed it was the country's destiny to stretch from the Atlantic Ocean to the Pacific Ocean. This belief helped fuel and justify westward expansion, wars, land purchases, treatment of the Native Americans, and economic development. Still, it was not a conviction supported by everyone. Some Americans, most notably members of the Whig party, did not believe that it was America's divine right to expand; rather, the United States should be a virtuous example of democracy for others to follow. However, Jefferson's purchase of the Louisiana territory in 1803, netting 827,000 square miles of land west of the Mississippi River for $15 million, created conditions to support America's westward growth and development.

Results of Westward Expansion

As America grew in the 19th century, so did its need for resources, land, and expansion. European settlers had originally claimed much of the terrain, although Native Americans had long-established territories of their own. Therefore, when land was garnered through agreements (e.g., the Louisiana Purchase from the French), annexation (e.g., Texas), and war (e.g., with Mexico), the American people expected that they had a right to the land. Acquiring more land made the country stronger economically. For example, more crops could be grown to provide a food source for American cities or to be exported to other countries. The natural resources fueled the country's industrial power. The **Transcontinental Railroad** was built to move resources and people across the nation and thus tied the nation together from the East Coast to the West Coast. The railroad was pivotal to the economic growth and development of the United States and to the rapid settling of the West.

Expansion came at great cost to the Native Americans. Some Native Americans may have coexisted peacefully with settlers when peace agreements were made and kept. Others groups, such as the Comanche and Apache, were more aggressive and given to war. The expansion of American settlements in the 1800s caused tensions to increase between Native Americans and settlers. In the end, Native Americans were forced to give up their lands and eventually their way of life. The American government set aside reservations, land specifically designated for these groups. However, this land was typically poor quality and unwanted by both Americans and Native Americans. This forced Native Americans into a state of dependency and poverty. If life on the reservation was refused, war ensued to compel Native Americans to comply. In many cases, Native Americans were killed in raids or in war. Native Americans also attacked settlers, which added to the distrust and increased military action.

One of the most controversial actions occurred in 1830 when Andrew Jackson signed the Indian Removal Act, which forced Native Americans out of the cotton-producing lands in the South, east of the Mississippi River. Although this action did not follow the legal negotiation of a fair removal of the treaty with the Indians, Jackson's administration wanted all Native Americans out of the economically productive Eastern part of the country. The Indian removal process, also known as the Trail of Tears, forced Native Americans to vacate their homes in the southeastern part of the United States to lands in the West, mainly in what is now Oklahoma. The U.S. Army crushed any resistance to removal.

With the West cleared, Westerners focused on developing new methods of transporting their goods to market. The canal and railroad systems, which were developed in the North, facilitated a much larger volume of trade and manufacturing while greatly reducing costs. Great cities sprang up throughout the North and Northwest, bolstered by the improvement in transportation.

After the Midwest had been substantially developed, the national focus turned toward the far West. The territory of Texas, controlled by the Spanish, was settled by Americans, who eventually undertook the Texas Rebellion in efforts to win independence. When the United States admitted Texas to the Union in 1845, the Mexican government was outraged, and from 1846 to 1848, the two nations squared off in the Mexican War. As a result of this war, the United States gained control of Texas, New Mexico, and California. When the Oregon Territory was annexed in 1846, the U.S. stretched all the way to the Pacific Ocean.

As the population of the West soared and the prospects of statehood for western territories appeared clearer and clearer, the nation battled over the future of slavery in the West. This battle was one reason for the Civil War, which slowed the acceleration of expansion. However, the last three decades of the 19th century saw the return of accelerated expansion due to the successful struggle to contain the Plains Indians in reservations, and the completion of the **Transcontinental Railroad** in 1869. By the early 20th century, the organization of the West was complete, and the United States consisted of 48 contiguous states.

Slavery in the United States

As the nation grew, so did local, state, and national politics. The issue of slavery was a constant concern. Agreements were made to limit the number of states that did or did not allow slavery. Expanded territories became states as the population increased, thereby adding to the number of members of Congress in the Senate and House of Representatives. The influx of legislators affected laws and policies. These legislative decisions included laws about Native Americans, slavery, and big businesses (e.g., railroads, steel, meatpacking industries, etc.).

The Dutch brought the first African slaves to Virginia in 1619 to work on plantations. From 1640 to 1680, large numbers of slaves were brought to the Americas. With the invention of Eli Whitney's cotton gin, cotton became the economic mainstay of the South, and the demand for labor increased the slave trade. From 1798 to 1808, more than 200,000 African slaves were brought to America, mostly to the southern region.

Beginning in 1774, the North began regulating and eventually prohibiting slavery. By 1804, New York and New Jersey had passed gradual emancipation laws. Meanwhile, the slave trade in the South grew to meet the economic needs of the area. Eventually, the issue of slavery, along with other economic and ideological differences between the regions, resulted in the American Civil War. In 1862, Abraham Lincoln issued the Emancipation Proclamation, granting freedom to slaves in the rebellious states. After the war, the 13th Amendment to the Constitution officially abolished slavery. Additionally, in 1866 the 14th Amendment gave African Americans full citizenship, and in 1870 the 15th Amendment granted voting rights to black men.

Compromises

The late 17th and early 18th centuries were marked by a number of compromises between the various regions. Most of the time these compromises were short-lived and broke down quickly. One of the compromises was the **three-fifths compromise** proposed at the Constitutional Convention of 1787. This compromise centered on how to count slaves in deciding the number of representatives for the House of Representatives and the amount of taxes to be paid. Residents of the South wanted to count the slaves for the purposes of representation, but not for taxation. Northerners, on the other hand, wanted the opposite. As a compromise, the two sides agreed to count three-fifths of the slave population for both taxation and representation purposes.

The **Missouri Compromise** was an agreement passed in 1820 between the pro-slavery and anti-slavery factions in the United States Congress, involving primarily the regulation of slavery in the western territories. In 1819, the United States had 21 states: 10 slave states and 11 free states. The Territory of Missouri allowed slavery; its admittance as a state into the Union would cause an imbalance in the number of U.S. senators. Alabama had recently been added to the Union, thus equalizing the representation of free and slave states at 22 senators each. To resolve the conflict, the first Missouri Compromise allowed Maine to be admitted as a free state to the Union along with Missouri as a slave state.

Additionally, the Missouri Compromise prohibited slavery in the former Louisiana Territory north of the parallel 36°30' except within the boundaries of the proposed state of Missouri. Prior to the agreement, the House of Representatives had refused to accept this compromise and a conference committee was appointed. Southern congressmen accepted this proposal since growing cotton on land north of this line was not profitable. One year after the first compromise was passed, tensions heated up again as Missouri's state constitution discriminated against free blacks. Antislavery advocates demanded that Missouri not be admitted to the union. Under the leadership of Henry Clay, known as the great compromiser, it was proposed that the Constitution of the United States guaranteed the protection and privileges of citizens in states and thus Missouri's state constitution could not deny any person these rights. This proposal was accepted in 1820 and Missouri was admitted to the Union.

The **Compromise of 1850** was another agreement crafted by Henry Clay and Stephen Douglas aimed at ending the continuing struggle between slave and non-slave states. This compromise included a series of five bills intended to stave off sectional strife over slavery. Its goal was to deal with the spread of slavery to territories in order to keep northern and southern interests in balance. The five bills are summarized below:

1. California was entered as a free state.

2. New Mexico and Utah were each allowed using **popular sovereignty,** or the idea that people living in territories or states should decide for themselves if slavery should be permitted.

3. The Republic of Texas gave up lands that it claimed in present-day New Mexico and received $10 million to pay its debt to Mexico.

4. The slave trade was abolished in the District of Columbia.

5. The **Fugitive Slave Act** made any federal official who did not arrest a runaway slave liable to pay a fine. This was the most controversial part of the Compromise of 1850 and caused many abolitionists to increase their efforts against slavery.

The **Kansas–Nebraska Act** of 1854 created the territories of Kansas and Nebraska, opened new lands that would help settlement in them, repealed the Missouri Compromise of 1820, and allowed settlers in those territories to determine via popular sovereignty if they would allow slavery within their boundaries. Designed by Democratic Senator Stephen Douglas, the Kansas-Nebraska Act created a huge controversy because of the popular sovereignty provision. Both pro- and anti-slavery supporters flooded into Kansas with the goal of voting slavery up or down. One group of northern abolitionists, led by **John Brown**, also flocked to the territory and set up their own government in Lawrence. A band of pro-slavery men, however, burned Lawrence to the ground in 1856. In revenge, an abolitionist gang killed five men in the **Pottawatomie Massacre**. In 1859, Brown and his followers seized the federal arsenal at Harper's Ferry in what is now West Virginia. Their purpose was to steal the guns in the arsenal, give them to slaves nearby, and begin a widespread rebellion. Brown and his men were captured by Colonel Robert E. Lee and found guilty. Brown was later hanged. These two events sparked an internal war so savage that many referred to the territory as **"Bleeding Kansas."**

The decision rendered in the ***Dred Scott v. Sandford*** Supreme Court case served to intensify the debate regarding the issue of slavery in the United States. Dred Scott was a slave whose owner had taken him from Missouri, a slave state, to Illinois and Minnesota, both free states, and back to Missouri. Scott petitioned the Supreme Court (after petitioning two lower courts) for his freedom based on his having resided in two free states, each with state laws that declared that slaves brought into the state were set free. The Supreme Court ruled that Scott and all other slaves were not citizens of any state or the United States and thus had no rights. A slave was deemed property, neither a person nor a citizen. Thus, Scott or other slaves had no right to sue in either state or federal court. Further, the court held that the federal government had no legal right to interfere with the institution of slavery. Slavery advocates were encouraged and began to make plans to expand slavery into all of the western territories and states, thus creating much of the tension that led to the Civil War.

Civil War (April 12, 1861–May 9, 1865)

Political, Economic, Social Differences

As the nation expanded and territories became states, each new state developed its own unique political, social, economic, and cultural identity. Over time, regional identities evolved, leading to regionalism or the political division of and loyalty to the interests of particular regions. Each region came to be defined by the economic and social institutions most prevalent in the area. In the North, the industrialized factory system created a division between factory owners who reaped huge profits and factory workers who were subjected to poor working conditions. The industrialized North had a boom in the number of factories and towns, while the South remained primarily agricultural where slaves and indentured servants worked on large plantations owned by wealthy whites. The South defended their economy on the basis that states had the right to self-determination with regard to their economic and social institutions. The West was a vast expanse of newly explored and settled land in which ranching became a mainstay. Settlers who traveled to the West were looking for land, wealth, and opportunity. Many settlers were from the South and brought slaves with them. As such, the identity of each of these regions was distinctly different, especially in the role of children, women, trade, religion, and labor systems. As might be expected, these differences led to conflicts among the inhabitants of each region.

Slavery and Sectionalism

The issue of slavery became a major issue between the North and South and created deep divisions for the young nation. By the 1800s, slavery had been virtually abolished in the North. The northern states' reasons for turning against slavery were primarily economic: the North had become more urban and industrialized than the South, and northern states received large numbers of immigrants who provided the necessary labor. Southern states remained mostly rural and received few immigrants, making slavery the foundation of their economy. This economic disparity coupled with the publication of Harriet Beecher Stowe's book *Uncle Tom's Cabin* as well as efforts by the national government to control trade between the regions created a huge rift between the North and the South. The disagreement over slavery, specifically over the issue of who was guaranteed the inalienable right to be free, led to sectionalism, or the excessive devotion to local interests and customs. This growing sectionalism would be a primary cause of the Civil War.

The issue of slavery became the main topic of the presidential election of 1860. The candidates were clearly aligned either in favor of or against slavery. The southern Democrats backed a strong proslavery candidate, John C. Breckinridge of Kentucky, while the new Republican Party selected a strong antislavery candidate in the figure of Abraham Lincoln. The election of Abraham Lincoln resulted in the secession of the southern states from the union (January 1861), the creation of the Confederacy, known as the Confederate States of America, and the start of the American Civil War (1861-1865). The southern states created the **Confederate States of America** in February 1861 and selected Jefferson Davis as president. For more information about events of the Civil War, see *http://www.historynet.com/civil-war-timeline*.

Secession

In response to the election of Abraham Lincoln, 11 southern slave states, led first by South Carolina, seceded from the Union and formed the Confederate States of America, or the Confederacy. Twenty-five states supported the federal government and remained part of the Union. Both sides began preparations for war. The North had a greater advantage over the South because of a larger population, financial security, industrial resources, increased means of transportation, and natural resources. The South, largely agricultural in nature, did not have the same caliber of resources or infrastructure as the North. The South, however, had some advantage in the sheer vastness of their territory and the know-how of their army leaders, many of whom were educated at West Point and had extensive experience in previous wars.

The major aim of the Confederacy's war efforts was to win independence, protect the institution of slavery, and earn the right to govern themselves. The war efforts of the North coalesced around protecting the sanctity of the union under the leadership of Lincoln. However, the abolition of slavery became an increasingly more important issue as the war continued.

Battle of Gettysburg

Hundreds of battles were fought in this war, but none was as devastating as the **Battle of Gettysburg**. Fought in 1863, this battle was the most disastrous event of the war and marked a major turning point; more than 50,000 soldiers from the North and the South lost their lives. In a speech delivered on the battlefield in November 1863, President Lincoln eulogized the fallen Union soldiers in what became the famous **Gettysburg Address**.

The American Civil War in Texas

Initially, Texas was divided about entering the Civil War. Texas had fought hard to get into the Union, but many Texans did not like the northern legislators' control of the government. Texans also did not like the antislavery sentiment, though only about one-fourth of its people owned slaves. Once in the war, the state provided many troops and was essential to westward expansion, protecting the Gulf Coast and supporting major battles in the Deep South. For more information visit the Texas State Historical Association, *https://www.tshaonline.org/handbook/online /articles/qdc02*.

The End of the American Civil War

In 1865, after five years of fighting, the loss of thousands of lives and millions of dollars in property, the commander of the Confederate army, General Robert E. Lee, surrendered to General Ulysses S. Grant, commander of the Union forces. The Civil War took more American lives than any other war in U.S. history. The South lost nearly one-third of its soldiers, while the North lost about one-sixth. More than 50% of the deaths were attributed to the terrible conditions of field hospitals and to disease.

The loss of human life was not the only devastation; the economic losses were significant for both sides. The physical destruction, almost all of it in the South, was enormous: burned or plundered homes, pillaged countryside, untold losses in crops and farm animals, ruined buildings and bridges, devastated college campuses, and neglected roads all left the South in ruins.

Reconstruction Era (1865–1877)

Post–Civil War physical reconstruction focused on the South because the war was primarily fought in this region. However, the emotional reconstruction and the reconstruction of American unity had to be done nationwide, and admission of rebel states back into the Union was not automatically granted. The Reconstruction period was characterized by hatred and violence. Because Lincoln was assassinated shortly after the end of the war, leadership of southern reconstruction fell to Lincoln's vice president, Andrew Johnson, a southerner who was disliked by both northerners as well as southerners. Eventually, Johnson was impeached and almost removed from power, surviving the removal vote in the U.S. Senate by one vote. One of the immediate changes to take place was to officially abolish slavery. Passed by Congress on January 21, 1865, and ratified by the states on December 6, 1865, the 13th Amendment to the Constitution formally ended slavery. Next, former slaves had to be granted due process, which came with the recognition of citizenship. On July 9, 1868, the 14th Amendment of the Constitution granted citizenship to "all persons born or naturalized in the United States."

A major obstacle to reunification were the restrictive laws enacted immediately after the Civil War by every southern legislature. These **Black Codes** barred the newly freed slaves from free assembly, regulated black labor, and, among other restrictions, denied **Freedmen** the right to vote, serve on juries, and testify against whites. After major electoral victories in the election of 1866, Republicans placed the South under military rule, and held new elections in which the Freedmen could vote.

By 1867, the U.S. Congress, still composed entirely of northerners, passed legislation to eliminate the Black Codes. On February 26, 1869, Congress passed the **15th Amendment of the Constitution** that provided universal male suffrage (right to vote), made the Bill of Rights applicable to the states recognizing all substantive and procedural rights under the law, and providing equal protection under the law to all people in their jurisdiction. The 15th Amendment was ratified on February 3, 1870. Furthermore, the U.S. Congress required that each state ratify the 13th, 14th and 15th Amendments as a prerequisite for reentry into the Union. Finally, in 1870, the last two states (Texas and Florida), having satisfied all requirements, were allowed back into the Union. For more information on the 13th, 14th, and 15th amendments go to *https://www.loc.gov/*.

Reconstruction in Texas

Reconstruction in Texas caused a great deal of political, economic, and social tension. The Union first moved a number of troops throughout the state to aid in the transition and to enforce Union rules. However, within a year, most of the troops were sent to the frontier, allowing more former secessionists to have political power. After much turmoil and the removal of key state and local legislators throughout the state, Texas ratified the new constitution, established the Bureau of Refugees, Freedmen, and Abandoned Lands (the Freedmen's Bureau), and accepted the 13th, 14th, and 15th amendments. However, violence became a problem as some areas developed the Black Codes (rules to control the African American population) and the rise of the Ku Klux Klan (KKK), a secret vigilante group whose members, according to the Texas State Historical Association, "were pledged to support the supremacy of the white race, to oppose the amalgamation of the races, to resist the social and political encroachment of carpetbaggers, and to restore white control of the government." Other issues facing Texas included the economy as well as the situation with Native Americans. Railroads were a major part of economic development in Texas because they would allow quick access to agriculture and textile markets. This industry needed financial support after the war, which caused tension within and between political parties. Additionally, the influx of immigrants as well as migrants from the Deep South who came to Texas for a better life taxed the ability of already overburdened systems to support the increase in population. For more information go to *https://tshaonline.org/handbook/online/articles/mzr01* and *https://texaspolitics.utexas.edu/educational-resources/.*

Ku Klux Klan

After first emerging as a secret society during Reconstruction, the **Ku Klux Klan** flourished in the 1860s and died out in the 1870s, only to reemerge in the 1920s and again in the 1950s and 1960s. During Reconstruction, Klan members enforced the Black Codes through violence and terror. Subsequent Klan activities, both overt and covert, upheld **Jim Crow laws** reinforcing segregation and spreading intimidation. Racial separation continued to characterize life in the South and other parts of the nation throughout most of the twentieth century.

Economic Development

After the reunification of the country, energy was redirected to the economic development and growth of the nation. New inventions, together with the development of the railroad, paved the way to economic recovery. The reconstruction that followed the war also played a vital role in the development of the United States as a solid economic and industrial nation.

In the late 19th and early 20th centuries, Americans recognized opportunities in cities. Migration to urban areas caused the cities to grow exponentially in size, population, and population density. This is called **urbanization**. The fast growth caused issues with housing, transportation, sanitation, and employment (De Blij & Murphy, 2005). People from diverse backgrounds were forced to live and work in proximity. The surrounding countryside was absorbed as an area grew. Poor areas, called shantytowns, sometimes developed on the periphery of the cities. The rapid increase in population provided more workers than needed for manufacturing, resulting in a surplus of labor. In Texas, the greatest examples of urbanization occurred in cities that served as major transportation and economic centers. They include Galveston, Houston, Corpus Christi, El Paso, San Antonio, Austin, Dallas, Fort Worth, and Amarillo. Urbanization also led to urban sprawl, the multidimensional expansion of a city. Urban sprawl may not always coincide with proper coding and planning.

In the 19th and 20th centuries, American farmers used exploitive agricultural methods that rarely conserved the soil. Overgrazing, expanding farmland, and new mechanized practices increased production, but also created a problem: The land could not replenish the nutrients at the same rate they were being used. In the 1930s, the area encompassing the Texas and Oklahoma panhandles, as well as parts of Kansas, Colorado, and New Mexico, suffered from a severe drought. The thin, dry soil did not have enough plants to anchor the topsoil. Strong winds blew the topsoil into dust storms. The affected region was called the Dust Bowl.

Temperance Movement—Prohibition

Early Americans drank alcohol in enormous quantities. Their yearly consumption at the time of the American Revolution has been estimated at the equivalent of three-and-a-half gallons of pure, 200-proof alcohol for each person. After 1790, American men began to drink even more. By the late 1820s, imbibing had risen to an all-time high of almost four gallons per capita. This pattern went unchallenged until early in the 19th century, when local efforts to curb drinking by individual clergymen were amplified by the founding of the American Temperance Society in 1826, sponsored by a wide range of groups and individuals. Temperance reformers acted for a variety of reasons, but we can describe four powerful perspectives on temperance that motivated most advocates and shaped their arguments and campaigns. For many of them, of course, all four viewpoints were linked together.

1. *Social order.* Many reformers feared that drunkenness—particularly the increasing prevalence of binge drinking—was a threat to law-abiding society and economic prosperity. How could men act as responsible workers and vote as responsible citizens if they were insensible with drink?

2. *Evangelical religion.* Religiously motivated temperance advocates came to see drinking as a sin—a way of giving in to the animal or depraved self that was incompatible with Christian morals, self-control, and spiritual awakening.

3. *Damage to the family.* Looking at family destitution and violence, reformers reckoned the cost to American wives, mothers, and children of heavy drinking by their husbands and fathers. The Woman's Christian Temperance Union, founded in 1874, brought the concerns of religion and family together in the battle to outlaw alcohol.

4. *Medical.* Health-minded reformers popularized a radically new way of looking at alcohol. Americans had traditionally considered strong drink to be healthy and fortifying; but after 1810, many physicians and writers on health were telling their patients and readers that alcohol was actually a poison.

By the end of the 19th century and the beginning of the 20th century, alcohol abuse had reached such heights that the movement focused on an outright prohibition of its consumption. In 1919, the U.S. Constitution was amended to prohibit alcohol consumption at the national level; this marked the adoption of the **18th Amendment** (Cardinale, 2007). However, the prohibition was never fully enforced. Battles between law enforcements agents, like Eliot Ness, and organized crime characterized the prohibition era. Leaders of organized crime, like Al Capone, made millions bootlegging alcohol. After 14 years of prohibition and unsuccessful attempts to enforce the law, the 18th Amendment was finally repealed in 1933 with the **21st Amendment**.

Prohibition in Texas

Texas politics was affected by the Prohibition movement for nearly a century (1840s–1930s). Initially, Prohibition resonated with fundamental Christians, and later gained local and state support.

Local communities determined whether they would be "dry" (that is, prohibit the production and sale of alcohol). The Legislature passed laws limiting and disallowing alcohol before the adoption of the 18th Amendment to the U.S. Constitution. After the repeal of the 18th Amendment, Texas reverted to allowing local governments to determine whether to allow the sale of alcohol in their communities. Texas still has some dry counties and cities. Since the 1980s, laws dictate when the legal drinking age begins, and warning labels are required on alcohol products. For more information, visit the Texas State Historical Association, *https://tshaonline.org/handbook/online/articles/vap01*.

Civil Rights Movement

In the United States, the Constitution and the Bill of Rights guarantee civil rights to American citizens and residents. The first 10 amendments to the U.S. Constitution are known as the **Bill of Rights**. Following these initial amendments and as a result of the American Civil War, three additional amendments were ratified.

1. The 13th Amendment freed all the slaves without compensation to slave owners.

2. The 14th Amendment declared that all persons born in the United States were citizens (excluding Native Americans, due to their legal sovereignty) and, that all citizens were entitled to equal rights, and that their rights were protected by due process.

3. The 15th Amendment granted universal male suffrage, thereby granting black men the right to vote.

Even after the 13th, 14th, and 15th Amendments extended constitutional protections, blacks continued to be denied full civil rights through discriminatory state and local laws and practices. These laws, known as Jim Crow laws, reinforced a strict racial separation in the South. African Americans were kept from voting by poll taxes and literacy tests. Segregation rules restricted blacks to separate facilities in public places such as theaters, restaurants, buses, restrooms, and schools. In 1896, ***Plessy v. Ferguson*** legalized segregation, allowing "separate but equal facilities" for black and white students.

In response to the horrific practice of lynching that undergirded the program of terror to enforce Jim Crow laws, and specifically in reaction to the 1908 race riots in Springfield, Illinois, a group of white liberals issued a call for a meeting to discuss racial justice. Sixty people, seven of whom were African American (including W.E.B. Du Bois, Ida B. Wells-Barnett and Mary Church Terrell), signed the call, which was released on the centennial of Lincoln's birth. This heralded the birth, on February 12, 1909, of the **National Association for the Advancement of Colored People (NAACP)**. Throughout the early 20th century, the NAACP saw enormous growth in membership, recording roughly 600,000 members by 1946. It continued to act as a legislative and legal advocate, pushing for a federal anti-lynching law and for an end to state-mandated segregation.

Several historic events marked the beginning of what is today known as the **Civil Rights Movement**. In 1947, Jackie Robinson became the first African American to play baseball on a Major League team. In 1948, President Truman ordered the desegregation of the armed forces and introduced civil rights legislation in Congress. In 1954, the NAACP Legal Defense and Educational Fund, headed by Thurgood Marshall, secured an important milestone through the landmark Supreme Court ruling in *Brown v. Board of Education of Topeka* (1954), which outlawed segregation in public schools.

The **Montgomery Bus Boycott** began in December 1955 when **Rosa Parks**, a well-known NAACP activist and respected citizen of Montgomery, Alabama, refused to give up her seat on a bus to a white man as Alabama's Jim Crow laws required. She was arrested and consequently sent to jail. Her actions prompted local community leaders of the NAACP to form a new organization called the Montgomery Improvement Association.

The association chose a young Baptist minister, **Dr. Martin Luther King, Jr.**, to lead the organization and to direct a boycott of the Montgomery bus company. The boycott began in December 1956 and ended about a year later when the Supreme Court ruled segregation on buses unconstitutional. This victory gained national attention and Dr. King became one of the most prominent figures of the civil rights movement. He founded the Southern Christian Leadership Conference (SCLC) with other African American leaders. The SCLC favored nonviolent forms of protest such as sit-ins, boycotts, freedom rides, and protest marches. On August 28, 1963, a march in Washington in support of the Civil Rights Act culminated in Dr. King's influential and memorable "I Have a Dream" speech. The eloquent speech and orderly, large-scale demonstration gained more supporters for the cause.

President **John F. Kennedy** proposed new civil rights laws as well as programs to help the millions of Americans living in poverty. After his assassination in Dallas in 1963, President **Lyndon B. Johnson** urged Congress to pass the laws in honor of Kennedy, persuading the majority of Democrats and some Republicans. The **Civil Rights Act**, passed in 1964, prohibited segregation in all public facilities and outlawed discrimination in education and employment. On April 4, 1968, Martin Luther King was assassinated in Memphis, Tennessee, taking his place alongside the other martyrs who lost their lives in the struggle for freedom during the modern Civil Rights Movement, which extended from 1954 to 1968.

The Mexican American Civil Rights Movement

During the 1960s, Mexican Americans were engaged in the struggle for human rights. As part of the process, the Mexican-American leaders initiated a movement called the **Chicano Movement**. This movement was cultural as well as political (Rosales Castañeda, n.d.). It embraced four main goals: the restoration of land grants, farm workers' rights, and education and political rights (Mendoza, 2001). The movement also sought to rescue the cultural and linguistic identity of Mexican Americans.

Activist **Reies López Tijerina** initiated the Chicano Movement in New Mexico with the land grant movement, which sought to recover the land taken from the Mexican Americans as a result of the Guadalupe Hidalgo Treaty of 1848 and the eventual annexation of the American Southwest. In Colorado, Rodolfo "Corky" Gonzales founded the Crusade for Justice as a platform for the political movement (Mendoza, 2001). He also defined the movement through his epic poem "Yo Soy Joaquín/I Am Joaquin." In this poem he provided a historical development of Mexican-American identity and described their struggles in the United States.

As part of the effort to support the rights of farm workers, human rights leaders **Cesar Chávez** and **Dolores Huerta** founded the **United Farm Workers (UFW)** union. Through the UFW they fought for better working conditions and fair compensation for agricultural workers.

In Texas, the movement focused its attention on the educational and political rights of Mexican Americans. In Crystal City, students took a leadership role by organizing Mexican-American voters and joining the political process. As part of this process, **Mexican American Youth Organization (MAYO)**, under the leadership of **José Ángel Gutiérrez** and **Mario Compean**, founded the **Raza Unida Party (RUP)** in 1970. Through the RUP, they sought to bring greater economic, social, and political autonomy to Mexican Americans (Acosta, n.d.). As a result of this movement, the RUP nominated candidates for mayor, city councils, and school boards in three South Texas cities—Crystal City, Cotulla, and Carrizo. In these communities, the RUP won 15 seats. This political awakening of the Mexican-American voters in Texas paved the way for better schools and programs for Mexican-American and minority children in general.

Civil Rights in Texas

Texas civil rights issues center mainly on African Americans and Mexican Americans, the largest ethnic minority groups. Although both parties have fought for equal treatment since the mid-1800s, true change did not occur until the 20th century. This change was fraught with violence and intimidation from such factions as the Ku Klux Klan, the White Caps, community leaders, law officials, and the Texas Rangers. Such factors as the poll-tax and Jim Crow laws limited African American and Mexican American involvement in politics and society. Schools and communities were segregated by ethnicities until the *Brown v. Board of Education* (1954) decision started a move toward integrated schools. Civil rights transformation was a long, arduous process. It required laws to change, and communities to modify their cultural customs, traditions, and mindsets. Much support for civil rights came from the middle class. After World War II, many Mexican or African American men pushed for equal treatment, which influenced the tumultuous 1960s when many men and women spoke out against inequalities. These ethnic groups have made gains in their struggle for civil rights and continue to work to ensure that they are treated equally by the law and within their Texas communities. To learn more, read the information contained in the following link: *https://www.tshaonline.org/handbook/online/articles/pkcfl*.

Women's Rights

While the **19th Amendment** to the Constitution guaranteed women the right to vote in 1920, women remained the subject of discrimination. The civil rights movement provided a backdrop for the women's movements of the 1960s as women of varying classes and races, working in the civil rights movement and in the anti-war movement, began to recognize their own second-class status. The liberal women's movement attained better employment and professional opportunities for women through legislation such as the Equal Pay Act of 1963, the Civil Rights Act of 1964, the Equal Credit Opportunity Act (1974), and the Pregnancy Discrimination Act of 1978. All this legislation prohibited discrimination based on gender. In 1966, **Betty Friedan**, author of *The Feminine Mystique*, and other women leaders founded the **National Organization for Women (NOW)**, and the 1970s saw an exponential growth of organizations and associations formed to promote women's equality.

Woman Suffrage Movement in Texas

The Woman Suffrage Movement in Texas was a long fight of determination that began in the 1860s. Although women worked and paid taxes like men, they did not have the right to vote for leaders and rarely participated in government and politics. Opponents of woman suffrage feared that allowing a change in women's status would challenge cultural customs and traditions. In fact, recent male immigrants could vote before women could. Women not only had to convince political leaders to stop the disenfranchisement of women, they also had to persuade people, including other women, that women's roles at home, in the community, and at work would not change simply because they could vote. The Texas legislature considered and/or voted on women's suffrage multiple times from the 1860s to the early 1900s. In June 1919, the **19th Amendment** to the U.S. Constitution, giving women the right to vote nationally, was submitted to the states for ratification. On June 28, 1919, Texas became the ninth state to ratify it. To learn more, see *https://www.tshaonline. org/handbook/online/articles/viw0*.

Conflicts and Wars

Spanish-American War of 1898

The war between Spain and the United States in 1898 made the United States a world power. Setting the tone for the **Spanish-American War** were blaring headlines accompanied by sensationalized reporting of the sinking of the *U.S.S. Maine*. Though it's too much to claim that the newspapers started the war, what came to be known as "yellow journalism" certainly helped sound the drumbeat for war. As a result of this war, the United States established its power and influence in the Caribbean Sea and Pacific Ocean. Cuba became an independent nation, and the United States gained control of the Philippines, Guam, and Puerto Rico. Eventually, the Philippines became an independent nation, while Puerto Rico and Guam remained U.S. territories. Eventually, the people from Guam and Puerto Rico became American citizens.

World War I

The first global war, **World War I**, began in Europe and involved two alliances: the Allies and the Central Powers. The **Allies** were England, France, Russia, and Italy. The **Central Powers** were Germany, the Austria-Hungary Empire, Turkey, and Bulgaria. Initially, the Americans remained neutral and benefited extensively from trading with the Allies. America's neutrality was challenged, however, when the Germans developed a new weapon, the submarine, and used it successfully to destroy Allied ships. In 1915, the Germans sank a British liner, the *Lusitania*, killing more than 1,100 passengers, including 128 Americans. Additionally, American cargo ships were sunk, which forced President Wilson to ask Congress to declare war against Germany and the Central Powers. The influx of fresh American forces fostered the Allies' victory in 1918.

With the **Treaty of Versailles**, the war officially ended. In this treaty, the Central Powers were severely punished and forced to pay for the war. Additionally, the Austria-Hungary Empire was dismembered and new countries created. The punitive conditions of the Treaty of Versailles created the resentment among the Germans that eventually led to the second global confrontation, World War II.

The Bolshevik Revolution in Russia

In 1917, the Communists, led by Vladimir Lenin, took over the Russian Empire in what was called the **Bolshevik Revolution**. To address the unrest at home, Russia withdrew from World War I. As a result of this revolution, or civil war, the Russian Empire ceased to exist and the **Union of Soviet Socialist Republics (USSR)** was established (1922). The USSR is also referred to as the Soviet Union. The USSR underwent a period of governmental reconstruction to incorporate the communist philosophy. (**Note:** Often *Russia* and *USSR* are used interchangeably. Teachers should be aware of this misconception and use these terms correctly.)

The Great Depression

After World War I, the United States enjoyed a period of prosperity, the golden 1920s. However, it all came to an abrupt end on October 29, 1929, when the stock market crashed, initiating a ten-year period that we now call the **Great Depression**. During the Depression, millions of people lost their capital and jobs. Between 1933 and 1937, **President Franklin D. Roosevelt** implemented a series of government-sponsored programs called the **New Deal**, designed to revitalize the economy and alleviate poverty and despair caused by the Depression.

World War II

The emergence of totalitarian countries like the USSR, Germany, and Italy created instability in Europe and led to war. The Communist Soviet Union under **Joseph Stalin** became a threat to European countries. Italy, ruled by **Benito Mussolini** was a fascist, belligerent state where individual liberties were ignored. Germany under **Adolf Hitler** was ready to avenge the humiliating treatment it suffered as a result of World War I. In the Pacific, meanwhile, Japan was building an empire that had already conquered parts of China. These conditions promoted the creation of military alliances that led to **World War II**. Germany, Italy, and Japan created the **Axis Powers**, and the USSR, France, and England became the Allies. The war started with the German invasion of Poland in 1939. Two days later, France and England declared war against Germany. Hitler conquered most of Europe in a short time. France was occupied, and England was brought close to submission. The United States supported the Allies with supplies and weapons, but did not send troops. Although it remained neutral for the first few years of the war, the United States joined the Allies when Japan attacked its naval base in Pearl Harbor, Hawaii, in 1941. Three days later, Hitler declared war on the United States. Believing Germany to be the greater threat, the United States concentrated on the war in Europe before turning its attention to Japan.

D-Day

With Hitler in full control of Europe, the United States joined England and representatives of the French government to plan and execute the invasion of Europe in 1944. On June 6, **General Dwight D. Eisenhower**, together with a quarter of a million Allied soldiers, crossed the English Channel into France and launched one of the largest offensives ever seen against the German occupying forces. This massive attack was known as **D-Day**. As a result of the collective effort of the Allies, France was freed from German occupation. With the combined forces of England, Russia, Canada, and the United States, Hitler and the Axis forces were finally defeated. **Victory in Europe** day, or **VE Day**, occurred on May 8, 1945. **Victory over Japan** day, or **VJ Day**, occurred on August 15, 1945.

Yalta Conference

The Allies met in Yalta, Russia, to discuss the terms of the treaty to end the war in Europe. In this meeting, the leaders of the Allied forces—Winston Churchill, Joseph Stalin, and Franklin D. Roosevelt—met to discuss peace. Under the terms of peace agreed to at Yalta, Germany was to be divided into four sections, each controlled by an Allied country—Britain, France, Russia, and the United States. The Germans were to pay the Russians for war reparations in money and labor. Poland was divided, and the Russians received control of one section (later they took full control of the nation). Finally, plans were set to organize the United Nations to prevent future conflicts in the world.

Hiroshima and Nagasaki

The United States was fighting the war on two fronts, and the Japanese appeared to be invincible. The best available option seemed to be the atomic bomb. An island nation, Japan had gained control of much territory in the Pacific, most of it islands. Securing each island would take much time and cost many American soldiers' lives. After asking for the Japanese to surrender, by the order of **President Harry Truman**, the United States dropped two atomic bombs, one each on the cities of Hiroshima and Nagasaki. The death and destruction caused by these two bombs forced the Japanese government to surrender in 1945, which officially ended World War II.

Marshall Plan

The **Marshall Plan** was a U.S.-supported program to rebuild the economic infrastructure in Europe. The United States provided money and machinery for the reconstruction of the continent.

The Holocaust and Creation of Israel

During World War II, Hitler devised a "master plan" to exterminate the Jewish population. Germany placed European Jews in concentration camps and systematically killed millions. This act of genocide is known today as the **Holocaust**. At the end of the war, under the leadership of Great Britain, the United States, and the United Nations, the state of Israel was created in Palestine. On that same day, the Arab Liberation Army (ALA) was created to fight the Jewish state. This liberation movement has resulted in several wars between Israel and the Arabs. Today, this conflict has expanded to include Europe and the United States, with many terrorist attacks committed during the twenty-first century.

Truman Doctrine

In response to the threat of the Soviets, Harry Truman issued a proclamation warning communist countries that the United States would help any nation in danger of falling under communist control. This declaration was called the **Truman Doctrine**. As a result of this doctrine, the United States became involved in two major military conflicts: the **Korean War** and the **Vietnam War**.

Cold War

As a result of the Yalta agreement, Russia became the most powerful country in the region. After taking over Poland and East Berlin, and building the Berlin Wall, a new war emerged between the Soviet Union and the United States—the **Cold War**. Although war was never formally declared between the two nations, confrontations occurred from 1945 to 1991. In 1963, the two nations were on the verge of nuclear war after **Premier Nikita Khrushchev** ordered the deployment of nuclear missiles to Cuba. An intense negotiation between Premier Khrushchev and President Kennedy avoided war between the two countries. This most intense confrontation of the Cold War was called the **Cuban Missile Crisis**.

The Cold War finally ended with the fall of the Soviet Union under the leadership of **Mikhail Gorbachev**. The fall of the Soviet empire resulted in the reunification of Germany and the creation of multiple smaller countries in Russia that gained independence.

War on Terrorism

On September 11, 2001, terrorists from abroad attacked Americans on American soil. The assailants hijacked four domestic aircraft and used two of them as missiles to crash into the twin towers of the World Trade Center in New York and a third to strike the Pentagon just outside Washington D.C. A fourth plane crashed in Shanksville, Pennsylvania, as passengers tried to wrest control of the plane from the hijackers. The attacks killed nearly 3,000 people. As a result of the attacks, the United States declared war on terrorism and attacked and ultimately toppled the ultra-conservative Taliban regime early in the course of the Afghanistan War (2001–2014). The Taliban had harbored al-Qaeda, the terrorist group that planned the 9/11 attacks. Al-Qaeda's leader, Osama bin Laden, the mastermind of the 9/11 attacks, was hunted for nearly a decade and was killed by U.S. special forces on May 2, 2011, in his Pakistani compound. The search for alleged weapons of mass destruction (WMD), as well as Iraq's support of terrorist organizations, led the United States into the Iraq War (2003–2011). In 2015, the U.S. was still fighting to stabilize the region. Weapons of mass destruction were never found, and this topic continues to stir debate. In hindsight, the American government came to recognize that faulty intelligence paved the way for the rationale for the Iraq invasion. Once elected, President Obama worked to reduce the number of troops in this region. He formally declared the war in Iraq over in October 2011.

War in Syria

The recent war in Syria has given rise to the Islamic State, also known as the Islamic State of Iraq and Syria (ISIS), an extreme al-Qaeda faction from Iraq. The Syrian conflict began in March 2011 with pro-democracy protests that ended when demonstrators were shot by Syrian security forces. This action triggered protests across the nation, while some opponents fought back. The violence and fighting continued to escalate from 2012–2014, with 2014 being the deadliest year. The conflicts grew to be more than issues with President Assad. The Sunni majority was against the Shia Alawite sect supporting the president. Neighboring countries and key world powers were drawn in as well. The United Nations Commission of Inquiry on the Syrian Arab Republic found human rights violations on both sides. The Islamic State grew in power and was accused of intimidating the public, killing Syrian security forces, and engaging in the mass murder of religious minorities. Although President Assad agreed to destroy his chemical weapons, evidence indicated these weapons were used against his opponents. According to the BBC, the Islamic State capitalized on the turmoil to seize large amounts of territory in Iraq and Syria. "In September 2014, a United States-led coalition launched air strikes inside Iraq and Syria in an effort to 'degrade and ultimately destroy' ISIS." (BBC, 2016). In January 2014, a conference among the United States, Russia, and the UN tried unsuccessfully to agree on the implementation of the 2012 Geneva Communiqué to establish a governing body in Syria. The conflict continues, with Iran and Russia supporting the Alawite-led government. Turkey, various

Arab states, the United States, the United Kingdom, and France have been supporting the Sunni-led opposition. While fighting continued, the Geneva peace talks on Syria took place between February 23 and March 3, 2017. The peace talks were successful in that neither of the opposing sides walked away during the conference, but there was never face-to-face negotiations. Each side concluded with an agreed agenda, but no breakthrough negotiation came from the peace talks. A few weeks after the Geneva peace talks on Syria, the Syrian government deployed an airstrike containing chemical weapons on the town of Khan Sheikhoun in northwestern Syria. The bombing killed more than 80 people, including women and children, and injured over 500. This led to the United States deploying multiple airstrikes to Syria and attacking towns occupied by the Syrian government. For more information, see *http://www.bbc.com/news/world-middle-east-39500947* and *http://www.bbc.com/news/world-middle-east-39037609.*

Arab Spring

The **Arab Spring** is the democratic uprising that took hold of the Middle East and northern parts of Africa. The uprising first took place in Tunisia in December 2010 with the Tunisian Revolution. Unrest quickly spread to other countries, including Egypt, Syria, Libya, Yemen, Bahrain, Jordan, and Saudi Arabia. The rebellions continued throughout 2011 until fading during mid-2012. These uprisings gave way to larger political tension, which eventually led to the Syrian Civil War, Iraqi insurgency and civil war, the Egyptian Crisis and coup, the Libyan Crisis, as well as the Crisis in Yemen. The Arab Spring sparked the ongoing battle for power between the religious elites and the wave of support for democratic leadership in Muslim-majority states. For more information, see *http://www.bbc.com/news/world-middle-east-30003865.*

Brexit

"Brexit" is the term for when the people of United Kingdom voted to leave the **European Union** (EU). The European Union is the partnership among 28 European countries connected economically and politically. The decision to leave the EU was made by a referendum, a poll in which every person of legal voting age within the United Kingdom was able to vote. Thirty million people voted, and even though Ireland and Scotland voted against leaving, the majority of people in the United Kingdom, 51.9 percent, voted for leaving the EU. It can be argued that this decision was influenced by the threat of immigration. People of the United Kingdom were worried about their cultural identity, what immigration had done to their society, and what it could possibly do in the next 20 years. For more information, see *http://www.bbc.com/news/uk-politics-32810887* and *http://www.bbc.com/news/uk-politics-eu-referendum-36574526.*

Texas History

Timeline

1519	Álonso Alvarez de Pineda explores and maps the Texas coastline
1528	Spanish explorer Álvar Núñez Cabeza de Vaca explores the Texas interior on his way to Mexico
1685	French explorer, René-Robert Cavelier, Sieur de La Salle establishes Fort St. Louis at Matagorda Bay, establishing French claim to Texas territory
1688	French colony is massacred
1689	The French continue to claim Texas but no longer physically occupy any of the territory
1690	First mission in East Texas established by Alonso de Leon
1700s	Spain establishes Catholic missions throughout Texas
1718	Mission San Antonio de Valero (the Alamo) founded
1762	As a result of the The Seven Years War (French and Indian War) the French give up their claims to Texas and cede Louisiana to Spain until 1800
1800	North Texas territory is returned to French and later sold to the U.S. in the Louisiana purchase (1803)
1821	Texas becomes a Mexican state as Mexico becomes free from Spain
1823	Stephen Austin establishes the Old Three Hundred colony along the Brazos River
1830	Mexico bans emigration into Texas by settlers from the United States
1832	Battle of Velasco—first casualties of the Texas Revolution
1835	The Texas Revolution official begins at the Battle of Gonzales
1835	Texans lead by Jim Bowie win the Battle of Concepcion, near San Antonio
1836	The Convention of 1836 signs the Texas Declaration of Independence at Washington on the Brazos
1836	The Alamo—Texans under Colonel William B. Travis were defeated by the Mexican army after a two-week siege at the Battle of the Alamo in San Antonio
1836	The Battle of San Jacinto—Texans under Sam Houston defeat Santa Anna and win independence
1837	Sam Houston, the first President of the Texas Republic, begins operating the seat of government from Houston
1839	Austin becomes the capital of the Republic of Texas
1845	Texas admitted as the 28th state in the Union.

1846	The Mexican-American War due to disputes over claims to Texas boundaries. The outcome fixed the southern boundary at the Rio Grande River.
1850	The compromise of 1850 adjusts the state boundary and assumes Texas' debts
1861	Texas secedes from the Union and becomes part of the Confederacy
1865	Texas slaves freed after Union soldiers land in Galveston and put the Emancipation Proclamation into effect
1870	Texas is readmitted into the United States
1900	Hurricane destroys Galveston and kills over 6,000 people
1901	Oil discovered at Spindletop

Before European Colonization

Several Native American groups inhabited the territory known today as Texas. They adopted different customs, different farming, hunting, and gathering methods, and made slightly different weapons. At times they fought against one another, and at other times they lived in cooperation. It is important to recognize that Native American tribes had established important cultural, social, and economic systems in the United States long before European colonizers arrived on the continent.

Archeologists have found evidence of Native American civilization in Texas dating back to at least 9,200 BCE. The three groups living in the coastal plains—the Coahuiltecans, Karankawas, and Caddos—were food gatherers, fishermen, and farmers. When the Spanish arrived in Texas, they made initial contact with these groups. The name *Texas* came as a result of contact with the Caddos. Attempting to communicate to the Spaniards that they were not hostile, some Caddos identified themselves with the word *taysha*, which in their language meant "friend" or "ally." When the Spaniards heard the word *taysha*, they thought the Caddos were identifying the name of the region. From that exchange, the name Texas and the state motto, "Friendship," emerged.

A fourth group, the Jumanos, lived in the mountains and basins of West Texas. The information about this group is limited because they virtually disappeared before the Spaniards arrived in the area. The last two groups are the Comanches and the Apaches. These two groups coexisted with Europeans and resisted colonization efforts. After they domesticated horses, previously introduced by the Spanish, the Comanches and Apaches became fearless warriors and successful buffalo hunters. The domestication of the horse allowed the development of the culture of the buffalo. When buffalo were later annihilated in the area, these two groups became practically extinct. Table 5-2 presents a summary of Native American groups in Texas.

Table 5-2
Native American Groups in Texas

Regions	Native Group
Coastal plains, flatland	**Coahuiltecan** (Rio Grande Valley) **Economic Activity:** Food gatherers and hunters—roots, beans of the mesquite tree, rabbit, birds, and deer **Features:** Lived in family groups
	Karankawa (Southeastern Texas) **Economic Activity:** Fishing and food gathering **Features:** Lived as nomads and used canoes for fishing
	Caddo (East Texas, Piney Woods) **Economic Activity:** Farming—squash, pumpkins, tobacco, and corn (good food supply) **Features:** Built villages and lived in groups
Central plains, flatland, and hills	**Apache** (Central and western Texas) **Economic Activity:** Farming and hunting **Features:** Lived as nomads, built portable housing called tepees, domesticated horses, and hunted bison
Great Plains, flatland, and hills	**Comanche** **Economic Activity:** Hunters **Features:** Lived as nomads and built portable housing; also domesticated the horse and hunted the buffalo
Mountains and basins	**Jumano** (West Texas) **Economic Activity:** Farming and hunting **Features:** Mostly sedentary and built homes of adobe

European Colonization

Cabeza de Vaca

The Spanish exploration of the territory known today as Texas began in 1528, when *Álvar Núñez Cabeza de Vaca* and three companions landed in the territory. The four Spaniards made contact with the Caddo in the southeastern part of the state, near modern-day Houston. In his account of the meeting, de Vaca described the Caddo as a very sophisticated Native American group. From there, de Vaca continued exploring the region of modern-day New Mexico and Arizona. No other significant events happened in the region until 1541, when **Francisco Vázquez de Coronado** explored Texas.

Francisco Vázquez de Coronado

In response to reports of the mythical Seven Cities of Cibola, Coronado led an expedition of almost a thousand men in search of the golden cities. The expedition left Mexico City and explored the southwestern United States and northern Texas. In 1542, Coronado returned to Mexico empty-handed. For the next 140 years, the Texas region remained isolated, and no other attempts were made to colonize it.

Juán de Oñate

In 1595, Oñate received permission from King Philip II of Spain to colonize New Mexico. In 1598, he founded the first European settlement west of the Mississippi in New Mexico.

First Mission in Texas

In 1682, the Spanish established the first permanent settlement in Texas—the mission of Ysleta del Sur near what is now El Paso. After this mission, no serious efforts were made to colonize the area until the French threatened the Spanish hegemony in East Texas in the late 1600s and early 1700s.

Robert de La Salle and French Influence over Texas

In 1685, **Robert de La Salle**, a French explorer, established a French settlement at Matagorda Bay called Fort St. Louis in East Texas. This settlement established France's claim on this region of Texas. A few years later, the French colony was massacred by Native Americans. Spain then established a series of missions in East Texas to control the French threat in the region. The French continued to claim Texas for decades following the massacre, even though they had no physical presence in the region. In 1762, France relinquished its claim on Texas, turning it over to Spain.

Catholic Missions in Texas

In 1682, the Spanish began establishing missions throughout Texas beginning with the Ysleta del Sur near the present-day city of El Paso. In 1690, **Alonso de Leon** established the San Francisco de los Tejas Mission in East Texas. Spain continued to establish missions throughout Texas through the 18th century. In 1718, the Spanish established a mission and a fort—San Antonio de Valero and Fort San Antonio de Bexar—near what is now the city of San Antonio. The Spanish missions were designed not only to promote religious conversion, but to provide territorial claim and protection over Texas. The Catholic missions established throughout Texas helped the Spanish maintain control over the region from 1682-1821.

Mexican War of Independence

During the first part of the 19th century, the Spanish empire began crumbling. Mexico obtained its independence in 1821 and took control of the colony of Texas. Up until this point, Texas had been a sparsely populated area that served as a buffer between the territories claimed by France and Spain. To encourage settlement in this area, Mexico invited European and American settlers to move to the region.

Stephen F. Austin and Anglo Presence in Texas

In 1821, Moses Austin received permission from the Spanish government to bring Anglo-American families to settle in Texas. This agreement was voided when Mexico took control of the territory. Later, Austin's son, Stephen, negotiated with the Mexican government and obtained a similar agreement to allow Anglo-Americans to settle in Texas. Stephen F. Austin established a colony called the *Old Three Hundred* on the Brazos River, which opened the way for further settlement in this area. By 1835, the settlers were the majority in the region, which antagonized the Mexican government and eventually resulted in war.

The Texas War for Independence

Conflicts between Texans and the Mexican government started as early as 1830. The colonists felt that the government was not providing adequate support and protection to Texas. Initially, they wanted to negotiate with the new president, **Santa Anna**, and sent Stephen Austin to Mexico City to represent the colony. The Mexican government was not willing to negotiate and jailed Austin for a year.

Battle of Gonzales

The power struggle between the Mexican government and Texas settlers continued to escalate. The town of Gonzales had a cannon to protect the colonists from Native Americans. By order of the government, Mexican soldiers came to take the cannon from the colonists in October 1835. The Texans refused to relinquish their weapon and fired the cannon against the Mexican soldiers. The soldiers were told to "come and take it!" Although the battle was lost, the motto "Come and take it" became a symbol of Texas independence and a rallying cry for the soldiers. With this incident in Gonzales, the war for Texas independence began.

Sam Houston

A delegation of Texans traveled to Washington, D.C., to secure support from the U.S. government. Sam Houston, a former governor of Tennessee, volunteered to fight for Texas and would become the commander-in-chief of the Texas army.

Battle of the Alamo and Goliad

The next major battle of the Texas War for Independence took place near the present-day city of San Antonio in a small mission and fort known as the Alamo. When the battle began, fewer than 200 men, led by **Colonel William Travis**, protected the Alamo. Eventually, James Bowie and Davy Crockett joined Travis in defending the fort. In 1836, **General Antonio López de Santa Anna** and the Mexican army took the fort and killed all its defenders, including Texans of Mexican ancestry. Following this victory, Santa Anna continued marching against the rebels and took the city of Goliad, where more than 300 rebels were killed. These two battles provided the battle cry that resulted in the creation of a Texas army, led by Sam Houston.

Texas Declaration of Independence

As fighting grew worse, another Convention of Texas delegates was called in 1836 at Washington-on-the-Brazos. This convention led to the creation of the Texas Declaration of Independence, which established the Republic of Texas and the *Ad Interim* government with **David G. Burnet** as president and **Lorenzo de Zavala** as vice president. This document was signed on March 2, 1836, two days before the Battle of the Alamo ended.

Battle of San Jacinto

While the colonists were fighting the Mexican army at the Alamo and in Goliad, General Sam Houston was strengthening the army of the new republic. The Texan army continued retreating ahead of the Mexican forces until they reached the San Jacinto River, near the city of Houston. In a battle that lasted less than 20 minutes, Houston's troops defeated the Mexican army and captured General Santa Anna. Texas President Burnet and Mexican President Santa Anna signed the Treaty of Velasco, with Santa Anna agreeing to withdraw his troops from Texas in exchange for safe conduct back to Mexico, where he would lobby for recognition of Texas independence. Santa Anna's commitment never materialized, and the Mexican government refused to recognize Texas as an independent republic. Nevertheless, Sam Houston became the president of the new republic, and from 1836 to 1845, Texas functioned as an independent nation. However, the Mexican government still considered it one of its rebellious provinces that it could one day reclaim (Barker & Pohl, 2009).

The Republic Period (1836–1845)

Despite the economic hardship typical of new nations, Texas managed to remain independent for 10 years and was recognized by several nations in the world, including the United States. This period was marked by tensions between those who wished to remain independent and those who wished to become part of the United States. Sam Houston was one who advocated for Texas to join the union. Unable to secure its borders and reverse its financial situation, Sam Houston's vision would grain traction as the Republic of Texas sought the support of the United States.

Texas Joins the United States

In 1845, Texas became the 28th state of the American Union. Texas was admitted as a slave state. Immediately, the U.S. government sent troops to the Rio Grande (which Mexicans considered their territory) to secure the Texas border. The ensuing clashes between Mexican and U.S. forces resulted in Congress declaring war in May 1846.

Mexican-American War

Between 1846 and 1848, Mexico and the United States waged a war that ended with a decisive victory and tremendous land acquisitions for the United States. As a result of the Treaty of Guadalupe Hidalgo, Mexico withdrew its claim over Texas and established the Rio Grande, or *Rio Bravo*, as it is known in Mexico, as the official border between the two countries. Mexico also ceded California and the territory known today as the American Southwest to the United States. Figure 5-1 presents a timeline of important events in Texas history from 1528–1861.

Figure 5-1
Texas Timeline from 1528 to 1861

1528	1541	1682	1682	1690	1718	1820
Cabeza de Vaca lands in Texas	Coronado explores Texas	Mission founded in El Paso	La Salle (French) lands in Texas	First mission in East Texas San Francisco de los Tejas	Mission and fort founded in San Antonio	Austin arrives in San Antonio

1861	1848	1846	1845	1836	1835	1833
Texas secedes from the union	Treaty of Guadalupe Hidalgo	Mexican-American War begins	Texas becomes the 28th state in the union	Battle of San Jacinto; Texas declares independence	Battle of Gonzales marks beginning of Texas revolution	Santa Anna becomes president of Mexico

Confederacy Period (1861–1865)

At the onset of the American Civil War, Texas left the Union and joined the Confederacy as a proslavery state. Sam Houston, the governor of the State of Texas, refused to declare allegiance to the Confederacy and was thus replaced. After five years of war, the Confederate army, led by General Robert E. Lee, surrendered to General Ulysses S. Grant, the leader of the Union forces. With the Union victory came freedom for slaves. In June 1865, news of the Emancipation Proclamation, which abolished slavery, reached Galveston. "**Juneteenth**" is a holiday that celebrates this event.

Reconstruction Period (1865–1877)

After the war, the Union forces occupied the South for a period of 12 years (1865–1877). This era was called the Reconstruction Period. During Reconstruction, Texas was briefly under occupation by U.S. troops. Texas was allowed to rejoin the union in 1870. The Ku Klux Klan became very active at this time, terrorizing African Americans in Texas and across the South.

Economic Development after Reconstruction

After Reconstruction, the Texas economy flourished, largely based on the growth of the cattle industry. Barbed wire was introduced in 1880, and ranchers began using scientific cattle breeding to increase production and improve the quality of meat.

Boom or Bust Economic Cycles in Texas

As Texas developed in the latter part of the 19th into the 20th and 21st centuries, it experienced a number of "boom-or-bust" economic cycles. They included railroads, the cattle industry, oil and gas production, cotton, real estate, banking, and computer technology. A "boom-or-bust" economy undergoes sharp fluctuations from boom, a period of strength and wealth, to bust, a period of weakness and poverty. These variations affect the stability of the economy and the ability for the state to plan its future.

Cattle

Cattle that were left untended during the Civil War greatly multiplied. After the war, they were rounded up and driven to major rail lines to be shipped to the east where the demand for beef was the greatest and where they were willing to pay about 10 times more than the prices in Texas. Many of these cattle trails followed old Indian paths and some formed the route for major roads today. See also *https://tpwd.texas.gov/education/resources/* (search "vaqueros and cowboys"), *http://www.historynet.com/* (search "Texas Longhorns: A Short History"), and *https://texasourtexas.texaspbs.org/* (search "The Eras of Texas: Cotton, Cattle, Railroads").

Railroads

Railroads changed the way Texas farms. With increased access to railroads, farmers could ship their surplus goods to market and ranchers could ship cattle to other states. As such, the building of rail lines in Texas led to an increase in both commercial agriculture and cattle ranching.

Oil

In 1901, oil was discovered in the Spindletop Oil Field near Beaumont. The ensuing development of the oil industry catapulted Texas to its position as the leading producer of oil in the United States. As a result of this boom, cities like Houston and Dallas became large urban and industrial centers.

Military and Wartime Industry

As a result of World War I, Texas emerged as a leading military training center. Several military bases were established in the state, bringing economic growth. The rapid development of the aircraft industry and highly technological businesses led to rapid industrialization in the state. By World War II, Texas was a leading state in the defense industry. The modern economy of Texas still relies on agriculture, ranching, and oil production, but new high-tech industries are rapidly becoming the top economic forces in the state. More factories are moving to Texas and other places in the South because land is abundant and cheap, and the labor costs and regulations are fewer than the Northeast.

Six Flags over Texas

The phrase "Six flags over Texas" describes the different countries that have exerted control in Texas from 1519, when the first European exploration of the region by Cortés took place, to the present:

- Spain (1519–1821)

- France (1685–1690)

- Mexico (1821–1836)

- Republic of Texas (1836–1845)

- United States (1845–1861)

- Texas in the Confederacy (1861–1865)

- Back to the American union (1870–present)

State Facts and Symbols

Texas has adopted the following symbols to represent the state:

- State flower   Bluebonnet

- State bird   Mockingbird

- State tree   Pecan

- State motto   Friendship

- Border states   Oklahoma, Louisiana, Arkansas, and New Mexico

- State song   "Texas, Our Texas," by William J. Marsh and Gladys Yoakum Wright.

  Here are the lyrics to "Texas, Our Texas":

  Texas, our Texas!
  All hail the
  mighty State!
  Texas, our Texas!
  So wonderful so great!

  Boldest and grandest, withstanding ev'ry test;
  O Empire wide and glorious, you stand supremely blest.

  [Refrain]
  God bless you Texas! And
  keep you brave and strong,
  That you may grow in
  power and worth, thro'out
  the ages long.

- United States Pledge of Allegiance

  I pledge allegiance to the Flag of the United States of America, and to the Republic for which it stands, one Nation under God, indivisible, with liberty and justice for all.

- Texas Pledge of Allegiance

  Honor the Texas flag; I pledge allegiance to thee, Texas, one state under God, one and indivisible.

COMPETENCY 002: GEOGRAPHY

The teacher understands and applies knowledge of geographic relationships involving people, places, and environments in Texas, the United States, and the world, as defined by the Texas Essential Knowledge and Skills (TEKS).

The beginning teacher:

A. Understands and applies the geographic concept of region.

B. Knows how to create and use geographic tools and translate geographic data into a variety of formats (e.g., grid systems, legends, scales, databases, construction of maps, graphs, charts, models).

C. Knows the location and the human and physical characteristics of places and regions in Texas, the United States and the world.

D. Analyzes ways in which humans adapt to, use and modify the physical environment.

E. Knows how regional physical characteristics and human modifications to the environment affect people's activities, settlement, immigration and migration patterns.

F. Analyzes ways in which location (absolute and relative) affects people, places and environments.

G. Demonstrates knowledge of physical processes (e.g., erosion, deposition and weathering; plate tectonics; sediment transfer; the flows and exchanges of energy and matter in the atmosphere that produce weather and climate) and their effects on environmental patterns.

H. Understands the characteristics, distribution and migration of populations in Texas, the United States and the world.

I. Understands the physical and environmental characteristics of Texas, the United States and the world, past and present, and how humans have adapted to and positively and negatively modified the environment (e.g., air and water quality, building of dams, use of natural resources, the impact on habitats and wildlife).

J. Analyzes how geographic factors have influenced settlement patterns, economic and social development, political relationships and policies of societies and regions in Texas, the United States and the world (e.g., the Galveston hurricane of 1900, the Dust Bowl, limited water resources, alternative energy sources).

K. Analyzes interactions between people and the physical environment and the effects of these interactions on the development of places and regions.

L. Understands comparisons among various world regions and countries (e.g., aspects of population, disease and economic activities) by analyzing maps, charts, databases and models.

Geographic Concepts

Geography

Geography studies the Earth's surface, the organisms that populate it, and their interaction within the ecosystem by examining spatial patterns, processes, and relationships from a local to global scale. Geography can be divided into two main areas: physical and cultural. **Physical geography** refers to the physical characteristics of the surface of the Earth and how those features affect life (e.g., plate tectonics, landforms, bodies of water, climate, biomes, weathering, erosion, etc.). **Cultural, or human geography** deals with the interaction of humans with their environment and how that interaction produces changes. Humans can alter the physical environment of the Earth, but the physical environment can also shape humans and their culture. For example, the Incas built the capital of their empire, Cuzco, in the Andes Mountains in what is now Peru. This city has an altitude of 11,152 feet above sea level, where oxygen is scarce and agriculture is a challenge. However, the Incas managed to live and flourish. They carved the land for agriculture and built roads and cities. In turn, the environment changed the Incas, who had to evolve to tolerate the low levels of oxygen. Studies conducted on the Indians from Peru suggest that people of the Andes developed genetic adaptations for high-altitude living (Discovery Channel, March 10, 2004). By adapting to environmental conditions, the inhabitants not only survived but also flourished in less-than-ideal conditions.

Physical Geography Influences Settlement Locations

People typically settle where there is good land, good climate, and good, clean water. The location of such renewable and nonrenewable natural resources as fresh water, fossil fuels, fertile soils, and timber affect decisions about where to build a community. For example, the settlement patterns in Texas and in the United States show that people did not simply settle where the climate was good for crops, or along the coast where land was easily accessed. People also settled away from the coast along waterways. This provided a fresh source of water as well as a resource for food and transportation. However, settlement decisions can also cause stress on the natural resource. For example, in San Antonio the Edward's Aquifer is one of the most prolific underground sources of water in the world. The demand for the water may become greater than the capacity of the aquifer, which will affect the livelihood of the people as well as the potential development of urban areas in the region.

Locating Places and Regions on a Map

Maps have two categories: reference and thematic. **Reference maps** show the locations of places, boundaries of countries, states, counties, towns, landforms, and bodies of water. They are sometimes referred to as political and physical maps. A **physical map** shows the topography of the Earth, including land features and elevations. A **political map** shows how a country is organized. Atlases are examples of reference maps. **Thematic maps, or special purpose maps,** show such specific topics as population density or distribution of world religions as well as physical, social, economic, political, agricultural, or economic features. An *economic map* shows the important resources of a country or region. A **historical map** shows the location of historical events. **Population maps** show where people live.

A globe is a scale model of the Earth shaped like a sphere. Because a globe models the shape of the Earth, it shows sizes and shapes accurately. The Mercator projection map is a flat representation of the Earth, and it thus distorts the shape, size, and/or distance in some way. This projection, used initially for shipping, is most accurate nearest the equator. The portability of maps makes them more useful than globes. The position of people, places, and things can be identified using relative or absolute location. **Relative location** uses references to help describe where something is. For example, a house may be located next to a big soccer field. **Absolute location** provides the exact position of the destination. This could be as simple as an address for a house or the coordinates of the location using latitude and longitude. It is important to say "latitude and longitude" in that order because the coordinate system identifies latitude first. For example, Dallas is located at 33°N, 97°W.

The Grid System

A grid system is a network of horizontal and vertical lines used to locate points on a map or a chart by means of coordinates. This grid shows the location of places. Latitude and longitude lines form divisions in this grid system that consist of geometrical coordinates used in designating the location of places on the surface of the Earth on a globe or map. The lines measure distances in degrees.

Latitude lines are horizontal lines that run parallel around the Earth measuring the distance north and south of the equator. The equator is identified as the 0 degree line of latitude, and it divides the Earth into the Northern and the Southern hemispheres. The United States is located in the Northern Hemisphere, while Brazil, for example, is located in the Southern Hemisphere. Longitude lines are vertical lines that run north and south going east and west. The 0 degree line of longitude is known as the prime meridian. It goes through Greenwich, England, and it divides the Earth into the Eastern and Western hemispheres. The United States is in the Western Hemisphere and Japan in the Eastern Hemisphere.

Geographic Symbols

A **compass rose** is a design printed on a chart or map for reference. It shows the orientation of a map on Earth and shows the four cardinal directions (north, south, east, and west). A compass rose may also show in-between directions such as northeast or northwest. Symbols are used for a map to contain a large amount of information that can be easily understood. Common symbols used on a map include dots, stars, and small pictures to represent cities or places. Some maps use different colors to represent features such as elevations and divisions. These symbols and colors are defined in the map's key, or legend. A map scale shows the distance between two places in the world. The scale to which a map is drawn represents the ratio of the distance between two points on the Earth and the distance between the two corresponding points on the map. When teaching cardinal and intermediate directions, teachers sometimes label walls with N, S, E, W to aid students when giving directions. Teachers need to take precautions to assure that each wall is labeled accurately. This means that the wall that faces north is labeled "North." If North is in a corner, label the corner North. The wall can then have a sign for the correct intermediate direction.

Time Zones

Time zones are established based on the lines of longitude, or meridians. These lines run from north to south. The prime meridian, or the meridian at 0 degrees, has been set in Greenwich, England. On the other side of the globe is the 180th meridian along which the International Date Line (IDL) generally follows. The prime meridian divides the Earth into the Western and Eastern hemispheres. Following the sunlight as it travels along the rotating Earth, the time decreases moving from east to west. Crossing the IDL eastward, you subtract a day, whereas moving westward means you add a day. So in the first example, Monday would become Sunday; in the second case, it would be Tuesday.

The United States is divided into six time zones, all one hour apart—Eastern, Central, Mountain, Pacific, Alaska, and Hawaii. Figure 5-2 represents the six time zones in the United States with a key city for each zone. Technically, the United States has four time zones in the contiguous 48 states, five in the continental U.S. with the addition of Alaska, and when we add Hawaii, we add the sixth time zone. For more information about time zones, go to the website provided by the National Institute of Standards and Technology (an agency of the U.S. Department of Commerce) and the U.S. Naval Observatory at *http://time.gov/aboutB.html*.

Figure 5-2
Time Zones in the United States

West ←					→ East
Hawaii	Alaska	Pacific	Mountain	Central	Eastern
1:00 PM	2:00 PM	3:00 PM	4:00 PM	5:00 PM	6:00 PM
Honolulu	Anchorage	Los Angeles	Phoenix	Dallas	New York City

Locations and Human and Physical Characteristics of Places and Regions

Texas

As measured by area, Texas is the second-largest state in the United States. Only Alaska is larger. Covering 268,601 square miles, the state contains five geographic regions within its boundaries. Table 5-3 lists the regions and the key cities and main economic activities of each.

Table 5-3
Regions and Economic Activity in Texas

Region	Key Cities	Main Economic Activities	Key Statistics
Coastal plains, flatland	Dallas, Houston, San Antonio, Austin, Corpus Christi, Laredo	**Lumber:** East Texas (Piney Woods) **Oil:** Refineries in Houston **Farming:** Rice, oranges, cotton, wheat, milo **Ranching:** Cattle in Kingsville **Shipping:** Houston	**Population:** High: 1 of 3 Texans **Rainfall:** High **Distinguishing Mark:** Hurricanes
Central plains, flatland and hills	Fort Worth, Arlington, San Angelo, Abilene	**Ranching:** Cattle, wool (mohair), sheep **Farming:** Grains	**Population:** High **Rainfall:** Medium **Distinguishing Marks:** Tornadoes, northerlies (cold winds), hailstorms; large ranches
Great Plains Flatland and hill country	Midland, Odessa, Lubbock, Amarillo, Texas Panhandle	**Ranching:** Cattle, sheep **Minerals:** Graphite **Oil:** Odessa and Midland **Farming:** Wheat	**Population:** Average **Rainfall:** Medium **Distinguishing Marks:** Snowstorms, dust storms, windmills, use of aquifers
Mountains and basins, Rocky Mountains, Davis, Chisos, and Guadalupe	El Paso	**Ranching:** Limited large ranches	**Population:** Low **Rainfall:** Low; hard rain wears out the rocks and land **Distinguishing Mark:** Big Bend National Park
Chihuahuan Desert		**Maquiladoras:** Factories at Mexico-U.S. border that import and assemble duty-free components for export	

The United States

The concept of regions facilitates the examination of geography by providing a convenient and manageable unit for studying the Earth's human and natural environment.

Regions in the United States

The continental United States is typically divided into eight broad geographic regions:

- **Laurentian Highlands** are part of the Canadian Shield that extends into the northern United States and the Great Lakes area. This area has a hard winter, and agriculture is very limited.

- **Atlantic–Gulf Coastal Plains** are the coastal regions of the eastern and southern states. It includes New York in the North, the Mid-Atlantic states to Florida in the South, and all the way west to Texas on the Gulf Coast.

- **Appalachian Highlands** covers the Appalachian Mountains, the Adirondack Mountains, and New England—the states of Connecticut, Maine, Massachusetts, New Hampshire, Rhode Island, and Vermont.

- **Interior Plains and the Great Plains** cover the interior part of the United States. Included in this area are the states west of the Appalachians, south of the Great Lakes, and as far west as Montana, Wyoming, Colorado, New Mexico, and northwestern Texas. Most of the nation's wheat, corn, and feed crops are grown in this area.

- **Interior Highlands** are also part of the interior continental United States. This area includes the Ozark Mountains and the states of Missouri, Arkansas, Kentucky, and part of Oklahoma and Kansas.

- **Rocky Mountain System** is in the western United States and Canada, extending from British Columbia to Montana, Utah, Colorado, and New Mexico. The mountain range is called the **Continental Divide**, because it separates the eastward-flowing rivers from the westward-flowing rivers. The waters that flow eastward empty into the Atlantic Ocean, and those that flow westward empty into the Pacific Ocean.

- **Intermontane Plateaus** is a large region that includes the Pacific Northwest, the Colorado Plateau, and the basins of the southwestern United States. This area covers the states of Washington, Oregon, Idaho, part of Utah, New Mexico, and Arizona. Included are the areas of the Grand Canyon and Death Valley.

- **Pacific Mountain System** covers the west coast of the United States. This area extends from the Cascade Mountains in the north down the entire west coast through the states of Washington, Oregon, and California.

Rivers in the United States

These are the largest and most important rivers in the United States:

- The **Mississippi** is the longest river in the United States and the 14th longest in the world. It begins in Minnesota and ends in the Gulf of Mexico.

- The **Ohio River** begins near Pittsburgh and runs southwest, ending in the Mississippi River on the Illinois and Missouri borders.

- The **Rio Grande** begins in the San Juan Mountains of southern Colorado and ends in the Gulf of Mexico. The river is the official border between the United States and Mexico, where it is known as the **Rio Bravo**.

- The **Colorado River** begins in the Rocky Mountains and flows to the wetlands of northwestern Mexico and the Gulf of California.

- The **Missouri River** begins in the Rocky Mountains, flowing north first and then generally southeast across the central United States, ending at the Mississippi River, just to the north of St. Louis, Missouri.

For information about significant rivers in the continental United States, visit *http://www.worldatlas.com*.

Regions of the World

A world region is an area of the world that shares similar, unifying cultural or physical characteristics that are different from those of surrounding areas. The physical features refer to topographic characteristics like elevation, rivers, and mountains. The cultural features include all the features that distinguish different groups of people, for example: language, religion, government, economics, food, architecture, shared values, and family life.

Geographers divide the world into ten regions: North America, Central and South America, Europe, Central Eurasia, the Middle East, North Africa, Sub-Saharan Africa, South Asia, East Asia, and Australasia. These divisions are based on physical and cultural similarities. North America consists of Canada, the United States, and Mexico. It is the third-largest continent, and it is located between the Arctic Circle and the Tropic of Cancer. The Europeans colonized the North American region. Table 5-4 presents an overview of the world regions by physical and cultural features. World region names and scope can vary depending on the purpose of those defining the area. For example, when discussing North America and Latin America, North America in this instance only refers to Canada and the United States, while Latin America consists of everything south of the United States (Mexico, Central America, the Caribbean, and South America).

**Table 5-4
World Regions**

World Region	Physical Features	Cultural Features
North America	• Consists of Canada, the United States, and Mexico. • The United States is the fourth-largest country in the world. • Oil is an important resource in the U.S. • Most of the U.S. has a humid-continental or humid-subtropical climate • Most of Canada has a subarctic or tundra climate. • Over 75% of Canadians live along the southern border. • The areas of greatest concentration of population in the U.S. are along the East Coast and California. • The climate of Mexico ranges from humid tropical and subtropical to desert and highland. • Mexico has rich mineral resources including oil.	• Europeans colonized this region. • Languages spoken are predominantly English, Spanish, and French. • Most people hold Christian beliefs.
Central and South America	• Includes the countries of Central America, the Caribbean islands, and South America. • The majority of this continuous mass of land is south of the Equator. • South America extends from Point Gallinas in Colombia to Cape Horn. • Part of South America lies closer to the South Pole than any other land mass of this size. • Venezuela is one of the world's leading exporters of oil. • Most of Eastern Central America and equatorial South America have a humid tropical climate.	• Most people speak Spanish, but many other languages are spoken: Portuguese, French, Dutch, English, and several Native American languages and dialects. • Christian beliefs, the Roman Catholic religion is predominant. • Architecture, law, religion, traditions, and language are strongly influenced by Europe's colonial rule of this region. • The many ethnic groups in this region are separated by geographical barriers such as the Andes and the Amazon.

(continued)

World Region	Physical Features	Cultural Features
Europe	• Western section of the Eurasian continent • Shares a mountain chain, the Alps. • Most of Europe has a temperate climate. • Europe's irregular coastline has many harbors that are important manufacturing and trade centers. • The rivers of Europe are important resources for trade, water, and hydroelectricity. • European population growth rates are the smallest in the world.	• Shares a common history in the Roman Empire and later the Catholic Church and Latin language. • English is the most spoken language in Europe, German and French are also widespread. • Cultural diffusion or shared cultural traits spread throughout Europe. • Ninety percent of all adults ages 15–24 speak a second language and some countries are considered multilingual. • Europeans practice many different religions. • Roman Catholicism is the predominant religion of many European countries. • Most of Northern and Central Europe is Protestant. • Jews live in many parts of Western Europe.
Central Eurasia	• Central Asia and Eastern Europe • United around one continuous mass of land located in the middle of the continent. • Little access to the sea • The borders of Eastern European countries have changed many times. • From WWII to the late 1980s, the Soviet Union controlled Eastern Europe and introduced communism to the region.	• Conquered at different times by the Persians, Mongolians, Tartars, the French, the Germans, and the Russians. • Slavic languages are predominant. • Most people in the Eastern part of the region follow the Eastern Orthodox church; people in the Northern area are mostly Roman Catholic.

World Region	Physical Features	Cultural Features
Middle East	• Consists of the area of southwest Asia and North Africa. • Access to sea water • The majority of the land is desert. • Rich in oil	• While the majority of people follow the religion of Islam there are also groups that follow Christianity and Judaism. • The religion defines the law in many places. • The most ancient of human civilizations. Egyptians, Assyrians, Babylonians, Persians, Greeks, and Romans have left their mark in this region. • This region has been the fighting ground for many religious battles.
North Africa	• Part of the African continent • Includes Egypt, Libya, Tunisia, Algeria, and Morocco • Extensive coastline • The Sahara desert and the Nile river are two important physical features of this area. • Rich in oil • Egypt is undergoing rapid growth, urbanization, and industrialization.	• The majority of people follow the religion of Islam. • People speak Arabic predominantly. • Religious issues influence the politics of this area.
Sub-Saharan Africa	• Consists of Africa south of the Sahara • Most of the area is a savanna. • Has abundant rain • Extensive coastline • Fertile land • Most people live in the forest zone and the dry savannas. • Agriculture is the predominant activity in West Africa. • Livestock is the predominant economic activity in the northern area.	• Cultural diversity reflects indigenous, Arab, and European influences. • Majority follows tribal beliefs, Christianity, or a combination of both. • Most people speak native African or European languages. • Over 500 ethnic groups live in this region.

(continued)

World Region	Physical Features	Cultural Features
South Asia	• Consists of a large Indian peninsula that extends into the Indian Ocean. • Abundant rainfall • Strong seasonal winds called monsoons • Rice is an important crop. • One of the most populated regions in the world. • The world's highest mountains are located in the northern area of this region. • Many major manufacturing and trade centers are located along the coast.	• People in South Asia speak many languages. • Predominant beliefs are of Eastern origins such as Buddhism and Hinduism. • Many South Asians are farmers who live in small villages. • Many cultural influences • Through the efforts of Mohandas Gandhi the region gained its independence from Britain in 1947.
East Asia	• Consists of China, Korea, Taiwan, and Japan. • It is the most densely populated region in the world. • Large expanse of coastline.	• Buddhism and Taoism are predominant religions. • Confucian philosophy • People speak Chinese, Japanese, Korean, Mongolian, and many other languages. • Chinese Script or characters influence many of the writing systems of these languages. • Culturally, China has had a major influence in this region.
Australasia	• It is composed of the Australian continent and surrounding islands. • South of the equator	• English is the predominant language of most of the nations in this region • Population contains a large Christian majority.

World Mountains

With the notable exception of the peak known as K2, which is part of the Karakoram Range, the tallest mountains in the world are located in the Himalayas, ranging across the countries of China, Pakistan, Nepal, and Tibet. Table 5-5 lists the top ten tallest mountains in the world. For additional information about the world's mountains, see *http://www.infoplease.com/ipa/A0001771.html*.

Table 5-5
Tallest Mountains in the World

Mountain	Location	Height (in feet)
Everest	Nepal/Tibet	29,035
K2	Pakistan/China	28,250
Kanchenjunga	India/Nepal	28,169
Lhotse I	Nepal/Tibet	27,940
Makalu I	Nepal/Tibet	27,766
Cho Oyu	Nepal/Tibet	26,906
Dhaulagiri	Nepal	26,795
Manaslu I	Nepal	26,781
Nanga Parbat	Pakistan	26,660
Annapurna	Nepal	26,545

Compared to the world's tallest peaks, mountains in the United States are smaller, with the highest mountain being Mt. McKinley in Alaska, which is 20,310 feet high. The state of Alaska has the 16 highest peaks in the United States. A list of U.S. mountains with elevations of 16,000 feet or above is presented in Table 5-6.

Table 5-6
Tallest Mountains in the United States

Mountain	Location	Height (in feet)
Denali*	Alaska	20,310
Mt. St. Elias	Alaska	18,008
Mt. Foraker	Alaska	17,400
Mt. Bona	Alaska	16,500
Mt. Blackburn	Alaska	16,390
Mt. Sanford	Alaska	16,237

*Also called Mt. McKinley. Denali's official elevation was established by the U.S. Geological Survey in 2015.

Deforestation

Deforestation can increase soil erosion and lead to tragedies like the mudslides that occurred in 2006 in the Philippines, where thousands of people were buried alive. The rate of soil erosion is most likely to exceed the rate of soil formation in areas like Brazil, where people have cut forests to clear land for farming.

Deposition

Deposition is the process of carrying soil from one place to another, usually by means of water or wind. This process is responsible for the creation of beaches, sand dunes found in desert areas, and landforms created by glaciers.

Human Adaptation, Modification, and Use of the Physical Environment

Humans can alter the physical environment of the Earth, but the physical environment can also shape humans and their culture. For example, the Incas built the capital of their empire, Cuzco, in the Andes Mountains in what is now Peru. This city has an altitude of 11,152 feet above sea level, where oxygen is scarce and agriculture is a challenge. However, the Incas managed to live and flourish under these conditions. They carved the land for agriculture and built roads and cities. In turn, the environment changed the Incas, who had to evolve to tolerate the low levels of oxygen. Studies conducted on the Indians from Peru suggest that people of the Andes developed genetic adaptations for high-altitude living (Discovery Channel, 2004 March 10). By adapting to the conditions of their environment, inhabitants of the area not only survived but also flourished in less-than-ideal conditions.

How Regional Physical Characteristics and Human Modifications to the Environment Affect People's Activities and Settlement Patterns

The intended and unintended consequences of how humans modify the physical environment result in constant change to the human and physical world.

Advances in technology can bring a continuum of positive to negative consequences for people and for the environment. For example, humans often supply their energy needs from the Earth. The United States has long relied on coal as an energy source. Much of U.S. coal comes from Pennsylvania and West Virginia. Humans cannot have the energy benefits of coal without altering the physical landscape from which the coal is taken. This physical reshaping of mining the Earth changes how rainfall runs, where people can build homes, and how they maintain safe drinking water.

Supplying human energy needs often comes at great human and ecological costs. For example, people in Japan rely primarily on nuclear energy to meet their needs. However, events such as tsunamis and earthquakes can jeopardize the stability of plants that produce this main energy source. In 2011, a nuclear energy accident at the Daiichi Nuclear Power Plant in Fukushima, Japan, led to three nuclear meltdowns and the release of radioactive material. Other nuclear incidents around the world serve as examples, such as those at Chernobyl, Ukraine, and Three Mile Island, Pennsylvania.

Humans often redefine environmental systems and reshape the Earth in order to plant and harvest food. Some farming methods, such as intercropping, feature greater measures for sustainability, while other methods maintain focus on maximizing yield and are more detrimental to the environment.

How Location (Absolute and Relative) Affects People, Places and Environments

Both relative and absolute location tell us about where we are in the world. We use latitude and longitude to determine a global location. We use a street address to determine local location. Both of these are examples of absolute location. Often we describe a location by what is around a location. This is relative location. Referencing a landmark or the distance a location is from another well-known location would be examples of giving a relative location.

Most of us interact daily with our environment. Dolphin-safe tuna, bottled water, and sunscreen, are all real-life examples of products people create to interact safely and sustainably with their environment. Geography, in part, contributes to the pattern of how people organize space on the Earth. People use location, place, territory, geopolitics, migration, gender, race, language, economic change, and power to manage their relationship to the space around them. All of these have both local and worldwide effects.

Characteristics, Distribution, and Migration of Populations

The global population is more than seven-and-a-half billion people, with much of the growth occurring in the last two centuries. Population density of hyper-urban areas is also growing. For example, Tokyo, Japan, has over 36 million people. The New York and Sao Paulo, Brazil, metropolitan areas both have over 20 million people. Mumbai and Delhi, both urban areas in India, have over 21 million people each! Increases in population places strains on cities, regions, countries, and the Earth to keep up with the daily needs and wants of people, from access to clean water and medical care, to maintaining and growing schools and industry to support basic to extended quality of life. Population growth sometimes causes migration. Some migration is voluntary, as when humans search for a better quality of life. Other migration is involuntary, as when humans must move to maintain their culture or life, as in the face of famine, war, or ecological devastation. World events, as varied as war or the use of vaccines, can also affect population. Shifts in population density affect supply and demand of goods and services for people.

Culture

The culture of a group is reflected in what its people write, create, and wear as well as their government, decisions, customs and ceremonies, way of life, and dwellings. Humans share their culture through oral traditions, stories, real and mythical heroes, music, paintings, and sculptures. Significant historical periods represent cultural ideals at a given time and may continue to influence following generations as well as other regions of the world. For example, the Renaissance, Baroque, Classicism, Neoclassicism, and Romanticism are key historical periods that gave birth to influential literature, art, and music. The **Renaissance**, or "rebirth," was a time of great creativity. **William Shakespeare**'s plays explored humanity in plays that are still read and performed. **Leonardo da Vinci** created inspiring painting and sculptures. He also was known as the "Renaissance Man" who learned about and pursued different disciplines that enabled him to follow his interest in science and inventions as well. Literature and art often also reflect their time as well as the societies in which they are produced. The Renaissance also reflected reformation of attitudes toward political authority, which was mainly embodied in the church and monarchs. Society questioned and challenged decisions made by the church—as well as the monarch's rule. (For more information go to *http://www.britannica.com/EBchecked/topic/497731/Renaissance*.)

In the United States, the American Renaissance occurred in literature from the 1830s through the Civil War and into the 1880s. As with the European renaissance, literature and the arts explored humanity and challenged beliefs in the church, politics, and society. It was a period of time that was greatly governed by Transcendentalism. **American Transcendentalism**, a term derived from the philosopher Kant, was heavily influenced by the great minds of England and Germany. In America, this philosophy, or belief, was idealistic in nature, rooted in faith, and had a visionary bent. As stated by Thomas Hampson and Carla Maria Verdino-Süllwold in the PBS "Song of America" program, it was a collection of complex beliefs "that the spark of divinity lies within man; that everything in the world is a microcosm of existence; that the individual soul is identical to the world soul, or Over-Soul, as Emerson called it. . . . By meditation, by communing with nature, through work and art, man could transcend his senses and attain an understanding of beauty and goodness and truth." (see *http://www.songofamerica.net/library/ami/the-american-renaissance-and-transcendentalism*) This philosophy permeated American life through literature, poetry, artwork (e.g., painting, sculpture), architecture, and music. Well-known authors in American Transcendentalism include Emerson, Thoreau, Hawthorne, Whitman, and Dickinson. The renaissance is just one example of how creative expression is influenced by societal issues, and how it can transcend the societal boundaries with art, music, and literature and explore such universal ideas as religion, justice, and the passage of time.

Culture can be also analyzed by the effects of race, gender, socioeconomic class, and status and stratification on the ways of life. Historically, individuals differentiate themselves, and this affects their societies. For example, race has been used as a way to segment society and to allow certain groups to achieve status or some reward over another group. Race groups people according to such common features as hair, eye, or skin color. Ethnicity identifies a group of people by cultural traits. During World War II, Adolf Hitler, the leader of Germany, identified Jews as the reason for the economic and social crisis Germany was facing. He gradually stratified society by Jew and non-Jew. Although he referred to the Jewish ethnic group, Jews were recognized by characteristics that Hitler identified as the Jewish race. In the United States, people have recognized race as both unifying and divisive. For example, enclaves developed in cities where people with similar ethnic backgrounds lived. In this way, the immigrants felt at home and could ease into American culture. However, cultural differences sometimes have divided people. After a series of potato famines in Ireland, Irish immigrants moved to America to find a new life—and were met with such signs as "Don't hire Irish" and such comments as "dirty Irish." Texas was settled by cultural groups who created towns to reflect their German, Polish, Mexican, and other heritages. At the same time, societies were often stratified by race, gender, and socioeconomic class.

Cultural Diffusion

The term **cultural diffusion** describes the exchange or transmission of cultural information and lifestyles from people around the world. For example, most people in the world use cotton, a fabric developed in India; and silk, developed in China. Chickens and pigs were originally domesticated in Asia, but by the process of cultural diffusion, these animals are common today in most countries in the world. Many countries are predominantly Christian today, but Christianity was born in the Middle East, a place where most people are Muslim. The Romans facilitated the cultural diffusion of Christianity around the ancient world. Travelers visiting Morocco, a Muslim country in North Africa, may be surprised to hear Puerto Rican salsa and Jamaican reggae music being played in local nightclubs. The popularity of Latin and Caribbean rhythms in a predominantly Muslim country is an example of the powerful effect of cultural diffusion.

Cultural diffusion influences the development of multicultural societies, which may have unifying and divisive qualities. The influx of people can aid the social and economic development of a nation. All cultures have unique characteristics and knowledge that can add to a society. These include inventions, art, music, and technology as well as production techniques. However, tensions can rise when people compete for housing, jobs, and land. Large cultural groups also may seek to dominate and exploit smaller, weaker cultural groups. Conflict also may occur if cultural groups try to force their way of life on others.

Relationships among cultural groups are dynamic. The relationships are influenced by conflict, cooperation, and change and are based on such factors as race, ethnicity, and religion. For example, in the 1960s tensions between the Caucasian and African-American races in the United States brought about much change. Although in the South some conflicts occurred in the form of riots, protests, and attacks, both races also cooperated through marches, speeches, peaceful demonstrations, and, eventually, new laws. Religion can also cause tensions. For example, in Northern Ireland, Catholics and Protestants have fought for many years. Although both groups are Christian, their religion has come to symbolize geopolitical issues.

Improved communication, transportation and economic development can also impact cultural change. For example, the country of Malawi, on the continent of Africa, has a poor infrastructure resulting in a few people owning a telephone in their house or village. Telephones with landlines require electricity, wiring under or above ground, and other infrastructure. However, satellites allow farmers in this country to operate satellite mobile telephones that need little infrastructure. The people in Malawi, like many African cultures, have a strong oral tradition, meaning they learn by listening as experienced elders pass knowledge and traditions. Many cannot read and write. Satellite phones let members of this society gain new knowledge to improve their agriculture by using their oral traditions rather than written language.

Geographical Tools

Social scientists (e.g., geographers, historians, political scientists, and economists) use an assortment of geographical tools to help examine physical and cultural geographic data. First, the globe is recognized as a mathematical model of the world and is important to students' development of spatial thinking. It shows accurate distance, shape, and size of continents and bodies of water. As will be discussed, colors are used to symbolize elevation or other concepts. The complexity of the globe increases with the grade level. Maps are a flat representation of the world or a region of the world. As with globes, the complexity of maps increases developmentally with the grade level. Charts, graphs, and diagrams are also used to analyze data. Some mathematical representations, such as Dot Plots, offer an opportunity to reinforce mathematical concepts while examining cultural and historical data sets. Digital geospatial tools can offer teachers an alternative to paper maps and allow for more depth and rigor when used appropriately. These tools can provide an easy way to explore data spatially, such as in the Annie E. Case Foundation KIDS COUNT website (*http://datacenter.kidscount.org/*) and the Census Bureau webpage for kids (*http://www.census. gov/schools/census_for_kids*). Others provide interactive online maps such as *http://mrnussbaum. com/united-states/amwest/* or *http://mrnussbaum.com/united-states/southwest/*. A popular digital globe is Google Earth (*https://https://www.google.com/earth/*), which allows users to add data layers and to spatially analyze data from a local to global scale. Finally, ArcGIS Online (*http://www. arcgis.com/features/*) offers an online tool that facilitates inquiry-based discussions and lets students and teachers explore data and create maps.

Map Skills by Grade—Scope and Sequence

Students should create and interpret maps of places and regions of the world that contain developmentally appropriate map elements and symbols. A compass rose and grid system should be used to locate places on maps and globes as well. Place location, or memorizing countries, cities, bodies of water, and landforms on a map, is critical to learning geography and other social studies. It provides a foundation on which content about Texas, the United States, and the World can be built. Its importance is akin to the multiplication tables in mathematics. Maps may be provided through an online or desktop digital source or on paper. Paper maps may already have an outline of a region or require students to sketch the area. Sketch maps are important because they require students to create a mental image, or map, of the area. Doing so will help them visualize the region when learning about social studies, and it will also help them to make connections to other content, including literature and science.

In addition to knowing the specific knowledge and skills required at each grade level in the Texas Essential Knowledge and Skills (TEKS), it is important to be aware of areas in the curriculum for vertical alignment. For example, in each grade level in elementary school, the following skills are reinforced. Savvy elementary teachers would work together to ensure that these skills are supported and extended to appropriately challenge students. As you read the geography knowledge and skills for each grade level, consider ways you can continue to build and develop curriculum to make it rigorous and relevant while preparing students for their next grade level.

Middle Grades Knowledge and Skills for Social Studies

- Understands and uses terms related to location, direction, and distance (e.g., *up, down, left, right, here, near, far*).

- Recognizes a globe as a model of the Earth.

- Recognizes and uses terms that express relative size and shape (e.g., *big, little, large, small, round, square*).

- Identifies school and local community by name.

- Recognizes and uses models and symbols to represent real things.

- Identifies bodies of water—oceans, seas, lakes, rivers, ponds, and bayous (TEKS).

- Identifies landforms—plains, mountains, deserts, hills, and canyons (TEKS).

- Identifies natural resources—water, soil, trees, metals, and fish (TEKS).

Grade 4 Knowledge and Skills for Social Studies

- Interprets pictures, graphs, charts, and tables.

- Works with distance, directions, scale, and map symbols.

- Relates similarities and differences between maps and globes.

- Uses maps of different scales and themes.

- Recognizes the common characteristics of the map grid system.

- Compares and contrasts regions on a state, national, or world basis.

- Understands such concepts of adaptation and modification as changing the landscape to meet survival needs and building to adjust to a new environment (TEKS).

- Identifies elements that affect the climate (TEKS).

- Uses a compass rose to find true directions.

- Identifies key explorers and their achievements (TEKS).

- Identifies how geography affects the settlement and development of places.

- Understands the connection between climate and vegetation.

- Identifies global divisions, like the prime meridian, the equator, and the four hemispheres. (TEKS).

Grade 5 Knowledge and Skills for Social Studies

- Uses geographic tools to collect, analyze, and interpret data (TEKS).

- Applies such geographic tools as grid systems, legends, symbols, scales, and compass roses to make and interpret maps (TEKS).

- Translates geographic data into such formats as graphs and maps (TEKS).

- Understands the concept of regions and can describe regions in the U.S. that result from patterns of human activity, including political, population, and economic regions as well as from physical characteristics, including landform, climate, and vegetation regions (TEKS).

- Locates the 50 states on a map and identifies regions made by groups of states, such as New England and the Great Plains (TEKS).

- Understands and describes location and patterns of settlement as well as their distribution (TEKS).

- Analyzes the location of U. S. cities, including state capitals (TEKS).

- Understands how people adapt and modify their environment to meet human needs (TEKS).

- Analyzes the consequences of human modification of the environment in the United States (TEKS).

Grade 6 Knowledge and Skills for Social Studies

- Uses maps, globes, graphs, charts, models, and databases to answer geographic questions.

- Creates maps, graphs, models, and databases (TEKS).

- Poses and answers questions about geographic distributions and patterns from selected world regions and countries (TEKS).

- Compares selected world regions and countries by using data from maps, graphs, charts, databases, and models (TEKS).

- Understands the characteristics and relative locations of major historical and contemporary societies (TEKS).

- Locates major historical and contemporary societies on maps and globes (TEKS).

- Identifies and explains how geography affects patterns of population in places and regions (TEKS).

- Understands how geography influences the economic development, political relationships, and policies of societies (TEKS).

- Understands the impact of physical processes on patterns in the environment (TEKS).

- Understands the impact of interactions between people and the physical environment on the development of places and regions (TEKS).

Grade 7 Knowledge and Skills for Social Studies

- Uses geographic tools to collect, analyze, and interpret data (TEKS).

- Creates and interprets thematic maps, graphs, charts, models, and databases (TEKS).

- Analyzes and interprets geographic distributions and patterns (TEKS).

- Locates the mountains and basics, Great Plains, North Central Plains, and Coastal Plains regions and places of importance (TEKS).

- Compares places and regions in terms of physical and human characteristics (TEKS).

- Analyzes the effects of physical and human factors (TEKS).

- Identifies ways people have modified and adapted to the environment (TEKS).

- Analyzes positive and negative consequences of modifications (TEKS).

- Explains ways in which geographic factors have affected political, economic, and social development (TEKS).

- Analyzes why immigrants moved and where they settled (TEKS).

- Analyzes how immigrants and migrants influenced Texas (TEKS).

- Analyzes the effects of changing population distribution and growth (TEKS).

- Describes the structure of the population (TEKS).

Grade 8 Knowledge and Skills for Social Studies

- Understands United States history from early colonial period in the 16th and 17th century through Reconstruction in the 19th century.

- Understands the location and characteristics of places and regions of the U.S., past and present (TEKS).

- Locates places and regions of importance (TEKS).

- Compares places and regions in terms of physical and human characteristics (TEKS).

- Understands the physical characteristics of the U.S. and how humans adapted and modified the environment (TEKS).

- Analyzes how physical characteristics influenced population distribution, settlement patterns and economic activities (TEKS).

- Analyzes positive and negative consequences of modifications (TEKS).

- Analyzes how different immigrant groups interacted with the environment (TEKS).

COMPETENCY 003: ECONOMICS

The teacher understands and applies knowledge of economic systems and how people organize economic systems to produce, distribute, and consume goods and services, as defined by the Texas Essential Knowledge and Skills (TEKS).

The beginning teacher:

A. Understands that basic human needs are met in many ways.

B. Understands and applies knowledge of basic economic concepts (e.g., goods and services, free enterprise, interdependence, needs and wants, scarcity, economic system, factors of production).

C. Demonstrates knowledge of the ways in which people organize economic systems and the similarities and differences among various economic systems around the world.

D. Understands the value and importance of work and purposes for spending and saving money.

E.   Demonstrates knowledge of occupational patterns and economic activities in Texas, the United States and the world, past and present (e.g., the plantation system, the spread of slavery, industrialization and urbanization, transportation, the American ideals of progress, equality of opportunity).

F.   Understands the characteristics, benefits and development of the free enterprise system in Texas and the United States.

G.   Analyzes the roles of producers and consumers in the production of goods and services.

H.   Understands the effects of government regulation and taxation on economic development.

I.   Demonstrates knowledge of how businesses operate in the U.S. free enterprise system and international markets (e.g., government regulation, world competition, the importance of morality and ethics in maintaining a functional enterprise system).

J.   Applies knowledge of the effects of supply and demand on consumers and producers in a free-enterprise system.

K.   Demonstrates knowledge of categories of economic activities and methods used to measure a society's economic level.

L.   Uses economic indicators to describe and measure levels of economic activity.

M.   Understands the causes of major events and trends in economic history (e.g., factors leading societies to change from agrarian to urban, economic reasons for exploration and colonization, economic forces leading to the Industrial Revolution, processes of economic development in world areas, factors leading to the emergence of different patterns in jobs, economic activity in regions of the United States).

N.   Analyzes the interdependence of Texas, United States and world economies.

O.   Understands how geographic factors such as immigration, migration, location, climate and limited resources have influenced the development of economic activities in Texas, the United States, and the world.

P.   Applies knowledge of significant economic events and issues and their effects in Texas, in the United States and the world.

Basic Principles of Economy

Economics, the subject covered by Competency 003, is a social science that analyzes the principles that regulate the production, distribution, and consumption of resources in society. It emphasizes how these principles operate within the economic choices of individuals, households, businesses, and governments. Economics can be divided into two main areas: macroeconomics and microeconomics. Macroeconomics is the study of the economy at the world, regional, state, and local levels. Some of the topics include reasons and ways to control inflation, causes of unemployment, and economic growth in general. Microeconomics deals with specific issues related to the decision-making process at the household, firm, or industry levels.

The study of economics can be summarized into several key principles.

1. People choose.

2. People's choices have costs.

3. People respond to incentives in predictable ways.

4. People create economic systems that influence individual choices and incentives.

5. People gain when they trade voluntarily.

6. People's choices have consequences that lie in the future.

Scarcity

Economics centers on the notion of scarcity. Scarcity refers to the reality that there are limited resources despite consumer's unlimited wants. The result is that people must choose among competing alternatives. The choices people make about which alternative to choose are generally purposeful and based on their desire to obtain the most utility or satisfaction from their choices. Time, money, and natural resources are all examples of scarce resources.

Opportunity Costs

All choices have benefits and costs. Every time an investor, saver, consumer, or producer makes a decision, there is an alternative course of action that could be taken. Economists refer to the best alternative forgone as the opportunity cost of a decision. Opportunity costs are both monetary and nonmonetary in nature, and are an important consideration in the choices people make. Let's consider your decision to read this book and study for the TExES exam. There are probably several other things you could be doing rather than reading this book and studying for the TExES exam, such as watching television, spending time with family or friends, or exercising. If you were to rank your alternatives in order, the alternative ranking right behind your decision to read this book is the opportunity cost of your choice.

For instance, if you were to rank your choices in the following order, the opportunity cost of your decision to read this book would have been exercising.

1. Read this book (choice)

2. Exercise (opportunity cost: best alternative forgone)

3. Watch television

4. Spend time with family and friends

Theory of Supply and Demand

This theory states that prices vary based on the balance between the availability of a product or service at a certain price (supply) and the desire of potential purchasers to pay that price (demand). This balance of supply and demand can occur naturally or be created artificially. An example of an artificially created balance is the intentional destruction of a surplus of a given product on the world market to maintain the price level. Another way is to control the production and availability of the product to create a scarcity of a product. For instance, the Organization of Petroleum Exporting Countries (OPEC) often reduces its production of oil to cause an increase in price.

Goods and Services

The use of machines increases the availability of goods and services to the population. This kind of production can decrease the cost of producing the goods and consequently its price. For example, as a result of the division of labor and the use of assembly lines developed by Eli Whitney in 1799, production costs of manufactured goods decreased and productivity increased. Mass production that came as a result of the Industrial Revolution made contemporary families and children more likely to become consumers rather than producers. However, before the Industrial Revolution, especially in colonial America, children were used to produce goods and contribute to the group.

Economic activities are categorized into five major categories: primary, secondary, tertiary, quaternary, and quinary. *Primary* economic activities directly use natural resources by such activities as farming, mining, logging, etc. *Secondary* economic activities take the primary goods and change, or manufacture, them in some way. For example, fresh vegetables are canned or put into a frozen dinner. *Tertiary* activities typically refer to the service industry. To carry the previous examples further, the grocery store where canned and frozen foods are bought is considered part of the tertiary sector. *Quaternary* activities typically require specialized knowledge or technical skills and refer to the "collection, processing, and manipulation of information and capital (finance, administration, insurance, legal services, computer services, etc.)" (de Blij & Murphy 1999, 320). Finally, the *quinary* sector "denotes activities that facilitate complex decision making and the advancement of human capacities (scientific research, high-level management, etc.)" required for jobs like "research professors, the heads of corporations, and top government officials." (de Blij & Murphy 1999, 320).

Factors of Production

The resources required for the production of goods and services are generally classified into four categories: natural resources, labor, capital, and entrepreneurship.

Natural resources include timber, land, fisheries, farms, oil, and other similar natural resources. Natural resources are generally a limited resource for many economies. Although some natural resources, such as timber, food and animals, are renewable, the physical land is usually a fixed resource. Nations must carefully use their natural resources by creating a mix of natural and industrial uses.

Labor represents the human capital available to transform raw or national resources into consumer goods. Human capital includes all able-bodied individuals capable of working in the economic system and providing various services to other individuals or businesses. This factor of production is a flexible resource as workers can be allocated to different areas of the economy for producing consumer goods or services. Human capital can also be improved through training or educating workers to complete technical functions or business tasks when working with other economic resources.

Capital has two economic definitions as a factor of production. Capital can represent the monetary resources companies use to purchase natural resources, land and other capital goods. Monetary resources flow through an economic system as individuals buy and sell resources to individuals and businesses. Capital also represents the major physical assets individuals and companies use when producing goods or services. These assets include buildings, production facilities, equipment, vehicles and other similar items.

Entrepreneurship is considered a factor of production because economic resources can exist in an economy and not be transformed into consumer goods. Entrepreneurs usually have an idea for creating a valuable good or service and assume the risk involved with transforming economic resources into consumer products. Entrepreneurship is also considered a factor of production since someone must complete the managerial functions of gathering, allocating and distributing economic resources or consumer products to individuals and other businesses in the economy.

Gross Domestic Product (GDP)

The Gross Domestic Product is the total value of all goods and services produced in the country. In computing the GDP, only the value of the final goods and services are included. This means that only the value of the final product is included, excluding all the individual factors of production that went into making that product. A house, for example, would only have its own value included in the GDP, and not the lumber, brick, wire, glass, cement, and shingles that went into building it. GDP is part of macroeconomics and is a primary indicator of an economy's overall health.

GDP consists of four broad sectors: consumers, businesses, government, and the foreign sector. To tabulate GDP, an economy's output can be measured in two ways, both of which yield the same result: the expenditure approach and the incomes approach. In the expenditures approach, GDP is determined by the spending in each sector. GDP equals the consumer consumption (C) plus investment expenditures (I) plus government spending (G) plus the difference between exports and imports in foreign sector spending (X − M). This formula includes only final goods and services, and not the value of intermediate goods.

$$GDP = C + I + G + (X - M)$$

The less-used income approach to GDP is calculated by adding up total compensation to employees, gross profits for incorporated and non-incorporated firms, and taxes, less any subsidies. Regardless of how GDP is calculated, this macroeconomic measure is an important indicator of the standard of living in various economies. For instance, GDP per capita (using purchase power parity) in the U.S. is $47,200 and in Mexico is $13,900.

Economic Systems

Because resources are scarce and wants are unlimited, societies often devise economic systems to help regulate this divide between demand and supply. Economic systems are generally created based on three important questions:

1. What goods and services to produce?

2. How to produce these goods and services?

3. How are these goods and services allocated?

The way a society answers these questions determines the type of economic system they will create. The three main economic systems are:

1. Free enterprise or market economy (also referred to as capitalism)

2. Communism (or centrally planned economies)*

3. Socialism (or mixed economies)

Market Economy, or Free Enterprise

Free enterprise is an economic and political doctrine of the capitalist system. The concept is based on the premise that the economy can regulate itself in a freely competitive market through the relationship of supply and demand, and with minimum governmental intervention. This economic system allows entrepreneurship, or individually owned and operated businesses. One of the main benefits of free enterprise is the competition among businesses. This results in a greater choice and better prices for consumers as well as in increased specialization and trade. Americans believe strongly in equal opportunities for all. All citizens expect to be given an equal chance to succeed. Individual ownership and engagement in the free-market system comes with the responsibility and importance of employing moral and ethical business practices. The federal government sometimes needs to step in to protect workers, small businesses, and the consumer. For example, business cannot discriminate, or treat someone differently, based on such things as skin color,

---

*** Note:** Although *communism* is sometimes used to describe both an economic and political system in the context of strong government control, meaning that the government gives little power to the citizens of the country, it is more appropriately used to describe a system of government, i.e., an example of a totalitarian regime. This can be confusing for students. Be sure to be clear how you phrase your discussion with students. For more information, see *https://www.britannica.com/topic/command-economy.*

ethnicity, or gender. The United States government is also supposed to safeguard small business by preventing monopolies, which occur when one business controls part of the market. The U.S. government tries to encourage small businesses to flourish. Additionally, regulations are laws that require businesses to use safe practices. For example, in the early 20th century, President Theodore Roosevelt pushed through a meat inspection act to make sure that meat is packaged properly to prevent people from getting sick. The Food and Drug Administration now requires additional information, such as the expiration date, to inform consumers about a product.

The three questions of economic systems are answered in the marketplace by the interaction of buyers and sellers. One of the main benefits of the system of free enterprise is the competition among businesses that results in a greater choice and better prices for consumers. The system of free enterprise has led to **globalization**. Globalization can be defined as a continuous increase of cross-border financial, economic, and social activities. It implies some level of economic interdependence among individuals, financial entities, and nations. As a result of globalization, trade barriers have been eliminated and tariffs imposed on imported products have been largely discontinued. In a global market, it is difficult to determine the origins of products. For example, Japan-based Toyota, and U.S.-based Ford joined forces to build cars using parts and labor from Mexico. The concept of **economic interdependence** describes a positive, close connection between producers and consumers of goods and services within a nation or across nations. This economic interdependence has guided nations to establish large markets of free trade zones like the European Union (EU) trade agreement and the North American Free Trade Agreement (NAFTA) for Canada, Mexico, and the United States. The European Union went a step further; in 2002 they adopted a common currency for the Union—the *euro*. This alliance has resulted in the euro's ranking as one of the strongest currencies in the world.

Centrally Planned or Command Economy

The opposite of a market or free enterprise economy is called a **centrally planned economy**, also referred to as a command economy or centralized economy. In a planned economy, supply and price are regulated by the government rather than market forces (i.e., the interaction between consumers and businesses). Government planners answer the three questions of economic systems and decide which goods and services are produced and how they are distributed. Most planned economies direct resources into the production of capital and military goods leaving little resources for consumer goods. A planned economy discourages individualistic profit motives and consumeristic needs.

A **command economy** is the extreme form of a planned economy that discourages individualistic profit motives and consumeristic needs. Under such a planned system, rewards, wages, and perks are distributed based on the social value of the service performed. Certain sectors get preferential allocation at the expense of others, which may lead to shortages in some essential goods. Absence of profit motives precludes any need for competitiveness. This acts as a disincentive in individual contribution to collective efforts. The former Soviet Union was an example of a command economy. China also has a command economy, but, in recent years, it has brought changes allowing for some form of more open economies in certain regions. Today, countries using a command economy are rare. Remaining examples of countries with a command economy include Cuba and North Korea.

Mixed Economies

In between market and planned economies are mixed economies. A mixed economy, also referred to as a **socialist economy** or **socialism**, is an economic system that answers the three questions both in the marketplace and in the government. It is a system in which the central government controls the production and distribution of goods, services, and labor to some degree. Economic systems can be viewed as part of a continuum moving from strict government control (a command or communist economy) to one with little or no government control (free enterprise or market economy). Mixed, or socialist, economies can be anywhere along the continuum, in between command and market economies. Planning is usually used to direct resources at the upper levels of the economy, with markets being used to determine prices of consumer goods and wages. The former Yugoslavia was a mixed economy. Although the United States government plays a role in our economy, a mixed economy usually involves producers working closer with the government than they do in the United States, so the U.S. economic system is still a market economy.

Money and Banking

Under the presidency of Woodrow Wilson, the **Federal Reserve System** was established in 1913. The main purpose of this institution is to keep the banking industry strong to ensure a supply of currency. The Federal Reserve is run by the Federal Reserve Board of Governors, a seven-member body appointed to a four-year term, with the option of being reappointed to a maximum of fourteen-year terms. **Alan Greenspan** served as chairman of the Federal Reserve Board from 1987 to 2006. He finished an unexpired term and then served for a full fourteen-year term for a total of eighteen and a half years. He was followed by **Ben S. Bernanke** whose term was from 2006-2014, spanning the George W. Bush and Obama administrations. In 2014, **Janet Yellen** began her term as Fed chair under the Obama administration. Yellen was succeeded in 2018 by President Donald Trump's pick, **Jerome Powell**. The main function of the Fed, as it is commonly called, is to promote monetary stability and economic growth in the nation and to regulate inflation and deflation. The Board of Governors controls the flow of money and sets the interest rate that banks use to lend money. They increase the interest rate to control inflation and lower the interest rate when business slows down. To learn more about the Federal Reserve System go to *http://www.federalreserve.gov*.

Savings, Interest Rates, and Investment

All markets, including financial markets, function to create an efficient allocation of resources. In the financial market, the supply and demand of money is often tied to the loanable funds available to those who are willing to transact at the market price. The market price of loanable funds is the interest rate. The interest rate is determined by the Fed. The supply of loanable funds comes from savings. Savings represents the dollar amount of the postponed spending of business and individuals. In order to save, people must have some incentive to postpone their spending and save money. The incentive to save money comes in the form of an interest rate. The higher the interest rate, the more money people are willing to save and the more money that is available to be loaned. The lower the interest rate, the less incentive people have to save and the less loanable funds that are available. The interest rate represents an **opportunity cost**. At higher interest rates, the opportunity cost of not saving is higher than at lower interest rates. As such, the supply of loanable funds is an upward sloping curve.

The funds created from savings are needed for individuals and businesses to invest in the production of goods and services. Oftentimes individuals and businesses do not have the liquid funds available to invest, thus they must borrow funds. In order to borrow funds, investors must pay a price for what they borrow. This price is the interest rate. The lower the interest rate, the more money people are willing to borrow. This means that the demand for loanable funds is a downward sloping curve.

Investment is an important component of GDP. For economies to grow, individuals and businesses have to be willing to invest funds. Economies with higher rates of savings have higher rates of investment and therefore higher growth rates. When individuals save money, they free up resources for things such as investment, which leads to economic growth. Economies with lower investment rates have lower growth rates because there are fewer funds for investment and growth purposes.

Inflation and Deflation

Inflation reduces the purchasing power of money, which technically affects the value of the currency. Countries generally devalue their currency to keep up with inflation. Deflation is the opposite of inflation: the purchasing power of money increases, thereby lowering the prices of goods and services. In a period of deflation, consumers benefit but industry suffers. The Federal Reserve controls the flow of money and seeks to keep a healthy balance between inflation and deflation.

Economic Indicators

The health of an economy is determined by assessing indicators. An indicator is a statistic used to evaluate the strength of an economy to make economic predictions about the country or state. For example, a country's gross national product (GNP) or gross domestic product (GDP) explains the monetary value of the goods and services produced by a given country. (GDP is the value of goods and services produced within the geographic boundaries of a country in a year. GNP is a similar measure, but is an estimate that also includes goods and services by calculating the sum of its residents' personal consumption expenditures and investment income within and beyond the geographic boundaries of a country.) Other indicators may include unemployment, number of doctors, life expectancy, number of imports and exports, inflation and deflation.

Economic indicators reveal what is happening in the economy, including how well or poorly it is performing. Most measures of economic output are expressed in terms of dollars. However, the purchasing power of the dollar often changes due to inflation and economic growth. Thus, when comparing figures like GDP over time, there are fluctuations from year to year. To determine if these fluctuations are actual differences in output or if they are due to inflation or price changes, we must adjust for these possibilities in our calculation. To do so, we use what is called the **price index**. The price index equals the price in any year divided by the price in a base year multiplied by 100. This means we must select one year to be the base year and use that in our calculations to construct the price index. The Consumer Price Index (CPI) is a specific price index that measures the average change over time in the prices paid by consumers for a market basket of predetermined goods and services.

Price Index = (Price in any year/price in base year) × 100

Once we have established a price index, we can then adjust for inflation and growth in our GDP comparisons. Real GDP is GDP adjusted for inflation. Nominal or unadjusted GDP is reported in current dollar figures and has not been adjusted for inflation. By adjusting for inflation and growth, we can make meaningful comparisons of GDP across time.

Real GDP = (Nominal GDP/Price Index)

Another critical economic metric is the inflation rate. The inflation rate shows the decrease in purchasing power of the dollar in relation to the rise in the general level of prices. Essentially, the inflation rate simply means we cannot buy as much as we did before.

Inflation Rate =
(current year price index – previous year's price index)/previous year's price index

The unemployment rate refers to the percentage of the labor force that is not working. It is calculating via the following method:

Unemployment Rate =
(Number of people unemployed/number of people in labor force) × 100

The labor force only includes those people who are capable of working, are willing to work, and are working or actively seeking work. In the United States, the labor force is roughly one-half of the population.

Real GDP, inflation, and unemployment figures provide important information about the state of the economy. An economy in recession needs to be stimulated with expansionary monetary and fiscal (government policy over taxation and spending) policy and an economy that is expanding too rapidly with inflation needs to be slowed down with contractionary monetary and fiscal policy. Government official and economists use these figures to determine the best course of action to maintain the health of an economy.

Government Regulations and Taxation

City, state, and national governments regulate businesses to ensure safe, fair, and consistent practices as well as to create a framework for standardizing production of certain products. Taxes support regulations by providing the money to pay people to inspect products and practices as well as to enforce sanctions. Regulations are important to build consumer trust. For example, children's toys are not allowed to use lead-based paint because a child may put a toy in his or her mouth and become sick. Taxes pay for inspectors to monitor toy manufacturers as well as the people who take these cases to court. Buildings are also examined during construction to check that the frame and materials are up to code. When businesses fail to comply with regulations, the owners are fined or in some cases put in jail. However, if the regulations are viewed as burdensome to businesses, it can be said that the regulations will negatively affect business development or be too great of a tax burden for the community. A careful balance must be struck between providing a safe, consistent product and being too restrictive and thereby hindering businesses.

American Federal Income Tax System

In 1913, the 16th Amendment to the U.S. Constitution allowed the imposition of direct taxation of citizens. This direct taxation is known as the **federal income tax**. Federal income tax dollars are used to fund various government agencies and projects.

Major Events and Trends of State, National, and World Economies

It is important to understand the major events and trends that have shaped economic history. These events and trends helped create and shape the economic system of Texas, the United States, and the world.

Agricultural Revolution

The invention of the plow around 3500 BCE set in motion a significant transformation in the way people lived, and led to the agricultural revolution. The plow made mass agriculture possible and facilitated the development of agrarian societies. In addition to the plow, the invention of the wheel and formalized writing structures helped shift hunter/gatherer societies toward more agricultural societies that were self-sustaining.

The continued advances in agricultural technology led to the ability of societies to produce surplus goods. The surplus of goods created a trade market in which people trading their surpluses for other desired goods. As such, traders and trade routes developed between different communities and villages. Protecting these surplus goods became a prime concern of societies and led to the construction of fortified communities.

Economic History of the United States

Industrial Revolution

The industrial revolution of the 18th and 19th centuries led to even greater changes in human societies and increased opportunities for trade, production, and the exchange of goods and ideas. The first phase of the industrial revolution (1750–1830) included improvements in mining, the invention of the steam engine, improvements in transportation including canals and railroads, and the mechanization of the textile industry. The second phase of the industrial revolution (1830–1910) resulted in improvement in the mechanization of a variety of industries. Important innovations of this time period included the Bessemer steel process, the steamship, electricity, photography, hydroelectric power, and petroleum engineering. It was during this phase of the industrial revolution that these ideas and inventions spread to the United States.

The industrial revolution led to some major economic shifts including: an increase in productivity, specialization and division of labor, increase in global trade, mass production, growth in large corporations and monopolies. During this time, ideas and knowledge spread rapidly with the increase in mobility. Additionally, immigration to industrialized countries also increased. As immigration increased, so did the clashing and blending of cultures. In the United States, as the economy grew and developed, people began spreading north, south, and westward. Each of these regions developed unique economic systems. The southern states had economies based primarily on agriculture, plantations, and slave labor. The North developed into a primarily industrial economy.

The Roaring Twenties Give Way to the Great Depression

Prior to World War I, the United States remained fairly isolationist with few trade partners. Following the war, international trade became an increasingly common reality for the United States. After the war, the U.S. economy of the "Roaring Twenties" saw huge increases in mass production. Manufacturing output doubled during this period from 1918–1929. The building and loan sector also saw a huge boom. The stock market was booming, with investors buying and selling with borrowed money, or, on margin. Unfortunately, when stock prices fell in 1929, many speculators could not meet their margin demands and this shortfall eventually led to the Great Depression.

The Great Depression (1929 to about 1939) had devastating effects in virtually every country. Personal income, tax revenue, profits and prices dropped, while international trade plunged by more than 50 percent. Unemployment in the United States rose to 25 percent, and in some countries went as high as 33 percent. Cities around the world were hit hard, especially those dependent on industry. Construction was virtually halted in many countries. Farming and rural areas suffered as crop prices fell by approximately 60 percent.

World War II (1939–1945)

As America prepared to enter World War II, the nation's wartime efforts demanded the production of various wartime goods and services. This demand for increased production also led to increased employment opportunities. World War II drove a dramatic increase in GDP, the export of vast quantities of supplies to the Allies and to American forces overseas, the end of unemployment, and a rise in civilian consumption even as 40 percent of the GDP went to the war effort. This was achieved by workers moving from low-productivity occupations to high-efficiency jobs, improvements in productivity through better technology and management, by students, retired people, housewives, and the unemployed moving into the active labor force, and an increase in hours worked. FDR's New Deal relief programs helped stabilize the economy. Most durable goods became unavailable, and meat, clothing, and gasoline were tightly rationed. In addition, prices and wages were controlled, and individual savings eventually increased as the war effort kicked manufactoring into high gear.

Economy in the New Millennium

Although there was a recession and high oil prices in the 1990s, Americans were generally optimistic due to the rise of technology and Internet companies, referred to as the "dot-com boom." During this time, China bought a number of U.S. bonds—in effect, becoming a banker to the United States. The U.S. consumer-driven economy came to rely more on cheap China goods. Inflation, interest rates, and wage costs were artificially low, setting the stage for the recession in the early 2000s. As investments in technology slowed and interest rates increased, the economy began to slow with business failures and unemployment increasing. Unregulated lending practices and housing loans with adjustable-rate mortgages, created a housing bubble that made the economy seem stronger than it was. The housing market faltered, leading to a credit crisis. The U.S. government bailed out some banks to lessen the negative impact on the economy. Many Americans lost their homes to foreclosures, with poor minorities the hardest hit. Inheriting the economic crisis, President Obama's administration worked with Congress to commit millions in bailout money. Banks' lending practices were more closely regulated with stricter policies. The stimulus legislation, such as the American Recovery and Reinvestment Act of 2009, was controversial, but welcomed by many who sought relief. One concern was the increase in U.S. government debt, which rose to a new high of $11 trillion in 2009. Meanwhile, President Obama and Congress worked to curb rising unemployment. By the end of the Obama administration, unemployment had lessened and the housing market had stabilized. For more information regarding the U.S. economy, visit *http://www.america.gov* and *https://www.learner.org/series/econusa/Interactivelabs/economic-timeline*.

The Texas Economy

Texas continues to play a unique role in the U.S. economy and in the world. Texas interacts with other states and the national government through trade and commerce. Cattle, livestock, and agriculture were important factors in the development of the Texas economy. As railroads and cities developed, the Texas economy continued to expand. Dallas became a trading post for grain and cotton. Houston's port location was at the heart of the sugar trade and later the oil industry. In 1901, the discovery of oil at Spindletop also led to increased economic production in Texas as it became the leading producer of oil in the U.S. In the 1940s, the Texas economy continued to grow as major corporations relocated to Texas providing more jobs.

Today, the Texas economy is still highly bound up in agricultural and serves as the leading exporter of cattle and cotton in the U.S. High-tech industries, defense contracting, telecommunications, biotechnology, oil, and tourism are also important economic activities in Texas. A large percentage of these products are exported to NAFTA members—Mexico and Canada—and to world markets. The Texas economy relies heavily on exports of goods and services. From 2002 through 2005, Texas was ranked as the No. 1 state in terms of export revenues (BIDC, 2006). Without its exports, the Texas economy could not sustain its growth. Because of the interdependence of state and global economies, political turmoil and economic problems in the world can have a direct impact on the Texas economy. For example, because part of the economy of Texas is based on petroleum, the decisions of OPEC have a direct impact on the state's economy. The Texas economy weathered the Great Recession of 2008–2009 better than most states, but the unemployment rate in the state continued to climb even after the recession ended. In 2011, the jobless rate stood at almost 8.5 percent. Later, nonfarm employment found its footing again. With more factories and other businesses moving to the state, the housing market improved, especially in urban markets like the Dallas-Fort Worth area. In 2017, the unemployment rate stood at 4.8 percent, about half a percentage point higher than the national average.

COMPETENCY 004: GOVERNMENT AND CITIZENSHIP

The teacher understands and applies knowledge of government, democracy, and citizenship, including ways in which individuals and groups achieve their goals through political systems, as defined by the Texas Essential Knowledge and Skills (TEKS).

The beginning teacher:

A. Demonstrates knowledge of the historical origins of democratic forms of government, such as ancient Greece.

B. Understands the purpose of rules and laws; the relationship between rules, rights and responsibilities; and the individual's role in making and enforcing rules and ensuring the welfare of society.

C. Knows the basic structure and functions of the U.S. government, the Texas government and local governments (including the roles of public officials) and relationships among national, state and local governments.

D. Demonstrates knowledge of key principles and ideas in major political documents of Texas and the United States (e.g., Articles of Confederation, Declaration of Independence, U.S. Constitution, Bill of Rights, Texas Constitution) and relationships among political documents.

E. Understands early United States political issues, including those surrounding Alexander Hamilton, Patrick Henry, James Madison, George Mason; the arguments of the Federalists and Anti-Federalists; states' rights issues; and the nullification crisis.

F. Knows how American Indian groups and settlers organized governments in precolonial America, and during the early development of Texas and North America.

G. Demonstrates knowledge of how state and local governments use sources of revenue such as property tax and sales tax, and the funding of Texas public education.

H. Demonstrates knowledge of types of government (e.g., constitutional, totalitarian), their effectiveness in meeting citizens' needs and the reasons for limiting the power of government.

I. Knows the formal and informal process of changing the U.S. and Texas constitutions and the impact of constitutional changes on society.

J. Understands the impact of landmark Supreme Court cases (e.g., *Marbury v. Madison*, *Dred Scott v. Sandford*, *McCulloch v. Maryland*, *Gibbons v. Ogden*).

K. Understands components of the democratic process (e.g., voting, contacting local and state representatives, voluntary individual participation, effective leadership, expression of different points of view) and their significance in a democratic society.

L. Demonstrates knowledge of important customs, symbols, landmarks and celebrations that represent American and Texan beliefs and principles and that contribute to national unity (e.g., Uncle Sam, "The Star-Spangled Banner," the San Jacinto Monument, "Texas, our Texas").

M. Demonstrates knowledge of the importance, accomplishments and leadership qualities of United States and Texas leaders (e.g., presidents Washington, Adams, Jefferson, Madison, Monroe, Lincoln; U.S. senators Calhoun, Webster, Clay; Texas governors and local Texas representatives).

N. Analyzes the relationship among individual rights, responsibilities and freedoms in democratic societies.

O. Applies knowledge of the nature, rights and responsibilities of citizens in Texas, the United States, and various societies, past and present.

P. Understands the contributions and importance of political figures, members of Congress, military leaders and social reformers who modeled active participation in the democratic process in Texas and in the United States (e.g., Frederick Douglass, Susan B. Anthony, Sam Houston, Barbara Jordan, Henry B. González, Kay Bailey Hutchinson, Audie Murphy, William Carney, Philip Bazaar).

Forms of Government

Forms of government or political systems can be defined by the way nations govern themselves. The U.S. Department of State identifies 26 forms of governments in the world (CIA, n.d.). Three of the most common forms of government are democracy, monarchy, and totalitarian. A description of these types of government follows:

- **Democracy** is a form of government in which the majority rules. The government's power is limited, meaning that a constitution, or agreement with the people, delineates the authority that the government is allowed. Citizens in this government enjoy an abundance of civil liberties. In the United States, these civil liberties are unique because they are called "inalienable rights," meaning that they cannot be ever taken away from the citizens by the government or any other entity. Though rare, pure democracies, a form of government in which each individual votes on all decisions, exist in some places. In the United States, pure democracies are still used in some town hall meetings, where people meet to make decisions for their municipality. In practice, it becomes a representative democracy, in which the people elect candidates to represent them in the government. Democratic governments typically have either free enterprise or socialist economies.

- **Monarchy** is a system in which a king or queen leads the nation. The monarch gains power by inheriting it from his or her parents. The monarch can have supreme powers and control the entire government, or he or she can have limited or ceremonial powers circumscribed by a parliament or a constitution, as in a constitutional monarchy.

- **Totalitarian** is a form of government in which one person or a few people have all of the governing power and authority. The central government controls nearly all aspects of its citizens' political, social, cultural, and economic lives, including education, employment, housing, reproduction, and movement. This form of government typically has either a communist or socialist economic system. Additionally, citizens have few individual rights, while the government has unlimited rights. It can also be in the form of an oligarchy. Incidences of human rights violations, or abuses, are typically more frequent under this government. **Note:** Sometimes a totalitarian government is referred to as a communist government or a communist state. This means it is a country in which the state (government) controls the economic activity in the nation. The state rejects free enterprise; consequently, private ownership is discouraged and often prohibited. (See Economics section for more about communism.)

There are three broad classifications or forms of government based on the number of people in power—government by one person, a group, or by many people, and vary regarding the degree of limitations and freedom citizens experience.

Rule by One

In this form of government, one person becomes the supreme leader of the nation. Some of the terminology and concepts linked to this type of government are:

- **Autocracy:** Ruler has unlimited power, uses power in an arbitrary manner.

- **Monarchy:** A system in which a king or queen leads the nation. The monarch can have supreme powers and hold complete control over the subjects. Typically, the ruler is determined by birth or divine rights. Titles of monarchs may be King/Queen, Emperor/Empress, Tsar/Tsarina, etc. (For monarchs who have limited or ceremonial powers determined by a parliament or a constitution, see the section below titled "Ruled by Many, Parliamentarian Monarchy.")

- **Dictatorship:** The ruler holds absolute power to make laws and to command the army.

Ruled by a Few

In this system, a group of influential people takes control of the government. Traditionally, they appoint one of their own to function as the supreme leader of the government. Some examples of this type of government are:

- **Theocracy:** Ruled by a group of religious leaders, e.g., the Islamic Republic in Iran, or, the Taliban in Afghanistan.

- **Aristocracy:** A group of nobles controls the economy and the government.

- **Oligarchy:** A small group of people controls the government. Generally, power rests with an elite class distinguished by royalty, wealth, family ties, commercial, and/or military legitimacy.

- **Military:** A committee of military officers or a junta becomes the rulers of the nation.

Rule by Many

In this government, the citizens technically are the government because they make the decisions for the community being governed (e.g., cultural group, town, state, or nation). This is called a democracy. In its purest form, each person participates in voting on each decision made for the community. In practice, the citizens elect members to represent them and elected officials become the government. This is called a representative democracy. Today, most democracies are also a constitutional democracy, meaning that they are regulated by a constitution. Examples of representative governments include constitutional democracy and parliamentarian (or constitutional) monarchy.

The historical origins of democratic governance can be found in Ancient Greece where the cultures participated in pure and representational democracy and developed a court system with a jury. More information about Ancient Greece and the roots of democracy can be found online at *http://www.history.com/topics/ancient-history/ancient-greece-democracy*.

Some examples of this type of government are:

- **Democracy:** A form of government in which the majority rules. The citizens of the nation directly or through elected members make important decisions, and become part of the government. In practice, it becomes a representative democracy, in which the people elect candidates to represent them in the government.

- **Republic:** A representative democracy is led by someone who is not a monarch, such as a president. Example: the United States of America.

- **Constitutional Democracy:** It is a democratic form of government regulated by a constitution.

- **Parliamentarian Monarchy:** The monarch shares the power with the parliament. Often, the powers of the monarch are ceremonial in nature, like in the United Kingdom. This government is also referred to as a "constitutional monarchy" because the monarch's power is limited by the constitution for the given country.

- **Federal Republic:** A constitutional government in which the powers of the central government are restricted to create semi-autonomous bodies (states or provinces) with certain degrees of self-governing powers, e.g., the United States.

Government Power Structure

The structure of the governmental power can be designed so that either almost all of the decision-making capabilities are held within the centralized government (unitary government), such as the United Kingdom, or the power is shared between the central and local governing bodies (federal government), such as the United States.

The American Government

The governmental system of the United States has been identified as a federal republic and a constitutional representative democracy. It is a federal republic because the U.S. government is limited by law; in this case, the government is limited by the Constitution. It is a constitutional representative democracy because the citizens elect members of Congress to represent them in the bicameral (two house) system. (Senators are elected to the Senate. Representatives are elected to the House of Representatives. Both houses, together, are referred to as Congress.) This combination is referred to as a Constitutional Republic in the revised social studies TEKS.

The American democratic system is based on popular sovereignty. **Popular sovereignty** grants citizens the ability to participate directly in their own government by voting and running for public office. This ideal is based on the notion that all citizens have equal rights to engage in their own governance. Certainly, over time, this notion of equal rights has expanded to include a respect for minority rights, including women and ethnic minority citizens.

The American government is also based on majority rule. In public elections, the candidate who receives the most votes wins; in Congress, legislation is decided based on how the majority of the body votes. Majority rule ensures that authority cannot be concentrated in a small group of people. This majority rule system also shapes the two-party system of the U.S. government. There are two major political parties in the U.S.: the Republican and Democratic parties.

The Constitution is the supreme law of the nation. It contains a description of the government and the rights and responsibilities of its citizens. The document can be amended with the approval of two-thirds of the House and the Senate and the ratification of individual state legislatures. Amendments to the U.S. Constitution have made it more democratic than the original document.

Effective leadership in a constitutional republic is critical for the success of the country. The leader must collaborate with opposing parties to make the best possible decisions for the nation. The following links list U.S. presidents and Texas governors and describes their term in office *http://www.whitehouse.gov/about/presidents* and *https://www.tsl.texas.gov/ref/abouttx/governors*. Students can look up their members of Congress at *https://www.govtrack.us/congress/members*. To develop a better understanding of effective leadership, teachers can ask students to compare and contrast leaders, the decisions they made, and the long-term impact of those decisions.

The U.S. Constitution

The Constitution is the supreme law of the nation. It contains a description of the government and the rights and responsibilities of its citizens. The document can be amended with the approval of two-thirds of the House and the Senate and the ratification of three-fourths of the individual state legislatures. Amendments to the U.S. Constitution have made it more democratic than the original document. The first ten amendments to the Constitution are known as the Bill of Rights. For more on the Constitution go to *https://www.archives.gov/founding-docs/constitution*.

The U.S. Constitution was based on four fundamental principles, which are listed below.

1. *Federalism:* This is a system in which government powers are divided between the national and state governments. This established four types of governmental powers: 1) delegated or expressed—those directly listed; 2) implied powers—those not stated directly but suggested; 3) reserved powers—those not given to the national government but reserved for the people or for the states; and 4) concurrent powers—given to both national and state governments at the same time.

2. *Separation of Powers:* This constitutional principle is based on a system of checks and balances. The constitutional writers wanted to protect their new nation from tyranny or the possibility of one branch of government becoming more powerful and influential than another. Thus, they created a three-branch system of separation of powers and checks and balances.

3. *Protection of individual rights and liberties:* These provisions of the Constitution include: the prohibition of "ex post facto laws," or laws passed after the crime was committed, providing the penalty for an act that was not illegal at the time it was committed and "bills of attainder," or laws that mete out punishment to someone without a court trial first. Individual rights are protected through the "writ of habeas corpus" that required persons be released from jail if they had not been formally charged or convicted of a crime. The Bill of Rights also guarantees protection of individuals against federal action that would threaten their life, liberty, or property without proper legal proceedings.

4. *Adaptation to changing times and circumstances:* This allows governing bodies to meet the needs of changing times through the process of amendments. The necessary and proper or elastic clause also provides Congress the power to make additional laws needed to implement other powers.

In the United States, the national government makes decisions for the benefit of the country as a whole (e.g., laws, coin money, regulate trade and commerce, protection of rights, foreign affairs, declaration of war, banking regulations, education, taxation, postal services, etc.). Each state government makes decisions pertaining to the people and businesses within its borders. These include elections, business regulations, education, taxation, transportation and communication, and so on. The national, or federal, government's powers are delineated in the U.S. Constitution. All powers not mentioned belong to the states. Local governments provide direct governance of the people in an immediate area. Many duties of local government mirror those of the state (taxation, communication, transportation, business regulation, etc.) on a smaller scale. State legislatures determine local governments' power. The official White House website (*http://www.whitehouse.gov/our-government/executive-branch*) provides more details about the federal government. Government responsibilities and programs are largely funded by taxes. All Americans contribute a portion of their paycheck to the federal income tax. Each state decides whether to allow state and local taxes. Texas has no state and local taxes. Governments can also issue bonds, which are a mechanism to allow the government to borrow money from its citizens or from other countries. According to the U.S. Department of the Treasury, the U.S. outstanding debt was $20,493,344,333,189.55 (approximately $20.49 trillion) as of January 29, 2018, as stated on the website *https://www.treasurydirect.gov/NP/debt/current*.

Federalism: Power Sharing Between State and Federal Governments

One of the most significant principles of the U.S. Constitution is the concept of power sharing between the federal and state governments. Some of the powers reserved to the federal and state governments follow.

Powers Reserved for the Federal Government

- Regulate interstate and foreign commerce

- Print money and regulate its value

- Establish laws for regulation of immigration and naturalization

- Regulate admission of new states

- Declare war and ratify peace treaties

- Establish a system of weights and measures

- Raise and maintain armed forces

- Conduct relations with foreign nations

Powers Reserved for State Governments

- Conduct and monitor local, state, and federal elections

- Provide for local government

- Ratify proposed amendments to the Constitution

- Regulate intrastate commerce

- Provide education for its citizens

- Establish direct taxes like sales and state taxes

- Regulate and maintain police power over public health and safety

- Maintain control of state borders

Concurrent Powers of Federal and State Governments

- Both may tax

- Both may borrow money

- Both may charter banks and corporations

- Both may establish courts

- Both may make and enforce laws

- Both may take property for public purposes

- Both may spend money to provide for public welfare

In addition to the powers reserved to the states, the Tenth Amendment to the U.S. Constitution provides additional powers to the state. In this amendment, the powers not specifically delegated to the federal government are reserved for the states.

Separation of Powers: Branches of Government

The U.S. Constitution set up a federal system of government, dividing up power between the state and national governments. The national government is further balanced through the three branches of government that provide checks and balances on each other's power. The three branches of government are the executive, legislative, and judicial branches. To learn more, go to *https://www.usa.gov/branches-of-government*. Each of the branches is described in more detail below.

Executive Branch

The executive branch of the U.S. government is composed of a president and a vice president elected every four years by electoral votes. The president can be elected for a maximum of two terms. The president is the commander-in-chief of the armed forces. He or she appoints cabinet members, nominates judges to the federal court system, grants pardons, recommends legislation, and has the power to veto legislation. The president also appoints American representatives to carry out diplomatic relations in foreign lands and to serve in international organizations. The president also performs a variety of ceremonial duties.

Legislative Branch

The legislative branch is composed of the Congress, which is bicameral, or divided into two parts—the Senate and the House of Representatives. The Senate is composed of two senators from each state, for a total of a 100 members. Senators are elected for six-year terms. The composition of the House is based on the population of people in each state, for a total of 435 members, who each serve two-year terms. The Congress makes the laws of the nation, collects taxes, coins money and regulates its value, can declare war, controls appropriations, can impeach public officials, regulates the jurisdictions of federal courts, and can override presidential vetoes. The vice president presides over the Senate as its leader, while the Speaker of the House serves as the leader of the House of Representatives.

Judicial Branch

The judicial branch is composed of a federal court system that includes the Supreme Court and a system of lower courts—district courts, appeals courts, bankruptcy courts, and special federal courts. Federal judges are nominated by the president of the United States and confirmed by the Senate. All federal judges are appointed for life. The Supreme Court is composed of nine judges, and their ruling is considered final. Under a process called "judicial review" (set forth in *Marbury v. Madison*, 1803), the Supreme Court has the power to declare unconstitutional any executive orders or legislative acts of both the federal and state governments. Some of the major responsibilities of this body are to interpret the Constitution, resolve conflicts among states, and interpret laws and treaties.

System of Checks and Balances

The U.S. Constitution provides for a system of checks and balances among the three branches of the government. In this type of system, individual branches check the others to be sure that no one branch assumes full control of the central government. The legislative branch can check the executive branch by passing laws over presidential veto (by a two-thirds majority in both houses). This branch exerts control over the judicial branch by having to confirm the president's judicial appointments. The executive can check the legislative branch by the use of the veto and the judicial branch by appointing federal judges. The judicial branch can check the other two branches through the process of judicial review, which can declare legislation unconstitutional or illegal.

Protection of Individual Rights and Liberties: The Bill of Rights

After the U.S. Constitution was enacted in 1783, the founders felt that additional measures were necessary to preserve basic human rights. The first 10 amendments to the U.S. Constitution are called the **Bill of Rights**. A summary of those 10 amendments follows:

- *First Amendment*—separation of church and state; freedom of religion, speech and press; and the right to peaceful assembly

- *Second Amendment*—right to keep and bear arms

- *Third Amendment*—makes it illegal to force people to offer quarters to soldiers in time of peace

- *Fourth Amendment*—rights to privacy and unreasonable searches or seizures

- *Fifth Amendment*—rights of due process, protection against self-incrimination, and protection from being indicted for the same crime twice (double jeopardy)

- *Sixth Amendment*—rights to speedy public trial by an impartial jury and to counsel for one's defense

- *Seventh Amendment*—right to sue people

- *Eighth Amendment*—protection against cruel and unusual punishment

- *Ninth Amendment*—enumeration of specific rights in the Constitution cannot be taken as a way to deny other rights retained by the people

- *Tenth Amendment*—rights not delegated to the federal government by the Constitution are reserved to the states or to the people

Adapting to Change: The Amendment Process

When the Constitution was written, the writers knew their creation was not perfect. They knew that new ideas and changes would need to be considered. They wanted to make it possible to change the Constitution through a thoughtful and democratic process. Thus, the Constitution provides for an amendment process. An amendment to the Constitution is a change that can add to the Constitution or change a part of it. An amendment can even overturn a previous amendment, as the 21st Amendment overturned the 18th Amendment. There are several methods to amend the Constitution, but the most common is to pass an amendment through the Congress, on a two-thirds vote. After that, the amendment goes to the states; if three-quarters of the state legislatures pass the amendment, it has been ratified and is considered a part of the Constitution. To date, there are 27 amendments to the Constitution; the first 10 comprise the Bill of Rights.

Additional Key Amendments to the U.S. Constitution

- **13th Amendment**—Slavery abolished

- **14th Amendment**—Citizenship and rights: Citizenship to African-Americans including former slaves; reaffirmed privileges and rights for all citizens

- **15th Amendment**—Race, color, or previous servitude/No bar to vote: Right to vote for African American males

- **16th Amendment**—Ratified in 1913, it gives the federal government power to levy taxes

- **19th Amendment**—Women's suffrage (right to vote)

- **25th Amendment**—Presidential disability and succession

- **26th Amendment**—Voting age set to 18 years

For a detailed analysis of the U.S. Constitution and the 27 amendments, see the U.S. Constitution online at *http://www.usconstitution.net/const.html*.

Landmark Supreme Court Cases

Judicial Review Process—*Marbury v. Madison* (1803)

A dispute that occurred as the Thomas Jefferson administration came into power fundamentally altered the system of checks and balances of the American government. In this case, the judicial branch confirmed its power to review and assess the constitutionality of the legislation passed by Congress and signed by the president. This process is now called *judicial review*.

National Supremacy—*McCulloch v. Maryland* (1819)

A dispute occurred between the Bank of the United States and the State of Maryland in 1819. At that time, the United States still had a federal bank, the Bank of the United States (which has since died out). The State of Maryland voted to tax all bank business not done with state banks. This was meant to be a tax on people who lived in Maryland but did business with banks in other states, and with the federal bank. Andrew McCulloch, who worked in the Baltimore branch of the Bank of the United States, refused to pay the tax. The State of Maryland sued, and the Supreme Court accepted the case. Chief Justice Marshall wrote in his opinion that the federal government did indeed have the right and power to set up the federal bank. He wrote that the state did not have the power to tax the federal government.

Federal Regulation of Commerce—*Gibbons v. Ogden* (1824)

The New York Legislature in 1808 granted Robert Livingston and Robert Fulton a 20-year monopoly to operate steamboats in New York waters. In 1811, Fulton in turn granted Aaron Ogden a license to operate steamboats between New York and New Jersey. In 1818, the U.S. Congress, using the power given it by the commerce clause of Article I, Section 8 of the Constitution, granted Thomas Gibbons a license to engage in the coastal trade and operate steamboats between New York and New Jersey. Claiming that his monopoly rights were being violated, Ogden obtained an injunction from a New York court forbidding Gibbons from continuing to operate his steamboats in these U.S. Supreme Court. The majority opinion, written by Chief Justice Marshall, said that the U.S. Constitution had a commerce clause that allowed the federal government to regulate commerce, in this case trade, wherever it might be, including within the borders of a state. Previously, it was thought that the federal government had power over only *interstate commerce*. However, Marshall's opinion said that the commerce clause applied here, too. Thus, the Supreme Court extended the definition of interstate commerce and cemented the power of the federal government over the states when laws conflicted.

Federal vs. States Rights in Indian Affairs—*Worcester v. Georgia* (1832)

In December 1829, President Andrew Jackson announced his Indian removal proposal in an address to the U.S. Congress. In 1830, the Congress passed the Indian Removal Act, which authorized the president to grant the Indians unsettled lands west of the Mississippi River in exchange for Indian lands within existing state borders. The Georgia legislature had passed a law requiring anyone other than Cherokees who lived on Indian territory to obtain a license from the state. Samuel Worcester and several other non-Cherokee Congregational missionaries settled and established a mission on Cherokee land at the request of the Cherokees, and with permission of the United States government. The state of Georgia charged them with residing within the limits of the Cherokee nation without a license. They were tried, convicted, and sentenced to four years of hard labor. Worcester and the other missionaries appealed their convictions to the U.S. Supreme Court. The Supreme Court ruled in favor of Worcester and the Cherokees arguing that the Cherokee nation was a "distinct community" with self-government "in which the laws of Georgia can have no force." It established the doctrine that the national government of the United States, and not individual states, had authority in American Indian affairs.

Slavery/Due Process—*Dred Scott v. Sandford* (1857)

Dred Scott, a slave in Virginia, was moved by his owner to Illinois, a non-slave (free) state. In 1836, they moved to Minnesota, which was part of the non-slave Wisconsin territory, before being moved to Missouri. Then, Dred Scott sued his owners, claiming that he was no longer a slave because he had become free when he lived in a free state. The jury decided that Scott and his family should be free. His owners did not like the decision and appealed to the Missouri Supreme Court in 1852. That court said that Missouri does not have to follow the laws of another state. As a slave state, Missouri's laws meant that Scott and his family were not free. Scott finally took his case to the U.S. Supreme Court, which ruled that Scott and all other slaves were not state or U.S. citizens, and thus had no rights. A slave was considered property, not a person or a citizen. Thus, Scott or any other slave, had no right to sue in state or federal court. Further, the court ruled that the federal government had no legal right to interfere with the institution of slavery.

Separate but Equal—*Plessy v. Ferguson* (1896)

In 1890, Louisiana passed a law called the Separate Car Act. This law said that railroad companies must provide separate but equal train cars for whites and blacks. Two parties wanted to challenge the constitutionality of the Separate Car Act. A group of black citizens who raised money to overturn the law worked together with the East Louisiana Railroad Company, which sought to terminate the law largely for monetary reasons. They chose a 30-year-old shoemaker named Homer Plessy, a citizen of the United States who was one-eighth black and a resident of the state of Louisiana. On June 7, 1892, Plessy purchased a first-class passage from New Orleans to Covington, Louisiana, and sat in the railroad car for white passengers. The railroad officials knew Plessy was coming and arrested him for violating the Separate Car Act. Plessy argued in court that the Separate Car Act violated the 13th and 14th Amendments to the Constitution. The 13th Amendment banned slavery and the 14th Amendment requires that the government treat people equally. After both a lower court and the Supreme Court of Louisiana found Plessy guilty, he took his case to the Supreme Court of the United States. The high court upheld the decisions of the two lower courts, arguing that separate but equal practices were constitutional. This decision legitimized the move towards segregation practices begun earlier in the South and provided an impetus for further segregation laws.

Desegregation—*Brown v. Board of Education of Topeka* (1954)

In the early 1950s, many students went to different schools based on their race. Many other public facilities were also segregated. Segregation was legal because of the *Plessy v. Ferguson* case. Under segregation, all-white and all-black schools sometimes had similar buildings, buses, and teachers. Sometimes, the buildings, busses, and teachers for the all-black schools were lower in quality. Often, black children had to travel far to get to their school. In Topeka, Kansas, a black student named Linda Brown had to walk through a dangerous railroad switching station to get to her all-black school. Her family believed that segregated schools should be illegal. The Brown family sued the school system (Board of Education of Topeka). After losing their cases in two lower courts, the Browns took their case to the U.S. Supreme Court, which unanimously ruled that "separate educational facilities are inherently unequal." This case paved the way for integration and the civil rights movement.

Local and State Governments

Most states in the United States follow the type of government established for the federal government in the U.S. Constitution. State governments generally have three branches—executive, legislative, and judicial. The main difference is that the executive branch is led by a governor and the judicial branch is composed of a state court system subordinate to the federal court system. The city government is generally headed by a mayor or city manager with the support of a city council.

Citizenship in the U.S.

Citizenship is membership in a political state such as a country or state. Citizenship confers the right to participate politically in a society. Anyone born in the United States is a U.S. citizen, regardless of the nationality or citizenship of his or her parents. Additionally, children who are born on foreign soil, but whose parents are U.S. citizens, are also citizens of the United States.

Citizenship in the United States provides individuals with certain rights, including the right to life, liberty, and the pursuit of property. Along with rights, however, come specific responsibilities. In the United States, citizens have the right to vote at the age of 18. With this right comes the responsibility to be an informed voter who makes wise decisions. Citizens of the U.S. are also eligible to run for public office. With this right comes the responsibility of representing one's constituents as well as possible. The right to free speech is also given to citizens of the United States. This means that citizens also have the responsibility to allow others to speak freely. Additionally, the U.S. Constitution guarantees freedom of religion. This means that citizens have both the right to choose their religious affiliation and the responsibility to allow others to practice their religion. Being a good citizen means exercising one's own rights, meeting one's responsibilities, and allowing others to do the same.

Citizenship rights and responsibilities in Texas and the United States include obeying local, state, and national laws; paying taxes; and voting in elections. Good citizens should also develop a respect that recognizes and values the feelings, interests, beliefs, and values of others. While citizenship involves being respectful of one another and obeying the laws of the land, it does not mean that we need to teach students to simply comply and conform. Dissent is an important part in any governmental system and provides necessary checks and balances on governmental authority. Dissent may be expressed in a number of ways, including voting, protesting, writing to one's legislator, etc. Certainly, there are some forms of dissent that are more socially and politically acceptable.

The development of civic ideas and practices is a lifelong process that begins in school by observing patriotic holidays, learning about the contribution of historical characters, and pledging allegiance to the American and Texas flags each day, unless excused. Students should develop foundational knowledge about what each pledge means, as well as the history of their development and why the pledges are important to American citizens. In this way, saying the pledge will be meaningful rather than rote memorization and recitation of words that students do not understand. In lower elementary, encouraging good citizenship continues with the introduction of the American anthem and the mottoes of Texas and the United States, which should be reinforced in later grades as well. Civic education and the principles of democracy are infused through active participation in community activities. To promote civic responsibility, students can get involved in discussions about issues that affect the community. Teachers guide students to suggest possible solutions to community problems, while students are guided to listen and analyze contributions.

Through this exchange, students are guided to practice principles of democracy and to value individual contributions to solve community problems.

Children in these grade levels should be developing **civic responsibility**. Teachers can promote this sense of responsibility by involving students in real-life situations in which they take civic responsibility. For example, teachers can make children aware of how producing trash can affect the environment. As part of this process, students can be guided to examine the amount of trash that they produce daily and explore ways to reduce it. Promoting a sense of responsibility for the well-being of everyone constitutes the main principle for developing responsible citizenship.

Additionally, students should define "civic responsibility" (referred to in early grades as a "good citizen") and connect their definition with historical and contemporary examples from the community, state, and nation. Americans value such things as recognizing social responsibilities; helping each other; making sure everyone has food, shelter, and clothing; caring for the elderly; keeping the land clean; using things wisely; caring for others; being patriotic; respecting our men and women in uniform (e.g., military, police, firefighters); respecting our state and country flags and what they symbolize; and so on. Teachers can invite speakers from such organizations as food pantries, the Red Cross, Boy Scouts, Girl Scouts, and Meals on Wheels to show examples of good citizenship. Interdisciplinary service learning can be developed to help students explore this topic in-depth. Students can investigate ways that good citizens keep the land clean via recycling as well as with larger projects. For example, Chad Pregracke as a teenager was concerned about the trash in the Mississippi River. Realizing no one else was going to clean up the river, he began to fill his little boat with trash and haul it away. He developed an organization that now has over 70,000 volunteers who work to clean the rivers. (For more information, see *http://livinglandsandwaters.org/*.) Inspiring stories help students realize they can be good citizens as well. Clara Harlowe Barton was a teacher who risked her life to help soldiers during the Civil War. She later founded the American Red Cross. Teachers should help students recognize the values that made these people good citizens and show students how they can also be good citizens. (For more information go to *http://www.redcross.org/about-us/history/clara-barton.*)

In grades K–6, students should learn the meaning and importance of national holidays. Holidays with historic significance include Memorial Day, Labor Day, Columbus Day, Independence Day, Veterans Day, and Martin Luther King Jr. Day. Memorial Day honors members of the military who died in war. Labor Day recognizes the importance of workers and labor unions. Columbus Day commemorates the arrival of Christopher Columbus to the Americas. Independence Day commemorates the adoption of the Declaration of Independence. Often it is referred to as the "4th of July"; however, sometimes its purpose can be lost. By referring to it as "Independence Day," teachers can remind students of its meaning and historic importance. Martin Luther King Jr. Day honors the leader of the civil rights movement. Veterans Day celebrates those who have served in the country's armed forces.

American Symbols

American Patriotic Symbols

Patriotic symbols are visible signs of national pride. The U.S. National Flag, the Pledge of Allegiance, the Statue of Liberty, the Liberty Bell, and the White House are important examples of patriotic symbols for Americans.

The United States of America National Flag has 50 stars representing the 50 states of the Union. The color red represents hardiness and valor; the white symbolizes purity and innocence; and the blue symbolizes vigilance, perseverance, and justice. Congress approved a new flag with 13 red and white alternating horizontal stripes and 13 stars representing the original colonies in 1777. A star and stripe were added to the flag each time a state entered the union. Congress set the number of stripes at 13 in 1818 and decided to add one star for each new state. In Texas, the state flag is a symbol of state pride. It can fly equal to or below the United States flag because it was a sovereign nation when it entered the United States of America. Many Texans fly both flags as a symbol of their American patriotism.

The U.S. Pledge of Allegiance is a declaration of patriotism. First published in 1892 in *The Youth's Companion*, it was believed to have been written by the magazine's editor, Francis Bellamy. The original purpose for the pledge was as an activity by schoolchildren to celebrate the 400th anniversary of the discovery of America. The Pledge was widely used in morning school routines for many years and received official recognition by Congress on 1942. The phrase "under God" was added in 1954, along with a law indicating the proper behavior to adopt when reciting the pledge, which includes standing straight, removing hats or any other headgear, and placing the right hand over the heart.

The Star-Spangled Banner is the national anthem of the United States. It was originally a poem written by Francis Scott Key during the Battle of Baltimore in the War of 1812 against the British. In 1931, it was made the official national anthem of the United States.

The Statue of Liberty was a gift of friendship from the people of France to the people of the United States commemorating the 100th anniversary of the United States. It is a universal symbol of freedom, democracy, and international friendship.

The Liberty Bell is a symbol of freedom and liberty. The Pennsylvania Assembly ordered the Liberty Bell to commemorate the 50th anniversary of Pennsylvania's original constitution, the William Penn's Charter of Privileges. It is traditionally believed that it was rung to summon the people of Philadelphia to hear the Declaration of Independence. It became an icon when the abolitionists adopted it as a symbol of freedom. The abolitionists changed its name from The State House Bell to the Liberty Bell.

The White House was originally planned by President George Washington in 1791 and was completed in 1800 when its first resident, President John Adams, moved in with his wife, Abigail. It was originally called the President's House. President Theodore Roosevelt christened it The White House in 1901. For more than 200 years, it has been the home of U.S. presidents and their families. It is recognized as a symbol of the Presidency of the United States throughout the world.

The Great Seal of the United States consists of a bald eagle holding an olive branch and a bundle of arrows. The olive branch represents peace and the arrows represent military strength. The eagle holds a scroll in its beak with the nation's original motto, "E Pluribus Unum," which means "from many, one."

For additional information about symbols of the United States, see *http://www.ushistory.org.*, a website created and hosted by the Independence Hall Association in Philadelphia.

Texan Symbols

Texas Patriotic Symbols

Patriotic symbols are also signs of state pride. The Texas Flag, the Texas Pledge of Allegiance, bluebonnets, longhorns, oil rigs, and the state capitol are important symbols of Texas state pride. Such places such as King's Ranch, the Alamo, cattle trails, the Capitol, Gruene Hall, and the San Jacinto battlegrounds are examples of landmarks that are meaningful symbols. For additional information about symbols of Texas, go to *http://www.statesymbolsusa.org/Texas/state_symbols. html*. For additional information about national monuments and landmarks in Texas, go to *http:// texastimetravel.com/node/28774*.

COMPETENCY 005: CULTURE; SCIENCE, TECHNOLOGY AND SOCIETY

The teacher understands and applies knowledge of cultural development, adaptation and diversity and understands and applies knowledge of interactions among science, technology, and society, as defined by the Texas Essential Knowledge and Skills (TEKS).

The beginning teacher:

A. Understands basic concepts of culture and the processes of cultural adaptation, diffusion and exchange.

B. Analyzes similarities and differences in the ways various peoples at different times in history have lived and met basic human needs.

C. Applies knowledge of the role of families in meeting basic human needs and how families and cultures develop and use customs, traditions and beliefs to define themselves.

D. Demonstrates knowledge of institutions that exist in all societies and how characteristics of these institutions may vary among societies.

E. Understands how people use oral tradition, stories, real and mythical heroes, music, paintings and sculpture to create and represent culture in communities in Texas, the United States and the world.

F. Demonstrates knowledge of significant examples of art, music and literature from various periods in U.S. and Texas history (e.g., John James Audubon, Henry David Thoreau, transcendentalism, the painting American Progress, "Yankee Doodle," "Battle Hymn of the Republic," Amado Peña, Diane Gonzales Bertrand, Scott Joplin).

G. Understands the universal themes found in the arts and their relationship with the times and societies in which they are produced, including how contemporary issues influence creative expressions and how the arts can transcend the boundaries of societies (e.g., religion, justice, the passage of time).

H. Understands the contributions of people of various racial, ethnic and religious groups in Texas, the United States and the world.

I. Demonstrates knowledge of relationships among world cultures and relationships between and among people from various groups, including racial, ethnic and religious groups, in the United States and throughout the world.

J. Analyzes relationships among religion, philosophy and culture, and the impact of religion on ways of life in the United States and throughout the world.

K. Understands the concept of diversity within unity.

L. Analyzes the effects of race, gender, socioeconomic class, status and stratification on ways of life in the United States and throughout the world.

M. Understands the various roles of men, women, children and families in cultures past and present.

N. Understands how the self develops and the dynamic relationship between self and social context.

O. Demonstrates knowledge of the discoveries, technological innovations and accomplishments of notable inventors and individuals in the field of science from the United States, Texas and the world (e.g., Benjamin Franklin, Eli Whitney, Cyrus McCormick, Thomas Alva Edison, Alexander Graham Bell, Michael DeBakey, Millie Hughes-Fulford, Walter Cunningham, Denton Cooley, Michael Dell).

P. Applies knowledge of the effects of scientific discoveries and technological innovations on political, economic, social and environmental developments and on everyday life in Texas, the United States and the world in the past, present and future.

Q. Analyzes how science and technology relate to political, economic, social and cultural issues and events.

R. Demonstrates knowledge of the origins, diffusions and effects of major scientific, mathematical and technological discoveries throughout history.

S. Knows how developments in science and technology have affected the physical environment; the growth of economies and societies; and definitions of, access to and use of physical and human resources.

T. Knows how changes in science and technology affect moral and ethical issues.

The Role of Families in Meeting Basic Human Needs

While all young people need food, clothing, and shelter, families may have different ways of meeting these needs. Cultural, religious, and familiar traditions may influences families' preferences and choices in meeting basic needs.

How Families and Cultures Develop and Use Customs, Traditions, and Beliefs to Define Themselves

Educators should give students and families opportunities to share and express their culture throughout the social studies curriculum. Parents are children's first and constant teachers. Educators must realize that a student's cultural or religious beliefs could at times be incompatible with school activities and thus, students may opt not to participate in certain school events. Teachers should help students feel positively about their cultural differences. Family values and culture fuel children's self-esteem, identity, and pride surrounding who they are and who they aspire to become as educated adults. Schools should make space for students' cultural heritages to be respected, valued, and incorporated into their education.

Knowledge of Institutions that Exist in All Societies and How Characteristics of These Institutions May Vary among Societies

Geneva Gay, a professor of education at the University of Washington, defines culturally responsive teaching as using the cultural knowledge, prior experiences, and performance styles of diverse students to make learning more appropriate and effective for them; it teaches to and through the strengths of these students (Gay, 2000). All societies have norms, rules, and laws; however, these may differ from one society to the next.

Use of Oral Tradition, Stories, Real and Mythical Heroes, Music, Paintings, and Sculpture to Create and Represent Culture in Communities

Stories, art, and music help people express and share culture. While some mythic archetypes exist across cultures, such as the hero's journey, the trickster, the quest, and creation stories, cultural aspects of stories vary from one culture to the next.

In Texas

Texas has unique cultural traditions and celebrations, such as Juneteenth. Juneteenth is uniquely Texan, representing the oldest celebration commemorating the end of U.S. slavery. On June 19, 1865, two-and-a-half years after Lincoln's *Emancipation Proclamation*, Major General Gordon Granger landed in Galveston, Texas, and announced, "The people of Texas are informed that in accordance with a proclamation from the executive of the United States, all slaves are free."

In the United States

Thanksgiving, Memorial Day, and Independence Day on the Fourth of July are holidays unique to the United States. We have localized myths and folktales from various American Indian tales to frontier folklore such as Paul Bunyan and Babe the Blue Ox. In addition to mythical heroes, all cultures, including the United States, have real heroes of cultural expression. The Harlem Renaissance in the 1920s and 1930s represents a uniquely U.S. convergence of cultural expression with many real-life cultural leaders and heroes.

In the World

Cultural stories exist in any culture. Humans tell stories as part of cultural expression. *Beowulf*, *The Odyssey*, *The Aeneid*, *El Cid*, *Paradise Lost*, *Mahabharata*, *Metamorphoses*, and *Epic of Gilgamesh* all represent cultural stories from differing languages and origins that are still valued today.

Relationships among World Cultures, and Relationships between and among People from Various Groups, Including Racial, Ethnic and Religious Groups

According to the *Curriculum Guidelines for Multicultural Education* by the National Council for the Social Studies, "A democratic society protects and provides opportunities for ethnic and cultural diversity at the same time having overarching values—such as equality, justice, and human dignity—that all groups accept and respect." (Fullinwider, 2001)

Relationships among Religion, Philosophy, and Culture, and the Impact of Religion on Ways of Life in the United States and World Areas

Though the Harlem Renaissance is perhaps best known for its artistic and religious movements, Harlem also had significant political movements at this same time period. Marcus Garvey, who ascribed to a Black Nationalist philosophy, founded the Universal Negro Improvement Association, and was a proponent of a black migration back to Africa. He also founded African Orthodox Church. While Garvey advocated for separation, W.E.B. Du Bois favored integration. Du Bois was the leading African American politician and philosopher during the Harlem Renaissance. James Weldon Johnson was the first appointed African American officer in the NAACP. Louis Armstrong and Duke Ellington were noted musicians during this period.

Concept of Diversity within Unity

As we said earlier, "E Pluribus Unum" means "from many, one." In 1776, John Adams, Benjamin Franklin, and Thomas Jefferson proposed this Latin saying as the motto to be printed on the first Great Seal of the United States. While the original intent involved a single unified nation from many states, the motto stands the test of time and still affirms U.S. identity even though the U.S. national motto since 1956 has been "In God We Trust." James Banks (2001) and several co-authors, published a document entitled *Diversity within Unity Essential Principles for Teaching and Learning in a Multicultural Society*. It centered on 12 principles aligned to five key areas:

1. teacher learning

2. student learning

3. intergroup relations

4. school governance, organization, and equity

5. assessment

The concept of diversity within unity underscores that our cultural differences make society stronger. We achieve unity through civic ideals and practices and an acknowledged commitment to the greater good. As citizens of the United States, we share in common challenges and collective joys of our nation, bound by both geographic union and shared American identity, not by any law that would impose a forced unity. Americans uphold and affirm citizens' rights to decent lives and publicly speak against policy via peaceful protest. In part, it is our affirmation and respect of differences that hold us in our unity.

Effects of Scientific Discoveries and Technological Innovations

In Texas

Some Texas leaders in science and technology include:

- *Walter Cunningham*—NASA's second civilian astronaut, fighter pilot, retired military physicist

- *Michael DeBakey*—Surgeon who helped develop innovative treatments in heart and vascular surgery

- *Denton Cooley*—Native Houstonian known for heart surgery and transplants, as well as adept surgical work with children

- *Benjy Brooks*—Native Texan and the first female pediatric surgeon in Texas. She conducted research on congenital defects, burn treatment, spleen reparation, and the prevention of hepatitis. A foundation set up in her name has advanced the surgical care of young children in Texas.

- *Michael Dell*—Founder of Dell Computer Corporation. He is a native Houstonian known for technology, business, and philanthropy.

- *Howard Hughes Sr.*—Designer of a drill bit that could drill through hard rock. Previously, oil drillers could not reach large pockets of oil lying beneath hard rock. He co-founded the Sharp-Hughes Tool Company, which held the patent for the new drill bit, manufactured the bit, and leased the bit to oil companies.

Major Scientific, Mathematical, and Technological Discoveries throughout History

- *Archimedes*—One of the greatest mathematicians and scientists; worked in hydrostatics, static mechanics, the measurement of the volume or density; made key contributions to calculus

- *Copernicus*—Mathematician and astronomer; discovered that the Earth revolved around the sun, which was stationary in the center of the universe; created a conceptualization of our universe as a place where the distances of the planets from the sun had a direct relationship to the size of their orbits; often considered to be the initiator of the Scientific Revolution.

- *Eratosthenes*—A mathematician who worked on prime numbers and measuring the diameter of the Earth

- *Galileo*—Scientist who formulated basic laws of falling bodies; constructed a telescope to study lunar craters; discovered four of Jupiter's moons

- *Pythagoras*—Philosopher and mathematician; contributed to math systems; however, none of his writings are known, so his contributions are not distinctly defined

- *Robert Boyle*—Chemist and philosopher; worked toward establishing chemistry as based on a mechanistic theory of matter

- *Marie Curie*—Scientist who discovered the radioactive elements polonium and radium; first person awarded two Nobel prizes. Her work influenced the development of medical research and treatment.

- *Thomas Edison*—Scientist and inventor, most famous for developing the incandescent light bulb

- *Albert Einstein*—Physicist who heavily contributed to the modern vision of physics including his general theories of relativity.

- *Robert Fulton*—Artist, engineer, and inventor who made the steamboat designs viable and put this mode of transportation into actual practice

- *Sir Isaac Newton*—Philosopher, scientific theorist, and inventor of the infinitesimal calculus and a new theory of light and color. He transformed physical science through conceiving the three laws of motion and the law of universal gravitation.

- *Louis Pasteur*—Biologist, chemist, and humanitarian, known for germ and immunization theories; he uncovered origins of rabies, anthrax, chicken cholera, and silkworm diseases; contributed to the development of the first vaccines; he described the scientific basis for fermentation.

- *James Watt*—Engineer and inventor known for improvements made to Newcomen's atmospheric engine, which turned steam into the major power source of the Industrial Revolution

COMPETENCY 006: SOCIAL STUDIES FOUNDATIONS AND SKILLS

The teacher understands the foundations of social studies education and applies knowledge of skills used in the social sciences.*

The beginning teacher:

A. Understands the philosophical foundations of the social science disciplines and knows how knowledge generated by the social sciences affects society and people's lives.

---

* Social Studies Texas Essential Knowledge and Skills include eight strands of essential knowledge and skills that are intended to be integrated for instructional purposes. Typically, the last 3 to 5 Social Studies TEKS identify the Social Studies Skills students are to know. Constructing lessons based on one TEKS is a common error. Every Social Studies lesson should include a minimum of one Social Studies Skills and at least one other TEKS from another strand.

B. Understands how social science disciplines relate to each other.

C. Understands practical applications of social studies education.

D. Relates philosophical assumptions and ideas to issues and trends in the social sciences.

E. Knows characteristics and uses of various primary and secondary sources (e.g., databases, maps, photographs, media services, the Internet, biographies, interviews, questionnaires, artifacts) and uses information from a variety of sources to acquire social science information and answer social science questions.

F. Knows how to formulate research questions and use appropriate procedures to reach supportable judgments and conclusions in the social sciences.

G. Understands social science research and knows how social scientists locate, gather, organize, analyze and report information using standard research methodologies.

H. Evaluates the validity of social science information from primary and secondary sources regarding bias issues, propaganda, point of view and frame of reference.

I. Understands and evaluates multiple points of view and frames of reference relating to issues in the social sciences.

J. Knows how to analyze social science information (e.g., by categorizing, comparing and contrasting, making generalizations and predictions, drawing inferences and conclusions).

K. Communicates and interprets social science information in written, oral and visual forms and translates information from one medium to another (e.g., written to visual, statistical to written or visual).

L. Uses standard grammar, spelling, sentence structure, punctuation and proper citation of sources.

M. Knows how to use problem-solving processes to identify problems, gather information, list and consider options, consider advantages and disadvantages, choose and implement solutions and evaluate the effectiveness of solutions.

N. Knows how to use decision-making processes to identify situations that require decisions, gather information, identify options, predict consequences and take action to implement decisions.

O. Knows how to create maps and other graphics to present geographic, political, historical, economic and cultural features, distributions, and relationships.

P. Analyzes social science data by using basic mathematical and statistical concepts and analytical methods.

Q. Knows how to apply skills for resolving conflict, including persuasion, compromise, debate and negotiation.

R. Understands and uses social studies terminology correctly.

Social Studies Inquiry

Research in social studies involves the use of systematic inquiry. Engaging students in inquiry involves the ability to acquire information from various resources. Inquiry involves the ability to design and conduct investigations, which requires students to develop an understanding of key information in social studies content. To gather content information, students should become familiar with the various resources used in social sciences research. Those resources include primary and secondary sources, encyclopedias, almanacs, atlases, government documents, artifacts, and oral histories. Students need to apply critical-thinking skills to organize and use information acquired from a variety of sources including electronic technology.

Information about social studies is available from the Internet; however, students need to evaluate the scholarship of the many sources available and use only those known to be reliable. Teachers should equip middle-grade social studies students to think, research, and communicate like historians, sociologists, geographers, economists, political scientists, and other social studies processionals. Asking and answering appropriate levels of higher-order questions is imperative to teaching students to think like a social scientist. For more information, see *http://www.nscsd. org/webpages/jennisullivan/files/questioning-strategies.pdf* and *http://www.esc4.net/users/0001/ docs/107-DWilliamsTCSS2005.ppt.* Inquiry is the mechanism to achieve professional-level social studies skills.

The Problem-Solving Process

Just like scientists, social scientists utilize the basics of the scientific method. Educators should guide students to:

1. Identify a social science problem.

2. Formulate research questions and hypotheses.

3. Gather and analyze information, look for patterns.

4. Raise discipline-appropriate question, identify possible positive and negative consequences, and use data to support ideas.

5. Test and report findings.

Data (facts) must be used to support one's conclusions. In a democracy, an informed citizenry must be able to make statements and support (or defend) them with evidence (data) from multiple perspectives. Social studies education seeks to develop content knowledge and skills communities expect their citizens to have. In America, we strongly value being able to articulate well-reasoned conclusions, thoughts, and beliefs that consider different points of view. Social studies classrooms in the United States prepare youth to be able to function in an active participatory democracy.

Professionally Modeled Thinking

When studying history, an educator should guide students to think like historians. Likewise, when studying geography or culture, the teacher will prompt students to work like geographers and anthropologists. This approach builds core social studies skills while simultaneously preparing students with college and career readiness skills. Professionals who work in the field of social studies do not rely on memory skills alone, nor should students in the middle grades. Professionally modeled thinking involves leading students through the interrogation of primary and supporting secondary sources to test hypotheses. Often, students may come away with more questions than they started with in their initial hypothesis, which is natural for this type of educational experience. Professionally modeled thinking prompts students to be critical consumers of information and it empowers them to think critically about the social worlds around them. Students acquire life-long learning skills through classroom activities that foreground professionally modeled thinking. Social studies teachers do not always recognize how to or what to model. Modeling how to think and reason in various situations or about different issues is critical. Social studies teachers can do this using think-aloud strategies. Teachers need to be cautious when thinking through events and issues to use the different Social studies "hats"—history, geography, political science, and economics to develop a complete understanding of the topic at hand.

How Social Science Disciplines Relate to Each Other

Social studies is an umbrella term used to encompass the disciplines of history, geography, civics and government, economics, and psychology. All five components are intertwined with the standards or strands developed by the National Council for the Social Studies in 1997 (NCSS, 2018). The Texas Education Agency (TEA) used these strands and curriculum standards as a foundation to develop the state social studies curriculum for kindergarten through grade 12. In many ways, social studies is a hub at the center of all other disciplines. Social studies brings together reading, writing, and other linguistic processing skills with mathematical reading and thinking skills as students read and interpret maps, charts, and other social science data immersed in both linguistic and numerical data. Social studies subjects also relate to students' everyday life interactions with all subject areas. For example, when students encounter chemistry and health in the real world, it often takes laboratory science to the everyday social setting of the breakfast table where nutritional charts inform them about their own eating choices and where digestion becomes an internal body chemistry validation of what they read. When teachers overtly connect all the other disciplines linked to students' everyday worlds through their study of the social studies, then students begin to understand the applicability of the entire curriculum through the study of their own and others' social lives. Social studies can become the real-world connection hub for all other disciplines.

Relates Philosophical Assumptions and Ideas to Issues and Trends in the Social Sciences

Core philosophical assumptions align with various historical and social traditions. For example, the Enlightenment pulls ideas from Jefferson, Locke, and Rousseau. The scientific revolution relies on ideas from Copernicus (Ptolemaic Astronomy; Earth's revolution around the sun), Galileo (refracting telescope, objects of various weights descend at the same rate), and Newton (universal gravitation, calculus, laws of motion). Political science origins rely on Aristotle, Plato, and Aquinas. Machiavelli and Hobbes contribute to ideas of power. Historical and philosophical trends go hand-and-hand. Students begin to understand the works of philosophers like Heidegger and Arendt more fully when they can process the information within the historical backdrop of that period in time.

In part, people think about philosophy as they do because of what is going on in the world around them. In powerful and transformative social studies classrooms, educators help students to explore and make sense of how social theory, philosophical development, and history intermingle and influence one another. Students can then apply the continuity of historical and philosophical ideas to the worlds of today and tomorrow.

Sources of Information

Teachers should use various primary and secondary sources (e.g., databases, maps, photographs, media services, the Internet, biographies, interviews, questionnaires, artifacts, works of historical fiction, interviews, etc.) and information from a variety of sources to acquire social science information and answer social science questions. Students and teachers must evaluate the validity of social science information from primary and secondary sources regarding bias issues, propaganda, point-of-view, and frame of reference.

Educators should help students to formulate social studies research questions and use appropriate procedures to reach supportable judgments and conclusions in the social sciences, as well as analyze social science information (e.g., by categorizing, comparing and contrasting, making generalizations and predictions, drawing inferences and conclusions). Students should be able to pull together, synthesize, apply, and evaluate contemporary Internet resources alongside historical sources. Teachers should always consider students' everyday worlds as sources or comparative sources to help make the study of social studies meaningful to students' lives. Likewise, educators should include familial and local oral histories and other historical and cultural documents and artifacts that make students' immediate geographies and histories relevant to the majority of the social studies curriculum.

See the National Archives (*www.archives.gov*) for more information on locating primary sources and lesson ideas related to social studies.

Spatial Thinking

Social scientists continually use space and place as vehicles for analyzing patterns, relationships, and processes within and between places from multiple perspectives (i.e., historical, geographical, political, economical, etc.). These professionals seek to organize and understand the world around them. Using a spatial perspective is a vital part of what they do. Educators must model for students how to think spatially and show them how this analysis differs on a local, state, national and global scale. Recently, methods of spatial analysis have been enhanced through geospatial tools such as digital globes (i.e., Google Earth) and geographic information systems (GIS). Due to the participation of Esri, a mapping and spatial data analytics supplier, in President Obama's 2013 ConnectED initiative, the online, cloud-based ArcGIS software is available to all educators in the U.S. Educators can create an account for their school from which each teacher can have a space for students to interact with, create, and upload maps using GIS. For more, go to *http://www.esri.com/connected* and *http://geospatialrevolution.psu.edu/*. By visualizing data, educators can teach students how to better understand the patterns, relationships, and connections throughout time and place.

COMPETENCY 007: SOCIAL STUDIES INSTRUCTION AND ASSESSMENT

The teacher plans and implements effective instruction and assessment in social studies.

The beginning teacher:

A. Knows state content and performance standards for social studies that are used in the Texas Essential Knowledge and Skills (TEKS).

B. Understands the vertical alignment of the social sciences in the Texas Essential Knowledge and Skills (TEKS) from grade level to grade level, including prerequisite knowledge and skills.

C. Understands the implications of stages of child growth and development for designing and implementing effective learning experiences in the social sciences.

D. Understands the appropriate use of technology as a tool for learning and communicating social studies concepts.

E. Selects and uses effective instructional practices, activities, technologies and materials to promote students' knowledge and skills in the social sciences.

F. Knows how to promote students' use of social science skills, vocabulary and research tools, including technological tools.

G. Knows how to communicate the value of social studies education to students, parents/caregivers, colleagues and the community.

H. Knows how to provide instruction that relates skills, concepts and ideas in different social science disciplines.

I. Provides instruction that makes connections between knowledge and methods in the social sciences and in other content areas.

J. Demonstrates knowledge of forms of assessment appropriate for evaluating students' progress and needs in the social sciences.

K. Uses multiple forms of assessment and knowledge of the Texas Essential Knowledge and Skills (TEKS) to determine students' progress and needs and to help plan instruction that addresses the strengths, needs and interests of all students, including English-language learners.

Educators have a crucial responsibility because they lay the foundation of American core values, citizenship, democracy, and patriotism. Social studies often gets less attention in the classroom than the intended state curriculum calls for. Teachers must learn to find ways to infuse their curricula with social studies lessons and recognize that social studies strongly supports literacy and other content areas. Understanding maps, diagrams, charts, and graphs as well as analysis of spatial patterns and relationships support students' spatial and mathematical reasoning capabilities.

The middle-grades teacher should plan and implement effective instruction and assessment in social studies, aligned to state content and performance standards for social studies that comprise the TEKS. Additionally, educators must understand the vertical alignment of the social sciences in the TEKS from one grade level to the next, including prerequisite knowledge and skills. Educators should account for the implications of stages of child growth and development for designing and implementing effective learning experiences in the social sciences and understand the appropriate use of technology as a tool for learning and communicating social studies concepts.

Educators should select and use effective instructional practices, activities, technologies and materials to promote students' knowledge and skills in the social sciences in order to promote students' use of social science skills, vocabulary and research tools, including technological tools. Prepared educators know how to communicate the value of social studies education to students, parents/caregivers, colleagues, and the community and how to provide instruction that relates skills, concepts, and ideas in different social science disciplines.

Optimally, educators should provide instruction that makes connections between knowledge and methods in the social sciences and in other content areas. Teachers must demonstrate knowledge of forms of assessment appropriate for evaluating students' progress and needs in the social science and use multiple forms of assessment and knowledge of the TEKS to determine students' progress and needs and to help plan instruction that addresses the strengths, needs, and interests of all students, including English language learners.

Texas Essential Knowledge and Skills (TEKS) in Social Studies

As the state curriculum for kindergarten to grade 12, the TEKS organizes the social studies content inductively, from the known to the unknown. In this vertical alignment, children begin learning about the self in kindergarten and expand their knowledge with each successive grade, eventually encompassing the community, the state, the nation, and the world. This is sometimes referred to as thinking on a local to global scale. Secondary grade-level social studies courses build and rely on the foundation laid by 4–8 teachers. Social Studies nationally is divided into 10 strands that are infused throughout each of the social studies disciplines (See Figure 5-3 below). This is reflected in the Social Studies Texas Essential Knowledge and Skills (TEKS), where eight strands are present in the social studies course for each grade level. In Texas, social studies is built on the foundation of the following strands: history, geography, economics, government, citizenship, culture, science, technology, and society, and social studies skills.

**Figure 5-3
Social Studies Strands**

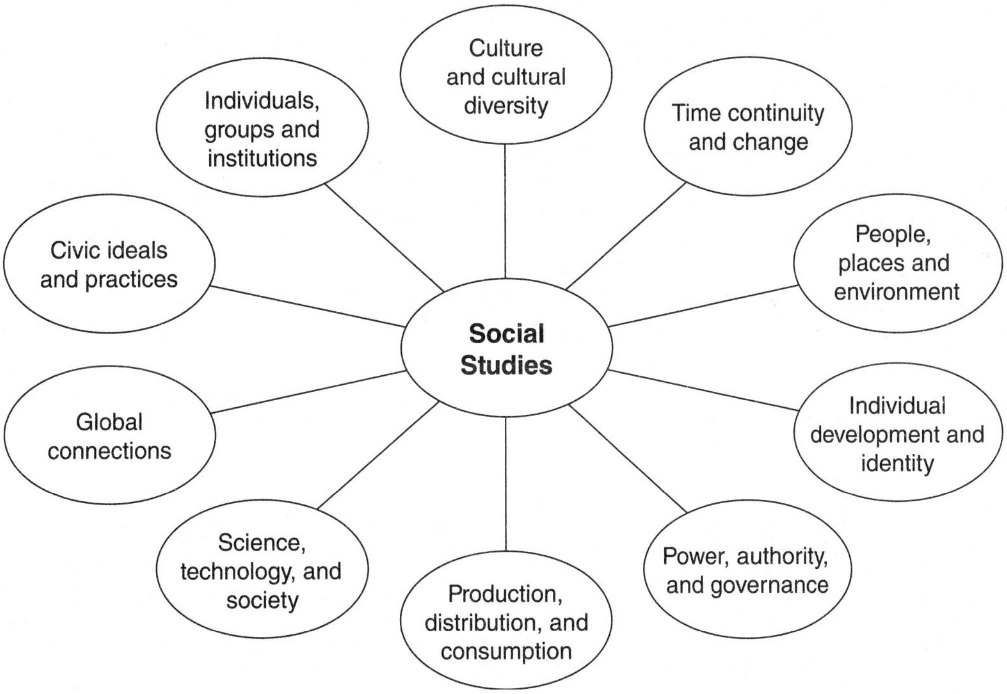

A summary of the key components of the social studies curriculum covered in Grades 4–8 follows.

Grades 4 & 7 Focus—History of Texas

- History of Texas from its beginning to the present. Several Native American groups inhabited the territory that became Texas.

- Geographic regions of Texas (i.e., location, biomes, resources, economic products, settlements, groups of people)

- Events and individuals of the 19th and 20th centuries

- Human activity and physical features of regions in Texas and the Western Hemisphere

- Native Americans in Texas and the Western Hemisphere (i.e., tribes, customs, location, time period, movement, interaction with other people)

- European exploration and colonization

- Types of Native American governments

- Characteristics of Spanish and Mexican colonial governments

- Anthems, mottoes, and pledges of Texas and the United States

Grades 5 & 8 Focus—United States History

- Anthem, motto, and pledge of the United States of America

- History of the United States from its early beginnings to the present

- Major events and significant individuals of the late 19th and 20th centuries including contributions of famous inventors and scientists

- Regions of the United States that result from physical features and human activity

- Characteristics and benefits of the free enterprise system

- Roots of representative government

- Important ideas in the Declaration of Independence

- Meaning of the Pledge of Allegiance

- Fundamental rights guaranteed in the Bill of Rights

- Customs and celebrations of various racial, ethnic, and religious groups in the nation

Grade 6—People and Places of the Contemporary World

- This part of the curriculum is designed to introduce students to the concepts of cultural geography. The discipline of geography explores patterns, relationships, and processes at local to global scale.

- People and places of the contemporary world

- Societies from the following regions in the world: Europe, Russia and the Eurasian republics, North America, Middle America, South America, Southwest Asia-North Africa, Sub-Saharan Africa, South Asia, East Asia, Southeast Asia, Australia, and the Pacific Realm

- Influence of individuals and groups from various cultures on selected historical and contemporary events

- Different ways of organizing economic and governmental systems

Different Ways of Organizing Economic and Governmental Systems

Using Maps and Globes

Symbolic representation can pose challenges for students through grade 4, and even students in grades 5 and 6. Maps and globes are tools for representing space symbolically. Globes are a mathematical model of the Earth and show correct, unaltered (not distorted) distance, size, and shape of continents and bodies of water. Maps are a flat representation of the world and distort the distance, size, or shape of continents and bodies of water. This distortion can confuse the young learner. In the early grades, the main purpose for using globes is to familiarize children with the basic roundness of the Earth and to begin developing a global perspective. It can also be used to study the proportion of land and water. In grades 4 through 6, students can use a 16-inch globe containing additional details. Generally, seven colors are used to represent land elevation and three colors to represent water depth. For ideas for lessons, and for personal practice, go to *http://www. nea.org/tools/lessons/teaching-with-maps.html*. For creating online maps go to *http://www.arcgis. com/features/index.html* or *https://www.google.com/help/maps/education/*.

Activities for Students in Grades 4–8

Teaching map concepts in grade 4 should include the following activities:

- Stress that the globe is a very small representation that is a model of the Earth.

- Stress that the map is a flat representation of the Earth and why maps are used more often than globes.

- Show children different kinds of maps of Texas (i.e., climate, precipitation, resources, vegetation, physical, population, etc.) as well as from different time periods throughout the year (i.e., Indian tribe locations, exploration paths, settlement patterns, battles, land acquisition, etc.) to better understand place and change over time.

- Show children how land areas and water bodies are represented on the globe.

- Identify major landforms and water bodies.

- Show and explain the location of the North Pole and the concept of the Northern Hemisphere, where most of the world's land is located.

- Show and explain the location of the South Pole and the concept of the Southern Hemisphere, where most of the world's water is located.

- Show the relationship and location of the Earth in the solar system.

- Use the globe to find the continent, the country, the state, and the city where the children live.

- Encourage children to explore the globe and maps to find places by themselves as well as the connections between places.

- Compare the size of the continents represented on a globe with their representation on a Mercator projection—the flat representation.

Teaching map concepts in grades 5 and 6 should include the following activities:

- Identify countries, capitals, and other major cities in the United States and the world.

- Identify major landforms and bodies of water.

- Create and interpret maps.

- Use maps and globes to pose and answer questions.

- Locate major historical and contemporary societies on maps and globes.

- Use maps to solve real-life problems, i.e., using road maps to plan a route to a specific destination.

Latitude and Longitude—Developmental Considerations

The concepts of **latitude** and **longitude** are generally covered in grade 4 and up. However, students may have difficulty understanding the mathematics involved in the grid system. Children might get confused with these concepts:

- The length of the meridians of longitude and the parallels of latitude on a globe and Mercator projection look different. Note the difference on other projections such as the Robinson projection.

- The meridians of longitude have a consistent size, but the parallels of latitude vary in size, becoming smaller as they move away from the equator. However, lines of longitude meet at the poles.

- Lines of latitude are measured in degrees based on the angle formed when measured from the equator, zero degrees latitude. Lines of longitude are measured in degrees based on time. (For more information on the history of measuring longitude, visit the *National Geographic* website at *http://education.nationalgeographic.com/encyclopedia/longitude*.)

Using Technology Information in Social Studies

Research in social studies involves the use of systematic inquiry. Engaging children in inquiry involves the ability to acquire information from various resources. Inquiry involves the ability to design and conduct investigations, which requires students to develop an understanding of key information in social studies content.

To gather information, students should learn about the sources used in social sciences research. They should learn to distinguish between primary and secondary sources as they become familiar with encyclopedias, almanacs, atlases, government documents, artifacts, and oral histories. Students should apply critical-thinking skills to organize and use information acquired from sources including electronic technology. Information about social studies is available from the Internet; however, students need to evaluate the scholarship of the many sources available and use only those known to be reliable. Students can use commercially developed programs like *Oregon Trails* and *Where in the World is Carmen San Diego?* Digital globes, such as Google Earth (*https://www.google.com/earth/*), National Geographic's Map Machine (*maps.nationalgeographic.com/map-machine*), and ArcGIS Online (*http://www.arcgis.com/features/index.html*) are **geospatial**

technologies that provide a forum to analyze relationships and patterns at a local to global scale. Another excellent recourse is MapStats for Kids that allows students to experience the dynamic relationships of charts, diagrams, and maps as they work to achieve a goal (*https://www.geovista. psu.edu/grants/MapStatsKids/MSK_portal/*). These interactive programs expose students to problem-solving skills and social studies content in a fun and supportive environment. These kinds of interactive programs can expose students to problem-solving skills and social studies content in a fun and supportive environment.

Integration of Social Studies

As mentioned earlier, the teaching of social studies by definition implies integration of content from five disciplines: history, geography, civics and government, economics, and psychology. However, teachers can go beyond this integration and add components from other content areas. The use of a literature-based approach is an ideal way to integrate social studies with language arts. Using authentic multicultural literature, teachers can expose children to quality reading and the cultures of the many ethnic and linguistic groups living in the United States. Social studies is strongly linked with English Language Arts and Reading. It not only requires strong reading and writing skills but also supports reading by providing an understanding of the history as well as the physical and cultural characteristics of a place.

The use of thematic units can also help teachers to integrate the content areas. In this approach, a teacher or teachers select a theme and organize content area instruction around it. Thematic instruction can be done in a self-contained classroom or in a departmental format in which several teachers teach the content. However, units may be organized by key time periods in history or regions of the world with key themes serving as "big ideas" or "guiding questions" to drive instruction. This method allows learners to "chunk" the material historically or geographically while simultaneously analyzing major themes or "big ideas" that connect to other units of instruction. Some educators may prefer this method because it divides content into units familiar to both the educator and students.

Thematic instruction is ideal for English language learners because the use of a common theme in multiple content areas makes content more cognitively accessible for them. For example, in a unit on the **solar system**, the names of the planets and the terminology used to describe the system can be introduced and repeated in several subjects through the duration of the unit. The presentation and repetition of content in different subjects and conditions allow students the opportunity to develop English vocabulary while learning content.

Graphic Representations of Historical Information

Information in social studies can be presented in a visual form with graphs and charts to make content accessible to all children, including ELLs.

Graphs

The most commonly used graphs are the pictorial graph, the bar graph, the pie or circle graph, and the line graph. The **pictorial graph** is the most concrete type of graph because it uses a picture of the object being represented. **Bar graphs** are more concrete than pie graphs (also known as pie charts or circle graphs). In elementary school, social studies teachers can use a **Dot Plot** from mathematics, which is a simple histogram-like chart that is similar to a bar graph. A common bar graph in social studies is the population pyramid, which shows the number of males and females for each age group in a community. The population pyramid is appropriate for upper elementary because it uses percentages as well as whole numbers. Visit the U.S. Census Bureau's website for more information at *http://www.census.gov/population/ metro/data/pop_pyramid.html*. When possible, teachers should also incorporate such charts and graphs common to other disciplines as the dot plots in mathematics, to reinforce concepts and show that learning is continuous and can be applied in different ways.

Although the **pie graph** appears to be simple, students need to understand the concept of percentages to interpret correctly the meaning of this type of graph, and the concept of percentages is not acquired until late in the elementary grades. Teachers can use more sophisticated graphs like the pie graph to represent research information. For example, children can take 5 to 10 minutes a day to observe the types of transportation used by people in the neighborhood. Teachers can use this information to guide children to make inferences about the information contained in the graph. Why are so many people using pickup trucks as a mode of transportation? Why are only a small number of people walking? Graphs provide a great opportunity to integrate social studies into mathematics and vice versa.

Charts

Charts can be used to record information and present ideas in a concise way. Charts are ideal for promoting concept formation in a concrete fashion. **Data retrieval charts** are used to gather and keep track of data gathered from research, observation, or experimentation. This type of chart is constructed to allow the easy comparison of two or more sets of data. An example of a data retrieval chart appears below in Table 5-7.

Table 5-7
Data Retrieval Chart—Country Leaders

Country	Head of the Government	Type of Government
United States	President	Constitutional Federal Republic
United Kingdom	Prime Minister	Parliamentary Constitutional Monarchy
Saudi Arabia	King and Prime Minister	Absolute Monarch

Source: The CIA World Factbook (*https://www.cia.gov*)

Narrative charts are used to show events in a sequence. For example, students can develop charts showing the steps in making their favorite dishes. A narrative chart can also be used to present a timeline of historical events. An example of a simple timeline is Figure 5-4 below, which shows a child's personal history.

Figure 5-4
Timeline—My History

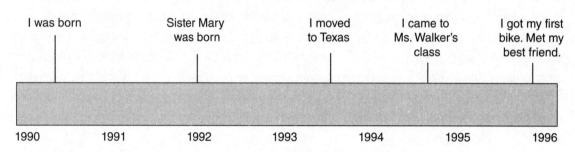

A **tabulation** or **classification** chart provides an orderly columnar display of information for comparison. For example, Table 5-8 compares data based on the 2010 United States census.

Table 5-8
Tabulation or Classification Chart—U.S. and Texas Populations by Group

Race/Ethnic Group Population	Percentage of U.S. Population	Percentage of Texas Population
Caucasian/not Hispanic	62.6%	44.0%
African American	13.2%	12.4%
Asian	5.3%	4.3%
Hispanic or Latino	17.1%	38.4%
American Indian/Alaskan Native	1.2%	1.0%
Native Hawaiian/Pacific Is.	0.2%	0.1%

Source: U.S. Census Bureau (2013): online *http://quickfacts.census.gov/qfd/states/00000.html*
Texas Quick Facts online: *http://www.census.gov/quickfacts/table/PST045214/48,00*

Using developmentally appropriate vocabulary, teachers can guide students to recall and infer data from the chart. It is important to move between various social studies tools (i.e., maps, graphs, charts, diagrams, and pictures) to help build learners cognitive ability and skills that increase in complexity with age and grade level.

A **flowchart** shows a process involving changes at certain points.

Figure 5-5
Flowchart for Program Completion

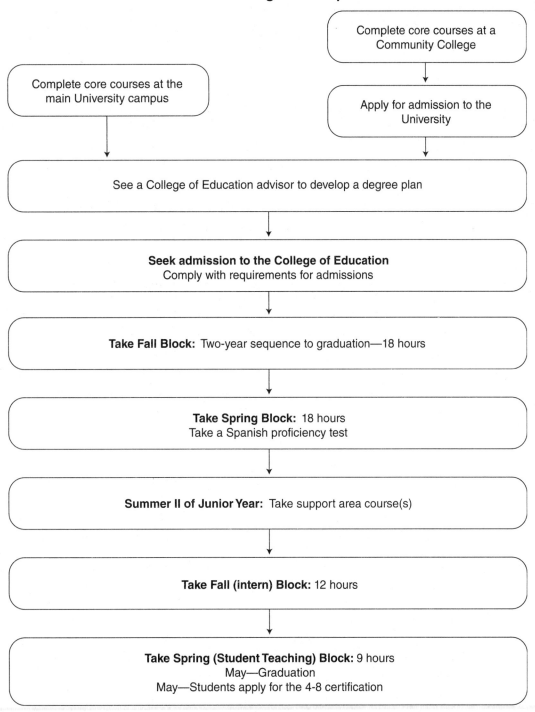

Addressing the Needs of English Language Learners

English language learners can find social studies instruction quite challenging; thus, teachers need to modify instruction to make the content comprehensible for this group. Some textbooks have been written with ELLs in mind. These books use numerous visual and graphic representations to make the content cognitively accessible to children learning English. For example, *Adventure Tales of America*, written by Jody Potts (1994), is an American history book that uses cartoons and illustrations to explain complex concepts like the processes of electing the president and making a bill into law. It also uses concrete timelines to represent the historical development of the nation. The illustrations give ELLs the fundamental meanings of important concepts from which teachers can develop lessons. Other books integrate language instruction with content to deliver both components in a contextualized format. One example is the English as a Second Language (ESL) series titled *Avenues*, published by Hampton Brown (Schifini et al., 2004). This set of books presents ESL lessons in conjunction with content from other disciplines. The integration of content and language is one of the most effective strategies to promote content area mastery and language development.

Cognates and Suffixes

English and most Western languages have been heavily influenced by the Greek and Roman civilizations. The association has resulted in the creation of multiple cognates—words that are similar in two languages. Most of the sophisticated English words in the content areas and especially in social studies are cognates of Spanish and other Western languages. Teachers can use these similarities to expand the vocabulary of students and enhance content area comprehension. Table 5-9 below presents examples of the connection between English and Spanish words (Rosado & Salazar, 2002–2003).

Table 5-9
Common Greek and Latin Roots and Affixes

Roots/Affixes	Meaning	English/Spanish Cognates
Phobia Xeno	Fear of Foreigners or strangers	Xenophobia/Xenofobia
Phono Logy(ia)	Sound Study of	Phonology/Fonología
Photo Graphy	Light Graph, form	Photography/Fotografía

Roots/Affixes	Meaning	English/Spanish Cognates
Homo Sapiens	Same, Man Able to think	Homo sapiens/homo sapiens
Demo Cracy	People Government	Democracy/Democracia

Instructional Techniques to Support English Language Learners

Teachers need to implement a variety of activities to teach the state curriculum to English language learners (ELLs) at the grade level and complexity required of native English speakers. Scaffolding was originally used to describe the way in which adults support children in their efforts to communicate in the native language (L1). The same concept can be used to facilitate language and content development for ELLs. The term *scaffolding* alludes to the provisional structure used to provide support during the construction of a building. This support is eliminated when the structure is complete. Following this analogy, ELLs receive language support to make content cognitively accessible to them until they achieve mastery in the second language (L2); once that mastery is accomplished, the language support is eliminated. In education, the term "scaffold" is based on research by Jerome Bruner and influenced by Lev Vygotsky. According to Bruner, scaffolding is the helpful interaction between teachers (or other adult) and the learner so that the learners can move from one idea to a more complex one or to achieve a goal. (For more, see *http://www. teachthough.com/learning/learning-theories-jerome-bruner-scaffolding-learning/* or *https://www/ simplypsychology.org/bruner.html*) When giving a lecture, remember to keep it to 4- to 10-minute segments. Younger children have shorter attention spans; lectures should be kept to a minimum. Preview vocabulary and key concepts prior to lecture. Use plenty of visuals. Refrain from creating busy or text-heavy presentation slides. After the lecture, provide a minimum of two minutes for students to discuss or otherwise interact with the lecture content.

Graphic organizers are visuals used to show relationships and are important to use with all learners. However, they are particularly helpful with ELLs as they learn to break down the language when learning new concepts. These are the most common graphic organizers:

- A **semantic web** or **tree diagram** shows the relationship between main ideas and subordinated components.

- A **timeline** presents a visual summary of chronological events and is ideal for showing historical events or events in a sequence.

- A **flowchart** shows cause-and-effect relationships and can be used to show steps in a process, like the process for admission to a school or program.

- A **Venn diagram** (Figure 5-6) uses circles to compare common and unique elements of two or three distinct components, such as properties of numbers, elements of stories, or events, or civilizations.

Figure 5-6
Venn diagram—Three Civilizations

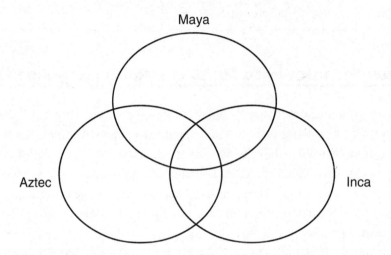

The **SQ4R** is a study strategy in which the learner is engaged in the entire reading process. The acronym stands for **survey**, **question**, **read**, **reflect**, **recite**, and **review**. During the **survey** part, readers examine the headings and major components of the text to develop predictions and generate questions. Through these **questions**, students establish the purpose for reading. As they **read**, students look for answers to the questions they generated. They monitor their comprehension as they **reflect**, write a summary, and **recite** the content they learned. Finally, they **review** to evaluate how much they learned about the content.

Academic Vocabulary in Social Studies

Academic vocabulary is the vocabulary needed to understand the concepts of school. In other words, it is the vocabulary of teaching and learning. Marzano and Pickering (2005) emphasize the importance of teaching academic vocabulary to English language learners and recommend a six-step systematic approach that includes direct instruction as well as practice and reinforcement. The steps to teach academic vocabulary are presented next.

- The teacher provides a description, explanation, or example of the new term.

- Students restate the description, example, or explanation in their own words.

- Students create a representation of the word by drawing a picture, symbol, or graphic of the word.

- Students periodically participate in activities that help to add to their knowledge of terms.

- Students discuss terms with one another.

- Students participate in games and activities that reinforce the new term.

Cooperative learning is a teaching strategy designed to create a low-anxiety learning environment in which students work together in small groups to achieve instructional goals. As a result of this instructional arrangement, students with different levels of ability or language development work collaboratively to support each other to ensure that each member masters the objectives of the lesson. This approach can easily be used to deliver content and language instruction. Traditionally, the strategy is delivered in specific steps (Arends, 1998):

1. **Present Goals**—The teacher goes over the objectives of the lesson and provides the motivation.

2. **Present Information**—The teacher presents information to students either verbally or with text.

3. **Organize Students into Learning Teams**—The teacher explains to students how to form learning teams and helps groups make an efficient transition.

4. **Assist Teamwork and Study**—The teacher assists learning teams as they do their work.

5. **Test Students on the Content**—The teacher tests students' knowledge of learning materials as each group presents the results of its work.

6. **Provide Recognition**—The teacher finds ways to recognize both individual and group efforts and achievements.

To emphasize the cooperative nature of the strategy, specific methods were developed to enrich the lessons such as Student Teams Achievement Division (STAD), Group Investigations, Think-Pair-Share, and Numbered Heads Together. These specialized methods are described in the sections that follow.

Student Teams Achievement Division (STAD)

1. The teacher presents new academic information to students.

2. Students are divided into four- or five-member learning teams.

3. Team members master the content and then help each other learn the material through tutoring, quizzing one another, or carrying on team discussions.

4. Each student receives an improvement score that helps show the growth he or she has made.

5. Daily or weekly quizzes are given to assess mastery.

6. Each week, through newsletters or a short ceremony, groups and individual students are recognized for showing the most improvement (Slavin, 1986).

Think-Pair-Share

This activity was developed as a result of the wait-time research. Wait-time research suggests that pausing for a few seconds to allow children to reflect on the question can improve the quality of the response and the overall performance of children (Rowe, 1986).

1. **Think**—The teacher poses a question and asks students to spend a minute thinking alone about the answer. No talking or walking is allowed.

2. **Pair**—Students pair off and discuss what they have been thinking about, sharing possible answers or information.

3. **Share**—Students share their answers with the whole class. The teacher goes around the classroom from pair to pair until a fourth to a half of the class has a chance to report (Lyman, 1981).

Numbered Heads Together Cooperative Learning Strategy

This activity was designed to involve more students in the review of materials covered in class.

1. **Number**—The teacher divides the students into teams with three to five members each and assigns a number to each member.

2. **Question**—The teacher asks a question.

3. **Heads Together**—Students put their heads together to figure out the answer and to be sure everyone knows the answer.

4. **Answer**—The teacher calls a number, and students who have that number from each group raise their hands and provide the answer (Kagan, 1985).

Inquiry

Inquiry as an instructional technique has gained popularity as a relevant way to connect students to authentic careers within given disciplines. Social studies is no different. Inquiry is viewed as fundamental to social studies. At the national level, the National Council for the Social

Studies (NCSS) published the new College, Career, and Civic Life (C3) Framework for the Social Studies State Standards (*https://www.socialstudies.org/c3*). Here, the NCSS presents the Inquiry Arc, which consists of four parts:

1. Developing questions and planning inquiries

2. Applying disciplinary concepts and tools

3. Evaluating sources and using evidence

4. Communicating conclusions and taking informed action

Inquiry is built on the premise that all children and adolescents are inherently curious. Inquiry helps students understand the world, what people do, and why they take the action that they do. The Minnesota Center for Social Studies Education explains inquiry as "an intellectual process used by social scientists to address authentic issues. Inquiry-based instruction gives students practice being political scientists, economists, geographers, and historians" (*http://www.mncsse.org/instruction/inquiry*). According to Edutopia, inquiry-based learning "uses student inquiries, questions, interests and curiosities to drive learning," which makes learning more relevant (*https://www.edutopia.org*). The teacher must carefully select resources and plan for the development of critical thinkers. Evidence is critical when studying the social studies disciplines. Students must be trained to support their statements and conclusions with evidence (data, facts, information). Further refined questions may be warranted to truly understand an issue, a group of people, or phenomenon. Throughout this process, be aware of myths and/or misconceptions so that they can be avoided and explained.

References

Acosta, T.P. (2009). Raza Unida Party. *The Handbook of Texas Online. Texas State Historical Association.*

Arends, R. (1998). *Learning to Teach.* (4th ed.). Boston: McGraw-Hill.

Banks, J.A., P. Cookson, G. Gay, W.D. Hawley, J.J. Irvine, S. Nieto, J.W. Schofield, and W.G. Stephan. 2001. Diversity within unity essential principles for teaching and learning in a multicultural society. Phi Delta Kappan. Retrieved from *http://www.uwyo.edu/education/_files/documents/diversity-articles/banks_2001.pdf.*

Barker, E.C., & Pohl, J.W. (2009). Texas Revolution. *The Handbook of Texas Online. Texas State Historical Association. Retrieved from http://www.tshaonline.org/online/articles/qdt01.*

Castaneda, O.R. 2006. The Chicano Movement in Washington State 1967-2006. Seattle Civil Rights and Labor History Project. Retrieved from *http://depts.washington.edu/civilr/Chicano-movement_part1.htm.*

Central Intelligence Agency. Central Asia: Russia. *World Factbook*. Retrieved from *https://www. cia.gov/library/publications/the-world-factbook/geos/rs.html*

De Blij, Harm & Murphy, A. B. 1999. Human Geography: Culture, Society, and Space. (7th Ed.) Wiley: New York.

Echevarria, J., Vogt, M., and Short, D. (2000). *Making content comprehensible for English language learners: The SIOP model*. Needham Heights, MA: Allyn and Bacon.

Fry, P. L., *Texas State Historical Association*. (n.d.). Origin of Name. *The Handbook of Texas Online. Retrieved from https://tshaonline.org/handbook/online/articles/pft04*.

Fullinwider, Robert K., International Journal of Educational Research, vol. 35, issue 3, 2001, pp. 331–343, Multicultural Education and Cosmopolitan Citizenship.

Ganeri, A., Martell, H. M., Williams, B. (1999). *The World History Encyclopedia*. Bath, UK: Parragon.

García, E. & García, E.E. Villamil, J. (2003). *Avenues: Success in language, literacy and content*. Carmel, CA: Hampton-Brown.

Gay, G. (2000). *Culturally Responsive Teaching: Theory, Research & Practice*. New York: Teachers College Press.

Kagan, S. (1985). *Cooperative learning resources for teachers*. Riverside, CA: Spencer Kagan.

Kerr, A., History Department, Ohio State University. (n.d.). Temperance and prohibition. Retrieved from https://prohibition.osu.edu.

Lister, T.R. Sanchez, M. Bixler, S. O'ley, M. Hogenmiller, & M. Tawfeeq (2018). ISIS goes global: 143 attacks in 29 countries have killed 2,043. CNN. Retrieved from *https://www.cnn. com/2015/12/17/world/mapping-isis-attacks-around-the-world/index.html*.

Lyman, F.T. (1981). The responsive classroom discussion: The inclusion of all students. In A.S. Anderson (Ed.), *Mainstreaming Digest (*e109–113). College Park, MD: University of Maryland Press.

Marzano, R., & Pickering, D. (2005). *Building academic vocabulary: Teacher's manual*. Alexandria, VA: Association for Supervision and Curriculum Development (ASCD).

National Council for the Social Studies (NCSS). (2006). National Curriculum Standards for Social Studies—Executive Summary. Retrieved from *https://www.socialstudies.org/standards/ execsummary*.

National Council for the Social Studies (2010). National Curriculum Standards for Social Studies: A Framework for Teaching, Learning, and Assessment. Retrieved from *https://www.social-studies.org/standards/curriculum*.

National Council for the Social Studies (NCSS), The College, Career, and Civic Life (C3) Framework for Social Studies State Standards: Guidance for Enhancing the Rigor of K–12 Civics, Economics, Geography, and History (Silver Spring, MD: NCSS, 2013).

Nieto, S. (1996). *Affirming diversity: The sociopolitical context of multicultural education* (2nd ed.). White Plains, NY: Longman.

Parker, W.C. (2001). *Social Studies in Elementary Education* (11th ed.). Columbus, OH: Merrill Prentice-Hall.

Potts, J. (1994). *Adventure Tales of America*. Dallas, TX: Signal Media.

Rodgers, L., D. Gritten, J. Offer, and P. Asare. (March 11, 2016). "Syria: The story of the conflict." BBC News. Retrieved from *http://www.bbc.com/news/world-middle-east-26116868*.

Rosado, L., & Salazar, D. (2002–2003). La Conexión: The English/Spanish connection. *National Forum of Applied Educational Research Journal 15*(4): 51–66.

Rosado, L., Hellawell, M. & Zamora, B.E. (June 6, 2011). An Analysis of the Education System in Mexico and the United States from Pre-Kindergarten to 12th Grade. Education Resources Information Center (ERIC #520900). Available: *http://www.eric.ed.gov/PDFS/ED520900.pdf*.

Rosales Castañeda, O. (2006). *The Chicano Movement in Washington State: Political activism in the Puget Sound and Yakima Valley regions, 1960s-1980s.* Retrieved from *http://historylink.org/File/7922*.

Rowe, M.B. (1986). *Wait Times: Slowing down may be a way of speeding up. Journal of Teacher Education, 37*, 43–50.

Schifini, A. (1985). *Sheltered English: Content area instruction for limited English proficiency students.* Los Angeles, CA: Los Angeles County Office of Education.

Seattle Civil Rights and Labor History Project. 2006.

Sheppard, D.E. (n.d.) *Cabeza de Vaca in North America.* Spanish exploration and conquest of Native America. Retrieved from *http://floridahistory.com*.

Slavin, R. (1986). *Student Learning: An overview and practical guide.* Washington, DC: Professional Library, National Education Association.

Strayhorn, C.K. (2004), Fall. "The Rebound is Here." Texas Economic Update. Window on State Government. Retrieved from *http://www.window.state.tx.us/ecodata/teufall04/*.

Subject Test IV: Science (809)

OVERVIEW OF SUBJECT TEST IV: SCIENCE

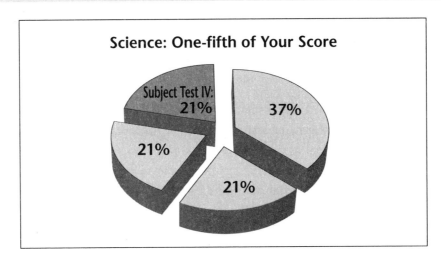

Science: One-fifth of Your Score

Subject Test IV: Science, as is the case with the Mathematics and Social Studies subject tests, represents approximately one-fifth of the Core Subjects 4–8 test. You'll have 50 minutes to answer 42 test items. As with Social Studies, this gives you slightly more than one minute for each question. Each of the four subject tests that make up the Core Subjects 4–8 test is individually timed.

The Science subject test assesses 11 Texas educator standards for teaching middle school science, including that the teacher:

1. Manages classroom, field, and laboratory activities to ensure the safety of all students and the ethical care and treatment of organisms and specimens;

2. Understands the correct use of tools, materials, equipment and technologies;

3. Understands the process of scientific inquiry and its role in science instruction;

4. Has theoretical and practical knowledge about teaching science and about how students learn science;

5. Knows the varied and appropriate assessments and assessment practices to monitor science learning;

6. Understands the history and nature of science;

7. Understands how science affects the daily lives of students and how it interacts with and influences personal and societal decisions;

8. Knows and understands the science content appropriate to teach the statewide curriculum (Texas Essential Knowledge and Skills) in physical science;

9. Knows and understands the science content appropriate to teach the statewide curriculum (Texas Essential Knowledge and Skills) in life science;

10. Knows and understands the science content appropriate to teach the statewide curriculum (Texas Essential Knowledge and Skills) in Earth and space science; and

11. Knows unifying concepts and processes that are common to all sciences.

This subject test embraces 23 competencies, which broadly define, as the Texas Education Agency puts it, "what an entry-level educator in this field in Texas public schools should know and be able to do." These competencies are covered in turn in this chapter. As part of your preparation, we encourage you to drill down in the official test framework to the descriptive statements, which describe the finer points of the knowledge and skills for which you are accountable.

The National Science Teachers Association (NSTA) Standards for Science Teacher Preparation (2012) list the following standards for effective science teaching (from: *http://www.nsta.org/preservice/docs/2012NSTAPreserviceScienceStandards.pdf*):

1. Effective teachers of science understand and articulate the knowledge and practices of contemporary science. They interrelate and interpret important concepts, ideas, and applications in their fields of licensure.

2. Effective teachers of science understand how students learn and develop scientific knowledge. Preservice teachers use scientific inquiry to develop this knowledge for all students.

3. Effective teachers of science are able to plan for engaging all students in science learning by setting appropriate goals that are consistent with knowledge of how students learn science and are aligned with state and national standards. The plans reflect the nature and social context of science, inquiry, and appropriate safety considerations. Candidates design and select learning activities, instructional settings, and resources—including science-specific technology, to achieve those goals; and they plan fair and equitable assessment strategies to evaluate if the learning goals are met.

4. Effective teachers of science can, in a P–12 classroom setting, demonstrate and maintain chemical safety, safety procedures, and the ethical treatment of living organisms needed in the P–12 science classroom appropriate to their area of licensure.

5. Effective teachers of science provide evidence to show that P–12 students' understanding of major science concepts, principles, theories, and laws have changed as a result of instruction by the candidate and that student knowledge is at a level of understanding beyond memorization. Candidates provide evidence for the diversity of students they teach.

6. Effective teachers of science strive continuously to improve their knowledge and understanding of the ever-changing knowledge base of both content, and science pedagogy, including approaches for addressing inequities and inclusion for all students in science. They identify with and conduct themselves as part of the science education community.

These standards are the hallmark of good science teaching agreed upon by science teachers and experienced professionals in the field. Essentially, for students to learn science, they must be consistently engaged in hands-on, manipulative activities. Teaching practices focusing on experience and direct investigation will best promote students' science learning. It is the teacher's responsibility to plan active learning experiences that engage the students in constructing new understandings of scientific phenomena, effectively measure learning, and provide a safe and interactive learning environment for all students.

NSTA strongly supports the idea that scientific inquiry should be a basic component of the curriculum in every grade in American schools (NSTA 2002). The 2016 NSTA position paper, *Science Education for Middle Level Students* (from: *http://static.nsta.org/pdfs/PositionStatement_Middle-Level.pdf*) acknowledges the uniqueness of students in the middle grades with the statement, "The middle school years, grades 5 through 9, are a time of tremendous physical, emotional, and cognitive changes for students. It also is a pivotal time in their understanding of and enthusiasm for science." (p. 1). It is important therefore that teachers gain sound knowledge of the content; however, it is equally important that they teach this content in ways that are motivating, interesting, and meaningful to students—focusing primarily on students having direct, hands on inquiry based learning experiences and connecting what they learn to everyday life.

Accordingly, teachers must consistently do the following in teaching science to middle level students (2016 *Science Education for Middle Level Students*, NSTA Position Paper, p. 1):

- Nurture curiosity about the natural world.

- Provide opportunities for students to engage in science and engineering experiences.

- Engage students in multiple laboratory investigations every week.

- Help students understand the nature of science by experiencing inquiry-based science in the classroom.

- Provide opportunities for students to work both independently and in collaborative groups.

- Integrate science learning with other subjects across the curriculum.

- Provide opportunities for and encourage critical thinking, reasoning, and analyses of evidence-based results.

- Give students experience in communicating and sharing ideas with others.

It is also important that science teaching utilizes scientific findings and advances of people from a variety of cultures and ensures equitable learning among all students.

Further, the National Academies report titled *A Framework for K–12 Science Education: Practices, Crosscutting Concepts, and Core Ideas* (National Research Council [NRC], 2012) emphasizes that "one of the principal goals of science education has been to cultivate students' scientific habits of mind, develop their capability to engage in scientific inquiry and teach them how to reason in a scientific context" (p. 3–1). It is important that teachers provide direct experiences so students may develop the knowledge they need through these experiences. Accordingly, "a narrow focus on content alone has the unfortunate consequence of leaving the students with naive conceptions of the nature of scientific inquiry and the impression that science is simply a body of isolated facts" (NRC 2011, p. 3–4). To be most effective in helping students learn science, teachers need to understand both the content and process of science. Importantly, teachers must understand and develop skill in implementing experiential, inquiry-based science as the primary teaching practice in all K–12 classrooms.

COMPETENCY 001

The teacher understands how to manage learning activities to ensure the safety of all students.

The beginning teacher:

A. Understands safety regulations and guidelines for science facilities and science instruction.

B. Knows procedures for and sources of information regarding the appropriate handling, use, disposal, care, and maintenance of chemicals, materials, specimens, and equipment.

C. Knows procedures for the safe handling and ethical care and treatment of organisms and specimens.

Teachers need to develop and communicate safety guidelines to students, model and implement safe practices in the classroom, and ensure all students follow the safety guidelines at all times. Teachers should prepare a safety contract for students listing all guidelines and behavioral expectations to be read aloud in class, and signed by both the student and parents or guardians. Safety rules should be clearly posted in the classroom and periodically reviewed, particularly before engaging in laboratory activities. Safe practices to consistently implement and enforce in the classroom include the following:

- Require students to use appropriate personal protective gear, like goggles, laboratory coats, and gloves.

- Use appropriate procedures for cleaning and disposing of materials.

- Adhere to appropriate disciplinary procedures to avoid accidents; for example, do not allow children to play with water or other lab materials.

- Substitute less hazardous equivalent materials when possible; for example, use cleaning products instead of chemicals in their pure form; use mild acids such as vinegar instead of more dangerous acids if appropriate.

- Use polyethylene or metal containers in place of glass.

- Advise children to avoid tasting or ingesting substances or materials.

- Label containers appropriately to avoid confusion.

- Control the distribution of materials to students and provide appropriate containers to safely transport materials.

- Control the use of sharp objects that can puncture the skin, providing strict rules and monitoring behavior at all times.

- Supervise the use of living organisms and ensure humane treatment of organisms is practiced.

- Monitor the cleaning of instruments used to ensure proper sanitation and avoid breakage.

- Avoid experimenting with human cells and bodily fluids.

- Share the responsibility for the safety of the students with the whole group; that is, students should motivate each other to follow safety procedures.

- Make provisions for the movement and handling of equipment and materials for students with special needs.

- Prepare, review, and send home an age-appropriate safety contract requiring parent/guardian signature.

- Organize all materials to be used in class by placing them in separate bins for a member of each student group to pick up for use for the lab activity and for returning materials after the lab activity.

- Clearly label and demonstrate the use of safety equipment with students, such as the eyewash station and fire blanket.

- Prepare and practice an emergency plan with students should an accident occur.

- Document all accidents, regardless of how minor, and have another teacher sign as witness if possible.

- Clearly write and read to students the safety precautions for the laboratory before beginning the activity. Ensure all students understand by responding to their questions before beginning.

- Place posters around the room emphasizing the safety rules of the classroom and laboratory.

- Keep all chemicals, glassware and other laboratory materials in locked cabinets with no unsupervised student access.

- Maintain regular inventory of all laboratory materials and chemicals.

- Store acids and other caustic chemicals in cabinets close to the floor in case they fall when retrieving for use.

- If using an open flame, such as lit candles, students must tie long hair back and tape or roll up loose sleeves to avoid contact with the fire.

- Caution students on the use of hot plates and placing materials on the hot plates reminding students that it remains warm long after it has been turned off.

The use of dangerous chemical substances in the middle level classroom may be generally limited in scope. Many laboratory chemicals can be substituted with household products. However, care needs to be taken even when handling household chemicals. It is important to demonstrate safe laboratory procedures for the classroom because household products are still chemicals and pose some level of risk to students. Safety management of chemicals in the classroom requires teachers to have knowledge of those chemicals and their properties. For example, teachers need to be aware that a simple tool like a mercury thermometer can break and pose a danger to students.

The National Science Teachers Association has an official position and guidelines on animals in the classroom. This information can be found at: *www.nsta.org/about/positions/animals.aspx*. NSTA contends that using animals in the classroom sparks interest and curiosity among students, and is therefore important to their science education experience. However, animals must be cared for and treated in a humane and ethical manner. This includes all animals that are sometimes not recognized as falling within these guidelines, from ants in ant farms, to mealworms, to guinea pigs and rabbits. Below are a few important guidelines in the treatment of animals in the classroom.

- Send permission slips home to be signed by parents or guardians if you anticipate the children will be handling the animals. This permission can go along with the safety contract previously described.

- Research and learn as much as possible about the animals, their typical behaviors, diet, sleep patterns, and habitats in advance of housing the animals in the classroom.

- Instruct students on how to handle animals and monitor their handling of animals at all times.

- Ensure the animals' habitats, including cages or other living quarters, are clean and regularly maintained. With instruction, cleaning animal housing can be done on a rotating basis by the students, teaching them important lessons on responsibility and fulfilling necessary chores.

- Feed and water the animals on a regular schedule according to the dietary needs of the animal.

- Demonstrate safe and humane treatment, and strictly enforce this treatment among all who have access to the animals.

When animals are used in dissection, it is critical that students learn to respect that this animal was a once a living organism, and that the dissection is for their learning. Monitor the dissection to ensure students treat the specimen with respect (e.g., do not "play" with internal organs). Have a back-up plan for students who may object to participating in animal dissection, or have low tolerance for the activity.

In addition to NSTA, the American Psychological Association provides guidelines for the ethical treatment of animals. These guidelines can be found at: *www.apa.org/science/leadership/care/ guidelines.aspx*. Most of the information presented deals with using animals in scientific research; however, the guidelines also present useful information on caring for animals.

COMPETENCY 002

The teacher understands the correct use of tools, materials, equipment, and technologies.

The beginning teacher:

A. Selects and safely uses appropriate tools, technologies, materials, and equipment needed for instructional activities.

B. Understands concepts of precision, accuracy, and error with regard to reading and recording numerical data from a scientific instrument.

C. Understands how to gather, organize, display, and communicate data in a variety of ways (e.g., charts, tables, graphs, diagrams, written reports, oral presentations, maps, satellite views).

D. Understands various units of measure such as the International System of Units (SI or metric system), light years, and degrees Celsius, and performs unit conversions within measurement systems (e.g., grams to kilograms, meters to millimeters).

Scientific experimentation requires careful observation and precise measures beyond what we can determine through our senses alone. To extend what can be observed with our senses scientific instruments are used such as balances, microscopes, beakers, electronic probes, and graduated cylinders to allow precise observations and measurements are made. Science requires the use of standard measuring devices to be sure that the information is clear, accurate, and able to be replicated in experimental settings.

In selecting the appropriate tools to use for a given observation and measurement consider the task that is needed and match that with the instrument as follows.

- To take an object's **mass** (amount of matter in an object) use triple beam or electronic balance and obtain the measurement in grams or kilograms. If taking the mass of a liquid or object that will not stay on the balance or scale, use a container such as a beaker or plastic cup in which to place the liquid or object. First measure and record the mass of the container minus the liquid or object. Then place the liquid or object in the container and measure the mass of both objects together. Subtract the mass of the container from the mass of both the container and liquid or object together to obtain the measure of only liquid or object. Regardless of the device used to measure mass, whether triple beam or electronic balance, the device must be zeroed out before placing the object on the device. This will ensure the mass measured is accurate.

- To measure the **volume** (amount of space something occupies) of a liquid, use a graduated cylinder for a precise measure in milliliters. Liquids that are polar molecules such as water cling to the walls of the container forming a downward arc shape or meniscus. The lowest point in the arc or meniscus is the accurate reading of liquid volume. It is best to have students view the meniscus at eye level to obtain an accurate reading.

- To measure the volume of an irregular object such as a rock, place water in a graduated cylinder to allow room for the object when dropped into the liquid, typically up to about half-way to three-quarters of the way to the top. Measure the water level as described above, reading and recording the water level at the meniscus. Then place the object into the graduated cylinder, being careful not to allow water to splash. The water will rise to a new level according to the volume of water that was displaced by the object. Measure the new volume of water with the object in the graduated cylinder then subtract the beginning volume of water to obtain the volume of the irregular object. One milliliter (ml) is a liquid volume measure that is equal to one cubic centimeter (cc or cm^3) that is a solid volume measure.

- Measuring the volume of a cube is accomplished by taking the length × width × height of the object using a metric tape measure or meter stick. The volume is typically recorded in cubic centimeters (cc or cm^3).

- Beakers are usually used to hold liquids, with a less precise measure of volume. Beakers are useful in making solutions.

- **Compound light microscopes** are used in observing very small specimens, and provide fairly high magnification. Specimens must be very thin when placed on a slide on the stage of the microscope in order that light may pass through.

- **Dissecting microscopes** have lower magnification than compound microscopes and are used for observing larger specimens such as whole insects, leaves, and rock minerals.

The United States uses a combination of the English system of measurement (standard) and the International System of Units (SI), also known as the metric system. The United States is the only technologically developed country in the world that uses the English system for business transactions and for day-to-day activities. However, for international business, engineering, and natural sciences, all countries use the more standardized, precise system of weights and measurement, the metric system. The English system uses pounds, gallons, and inches for measurement, while the metric system uses degrees Celsius, grams or kilograms, liters, and meters. The metric system uses a system of fractions and multiples of units that are related to each other by powers of 10, allowing conversion and comparison of measures simply by shifting a decimal point, and avoiding the lengthy arithmetical operations required by the English system. Examples of metric conversions include: 1.0 kilograms is equivalent to 1,000 grams and 1.0 meter is equivalent to 1,000 millimeters. The TEKS requires the teaching of both the metric and the English systems; however, all scientific data are to be reported using the metric system. In addition to the English and metric systems, students should be familiar with the light year as a unit of measurement. It is important to understand that light years are used to measure astronomical distances for objects in outer space and NOT a measure of time (as the term "years" may imply).

It is best that students become comfortable with using metric measurements. To help them learn metric, it is important to show them exactly what a gram or kilogram for example, looks and "feels" like, along with meters, centimeters, liters and milliliters. Have students measure and make items according to these standards as a reference for all to use in the classroom.

In addition to gathering data, such as measurements, students should be able to display their data appropriately. Teachers should be familiar with the varied ways to display data, which include: charts, tables, graphs, diagrams, written reports, oral presentations, maps, and satellite views.

COMPETENCY 003

The teacher understands the process of scientific inquiry and the history and nature of science.

The beginning teacher:

A. Understands the characteristics of various types of scientific investigations (e.g., descriptive studies, comparative data analysis, experiments).

B. Understands how to design, conduct and communicate the results of a variety of scientific investigations.

C.   Understands the historical development of science (e.g., cell theory, plate tectonics, laws of motion, universal gravity, atomic theory) and the contributions that diverse cultures and individuals of both genders have made to scientific knowledge.

D.   Understands the roles that logical reasoning, verifiable evidence, prediction, and peer review play in the process of generating and evaluating scientific knowledge.

E.   Understands principles of scientific ethics (e.g., honest and complete reporting of data, informed consent, legal constraints).

F.   Develops, analyzes, and evaluates different explanations for a given scientific result.

G.   Demonstrates an understanding of potential sources of error in an investigation.

H.   Demonstrates an understanding of how to communicate and defend the results of an investigation.

I.   Demonstrates an ability to identify, review, and evaluate legitimate sources of scientific information.

One common misunderstanding about scientific inquiry is that scientific investigations are limited to one method, the scientific method. Many science classrooms support this idea with a poster that describes this single method, the experimental method. These posters often describe a number of "steps" including a hypothesis, control, and variable to be manipulated. However, science has more than one way to carry out investigations, with experimental science as just <u>one</u> of several recognized forms of scientific inquiry accepted by the scientific community. Some of these forms of scientific inquiry include: *descriptive studies*, *comparative data analysis*, and as mentioned, *experiments*. **Descriptive studies** are those where the purpose of the inquiry is to explain or describe observations. For example, in an animal dissection, the students would describe observations of the internal systems and organs of the animal. The students would observe, illustrate, and label organs and make inferences on their functions or study them more in-depth. The students would record observations through illustrations, labels, and anatomical (appearances), as well as physiological (functions) descriptions. An astronomer, geologist, and ecologist may also use descriptive studies in their work; still engaging in scientific inquiry. For example, an astronomer would describe planetary motions, a geologist may describe rocks and rock layers, and an ecologist would describe interrelationships among living organisms in the natural environment. Descriptive studies simply explain "what is." For more information, see: *http://www.visionlearning.com/en/library/Process-of-Science/49/Description-in-Scientific-Research/151*

Comparative investigations are more open than descriptive studies; observations and data collected are compared among different existing situations, such as comparing and contrasting data collected on two different populations. Comparative investigations may have students compare the functions of the gills in fish with the lungs of a fetal pig, for example, viewing cross sections of each under the microscope. Comparative studies have some features of descriptive studies and some features of experimental studies. As with experimental studies, the researcher attempts to find the relationships between variables by observing and recording differences and similarities; for example, between different organisms, rock types, stars, and/or populations. However, unlike experimental studies, comparative studies do not involve setting up "treatments" or "controls." Like descriptive studies, comparative investigations describe what exists, making inferences about similarities and differences based on observations and data. Note, however, that simple comparative studies are not simple notations of similarities and differences—there must be "systematic cataloguing of the nature and/or behavior of two or more variables, and the quantification of the relationships between them." For more information, see *www.visionlearning.com/en/library/Process-of-Science/49/ Comparison-in-Scientific-Research/152.*

Experiments attempt to find relationships among variables within a particular phenomenon. Scientists using the experimental method; for example, a chemist experimenting on the effects of a certain chemical on bacterial growth may start with a hypothesis and experimental controls in a more structured manner. Experimental controls mean that all variables are constant between two different situations or groups except the variable being tested. For example, to determine whether or not "plants need light to survive and grow" the experiment would involve starting with two sets of plants of the same kind (e.g., bean plants) in the same types of pots, with the same amount and type of soil, under the same temperature conditions, receiving the same amount of water, and the same amount of light. These are the **independent variables** because they are the same for all plants. Consistency among the independent variables can also be determined by measuring and recording beginning experiment plant heights, number of leaves, and quality of color, for example. Photos or drawings would also add data to the experiment. Before beginning the experiment, often but not always, the researcher prepares a hypothesis to logically state what he or she predicts will be the result. Then the experiment begins: the researcher keeps one set of plants in the light, and takes one set of equivalent plants and places them in the dark. The set of plants in the light are the experimental "control" group because conditions are not changed. The second set of plants placed in the dark are the "treatment" group—these plants are subjected to only *one* different variable, also called the *dependent* variable—and that is they are no longer exposed to light. The **dependent variable** is the one aspect that is changed or different between one group and another. The plants would be observed and measured over time, still receiving the same amount of water, air, and heat (placed within the same temperature range), and data would be recorded on observed differences between the plants in the light and in the dark. The observed differences would be used to accept or fail to accept the hypothesis. For more information on experimental research in science, see: *http://www. visionlearning.com/en/library/Process-of-Science/49/Experimentation-in-Scientific-Research/150.*

It should be noted that experiments do not always precisely follow the linear set of steps of the scientific method from hypothesis to the reporting of results. Instead, the process is often a cyclical and nonlinear endeavor to establish relationships between variables, and sometimes to attempt to determine cause and effect. Regardless of the type of inquiry investigation being conducted (descriptive, comparative, experimental), all scientific investigations share at least one aspect: a question. The type of scientific inquiry to engage in is always dependent upon the nature of the question(s) and the best way to respond to the question(s).

In the classroom there are multiple ways to implement inquiry science, often referred to as structured, guided, or open. These instructional methods vary primarily in the amount of control of the teacher in the inquiry process, along with the nature of the scientific research question. Teachers often begin the school year with more structured investigations; then, as students learn the routines and rules of the classroom and laboratory, teachers turn more control over to students to engage in more open inquiry. Allowing more student-directed open inquiry should be a goal of every science teacher in order for students to be able to experience the true nature of the scientific discipline and understand what scientists do! In helping students understand and become immersed in what scientists do in the profession, teachers must also incorporate practice in developing students' communication skills. In the global scientific community, scientific research and information is always shared with and disseminated to other scientists and the general public using strong communication skills. Therefore, it is critical that students learn to effectively communicate their work to others, learning to effectively argue their reasoning and defend the results and explanations derived from their investigations. Students must use logical scientific reasoning and present sound arguments for their findings, not based on opinion, but based on **experimental evidence**. These communication skills can best be developed and promoted by engaging students in collaborative, inquiry-based science in the classroom, and providing them with regular opportunities to present findings in written and oral forms using a variety of delivery mechanisms (posters, technical papers, technology). Students should also be familiar with peer review—meaning that their investigations and findings are always subject to the critical review of others. In the scientific community, results of investigations are never published before they are carefully and critically reviewed and scrutinized by peers in the same field of study. Communicating results and allowing peer review in a scientific (not personal) manner should be practiced in the science classroom. The National Research Council promotes the need for strong communication among students as stated in the publication *Inquiry and the National Science Education Standards* (NRC, 2000). In this document, the NRC (2000) specifically states that students' scientific explanations "must adhere to criteria such as: a proposed explanation must be logically consistent; it must abide by the rules of evidence; it must be open to questions and possible modification; and it must be based on historical and current scientific knowledge" (p. 20). The book addresses several of the ideas and responsibilities encountered by students while conducting scientific inquiry. Further, according to the Next Generation Science Standards (NGSS), the practices of science involve the following activities. For more information see: *https://www.nextgenscience.org/*.

1. Asking questions (for science) and defining problems (for engineering)

2. Developing and using models

3. Planning and carrying out investigations

4. Analyzing and interpreting data

5. Using mathematics and computational thinking

6. Constructing explanations (for science) and designing solutions (for engineering)

7. Engaging in argument from evidence

8. Obtaining, evaluating, and communicating information

Teachers should understand the historical development of science (such as the development of cell theory and plate tectonics) and the contributions that diverse cultures and individuals of both genders have made to scientific knowledge. Although the "modern science" we practice today finds its origins in the European Renaissance, it was the "reawakening" to the work of many non-Western cultures (e.g., Arab philosophers and scholars) that led to the knowledge and technological advances of today in medicine and nearly all other fields of science. These contributions and contributions from the diverse populations and regions of the world need to be regularly introduced and discussed in the classroom. Teaching the history of science will help students better understand how we use what has been learned to build new conclusions and make new discoveries today, and help them realize that they are the scientists of the present and future.

Important history of science topics for teachers to understand and to incorporate into their teaching are shown in Table 6.1.

It is important to demonstrate to students that women have made tremendous contributions to the body of scientific knowledge. For example, it was astronomer Cecilia Payne (1900–1979) who challenged the assumptions of the prevailing opinion that the sun was composed primarily of iron. It was her spectroscopic work that suggested the sun was actually composed primarily of hydrogen and helium. As it was then, her work is often ignored in the classroom today. Yet, she is credited with providing a basis for the discovery of how the sun produces its energy (i.e., through fusion).

It is necessary for teachers to know and use the history of science in teaching, and to integrate the diverse number of scientists who made scientific contributions throughout history and in present-day science. The incorporation of scientists who have made important contributions to present-day scientific understandings and advances must be done with attention to equity. At the core of this competency is the premise that teachers must provide equitable science learning opportunities for their students. That is, science and science education is for *all students* regardless of gender, culture, ethnicity, physical ability, or learning exceptionality. Teachers must ensure that the examples they provide, the students called upon to respond, the opportunity to experience inquiry, and treatment of all students is equitable and fair at all times. It is important for the students to see *themselves* as scientists and as fully capable of solving problems and engaging in the inquiry process.

Table 6.1
History of Important Science Concepts to Use in Classroom Teaching

Concept	Description	Who	Timeframe	Resource
Cell theory	All living things are made up of cells and all cells have arisen from other existing cells.	Robert Hooke Henri Dutrochet	1635–1703 1776–1847	http://www.biologyreference.com/Gr-Hi/History-of-Biology-Cell-Theory-and-Cell-Structure.html
Plate Tectonics	Continents on Earth today were long ago formed together in a single landmass.	Alfred Wegener	1880–1930	http://www.scec.org/education/k12/learn/plate2.htm
Laws of Motion	1. An object at rest will remain at rest unless acted on by an unbalanced force. An object in motion continues in motion with the same speed and in the same direction unless acted upon by an unbalanced force. This is known as the law of inertia. 2. Acceleration is produced when a force acts on a mass. The greater the mass, the greater the amount of force needed (to accelerate the object). 3. For every action there is an equal and opposite reaction.	Sir Isaac Newton	1643–1727	http://teachertech.rice.edu/Participants/louviere/Newton/index.html
Universal Gravity	Every object in the universe attracts every other object with a force directed along the line of centers for the two objects that is proportional to the product of their masses and inversely proportional to the square of the separation between the two objects.	Sir Isaac Newton	1643–1727	http://csep10.phys.utk.edu/astr161/lect/history/newtongrav.html
Technology	The invention and development of systematic techniques and/or tools for making and doing things.	Various Scientists and Inventors	2.5 Million Years Ago to the Present	http://www.historyworld.net/wrldhis/PlainTextHistories.asp?historyid=ab11

Ethical standards are an important aspect of science to preserve the scholarship and rigor of the discipline. As such, scientists' research and reporting of research is guided by a strict code of ethics; this practice should also be followed in the classroom. The following list is a summary of ethics that apply to the middle school classroom (Resnik, 1993; Resnik, 2015):

1. **Scientific Honesty:** Do not commit scientific fraud, i.e., do not fabricate, fudge, trim, cook, destroy, or misrepresent data.

2. **Carefulness:** Strive to avoid careless errors or sloppiness in all aspects of scientific work.

3. **Intellectual Freedom:** Scientists should be allowed to pursue new ideas and criticize old ones. They should be free to conduct research they find interesting.

4. **Openness:** i.e., share data, results, methods, theories, equipment, and so on.

5. **Acceptance of Criticism:** Allow people to see your work; be open to criticism.

6. **Assignment of Credit:** Do not plagiarize the work of other scientists; give credit where credit is due (but not where it is not due).

In addition to these six principles, scientists must also:

- Report findings in a complete and thorough manner.

- Consider the principles of informed consent and legal constraints when conducting experiments.

Informed consent pertains to experiments, including surveys conducted with human beings. Informed consent means individuals participating in the experiment or research study have full knowledge of what they will be required to do as part of the study/experiment, including any harmful side effects, and that they understand they may withdraw their participation at any time.

Legal constraints for scientists include the ethical treatment of both humans and animals that participate in the experiment or study. There are multiple laws in place to ensure the safety of humans and animals involved in experimentations.

Teachers should understand the potential sources of error or uncertainty in inquiry-based investigations. Two common sources of error that students might encounter are systematic and random error. Systematic errors, for example, are due to faulty instruments. Random errors are not predictable and could be due to a variety of causes, including human error in interpreting data, recording data incorrectly, or inaccurate readings of measurements.

In addition, teachers should be knowledgeable when it comes to reliable sources of scientific information. Teachers should be able to recognize sources that adhere to the above principles and those that do not. Websites and journal articles published by professional associations are generally reliable, peer-reviewed sources of information; for example, the journal titled *Science* is published by the American Association for the Advancement of Science. Websites that are sponsored by legitimate agencies such as NASA, the National Science Foundation (NSF), and the National Institutes of

Health (NIH) are also reliable. The research reported and other content is screened for accuracy and quality prior to publishing through a rigorous, peer-reviewed process. It is always good practice to review several sources of information before arriving at conclusions as to the saliency of the information presented. A single source is unacceptable as it may provide a narrow view, may have promotional or self-interests at stake, and/or may provide one-sided or biased information. For example, if conducting research on causes and treatments of cancer, it is best to seek several legitimate sources for information and consistency in findings presented by these sources. The World Health Organization (WHO), NIH, and sources such as a renowned medical facility like the Mayo Clinic are more reliable than unknown sources. It would not be acceptable to only cite research backed by the pharmaceutical company that holds the share of the market on the drugs sold to treat the disease.

COMPETENCY 004

The teacher understands how science impacts the daily lives of students and interacts with and influences personal and societal decisions.

The beginning teacher:

A. Understands that decisions about the use of science are based on factors such as ethical standards, economics, and personal and societal needs.

B. Applies scientific principles and the theory of probability to analyze the advantages of, disadvantages of, or alternatives to a given decision or course of action.

C. Applies scientific principles and processes to analyze factors that influence personal choices concerning fitness and health, including physiological and psychological effects and risks associated with the use of substances and substance abuse.

D. Understands concepts, characteristics, and issues related to changes in populations and human population growth.

E. Understands the types and uses of natural resources and the effects of human consumption on the renewal and depletion of global resources (e.g., energy, sustainability).

F. Understands the role science can play in helping resolve personal, societal, and global challenges (e.g., water quality, public health, climate change).

Teachers need to remain knowledgeable of the influences of science and technology on the lives of students and the extent to which these fields permeate students' lives. The functioning of their bodies, the potential threat of diseases, issues of sustainability and the natural environment around them, and their everyday use of electrical appliances, computers, and cell phones are examples of biological and physical science in their lives. Many of these topics and technologies can be used productively in classroom science instruction, as they are intertwined in the lives of students. However, teachers need to be aware that students tend to keep the science they learn in school separate from the science they experience in everyday life. Instead of teaching science and technology in isolation and maintaining this pervasive separation, teachers need to help students connect the science they are learning in school to the world around them. Integrating everyday life experiences and personal and societal topics into the classroom through science teaching will broaden students' conceptual understandings and promote the usefulness, value, and applicability of science. In inquiry science, the optimal time to make connections with everyday life phenomena is either after or while students experience a hands-on lab activity and construct an understanding of the concept. To make sense of science, the student must have the background needed to relate the newly learned concept to their everyday lives and see how the concept works in differing contexts. Connecting newly learned concepts to the students' life experiences makes the learning more meaningful for students and helps them retain understanding of the concept for later use. Relating science to what students already know and experience in life helps bridge the disconnections between "school science" and science they observe and experience in everyday life.

Another approach is to place the entire societal and everyday life connections in the context of science through Project Based Learning or PBL (Krajcik et al., 1994). In PBL, a societal topic is selected as the overarching theme, and the teacher leads the students in, or the students initiate their own, inquiry-based science experiences connected to the overarching theme, or project. Project Based Learning engages students in authentic learning activities that are motivating and designed to answer a question or solve a problem. PBL provides students with experiences that are consistent with learning and workplace activities that are present in the everyday world. More specifically, PBL is defined as: "a systematic teaching method that engages students in learning essential knowledge and life-enhancing skills through an extended, student-influenced inquiry process structured around complex, authentic questions and carefully designed products and tasks" (The Buck Institute for Education and Boise State University, 2012).

Science has brought society many advantages that have served to increase the health and longevity of human lives, and to improve the quality of life for all. However, there may be consequences, often unforeseen, to scientific discovery and invention that impacts society and the natural environment, as well as the habitats and survival of the living organisms that share this planet. To better understand these issues, students need to gain scientific knowledge and evidence of what is known. Armed with appropriate background knowledge, students will be in the position to weigh the pros and cons of various scientific discoveries and debate issues that prevail in our global community. Students should be apprised of issues such as global warming, for example; but before taking a position on the topic, they must be prepared with accurate scientific information on the topic. When students are given opportunities to use scientific concepts as support for sound logic and reasoning to debate or evaluate a scientific issue, they are operating at high cognitive levels important to their intellectual development. Equally important is student awareness of the ethical, personal, societal, and economic implications of science, from both positive and negative perspectives. Students need to realize the trade-offs often present in scientific discovery and experimentation: for example, laboratory testing on animals. Many new and important discoveries have improved the quality of human life at the cost of animals' lives. It is important for students to understand and weigh the costs versus benefits of research from not only financial, but also social and ethical, standpoints.

In order to best understand the complexity of how science interfaces with personal and societal issues, students need to be engaged in electronic and library research on impactful science topics and take part in discussion with peers and experts in the science fields. Topics such as cloning, global warming, alternative and fossil fuels, and space exploration are just a few additional topics tied to ethical, personal, societal, and economic concerns. It is important that students fully understand the scientific knowledge that underlies all such complex issues, and can formulate decisions based on this knowledge.

The scientific processes are skills that last a lifetime, applicable to a vast array of everyday life decisions and experiences. Teachers need to help students apply the scientific processes to real world situations. Making careful observations, experimenting, collecting data and information, and drawing conclusions, as examples, are important in everyday life decisions. Determining which presidential candidate to vote for, which doctor to see and after, knowing if the diagnoses are correct, what product to buy, or what to determine is true as presented in the media all require proficiency in using scientific processes and the associated reasoning skills. Teachers must provide students with opportunities to apply scientific processes in everyday life decisions so they may see the importance and benefits of learning these skills.

Natural resources and the consumption of natural resources have been dominant issues in society over the past 100 years. In today's society, the most pressing issue is the economic and environmental impacts of obtaining natural resources for use as fuel and electricity. It is important to know about fossil fuels, their origin, how they are obtained, and how they are used for energy. Since fossil fuels are nonrenewable and will one day be expended, science is continuing to develop and improve upon alternative sources of energy, such as wind, solar, hydroelectric, and geothermal. Teachers must be knowledgeable about these other sources of energy and be able to guide students toward understanding how these renewable energy sources are used, and how they impact our society's energy needs. This understanding must include the concepts of sustainability of global resources and energy sustainability. Teachers should allow students to discover and analyze how energy is used in the United States and in other countries; for example, the type of energy sources that each country is most dependent upon (nonrenewable, renewable). Energy dependency is a worldwide issue since consumption of resources that cannot be renewed will impact many nations across the globe. Non-regulation of pollutants produced in generating energy impacts more than those within the non-regulated nation; it also has implications on a global scale, including worldwide concerns of global warming due to unchecked carbon dioxide emissions.

A significant impact of science on a student's daily life relates to fitness and health. Childhood obesity is a serious crisis in the United States, and teachers can play an important role in educating children on the negative health issues associated with poor nutrition and a lack of exercise. Teachers need to help students learn about factors that impact physical and psychological health and about how to make good choices regarding nutrition, hygiene, physical exercise, smoking, drugs, and alcohol. Understanding human biology will help students realize how obesity and other factors such as substance use/abuse affect their physical and mental health. The topics of heart disease, diabetes, and cancer should be included in the curriculum as ways to help students understand the detrimental effects of unhealthy life choices.

Science can also impact societal and global challenges, including water quality and climate change. Scientists regularly share findings from their research on these issues in order to find solutions to solve problems and replicate research to determine consistency in results. For example, science has found innovative solutions to inexpensively produce clean water in societies where clean water is scarce. See solutions for clean water: *https://www.forbes.com/sites/patrickcox/2016/12/06/biotech-has-a-solution-for-the-clean-water-crisis/* and solutions for global warming: *http://www.climatehotmap.org/global-warming-solutions/* as examples.

COMPETENCY 005

The teacher knows and understands the unifying concepts and processes that are common to all sciences.

The beginning teacher:

A. Understands how the following concepts and processes provide a unifying explanatory framework across the science disciplines: systems, order and organization; evidence, models and explanation; change, constancy, and measurements; evolution and equilibrium; and form and function.

B. Demonstrates an understanding of how patterns in observations and data can be used to make explanations and predictions.

C. Analyzes interactions and interrelationships between systems and subsystems.

D. Applies unifying concepts to explore similarities in a variety of natural phenomena.

E. Understands how properties and patterns of systems can be described in terms of space, time, energy and matter.

F. Understands how change and constancy occur in systems.

G. Understands the complementary nature of form and function in a given system.

H. Understands how models are used to represent the natural world and how to evaluate the strengths and limitations of a variety of scientific models (e.g., physical, conceptual, mathematical).

Science is a way of knowing, a process—it is a systematic way of looking at the world and how it works. This competency focuses on how science uses a regular, consistent method of collecting and reporting data about scientific phenomena. Science is a way of organizing observations and then seeking patterns and regularity in order to make sense of the world. In science we organize evidence, create models, and explain observations in a logical form. We may make predictions and hypotheses and test our predictions and hypotheses through controlled experimentation, meaning all variables of the experiment remain constant except for the variable being tested. We repeat experiments multiple times and seek constancy in our findings in form and/or function. We seek patterns and consistency in our observations and data in order to construct explanations and make new predictions. We employ different forms of scientific inquiry to best respond to our research questions, including experimental, descriptive, and comparative methods, recognizing that experiments do not always progress as planned.

Science embraces a broad spectrum of subject matter, such as life science, physical science, and earth science, all of which is interrelated. For example, in studying the ecosystem, teachers must understand the biological aspects (e.g., the living organism) and how they interact, as in predator-prey relationships and symbiotic relationships (e.g., parasitism, commensalism), as well as the chemical aspects of the ecosystem (e.g., nitrogen cycle), the geologic or earth science aspects (e.g., the landscape, the water, and the climate) and the physics aspects (e.g., energy transfer, motion). Ecosystems, for example, regardless of location on Earth, share unifying components and characteristics, and teachers must understand this unity. In life science, there is unity of what makes organisms "living"—they all must carry on life functions and are composed of one or more cells. These are the criteria that unify life forms and classify something like a virus, for example, as non-living (it does not carry on the life functions and is not composed of cells).

All scientific observations can be described by their characteristics or "properties." These properties organize the observations according to commonalities, or classification. Observed properties and patterns are centered on space, time, energy, and matter. Unifying concepts in teaching science in Texas at each grade level are articulated in the *Texas Essential Knowledge and Skills for Science* document, found at: *www.tea.state.tx.us*.

COMPETENCY 006

The teacher understands forces and motion and their relationships.

The beginning teacher:

A. Demonstrates an understanding of properties of universal forces (e.g., gravitational, electrical, magnetic).

B. Understands how to measure, graph, and describe changes in motion using concepts of displacement, velocity, and acceleration.

C. Understands the vector nature of force.

D. Identifies the forces acting on an object and applies Newton's laws to describe the motion of an object.

E. Analyzes the relationship between force and motion in a variety of situations (e.g., simple machines, blood flow, geologic processes).

Universal forces include gravity, electricity, and magnetism, which are important to understanding this competency.

Force is defined as the action of moving an object [...] object to move at a constant speed or to accelerate. W[...] done. Work is the product of the force acting in the [...] ment. Energy is defined as the ability to do work; whe[...] it to a different location, energy is used and work is [...] important to understand in fulfilling this competency. [...] remain at rest unless acted upon by an (unbalanced) [...] to stay in motion with the same speed and in the sa[...] anced) outside force. This first law is also called ine[...] is produced when a force acts on mass and the great[...] greater the amount of force needed to accelerate tha[...] for every action there is an equal and opposite react[...]

[handwritten note: equal mass, acceleration = & opposite. acceleration depends on mass & applied force. What happens?]

Force and motion, as well as changes in motion [...] in which variables such as time, speed, distance, and direction can be recorded and graphed, and teachers need to know how to do so. For example, teachers can have students experience and record what happens when an object with higher mass (such as a large marble or ball bearing), collides with an object with less mass (e.g., a small marble or ball bearing). Teachers should also know what happens when the rate of speed is high when the objects collide compared to when the rate of speed is low. The game of pool or billiards is a good example. When forces are unbalanced, it may cause the object to change its motion or position.

Magnetism is the force of attraction or repulsion between objects that results from the positive and negative ionic charges of the objects. Usually, the objects are metals, such as iron, nickel, and cobalt. Magnets have two poles that have opposing charges or forces: north (+) and south (−). When the north pole of a magnet is placed close to the north pole of a second magnet, repulsion occurs. When poles of different kinds (north and south) are placed close, they attract one another. The strength of the forces depends on the size and the proximity of the magnets. The charged area around a magnet is called a magnetic field. The Earth is like a large magnet, with opposing forces—the North Pole and South Pole, and the magnetic field of attraction of Earth that we know as gravity is like that of a magnet. Without gravity, all objects on Earth, including the atmosphere, would not be held onto its surface. Planets and other celestial objects that are more massive than Earth, such as Jupiter, have stronger gravitational forces, and those that are less massive and/or dense, such as our moon, have weaker gravitational forces.

A machine is something that makes work easier. Machines can be as simple as a wedge or a screw or as sophisticated as a computer or gas engine. A simple machine has few or no moving parts and can change the size and direction of a force. A screw, hammer, wedge, and incline plane are examples of simple machines. Simple machines are part of our daily activities. For example, children playing on a seesaw are using a simple machine called a lever. Thus, teachers and their students should know the practical use of these simple machines in everyday life. A complex machine is two or more simple machines working together to facilitate work. Some of the complex machines used in daily activities are a wheelbarrow, a can opener, and a bicycle.

Force and motion is what keeps the sun, Earth, moon, and planets in their orbits and explains the structure and changes of the universe. On Earth, force and motion are found in all geologic processes, explaining phenomena such as tides and tsunamis.

COMPETENCY 007

The teacher understands physical properties of, and changes in, matter.

The beginning teacher:

A. Describes the physical properties of substances (e.g., density, boiling point, solubility, thermal and electrical conductivity).

B. Describes the physical properties and molecular structure of solids, liquids, and gases.

C. Describes the relationship between the molecular structure of materials (e.g., metals, crystals, polymers) and their physical properties.

D. Relates the physical properties of an element to its placement in the periodic table.

E. Distinguishes between physical and chemical changes in matter.

F. Applies knowledge of physical properties of and changes in matter to processes and situations that occur in life science and in Earth/space science (e.g., evaporation, changes in air pressure).

Matter has physical, thermal, electrical, and chemical properties. These properties are dependent upon the molecular composition of the matter.

The physical properties of matter are the way matter looks and feels. It includes qualities like color, density, hardness, and conductivity. Color represents how matter is reflected or perceived by the human eye. Density is the mass that is contained in a unit of volume of a given substance. Hardness represents the resistance to penetration offered by a given substance. Conductivity is the ability of substances to transmit thermal or electric current.

Matter is sensitive to temperature changes. Heat and cold produce changes in the physical properties of matter; however, the chemical properties remain unchanged. For example, when water is exposed to cold temperature (release of heat), it changes from liquid to solid; and when water is exposed to heat, it changes from solid to liquid. With continued heat, the water changes from liquid to gas (water vapor). Water vapor can be cooled again and turned back into liquid. However, through all these states, water retains its chemical properties—two molecules of hydrogen and one molecule of oxygen, or H_2O.

Matter can be classified as a conductor or nonconductor of electricity. Conductive matter allows the transfer of electric current or heat from one point to another. Metals are usually good conductors, while wood and rocks are examples of nonconductive matter.

Matter can exist in four distinct states: solid, liquid, gas, and plasma. Most people are familiar with the basic states of matter, but they might not be familiar with the fourth one, plasma. Plasmas are formed at extremely high temperatures when electrons are stripped from neutral atoms (University of California, 2006). Stars are predominantly composed of plasmas. Solids have mass, occupy a definite amount of space, or *volume,* or have a definite shape, and are denser than liquids. Liquids have mass, occupy a definite volume, do not have a definite shape, but instead take the shape of their container. Gases have mass, do not have a definite volume, have no definite shape but take the shape of their container, and are the least dense of the three states of matter. Plasma has no definite shape or volume, and is a substance that cannot be classified as a solid, liquid, or gas. When substances change from one state of matter to another, such as ice melting, it is a physical change, and not a chemical change.

A physical change is a change in a substance that does not change what that substance is made of. Examples of physical changes are melting ice, boiling water, tearing paper, chopping wood, writing with chalk, and mixing sugar and water together. In the mixing of sugar with water, or salt with water, even though the sugar or salt may not be visible to the naked eye in the water, it is still there and still has the same composition—that is, the molecules that make up the sugar or salt and water are still the same as when you mixed them. You can evaporate the water and you will recover your sugar or salt crystals. Students should be aware of the physical changes that occur in the life and Earth/space sciences. An example of a physical change in life science is when food is broken into smaller pieces during the process of chewing, which begins the process of food digestion in the body. An example of a physical change in Earth/space science would be evaporation during the water cycle. During evaporation, liquid water is heated enough that it becomes water vapor.

COMPETENCY 008

The teacher understands chemical properties of, and changes in, matter.

The beginning teacher:

A. Describes the structure and components of the atom.

B. Distinguishes among elements, mixtures, and compounds and describes their properties.

C. Relates the chemical properties of an element to its placement in the periodic table.

D. Describes chemical bonds and chemical formulas.

E. Analyzes chemical reactions and their associated chemical equations.

F. Explains the importance of a variety of chemical reactions that occur in daily life (e.g., rusting, burning of fossil fuels, photosynthesis, cell respiration, chemical batteries, digestion of food).

G. Understands applications of chemical properties of matter in physical, life, and Earth/space science and technology (e.g., materials science, biochemistry, transportation, medicine, telecommunications).

Matter is anything that takes up space and has mass. The mass of a body is the amount of matter in an object or thing, and volume describes the amount of space that matter takes up. Mass is also the property of a body that causes it to have weight. Weight is the amount of gravitational force exerted over an object. It is important not to confuse mass and weight. What students are measuring on their balances in the laboratory is an object's **mass**. Weight changes as an object goes from one level of gravitational force to another—for example, from Earth to the moon—because the amount of "pull" on that object is different. The mass of the object—how much matter or material is in the object—does not change unless we do something to actually take away or add matter to that object.

There are 118 basic kinds of matter, called elements, which are organized into the periodic table. An element is composed of sub-microscopic components called **atoms**. Atoms are made up of particles called electrons, neutrons, and protons. The mass of the atom is located mostly in the nucleus, which is made up of protons, which have a positive charge, and neutrons, which are neutral or have no charge. The atomic mass of the atom is its protons plus neutrons, where each has a mass of 1 atomic mass unit (AMU). The electron contains little mass (which has a negligible contribution to the overall atomic mass), carries a negative charge, and follows an orbit with a specific distance and shape around the nucleus (electron energy level or shell). The atomic number is the number of protons in the nucleus of the atom. The number of protons is the distinction between one type of atom and another, e.g., hydrogen, which has 1 proton, and helium, an entirely different atom with different properties, which has 2 protons. The number of electrons is equal to the number of protons in a stable atom, so the negative and positive charges are balanced. An ion is an atom or molecule that has lost or gained one or more electrons and thus has negative or positive charge (because there are either more or less protons, or positive charges, compared to electrons, or negative charges). It is these chemical properties that determine an element's location on the periodic table. Elements with the same number of electrons in their outer shell (or valence electrons) will be in the same vertical column or group. Elements in the same period, or horizontal row, have fewer properties in common. However, as you move from left to right across a period, the atomic numbers always increase.

Molecules are two or more atoms bonded together in a chemical bond. There are two types of chemical bonds, ionic bonds and covalent bonds. In ionic bonds electrons are transferred from one atom to the other that it is bonding with, for example Na (sodium) gives its outer shell electron to Cl (chlorine) to make NaCl (sodium chloride) or table salt. In covalent bonding electrons are shared, equally or unequally, between the different atoms in the molecule. For example, carbon and two oxygen atoms share outer shell electrons to form covalent bonds to the molecule CO_2 (carbon dioxide). In bonding, the atoms are chemically seeking to fill their outer shell of electrons, usually with the full complement of 8 electrons (2 electrons in the case of hydrogen).

The atoms of a molecule can be more than one of the *same kind* of atom, as in the naturally occurring oxygen molecule, O_2, or a molecule can be two or more *different kinds* of atoms as in carbon dioxide (CO_2), ammonia (NH_3), and glucose ($C_6H_{12}O_6$). Compounds are when you have two or more *different* kinds of atoms in the molecule and you have a given amount of that substance. In other words, compounds consist of matter composed of atoms that are chemically combined with one another in molecules in definite weight proportions. An example of a compound is water; water is oxygen and hydrogen combined in the ratio of two hydrogen molecules to one molecule of oxygen (H_2O). So, you can also call *one* H_2O a molecule.

The chemical properties of one type of matter (element) can react with the chemical properties of other types of matter. In general, elements from the same groups will not react with each other, while elements from different groups may. The more separated the groups, the more likely they will cause a chemical reaction when brought together. A type of matter can be chemically altered to become a different type of matter; for example, a metal trash can will rust if it is left out in the rain.

Mixtures are combinations of two or more substances (where each substance is distinct from the other) that are made up of two or more types of molecules and not chemically combined. The two substances in the mixture may or may not be evenly distributed, so there are no definite amounts or weight proportions. Mixtures may be **heterogeneous**, which means an uneven distribution of the substances in the mixture throughout. A mixture may be **homogeneous**, which means the components are evenly distributed throughout. Examples of mixtures include milk, which is a heterogeneous mixture of water and butterfat particles. The components of a mixture can be separated physically. For example, milk producers and manufacturers remove the butterfat from whole milk to make skim milk.

Solutions are *mixtures* that are *homogeneous*, which means that the components are distributed evenly and there is an even concentration throughout. The solute is the substance in the smaller amount that dissolves and that you add into the substance that is in the larger amount — the solvent. Water is a common solvent. Solids, liquids, and gases can be solutes. Examples of solutions are seawater and ammonia. Seawater is made up of water and salt, and ammonia is made up of ammonia gas and water. In these examples, the salt and the ammonia (NH_3) are the solutes; water is the solvent.

A chemical change is when the substances that were combined are no longer the same molecules — they have changed to new substances. For example, burning wood, mixing baking soda and vinegar, or a rusting nail, which is when the iron of the nail (Fe) combines with oxygen (in the presence of water) to form a new substance — that is, a new molecule is formed: iron oxide, or Fe_2O_3.

Physical changes can be reversed, whereas chemical changes generally cannot be reversed. Evidence of a chemical change include that the combination of the substances gives off a gas (bubbles are observed), it changes color (not always a chemical change, but may be if the other evidences are also present), gives off heat and becomes warmer, or absorbs heat and becomes colder (temperature change), and forms a precipitate (a solid substance). When heat is given off in a chemical change, it is an **exothermic** reaction; and when heat is absorbed in a chemical change (the combination becomes colder), it is an **endothermic** reaction. Everyday examples of exothermic reactions are firewood burning or the use of a hand warmer by many mountain climbers and snow skiers. Examples of endothermic reactions are a cold pack used for sports injuries or the combination of baking soda and vinegar (try it with a thermometer in the vinegar during the reaction and see!).

Chemical reactions occur in everyday life and are an essential part of our physical and biological world. The burning of gasoline in automobiles is a chemical change—as is burning of any kind. Burning is the combination of oxygen from the atmosphere with substances containing the carbon atom. The proper temperature has to be reached in order to begin this exothermic reaction, but once started, the chemical reaction can continue until the oxygen is used up or is prevented from entering into the reaction. So since gasoline is a fossil fuel (a once living organism), it contains carbon. When we provide the energy it needs to begin the reaction, called activation energy, as long as oxygen is present, the carbon substance will burn. Burning is a chemical reaction because the carbon and oxygen combine to form new substances such as carbon monoxide (CO) and carbon dioxide (CO_2). The same reaction occurs in burning wood, candles, and even in cell respiration—the oxygen we breathe and carry through our bloodstream is combined in our cells with carbon-containing glucose molecules in a type of "controlled" burning. Our bodies give off heat from this reaction, which is why we are able to maintain a fairly high temperature of about 98.6 degrees Fahrenheit. Other examples of chemical reactions in everyday life include chemical batteries, the digestion of food, and cooking/baking. Moreover, the process of photosynthesis, where plants use sunlight to convert carbon dioxide gas and water into food for the plant known as glucose (a simple sugar), is also an important chemical reaction responsible for providing food for and sustaining all life on Earth.

COMPETENCY 009

The teacher understands energy and interactions between matter and energy.

The beginning teacher:

A. Describes concepts of work, power, and potential and kinetic energy.

B. Understands the concept of heat energy and the difference between heat and temperature.

C. Understands the principles of electricity and magnetism and their applications (e.g., electric circuits, motors, audio speakers, nerve impulses, lighting).

D. Applies knowledge of types (longitudinal, transverse); properties (e.g., wavelength and frequency); and behaviors (e.g., reflection, refraction, dispersion) to describe a variety of waves (e.g., water, electromagnetic, sound, seismic waves).

E. Applies knowledge of properties and behaviors of light to describe the function of optical systems and phenomena (e.g., camera, microscope, rainbow, eye).

F. Demonstrates an understanding of the properties, production, and transmission of sound.

Energy is available in many forms, including heat, light, solar radiation, chemical, electrical, magnetic, sound, and mechanical energy. It exists in three states: potential, kinetic, and activation energies. An object possessing energy because of its ability to move has kinetic energy. The energy that an object has as the result of its position or condition is called potential energy. The energy necessary to transfer or convert potential energy into kinetic energy is called activation energy. All three states of energy can be transformed from one to the other. A vehicle parked in a garage has potential energy. When the driver starts the engine using the chemical energy stored in the battery and the fuel, potential energy becomes activation energy. Once the vehicle is moving, the energy changes to kinetic energy.

Heat is a form of energy. Temperature is the measure of heat. The most common device used to measure temperature is the thermometer. Thermometers are made of heat-sensitive substances— mercury and alcohol—that expand when heated.

The most common form of energy comes from the sun. Solar energy provides heat and light for animals and plants. Through photosynthesis, plants capture radiant energy from the sun and transform it into chemical energy in the form of glucose. This chemical energy is stored in the leaves, stems, and fruits of plants. Humans and animals consume the plants or fruits and get the energy they need for survival. This energy source is transformed again to create kinetic energy and body heat. Kinetic energy is used for movement and to do work, while heat is a required element for all warm-blooded animals, like humans. Cold-blooded animals also require heat, but rather than making it themselves through the transformation of plant sugar, they use solar energy to heat their body. Energy transformation constitutes the foundation and the driving force of an ecosystem. In addition to heat and solar radiation, energy is available in the forms of electricity and magnetism.

When you arrange an energy source, such as a battery, a wire, and a light bulb (or motor, or bell, or any electrical device) such that all metal parts are touching (metal is a good "conductor" of energy) in a circle—the bulb will light (the motor will run, the bell will ring, and so on). What has been created by arranging the items in this circle is known as an "electric circuit." The energy from the battery or other energy source is able to "flow" or be transferred through the metal wires and parts of the circuit. A closed circuit is when all metal parts are touching and the electrical charge is able to continue to be transferred through the circuit. A light switch or other "on button" closes the circuit and allows the electricity to flow. An open circuit is when there is a break someplace in the flow of electricity through the circuit. A switch or "off button" opens the circuit and stops the electricity flow. When you ring a door bell, you are closing the circuit or allowing all metal parts to touch and send electricity through it to make the bell ring; when you let go of the doorbell button, the circuit is open, and so the flow of electricity stops and so does the bell's ringing.

Lightning is a form of static electricity, which means it is not "flowing" or being transferred in the way it is through a metal wire, but is instead caused by friction, much the same as walking across a carpet in socks and getting a shock when a metal doorknob is touched. In both kinds of electricity, the electrons in the atoms of the substance, which are negatively charged, are pulled away from their atom's nucleus, giving the object, or cloud, a negative charge. The negative charge is quickly attracted to a positive charge—in the case of lightning, that positive charge could be something (or someone!) on the ground. The positive charge quickly jumps toward the negative charge and the negative charge quickly jumps toward the positive charge, and a flash of lighting and clap of thunder is heard; or in the case of the doorknob, a spark and a snap sound. Electric circuits are just a way to channel the electricity and the opposing charges through a conductor such as metal wires to allow us to use the energy to do work and to transform the energy into different forms such as sound (a radio), light (light bulbs), mechanical (machinery), and/or heat energy.

Light energy, and all energy for that matter, travels in waves and in a straight-line path. The electromagnetic spectrum shows the different wavelengths and frequencies of energy, including the small portion that is visible light. The electromagnetic spectrum includes, for example, microwaves, x-rays, radio waves, infrared radiation, visible light waves, and ultraviolet radiation, all of which have different wavelengths and frequencies that distinguish one type of wave from another.

Visible light is the wavelength of light we can see, which our eyes see as white light. However, this white light is composed of a host of other wavelengths of light that our eyes cannot always distinguish, which we know as the visible light spectrum, or a rainbow. The colors of white light include red, orange, yellow, green, blue, indigo, and violet (although some sources now eliminate indigo as separate from violet), or ROYGBIV. When light traveling in a straight line hits an object or substance and is bent, it is called **refraction**. The bending of light waves may result in the colors of light in the spectrum becoming visible, as when we see a rainbow in the sky (the water molecules in the air bend the light) or when light travels through cut glass such as with a prism. Reflection is when light waves bounce back, as when looking in a mirror. The principles of reflection and refraction are used in periscopes and telescopes in order to be able to see objects we may otherwise not be able to see. They are often popular in magic shows when objects are said to "disappear." In actuality, the light of the object has been refracted or reflected to a place away from our eyes so that we can no longer see it.

Refraction is also used to our advantage through concave and convex lenses. Concave or convex lenses work such that when light passes through it changes the focal point. The eye contains a lens, but when light passing through the eye cannot properly focus on the "screen" known as the retina, the object being viewed may be blurred. Concave or convex lenses are used in eyeglasses to adjust and correct the focal point. These lenses are also used in cameras, microscopes, and telescopes. A spoon is an example of both a concave and a convex lens—if you look into the concave side, you will see yourself upside down. If you look into the convex side of the spoon, you will see yourself right side up. This is due to refraction (and reflection) of light.

Sound also travels in waves. Sounds are caused by vibrations, such as a guitar string (or a rubber band), or banging on a drum or cymbal. Sound has a certain wavelength, frequency, pitch, and amplitude (loudness). Sound waves must travel through a medium, which may be solid, liquid, or gas. Sound travels best through solids because there are more molecules (particles) to vibrate, and least well through gases.

The types of sound waves are longitudinal and transverse. Longitudinal waves move parallel to the direction the wave moves, and transverse waves move perpendicular to the direction of the wave. Seismic waves are both longitudinal and transverse, as they travel in all directions from the source of the earthquake. An electromagnetic wave moves in a direction that is at a right angles to the vibrations of both the magnetic and electric fields, which are perpendicular to each other.

COMPETENCY 010

The teacher understands energy transformations and the conservation of matter and energy.

The beginning teacher:

A. Describes the processes that generate energy in the sun and other stars.

B. Applies the law of conservation of matter to analyze a variety of situations (e.g., the water cycle, food chains, decomposition, balancing chemical equations).

C. Describes sources of electrical energy and processes of energy transformation for human uses (e.g., fossil fuels, solar panels, hydroelectric plants).

D. Understands exothermic and endothermic chemical reactions and their applications (e.g., hot and cold packs, energy content of food).

E. Applies knowledge of energy concepts in a variety of situations (e.g., the production of heat, light, sound, and magnetic effects by electrical energy; the process of photosynthesis; weather processes; food webs; food/energy pyramids).

F. Applies the law of conservation of energy to analyze a variety of physical phenomena (e.g., specific heat, heat transfer, thermal equilibrium, nuclear reactions, efficiency of simple machines, collisions).

G. Understands applications of energy transformations and the conservation of matter and energy in life and Earth/space science.

The sun is the source of energy that sustains life on Earth. It is one of billions of stars in our galaxy, the Milky Way, and of the countless trillions of stars in the universe. The sun is actually quite an ordinary star, falling somewhere in the middle range in size. The sun is largely composed of the gases hydrogen and helium and generates energy by nuclear fusion, or the combining of atoms in high speed collisions releasing tremendous amounts of energy.

Electricity is the flow of electrons or electric power or charge. The basic unit of charge is based on the positive charge of the proton and the negative charge of the electron. Energy occurs naturally in the atmosphere through light. However, it is not feasible to capture that type of energy. The electricity that we use comes from secondary sources because it is produced from the conversion of primary (natural) sources of energy like fossil fuels that are nonrenewable (natural gas, coal, and oil) and nuclear, and renewable resources such as wind and solar energy. All sources of energy are used to produce a common result—to turn a turbine that generates electricity. Electricity that is generated can then be sent through wires for human use, and can be transformed into other forms of energy, including sound, light, heat, and force.

The main principle of energy conservation states that energy can change form but cannot totally disappear. For example, the chemical energy stored in a car battery is used to start the engine, which in turn is used to recharge the battery. Another example of energy conservation is placing merchandise on shelves. Energy was used to do the work (placing merchandise on a shelf) and it was stored as potential energy. Potential energy in turn can be converted to kinetic energy when the merchandise is pushed back to the floor. In this case, work was recovered completely, but often the recovered energy is less than the energy used to do the work. This loss of energy can be caused by friction or any kind of resistance encountered in the process of doing the work. For example, as a vehicle's tires roll across the pavement, doing the work of moving forward, they encounter friction. This friction causes heat energy to be released, as well as kinetic energy.

In essence, energy cannot be created or destroyed, only changed in form (law of conservation of energy). Likewise, matter cannot be created or destroyed, only changed in form (law of conservation of matter). Thus, energy from the sun is changed, for example, to chemical energy when plants use the energy to make glucose in photosynthesis. The energy from the sun is stored in the chemical bonds of the glucose molecule and will be released for use by the organism—the plant itself, or any organism that eats the plant and its glucose—when the molecule's chemical bonds are "broken" by oxygen in cell respiration and/or stored in another chemical form known as ATP. Likewise, electrical energy comes from burning, or breaking the bond of carbon-based molecules as in fossil fuels. This electricity generated is then transformed to another form by first capturing and sending that electrical energy through metal wires originating at the power generating plant, and sending it in a complete, closed circuit to homes, businesses, and industries. There the electrical energy may be transformed to sound, heat, light, and/or mechanical energy. In all cases the energy is not lost it is changed in form.

It is important to conserve matter and energy generated from fossil fuels as these are nonrenewable sources and will one day be expended. It is also important to continue exploring alternative, renewable forms of energy and electricity generation to meet our society's energy demands and maintain our Earth's clean air and water supplies.

COMPETENCY 011

The teacher understands the structure and function of living things.

The beginning teacher:

A. Describes characteristics of organisms from the major taxonomic groups.

B. Analyzes how structure complements function in cells.

C. Analyzes how structure complements function in tissues, organs, organ systems and organisms.

D. Identifies human body systems and describes their functions.

E. Describes how organisms obtain and use energy and matter.

F. Describes the composition, structure, and function of the basic chemical components (e.g., proteins, carbohydrates, lipids, nucleic acids) of living things.

Major Taxonomic Groups

Living things are divided into five groups, or kingdoms: Monera (bacteria), Protista (protozoans), Fungi, Plantae (plants), and Animalia (animals).

Monera consists of unicellular organisms. It is the only group of living organisms made of prokaryotic cells—the cells with a primitive organization system. Some examples of this organism are bacteria, blue-green algae, and spirochetes.

Protista contains a type of eukaryotic cell with a more complex organization system. This kingdom includes diverse, mostly unicellular organisms that live in aquatic habitats, in both freshwater and saltwater. They are not animals or plants but unique organisms. Some examples of Protista are protozoans and algae of various types. The Amoeba, Paramecium, and Euglena are in the Protista Kingdom.

Fungi are multicellular organisms with a sophisticated organization system—that is, containing eukaryotic cells. Fungi exist in a variety of forms and shapes. Because they do not have chlorophyll, they cannot produce food through photosynthesis. Fungi obtain energy, carbon, and water from digesting dead materials. Some examples of these types of organisms are mushrooms, mold, mildews, and yeast.

Plants are multicellular organisms with a sophisticated organization system. In addition to more familiar plants, moss and ferns also fall under this category. Plant cells have chloroplasts, a component that allows them to trap sunlight as energy for the process of photosynthesis. In photosynthesis plants use carbon dioxide from the atmospheric environment and as the by-product of this process, supply the oxygen needed for the survival of animals.

Animals are also multicellular with multiple forms and shapes, and with specialized senses and organs. The Animalia kingdom is composed of organisms like sponges, worms, insects, fish, amphibians, reptiles, birds, and mammals. Animals are the most sophisticated type of living organisms and represent the highest levels of evolution. Animals live in all kinds of habitats, and they are as simple as flies or as sophisticated as humans.

For additional information about living things, go to the website of the Behavioral Sciences Department of Palomar College, San Marcos, California, at *http://anthro.palomar.edu/animal/default.htm.*

There are relationships between the characteristics, structures, and functions of organisms and corresponding taxonomic classifications. **Homologous** structures refer to different living organisms with structural or anatomical features that look or function in a similar way. Because these organisms have a common ancestor, their homologous structures are of the same origin but have different functions. For example, the bone structure of the wing of a bat is very similar to the bone structure of the human arm. **Non-homologous** structures between two organisms are similar in structure and function, but arose independently and not from a common ancestor. **Parallelism** is when there are similar structures between two organisms in different species that arose after diverging from a common ancestor. The common ancestor did not have the structure, but had the beginning features of that structure. **Convergence** is when similar structures developed after diverging from a common ancestor, but the common ancestor did not have the trait or the beginnings of the trait. **Analogous** structures have the same structure or function but arose from different ancestors. That is, analogous structures developed from unrelated evolutionary lines, but the structure was a positive adaptation to the environment, so both survived and were carried on to offspring in their respective species. An example of analogous structures is the wing of a bird and the wing of a butterfly. Both serve as a beneficial adaptation, even though the species are not related.

For more detailed information see: *http://anthro.palomar.edu/animal/animal_2.htm* and *http://www.majordifferences.com/2013/05/difference-between-homologous-and.html - .WW_RQdPys6t*

Life Functions and Cells

All living things carry on life functions, such as respiration, nutrition, response, circulation, growth, excretion, regulation, and reproduction, all of which characterize them as living as opposed to nonliving. In addition, all living things are composed of the basic unit of life known as **cells**. Organisms, as well as individual cells of an organism and single-celled organisms, carry on these life functions using specialized structures. For example, earthworms carry on respiration through their moist skin; plants excrete gases from tiny pores on the underside of leaves called stomata; a single-celled Amoeba ingests food by use of a "false foot" or pseudopodia; and insects respond to chemical attractants called pheromones of the opposite-sex insect for mating.

Cells are the basic unit of all living organisms. Within cells there are specialized organelles that carry on all of the life functions at a microscopic/chemical level. For example, the mitochondria carries on cell respiration, and ribosomes assemble proteins for use both inside the cell and out. Teachers should know the parts of the cell, called organelles, and their functions, particularly, the nucleus, mitochondria, chloroplasts (plants only), ribosomes, Golgi, endoplasmic reticulum, vacuoles, and cell membranes.

Animal and plant cells are similar in appearance, but they do have certain distinctions. Animal cells contain mitochondria, small round or rod-shaped bodies found in the cytoplasm of most cells. The main function of mitochondria is to produce the enzymes for the metabolic conversion of food to energy. This process consumes oxygen and is termed aerobic respiration.

Plants cells also contain mitochondria, which allow plants to carry on respiration where they use oxygen and excrete carbon dioxide and water just like animals. However, plants also have specialized organelles called chloroplasts that are used for taking in sunlight and using this energy to convert the gas, carbon dioxide, and water taken in from the roots to make glucose—a simple sugar that is the food for the plant. Chloroplasts contain chlorophyll, which is used in this process of converting light into chemical energy. This process is called photosynthesis. Photosynthesis is the process by which chlorophyll-containing organisms convert light energy to chemical energy. Through the process of photosynthesis, a plant containing chlorophyll captures energy from the sun and converts it into chemical energy. Part of the chemical energy is used for the plant's own survival, and the rest is stored in the stem and leaves.

The cell is the basic unit of living organisms and the simplest living unit of life. Living organisms are composed of cells that have the following common characteristics:

- Have a membrane that regulates the flow of nutrients and water that enter and exit the cell

- Contain the genetic material (DNA) that allows for reproduction

- Require a supply of energy

- Contain basic chemicals to make metabolic decisions for survival

- Reproduce and are the result of reproduction

There are two kinds of cells—prokaryotic and eukaryotic. Prokaryotic cells are the simplest and most primitive type of cells. They do not contain the structures typical of eukaryotic cells. Prokaryotic cells lack a nucleus and instead have one strand of deoxyribonucleic acid (DNA). Some prokaryotic cells have external whip like flagella for locomotion or a hair-like system for adhesion. Prokaryotic cells come in three shapes: cocci (round), bacilli (rods), and spirilla or spirochetes (helical cells). Bacteria (of the Kingdom Monera) are prokaryotic cells.

Eukaryotic cells evolved from prokaryotic cells and in the process became structurally and biochemically more complex. The key distinction between the two cell types is that only eukaryotic cells contain many structures, or organelles, separated from other cytoplasm components by a membrane. The organelles within eukaryotic cells are the nucleus, mitochondria, chloroplasts, and Golgi apparatus. The nucleus contains the deoxyribonucleic acid (DNA) information. The mitochondria have their own membrane and contain some DNA information and proteins. They generate the energy for the cell. The chloroplast is a component that exists in plants *only*, allowing them to trap sunlight as energy for the process of photosynthesis. The Golgi apparatus secretes substances needed for the cell's survival.

An organism may consist of only one cell, or it may comprise many billions of cells of various dimensions. For example, cells are complete organisms, such as the unicellular bacteria; others, such as muscle cells, are parts of multicellular organisms. All cells have an internal substance called cytoplasm—a clear gelatinous fluid—enclosed within a membrane. Each cell contains the genetic material containing the information for the formation of organisms. Cells are composed primarily of water and the elements oxygen, hydrogen, carbon, and nitrogen.

Structures and Functions

Moving outward from the cell, it is important to know that cells communicate with one another on a chemical level and work together to perform specific functions. The shape of these groups of cells and activity levels differ according to their particular function in the body; for example, muscle cells are long and narrow so they may better respond to stimuli and contract. Groups of cells with similar functions are called **tissues**. Tissues are organized together to perform a specific life function. A complex system of tissues working together to carry on one of the body's life functions is an **organ**. A group of different organs working together to support and help carry out a life function and keep the organism alive is called an **organ system**. Examples of systems include the digestive system, the respiratory system, the immune system, the muscular system, the skeletal system, the nervous system, and the circulatory system. Organ systems are organized into an *organism*. The order of organization is as follows:

Cells → Tissues → Organs → Systems → Organ Systems → Organism

Musculoskeletal System

The human skeleton consists of more than 200 bones held together by connective tissues called ligaments. Movements are effected by contractions of the *skeletal muscles*, and skeletal muscles are arranged in pairs, such as the biceps and triceps of the upper arm. When one of the pair contracts, it causes a certain movement of the bones; in the meantime the opposing muscle relaxes. When the opposing pair of muscle contracts, a different movement of the bones occurs, and the original muscle of the pair relaxes. For example, when the biceps (the muscle on top of the upper arm) contracts, the arm bends upwards; when the opposing muscle of the pair, the triceps, contract, the arm extends. Skeletal muscles are attached to bones with specialized connective tissue called tendons.

The specialized connective tissue that attaches bones to other bones is called ligaments. The soft spongy tissue on the ends of bones is called cartilage. Muscular contractions are controlled by the nervous system.

In addition to skeletal muscle, the body also has muscles that are not part of the musculoskeletal system, thus not attached to bones. One such muscle type is called *smooth muscle*. Smooth muscle forms the inner linings of our digestive system and is controlled involuntarily by our autonomic (automatic) nervous system. A third type of muscle is *cardiac muscle*, which is the muscle of the heart, and is also controlled by our autonomic nervous system.

Nervous System

The nervous system has two main divisions: the somatic and automatic. The somatic allows the voluntary control of skeletal muscles, and the automatic, or involuntary, controls cardiac and glandular functions. Voluntary movement is caused by nerve impulses sent from the brain through the spinal cord to nerves to connecting skeletal muscles. Involuntary movement occurs in direct response to outside stimulus. Involuntary responses are called reflexes. For example, when an object presents danger to the eye, the body responds automatically by blinking or retracting away from the object.

Circulatory System

The circulatory system follows a cyclical process in which the heart pumps blood through the right chambers of the heart and through the lungs, where it acquires oxygen. From there it is pumped back into the left chambers of the heart, where it is pumped into the main artery (aorta), which then sends the oxygenated blood to the rest of the body using a system of veins and capillaries. Through the capillaries, the blood distributes the oxygen and nutrients to tissues, absorbing from them carbon dioxide, a metabolic waste product. Finally, the blood completes the circuit by passing through small veins, which join to form increasingly larger vessels. Eventually, the blood reaches the largest veins, which return it to the right side of the heart to complete and restart the process.

Immune System

The main function of the body's immune system is to defend itself against foreign proteins and infectious organisms. The system recognizes organisms that are not normally in the body and develops the antibodies needed to control and destroy the invaders. When the body is attacked by infectious organisms, it develops what we know as a fever. Fever is the body's way of fighting invading molecules. The raised temperature of a fever will kill some bacteria. The major components of the immune system are the thymus, lymph system, bone marrow, white blood cells, antibodies, and hormones.

Respiratory System

Respiration is carried out by the expansion and contraction of the lungs. In the lungs, oxygen enters tiny capillaries, where it combines with hemoglobin in the red blood cells and is carried to the tissues through the circulatory system. At the same time, carbon dioxide passes through capillaries into the air contained within the lungs.

Animals inhale oxygen from the environment and exhale carbon dioxide. Carbon dioxide is used by plants in the process of photosynthesis, which produces the oxygen that animals use again for survival.

Digestive and Excretory Systems

The energy required for sustenance of the human body is supplied through the chemical energy stored in food. To obtain the energy from food, it has to be fragmented and digested. Digestion begins at the moment that food is placed in the mouth and makes contact with saliva. Fragmented and partially digested food passes down the esophagus to the stomach, where the process is continued by the gastric and intestinal juices. Thereafter, the mixture of food and secretions makes its way down the small intestine, where the nutrients are extracted and absorbed into the bloodstream. The unused portion of the food goes to the large intestine and eventually is excreted from the body through defecation.

Reproductive System

Students in the middle grades should know some basic biological facts about human reproduction. They should know that the body matures and develops in order for child-bearing to occur. The menstrual cycle should be understood by students, including what occurs in ovulation to prepare the egg cell, namely, the process of meiosis. In males, the process of meiosis occurs to produce the sperm cell. Students should know that these specialized cells, called gametes (egg and sperm), unite to form a fertilized egg, which grows and develops in distinct stages to produce new offspring.

Energy and Matter

Plants make glucose during the process of photosynthesis. Plant cells' chloroplasts capture energy from the sun, take in carbon dioxide (CO_2) from the atmosphere, and absorb water (H_2O) up through its roots and restructuring these molecules into glucose ($C_6H_{12}O_6$). The glucose is used to make its own body structures and stored in chains, which when assembled together make carbohydrates or starch. The starch is stored in roots, stems and leaves, and may also be transformed into other substances made by the plant such as oils, waxes, and fruits. Photosynthesis is the way plants make food, but it is *not* the way they metabolize food for energy. The sugars plants make are metabolized by oxygen in respiration to produce the energy needed for plants to carry on their own life functions (excretion, growth). Thus, it is important to know that similar to animals, *plants carry on respiration* (along with photosynthesis) taking oxygen into their cells and into the mitochondria — the respiratory centers of their cells — where they break the bonds of the glucose molecule ($C_6H_{12}O_6$) to release stored energy in the form of ATP. Note that it is a common misconception of students who may think that plants only carry on photosynthesis – plants also carry on cellular respirations just like animals. Note however that the processes of photosynthesis and respiration are the reverse of one another, only with sunlight as the source of energy in photosynthesis, and energy in the form of ATP being produced in respiration.

Animals need the sugars and stored starches made by plants in order for its own cells to carry on life functions and produce the energy needed to sustain the animal's life. Animals therefore must ingest food from plants, or from animals that had ingested plants. Once the food is digested into its smallest components in the small intestine, the glucose enters the bloodstream and is carried to the cells. In the cells, and inside the mitochondria of the cells, oxygen that entered the bloodstream and ultimately the cells through respiration combines with the glucose to break the chemical bonds of the molecule and produce energy in the form of ATP. This energy is needed for the animal to sustain its own life functions.

Photosynthesis

(Chloroplasts of plant cells)

Sunlight energy + $6CO_2$ + $6H_2O \rightarrow C_6H_{12}O_6$ + $6O_2$

Plant *and* Animal Respiration

(Mitochondria of both plant and animal cells)

$C_6H_{12}O_6$ + $6O_2 \rightarrow 6CO_2$ + $6H_2O$ + ATP energy

In addition to aerobic cellular respiration, which requires the use of oxygen in the process, organisms or certain cells of organisms may carry on anaerobic respiration, a form of respiration that does not use oxygen. Anaerobic respiration occurs in organisms such as yeast, called fermentation, and in the muscle cells of animals when the demands for energy are high, as during strenuous exercise. Anaerobic respiration yields less energy than aerobic respiration; therefore, it occurs in small organisms (yeast, certain bacteria). In animals, it provides a little extra energy to the muscles in the form of ATP during exercise when extra energy is needed. The by-products in anaerobic respiration for yeast and certain bacteria (e.g., those used in making wine) are different than in muscle cells. In yeast and wine-making bacteria anaerobic respiration is called fermentation and the by-products are alcohol and carbon dioxide gas. The carbon dioxide gas is what makes bread dough containing yeast to rise (the alcohol burns off during baking). In the muscle cells the anaerobic respiration that takes place during strenuous exercise results in the production of lactic acid.

Anaerobic Respiration in Yeast and Certain Bacteria (as Fermentation)

$C_6H_{12}O_6$ (Glucose) is broken down to $\rightarrow$ Energy (ATP) + Ethanol + Carbon dioxide (CO_2)

Anaerobic Respiration in Muscle Cells

$C_6H_{12}O_6$ (Glucose) is broken down to $\rightarrow$ Energy (ATP) + Lactic acid

Chemical Compounds of Life

All living things contain and/or need four main carbon-based compounds for life, also known as organic molecules. These four compounds or organic molecules are carbohydrates, proteins, lipids, and nucleic acids. The composition of these life molecules are always carbon, hydrogen, and oxygen as the backbone, with nitrogen, phosphorous, and sulfur appearing in some of these molecules as well. These molecules can be remembered with the acronym: SPONCH (sulfur, phosphorous, oxygen, nitrogen, carbon, and hydrogen).

Carbohydrates are stored as starches, with the simplest form or basic building block a simple sugar or monosaccharide, such as glucose. Carbohydrates are ultimately digested into simple sugars and used in cellular respiration to produce energy for all life functions. The type of carbohydrate or starch is a factor of the number of monosaccharides in the chain, along with the types of monosaccharides. Plant substances contain starch in their roots, stems, leaves, and fruit in particular, with an abundance of starch often stored in the roots. Potatoes, carrots, turnips, corn, peas, celery, spinach and apples are examples of foods that store sugars and starches, or carbohydrates. Carbohydrates are composed of carbon, hydrogen, and oxygen atoms.

Proteins are complex molecules that are made of a repeating, and often turned and twisted, chain of its smallest component, amino acids. Proteins can be immense in size and perform a variety of essential functions and purposes in the body. Proteins are in cell membranes, and make up connective tissue, bones and muscles, and are the enzymes and hormones that control the body's metabo[...] are 20 different amino acids that exist on Earth t[...] gs, and cheese, as examples. In addition to carbon[...] itrogen.

Lip[...] the basic building block or smallest component is one to three fatty acid molec[...] [...] [...] Lipids are stored as energy reserves in the fat of a[...] [...] in the form of oils in place [...] pids stored in the body provide insulation for ani[...] [...] [...] [...] e important for brain development. Lipids can be [...] [...] like butter and oils. Lipids contain carbon, hydrog[...]

Nu[...] [...] [...] [...] [...] (DNA) and ribonucleic acids (RNA) found inside of cells [...] [...] hereditary information and instructions or "blueprints" that direct the cel[...] [...] [...] component of DNA and RNA are nucleotides, which consist of a suga[...] [...] [...] [...] A the sugar is deoxyribose and the nitrogen base in a nucleotide can be adenine (A), thymine (T), cytosine (C), or guanine (G). DNA is shaped as a "double helix," or twisted ladder, with the rungs of the molecular ladder being paired nitrogen bases, and the sides being the sugars and phosphate groups. The nitrogen bases from one side of the ladder are weakly bonded or attracted to the nitrogen bases on the other side of the ladder by hydrogen bonds. The pairing of nitrogen bases is important: DNA nucleotides with the nitrogen base **thymine** only bonds in the center of the ladder with nucleotides carrying the nitrogen base **adenine**, whereas nucleotides with **cytosine** only bond with nucleotides that have the nitrogen base **guanine** (A-T or G-C). The differing sizes of the nitrogen bases, A, T, G, and C, cause the ladder to twist, thus forming the twisted double-helix shape. The particular sequence of DNA nucleotides with their nitrogen bases code for traits and characteristics of the organism. The sequence in a section of DNA that codes for a trait is called a **gene**.

Ribonucleic acid (RNA) is similar to DNA, only it is single-stranded rather than double, the sugar in the nucleotide is ribose instead of deoxyribose, and the nitrogen bases are adenine, uracil, cytosine, and guanine (no thymine). In RNA adenine pairs with uracil, and cytosine pairs with guanine. RNA is important in making proteins (e.g., enzymes, hormones) in the cell to be used for a

[Handwritten note overlaying text:]

DNA, A,T,G,C
T-A
G-C

RNA - A,U,C,G
A-U
C-G

particular life function such as making the enzyme lipase in pancreatic cells to digest the sugar in milk known as lactose.

Nucleic acids are composed of carbon, hydrogen, and oxygen, and also phosphorus, nitrogen, and sometimes sulfur.

COMPETENCY 012

The teacher understands reproduction and the mechanisms of heredity.

The beginning teacher:

A. Compares and contrasts sexual and asexual reproduction.

B. Understands the organization of hereditary material (e.g., DNA, genes, chromosomes).

C. Describes how an inherited trait can be determined by one or many genes and how more than one trait can be influenced by a single gene.

D. Distinguishes between dominant and recessive alleles and predicts the probable outcomes of genetic combinations (i.e., genotypes and phenotypes).

E. Evaluates the influence of environmental and genetic factors on the traits of an organism.

F. Describes current applications of genetic research (e.g., related to cloning, reproduction, health, industry, agriculture).

Asexual and Sexual Reproduction

There are two forms of reproduction: asexual and sexual reproduction. Asexual reproduction has one parent cell that divides by a process called mitosis or binary fission into two daughter cells with identical DNA as the parent, and as each other. This type of reproduction occurs in simple, one-celled organisms and in body cells when they undergo growth and repair, and takes place through a series of steps in the cell's life cycle. Growth in most organisms is caused by mitosis. The importance of mitosis is that the offspring cells, or "daughter" cells, are each an exact copy of the original. Through mitosis, new cells are made; for example, to form a scar after an injury, new bone cells, muscle cells, blood cells, and any cell that is needed by the body throughout life and growth. In single-celled organisms, mitosis is the cell's form of reproduction—making exact copies of the DNA in each of the two daughter cells, and is often called binary fission. Only one organism (the single cell) is involved, and there is no exchange of genetic material or DNA. Thus, the two offspring cells, or daughter cells, are identical to the original, or parent cell.

In mitosis, the entire DNA within each chromosome in the cell makes a copy of itself (replicates). The replicated chromosomes containing DNA line up along the equatorial plane of the cell, and through a series of events, prepare to be separated from each other. When the cell divides, one copy of each strand or chromosome of DNA goes into one of the daughter cells, and one goes into the other daughter cell. This process preserves the DNA of the parent, but does not allow for much variation in the offspring (daughter cells).

Sexual reproduction requires two parent cells, and the combination DNA from parent with the DNA from the other parent in the new cell, or offspring. Sexual reproduction occurs in more complex organisms. The process of producing the cells that will ultimately join together to form the new offspring is meiosis. Meiosis occurs only in specialized cells of the parents—namely, within the sex organs, or gonads, known as the ovary in females and testicles in males. Meiosis is somewhat similar to mitosis, but there are important distinctions. Meiosis is how sperm and egg cells are formed in preparation for being combined in the process of fertilization.

Each species of organism has a certain number of chromosomes (containing DNA and thus the genetic code) in each of its cells; for example, humans have 46 chromosomes, arranged in 23 pairs. Any new offspring of that species must have the same number of chromosomes as the parent cells. Thus, in the case of humans, the specialized beginning cells (oocytes and spermatocytes) in the gonads have 46 chromosomes, but they must make cells that have half the number of chromosomes (23 in total), which are called **gametes**. This reduction to half the number of chromosomes occurs because when the gamete from one parent (female egg or ovum) combines with the gamete from the other parent (male sperm cell) the full number of 46 chromosomes (arranged in 23 pairs) is restored in the fertilized egg. In sum, meiosis is the process that reduces the number of chromosomes in half to prepare the new daughter cell(s), namely the egg cell in females and sperm cell in males, to join together in the process known as fertilization to produce a new offspring.

In **meiosis**, the chromosomes duplicate as they do in mitosis; however, the cell divides twice, preserving one of each pair of chromosomes in the resulting four daughter cells (in humans, 23 chromosomes). The result of meiosis, therefore, is four cells with half the number of chromosomes as the original parent cell. In the female, only one of the four daughter cells becomes a viable egg cell, whereas in males all four daughter cells are viable sperm cells. After the egg cell has been fertilized by the sperm, it is called a zygote. The zygote immediately begins to divide by **mitosis** to grow and develop into a new offspring; first forming a structure called the morula, then a blastocyst (ball of cells) and then differentiating its cells into what will become the various structures and organs of the new offspring, called the **gastrula**. Soon the gastrula, with its rapidly dividing and differentiating cells, becomes an embryo, and later a fetus that is growing and developing (by mitosis) into the new offspring.

Sexual reproduction allows for more variation in offspring because they have a combination of genetic material (DNA) from each parent. Many animals carry out sexual reproduction and therefore come from eggs. For some animals, the egg is inside the female animal and is fertilized by the male sperm cells within the body. For other animals such as most fish species, the eggs are fertilized by the male after they have been expelled from the female's body. When fertilized internally, the fertilized egg may be laid externally from the female as in many insects, reptiles, and birds, or it may remain in the body of the female until birth. The egg has an outer lining to protect the animal growing inside. Bird eggs have hard shells, while the eggs of amphibians, like the turtle, have hard but flexible coverings. With the appropriate care and heat, an egg will hatch. After hatching, in some species, the parents protect and feed the newborn until it can survive on its own; in other species, the eggs are left on their own to survive. On reaching adulthood, females begin laying eggs, and the cycle of life continues. Mammals are also conceived through egg fertilization, but the resulting embryo is kept inside the mother until it is mature enough for life outside the womb.

The reproduction of plants can also be divided into asexual and sexual mechanisms. Asexual reproduction of plants takes place by cutting portions of the plant and replanting them. Tubers or the eyes of potatoes and the bulbs of tulips grow into roots and are also a form of asexual reproduction.

Sexual reproduction in plants involves seeds produced by flowers of female and male plants, which are cross-pollinated with help from insects or other animals. The flower is the reproductive organ of the plant and consists of several parts that are the male and female reproductive organs. Some flowers may have only the male part, and likewise, some flowers contain only the female part of the same species of plant/tree. So, for example, there actually can be a "male" tree and a "female" tree. In the flower, the male reproductive organ is the **stamen**, which is divided into filament and anther. The filament simply holds up the anther, and the anther contains the pollen in which the sperm nuclei are found. Flowers may also contain the female reproductive organ, the **pistil**, which consists of the ovary, style, and stigma. The ovary contains the egg cells, which in the flower are called ovules. The style is the tube above the ovary, and the stigma is the top of the style, which has a sticky substance. The pollen needs to either be manually placed on the stigma, or blown there by the wind. Another mode of transfer, which is what usually happens, is that the pollen sticks to the body of a bee or butterfly (who are actually in search of sugary nectar in the flower, and not the pollen). When the pollen sticks to the body of the insect, it may then be transferred from the anther (male part) to the stigma (female part). In essence, the sperm nuclei then travel down the style to reach the ovules, where fertilization occurs. The fertilized egg then becomes the seed. The ovary of the flower may swell and become the fruit (as in a peach or apple). This process helps protect the seeds, and also helps with seed dispersal. Animals eat the fruit and excrete the seed unharmed in their fecal matter (the seed has a seed coat that protects it, making it indigestible). Seed germination — where the seed sprouts into a plant — requires the appropriate quantity of air, water, and heat.

Heredity

Hereditary information is contained in the specific sequence of DNA in areas called genes, on chromosomes within the cells of organisms. Traits are inherited from the parent cells to the off-spring according to the genes the offspring receive from the parents for particular traits. More than one trait can be determined by a single gene, and one or many genes can determine a particular trait. For example, the gene for human eye color is located on several genes. However, there may be several different physical expressions of genes, such as eye color, with brown, blue, green and hazel eye colors appearing in offspring, as examples. Alleles are the different varieties of a gene that exist for a trait. There may be two or more alleles for a given trait. For example, there are three genes, called alleles, for blood type in the human population: A, B, and O. The National Human

Genome Institute explains that though an allele is one of two or more versions of a gene, offspring can only inherit two alleles for each gene (one on each paired chromosome). That is, one allele can be inherited from each parent: one allele from the original sperm cell, and one allele from the original egg cell. For a brief video on alleles, see: *https://www.brightstorm.com/science/biology/mendelian-genetics/alleles/*.

Recall that sperm and egg cells each contain one of each pair of chromosomes from the original parent cell. When the egg is fertilized, the pairs are restored in a random combination from the mother (egg) and father (sperm). The genes inherited from the parent cells may be **dominant** or **recessive** for certain traits in the offspring. In the pair of chromosomes, dominant gene is the trait that is expressed in the offspring when paired with another dominant gene or with a recessive gene. The recessive gene is only expressed when paired with another recessive gene for a trait. Gene pairs are often shown in science as letters; for example, brown fur color = B (dominant is shown as a capital letter), and white fur color = b (recessive is shown as a lower case letter of the dominant gene).

Genetic problems are solved using **Punnett square** diagrams. These Punnett diagrams help predict the gene combinations and expressed traits in the offspring. The genotype is the actual gene combination, and the phenotype is the trait that is expressed or that "shows up" in the offspring. Recall that the egg or sperm cell will have only one of each allele, whereas the fertilized egg (offspring) will have two, and that number will be maintained in every cell in the offspring throughout its lifetime (except for its own sperm and egg cells when an adult). Two dominant traits may be shown as two capital letters (BB); a dominant and recessive pair may be shown as a capital letter with a lower case (Bb); and two recessive genes are shown as two lower case letters (bb). Two of the same genes, e.g., two dominant genes or two recessive genes, is called homozygous for that trait; and one dominant and one recessive together is termed heterozygous (hybrid).

A Punnett square problem is solved by placing the egg cell genes along one top (or side) of the diagram, and sperm cell genes along the side (or top). Then the genes are combined within the boxes of the diagram, representing fertilization, to predict the probabilities of certain gene combinations occurring in the offspring.

B = dominant for brown fur

b = recessive for white fur

A mother guinea pig is homozygous dominant for brown fur. She is mated with a heterozygous male with brown fur color. What are the expected genotypes and phenotypes of the offspring? The solution is shown in the Punnett square diagram below.

father	mother	
	B	B
B	BB	BB
b	Bb	Bb

In this problem, the mother's genotype is BB, and she has brown fur. The father's genotype is Bb, and he also has brown fur; however, the father carries the gene for white fur. Fifty percent of the offspring will be homozygous dominant (BB), and fifty percent will be heterozygous (Bb). One hundred percent of the offspring will have the phenotype of brown fur color.

In addition to the genotype and phenotype directly inherited in offspring, environmental factors may contribute to how, or sometimes even whether, the gene is expressed. Some genes may not be expressed until an environmental condition or stressor triggers the gene into action. It is believed that autoimmune diseases, a situation where antibodies are formed to attack otherwise normal body cells, as in certain forms of hypothyroidism, are triggered by environmental stressors. In addition, factors in the environment, such as viruses or carcinogens, may activate susceptible inherited genes in an individual in the development of certain cancers, food intolerances, or allergies.

Genetics has somewhat recently been transformed into an industry, where crops and cattle are genetically engineered to produce, for example, greater-quality specimens at higher yields. The health industry has been able to use genetics to produce vaccines and medications that have vastly improved the quality of human life; however, sometimes they have impinged on socially controversial areas, such as stem cell research and cloning. By changing the DNA sequence in genes, scientists may, for example, be able to grow limbs and organs to replace those lost; develop humans with pre-specified desired characteristics; or increase the human lifespan. Thus, genetics has been beneficial to the quality of life; however, if unchecked, it could also create controversy and possibly dangerous results.

COMPETENCY 013

The teacher understands adaptations of organisms and the theory of evolution.

The beginning teacher:

A. Describes similarities and differences among various taxonomical groups and methods of classifying organisms.

B. Describes adaptations in a population or species that enhance its survival and reproductive success.

C. Describes how populations and species may evolve through time.

D. Applies knowledge of the mechanisms and processes of biological evolution (e.g., diversity, variation, mutation, environmental factors, natural selection).

E. Describes evidence that supports the theory of evolution of life on Earth.

Survival in the Environment

Genetics plays an important role in the ability of organisms to be able to survive and thrive in their environment and, ultimately, produce new offspring such that they pass on similar genetic material, *like* that which allowed them to survive and thrive, and maybe survive and thrive even better. Some inherited traits, called **adaptations**, could allow the organisms to better survive in their environment or could lead to their demise (and thus prevent the prospect of future offspring). It is important to understand that adaptations do not suddenly arise or develop in the lifetime of organisms. They occur gradually in the species over time. For example, if a certain deer-like animal thousands of years ago were particularly fast—that is, it was born with stronger muscle tissue than most, and a better bone and muscle physical structure—perhaps it was better able to run away from predators and survive. Therefore, this deer-like animal was able to survive long enough for it to have offspring with similar genetic material. At the same time, those deer-like animals that were not born with the same muscular and structural soundness as this one were killed as prey before they could reproduce. In time, those animals that are best suited in these qualities, as well as others, are the organisms who survive, as do their offspring. Those not well-adapted perish.

It is also the case that the organism that survives will breed with another that also has better-adapted characteristics, and was also able to survive in the natural environment. A change or mutation in the genetic material, that is, the genes that direct the development of a trait, may give rise to a new characteristic that either is or is not better suited for the environment. In the case that it is better suited, the organism will survive and produce offspring with this same mutation. Over the years, mutations that are better suited to the environment may make the organism appear quite different than it did hundreds, thousands, and millions of years earlier. If the environment itself changes, however, organisms that were able to survive under the previous conditions (climate, water supply, vegetation, landscape) may be unable to survive in the new environmental conditions. Thus, a catastrophic event, such as perhaps a large asteroid striking the Earth, could change the environmental conditions and either lead to the extinction of organisms, or the survival of organisms that would not have survived under the conditions before the strike. Likewise, selective breeding, which is human selection of which organisms breed with another, and which controls the genetic material that is passed onto offspring, also affects the change over time of organisms. The combination of genetics, adaptations, changes over time, mutations, selective breeding, and environmental conditions/changes contribute to the concept known as **evolution**.

It is important to know that adaptations come about in a random manner. Though it was not known how adaptations occurred in Darwin's writings or Gregor Mendel's studies (the father of heredity), it was later discovered that adaptations occurred due to random mutations of gene sequences that code for certain traits. For a multitude of reasons, including chance, environmental conditions, or exposure to toxic material, genetic codes may change. The change in genetic code may give rise to a variation in a trait that turns out to be more favorable that the original trait. If the change prolongs the life of the species with the mutation, then the mutated species is more likely to survive long enough to produce new offspring with the same favorable mutation.

There are several lines of evidence for evolution. Paleontology contributes to our understanding of past organisms, specifically fossils.

- Fossils found in more recent layers of rock are similar or identical to existing organisms.

- In older rock layers, fossils significantly differ from present day organisms.

- Discoveries are regularly being made that fill gaps in the fossil record.

- Scientists are finding fossils that have the features they predicted based on known, older and younger fossils

- Fossils of any species have only been found in rock layers younger than their ancestor species, and not found in rock layers older than their ancestors.

Because the Earth is constantly changing, plates shifting and colliding, continents being uplifted, and seas being buried, fossils of once-living organisms have been found in all places over the Earth, called biogeography. Scientists have been able to reveal from fossils that species originate in one place and spread out to other places from that source. Fossils have been found to do exactly that—where a fossil is found it can be traced back to its source point.

Another source of evidence of evolution, known as developmental biology, studies how vertebrate embryos develop. During their development from embryos, all vertebrates tend to share common features. Some of these features, such as a tail, appear only in the embryo stage of some species and then disappear or are incorporated into the body, whereas the same feature may remain in another species.

Animals can be grouped according to commons physical structures or morphology. Organisms are grouped, for example, as vertebrates and invertebrates due to the presence or absence of a backbone, as described earlier in the discussion of taxonomic groups. There is also enormous diversity among living things. For more information refer to: *http://anthro.palomar.edu/animal/animal_1.htm*

With more precise and detailed information now available on genomes and particular gene sequences that make an organism's genetic code, we are better able to show how closely species may be related due to similarities and differences in the sequence. For example, because of similarities in the genetic code, humans have been found to be more closely related to chimpanzees than to gorillas—a finding that was at first surprising.

COMPETENCY 014

The teacher understands regulatory mechanisms and behavior.

The beginning teacher:

A. Describes how organisms respond to internal and external stimuli.

B. Applies knowledge of structures and physiological processes that maintain stable internal conditions (homeostasis).

C. Demonstrates an understanding of feedback mechanisms that allow organisms to maintain stable internal conditions.

D. Understands how evolutionary history of a species affects behavior (e.g., migration, nocturnality, territoriality).

Response to Stimuli

All living organisms respond to stimuli from within and outside in the environment. Stimuli within the organism are internal stimuli, including feeling hungry or needing food; stimuli outside of the organism are external stimuli such as warmth or cold, light, or dark. Even the tiniest organisms such as bacteria have sensory mechanisms called chemoreceptors in their cell membrane that allow them to sense and move toward food in their environment. Plants have chemical hormone substances called auxins, which cause a variety of growth and movement patterns called tropisms. Auxins in plants root tips sense and cause the roots to grow toward water, called hydrotropism, and downward toward gravity (geotropism). Auxins in the stem tips sense light and cause the stems and leaves to grow toward light (phototropism). Other auxins cause plants twining plants to seek anchors, some flowers to open during the day and close at night, and growth patterns called circadian rhythms.

Animals respond to external stimuli using their senses, with many responses to stimuli being automatic, such as the pupils of the eyes dilating in the dark and constricting in light (external stimuli). The nervous system in animals controls responses, sending signals to the spinal cord (if present in the organism) and/or to the brain, which then instructs the appropriate muscles or organs to respond. For example, if one accidentally touches a hot stove with the hand, the nervous system immediately sends a signal to the spinal cord, which sends a signal to the correct muscle (biceps) to pull the hand away. It is only after the hand is pulled away from danger that the signal is sent on to the brain and that the hand was burned is realized. Once the individual verbalizes pain (ouch!), the hand has already been pulled away. The action of the nerves in the hand to the spinal cord to the muscle is called a "reflex" arc. The purpose of the reflex arc is for protection.

Maintaining Stable Internal Conditions

Organisms respond to stimuli to maintain a stable internal condition called **homeostasis**. Homeostasis is the regulation and maintenance of bodily functions, such as temperature, blood sugar levels, water content, and amount of carbon dioxide. Homeostasis mechanisms also include maintaining proper and stable pH, respiratory rates, and other important factors that protect the balance of life functions in the organism. Maintaining homeostasis is important for an organism's survival. For more information see: *http://www.bbc.co.uk/education/guides/ z4khvcw/revision*

In addition to the nervous system, hormones within the body also act to regulate life functions and maintain homeostasis. Hormones are produced in glands in the body within the endocrine system. For example, adrenalin is secreted from the adrenal glands (located on top of the kidneys) in high stress or fear situations, such as being chased by a vicious dog, that triggers a series of other responses in the body to that allow the organism to experience "flight or fight" reactions. For example, respiration and heart rate is increased, and the brain is more alert. Some have reported sudden bursts of strength in such situations allowing them to survive or escape the stressful or fearful situation. Other hormones, such as those secreted by the thyroid and pituitary gland, control growth and metabolism. In females, hormones, including estrogen and progesterone, control menstrual cycles and pregnancy.

Feedback Mechanisms

Regulatory feedback mechanisms can be positive or negative. Positive feedback mechanisms causes reactions to increase, such as eating when hungry, whereas negative feedback causes reactions to slow down, such as stopping eating when full. Some examples described in this section, such as the secretion of adrenalin in the body, describe feedback mechanisms. Adrenalin secretion is an example of a positive feedback mechanism in which a stimulus causes a reaction, rather than slowing or stopping a reaction.

Evolution and Behavior

Organisms have long developed and displayed behaviors that contribute to their survival as a species. In ant colonies, for example, individual organisms have specific roles that ensure the survival of the entire colony, e.g., workers, soldiers. A variety of behaviors that serve important roles in survival have evolved over time, such as mating dances of some animals, echolocation in bats, differing bird calls, migratory patterns, territoriality, and nocturnality.

Migration is when organisms move as a group to different places for reasons such as seasonal climate changes, food sources, mating opportunities, or other causes that support their survival. Many species migrate, including birds, whales, butterflies, and others. For more information on migration, go to *https://www.livescience.com/10235-animals-migrate.html*.

Territoriality refers to defending the area where the organism or species live. Living things have many different defenses against intruders into their territory. For example, bees defend their hive by stinging intruders. The more effective they are at defending and protecting their territory, the more likely they are to survive. For more information on territoriality, see: *https://hewittapbiology.wordpress.com/2012/08/06/territorial-behavior/*

Nocturnality is an adaptation of some animals that are awake and active during nighttime, and inactive or asleep during the day. Nocturnal species are either in search of food or seeking the safety of darkness. Raccoons, bats, mice, moths, and other organisms, both predators and prey, are nocturnal. Nocturnal animals have certain adaptations that support their survival, such as enhanced eyesight and/or hearing. For more information on nocturnal organisms, see: *http://www.enchant-edlearning.com/coloring/nocturnal.shtml*

COMPETENCY 015

The teacher understands the relationships between organisms and the environment.

The beginning teacher:

A. Identifies the abiotic and biotic components of an ecosystem.

B. Analyzes the interrelationships among producers, consumers and decomposers in an ecosystem.

C. Identifies factors that influence the size of populations in an ecosystem (e.g., limiting factors, growth rate).

D. Analyzes adaptive characteristics that result in the unique niche of a population or species in an ecosystem.

E. Describes and analyzes energy flow through various types of ecosystems.

F. Knows how populations or species modify and affect ecosystems.

Ecology studies the relationship of organisms with their physical environment. The physical environment includes light, heat, solar radiation, moisture, wind, oxygen, carbon dioxide, nutrients, water, and the atmosphere. These factors of the physical environment are the **abiotic** (nonliving) components of the ecosystem. The **biotic** components are the living and nonliving organisms in the ecosystem. There are three main biotic components of an ecosystem:

• **Producers** are green plants that produce oxygen and store chemical energy for consumers.

• **Consumers** are animals, both herbivores and carnivores. The herbivores take the chemical energy from plants, and carnivores take the energy from other animals or directly from plants.

• **Decomposers**, like fungi and bacteria, are in charge of cleaning up the environment by decomposing and freeing dead matter for recycling back into the ecosystem.

A successful ecosystem requires a healthy balance among producers, consumers, and decomposers. This balance relies on natural ways to control populations of living organisms and is maintained mostly through competition and predation. Predation is the consumption of one living organism, plant or animal, by another. It is a direct way to control population and promote natural selection by eliminating weak organisms from the population. As a consequence of predation, predators and prey evolve to survive. If an organism cannot evolve to meet challenges from the environment, it perishes.

Living organisms like plants and animals need to have ideal conditions for their survival. They need nutrients, the appropriate temperature, and a balanced ecosystem to survive and reproduce. A healthy ecosystem must contain an appropriate system for energy exchange or a food chain. The right combination of herbivorous and carnivorous animals is necessary for a healthy ecosystem. The food chain generally begins with the primary source of energy, the sun. The sun provides the energy for plants; plants in turn are consumed by animals; and animals are consumed by other animals. These animals die and serve as food sources for decomposing bacteria, fungi, and plants. In the food chain, or more accurately, food web, energy from the sun is captured by plants in photosynthesis to make sugars stored as starches. Some of this energy is transferred to the consumers when eaten; however, energy was lost to the plant itself when used in its own life processes. Each level along the food chain receives less and less energy because of the use of some of the energy by the organism itself to sustain its life functions. It is estimated that each level of consumer only receives about 10 percent of the energy from the producer or consumer it ingests, whereas 90% was used in that organism's own life functions. A food chain is shown as follows. Decomposers digest dead organisms and return them to soil so that, with proper sunlight and water conditions, new producers may begin the food chain/web again.

Food chain/web:

Sun → producers → 1st order consumers → 2nd order consumers →
3rd order consumers → decomposers

Example:

Sun → wild corn → mouse → snake → hawk → decomposing bacteria

When the balance of the ecosystem's food chain/web is disrupted either by the removal of organisms or the introduction of nonnative species, the ecosystem is affected, forcing animals and plants to adapt or else die. Thus, the common basic needs of all living organisms for survival are: *air, water, food,* and *shelter.* When a shared resource is scarce, organisms must compete to survive. The competition, which occurs between animals as well as between plants, ensures the survival of the fittest and the preservation of the system.

Changes in the environment have led to certain adaptations to arise in organisms that are favorable to the new environment, and did allow the organisms without that adaptation to survive. The behaviors or physical features of organisms that developed due to mutations that were more favorable to the changes in the environment allowed greater chances of survival and so were carried on to future generations. For example, over thousands of years, the anteater species and its offspring were able to survive better if they had a long snout to be able to reach for ants, and frogs developed a long, sticky tongue to catch flies. Adaptation for animals, plants, and even humans is a matter of life and death. As another example, in analyzing the skulls of predators versus prey, a pattern in the placement of the eye sockets and shapes of teeth becomes clear.

Predators such as wolves, foxes, and lions have eye sockets in the front of their skull, which helps them focus on their prey when hunting. Prey, such as rabbits and squirrels, have eyes on the sides of their skull, which helps them see on both sides of their body at once in order to escape predation. Predators have sharp, pointed teeth for tearing the flesh of their prey, whereas prey (those that are primary or first-order consumers) have flat teeth for chewing and grinding plants they consume. It is important to note that plants and other non-animal organisms also adapt to their environment. For example, coniferous trees have thin but strong needles rather than leaves to protect it against the cold, whereas plants in the tropics have broad leaves allowing it to absorb the abundant sunshine for photosynthesis and release excess water through transpiration. In bacteria, a mutation in its genetic code may result in the bacteria being resistant to antibiotics; bacteria without the mutation are killed by the antibiotic, whereas the mutated variety survives. When the bacterium divides in binary fission, its offspring, or replicated bacteria, contains the mutated DNA, and so is also resistant to the antibiotic. This new, mutated variety of bacteria becomes predominant, whereas the former variety dies off. Scientists work to make new and different antibiotics in order to eliminate the new mutated species of bacteria.

Changes in the food chain of animals often lead to modifications in behaviors and the predominance of certain inherited traits that are favorable adaptations to new conditions. For example, because their habitats are destroyed when land is developed by humans, raccoons and opossums have learned to coexist with humans and to get new sources of food. Bears have managed to successfully adapt to colder climates by hibernating during the winter and living on the fat they accumulate during the rest of the year. Other animals, like the chameleon and the fox, have developed camouflage to hide from predators. Humans are not exempt from the need to adapt to new situations. For example, humans have had to adapt and use tools to produce, preserve, and trade the food supplies they needed to sustain them. All these examples represent ways in which organisms adapt to deal with challenges in their ecosystem.

All species of organisms have limiting factors that impact their population growth. These factors may be biotic, such as the availability of food, or abiotic such as the amount of freshwater available. A drought for example, would impact the growth of plants, which in turn would impact both the food (biotic) and water (abiotic) factors necessary for survival and growth in the population. For more information see: *https://biologydictionary.net/limiting-factor/*.

COMPETENCY 016

The teacher understands the structure and function of Earth systems.

The beginning teacher:

A. Understands the composition and structure of Earth (mantle, crust and core) and analyzes constructive and destructive processes that produce geologic change (e.g., plate tectonics, weathering, erosion, deposition).

B. Understands the form and function of surface water and ground water.

C. Applies knowledge of the composition and structure of the atmosphere and its properties.

D. Applies knowledge of how human activity and natural processes, both gradual and cata-strophic, can alter Earth systems.

E. Identifies the sources of energy (e.g., solar, geothermal) in Earth systems and describes mechanisms of energy transfer (e.g., convection, radiation).

The formation of deserts, mountains, rivers, oceans, and other landforms can be described in terms of geological processes. Mountains are formed by colliding plates. For example, the Appalachian Mountains in the United States were formed 250 million years ago when the tectonic plate carrying the continent of Africa collided with the plate carrying the North American continent (Badder et al., 2000). Rivers and natural lakes form at low elevations where rainfall collects and eventually runs down to the sea. The sediment gathered by the rivers in turn accumulates at river mouths to create deltas. These are both constructive and destructive processes that form the Earth. **Constructive processes** include those that build mountains, such as the gradual (over millions of years) collision and crushing together of the Earth's tectonic plates. **Destructive processes** include weathering and erosion—the wearing down of mountains and rock by forces such as water, wind, and ice.

Layers of the Earth

The average circumference of the Earth at the equator is 25,902 miles, and its radius is about 3,959 miles. The Earth is divided into three main parts:

*   The crust is the outer portion of the Earth where we live. The thickness of the crust varies from about 3 miles to 40 miles, depending on the location. It contains various types of soil, metals, and rocks. The crust is broken down into several floating tectonic plates. Movements of these plates cause earthquakes and changes in landforms.

*   The mantle is the thickest layer of the Earth located right below the crust. It is composed mostly of rocks and metals. The heat in the mantle is so intense that rocks and metals melt, creating magma and the resulting lava that reaches the surface.

*   The core is the inner part of the Earth. It is composed of a solid inner core and an outer core that is mostly liquid. The inner core is made of solid iron and nickel. Despite temperatures in the inner core that resemble the heat on the surface of the sun, this portion of the Earth remains solid because of the intense pressure there.

Continental Drift

In 1915, the German scientist Alfred Wegener proposed that all the continents were previously one large continent but then broke apart and drifted through the ocean floor to their present locations. This theory was called the Continental Drift, and it was the origin of today's concept of plate tectonics.

Tectonic Plates

Based on the theory of plate tectonics, the surface of the Earth is fragmented into large plates. The upper crust, or lithosphere, rides on top of the layer beneath, called the asthenosphere. The lithospheric plates are in continuous motion, floating on more liquid-like asthenosphere and always changing in size and position. The edges of these plates, where they move against each other, are sites of intense geologic activity, which results in earthquakes, volcanoes, and the creation of mountains. The generator for the movement of the continents/Earth's plates is the Mid-Atlantic Ridge—a huge volcanic mountain range on the floor of the Atlantic Ocean that is continuously erupting and pushing the plates apart in opposite directions from each other.

Forces That Change the Surface of the Earth

Three main forces and processes change the surface of the Earth: weathering, geological movements, and the creation of glaciers.

Weathering

Weathering is the process of breaking down rock, soils, and minerals through natural, chemical, and biological processes. Two of the most common examples of physical weathering are exfoliation and freeze-thaw.

- Exfoliation occurs in places like the desert when the soil is exposed first to high temperatures, which cause it to expand, and then to cold temperatures, which make the soil contract. The stress of these changes causes the outer layers of rock to peel off.

- Freeze-thaw breaks down rock when water gets into rock joints or cracks and then freezes and expands, breaking the rock. A similar process occurs when water containing salt crystals gets into the rock. Once the water evaporates, the crystals expand and break the rock. This process is called salt-crystal growth.

Weathering can be caused by chemical reactions. Two of the most common examples of chemical weathering are acid formation and hydration. Acid is formed under various conditions. For example, sulfur and rain are combined to create acid rain, which can weather and change the chemical composition of rock. Hydration occurs when the minerals in rock absorb water and expand sometimes changing the chemical composition of the rock. For example, through the process of hydration, a mineral like anhydrite can be changed into a different mineral, namely gypsum.

Erosion

After weathering, a second process called erosion can take place. Erosion is the movement of sediment from one location to the other through the use of water, wind, ice, or gravity. The Grand Canyon was created by the processes of weathering and erosion. The water movement (erosion) is responsible for the canyon being so deep, and the weathering process is responsible for its width (Houghton Mifflin, 2000).

Deposition

When the forces moving the sediment (water, wind, gravity) stop or slow down, the sediment is dropped. For example, when a river flows into a larger body of water, it slows down. The result of this slowdown is the sediment is deposited. When layer upon layer of sediment is deposited, a delta forms.

Earthquakes and Geologic Faults

The movement of the Earth's plates has forced rock layers to fold, creating mountains, hills, and valleys. This movement causes faults in the Earth's crust, breaking rocks and reshaping the environment. When forces within the Earth cause rocks to break and move around geologic faults, earthquakes occur. A fault is a deep crack that marks the boundary between two plates. The San Andreas Fault in central California is a well-known origin of earthquakes in the area. The epicenter of an earthquake is the point on the surface where the quake is the strongest. The Richter scale is used to measure the amount of energy released by the earthquake. The severity of an earthquake runs from 0 to 9 on the Richter scale. Small tremors occur constantly; but generally every few months, a major earthquake occurs somewhere in the world. Scientists are researching ways to predict earthquakes, but their predictions are not always accurate. There are various types of earthquake faults lines. These fault lines include normal fault, thrust fault, and strike-slip fault and are named according to how the two sides of the fault interface to cause the earthquake.

Volcanoes

Volcanoes are formed by the constant motion of tectonic plates. This movement creates pressure that forces magma from the mantle to escape to the surface, creating an explosion of lava, fire, and ash. The pressure of the magma and gases creates a monticule, or a small cone, that eventually grows to form a mountain-like volcano. Volcanic activity can create earthquakes, and the fiery lava can cause destruction. There are several types of volcanoes with different characteristics, including cinder cones, composite volcanoes, shield volcanoes, and lava domes.

Gravity

Gravity is the force of attraction that exists between objects. Gravity keeps the Earth in its orbit by establishing a balance between the attraction of the sun and the speed at which the Earth travels around it. However, gravity is also responsible for many of the Earth's forces that change the land. For example, when ice melts on the tops of mountains, it is because of gravity that the water will form streams and rivers that flow down the mountain, eventually making its way to the lowest point. Some of the main functions of gravity are listed here:

- Keeping the Earth's atmosphere, oceans, and inhabitants from drifting into space

- Pulling the rain to the rivers and eventually to the sea

- Guiding the development and growth of plants

- Affecting the way that our bones and muscles function

For information about the Earth and space, go to the official website of the National Aeronautics and Space Administration (NASA) at *www.nasa.gov*. The site includes special sections for students from kindergarten through grade 12 and teachers.

Surface Water and Groundwater

Surface water is the water in streams, lakes, rivers, and all water that is on the surface of the land. Groundwater is water that seeps beneath the surface of the land and forms an underground "river" of water. The groundwater seeps into the soil until it reaches an impermeable layer of rock. The water stays on top of this layer and is a source of drinking water. This water may be tapped into via aquifers and wells.

The Earth's Atmosphere

The Earth is surrounded by a large mass of gas called the atmosphere. Roughly 348 miles thick, this gas mass supports life on the Earth and separates it from space. Among the many functions of the atmosphere are these:

- Absorbing energy from the sun to sustain life

- Recycling water and other chemicals needed for life

- Maintaining the climate, working with electric and magnetic forces

- Serving as a vacuum that protects life

The atmosphere is composed of 78 percent nitrogen, 21 percent oxygen, and 1 percent argon. In addition to these gases, the atmosphere contains water, greenhouse gases like ozone, and carbon dioxide. The Earth's atmosphere has five layers. The layer closest to the Earth is called the troposphere, and the weather we experience occurs in this layer.

Natural and Human Influences on Earth Systems

It is important to understand that many natural processes on Earth can change its systems. For example, earthquakes and volcanoes can be destructive and change the structure and composition of the landscape. It is caused by earthquakes under bodies of water such as oceans. Tsunamis, an enormous wall of water that crashes into shorelines can create a dramatic change in that shoreline.

However, human influences may also change Earth systems. The destruction of the rainforests, called deforestation, can change the structure and composition of the land. On a larger scale, deforestation can affect the balance of atmospheric gases, including carbon dioxide and oxygen levels. Carbon dioxide emissions from factories, automobiles, and airplanes, as examples, may play a role in changing the atmospheric composition as well. Carbon dioxide, called a **greenhouse gas**, tends to trap heat energy and result in an overall warming of the atmosphere, which has an impact on climate and plant growth that in turn affects all living organisms on Earth. There are many natural and human influences that contribute to the increase of greenhouse gases in the atmosphere producing what is known as **global warming**. Other greenhouse gases include methane (CH_4) and ozone, (O_3), which is the primary component of smog found at Earth's ground level.

It is important to distinguish global warming and the ozone that is in smog from the destruction of the ozone layer (hole in the ozone layer), which is a different phenomenon. Ozone forms a layer at the top of the atmosphere that blocks harmful ultraviolet rays from the sun from reaching the Earth's surface ("good ozone"). The "hole" in the ozone layer means there is a destruction of this ozone layer, and now harmful ultraviolet radiation is reaching Earth's surface where this hole is present. Chlorofluorocarbons, which are found in aerosols, contribute to the destruction of the ozone layer.

Energy Transfer

The transfer of heat is accomplished in three ways: conduction, radiation, and convection.

Conduction is the process of transferring heat or electricity through a substance. It occurs when two objects of differing temperatures are placed in contact with each other and heat flows from the hotter object to the cooler object. For example, in the cooling system of a car, heat from the engine is transferred to the liquid coolant. When the coolant passes through the radiator, the heat transfers from the coolant to the radiator, and eventually, out of the car. This heat transfer system preserves the engine and allows it to continue working.

Radiation describes the energy that travels at high speed in space in the form of light or through the decay of radioactive elements. Radiation is part of our modern life. It exists in simple states as the energy emitted by microwaves, cellular phones, and sunshine or as potentially dangerous energy as X-ray machines and nuclear weapons. The radiation used in medicine, nuclear power, and nuclear weapons has enough energy to cause permanent damage and death.

Convection describes the flow of heat through the movement of fluid matter, meaning gases and liquids, from a hot region to a cool region. In its most basic form, the concept of convection is that warmer gases or liquids rise, and colder gases or liquids sink. The colder gases or liquids contract and so are denser and sink; the warmer gases or liquids expand, meaning particles become more spread out, and so are less dense, and rise. Thus, convection occurs when the heating and circulation of a substance changes the density of the substance. A good example is the heating of air over land near coastal areas coupled with the influx of cooler sea breezes offshore. The heated air inland expands and thus decreases in density, causing the cooler, more dense air to rush in to achieve equilibrium. A more common example of convection is the process of heating water on a stove. In this case, heat is transferred from the stove element to the bottom of the pot by conduction, which heats the water. Heat is transferred from the hot water at the bottom of the pot to the cooler water at the top by convection. At the same time, the cooler, denser water at the top sinks to the bottom, where it is subsequently heated. This circulation creates the movement typical of boiling water. Convection currents created by the combining or colliding of cold and warm air masses is one factor responsible for storms and circular rotation of the air in tornados and hurricanes. Ocean currents are also caused by the collision of cold water and warm water masses in the oceans (Cavallo, 2001). Convection currents occur in the molten or partially molten rock of the mantle, causing plates to move and the crust to have seismic and volcanic activity.

COMPETENCY 017

The teacher understands cycles in Earth systems.

The beginning teacher:

A. Understands the rock cycle and how rocks, minerals, and soils are formed.

B. Understands the water cycle and its relationship to weather processes.

C. Understands biogeochemical cycles (e.g., carbon, nitrogen, oxygen) and their relationship to Earth systems.

D. Understands the relationships and interactions that occur among the various cycles in the biosphere, geosphere, hydrosphere, and atmosphere.

Rock Types

The hard, solid part of the Earth's surface is called rock. Rocks are made of one or more minerals. Rocks like granite, marble, and limestone are extensively used in the construction industry. They can be used in floors, buildings, dams, highways, or the making of cement. Rocks are classified by the way they are formed.

On earth there are three types of rock:

- **Igneous** rocks are crystalline solids that form directly from the cooling of magma or lava. The composition of the magma determines the composition of the rock. Granite is one of the most common types of igneous rocks and is created from magma (inside the Earth). Once magma reaches the Earth's surface, it is called lava. Lava that has cooled forms a rock with a glassy look, called obsidian.

- **Sedimentary** rocks are called secondary rocks because they are often the result of the accumulation of small pieces broken off from preexisting rocks and then pressed into a new form. There are three types of sedimentary rocks:

  ▸ Clastic sedimentary rocks are made when pieces of rock, mineral, and organic material fuse together. These are classified as conglomerates, sandstone, and shale.

  ▸ Chemical sedimentary rocks are formed when water rich in minerals evaporates, leaving the minerals behind. Some common examples are gypsum, rock salt, and some limestone.

  ▸ Organic sedimentary rocks are made from the remains of plants and animals. For example, coal is formed when dead plants are squeezed together. Another example is a form of limestone rock composed of the remains of organisms that lived in the ocean.

- **Metamorphic** rocks are also secondary rocks formed from igneous, sedimentary, or other types of metamorphic rock. When hot magma or lava comes in contact with rocks, or when buried rocks are exposed to pressure and high temperatures, the result is metamorphic rocks. For example, exposing limestone to high temperatures creates marble. The most common metamorphic rocks are slate, gneiss, and marble.

Rock Cycle

The formation of rock follows a cyclical process. For instance, rocks can be formed when magma or lava cools down, creating igneous rocks. Igneous rocks exposed to weathering can break into sediment, which can be compacted and cemented to form sedimentary rocks. Sedimentary rocks are exposed to heat and pressure to create metamorphic rocks. Finally, metamorphic rocks can melt and become magma and lava again (Badder et al., 2000). For more information on the rock cycle, including an explanatory diagram of the process, please refer to the following website: *www. mineralogy4kids.org/rock-cycle*.

Minerals

Minerals are the most common form of solid material found in the Earth's crust. Even soil contains bits of minerals that have broken away from rock. To be considered a mineral, a substance must be found in nature and must never have been a part of any living organism. Minerals can be as soft as talc or as hard as emeralds and diamonds. Dug from the Earth, minerals are used to make various products:

- Jewelry—Gemstones, such as amethysts, opals, diamonds, emeralds, topazes, and garnets, are examples of minerals commonly used to create jewelry. Gold and silver are another type of mineral that can be used to create jewelry.

- Construction—Gypsum boards (drywall) are made of a mineral of the same name—gypsum. The windows in homes are made from the mineral, quartz.

- Personal Use—Talc is the softest mineral and it is commonly applied to the body in powder form.

Water Cycle

The hydrologic cycle describes a series of movements of water above, on, and below the surface of the Earth. This cycle consists of four distinct stages: storage, evaporation, precipitation, and runoff. It is the means by which the sun's energy is used to transport, through the atmosphere, stored water from the rivers and oceans to land masses. The heat of the sun evaporates the water and takes it to the atmosphere from which, through condensation, it falls as precipitation. As precipitation falls, water is filtrated back to underground water deposits called aquifers, or it runs off into storage in lakes, ponds, and oceans.

Tides

The word *tides* is used to describe the alternating rise and fall in sea level with respect to the land, produced by the gravitational attraction of the moon and the sun. Additional factors such as the configuration of the coastline, depth of the water, the topography of the ocean floor, and other hydrographic and meteorological influences may play an important role in altering the range, interval, and times of the arrival of the tides.

Biogeochemical Cycles

Biogeochemical cycles include the carbon, nitrogen, and oxygen cycles. The carbon cycle is the capture of carbon from carbon dioxide in the atmosphere by plants to make glucose. When this glucose is used as food for the plant or other organisms, it is digested, then by respiration, broken apart again into carbon dioxide and returned back to the atmosphere. The process continues in a life sustaining process.

For the nitrogen cycle it is important to recognize that most of the air we breathe is nitrogen, but it is not useful to us in that form, so it is exhaled. Lightning causes nitrogen in the air to combine with oxygen. Certain bacteria that live on the roots of certain plants, called nitrogen-fixing bacteria, are able to take nitrogen in this combined form with oxygen and make it available for use by plants. The plants can incorporate the nitrogen into their plant structure, and when eaten by animals and other organisms, this nitrogen becomes available for use. The nitrogen returns to the soil when the plant or other living organism dies and decays, releasing nitrogen gas back into the atmosphere. Nitrogen is important to all living things because it is a major component of DNA, RNA, and amino acids, which are the building blocks of proteins.

In the oxygen cycle, plants and animals use oxygen to complete the process of respiration where it is returned to the air in water and carbon dioxide. Carbon dioxide is then taken up by green plants and algae, allowing for photosynthesis, in which oxygen is a by-product. It is important for students to understand how the biogeochemical cycles interact with each other, as well as with the biosphere, geosphere, hydrosphere, and atmosphere.

COMPETENCY 018

The teacher understands the role of energy in weather and climate.

The beginning teacher:

A. Understands the elements of weather (e.g., humidity, wind speed, pressure, temperature) and how they are measured.

B. Compares and contrasts weather and climate.

C. Analyzes weather charts and data to make weather predictions (e.g. fronts, pressure systems).

D. Applies knowledge of how transfers of energy among Earth systems affect weather and climate.

E. Analyzes how Earth's position, orientation and surface features affect weather and climate (e.g., latitude, altitude, proximity to bodies of water).

Weather

The elements of weather include interactions between wind, water (precipitation), wind speed and direction, air pressure, humidity, and temperature. Wind is caused by air masses that have different amounts of heat (temperatures); for example, when a warm air mass moves toward a cold air mass. Air pressure is related to both the amount of water in the air mass and its temperature (heat content). Warm air has higher pressure than cold air; thus, warm, high pressure air masses move toward cold, low pressure air masses. One simple rule is that energy always moves from *warmer to colder*. So, if you open a window on a hot summer day when your air conditioning is on, the cold does not go out—the warm air comes in. The same is true with larger-scale warm and cold air masses.

Humidity is a measure of the percentage of water that is in the air. Dew point is the temperature of the air at which water condenses out of it in liquid form as precipitation and may be observed as "dew." In other words, air has a certain amount of water vapor (water in the gas state) in it (the percent is measured as humidity). That water vapor will turn to liquid water as temperatures drop overnight, in which we observe dew, or when a cold front moves in that lowers the temperature, which can result in a rainstorm or snowstorm.

Wind is measured by an instrument called an *anemometer*. Air pressure is measured by a **barometer**; **rain gauges** and other instruments measure precipitation. Temperature is measured by a **thermometer**. Relative humidity is measured by a *psychrometer*.

Climate

Weather is the conditions of the atmosphere at a given, relatively short period of time. Climate, however, is the long-term weather conditions in an area on a continuous, seasonal basis. The climate is more complex and can be measured by the average variety of weather conditions, such as temperature and precipitation, that occur seasonally in that geographic region of the world over a period of time.

Predicting Weather

Weather can be predicted by tracking weather patterns using maps and charts. These maps have special symbols that indicate, for example, warm and cold air masses, air pressure, and relative humidity in a region. By knowing how air behaves, such as the fact that cold air goes down and warm air rises, warmer air always moves toward colder air, and high pressure always moves outward toward lower pressure, we can track the weather and make predictions. Clouds are also an indication of the type of weather occurring in an area.

Interpreting weather maps is an important skill for weather prediction. It is important that teachers know the various symbols, including warm fronts, cold fronts, stationary fronts, wind speed and direction symbols, high and low pressure systems, and others.

The Earth's Surface and Position as a Factor in Weather and Climate

The Earth's surface is primarily water, and bodies of water affect the weather and climate of an area. Water has a high specific heat, which means that it takes longer to take in heat and longer to release the heat it has absorbed than any other material on Earth. Therefore, coastal areas tend to be warmer than areas inland or away from water, because the water moderates the temperature, even if the locations are at the same latitude. In the United States, for example, areas in the middle of the country will have greater extreme differences in the cold temperatures in the winter and warm temperatures in the summer compared to a location at the same latitude near the ocean.

Large lakes, such as the Great Lakes, also create a situation called "lake effect" in the winter — the air over the lake is relatively warm, and so can carry water vapor (evaporation). As soon as that air carrying water moves over land, however, it rapidly cools and releases its water (precipitation) in the form of snow over the land. Mountains and other landforms also have an effect on the weather. When air holding water hits a mountainside, it is forced upward, which makes the air cool and therefore rain (or snow) on that side of the mountain. This is typically the western side of the mountain in the United States, as in the mountain ranges of the Rocky Mountains. Once the precipitation is gone from that air mass, and the air mass crosses the mountain to the other side, it drops back down and warms; but at that point it is dry air and so may result in an arid region or desert. The Gobi Desert of the United States is a result of this phenomenon.

On a much larger scale, the tilt of the Earth itself—as a planet—is responsible for weather and climate. The Earth is on a 23.4-degree tilt on its axis in space. This tilt means the Earth's North Pole is pointed *away* from the sun when it is in one location in its orbit (path around the sun), and *toward* the sun when it is in the opposite orbital location. This tilt of the Earth results in the seasons, with extreme changes being in locations closer to the North and South poles, and in locations with a higher latitude. For example, when the North Pole is pointing toward the sun in its orbit, it is summer in the Northern Hemisphere; and when the North Pole is pointing away from the sun in its orbit, it is winter in the Northern Hemisphere. In addition to latitude, altitude has an effect on weather. At higher altitudes, air pressure is lower and thus temperatures are cooler.

COMPETENCY 019

The teacher understands the characteristics of the solar system and the universe.

The beginning teacher:

A. Applies knowledge of the Earth-Moon-Sun system and resulting phenomena (e.g., seasons, tides, lunar phases, eclipses).

B. Identifies properties of the components of the solar system.

C. Recognizes characteristics of stars, nebulas, comets, asteroids, and galaxies, and knows their distribution in the universe.

D. Demonstrates an understanding of evidence for the scientific theories of the origin of the universe.

The sun is the center of our solar system, which is composed of eight planets, many satellites that orbit the planets, several dwarf planets, and a large number of smaller bodies like comets and asteroids. Short definitions of these terms follow.

- Planets are large bodies orbiting the sun.

- Dwarf planets are small bodies orbiting the sun.

- Satellites are moons orbiting the planets. Our planet has one moon whereas other planets may have no moons (Mercury, Venus), or many moons (Jupiter, Saturn).

- Asteroids are small dense objects or rocks orbiting our star, the sun. The Asteroid Belt of our own solar system is located between Mars and Jupiter. Some theorize that the asteroids could be the remains of an exploded planet.

- Meteoroids are fragments of rock in space, most originating from the debris left behind by comets that burn up/vaporize upon entering Earth's atmosphere due to friction from the air molecules.

- Comets are small icy objects traveling through space in an elongated, elliptical orbit around the sun.

The objects in our solar system revolve around our star, which we call the sun. The **inner solar system** contains the planets Mercury, Venus, Earth, and Mars, in this order. The **outer solar system** comprises the planets Jupiter, Saturn, Uranus, and Neptune, and a number of dwarf planets, including Pluto, Ceres, Eris and others, with likely more yet to be found (see Table 6.2).

Table 6.2
Planets and Dwarf Planets of our Solar System

Inner Planets	Mercury, Venus, Earth, Mars
Outer Planets	Jupiter, Saturn, Uranus, Neptune
Dwarf Planets	Pluto, Ceres, Eris, Haumea, Makemake

Galaxies are large collections of stars, hydrogen, dust particles, and other gases. The universe is made up of countless galaxies. The solar system that includes Earth is part of a galaxy called the Milky Way.

Stars like the sun are composed of large masses of hydrogen pulled together by gravity. The hydrogen, with strong gravitational pressure, creates fusion inside the star, turning the hydrogen into helium. The liberation of energy created by this process causes solar radiation, which makes the sun glow with visible light, as well as forms of radiation not visible to the human eye. Nebulas are clouds of gas (mostly hydrogen) and dust in interstellar space. Stars and planetary systems are formed from this gas and dust.

Earth performs two kinds of movement: rotation and revolution. Rotation describes the spinning of Earth on its axis. Earth takes approximately 24 hours to make a complete (360°) rotation, which creates day and night.

While Earth is rotating on its axis, it is also following an orbit around the sun. This movement is called revolution. It takes a year, or 365¼ days, for Earth to complete one revolution. The tilt of Earth as it moves around the sun and its curvature create climate zones and seasons. The zones immediately north and south of the equator are called the tropics—Cancer (north) and Capricorn (south). The Arctic Circle (North Pole) and Antarctic Circle (South Pole) are the area surrounding Earth's axis points. Latitude lines are imaginary horizontal lines around the Earth, and longitude lines are likewise vertical lines around the Earth from the North to the South Poles.

These lines form a grid that helps us locate position and longitude.

During each lunar orbit around Earth (about 28 stages based on the portion of the moon visible fro of light but reflects the light from the sun. The sh Earth is between the sun and the moon, to a new n and Earth. When the Earth is between the sun ar sun to the moon, casting a shadow on the moon, between the sun and the Earth and the moon block a shadow on the Earth, this is called a solar ecli Earth, and moon result in tides on Earth.

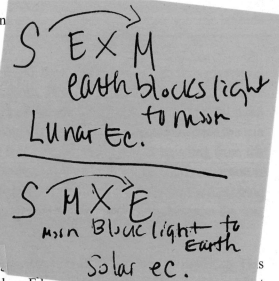

The most prominent scientific theory for the or theory is based on the observations of scientists such as Edwin Hubble. galaxies and other celestial objects appear to be moving away from a central point in our universe. Scientists theorize that a great explosion occurred 13.8 billion years ago as a result of the compression of all the matter and energy in the universe.

COMPETENCY 020

The teacher understands the history of the Earth system.

The beginning teacher:

A.   Understands dating methods and the geologic timescale as it relates to geologic processes.

B.   Demonstrates an understanding of theories about the Earth's origin and geologic history.

C.   Demonstrates an understanding of how tectonic forces have shaped landforms over time.

D.   Understands the formation of fossils and the importance of the fossil record in explaining the Earth's history.

Until the 18th century, it was commonly believed that the Earth was a few thousand years old. However, **radiometric dating** (the comparison of the amount of parent material to daughter material in a substance) has now placed the Earth at approximately 4.5 billion years old. This amount of time is difficult to imagine, especially since humans have only been on Earth for about 200,000 years. Geologic time is divided into **Precambrian** and **Cambrian** expanses of time, and further divided into **Eons**, **Eras**, **Periods**, and **Epochs**. The division of geologic time is based on geologic features of the Earth and events, and may also be characterized by the living organisms that dominated the Earth during that time.

The Earth originated from a cloud of dust that, as with all celestial objects, originated from the Big Bang and over time, rotated and condensed into its current form. The condensation of dust and rock particles in space that formed the Earth was caused by molecular attractions between the particles, just as dustballs seem to clump together on the floor of a home. More and more particles collided with Earth, also generating much heat. In its early history, the Earth consisted primarily of hot liquid, which cooled over time, as particle collisions subsided. It is believed that the first primitive living organisms, likely single-celled bacteria, originated on Earth 3 billion years ago.

As discussed in Competency 016, in the early 1900s, it was proposed that all the continents were previously one large continent but then broke apart and drifted through the ocean floor to their present locations. This theory was called the Continental Drift, and it was the origin of today's concept of plate tectonics, that is, that the surface of the Earth is fragmented into large plates. The collision of plates is the cause of many geologic features on Earth, and the cause of catastrophic events such as volcanoes and earthquakes. The edges or boundaries of the plates are the sites of much seismic activity and the location of most of the "fault lines" on Earth. The boundaries of the Pacific Plate, in particular, are known as the "Ring of Fire" because the seismic activity forms a circle around the edges of the continents surrounding the Pacific Ocean. This is where most volcanic and earthquake activity occurs.

As the plates collide they produce a variety of geologic results. One possible result that occurs when plates collide is that one plate is forced beneath the other, creating a subduction zone. The plate that rides over the top pushes upwards and forms mountains, whereas the plate that plunges underneath forms a deep sea trench. This type of boundary exists off the west coast of South America and is responsible for forming the Andes Mountains. In subduction zones, plates are destroyed. Another plate boundary is called a convergent zone, which is where island chains may arise.

As mentioned in Competency 016, the movement of the continents/Earth's plates is caused by a huge "generator" known as the Mid-Atlantic Ridge. This ridge is a significantly large volcanic mountain range on the floor of the Atlantic Ocean running north and south, extending through the center of Iceland. The mountains in the ridge are continuously erupting and pushing the plates apart in opposite directions from each other, at a rate of about 1 cm per year. Evidence exists that the Mid-Atlantic Ridge is responsible for pushing the continents apart when they were (at several times in geologic history) joined together as one large supercontinent.

The theory of Continental Drift was supported by the existence of common preserved remains of organisms along the continents, known as fossils. For example, according to the theory, the continents have been joined together at various times throughout history. Fossils of the same time period have been found on the western coast of Africa that are identical to fossils of the same time period found on the east coast of South America, where the two continents would have been joined. The continents when joined together formed a supercontinent, often referred to as Pangaea.

COMPETENCY 021

The teacher has theoretical and practical knowledge about teaching science and about how students learn science.

The beginning teacher:

A. Understands how the developmental characteristics, prior knowledge and experience, and attitudes of students influence science learning.

B. Selects and adapts science curricula, content, instructional materials, vocabulary, and activities to meet the interests, knowledge, understanding, abilities, experiences, and needs of all students, including English language learners.

C. Understands how to use situations from students' daily lives to develop instructional materials that investigate how science can be used to make informed decisions.

D. Understands effective ways to address common misconceptions in science.

E. Understands the use of active learning including the appropriate use of inquiry processes for students and other instructional models (e.g., collaborative learning groups).

F. Understands questioning strategies designed to elicit higher-level thinking and how to use them to move students from concrete to more abstract understanding.

G. Understands the importance of planning activities that are inclusive and accommodate the needs of all students.

H. Understands how to sequence learning activities in a way that allows students to build upon their prior knowledge and challenges them to expand their understanding of science.

Developmentally Appropriate Practices

Children's processing of scientific inquiry can begin as early as age 3 or 4. However, teachers must be aware of the stages of cognitive, social, and emotional development of children to appropriately introduce children to science concepts. For example, observing and experimenting with water and colors can easily be done by 3- or 4-year-olds, but using microscopes to observe and analyze animal or vegetable cells might be more appropriate for children in third and fourth grades. Students in grades 4–8 need direct experiences in order to understand concepts. According to Piaget (1964), children are transitioning through stages of development that require direct involvement to make sense of their experience. The model of teaching known as the learning cycle and 5-E model are based upon promoting the intellectual development of children. Thus, these models of teaching were designed to be consistent with the nature of science—and importantly, to match how children naturally learn (Marek and Cavallo, 1997; Renner and Marek, 1990). It is important that teachers understand the theory and research that underlie such models, as well as know how to use these models in teaching.

Misconceptions or alternative conceptions are a pervasive problem in science teaching and learning. Children tend to view the world from their own perspectives and draw conclusions based on their limited experiences. Once misconceptions are established in learners' minds, they are difficult to change. As such, misconceptions must be identified and addressed directly. It cannot be assumed that students will correct their misconceptions on their own. Therefore, teaching needs to allow children the opportunity for **direct experience** and collecting evidence on their own, through teacher-guided experimentation. The learning cycle/5-E model is a research-based and supported teaching model that promotes conceptual change, helps students resolve misconceptions, and leads to more scientifically accurate understandings (Sandoval, 1995). The learning cycle consists of three major phases: Exploration, Concept Invention, and Application (Lawson, Abraham, & Renner, 1989; Marek & Cavallo, 1997). It has been expanded into a five-phase sequence: Engage, Explore, Explain, Elaborate, and Evaluate (Bybee et al., 1989; Bybee, 2014).

In the learning cycle/5-E model, teachers begin lessons with direct, concrete activities, giving students experience with objects, observation, and the opportunity to collect data (exploration, or engage/explore phase). Students use these experiences and evidence-based data to construct the main concept of their explorations (concept invention or explain phase). The students' experimentation and construction of the main idea or concept from their experiences becomes the "anchor" for connecting other ideas and information in their minds, making new learning more meaningful. Students' direct experiences and construction of concepts based on their own findings guide them to developmentally progress from concrete to more abstract reasoners. For example, in learning the concept of density, it is important that students have objects to touch, feel, weigh (take the mass of) and measure in the exploration phase of the learning cycle/5-E model. From direct experience with the objects, students should construct the concept that "a certain amount of matter (mass) is packed into a given amount of space (volume)." The term that labels this concept is "density." It is important that the *label* or new scientific *vocabulary* is attached to the concept only after the students have had direct, hands-on experience and have constructed *meanings* from their experiences; that is, they have stated the scientific concept in their own words. The teacher guides students toward articulating and understanding the concept, but does not tell them. Instead, the teacher uses the students' findings and words, later substituting more scientific terms and definitions as necessary. This process helps students attach new labels to concepts only after they fully understand the meanings, a strategy that also helps English language learners, as well as fluent English-speaking students, learn new vocabulary. Next, the teacher takes this newly constructed concept and the vocabulary that labels the concept and helps students connect it to real-world experiences and to new scientific concepts (application or elaborate phase). Continuing with the density example, in this phase teachers would help students develop their abstract thinking abilities by having them solve problems using the formula for density, $D = M/V$.

Teachers need to select and design learning experiences such that concrete experiences are used first, leading the students to later use abstract reasoning. In doing so, teachers must focus on promoting students' scientific knowledge, skills, and use of inquiry. Further, the students must consistently use prior knowledge and understandings they have constructed (in this example, about density), to learn more extended, related concepts (e.g., buoyancy). Teaching this way also promotes more meaningful learning versus rote memorization. It also allows teachers to listen to students' thinking and observe their construction of understandings to better address possible misconceptions or misunderstandings. This example demonstrates the instructional knowledge and skills teachers need to have to prepare the best possible science learning experiences for students. The learning cycle/5-E model is consistent with the goals of this competency. (See Marek & Cavallo, 1997.)

Using collaborative groups in teaching also develops students' language, communication, vocabulary, and ability to articulate ideas to others in both written and oral forms. The learning cycle/5E model described here and further discussed in Competency 022 places students in groups throughout their experimentation so they may interact in sharing findings, ideas, and concepts. With teacher guidance, the students also learn skills of argumentation based on evidence. Project Based Learning is an extended, long-term inquiry model in which the instruction is based on a larger theme or problem. Students work in collaborative groups over a period of time to experientially learn concepts within the theme (e.g., through learning cycles/5E modules) and respond and/or present solutions to the problem. The National Education Association (NEA) supports Project Based Learning (PBL) and provides additional resources here: *http://www.nea. org/tools/16963.htm*. For additional information on PBL, also refer to *https://www.bie.org/about/ what_pbl*.

The use of good questions by the teacher is critical to promoting logical thinking and scientific reasoning among students. Good questioning causes students to reflect upon the logic of their data and observations with confidence and also identifies possible misinformation or misunderstanding of important concepts. Students learn to effectively use scientific argumentation and respond to challenges to their findings in order to support their conclusions. Teachers use questioning to reveal student learning and assess their progress in forming sound scientific frameworks of understanding. Questioning is the hallmark of scientific inquiry and should be used throughout inquiry-based instruction. In the learning cycle/5-E model, questioning must be designed to lead students toward being able to state the concept, so it is especially critical in the concept invention or "explain" phase.

Teachers can guide students at various levels of development to observe events; and through questioning, teachers can help students develop high-order thinking skills. For example, a teacher can lead children to make predictions while conducting experiments with objects that float or sink in water. By asking students to predict and explain why an object might sink or float, the teacher is leading students to analyze the properties of the object and the water to make an evaluative decision; that is, the children are using analysis and evaluation to complete that simple task. The following guide uses **Bloom's Taxonomy of Educational Objectives** to help teachers best promote and elevate logical thinking abilities among students.

Use key questioning terms aimed at the full range of the cognitive domain. (Bloom & Krathwohl, 1956; Anderson, Krathwohl et al., 2001; Krathwohl, 2002.)

Bloom's Taxonomy: Critical Thinking Skills

LEVEL 1: Remember

Recall factual information.

Examples

List the five Kingdoms.

Label the parts of the cell in the diagram provided.

Write the formula for density.

LEVEL 2: Understand

Communicate an idea in a different form.

Examples

Explain heat transfer through conduction.

Restate what an ecosystem is in your own words.

Submit a definition of photosynthesis in your own words.

LEVEL 3: Apply

Use what is known to find new solutions or apply in new situations.

Examples

Relate the concept of convection to plate tectonics.

Utilize your understanding of density to explain why pennies sink in water but battle-ships float.

Making use of the clothes you are wearing, how can you stay afloat for several hours?

LEVEL 4: Analyze

Break things and ideas down into component parts and find their unique characteristics.

Examples

Examine blueprints of the electrical circuitry of your school building and explain how it works to bring electricity to your laboratory station.

Study the diagram of human digestion and *reason* what the organ marked #7 might be and explain its function.

Using the given laboratory materials, *deduce* the identities of the substances labeled "A," "B," and "C."

LEVEL 5: Evaluate

Use what is known to make judgments and ratings; accept or reject ideas; determine the worthiness of an idea or thing.

Examples

Decide whether or not you agree with the production of more nuclear power plants and provide justification for your decision.

Make a ruling you would give to car manufacturers on global warming and provide support for your ruling.

Rank the top five greatest discoveries in scientific history and *explain* why you have chosen those discoveries and ranked them in that particular order.

LEVEL 6: Create

A. Use what is known to think creatively and divergently; make something new or original; pattern ideas or things in a new way.

Examples

Create a burglar alarm system for the classroom.

Build an interactive display for a hands-on science museum that demonstrates at least one important concept you have learned in science class this year.

Develop a plan for cleaning the pollutants in the Trinity River.

B. Avoid yes/no questions (unless part of a game) and questions with obvious answers.

Examples

Activity	Ineffective prompt - Yes/No	Better prompt - Critical Thinking
Students are shown a picture of a living cell.	Is this a cell?	What is this structure, and how do you know?
Students watch a chemical reaction in which the solution turns blue.	Did it turn blue?	What happened? What did you observe? Why did this happen?

C. Use questions beginning with the words *why, how, what, where,* and *when* that probe students' thinking.

> **Examples**
>
> How do you know?
>
> Why do you think that? Where did you see a change?
>
> What is your explanation for this observation? When did you notice the change occur?
>
> What do you think?

COMPETENCY 022

The teacher understands the process of scientific inquiry and its role in science instruction.

The beginning teacher:

A. Plans and implements instruction that provides opportunities for all students to engage in investigations.

B. Focuses inquiry-based instruction on questions and issues relevant to students and uses strategies to assist students with generating, refining and focusing scientific questions and hypotheses.

C. Instructs students in the safe and proper use of a variety of grade-appropriate tools, equipment, resources, technology and techniques to access, gather, store, retrieve, organize, and analyze data.

D. Knows how to guide students in making systematic observations and measurements, including repeating investigations to increase reliability.

E. Knows how to promote the use of critical-thinking skills, logical reasoning and scientific problem solving to reach conclusions based on evidence.

F. Knows how to teach students to develop, analyze and evaluate different explanations for a given scientific result.

G. Knows how to teach students to demonstrate an understanding of potential sources of error in inquiry-based investigation.

H. Knows how to teach students to demonstrate an understanding of how to communicate and defend the results of an inquiry-based investigation.

Planning and Implementing Scientific Inquiry

Scientific inquiry is promoted through students engaging in hands-on activities and experimentation. From their experiences conducting scientific experiments, students acquire information firsthand and develop problem-solving skills. Children in grades 4–8 are inquisitive and want to understand the environment around them. Teachers can use this interest to provide students with opportunities to use electronic and printed sources to find answers to their questions and to expand their knowledge about the topic. It is important for children to develop inquiry skills. This can only be accomplished by allowing them to experience science for themselves in hands-on investigations. By doing so, students develop important science inquiry and thinking skills (Table 6.3).

Table 6.3
Science Thinking Skills (Full Option Science System, 2000)

Observing: Using the senses to get information
Communicating: Talking, drawing, and acting
Comparing: Pairing and one-to-one correspondence
Organizing: Grouping, seriating, and sequencing
Relating: Cause-and-effect and classification
Inferring: Super-ordinate/subordinate classification, if/then reasoning, and developing scientific laws
Applying: Developing strategic plans and inventing

As introduced in Competency 021, the model of inquiry that best supports science learning is a model known as the *learning cycle*, consisting of three phases: *exploration*, *concept invention*, and *application* (Lawson, Abraham, & Renner, 1989; Marek & Cavallo, 1997). Over time, the learning cycle was extended with the addition of two new phases becoming what is known as the 5-E model (Engage, Explore, Explain, Elaborate, Evaluate) (Bybee, 1989). What follows is some history on the development of inquiry-based teaching via the learning cycle and 5-E model.

The original three-phase learning cycle model developed by Robert Karplus in the 1960s was based upon the following theoretical foundation (Karplus & Thier, 1967):

1. Science must be taught in a way that is *consistent with the nature of science*. Science is discovery and investigation, and that means science must be taught as an active pro-

cess—as something we *do*. The children need to have the opportunity to experience the true nature of science by doing science exploration for themselves through direct experiences and hands-on investigations.

2. Science teaching must be focused on promoting the main purpose of education, namely, to promote the development in our students the *ability to think*—to be critical and independent thinkers. Science must be taught in a way that promotes the students use of independent, critical, and higher-level thinking abilities (e.g., logic). Promoting this purpose of education is best accomplished by *not* giving or telling students the "answers" or information (e.g., as in giving a lecture); but instead by first giving students hands-on, direct experiences in which they use logic and reasoning to find "answers" or explanations for themselves; further discussion and teacher guidance can follow the students' direct experiences.

3. Science must be taught in a way that *matches how students learn,* described as the mental functioning model by Piaget (1964). How individuals learn is through mentally experiencing the following three-phase mental process.

- First, we **assimilate** or "take in" information with our senses from our environment and what we are experiencing in our environment. During assimilation, we may have a sense of "disequilibrium," which is confusion or "cognitive conflict" as we try to make sense of our experiences. When in disequilibrium, we need to go back and assimilate more information—make more observations and gather more data, for example.

- Second, when we have assimilated enough information and made sense of the information we have gathered, our minds experience **accommodation**. This is the "aha!" moment, the point when we ultimately feel "cognitive relief"—we figured it out, or what we have observed/experienced now makes sense!

- Third, our minds take that newly accommodated information and we **organize** it into our mental structures. That is, we connect the new idea or what we have just figured out/made sense of to what we already know, what we experience in everyday life, and/or to new related concepts.

The three phases of learning described by Piaget, assimilation-accommodation-organization, *match* the original learning cycle's three phases: Exploration-Concept Invention-Application. The logic in developing the learning cycle in these three phases was that, given what we know about how children (people) *learn*, we should be *teaching* in a sequence or way that matches this learning pattern. To do so, teachers should:

1. First, provide students with an *Exploration* phase in which they can assimilate information using their senses. Students may or may not experience disequilibrium, but teachers should guide them (not tell them!) through the sense-making process.

2. Teachers should then carry out a discussion in the *Concept Invention* phase in which students share their observations and findings. With careful questioning, teachers should guide students to review their data/observations toward helping them reach the "aha!" moment, or accommodation. The summarizing statement the students are to write, post on the board, and/or state aloud to others in this phase represents their accommodation, or understanding, of the concept.

3. The teacher then helps students organize the new concept by guiding them through *Application* of the concept in new contexts, in which students can connect the concept with what they observe in everyday life, or what they already know.

Teaching via the learning cycle, we are teaching in a way that is consistent with the nature of science—as an active, hands-on process characterized by investigation and discovery—and we are teaching in a way that supports the purpose of education, that is, we are promoting children's development of higher-level thinking abilities. The learning cycle and its origins and theory base is more fully described in a book by Marek & Cavallo (1997) titled *The Learning Cycle: Elementary School Science and Beyond*.

Over time, science educators added an additional phase to the learning cycle, namely, the *Engage* phase, with the idea that teachers need to do something that will gain the students' attention before beginning the *Exploration* phase. "Engage" can be a demonstration (without explanation) or the simple posing of a question, challenge, or problem. Thus, over time, the original learning cycle model's first phase, *Exploration*, became two phases: *Engage* and *Explore*.

Changing the names of two of the phases also helped refine the learning cycle. The *Concept Invention* phase's name was changed to *Explain*. To sustain the "E" alliteration, the *Application* phase name was changed to *Elaborate*. *Assessment*, or the measurement of learning, in the original three-phase model was to take place throughout the learning cycle. However, science educators at the time preferred to have assessment articulated as an additional phase; thus (again to sustain the "E" alliteration) *Assessment* was termed *Evaluate*. Consequently, the three-phase learning cycle model was expanded into a 5-E Model: *Engage, Explore, Explain, Elaborate, Evaluate*.

The two models (the original three-phase learning cycle model developed by Robert Karplus and the 5-E model that it grew into) are basically the same, and grew out of the same underlying philosophy and theoretical foundation. However, the three phases more closely follow the model of learning—assimilation, accommodation, and organization—as first described by Piaget; whereas the 5-E model incorporates two additional essentials of classroom teaching: (1) gaining students focus and attention, and (2) measuring student learning.

Most importantly, in both models—the Karplus learning cycle and 5-E model—students are *not told* the science concept or information before beginning the inquiry, but must discover the concept themselves through hands-on investigation, observation, and collection of data. In using the

TExES CORE SUBJECTS 4–8 (211)

Engage phase (from 5-E) the students' learning experience begins with the teacher posing one or more questions, giving an interesting demonstration, or providing a laboratory guide. In all of these approaches, this phase captures students' curiosity and motivates them to learn. Whether or not an *Engage* phase is used, students next (or first) experience an *Exploration* phase—and it must be a student-centered hands-on activity, investigation, or experiment. In the *Exploration* phase, students make observations and gather data on a science idea or topic area. In this phase, students can determine the experimental design or it can be pre-determined by the teacher. The main aspect, however, is that students are doing the lab activity themselves, and have not been told the expected outcome beforehand. For example, students may grow plants in the light and in the dark, and make observations, draw and/or take photos, and measure the plants grown under the two differing conditions over a period of time. All other variables are controlled (soil, water, air); only the light received by the plants is different, which is the variable.

After the observations have been made and data has been gathered by students, the teacher begins the next instructional phase called *Concept Invention*, or in the 5-E model, the *Explain* phase. In this phase the students present and share data with their classmates in a teacher-guided discussion of findings. The teacher uses questions to guide students' thinking and encourages the use of logic and reasoning as they interpret their data. For example, students may post the photos or drawings of plants grown in the dark and in the light, make line graphs of plant height over time, or share qualitative information about how the plant appeared after grown under the two conditions (e.g., plants in the light were green, whereas plants in the dark were yellow and pale). At the end of this phase, the students construct an overall statement that summarizes their data and observations, which is the central science *concept*. The science vocabulary is then linked to the concept students "invented."

Next, the teacher helps students through the *Application* (from the learning cycle) or *Elaborate* (from the 5-E model) in which students use the new concept they learned as it is applied in new contexts. For example, students can create new questions to investigate, or hypotheses to test based on what they just learned (the concept) and develop a way to answer their questions or test their hypotheses (e.g., what color of light is best for plants to grow?). They can also go to the Internet to learn more about the concept they just invented. In this phase the teacher can engage students in additional hands-on laboratories, readings, discussions, field trips, and/or writing activities that extend and expand upon the concept. These models of inquiry science teaching and learning are endorsed by NSTA (NSTA, 1998, 2003, 2012).

The diagram in Figure 6-2 shows the inquiry-based learning cycle model as it corresponds to the 5-E model of science teaching. The template shown in Table 6.4 explains each phase of the learning cycle as it relates to the 5-E Model for structuring inquiry-based science teaching for all students.

Figure 6.2
The Learning Cycle and 5-E Model

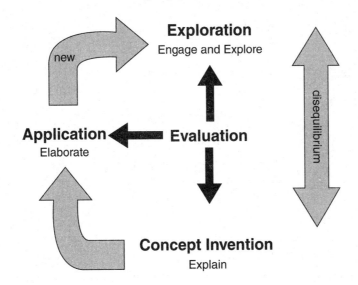

Table 6-4
Description of the Phases of the Learning Cycle and 5-E Model

5-E Definition	Teacher Behavior	Student Behavior
Engage		
• Generate interest • Access prior knowledge • Connect to past knowledge • Set parameters of the focus • Frame the idea	• Motivates • Creates interest • Taps into what students know or think about the topic • Raises questions and encourages responses	• Attentive in listening • Asks questions • Demonstrates interest in the lesson • Responds to questions demonstrating their own entry point of understanding

(continued)

Explore		
• Experience key concepts • Discover new skills • Probe, inquire, and question experiences • Examine their thinking • Establish relationships and understanding	• Acts as a facilitator • Observes and listens to students as they interact • Asks good inquiry-oriented questions • Provides time for students to think and to reflect • Encourages cooperative learning	• Conducts activities, predicts, and forms hypotheses or makes generalizations • Becomes a good listener • Shares ideas and suspends judgment • Records observations and/or generalizations • Discusses tentative alternatives
Explain		
• Connect prior knowledge and background to new discoveries • Communicate new understandings • Connect informal language to formal language	• Encourages students to explain their observations and findings in their own words • Provides definitions, new words, and explanations • Listens and builds upon discussion from students • Asks for clarification and justification • Accepts all reasonable responses	• Explains, listens, defines, and questions • Uses previous observations and findings • Provides reasonable responses to questions • Interacts in a positive, supportive manner

(continued)

Extend/Elaborate		
• Apply new learning to a new or similar situation • Extend and explain concept being explored • Communicate new understanding with formal language	• Uses previously learned information as a vehicle to enhance additional learning • Encourages students to apply or extend the new concepts and skills • Encourages students to use terms and definitions previously acquired	• Applies new terms and definitions • Uses previous information to probe, ask questions, and make reasonable judgments • Provides reasonable conclusions and solutions • Records observations, explanations, and solutions
Evaluate		
• Assess understanding (Self, peer and teacher evaluation) • Demonstrate understanding of new concept by observation or open-ended response • Apply within problem situation • Show evidence of accomplishment	• Observes student behaviors as they explore and apply new concepts and skills • Assesses students' knowledge and skills • Encourages students to assess their own learning • Asks open-ended questions	• Demonstrates an understanding or knowledge of concepts and skills • Evaluates his/her own progress • Answers open-ended questions • Provides reasonable responses and explanations to events or phenomena

Based on the 5-E Instructional Model presented by Dr. Jim Barufaldi at the Eisenhower Science Collaborative Conference in Austin, Texas, July 2002.

Interpreting Findings in Science Inquiry

In planning and conducting experiments, teachers should guide children to develop an appropriate procedure for testing hypotheses, including the use of instruments that can yield measurable data. Even at the early stages of scientific experimentation, the procedure must be clear and tangible enough to allow replication by other students or scientists. Help students understand the concept of controlling variables and testing only one variable at a time. Students need to learn to be precise in the collection of data and measurements. Ensure the use of the metric system in obtaining all measurement data.

Allowing students to gather their own data and observations for interpretation promotes their critical and logical thinking abilities. It also gives them experience with using appropriate tools, resources, and technology of science that will lead to accurate organization and analysis of data. The students will be able to experience and practice science skills by verifying their findings, basing findings on evidence, and analyzing sources of error. Having students collect and report their own data also brings the teacher opportunities to discuss scientific ethics with students. It is important to note that having students repeat investigations will increase the reliability of their results. In the scientific community, scientists repeat experiments possibly hundreds of times, and only report findings if/when they have consistent findings. Other research scientists also replicate experiments to determine if the same findings are produced independently of the original research. Thus, it is important to allow students opportunity to repeat experiments and share findings with other groups who have conducted the same experiments to more closely model the work of science and scientists.

In explaining data collection procedures and display of findings to English language learners, the teacher needs to demonstrate and provide a model of what the end results should look like. In using inquiry, students work in groups, which is particularly helpful for second language learners as they interpret and exchange ideas about data and scientific reasoning.

When students complete their experiments, teachers need to engage them in the process of analyzing their own, and other groups' data for similarities, differences, and variations including error. This occurs in the concept invention or "explain" phase of the learning cycle and 5-E model, and again in any application or "elaborate" activities in which data has been collected. After data has been collected from students' explorations, they display their data in charts and graphs, for example, and communicate their observations and, ultimately, concept statements to the class by posting them on the board and/or through an oral presentation. The data helps them develop conclusions and form new research questions or hypotheses as they evaluate their findings, setting the foundation for new explorations. Students should be able to present pertinent data using graphic representations, and communicate their findings in written and oral forms to others.

In using scientific inquiry as in the learning cycle and 5-E model, scientific vocabulary is introduced *after* students have had hands-on experiences in the (engage and) exploration phase *and* have used their observations and data to construct meaning from their experiences in the *concept invention* or "explain" phase. Once students have had the hands-on direct experience with the concept, and have stated the meaning of their observations, the scientific vocabulary or terms that label the concept can be introduced by the teacher. In the application or elaborate phase, the teacher and students use the new vocabulary in extended experimentation, discussion, readings, writing, and other learning activities. Introducing terms after students have directly experienced the science inquiry and constructed meaning from their experiences by making a concept statement is especially important for second language learners in facilitating the development of understanding of science concepts. For all students, but especially for second language learners, this helps them understand concepts when terms are later *re-introduced*. By giving students the experience — something they *do* — and then allowing them to form meaning from their experience in ways that make sense to them, then when the term that labels what they learned is introduced, they are able to link it to prior knowledge and learning experiences in their minds. The terms are now able to build their background knowledge, which is critical for second language learners to understand the language of science. Making a connection between the hands-on activities and scientific vocabulary is beneficial to all students but especially to English language learners (ELLs), who can link the actions with the appropriate concept and vocabulary words without engaging in translations.

Promoting Logical Thinking and Scientific Reasoning

Interpreting results is one of the most challenging phases of scientific inquiry for the middle grades. Students can easily discuss the observable results but might have difficulty interpreting their meaning. Teachers have to use developmentally appropriate practices to guide students to make extrapolations and infer information from the data, which involves the teachers' use of questioning, as addressed previously, in Competency 021.

Scientific Tools and Equipment for Gathering and Storing Data

Various tools or instruments are used in scientific experimentation in the middle level grades. The classroom should be equipped with measuring devices like graduated cylinders, beakers, scales, dishes, thermometers, meter sticks, and micrometers. They might also have anatomical models showing the body systems. Teachers need to learn to use these tools and equipment properly in order to help their students know how to use them and to collect accurate data in their inquiry investigations.

The TEKS requires students to gather information using specific equipment and tools. Examples of the tools required in grades 4 through 8 are presented in Table 6.5.

Table 6.5
Sample Tools and Equipment for the Middle Level Science Classroom

Tools and Equipment	4th	5th	6th	7th	8th
Nonstandard measurements					
Hand lenses	✓	✓	✓	✓	✓
Computers	✓	✓	✓	✓	✓
Balances	✓	✓	✓	✓	✓
Cups and bowls	✓	✓	✓	✓	✓
Thermometers	✓	✓	✓	✓	✓
Clocks	✓	✓	✓	✓	✓
Meter sticks	✓	✓	✓	✓	✓
Light Microscopes	✓	✓	✓	✓	✓
Dissecting Microscopes	✓	✓	✓	✓	✓
Safety goggles	✓	✓	✓	✓	✓
Magnets	✓	✓	✓	✓	✓
Compasses	✓	✓	✓	✓	✓
Timing devices	✓	✓	✓	✓	✓
Calculators	✓	✓	✓	✓	✓
Sound recorders	✓	✓	✓	✓	✓
Hot plates		✓	✓	✓	✓
Burners		✓	✓	✓	✓
Beakers		✓	✓	✓	✓
Graduated cylinders		✓	✓	✓	✓
Flasks (Erlenmeyer and Florence)		✓	✓	✓	✓
Test tubes and holders		✓	✓	✓	✓

COMPETENCY 023

The teacher knows the varied and appropriate assessments and assessment practices to monitor science learning in laboratory, field and classroom settings.

The beginning teacher:

A. Understands the relationships among science curriculum, assessment and instruction and bases instruction on information gathered through assessment of students' strengths and needs.

B. Understands the importance of monitoring and assessing students' understanding of science concepts and skills on an ongoing basis.

C. Understands the importance of carefully selecting or designing formative and summative assessments for the specific decisions they are intended to inform.

D. Selects or designs and administers a variety of appropriate assessment methods (e.g., performance assessment, self-assessment, formal/informal, formative/summative) to monitor student understanding and progress.

E. Uses formal and informal assessments of student performance and products (e.g., projects, lab journals, rubrics, portfolios, student profiles, checklists) to evaluate student participation in and understanding of the inquiry process.

F. Understands the importance of sharing evaluation criteria and assessment results with students.

Measuring Student Learning

Teaching cannot occur without student *learning*, and in order to determine that learning is occurring, student progress needs to be assessed on a regular basis. Assessment of learning should occur on some scale, large or small, *every class day*, to monitor students' progress in the learning of concepts, as in the learning cycle and 5-E models. Measuring learning as it is occurring is "authentic assessment" and allows teachers to adjust the instruction according to student learning and immediately and routinely address potential difficulties and/or misconceptions in learning. Alternative, **informal assessment methods**, in addition to the more traditional, **formal testing formats** (e.g., multiple-choice) should be used to obtain a full picture of what students know and do not know, or can and cannot do. Alternative assessments include techniques such as verbal reports, laboratory practical exams, story writing, developing advertisements or brochures, constructing concept maps, writing essays, creating drawings or models, and developing plays or skits. In each assessment, the concepts to be learned are represented in alternative ways—yet clearly communicate what students have learned and understand.

It is essential that teachers monitor and assess students' understanding of concepts and skills on a regular, consistent basis and use this information to adjust instruction. The results of frequent informal and formal/traditional and alternative assessments should be used as a tool for planning subsequent instruction. Teachers must communicate progress to students so they can learn to self-monitor their own learning and understand what is needed to achieve learning goals.

Formative assessments are assessments that take place during the learning process that allow teachers to regularly monitor learning, and provide measures of student learning at various times and in various manners throughout the process. Summative assessments are tests given at the end of instruction to measure learning, typically by an exam or standardized test. Formative assessments provide teachers with more information and insight into the students' thinking and learning compared to summative assessments, which provide a culminating measure of achievement. It is important that teachers use both forms of assessment, and prepare students on taking a variety of assessments, so the most accurate measure of their learning and accomplishments can be obtained.

Assessing the Science Curriculum

As part of the accountability system, Texas has a very comprehensive assessment system to measure the state uniform curriculum. This system, new in spring 2012, centers on the STAAR exam. Beginning in spring 2012, the State of Texas Assessments of Academic Readiness (STAAR) replaced the Texas Assessment of Knowledge and Skills (TAKS). On the STAAR, students are assessed on both content understanding and process skills (TEA, 2012).

In this system, students take the STAAR test in grades 3 through 12. However, the science component of STAAR is assessed only in grades 5, 8, and 10. For further information see: *http://tea.texas.gov/student.assessment/staar/science/*. The fifth grade and eighth grade science tests are available in Spanish; thus, Spanish-speaking ELLs can take the test in Spanish. In addition to the required science STAAR examinations, students are assessed through teacher- and district-developed tests in kindergarten through grade 12.

References

Anderson, L.W., Krathwohl, D.R., Airasian, P.W., Cruikshank, K.A., Richard E. Mayer, R.E., Pintrich, P.R., Wittrock, M.C. (2001). *A taxonomy for learning, teaching, and assessing: A revision of bloom's taxonomy of educational objectives*. Boston, MA: Allyn & Bacon (Pearson Education Group).

Houghton Mifflin. (2000). *Discovery works Texas*. Boston: Houghton Mifflin.

Bloom, B.S., & Krathwohl, D.R. (1956). *Taxonomy of educational objectives: The classification of educational goals, by a committee of college and university examiners. Handbook I: Cognitive domain*. New York, NY: Longmans, Green.

Bybee, R. (2014, April/May). The BSCS instructional model: Personal reflections and contemporary implications. Guest editorial. *Science and Children, 51*(8), 10–13.

Bybee, R., Buchwald, C.E., Crissman, S. Heil, D., Kuerbis, P., Matsumoto, C., & McInerney, J.D. (1989). *Science and technology education for elementary years: Frameworks for curriculum and instruction. Opinion paper.* Washington, DC: The National Center for Improving Science Education.

Cavallo, A.M.L. (2001). Convection connections: Integrated learning cycle investigations that explore convection—the science behind wind and waves. *Science and Children, 38*, 20–25.

Full Option Science System (FOSS). (2000). Lawrence Hall of Science, University of California, Berkeley, CA.

Karplus, R. & Thier, H.D. (1967). *A New Look at Elementary School Science*. Chicago: Rand McNally.

Krajcik, J., Blumfield, P., Marx, R., & Soloway, E. (1994). A collaborative model for helping middle grade science teachers learn project-based instruction. *Elementary School Journal, 94*, 483–97.

Lawson, A.E., Abraham, M.R., & Renner, J.W. (1989). *A theory of instruction: Using the learning cycle to teach science concepts and thinking skills.* NARST Monograph No. 1.

Marek, E.A., & Cavallo, A.M.L. (1997). *The learning cycle: Elementary school science and beyond* (rev. ed.). Portsmouth, NH: Heinemann.

National Science Teachers Association (2016). *Science education for middle level students.* Retrieved from *http://static.nsta.org/pdfs/PositionStatement_MiddleLevel.pdf*

National Science Teachers Association (2012). Standards for science teacher preparation. Retrieved from *http://www.nsta.org/preservice/docs/2012NSTAPreserviceScienceStandards.pdf*

National Science Teachers Association. (2003). *Standards for science teacher preparation: Skills of teaching* (revised edition.). Washington, DC: National Science Teachers Association.

National Science Teachers Association. (1998). *Standards for science teacher preparation: Skills of teaching*. Washington, DC: National Science Teachers Association.

National Research Council. (2012). *A framework for K–12 science education*. Washington, DC: National Academy Press.

National Research Council.(2011). *A framework for K–12 science education: Practices, crosscutting concepts, and core ideas*. Washington, DC: National Academy Press.

National Research Council. (2000). *Inquiry and the national science education standards*. Washington, D.C.: National Academy Press.

National Research Council. (1996). *National science education standards*. Washington, D.C.: National Academy Press.

Next Generation Science Standards (NGSS) Lead States (2013). Next generation science standards. Washington, DC: The National Academies Press. Retrieved from *https://www.nextgenscience.org/*

Piaget, J. (1964). Cognitive development in children: Piaget, development and learning. *Journal of Research in Science Teaching, 2*, 176–80.

Renner, J. W., and Marek, E.A. (1990). An educational theory base for science teaching. *Journal of Research in Science Teaching*, 27(3), 241–46.

Resnik, D. (1993). "Philosophical Foundations of Scientific Ethics," in *Ethical Issues in Physics: Workshop Proceedings*, Marshall Thomsen (ed.). Workshop: July 17–18, 1993, Eastern Michigan University, Ypsilanti, Michigan.

Sandoval, J.S. (1995). Teaching in subject matter areas: Science. *Annual Review of Psychology, 46*, 355–74.

Resnik, D.B. (2015). What is Ethics in Research & Why is it Important? *National Institute of Environmental Health Sciences*. Retrieved from: *https://www.niehs.nih.gov/research/resources/bioethics/whatis/index.cfm?links=false*.

Texas Education Agency (2010). *Title 19, Part II, Chapter 112: Texas Essential Knowledge and Skills for Science*. Texas Administrative Code (TAC*)*. Retrieved from *www.tea.state.tx.us*

Texas Education Agency. (2012). *STAAR science resources*. Retrieved from *www.tea.state.tx.us*.

University of California Santa Barbara (2017), Regents of the University of California (2017). *http://scienceline.ucsb.edu/getkey.php?key=3144*.

TExES Core Subjects 4–8 Practice Test 1: English Language Arts and Reading (ELAR) (806)

This pratice test plus an additional test are available at the online REA Study Center (*www.rea.com/studycenter*).

The TExES Core Subjects ELA and Reading (806) test is computer-based, so we strongly recommend that you take our online practice tests to simulate test-day conditions and to receive these added benefits:

- **Timed testing conditions**—Gauge how much time you can spend on each question.

- **Automatic scoring**—Find out how you did on the test, instantly.

- **On-screen detailed explanations of answers**—Learn not just the correct answer, but also why the other answers are incorrect.

- **Diagnostic score reports**—Pinpoint where you're strongest and where you need to focus your study.

English Language Arts and Reading
Practice Test 1: Answer Sheet

1. Ⓐ Ⓑ Ⓒ Ⓓ
2. Ⓐ Ⓑ Ⓒ Ⓓ
3. Ⓐ Ⓑ Ⓒ Ⓓ
4. Ⓐ Ⓑ Ⓒ Ⓓ
5. Ⓐ Ⓑ Ⓒ Ⓓ
6. Ⓐ Ⓑ Ⓒ Ⓓ
7. Ⓐ Ⓑ Ⓒ Ⓓ
8. Ⓐ Ⓑ Ⓒ Ⓓ
9. Ⓐ Ⓑ Ⓒ Ⓓ
10. Ⓐ Ⓑ Ⓒ Ⓓ
11. Ⓐ Ⓑ Ⓒ Ⓓ
12. Ⓐ Ⓑ Ⓒ Ⓓ
13. Ⓐ Ⓑ Ⓒ Ⓓ
14. Ⓐ Ⓑ Ⓒ Ⓓ
15. Ⓐ Ⓑ Ⓒ Ⓓ
16. Ⓐ Ⓑ Ⓒ Ⓓ
17. Ⓐ Ⓑ Ⓒ Ⓓ
18. Ⓐ Ⓑ Ⓒ Ⓓ
19. Ⓐ Ⓑ Ⓒ Ⓓ
20. Ⓐ Ⓑ Ⓒ Ⓓ
21. Ⓐ Ⓑ Ⓒ Ⓓ
22. Ⓐ Ⓑ Ⓒ Ⓓ
23. Ⓐ Ⓑ Ⓒ Ⓓ
24. Ⓐ Ⓑ Ⓒ Ⓓ
25. Ⓐ Ⓑ Ⓒ Ⓓ

26. Ⓐ Ⓑ Ⓒ Ⓓ
27. Ⓐ Ⓑ Ⓒ Ⓓ
28. Ⓐ Ⓑ Ⓒ Ⓓ
29. Ⓐ Ⓑ Ⓒ Ⓓ
30. Ⓐ Ⓑ Ⓒ Ⓓ
31. Ⓐ Ⓑ Ⓒ Ⓓ
32. Ⓐ Ⓑ Ⓒ Ⓓ
33. Ⓐ Ⓑ Ⓒ Ⓓ
34. Ⓐ Ⓑ Ⓒ Ⓓ
35. Ⓐ Ⓑ Ⓒ Ⓓ
36. Ⓐ Ⓑ Ⓒ Ⓓ
37. Ⓐ Ⓑ Ⓒ Ⓓ
38. Ⓐ Ⓑ Ⓒ Ⓓ
39. Ⓐ Ⓑ Ⓒ Ⓓ
40. Ⓐ Ⓑ Ⓒ Ⓓ
41. Ⓐ Ⓑ Ⓒ Ⓓ
42. Ⓐ Ⓑ Ⓒ Ⓓ
43. Ⓐ Ⓑ Ⓒ Ⓓ
44. Ⓐ Ⓑ Ⓒ Ⓓ
45. Ⓐ Ⓑ Ⓒ Ⓓ
46. Ⓐ Ⓑ Ⓒ Ⓓ
47. Ⓐ Ⓑ Ⓒ Ⓓ
48. Ⓐ Ⓑ Ⓒ Ⓓ
49. Ⓐ Ⓑ Ⓒ Ⓓ
50. Ⓐ Ⓑ Ⓒ Ⓓ

51. Ⓐ Ⓑ Ⓒ Ⓓ
52. Ⓐ Ⓑ Ⓒ Ⓓ
53. Ⓐ Ⓑ Ⓒ Ⓓ
54. Ⓐ Ⓑ Ⓒ Ⓓ
55. Ⓐ Ⓑ Ⓒ Ⓓ
56. Ⓐ Ⓑ Ⓒ Ⓓ
57. Ⓐ Ⓑ Ⓒ Ⓓ
58. Ⓐ Ⓑ Ⓒ Ⓓ
59. Ⓐ Ⓑ Ⓒ Ⓓ
60. Ⓐ Ⓑ Ⓒ Ⓓ
61. Ⓐ Ⓑ Ⓒ Ⓓ
62. Ⓐ Ⓑ Ⓒ Ⓓ
63. Ⓐ Ⓑ Ⓒ Ⓓ
64. Ⓐ Ⓑ Ⓒ Ⓓ
65. Ⓐ Ⓑ Ⓒ Ⓓ
66. Ⓐ Ⓑ Ⓒ Ⓓ
67. Ⓐ Ⓑ Ⓒ Ⓓ
68. Ⓐ Ⓑ Ⓒ Ⓓ
69. Ⓐ Ⓑ Ⓒ Ⓓ
70. Ⓐ Ⓑ Ⓒ Ⓓ
71. Ⓐ Ⓑ Ⓒ Ⓓ
72. Ⓐ Ⓑ Ⓒ Ⓓ
73. Ⓐ Ⓑ Ⓒ Ⓓ
74. Ⓐ Ⓑ Ⓒ Ⓓ

Practice Test 1: ELAR

TIME: 50 minutes
74 questions

> **Directions:** Read each item and select the best answer. Most items on this test require you to provide the one best answer. However, some questions require you to select all the options that apply.

1. During literature circle discussion, Mr. Smith's fourth graders bring a response journal with their ideas about the novel they read. In small groups, they share their ideas about the text in an open-ended discussion. The purpose of having students bring the written response journal to the group would be to develop the students' ability to

   A. express their thoughts in an imaginative way with others.

   B. plan and organize their thinking in writing before sharing their thoughts with the group.

   C. help them use grammar, spelling, and punctuation in conventional ways.

   D. assist less talkative students in sharing ideas.

2. Which of the following is the correct syllabication for the word *structure*?

   A. str-uc-ture

   B. struct-ure

   C. struc-ture

   D. stru-c-ture

3. To help her students acquire research skills, a fifth grade teacher wants them to evaluate credible sources of information from a variety of sources on the Internet. Which of the following lessons would help them most as they seek out multiple sources of information?

   A. Teach students how to critically evaluate sources of information for accuracy and credibility as potential sources.

   B. Teach students how to use multiple web browsers to search for different sources.

   C. Teach students how to summarize the article in a paragraph.

   D. Teach students how to read charts, tables, and graphs in different sources.

4. The writing process includes which of the following essential components?

   A. Brainstorming, mapping, rehearsal, drafting, editing

   B. Brainstorming, organizing, editing, spelling, grammar

   C. Brainstorming, drafting, revising, editing, publishing

   D. Brainstorming, sharing, listing, mapping, submitting

5. A teacher wants to help students properly cite sources as a component of academic integrity and to avoid plagiarism. Which of the following would NOT be acceptable as an instructional component for these objectives?

   A. Instruct students to locate images by going to a popular web browser and saving any image they need to use for a multimedia project.

   B. Provide instruction in how to properly cite sources and how to paraphrase in written reports.

   C. Give students written policies on avoiding plagiarism in a handbook.

   D. Explain to students different methods of how to keep track of research while gathering information so it can be properly cited later.

6. Ms. Rodriguez presents a writing sample to the class that contains common errors and then asks the class to help provide corrective feedback about the errors. Which of the following is her purpose in this instructional activity?

   A. Students will be able to develop their skills in writing an effective composition.

   B. Students will be able to identify correct writing conventions.

   C. Students will be able to construct coherent sentences.

   D. Students will be able to write for a particular audience.

7. Which of the following best helps foster early literacy development in English language learners at the emergent literacy stage of development?

   A. Provide opportunities for students to read decodable text without pictures.

   B. Provide chapter books for students to read silently.

   C. Provide opportunities for students to read short and simple text where the pictures closely match the printed words and story.

   D. Provide science and social studies textbooks for students to read independently.

8. A teacher provides opportunities for students to work in pairs on a collaborative project to support the English language learners in her class. This is an example of which of the following research-based language arts activities to support ELLs' oral language development?

   A. Peer-assisted learning

   B. Buddy reading

   C. Visual scaffolding

   D. Think-aloud protocol

9. A fifth grade student can read a grade-level passage aloud with 94% accuracy in decoding. This grade-level passage is the student's _____ reading level.

   A. frustrational

   B. independent

   C. comprehensive

   D. instructional

10. Mr. Smith is working with a group of fifth grade students who are below grade level in reading. He wants to monitor their progress every six weeks to get a comprehensive measure of both their decoding and comprehension skills. Which of the following assessment tools would best be used to monitor students' reading skills in these domains?

    A. An informal reading inventory

    B. A timed one-minute oral reading test

    C. A running record

    D. A phonics screening tool

11. In teaching viewing and representing, a language arts teacher might teach students to recognize and apply visual coherence to visual representations. The best definition of *visual coherence* is which of the following?

    A. The ways in which the overall design appeals to the viewer

    B. The ways in which the layout and use of color appeal to the viewer

    C. The ways in which the design of the visual creates a sense of unity

    D. The ways in which the layout creates a unique pattern

12. Which of the following activities fosters development in phonological awareness?

    A. Repeated reading

    B. Oral retelling

    C. Tongue twisters

    D. Think-pair-share

13. Mrs. Jones has three fourth graders who are at the early stages of their reading development. She wants to help her students to move from the emergent stage of reading to understanding some basic sight words and the conventions of print. She uses a technique called "shared writing" where students dictate their thoughts orally and she writes them down. This is followed by the group of students doing a repeated reading aloud of the shared text. The primary purpose in doing this activity with these students would be to

    A. demonstrate the conventions of writing such as punctuation, spelling, and grammar rules.

    B. engage students with a high-interest activity that will motivate them to want to write more.

    C. develop the students' ability to engage in listening, speaking, reading, and writing to further their reading development.

    D. foster a sight word vocabulary that will help them with spelling in future writing.

14. Ms. Ojeda wants her eighth grade students to understand how to use visuals to communicate meaning with an audience. Which of the following activities best develops this in her students?

    A. Provide students with a rubric detailing how they will be evaluated on their use of visuals.

    B. Ask students to write a paragraph describing why they chose their visuals.

    C. Have students display their visual work for other students to examine silently.

    D. Actively question and discuss with students about their choices and encourage them to provide reasons for their visual choices.

15. Mrs. Davis wants her students to read memoirs. This type of book would fall into the broader genre of which of the following?

    A. Science fiction

    B. Autobiography

    C. Traditional literature

    D. Folklore

16. Mr. Hart wants his students to write showing their own uniqueness and personal style. Mr. Hart wants his students to develop their skills in which of the following?

    A. Organization

    B. Ideas

    C. Focus

    D. Voice

17. In helping students to become more equipped with study skills, why might a teacher use a Venn diagram?

    A. It can help teachers to compare and contrast ideas across two different readings.

    B. It can help students to outline the main ideas of a text.

    C. It can help students as they make inferences about ideas.

    D. It can help students to identify the text structure of the reading.

18. During the writing process, students are encouraged to add, change, and/or delete ideas in their composition. This process is known as which of the following?

    A. Brainstorming

    B. Revision

    C. Editing

    D. Drafting

19. When seventh grade students are presenting a formal speech about research in class, they should be required to do which of the following, according to the Texas state curriculum (TEKS)?

    A. Include evidence that justifies the conclusions.

    B. Retell a personal narrative that relates to the findings.

    C. Share their report in a five-paragraph essay format.

    D. Provide information from only one source.

20. When teaching viewing and representing, the concept of design and selection of images to be used in a media presentation generally includes the study of which of the following? Select *all* that apply.

    A. Color

    B. Shapes

    C. Texture

    D. Hyperlinks

21. Mr. Jones wants to teach students to understand that learning to become literate involves being able to read and evaluate web-based media in addition to print-based text. Which of the following activities would best support this objective?

    A. Let students record their favorite song using a music-creation app or tool.

    B. Locate websites for students to print out and annotate using highlighters and pens.

    C. Curate a collection of books that discuss the role of technology in language arts instruction.

    D. Provide opportunities for students to browse and discuss in pairs information they read from pre-selected (bookmarked) news websites on smartphones and/or tablets.

22. As part of the writing process, eighth grade students are expected to be able to do which of the following? Select *all* that apply.

    A. Draft an essay with the audience in mind

    B. Develop coherence in a piece of writing

    C. Use compound and complex sentences

    D. Write primarily in narrative prose

23. A teacher wants to help English language learners at the intermediate stage of proficiency develop their fluency in reading using nonfiction text. Which of the following would best support this objective?

   A. Incorporate readers' theatre materials that connect to social studies topics that students are learning about.

   B. Have students read challenging text with vocabulary several levels above their reading level.

   C. Provide students worksheets with nonfiction text and fill-in-the-blank activities.

   D. Have students listen to a short nonfiction text and then ask them yes/no type of questions to assess their listening comprehension.

24. A seventh grade language arts teacher has her students write and respond to one another about a novel on a class blog (weblog). This way of having students represent information would primarily include which of the following types of media?

   A. Media literacy

   B. Print media

   C. Visual media

   D. Electronic media

25. The comprehension strategy of reciprocal teaching develops students' ability to discuss and analyze a shared text through use of which of the following?

   A. Summarizing, connecting, revising, sharing

   B. Summarizing, inferring, visualizing, recalling

   C. Summarizing, questioning, clarifying, and predicting

   D. Questioning, knowing, want to know, learned

26. During independent reading, Mr. Murphy encourages his students to self-select expository text in addition to narrative text. Which of the following is an example of expository text?

   A. A short story

   B. A poem from a poetry anthology

   C. A feature story in the daily newspaper

   D. A young adult novel

27. Ms. Conway wants to help her seventh graders to effectively give oral instructions to perform a task. Which of the following lessons would best help prepare students to be successful with this task?

   A. Model for students how to hold the audience's interest.

   B. Provide a blank graphic organizer for students to plan their speech.

   C. Pair students to practice their speech with a classmate.

   D. Teach students sequence words such as "first," "next," and "then" to organize their writing.

28. Mr. Chan is introducing a new novel to his seventh grade language arts class. He wants to do some effective pre-reading activities that will help the students to activate their background knowledge about the topic of immigration. Which of the following would best support this instructional objective of activating schema and background knowledge?

   A. Review new vocabulary that is related to the topic of immigration.

   B. Ask students to brainstorm about their experiences and knowledge about immigration and chart their responses as a class conversation.

   C. Provide a written summary about the topic to students and explain the main ideas of the topic.

   D. Watch a movie clip about immigrant experiences and have students write a summary.

29. The first stage of the writing process is known as which of the following?

    A. Revising

    B. Editing

    C. Publishing

    D. Brainstorming

30. Which of the following would be the best strategy to teach students so they can successfully read expository text?

    A. Teach them to look up all unknown words in the glossary before reading.

    B. Teach them to write a written summary after reading an expository text.

    C. Teach them to create a story grammar map during and after reading expository text.

    D. Teach them to read expository text more slowly than they would read narrative text.

31. A group of English language learners are at the beginning or emergent stage of language proficiency level. A task in class requires them to synthesize information from various written sources and write a short report. Which of the following instructional approaches would best support this group of students?

    A. Use visual images that accompany the key idea of the content and have students work in small groups with native English speakers to do collaborative peer work.

    B. Have students use graphic organizers to locate key words in the text to aid them as they synthesize information.

    C. Provide dictionaries to students so they can look up any new vocabulary words they may not know.

    D. Give students examples of written reports where information has been correctly synthesized and have students take turns reading the text aloud.

32. How can teaching students about morphology help them with their reading?

    A. It will help students to understand the overall meaning of the entire story or text.

    B. It will help students to unlock the meanings of words as they consider the meaning of prefixes, suffixes, or root words.

    C. It will help students to analyze the grammatical structure at the sentence level.

    D. It will help students to be able to react to the texts with a personal and interpretive response.

33. A teacher wants to read traditional stories to his class to help them learn more about this genre. Which of the following is another name for this larger genre that includes the sub-genre of traditional stories?

    A. Folklore

    B. Historical fiction

    C. Science fiction

    D. Poetry

34. Why is sight word practice important to reading instruction?

    A. It gives students a chance to decode CVC words and build word recognition.

    B. It builds vocabulary and helps students with their conceptual understanding of the text.

    C. It builds automaticity as sight words are not spelled in phonetically regular ways and must be memorized.

    D. It develops skills at problem-solving and higher-level comprehension.

35. Which of the following aspects of writing is used to assess whether the writer has engaged the reader sufficiently to keep the reader's attention?

    A. Organization

    B. Conventions

    C. Ideas

    D. Voice

36. Which of the following activities would best foster students' development of oral communication skills while using a tablet or smartphone device?

    A. Providing a bookmarked set of podcasts of interest for students to listen to

    B. Creating a podcast that other students can listen to and evaluate

    C. Directing students to watch videos about authors on a mobile device

    D. Listing apps that students can use to improve their reading comprehension

37. One activity used for pre-reading and post-reading is the KWL chart where students discuss and list what they know, what they want to know, and what they learned about the topic. A rationale for conducting this activity would be

    A. to help students to compare and contrast main ideas in the text.

    B. to provide a structured assessment tool to grade students' understanding of the text.

    C. to help students better understand the story grammar of the text.

    D. to activate students' background knowledge and generate interest in the text.

38. According to the sixth, seventh, and eighth grade Texas Essential Knowledge and Skills, the skills that should be taught as part of developing skills in making oral presentations do NOT include which of the following?

    A. Use of eye contact

    B. Enunciation

    C. A variety of natural gestures

    D. Including a personal story

39. While reading a novel with his seventh grade language arts class, Mr. McBride asks his students to analyze character. He asks the class, based on the actions and dialogue of the main character, to identify several character traits of the main character. He also asks them to refer back to direct evidence in the text for a specific example to support each character trait. Mr. McBride is helping his students to develop skills in which of the following?

    A. Connecting

    B. Inferencing

    C. Visualizing

    D. Synthesizing

40. Which of the following would indicate that a 10-year-old student is language-delayed?

    A. The student is not using courteous language when speaking.

    B. The student is still using short and simple sentences instead of complex sentences.

    C. The student is using a dialect when speaking.

    D. The student is frequently interrupting others.

41. Phonemic awareness helps literacy development in emergent and beginning readers primarily because of which of the following?

    A. It helps students to identify rhyming words.

    B. It is a predictor of learning to read.

    C. It aids in fluency development.

    D. It fosters comprehension.

42. Ms. Adams wants to assess her students' understanding by posing questions about the short story they are reading. She begins her questioning by asking some basic recall questions to check students' understanding. These types of questions are known as

    A. literal questions.

    B. evaluative questions.

    C. inferential questions.

    D. applied questions.

43. Ms. White wants to use a "mentor text" to exemplify the writing trait of voice. She selects several texts where the author uses dialogue and character development to teach this writing trait. What part of the language arts block would be most useful to model and share these examples of the selected writing trait?

    A. Guided reading

    B. Independent reading

    C. Read-aloud

    D. Partner reading

44. Students in fifth grade are practicing reading their readers' theatre scripts for a performance party on Friday. Their teacher encourages them to read with prosody, or expression. This instructional activity primarily fosters development in the key area of reading that is called

    A. comprehension.

    B. vocabulary.

    C. fluency.

    D. structural analysis.

45. A teacher wants to help students recognize high-frequency sight words. Which of the following instructional strategies would be most appropriate for achieving this?

    A. Determining the meaning of English words borrowed from foreign languages.

    B. Helping students to learn the definitions of multiple-meaning words.

    C. Teaching students to decode sight words phonetically.

    D. Having students practice recognizing sight words with flashcards.

46. According to the state standards, teaching sixth grade students about writing conventions is best when done

    A. in the context of meaningful writing and application.

    B. using isolated drill and practice editing techniques.

    C. through weekly editing tests.

    D. by using lots of corrective feedback and editing.

47. A teacher gives a one-minute timed fluency check each week for students who are reading below grade level to measure their reading rate and check for progress. What type of assessment technique is the teacher using?

    A. Criterion-based assessment

    B. Formal assessment

    C. Curriculum-based assessment

    D. Standardized assessment

48. The type of writing that explains and clarifies ideas about an informational topic is also known by which other general term?

    A. Narrative writing

    B. Expository writing

    C. Persuasive writing

    D. Letter writing

Use the information in this scenario to answer questions 49 and 50.

To foster authentic instruction, Mrs. Price has her sixth grade students work on developing their skills in editing while they are composing during writing workshop. She has students work together with partners using peer-editing checklists to help each other improve in writing conventions such as spelling, punctuation, and grammar. She notices that four students in particular are having trouble using the peer-editing checklist and are simply checking "OK" on all items on the checklist. She is concerned they are not understanding the purpose of the editing checklist.

49. What is the best approach to working with the group of students who are struggling with using the peer-editing checklist effectively?

    A. Take each student aside and tell them they are using it incorrectly while letting them know they will lose points on their assignment.

    B. Pull the four students aside for a small group intervention where the teacher models how to use the checklist with an example of student work followed by guided practice with the teacher's observation and feedback.

    C. Provide a picture-based checklist that is much simpler to understand so students have no excuse for why they are not using it effectively.

    D. Do not expect students to use the checklist for this task since they don't know how.

50. What additional strategy would best support the students who are struggling to use the peer-editing checklist effectively during writing workshop?

    A. Drill instruction and practice in editing sentences followed by periodic quizzes testing students on their knowledge of spelling and grammar.

    B. Assign additional homework for students so that parents can assist in reviewing remedial rules of grammar, punctuation, and spelling so that students can catch up.

    C. Provide additional resources for students such as sight-word lists, access to a mobile device with a dictionary tool, and increased use and access to anchor charts with basic editing techniques.

    D. Eliminate peer work for students who are struggling since they will not benefit from it.

51. What would be the most supportive tool for students to use to practice recording bibliographic information of articles they are reading in order to write a report?

    A. Have students copyedit each other's references when the report is complete.

    B. Provide a structured template for students to use to correctly cite needed information for citation of sources.

    C. Edit students' final bibliographic information with a pen to let them know the mistakes they made.

    D. Let students record bibliographic information in whatever style they choose.

52. An example of an informal way to assess students' written compositions and use of the writing process might include which of the following?

 A. Conferring with students individually about their written work

 B. Grading a student's errors and assigning a percentage grade

 C. Assessing students' use of an editing checklist

 D. Conducting an item analysis on a released form of a standardized test

53. Which of the following instructional activities would best assist students with the aspect of phrasing for fluency?

 A. Require students to explain why reading with expression is important.

 B. Have students read silently during guided reading groups.

 C. Provide a rubric for oral expression and reading and penalize students who deviate from the rubric.

 D. Model reading by doing expressive read-alouds.

54. Which of the following would help students to self-assess their correct use of writing conventions during the writing process?

 A. An editing checklist

 B. A retelling checklist

 C. A mentor text

 D. A revision checklist

55. To facilitate comprehension for the English language learners in his class, a language arts teacher wants to help students become more metacognitive at checking whether they understand what they read. The teacher asks students to practice "chunking" the text at designated stopping points and has them give what they read to a partner as a good way to support them with which of the following?

 A. Self-monitoring

 B. Increasing reading rate

 C. Motivating them to read more

 D. Developing their productive language skills

56. A teacher wants to meet with students individually during writing workshop time in her fifth grade classroom. A *primary* purpose of conferring with students would be to

 A. motivate students to want to write more.

 B. edit and proofread students' work for spelling and mechanics.

 C. give students a final grade for their finished product.

 D. check in with students to monitor their progress and assist their writing process.

57. While giving a reading assessment to his sixth graders to test their oral reading, Mr. Tompkins notes that one student, Gerald, consistently reads at a rate much slower than the grade-level norms. He also lacks confidence in reading. Which of the following activities would help him to develop his fluency in reading?

 A. Repeated reading of independent-level text

 B. Guided reading and pausing to discuss the meaning

 C. Repeated reading of frustrational-level text

 D. Guided reading and completion of a graphic organizer

58. Mr. Morrissey noticed his seventh grade students are consistently confusing the plural and the possessive in their written compositions. He wants to provide some guided practice to correct this error. Which of the following would best help practice this convention?

   A. Require students to complete practice worksheets with editing exercises.

   B. Provide direct instruction in the correct use of each, with specific examples, and have students practice writing sentences using each correctly.

   C. Model the correct use of each and deduct points each time students use it incorrectly.

   D. Emphasize to students that using correct grammar will help them to be more effective writers.

59. Which of the following is an example of an activity that fifth-grade students could engage in to conduct *primary research* for a social studies project?

   A. Do Internet research using encyclopedia databases.

   B. Conduct interviews to gather information.

   C. Synthesize facts from multiple informational texts.

   D. Evaluate websites for accuracy of information.

60. A way to use picture books to teach the Texas state curriculum (TEKS) that focuses on viewing might include which of the following?

   A. Examine the ways that the art and design impacts the mood of the story.

   B. Take turns discussing revision choices that students made during peer editing.

   C. Hold up the book during the read aloud so students can properly view the pictures.

   D. Have students discuss their favorite pictures within the story.

61. The purpose of having a teacher-led discussion prior to having students engage in small-group discussion might be primarily to do which of the following?

   A. The teacher wants to provide additional scaffolding for students who may need the explicit modeling prior to engaging in their own discussions.

   B. The teacher wants to be sure that behavior management is under control before she puts students into small groups.

   C. The teacher is unsure that students are capable of engaging in small-group discussion.

   D. The teacher wants to be in control of the lesson rather than have students take control of their conversations.

62. An eighth grade social studies teacher wants to develop her students' understanding of cause and effect in major historical events. Which of the following graphic organizers would best help to facilitate this type of comprehension?

   A. T-chart

   B. Venn diagram

   C. Semantic map

   D. Inquiry chart

63. Mr. Terry uses miscue analysis to assess each student's accuracy and types of miscues in decoding. He then looks for patterns in the types of miscues each student might make. Which of the following types of miscues are measured in the decoding part of such an assessment technique? Select *all* that apply.

   A. Substitution

   B. Omission

   C. Mispronunciation

   D. Prosody

64. Mr. Foster wants to help his fifth grade English language learners develop their reading comprehension. He is working with a group of students at the advanced intermediate level of proficiency in English. Which of the following strategies would best meet this objective with this group of students?

A. Provide a list of sight words for students to memorize to improve their fluency and comprehension of written text.

B. Explicitly and directly teach students comprehension strategies using the think-aloud approach to model active reading and encourage them to use the strategies.

C. Organize a shared reading group where students can improve their understanding of English grammar by listening to authentic text.

D. Teach students to analyze words using structural analysis to determine the meaning of the entire word.

65. Mrs. Jones wants to help her students use digital media such as movies to represent the key ideas about a novel they have read. She wants students to better understand how language, the medium, and presentation all inform the message of the digital media. Which of the following instructional approaches best supports this objective?

A. Conduct a mini-lesson where students learn the terminology of analyzing movies and discuss why directors made certain stylistic edits in different movie clips. Students then create their own storyboard for a video in small groups while discussing and explaining their reasons for making the storyboarding and editing decisions for the video.

B. Have students view several movie clips from different movies that connect to the novel read. Students then work in pairs to describe the plot of the movie.

C. Students work individually to write their reader responses to several movie clips. Students then share these in small groups while carefully listening and evaluating one another's reader response log.

D. Locate a movie version of the book read. After viewing the movie, students work in small groups to create a Venn diagram where they compare the book version to the movie version, focusing on explaining the key differences.

66. A teacher wants to develop students' understanding of literary terms such as types of figurative language in literary text. Which of the following is an example of figurative language?

A. Comparing two things using "like" or "as"

B. Using transition words to add coherence to an essay

C. The perspective of the narrator involved in a story

D. The word order or grammar of a sentence

67. Mrs. Lee wants her English language learners to use correct writing conventions in English during a writing workshop. Which of the following instructional strategies would best support this objective?

A. Give students a list of sight words to memorize so they can recognize and use these words correctly.

B. Use anchor charts to remind students to proofread their own work during writing workshop.

C. Use peer editing to allow students to give each other feedback on their written work.

D. Provide explicit modeling of English writing conventions such as punctuation and grammar, with opportunities for students to practice editing for conventions.

Use the information described in this scenario to answer questions 68, 69, and 70.

A seventh grade teacher is concerned that students are not closely evaluating the resources they are finding online for a report they are writing on current news events. She wants students to further their understanding of critically evaluating news sources while also determining what is "fake news" online.

68. What would be the best instructional approach to help students determine websites where they might encounter fake news (i.e. false articles that appear to be news)?

   A. Set up software to block fake news sites so students won't see them.

   B. When students come across a potentially fake news site, have them tell you so that you can add it to the blocked list.

   C. Instruction is not needed in this area because it doesn't relate to English language arts.

   D. Share examples of a few fake news websites that are designed for teaching and model various ways to verify information from a website to check for credibility.

69. In the course of gathering information from online sources, which of the following is the best way to help students enhance their inquiry skills so they are less likely to encounter news sources that are not credible?

   A. Identify some websites that are known as credible sources and explain and model what makes them credible.

   B. Require students to get permission to use certain websites before they can include them in their report.

   C. Have students read mainly from print books that are brought into the classroom by the teacher.

   D. Teach students to only read websites that are intended for the classroom.

70. Which of the following is a reason that students should be taught to determine which websites or other online sources of information might contain fake news?

   A. Students should know that the Internet is not the best place to locate information.

   B. Students will likely find multiple sources of information online and need to be able to select credible sources for inquiry.

   C. Students are only reading online sources of information.

   D. Students should be able to understand the main ideas of online text.

71. Which of the following activities best helps students to improve their reading comprehension with making inferences?

   A. Provide students with a short passage about a character and have students describe character traits using clues and evidence from the text.

   B. After reading a short text, have students list the central ideas and themes in the story in their writing notebooks.

   C. Have students take notes while the teacher reads aloud to them.

   D. Provide a graphic organizer for students to list the details from the text.

72. A sixth grade language arts teacher wants to start a series of lessons to help students learn how to produce a video. Which of the following is the first step the teacher should take to launch this unit?

   A. Teach students how to use the equipment to take different types of video shots.

   B. Provide examples of how to edit video with the audience in mind.

   C. Show students how to plan their video shoot using brainstorming and storyboarding.

   D. Model for students a variety of ways to use a green-screen to have a more interesting background in the video.

73. Ms. Weaver knows that her fifth graders need to have a solid understanding of text structure in order to better facilitate their reading and understanding of expository text. The types of text structure, for instance, can include: chronological, cause-and-effect, problem/solution, compare and contrast, and sequence. What types of instructional activity could help develop students' understanding and recognition of these types of text structure?

A. Stock the classroom library with a wide variety of reading materials that contain these types of text structures.

B. Model how to recognize the common types of text structures.

C. Demonstrate and practice with students the use of graphic organizers that align with the common text structures.

D. Discuss with students how text structure impacts the way the writer chose to organize the information.

74. Which of the following strategies would best support the objective of supporting students' correct use of syntax and grammar in composing their own written text?

A. Provide sentences for students to edit with feedback on the correct usage of grammar and syntax.

B. Use a red pen to edit each student's incorrect use of grammar and syntax.

C. Show examples of incorrect grammar pulled from student work in class.

D. Use indirect teaching techniques such as pointing out well-written sentences in read-alouds.

ELAR Practice Test 1: Answer Key

Test Item	Answer	Competency 806-
1.	B	001
2.	C	003
3.	A	009
4.	C	007
5.	A	007
6.	B	006
7.	C	002
8.	A	001
9.	D	004
10.	A	002
11.	C	008
12.	C	002
13.	C	002
14.	D	008
15.	B	005
16.	D	007
17.	A	009
18.	B	007
19.	A	001
20.	A, B, C	008
21.	D	002
22.	A, B, C	007
23.	A	003
24.	D	009
25.	C	004

Test Item	Answer	Competency 806-
26.	C	005
27.	D	001
28.	B	004
29.	D	007
30.	D	005
31.	A	009
32.	B	003
33.	A	005
34.	C	003
35.	D	007
36.	B	001
37.	D	005
38.	D	001
39.	B	004
40.	B	001
41.	B	002
42.	A	004
43.	C	007
44.	C	003
45.	D	003
46.	A	006
47.	C	002
48.	B	007
49.	B	006
50.	C	006

Test Item	Answer	Competency 806-
51.	B	009
52.	A	007
53.	D	003
54.	A	006
55.	A	004
56.	D	007
57.	A	003
58.	B	006
59.	B	009
60.	A	008
61.	A	001
62.	A	005
63.	A, B, C	003
64.	B	004
65.	A	008
66.	A	005
67.	D	006
68.	D	009
69.	A	009
70.	B	009
71.	A	004
72.	C	008
73.	C	005
74.	A	006

ELAR Practice Test 1: Detailed Answers

1. B.

The primary purpose of having a response notebook is to organize thinking about the key ideas and themes relating to the book. Organizing written notes also connects to students' ability to share these ideas orally. Choice (A) is incorrect because expression, while important, is not the primary purpose of the writing component and its connection with sharing ideas orally in the literature circles. Choice (C) is incorrect because grammar development and a focus on mechanics and conventions is not the primary objective of the written component. What is key is the ability to express ideas. Choice (D) is incorrect as writing and planning do not necessarily assist shy students in their ability to express themselves. **(Competency 806-001 Oral Language)**

2. C.

The word *structure* is syllabicated before the final stable syllable: *–ture*. Each syllable should also have one distinct vowel sound. **(Competency 806-003 Word Identification Skills and Reading Fluency)**

3. A.

Students need to critically evaluate and judge the credibility and accuracy of information that is online. This skill is critical in helping students to understand that not everything that is online is highly accurate. Choice (B) is incorrect because using multiple web browsers won't guarantee that students can critically examine and evaluate the text they are reading. Choice (C) is incorrect because summarizing also doesn't necessarily lead to the skills needed to judge or evaluate the credibility of a source. Choice (D) is incorrect because, though reading charts, tables, and graphs might develop overall comprehension of what is read, it also doesn't directly lead to the primary objective of critically evaluating the sources. **(Competency 806-009 Study and Inquiry Skills)**

4. C.

The writing process begins with brainstorming and ends with publishing or some type of written final product. Students work through the different aspects of the writing process but don't always have to go through them in the exact sequence specified in option (C). **(Competency 806-007 Written Language—Composition)**

5. A.

Choice (A) is correct because students should not be taught to go to an Internet web browser to save any images. Students need to know that some images are copyrighted and thus cannot be indiscriminately used. Choices (B), (C), and (D) are all good policies to teach students about multimedia and are therefore not correct possible choices since this question asks what would *not* be acceptable as an instructional component. **(Competency 806-007 Written Language—Composition)**

6. B.

A common practice used in classrooms to teach writing conventions is displaying or distributing sentences with errors in them. Students fix the errors, and then the corrections and reasons for making the corrections are discussed as a class. This is a teaching technique that can help students with identifying correct writing conventions. Choice (A) is incorrect because students don't always apply these skills to their actual compositions and this transfer can't always be assumed (as with spelling). Similarly, choices (C) and (D) are incorrect because while students may be able to identify incorrect writing conventions, the answer choices incorrectly assume students will be able to transfer the knowledge of conventions to the improvement in composing writing in general. **(Competency 806-006 Written Language—Writing Conventions)**

7. C.

Choice (C) is correct because it focuses on providing opportunities for learners to read text that best matches their proficiency level. The visuals provide a form of support for making sense of the text. Choice (A) is incorrect because decodable text doesn't always provide semantic cues for students to make sense of text. Choice (B) is incorrect because chapter books are not a good match for emergent readers who are ELLs. Choice (D) is incorrect because independent reading doesn't provide as much support for beginning readers and textbooks may be too difficult to be read independently at the emergent stage. **(Competency 806-002 Early Literacy Development)**

8. A.

Choice (A) is correct as peer-assisted learning facilitates language development for English language learners. Choice (B) is a more specific literacy technique that involves partner reading but it is not a general strategy. Choice (C) is not appropriate to this question and choice (D) is more teacher-centered rather than student-centered. **(Competency 806-001 Oral Language)**

9. D.

The instructional reading level is generally considered to be the level at which a reader can decode with 90%–95% accuracy. Below 90% is the frustrational reading level and above that is the independent reading level. **(Competency 806-004 Reading Comprehension and Assessment)**

10. A.

There are a variety of measurement tools that are used to assess reading growth and progress in decoding and comprehension. Thus, the correct choice is (A), an informal reading inventory, as it specifically measures both accuracy in decoding and comprehension of text at both the literal and inferential level. A timed test (B) is used to measure the fluency rate (accuracy and rate) of decoding but doesn't measure comprehension. A running record (C) is used more for beginning readers and usually measures just the decoding aspect of reading, although it can also give insight into the processes a stu-

dent uses to decode. Similarly, a phonics screening tool (D) might help the teacher to assess the decoding aspect, but would not let the teacher know how the student was developing in terms of comprehension. **(Competency 806-002 Early Literacy Development)**

11. C.

Visual coherence describes the overall unity of the way a visual representation is designed. The more unified it is, the more visually appealing it will be to the viewer. Choice (A) is incorrect because it describes visual impact. Choice (B) is incorrect because it is describing visual salience. Choice (D) is incorrect because it is describing the structure of the design rather than its impact on the viewer. **(Competency 806-008 Viewing and Representing)**

12. C.

Phonological awareness involves listening and the ability to hear and make distinctions in oral language. It includes the ability to hear distinct sounds, use alliteration, distinguish rhymes, and develop skills in phonemic awareness. Choice (B) is correct because tongue twisters involve alliteration, or the ability to hear and use words that begin with the same initial sound. Repeated reading primarily develops fluency, while oral retelling (B) and think-pair-share (D) help to develop comprehension. **(Competency 806-002 Early Literacy Development)**

13. C.

Shared writing is also known as Language Experience Approach. Its purpose is to integrate reading, writing, listening, and speaking in a holistic way for students who are making connections between speech and print. By engaging in this activity, students can learn about both the reading and writing process in an authentic and holistic way. Choices (A), (B), and (D) are incorrect as they focus on more narrow and specific aspects of the purpose of the activity. The broader and primary reason to do shared writing is therefore option (C). **(Competency 806-002 Early Literacy Development)**

14. D.

Choice (D) is correct because it shows the ways that a teacher can actively engage her or his students in critical thinking about design features. By asking students to explain their thinking, students will evaluate, judge, and critique their own work, drawing on higher orders of thinking. Choice (A) doesn't engage students in active learning and evaluation about their choices as much as choice (D) does. Choice (C) is incorrect because it doesn't focus specifically on the aspect of active discussion about design choices. **(Competency 806-008 Viewing and Representing)**

15. B.

Memoirs are a collection of stories written by the author to share aspects of her or his life. Memoir is, therefore, a type of autobiography. **(Competency 806-005 Reading Applications)**

16. D.

The writing traits each have a distinct focus in helping students to improve their composing process. The trait of voice (D) focuses on the writer's individual style and uniqueness. The other writing traits have a distinct focus other than individual style. **(Competency 806-007 Written Language—Composition)**

17. A.

Choice (A) is correct. A Venn diagram is designed to organize ideas that compare and contrast. It is ideal for comparing ideas across two texts. The other choices do not illustrate the primary use of a Venn diagram and would be better suited to other types of graphic organizers or study aids. **(Competency 806-009 Study and Inquiry Skills)**

18. B.

In the writing process, students are encouraged to proceed through four phases: brainstorming, revision, editing, and drafting. Revision (B) involves the adding, deleting, or changing of ideas. Editing (C) is incorrect as it involves changing the mechanics or conventions rather than the writer's ideas. Brainstorming (A) and draft-ing (D) are initial stages of writing in which the writer organizes ideas and produces a first draft. **(Competency 806-007 Written Language—Composition)**

19. A.

The ability to support an argument with evidence and facts is a key component of oral presentations. The ability to share a personal narrative (B) may not support the conclusion or thesis of the research and is more of an appeal to emotion. Choice (C) is incorrect because the structure of the essay doesn't relate to the criteria necessary to present research. Choice (D) is incorrect because students should support their research with multiple sources and not limit their support to one source. **(Competency 806-001 Oral Language)**

20. A., B., C.

The study of design includes the visual components of images. This would include what makes an image or picture visually appealing and so the consideration of color, shapes, and texture are important. However, hyperlinks are a functional tool that might or might not be used within a media representation. Therefore, it is not included and thus choice (D) should not be selected. **(Competency 806-008 Viewing and Representing)**

21. D.

Choice (D) is correct because it focuses on reading and evaluating web-based content. Additionally, students are actively engaged in evaluating the information. Choice (A) involves an engaging digital literacy-focused task; however, it doesn't involve evaluation of the recorded song. Choice (B) involves traditional text-based literacy. Choice (C) is incorrect because it also focuses on text-based literacy practices. **(Competency 806-002 Early Literacy Development)**

22. A., B., C.

Choices (A), (B), and (C) correctly focus on aspects of the writing process that are covered in the state TEKS standards. Choice (D) is the one option that does not fit because as part of the writing process, students should be able to compose in both narrative and expository types of prose. Students are held accountable to write in both forms of writing. **(Competency 806-007 Written Language—Composition)**

23. A.

Choice (A) is correct because readers' theatre provides opportunities to develop fluency. Using nonfiction topics that relate to a content area (e.g., social studies) helps to support learning about nonfiction text and helps to build background knowledge. Choice (B) is incorrect because the over-challenging vocabulary will not support the objective of fluency development. Choice (C) is incorrect because it is too passive and doesn't focus on fluency development. Choice (D) is also too limited and doesn't focus on the objective of fluency. **(Competency 806-003 Word Identification Skills and Reading Fluency)**

24. D.

Using the Internet to compose, read, or write is an example of electronic media. Choice (A) is a broader category that includes a wider variety of media and focuses more on how media is generally used. Choice (B), print media, focuses more on non-electronic media. Choice (C) includes both print and electronic media, while choice (D) is the most specific to the type of media used while reading and writing on the computer and the Internet. **(Competency 806-009 Study and Inquiry Skills)**

25. C.

Reciprocal teaching is a collaborative, small-group comprehension activity where students work together to read and discuss a selected text. Each student has a role in processing and leading a discussion about the text. The correct answer is choice (C). In these four roles, a student serves as the summarizer. Another student poses questions to the group and encourages other students in the group to do so as well. A third student leads the group in predicting before and throughout the reading, while the fourth student helps the group to clarify tricky or confusing parts of the text. Together, the students work together to comprehend the text at a deeper level. **(Competency 806-004 Reading Comprehension and Assessment)**

26. C.

Expository text means non-fiction or informational text. Examples used in the classroom typically include magazines with information-based text, newspapers with feature or news stories, and nonfiction books. The other choices are examples of narrative, or story-like text and, therefore, would not be examples of expository text. **(Competency 806-005 Reading Applications)**

27. D.

Choice (D) is the correct choice as it addresses using transitional language in order to sequence steps, making it a more effective, coherent, and cohesive "how-to" essay. The other choices suggest the type of instruction that is more generic to supporting speech instruction in general, but are not specifically related to the type of rhetorical tools that best support the oral structure of a "how-to" speech. **(Competency 806-001 Oral Language)**

28. B.

Pre-reading is designed to activate students' background and prior knowledge about a topic or theme(s) in a book prior to reading. Choice (B) best fosters this type of instructional goal. Through discussion, students can share background knowledge while also building new concepts by listening to others' ideas. The teacher can support understanding by monitoring and contributing to the pre-reading conversation. Choice (A) doesn't allow students to share background knowledge in a collaborative way. Choice (C) is too teacher-centered and doesn't facilitate active learning on the part of the students. Choice (D) is similarly passive and doesn't activate the students' specific background knowledge and schema. **(Competency 806-004 Reading Comprehension and Assessment)**

29. D.

The writing process, although not always linear, generally is sequenced in the following way: brainstorming, revising, editing, and publishing. Brainstorming is the beginning of the writing process. **(Competency 806-007 Written Language—Composition)**

30. D.

Expository text, or, informational text, often contains denser and more conceptually challenging ideas than encountered in narrative text. Therefore, students need to be taught to read this text more slowly so they can fully understand and monitor their own understanding about these denser ideas. Choices (A), (B), and (C) focus more on overall vocabulary and comprehension development. Choice (D) has the broadest application of use, while the other choices are instructional activities that could be used as follow-up work to develop comprehension. **(Competency 806-005 Reading Applications)**

31. A.

Choice (A) is correct because students at the beginning proficiency levels in English benefit from visual supports to help support their understanding of English. Choice (B) doesn't help with the process of synthesizing information. Choice (C) also focuses more on vocabulary development. Choice (D) suggests using text that may not be comprehensible to students and reading it aloud is not aligned with the task of synthesizing information. **(Competency 806-009 Study and Inquiry Skills)**

32. B.

Morphemes are the smallest units of meaning in a word. Examples include prefixes, suffixes, and roots that can change the meaning of a word. By drawing students' attention to morphemes through the study of morphology, students can consider word meaning and hence, their vocabulary. Choice (A) focuses on broader comprehension development; choice (C) focuses on the grammar of the sentence, which is not the focus of morphology; choice (D) is incorrect because it has an overall comprehension focus. **(Competency 806-003 Word Identification Skills and Reading Fluency)**

33. A.

Traditional stories are part of the larger genre of folklore. Folklore draws on both oral and written literature and includes traditional stories as well as legends, mythology, and tall tales. **(Competency 806-005 Reading Applications)**

34. C.

Sight words are words that are not spelled in phonetically regular ways. Learning them helps build automaticity in word recognition and overall fluency in reading. Examples might include "the," "of," and "many." They must simply be memorized. Choice (A) is incorrect as sight words are not CVC (consonant-vowel-consonant) words and are irregular. Choice (B) is incorrect because, while learning sight words can also help build vocabulary or knowledge of word meanings, it is not the primary focus of sight-word practice. Choice (D) is incorrect because sight-word practice is primarily a word recognition strategy and is only incidentally related to comprehension. **(Competency 806-003 Word Identification Skills and Reading Fluency)**

35. D.

When students write a composition, they are often assessed using a rubric that focuses on the key features of writing. The feature of writing that focuses on engaging the reader is the writer's voice. Writing with a strong voice allows the writer to have style. It is this style that engages the reader. Organization focuses on the arrangement of ideas in the text. Convention focuses on the writer's correct use of mechanics such as spelling, punctuation, and grammar. Ideas focus on the development of strong ideas, but might not necessarily engage the reader with style or voice. **(Competency 806-007 Written Language—Composition)**

36. B.

Choice (B) is correct because it involves students using oral language (speaking skills in this case) while using technology. Choice (A) fosters listening skills but is more passive than choice (B). Choices (C) and (D) similarly involve more passive listening skills rather than the production of oral language by students. **(Competency 806-001 Oral Language)**

37. D.

KWL stands for "Know," "Want to Know," and "Learned" and relates to the types of discussion and questioning that would take place before, during, and after a story was read. In the "know" part, the teacher guides students to consider what background knowledge they have that relates to the text. After these are shared, students pose questions about what they hope to learn and know from the text prior to reading it. After the text is read, or while it is read, the teacher can discuss with students what they are learning or learned as a result of reading the text. These activities help students to anticipate what it is they will be reading prior to reading it as well as activate their schema or background knowledge prior to reading. Choice (D) is the correct answer as it best fits this purpose of building and activating background knowledge while helping students to anticipate the key ideas in the text. The other choices don't directly relate to this purpose. **(Competency 806-005 Reading Applications)**

38. D.

Students are expected to use conventions of oral speaking such as eye contact, enunciating clearly, and to use gestures in a natural and effective way. However, the Texas state guidelines do not require that students include a personal narrative with their oral presentation. Although it is helpful and might hook the attention of the audience, it is not required as the other components are. **(Competency 806-001 Oral Language)**

39. B.

The ability to draw conclusions about character requires students to think beyond the literal meaning of the text. By being able to draw conclusions about apt descriptors that tell what a character is like, students are engaged in the comprehension strategy of making inferences. **(Competency 806-004 Reading Comprehension and Assessment)**

40. B.

Language delay can include delays in vocabulary, speaking, and in complexity of sentence structure, among other things. Using short sentences (B) is not developmentally typical for a child of that age (10 years old). Although the other answer choices indicate a lack of decorum when using language, they are not indicators of language delay. **(Competency 806-001 Oral Language)**

41. B.

Phonemic awareness is an important prerequisite skill in learning to read. It involves being able to hear, identify, and manipulate the smallest individual units of sound in words. As such, the ability to do this predicts (but is not the only predictor) for learning to read. Choice (A) is incorrect because rhyming words is part of the broader skill of phonological awareness. Choices (C) and (D) are incorrect because phonemic awareness is not directly related to fluency or comprehension development in reading text, as it is an auditory skill primarily. **(Competency 806-002 Early Literacy Development)**

42. A.

Basic recall questions in a narrative text assess whether a reader understands basic aspects of the story such as who was in it, what the main events were, and what happened. Evaluative questions (B) test what a reader's judgment is of a certain aspect of the story and tests a higher level of understanding. Choices (C) and (D) also test higher-order comprehension beyond the literal or basic understanding of the story. **(Competency 806-004 Reading Comprehension and Assessment)**

43. C.

The correct answer is choice (C) because read-aloud provides the best opportunity for the teacher to model the teaching focus of a writing mini-lesson using one or more mentor texts. During read-aloud, the teacher can point out different characteristics of quality writing and encourage students to apply these same characteristics in their own writing. **(Competency 806-007 Written Language—Composition)**

44. C.

Readers' theatre involves the act of repeated reading. Evidence from research suggests that repeated reading builds automaticity and fluency in reading. Therefore, readers' theatre fosters development in fluency. While comprehension (A) and vocabulary (B) might be developed incidentally, the act of repeated reading is primarily to develop fluency. Structural analysis (D) is a vocabulary tool used to decode and make sense of the meaning of individual words. **(Competency 806-003 Word Identification Skills and Reading Fluency)**

45. D.

Choice (D) is correct. High-frequency sight words must be memorized so they can be recognized automatically. Repeated exposure through printed or digital flashcards helps learners commit such words to memory. Choice (A) is incorrect because it involves analysis that is inappropriate to sight-word recognition. Choice (B) is incorrect because sight words by their nature need to be able to be recognized without having to use decoding skills—and such recognition does not necessarily help build vocabulary, though it does improve reading fluency. Choice (C) is incorrect because sight words generally fail to follow the rules of phonics. **(Competency 806-003 Word Identification Skills and Reading Fluency)**

46. A.

The state standards (Texas Essential Knowledge and Skills) emphasize that teaching about conventions should be done in the context of meaningful instruction. This would exclude choice (B) as it focuses on isolated skills practice. Choice (C) is incorrect because weekly tests don't focus on instructional practice. Choice (D) is incorrect because corrective feedback doesn't guarantee students can practice the use of mechanics in meaningful work, as specified in the state standards. The TEKS standards focus on student application of conventions. **(Competency 806-006 Written Language—Writing Conventions)**

47. C.

Choice (C) is correct because curriculum-based measurement uses a quick and efficient method of measuring an aspect of the learning process. Choices (A), (B), and (D) focus on other types of assessment techniques. **(Competency 806-002 Early Literacy Development)**

48. B.

Expository text is also known as informational text. It typically covers the content areas such as science, social studies, math, health, and other core academic areas. It usually is in the format of news stories, articles, biographies, textbooks, magazine articles, and other formats, including online reading. Narrative writing (A) usually consists of story-like text such as fiction. Choice (C) is a more specific type of expository text.

Choice (D) is incorrect because it is not a broad category of informational text. **(Competency 806-007 Written Language—Composition)**

49. B.

Choice (B) is correct because it focuses on instruction that is direct and targeted to the learning needs of the students. Intervention by the teacher with feedback is ideal for developing skills with using the editing checklist. The other choices are too simplistic or not targeted enough for an effective instructional intervention. **(Competency 806-006 Written Language—Writing Conventions)**

50. C.

Choice (C) is correct because additional specific resources are being provided for students that align with the area of intervention. The remaining choices are not direct interventions for students who face challenges in this area. **(Competency 806-006 Written Language—Writing Conventions)**

51. B.

Choice (B) is the best answer because it provides the most support for students in learning the process of citing sources correctly. Choice (A) provides little support and assumes that students have the background knowledge to help one another; it also doesn't help them during the process of recording sources during the writing phase. Choice (C) is very teacher-centered and doesn't provide students a chance to practice the process of recording their own bibliography. Choice (D) doesn't provide enough structure or instruction for students to correctly learn how to source information. **(Competency 806-009 Study and Inquiry Skills)**

52. A.

Choice (A) focuses on informal assessment that is most closely related to the content of students' composition and composition process. By conferring individually with students, the teacher can make observations (and record anecdotal notes), collect work samples, and ask students questions about their writing process or strengths and challenges they are facing. Choices (B), (C), and (D) are incorrect because they don't give insight into what the writing process is like for the student. **(Competency 806-007 Written Language—Composition)**

53.　D.

Modeled reading provides a powerful example of fluent reading, including rate, accuracy, and expression. The idea of phrasing for fluency involves many aspects of reading with expression including pausing, intonation, and adjusting reading rate. Students need to hear examples of phrasing to engage in it independently. By engaging in silent reading during read-aloud (B), students may not get the feedback they need to use the strategy effectively. A rubric alone (C) is not sufficient to give students the input and examples they need to engage in phrasing for fluency independently. The ability to explain something (A) does not mean that students will necessarily be able to engage in the task. **(Competency 806-003 Word Identification Skills and Reading Fluency)**

54.　A.

An editing checklist is typically used to assist students in using correct mechanics and conventions of writing. This includes spelling, grammar, and punctuation. A retelling checklist (B) is primarily used to check reading comprehension rather than check an aspect of the writing process. A mentor text (C) is a text used by the teacher to model effective writing but is not a tool used by students to check conventions. Choice (D) is incorrect because a revision checklist is more for adding, deleting, and changing ideas and composition in the text rather than mechanics and conventions only. **(Competency 806-006 Written Language—Writing Conventions)**

55.　A.

When students can regulate their own understanding of whether they comprehend a text, they are engaging in self-monitoring (A). Choice (B) is incorrect because students are attending more to comprehension than the development of fluency. Choice (C) is incorrect because motivation to read may or may not be related to the cognitive skill of being metacognitive while reading. Choice (D) is incorrect because the focus of the lesson is more on comprehension than oral speech production.

(Competency 806-004 Reading Comprehension and Assessment):

56.　D.

Conferring gives the teacher a chance to work with students for different purposes. A primary purpose is to give students individualized feedback on their written work. Choice (D) is the correct choice as it focuses on this chance to monitor individual student progress. **(Competency 806-007 Written Language—Composition)**

57.　A.

Repeated reading is the best approach to developing fluency in reading. By focusing on independent-level text, the reader is able to build upon success and is encouraged to continue reading the same text. **(Competency 806-003 Word Identification Skills and Reading Fluency)**

58.　B.

In developing editing skills, students would benefit most from clear and explicit instruction in the conventional use of both plural and possessive use of words. Having a direct application to a real sentence would provide the independent practice that is most closely related to using the correct form in their own writing. Choice (A) is incorrect because it doesn't ensure transfer to the student's own writing and composition. Choice (C) is incorrect because simply penalizing students doesn't promote the application and use of the correct written expression in the student's own writing. Choice (D) is incorrect because it is not direct enough to help students engage in guided practice or application of the rule to their own writing. **(Competency 806-006 Written Language—Writing Conventions)**

59.　B.

In doing primary research, the student should gather original information from either a primary source document or by gathering information directly from a person or persons. In this case, an interview would be primary research and a way of gathering information that was not collected by someone else. The remaining choices, (A), (C), and (D), are examples of secondary research, or using documents or information that has already been collected. **(Competency 806-009 Study and Inquiry Skills)**

60. A.

Choice (A) focuses on the skills students will need to view images and have a better understanding of the ways that images can be effectively used in text. It focuses on the teacher's intent in using a picture book with older students to teach viewing. Choice (B) focuses on an aspect of composition that is not related to the viewing standard. Choice (C) only focuses on properly displaying the text but doesn't have a clear instructional focus aligned with the state standards. Choice (D) fosters a reader response among the students; however, it also doesn't have a clear instructional focus aligned with the viewing standard. **(Competency 806-008 Viewing and Representing)**

61. A.

Choice (A) is correct because it fits with the concept that teachers need to first effectively model the types of discourse patterns and discussions they wish students to use in small group discussions. Choice (B) is incorrect because behavior management, though important, is not a primary consideration for choosing to use whole-class instruction. Choice (C) is incorrect because student discussion is an expectation of the state standards. Choice (D) is incorrect because teachers need to allow students the responsibility and expectation of engaging in small-group dialogue across different instructional activities to facilitate their development of oral language and expression. **(Competency 806-001 Oral Language)**

62. A.

Graphic organizers help students to represent the text structure and organization of the key ideas in the text. If a teacher wants students to understand some of the underlying ideas that relate to cause and effect, a T-chart would be the best way to organize the causes (on the left side of the T-chart) and the effects (on the right side of the T-chart). A Venn diagram (B) is typically used to show comparison and contrast, while a seman-

tic map (C) is more broadly used to conceptualize key ideas in the text, but not necessarily those that are causally related. Choice (D) is incorrect because an inquiry chart is used to show common aspects of a story or topic across multiple texts. **(Competency 806-005 Reading Applications)**

63. A., B., C.

Miscue analysis was designed to help teachers attend to the types of cues a student might use during the reading process. When a student is reading and says something other than what is printed in the text, it is termed a miscue. Choices (A), (B), and (C) focus on common types of miscues a student might make. Substitution (A) is when a student substitutes a real word for the printed word. Omission (B) is when a student leaves out a word. Mispronunciation (C) is when a student utters a nonsense word or a non-word while reading. Choice (D) is incorrect because it is not a type of miscue, but rather the aspect of fluency where students read with expression. **(Competency 806-003 Word Identification Skills and Reading Fluency)**

64. B.

Choice (B) is correct because students are learning active comprehension techniques through both teacher modeling and active practice of the technique. Choice (A) is more focused on automatic word recognition and not comprehension. It is indirectly related more to fluency than comprehension development. Choice (C) is incorrect because improving grammar is indirectly related to improvement in reading comprehension. Choice (B) is more directly related to comprehension development. Choice (D) is incorrect because it is more focused on vocabulary development. **(Competency 806-004 Reading Comprehension and Assessment)**

65. A.

Choice (A) is correct because it provides input and instruction on the process of creating and producing videos as a medium. Choice (B) is more focused on comprehending the plot but is much less aligned with the instructional objective in this question. Choice (C) focuses on literary meaning but is also not aligned with the objective. Choice (D) is more focused on comprehension but does not directly address the objective. **(Competency 806-008 Viewing and Representing)**

66. A.

Figurative language encompasses use of language such as metaphor, simile, hyperbole, and more. Choice (A) is correct because it focuses on simile (comparing two things using "like" or "as"). Choice (B) focuses more on coherence (text fitting around a central topic). Choice (C) focuses more on the point of view of a narrator, while choice (D) focuses on the syntax or grammar of language at the sentence level. Choice (A) is the best example of figurative language. **(Competency 806-005 Reading Applications)**

67. D.

Choice (D) is correct because it involves explicit instruction, which is important for English language learners when combined with opportunities to practice. The key focus is on connection of modeling and practice of writing conventions. Choices (B), (C), and (A) focus on indirect ways to improve writing conventions. Choice (A) might improve spelling, but it can't be guaranteed that students will use a resource while writing. Choice (B) is simply a reminder and less effective than modeling and practice. **(Competency 806-006 Written Language—Writing Conventions)**

68. D.

Choice (D) is correct because it involves teacher modeling and explicit instruction. Students are guided to note the ways that fake news articles can be verified—a key element of checking the source and credibility of online informational sources. Choice (A) is inappropriate as it doesn't teach critical thinking. Such software is also likely difficult to find. Choice (C) is inappropriate as it assumes students don't need instruction in this area and they do. Choice (B), like choice (A), doesn't foster critical thinking in students and so is incorrect. **(Competency 806-009 Study and Inquiry Skills)**

69. A.

Choice (A) is correct because it models and provides information on what makes a website credible. Choices (B), (C), and (D) do not provide that level of explicit instruction or limit the amount of information available to students. **(Competency 806-009 Study and Inquiry Skills)**

70. B.

Choice (B) is correct because it is likely students will encounter websites and online information (e.g., via social media) where sources are questionable. It is crucial that they know how to evaluate this information as they do research and inquiry. Answer choice (A) undermines the fact that increasingly we find information sources online. Answer choice (C) is incorrect because not all information is found online. Choice (D) is incorrect because understanding the main ideas is not the same as evaluating online information sources' credibility. **(Competency 806-009 Study and Inquiry Skills)**

71. A.

Choice (A) is correct because students must use multiple clues from the text to make inferences about a character. Choice (B) is incorrect because main idea is a different comprehension strategy focus than making inferences. Choice (C) is incorrect because while taking notes may help students attend to the text, it does not align with the objective of developing students ability to make inferences. Choice (D) is not correct because it does not have a specific comprehension strategy focus other than listing details. Listing details is more at the recall level of Bloom's Taxonomy and thus is not a higher-order thinking skill akin to inferential reasoning. **(Competency 806-004 Reading Comprehension and Assessment)**

72. C.

Choice (C) is the best response because it is involved in the pre-production (beginning and planning stages) of producing the video. Choices (A), (B), and (D) are involved in the production phase (during the process of producing). **(Competency 806-008 Viewing and Representing)**

73. C.

Choice (C) best promotes understanding of text structure. The types of expository text structure listed in this question are aligned with commonly used graphic organizers. The graphic organizer can help students to see how texts are typically organized. Choice (A) is too vague and doesn't provide direct instruction in identifying text structure. Similarly, choice (B) doesn't allow for student practice and so is less effective than choice (C). Choice (D) is less direct and less explicit than the correct answer choice. **(Competency 806-005 Reading Applications)**

74. A.

Choice (A) is the best answer because it involves instructive feedback on correct grammar. Choice (B) is more punitive and not as useful for instructive purposes. Choice (C) is not appropriate to creating a positive and supportive writing environment for students as it is also punitive. Choice (D) is incorrect because it is too indirect to be effective when students are composing their own text. **(Competency 806-006 Written Language—Writing Conventions)**

TExES Core Subjects 4–8 Practice Test 1: Mathematics (807)

This pratice test plus an additional test are available at the online REA Study Center (*www.rea.com/studycenter*).

The TExES Core Subjects Mathematics (807) test is computer-based, so we strongly recommend that you take our online practice tests to simulate test-day conditions and to receive these added benefits:

- **Timed testing conditions**—Gauge how much time you can spend on each question.

- **Automatic scoring**—Find out how you did on the test, instantly.

- **On-screen detailed explanations of answers**—Learn not just the correct answer, but also why the other answers are incorrect.

- **Diagnostic score reports**—Pinpoint where you're strongest and where you need to focus your study.

Mathematics Practice Test 1: Answer Sheet

1. Ⓐ Ⓑ Ⓒ Ⓓ   15. Ⓐ Ⓑ Ⓒ Ⓓ   29. Ⓐ Ⓑ Ⓒ Ⓓ

2. Ⓐ Ⓑ Ⓒ Ⓓ   16. Ⓐ Ⓑ Ⓒ Ⓓ   30. Ⓐ Ⓑ Ⓒ Ⓓ

3. Ⓐ Ⓑ Ⓒ Ⓓ   17. Ⓐ Ⓑ Ⓒ Ⓓ   31. Ⓐ Ⓑ Ⓒ Ⓓ

4. Ⓐ Ⓑ Ⓒ Ⓓ   18. Ⓐ Ⓑ Ⓒ Ⓓ   32. Ⓐ Ⓑ Ⓒ Ⓓ

5. Ⓐ Ⓑ Ⓒ Ⓓ   19. Ⓐ Ⓑ Ⓒ Ⓓ   33. Ⓐ Ⓑ Ⓒ Ⓓ

6. Ⓐ Ⓑ Ⓒ Ⓓ   20. Ⓐ Ⓑ Ⓒ Ⓓ   34. Ⓐ Ⓑ Ⓒ Ⓓ

7. Ⓐ Ⓑ Ⓒ Ⓓ   21. Ⓐ Ⓑ Ⓒ Ⓓ   35. Ⓐ Ⓑ Ⓒ Ⓓ

8. Ⓐ Ⓑ Ⓒ Ⓓ   22. Ⓐ Ⓑ Ⓒ Ⓓ   36. Ⓐ Ⓑ Ⓒ Ⓓ

9. Ⓐ Ⓑ Ⓒ Ⓓ   23. Ⓐ Ⓑ Ⓒ Ⓓ   37. Ⓐ Ⓑ Ⓒ Ⓓ Ⓔ Ⓕ

10. Ⓐ Ⓑ Ⓒ Ⓓ   24. Ⓐ Ⓑ Ⓒ Ⓓ   38. Ⓐ Ⓑ Ⓒ Ⓓ

11. Ⓐ Ⓑ Ⓒ Ⓓ   25. Ⓐ Ⓑ Ⓒ Ⓓ   39. Ⓐ Ⓑ Ⓒ Ⓓ

12. Ⓐ Ⓑ Ⓒ Ⓓ   26. Ⓐ Ⓑ Ⓒ Ⓓ   40. Ⓐ Ⓑ Ⓒ Ⓓ

13. Ⓐ Ⓑ Ⓒ Ⓓ   27. Ⓐ Ⓑ Ⓒ Ⓓ   41. Ⓐ Ⓑ Ⓒ Ⓓ

14. Ⓐ Ⓑ Ⓒ Ⓓ   28. Ⓐ Ⓑ Ⓒ Ⓓ   42. Ⓐ Ⓑ Ⓒ Ⓓ

Practice Test 1: Mathematics

TIME: 1 hour and 5 minutes
42 questions

> **Directions:** Read each item and select the best answer. Most items on this test require you to provide the one best answer. However, some questions require you to select all the options that apply.

1. The flu hit Star Elementary School very badly one week. The administration determined that 90 out of 360 students were absent that week. What percentage of students were present?

   A. 25%

   B. 90%

   C. 75%

   D. 40%

2. Nancy is 3 years older than Doug. Kim is 4 years younger than Doug. Nancy is 12 years old. How old are Doug and Kim?

   A. Doug is 8 and Kim is 5

   B. Doug is 9 and Kim is 4

   C. Doug is 9 and Kim is 5

   D. Doug is 8 and Kim is 4

3. Add the following fractions: $\frac{2}{3} + \frac{3}{5} + \frac{5}{6}$.

   A. $\frac{5}{7}$

   B. $1\frac{9}{10}$

   C. $2\frac{1}{30}$

   D. $2\frac{1}{10}$

4. The test scores from two different classes are shown below.

   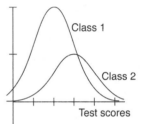

   If the scores for each class are normally distributed, which of the following statements is true?

   A. The mean score for class 1 is greater than the mean score for class 2.

   B. The median score for class 2 is greater than the median score for class 1.

   C. The mode for class 2 is less than the mode for class 1.

   D. The standard deviation for class 1 is much larger than for class 2.

5. Find the equation of the line with x-intercept $\frac{1}{2}$ and y-intercept $-\frac{1}{2}$.

   A. $y = -x$

   B. $2x + 2y = 0$

   C. $2x + 2y = 1$

   D. $2x - 2y = 1$

6. Jaxson's rectangular sandbox has a perimeter of 34 feet. The length of the sandbox is 9 feet. What is the width of the sandbox?

    A. 16 feet

    B. 9 feet

    C. 8 feet

    D. 72 feet

7. Which of the following statements is true?

    A. All quadrilaterals are squares.

    B. All rectangles are squares.

    C. A square is also a rhombus.

    D. Not all trapezoids are quadrilaterals.

8. Given the following tables of function values, which could NOT be a quadratic function?

    A.
x	$f(x)$
0	1
1	2
2	5
3	10

    B.
x	$f(x)$
0	1
1	4
2	7
3	10

    C.
x	$f(x)$
0	1
1	2
2	4
3	7

    D.
x	$f(x)$
0	−4
1	−1
2	0
3	−1

9. In a triangle PQR the measure of angle PQR is 60°, and the measure of angle QRP is 75°. What is the measure of angle RQP and what type of triangle is it?

    A. 60°, acute triangle

    B. 120°, obtuse triangle

    C. 90°, right triangle

    D. 45°, acute triangle

10. A right circular cone has radius 3 inches and height 6 inches. If the radius doubles and the height is halved, what is the percent change of the cone's new volume compared to its original volume?

    A. 100%

    B. 50%

    C. 200%

    D. 0%

11. Using the following right triangle, find the value of $\dfrac{\sin\theta - \cos\theta}{\tan\theta}$.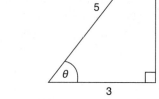

    A. $\dfrac{15}{4}$

    B. $\dfrac{4}{15}$

    C. $\dfrac{3}{20}$

    D. $\dfrac{20}{3}$

12. Which of the following was the advocate of Social Constructivism?

    A. Piaget

    B. Vygotsky

    C. Bruner

    D. Einstein

13. Find the mode for the following stem leaf plot:

    1: 2 2 3
    2: 5 6 6
    4: 7 8
    5: 1 3 5

    A. 26

    B. 12

    C. 12, 26

    D. None

14. Wayne is randomly pulling out golf balls from a bag which contains 3 Nike balls, 5 Srixon balls and 6 Titleist balls. What is the probability that he will pull out a Titleist ball?

    A. $\dfrac{3}{14}$

    B. $\dfrac{3}{7}$

    C. $\dfrac{3}{4}$

    D. $\dfrac{1}{2}$

15. Using the point-slope formula find the slope of a line passing through the points (5, 4) and (–1, 3).

    A. $\dfrac{1}{6}$

    B. $\dfrac{4}{7}$

    C. $-\dfrac{1}{6}$

    D. $\dfrac{1}{4}$

16. Which of the following is NOT a philosophy of differentiated instruction?

    A. Students work in groups that change membership to discuss problem solving strategies.

    B. Students are given choices in their reading and writing assignments.

    C. The entire class gets the same exam on a subject.

    D. A focus on big ideas when teaching.

17. Triangular flashcards can be used to help with what concept(s)?

    A. Place value

    B. Multiplication and Division

    C. Addition and Subtraction

    D. Both B and C

18. A deck consists of 1 orange, 3 blue, 1 green, 2 yellow, and 3 purple cards. If two cards are chosen randomly from the deck without replacing the first, find the probability P of both of them being purple.

    A. 6.7%

    B. 9.5%

    C. 22.2%

    D. 52.2%

19. What is the prime factorization of 280?

    A. $2^2 \times 5 \times 14$

    B. $2^3 \times 5 \times 10$

    C. $2^3 \times 5 \times 7$

    D. $2^2 \times 5 \times 7$

20. Five runners are competing in a 50-yard dash. If there are not any ties, how many different combinations are possible for a first, second, and third place?

    A. 15

    B. 20

    C. 120

    D. 60

21. In a middle school math class, students have begun activities exploring area relationships among rectangles, triangles, parallelograms, and trapezoids. The classroom teacher wants to identify any aspects of the content that challenges the students in order to adjust future lessons on this topic. Which of the following assessment methods would be most appropriate for achieving this goal?

    A. Regular observation and interviews between teacher and student

    B. Periodic peer review of partner work

    C. Pretest and posttest

    D. Pop quizzes after future lessons

22. The price of a bicycle was reduced from $60 to $45. By what percentage was the price of the bike reduced?

    A.   25%

    B.   15%

    C.   33.3%

    D.   40%

23. Kirk is driving on a highway whose speed limit is 60 mph. He passes a police car traveling at 50 mph. There is a speed trap set up and 2.5 miles down the road, he passes another police car 2 minutes after he passed the first police car. He is traveling at 50 mph when he passes the 2nd policeman as well. The police radio each other and discuss Kirk. What should they decide?

    A.   He gets a ticket because he definitely was speeding.

    B.   He gets a warning because he probably was speeding.

    C.   He does not get a ticket because he definitely was not speeding.

    D.   He is not stopped because there is not enough evidence to determine whether he was speeding.

24. How many ways can all the letters in the word "HAPPINESS" be arranged to form a sequence of 9 letters?

    A.   362,880

    B.   45

    C.   90,720

    D.   181,550

25. A net of a three-dimensional solid appears below. What is the volume of the solid?

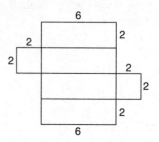

    A.   12

    B.   24

    C.   48

    D.   56

26. Given the graph of the function $f(x)$, what would be the result of graphing $-f(x)$?

    A.   Reflects the graph of $f(x)$ across the x-axis

    B.   Reflects the graph of $f(x)$ across the y-axis

    C.   Shifts $f(x)$ down vertically

    D.   Shifts $f(x)$ to the left horizontally

27. A deck of cards has numbers 1 through 10. It is shuffled completely. Which of the following represents a binomial experiment problem?

    A.   A card is chosen and not replaced and then another card is chosen. What is the probability of choosing two even numbers?

    B.   A card is chosen and replaced and then another card is chosen. What is the probability of choosing two even numbers?

    C.   A card is chosen and whether it is even is noted. It is not replaced and another card is chosen. We stop when two even cards have been chosen. We are interested in the average number of cards necessary to get two even cards.

    D.   A card is chosen and whether it is even is noted. It is replaced and another card is chosen. We stop when two even cards have been chosen. We are interested in the average number of cards necessary to get two even cards.

28. The graph of $f(x)$ is shown below.

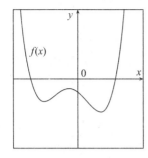

Determine how many of the features the graph has.

	Relative Minimum	Relative Maximum	Absolute Minimum	Absolute Maximum
A.	1	1	Yes	No
B.	1	2	No	No
C.	2	1	Yes	No
D.	2	1	Yes	Yes

29. A teacher asked one set of students to write $y = 3x^2 - 6x + 4$ in standard form while another teacher asked students to graph $y = 3x^2 - 6x + 4$ and report what they see. This is an example of:

    A. passive task vs active task

    B. specific task vs. parallel task

    C. closed task vs. open task

    D. flawed approach vs. effective approach

30. In order to measure the top wind speed of a hurricane, a special plane is needed to fly over the eye of the hurricane. The plane travels over the eye of Hurricane Jay at random times and samples the maximum wind speed. It finds that the maximum wind speed averages 105 mph with a margin of error of 7.5 mph for 95% confidence. Interpret the meaning of this.

    A. 95% of the samples had maximum wind speed between 90 mph and 120 mph.

    B. We are 95% confident that the maximum wind speed of Jay is between 90 mph and 120 mph.

C. The probability that the maximum wind speed of Jay is between 90 mph and 120 mph is 95%.

D. 95% of hurricanes have a maximum wind speed between 90 mph and 120 mph.

31. Which definition is incorrect?

    A. Variable—a letter that represents an unknown number.

    B. Exponent—the number of times a number is multiplied by itself

    C. Factor of a number—another number that divides into the original number

    D. All are correct

32. A number of cruises were sampled with a scatter plot made measuring the length of the cruise in days compared to the cost of the cruise using the same type of accommodations in thousands of dollars. A line of best fit is drawn. A new cruise is added that lasts 7 days and costs $6,000. If the line of best fit is redrawn, how will the relationship between the length of the cruise and the cost change?

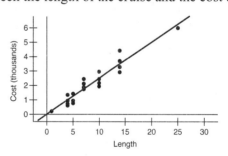

    A. It will become less strong.

    B. It will become stronger.

    C. It will become negative.

    D. No real change.

33. If triangle $A'B'C'$ is obtained when triangle ABC shown below is reflected over the line $x = 1$, which of the following would be the location of point B'?

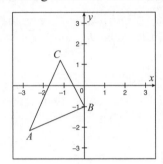

   A. $(0, -1)$

   B. $(1, -1)$

   C. $(2, -1)$

   D. $(1, 0)$

34. The size of a TV is measured by the distance of its diagonal from top left to bottom right. Larry purchased a new television for his family room. The base of the television is 35 inches and its height is 18 inches. What is the size of the television? Round to the nearest inch.

   A.   39 inches

   B.   53 inches

   C.   70 inches

   D.   106 inches

35. During a game of Expanded Form, Parker gave the following clues for his partners to figure out his number:

- The value of the digit 6 is (6×10)
- The value of the digit 5 is (5×100)
- The value of the digit 9 is $\left(9 \times \dfrac{1}{100}\right)$

Which number could fit Parker's description?

   A.   560.9

   B.   568.092

   C.   1,562.009

   D.   65.909

36. A teacher wants to demonstrate to students how to determine the total possible number of sundaes that can be made from 3 flavors of ice cream, 3 sauces, and 2 toppings, where a sundae is comprised of one flavor of ice cream with or without one sauce, and with or without one topping. Select the most effective method(s) to reach all learners.

   A.   Use the Multiplication Principle: Total sundaes = 3(3)(2) = 18

   B.   Use a tree diagram to list all possible combinations

   C.   Both of the above

   D.   Neither of the above

37. $f(x) = \left| 2^x - x^3 \right|$ is evaluated at certain values of x. Which of the following values of $f(x)$ are odd? Select *all* that apply.

   A. $x = 0$

   B. $x = 1$

   C. $x = 2$

   D. $x = 3$

   E. $x = 4$

   F. $x = 5$

38. Which of the following is an example of a formative assessment? Select *all* that apply.

   A.   A math teacher randomly checks several homework problems.

   B.   A math teacher gives a quiz after every topic that was taught.

   C.   A math teacher has students go to the board to show their solution to a problem.

   D.   A math teacher gives a final exam in geometry.

39. A bag of mulch covers 150 feet². Juan has a garden whose shape is a rectangle with a semicircle as shown at right. If he spreads mulch over the entire garden, how many bags must he purchase?

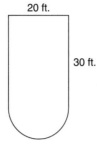

20 ft.

30 ft.

   A. 4

   B. 5

   C. 6

   D. 7

40. In isosceles triangle *PQR*, angle *P* measures 64° which represents the largest angular measurement in the triangle. What is the measure of angle *Q*?

   A. 116°

   B. 52°

   C. 58°

   D. Impossible to say

41. Express the number $0.00000008 \cdot 3{,}200{,}000$ in scientific notation.

   A. 2.56×10^{-3}

   B. 2.56×10^{-2}

   C. 2.56×10^{-1}

   D. 2.56×10^{0}

42. Which of the following is a list of prime numbers?

   A. 3, 5, 23, 33

   B. 1, 7, 13, 19

   C. 2, 17, 23, 51

   D. 5, 31, 53, 97

Mathematics Practice Test 1: Answer Key

Test Item	Answer	Competency 807-
1.	C	001
2.	C	016
3.	D	002
4.	B	012
5.	D	005
6.	C	009
7.	C	015
8.	B	006
9.	D	009
10.	A	010
11.	C	008
12.	B	017
13.	C	012
14.	B	013
15.	A	005
16.	C	018
17.	D	017
18.	A	013
19.	C	003
20.	D	003
21.	A	019

Test Item	Answer	Competency 807-
22.	A	004
23.	A	007
24.	C	003
25.	B	010
26.	A	011
27.	B	014
28.	C	007
29.	C	018
30.	B	014
31.	B	004
32.	A	012
33.	C	011
34.	A	008
35.	B	001
36.	B	016
37.	A, B, D, F	006
38.	A, B, C	019
39.	C	009
40.	D	015
41.	C	002
42.	D	002

Mathematics Practice Test 1: Detailed Answers

1. C.

$\frac{90}{360} = \frac{1}{4} = 25\%$. This is the percentage of students absent. Therefore, 75% were present. **(Competency 807-001: Teacher understands the structure of number systems.)**

2. C.

If Nancy is 12, then Doug is 3 years younger than 12 which is 9, and Kim is 4 years younger than Doug (9) which is 5. **(Competency 807-016: Teacher understands mathematical connections within and outside math.)**

3. D.

A lowest common denominator must be found, which is 30. All fractions must be multiplied by the fraction equivalent to 1 which gets the LCD.

$\frac{2}{3}\left(\frac{10}{10}\right) + \frac{3}{5}\left(\frac{6}{6}\right) + \frac{5}{6}\left(\frac{5}{5}\right) = \frac{20 + 18 + 25}{30} = \frac{63}{30} = \frac{21}{10} = 2\frac{1}{10}$.

Note that this can also be done using a common denominator of 90. **(Competency 807-002: Teacher understands number systems and computational algorithms.)**

4. B.

For mean and median, we are not concerned with the height of the curve which gives the frequency of each score. We are interested in the test score where the height of the curve is the highest. With normal distributions, the mean and median are the same and it is clear that the median for class 2 is greater than that of class 1. Without seeing the data scores, we have no idea what the mode is. The same is true for standard deviation but the fact that both classes seem to show the entirety of their curves in about 5 units along the axis is an indication that their standard deviations are very similar. **(Compe-**

tency 807-012: Teacher understands exploring data through graphical and numerical processes.)

5. D.

The points are $\left(\frac{1}{2}, 0\right)$ and $\left(0, -\frac{1}{2}\right)$. The slope m of the line is given by $m = \frac{\frac{-1}{2} - 0}{0 - \frac{1}{2}} = 1$. Using the point-slope equation $y - y_1 = m\left(x - x_1\right)$, substitute either point: $y + \frac{1}{2} = 1(x - 0)$. Multiplying each side by 2, we get $2y + 1 = 2x$ or $2x - 2y = 1$. An easier way is to substitute these points into all choices and see which one is true. **(Competency 807-005: Teacher understands linear functions.)**

6. C.

The perimeter formula for a rectangle is $P = 2L + 2W$. Therefore, $34 = 18 + 2W$ so $2W = 16$ and $W = 8$ feet. **(Competency 807-009: Teacher understands geometric relationships and formulas.)**

7. C.

A rhombus has four sides all the same length and is considered a square when all four angles are 90°. **(Competency 807-015: Teacher understands mathematical reasoning to solve problems.)**

8. B.

Investigate each table. Quadratic equations do not have a linear relationship; therefore there is not a constant rate of change between the y- and x-values. Option (B) is correct because the table shows a linear relationship. The y-values increase by 3 units for every 1-unit increase in the x-values. Hence the slope of the line is 3. Note that in Option (A), the y-values increase by 1, then 3, then 5. If this pattern is continued, the points form a quadratic function. The same is true in Option (C) as the y-values increase by consecutive integers 1, 2, and 3. Choice (D) is slightly different as the y-values increase by 3 and then 1. At that point, they decrease by 1. This signals a quadratic that reaches its high point at $x = 2$. This analysis is not necessary, though. Once choice (B) is determined as linear, it has to be the correct answer. **(Competency 807-006: Teacher understands non-linear functions.)**

9.　D.

The angles in a triangle add to 180°. Therefore, $180 - 75 - 60 = 45°$. Since all of the angles are less than 90°, the triangle is acute. **(Competency 807-009: Teacher uses geometric relationships.)**

10.　A.

$$V = \frac{1}{3}\pi r^2 h.$$

$$V_{\text{original}} = \frac{1}{3}\pi\left(3^2\right)(6) = 18\pi$$

$$V_{\text{new}} = \frac{1}{3}\pi\left(6^2\right)(3) = 36\pi$$

Change $= 36\pi - 18\pi = 18\pi$.

Percent change $= 100\%\left(\dfrac{V_{\text{change}}}{V_{\text{original}}}\right) = \dfrac{18\pi}{18\pi} = 100\%.$

(Competency 807-010: Teacher understands two- and three-dimensional figures.)

11.　C.

$$\sin\theta = \frac{\text{opposite}}{\text{hypotenuse}}$$

$$\cos\theta = \frac{\text{adjacent}}{\text{hypotenuse}}$$

$$\tan\theta = \frac{\text{opposite}}{\text{adjacent}}$$

$$\frac{\sin\theta - \cos\theta}{\tan\theta} = \frac{\frac{4}{5} - \frac{3}{5}}{\frac{4}{3}} = \frac{1}{5}\cdot\frac{3}{4} = \frac{3}{20}$$

(Competency 807-008: Teacher understands the use of measurement.)

12.　B.

Vygotsky extended Piaget's theories to include social interactions for increased student understanding. **(Competency 807-017: Teacher understands how children learn.)**

13.　C.

12, 26. A stem and leaf plot is read where the first number of the line is the stem (tens or hundreds place) and the following numbers are the ones place. Therefore, Line 5, for example, shows: 51, 53, 55, as the data. There are two 12's and two 26's, so therefore those are the mode. There can be more than one mode. **(Competency 807-12: Teacher understands exploring data through graphical and numerical processes.)**

14.　B.

The total number of balls is 14 and the number of Titleist balls is 6. $\dfrac{6}{14}$ reduces to $\dfrac{3}{7}$. **(Competency 807-013: Teacher understands the use of probability.)**

15.　A.

The slope of a line is given by $m = \dfrac{y_1 - y_2}{x_1 - x_2} = \dfrac{4 - 3}{5 - (-1)} = \dfrac{1}{6}$. **(Competency 807-005: Teacher understands linear functions.)**

16.　C.

Choices (A), (B), and (D) are hallmarks of differentiated instruction. Choice (C) is probably necessary in a math class, but it isn't differentiated instruction. **(Competency 807-018: Teacher understands planning, organizing and implementing instruction.)**

17.　D.

Factors and products are given for Multiplication and Division with three numbers, as are the addends and sums for Addition and Subtraction with three numbers. **(Competency 807-017: Teacher understands how children learn.)**

18. A.

There are 10 cards and 3 are purple. The probability of the first card being purple is $\frac{3}{10}$. For the second card, there are 9 cards remaining and 2 are purple. So, the probability of the second card being purple after you chose a purple card is $\frac{2}{9}$. Both events must happen, so multiply the probabilities. $P = \frac{3}{10}\left(\frac{2}{9}\right) = \frac{6}{90} = \frac{1}{15} = 6.67\%$. This can also be done using combinations: $P = \frac{_3C_2}{_{10}C_2} = \frac{3}{45} = \frac{1}{15} = 6.67\%$. **(Competency 807-013: Teacher understand the theory of probability.)**

19. C.

$2^3 \times 5 \times 7 = 8 \times 5 \times 7 = 280$. Choice (A) = 280, but 14 is a composite number. Choice (B) = 400 and 10 is a composite number. Choice (D) = 140, although all factors are prime. **(Competency 807-003: Teacher understands number theory.)**

20. D.

Any one of the 5 runners has the possibility of finishing first, which leaves 4 possible second-place finishers and 3 possible third-place finishers. Using the multiplication rule, there are 5(4)(3) = 60 possible combinations of how a runner may finish. Note that the word combination is used colloquially. Since order counts, we are calculating permutations. **(Competency 807-003: Teacher understands number theory.)**

21. A.

Frequent observation and interviewing students during observation provide a quick, informal opportunity to judge the progress of student learning, and then allows the teacher to decide whether adjustments to the lesson are necessary. Choice (B) is incorrect because periodic peer reviews of partner work will not allow the teacher to make adjustments to lessons early in a unit. Choice (C) is incorrect because a pretest will provide a teacher with information to plan lessons and a posttest shows what students know at the end of the unit. These types of assessments do not allow for adjustment during the lessons. Choice (D) is incorrect since the quizzes would occur after future lessons, and the adjustments need to happen before future lessons. **(Competency 807-019: Teacher understands assessment techniques.)**

22. A.

Percentage reduction $= \frac{\text{amount reduction}}{\text{original price}} = \frac{60 - 45}{60} = \frac{15}{60} = \frac{1}{4} = 25\%$. **(Competency 807-004: Teacher understands mathematical reasoning to identify patterns.)**

23. A.

This is a calculus problem in disguise. His average speed is $\frac{\text{total distance}}{\text{total time}} = \frac{2.5 \text{ miles}}{2 \text{ minutes}}$. Multiplying both numerator and denominator by 30 give 75 miles in 60 minutes or 75 mph. If Kirk averaged 75 mph in the 2 minutes, at some point in time he was traveling 75 mph despite his speed when passing the police cars. They are justified in giving him a ticket. **(Competency 807-007: Teacher understands the foundations of calculus.)**

24. C.

Since "HAPPINESS" has 9 letters and two sets of double letters, the answer may be found by computing $\frac{9!}{2!2!} = \frac{9(8)(7)(6)(5)(4)(3)(2)(1)}{(2)(1)(2)(1)} = \frac{362880}{4} = 90720$. **(Competency 807-003: Teacher understands number theory.)**

25. B.

The three-dimensional figure would be a rectangular prism that is 6 by 2 by 2. Its volume is 24.

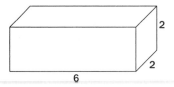

(Competency 807-010: Teacher understands two- and three-dimensional figures.)

26. A.

For instance, if $f(2) = 4, -f(2) = -4$. All points above the x-axis would shift below the x-axis and vice versa. **(Competency 807-011: Teacher understands the coordinate system and transformation.)**

27. B.

In a binomial experiment, every trial must have 2 outcomes: success or failure. For all 4 choices, an even card denotes success. There must be a fixed number of trials. That is not true for Choices (C) and (D) as we only stop choosing cards when two even cards have been chosen. The probabilities of success or failure must be the same for each trial. That is not true in choice (A). The probability of choosing an even number is initially $\frac{5}{10} = \frac{1}{2}$. If an even number is chosen, since the card is not replaced, the probability of an even number on the 2nd pick is $\frac{4}{9}$. In choice (B), since the card is replaced, the probability remains at $\frac{1}{2}$. **(Competency 807-014: Teacher understands sampling and statistical inference.)**

28. C.

A relative minimum is the bottom of a hill, and the graph has 2 of them. A relative maximum is the top of a hill and the graph has 1 of them. The curve has an absolute minimum if it has a lowest point, and this curve does. (Note that a relative minimum can also be an absolute minimum). The curve has an absolute maximum if it has a highest point. This curve does not as it goes up to infinity on both sides. **(Competency 807-007: Teacher understands the foundations of calculus.)**

29. C.

Writing the equation in standard form $y - 1 = 3(x - 1)^2$ tells the basic algebra student the vertex and if s/he doesn't know what standard form is, nothing can be done. This is a closed task. Asking them to graph it will tell them the vertex, how it opens, its width, and possibly its roots. This is an example of an open task where many pieces of information can be found. **(Competency 807-018: Teacher understands planning, organizing and implementing instruction.)**

30. B.

In this confidence interval, 95% of the data lies within the margin of error from the mean: $105 \pm 15 = 90$ to 120 mph. We are interested in the maximum wind speed of Jay, which is unknown. Choice (A) is incorrect as it makes no statement about this unknown top wind speed. Choice (C) is incorrect because the maximum wind speed of Jay is either between 90 mph or 120 mph or it isn't. Choice (D) is incorrect because the study is only about Jay. Choice (B) is the correct interpretation because based on the sample, we are willing to say that we are reasonably sure of the range of the maximum winds. **(Competency 807-014: Teacher understands sampling and statistical inference.)**

31. B.

The definition of an exponent is not quite correct. Since $3^2 = 3(3)$, the exponent 2 means 3 is multiplied by itself once and not twice. Since $3^3 = 3(3)(3)$, the exponent 3 means that 3 is multiplied by itself twice. **(Competency 807-004: Teacher understands mathematical reasoning to identify patterns.)**

32. A.

There is already a fairly strong positive relationship between length of cruise and cost (as length goes up, cost goes up) because the line of best fit is close to most of the points and it goes up to the right. This new point will be in the upper left. It acts as a magnet and the line of best fit will still go up to the right, meaning that there still is a positive relationship, but not as strong. **(Competency 807-012: Teacher understands data through graphical and numerical techniques.)**

33. C.

Reflecting triangle ABC across the line $x = 1$ will preserve the y-values but will change the x-values. Point B is at $(0, -1)$ which is a distance of 1 unit left of the point $(1, -1)$ so B' will be one unit to the right of $(1, -1)$ or $(2, -1)$. **(Competency 807-011: Teacher understands the coordinate system and transformation.)**

34. A.

This is solved by the Pythagorean Theorem.

$$c^2 = a^2 + b^2 \Rightarrow c^2 = 18^2 + 35^2 = 1549 \Rightarrow$$

$$c = \sqrt{1549} \approx 39.4 \text{ inches}$$

(Competency 807-008: Teacher understands the use of measurement to solve problems.)

35. B.

This is the only number in which the digits are in the correct place. **(Competency 807-001: Teacher understands the structure of number systems.)**

36. B.

The multiplication principle is true but the number of sundaes = 3(4)(3) = 36 as no sauce is a possibility as well as no topping. With differentiated instruction, a teacher should use a variety of methods to reach all learners. **(Competency 807-016: Teacher understands mathematical connections within and outside math.)**

37. A., B., D., F.

$$f(0) = \left|2^0 - 0^3\right| = \left|1 - 0\right| = \left|1\right| = 1 \text{ (odd)}$$

$$f(1) = \left|2^1 - 1^3\right| = \left|2 - 1\right| = \left|1\right| = 1 \text{ (odd)}$$

$$f(2) = \left|2^2 - 2^3\right| = \left|4 - 8\right| = \left|-4\right| = 4 \text{ (even)}$$

$$f(3) = \left|2^3 - 3^3\right| = \left|8 - 27\right| = \left|-19\right| = 19 \text{ (odd)}$$

$$f(4) = \left|2^4 - 4^3\right| = \left|16 - 64\right| = \left|48\right| = 48 \text{ (even)}$$

$$f(5) = \left|2^5 - 5^3\right| = \left|32 - 125\right| = \left|-93\right| = 93 \text{ (odd)}$$

(Competency 807-006: Teacher understands non-linear functions.)

38. A., B., C.

A formative assessment is a regularly planned checkup of student progress. Options (A), (B), and (C) fit this description while (D) is a summative assessment that generates a single score and shows what students know and learned over time. **(Competency 807-019: Teacher understands assessment techniques.)**

39. C.

The area of the garden is $20(30) + \dfrac{1}{2}\pi(10^2) =$
$600 + 157.08 = 757.08 \text{ ft}^2 \cdot \dfrac{757.08}{150} = 5.05$ bags, so he must purchase 6 bags. **(Competency 807-009: Teacher understands geometric relationships.)**

40. D.

The sum of the angles of a triangle is 180°. Subtracting 64° from 180° leaves 116° to be split evenly among Angles Q and R. So, each angle equals 58°. But it is possible that angle Q also equals 64° (which doesn't violate the terms of the problem). That would make angle R equal to 52°. So, there are two triangles that fit the criteria. **(Competency 807-015: Teacher understands mathematical reasoning to solve problems.)**

41. C.

$$0.00000008 = 8 \times 10^{-8}$$

$$3{,}200{,}000 = 3.2 \times 10^6$$

$$8 \times 10^{-8} \times 3.2 \times 10^6 = 25.6 \times 10^{-2} =$$

$$2.56 \times 10^1 \times 10^{-2} = 2.56 \times 10^{-1}$$

(Competency 807-002: Teacher understands number systems and computational algorithms.)

42. D.

Option (A) is incorrect because 33 is composite, choice (B) is incorrect because 1 is neither prime nor composite, and choice (C) is incorrect because 51 is a composite number. The numbers listed for choice (D) are all prime numbers. **(Competency 807-002: Teacher understands number systems and computational algorithms.)**

TExES Core Subjects 4–8 Practice Test 1: Social Studies (808)

This practice test plus an additional test are also available at the online REA Study Center (*www.rea.com/studycenter*).

The TExES Core Subjects Social Studies (808) test is computer-based, so we strongly recommend that you take our online practice tests to simulate test-day conditions and to receive these added benefits:

- **Timed testing conditions**—Gauge how much time you can spend on each question.

- **Automatic scoring**—Find out how you did on the test, instantly.

- **On-screen detailed explanations of answers**—Learn not just the correct answer, but also why the other answers are incorrect.

- **Diagnostic score reports**—Pinpoint where you're strongest and where you need to focus your study.

Social Studies Practice Test 1: Answer Sheet

1. Ⓐ Ⓑ Ⓒ Ⓓ

2. Ⓐ Ⓑ Ⓒ Ⓓ

3. Ⓐ Ⓑ Ⓒ Ⓓ

4. Ⓐ Ⓑ Ⓒ Ⓓ

5. Ⓐ Ⓑ Ⓒ Ⓓ

6. Ⓐ Ⓑ Ⓒ Ⓓ

7. Ⓐ Ⓑ Ⓒ Ⓓ

8. Ⓐ Ⓑ Ⓒ Ⓓ

9. Ⓐ Ⓑ Ⓒ Ⓓ

10. Ⓐ Ⓑ Ⓒ Ⓓ

11. Ⓐ Ⓑ Ⓒ Ⓓ

12. Ⓐ Ⓑ Ⓒ Ⓓ

13. Ⓐ Ⓑ Ⓒ Ⓓ Ⓔ

14. Ⓐ Ⓑ Ⓒ Ⓓ

15. Ⓐ Ⓑ Ⓒ Ⓓ

16. Ⓐ Ⓑ Ⓒ Ⓓ

17. Ⓐ Ⓑ Ⓒ Ⓓ

18. Ⓐ Ⓑ Ⓒ Ⓓ

19. Ⓐ Ⓑ Ⓒ Ⓓ

20. Ⓐ Ⓑ Ⓒ Ⓓ

21. Ⓐ Ⓑ Ⓒ Ⓓ

22. Ⓐ Ⓑ Ⓒ Ⓓ

23. Ⓐ Ⓑ Ⓒ Ⓓ

24. Ⓐ Ⓑ Ⓒ Ⓓ

25. Ⓐ Ⓑ Ⓒ Ⓓ

26. Ⓐ Ⓑ Ⓒ Ⓓ

27. Ⓐ Ⓑ Ⓒ Ⓓ

28. Ⓐ Ⓑ Ⓒ Ⓓ

29. Ⓐ Ⓑ Ⓒ Ⓓ

30. Ⓐ Ⓑ Ⓒ Ⓓ

31. Ⓐ Ⓑ Ⓒ Ⓓ

32. Ⓐ Ⓑ Ⓒ Ⓓ

33. Ⓐ Ⓑ Ⓒ Ⓓ

34. Ⓐ Ⓑ Ⓒ Ⓓ

35. Ⓐ Ⓑ Ⓒ Ⓓ

36. Ⓐ Ⓑ Ⓒ Ⓓ

37. Ⓐ Ⓑ Ⓒ Ⓓ

38. Ⓐ Ⓑ Ⓒ Ⓓ

39. Ⓐ Ⓑ Ⓒ Ⓓ

40. Ⓐ Ⓑ Ⓒ Ⓓ

41. Ⓐ Ⓑ Ⓒ Ⓓ

42. Ⓐ Ⓑ Ⓒ Ⓓ

Practice Test 1: Social Studies

TIME: 50 minutes
42 questions

> **Directions:** Read each item and select the best answer. Most items on this test require you to provide the one best answer. However, some questions require you to select all the options that apply.

1. Which of the following best describes the impact of Spindletop in Texas?

   A. Instrumental in moving Texas from an agrarian-based economy into the industrial age

   B. Major environmental disaster in 1901 that damaged grazing land and the beef industry

   C. Innovative amusement attraction that launched the tourist industry

   D. Caused a mass influx of prospectors that increased the Hispanic population

2. A globe is a scale model of the Earth shaped like a sphere. A globe shows sizes and shapes more accurately than which of the following?

   A. Compass rose

   B. Map

   C. Scale

   D. Grid system

3. A compass rose is printed on a map and used as a tool to

   A. show the orientation of a map of Earth.

   B. show the distance between two places in the world.

   C. represent features such as elevations and divisions.

   D. show the distance between two corresponding points.

4. The New England Colonies consisted of

   A. Virginia, North Carolina, South Carolina, and Georgia.

   B. Massachusetts, Connecticut, Rhode Island, and New Hampshire.

   C. New York, New Jersey, Delaware, Maryland, and Pennsylvania.

   D. North Carolina, Rhode Island, Delaware, and Maryland.

5. To apply the concept of time zones, students need to have a clear understanding of

   A. the International Date Line.

   B. the Earth's yearly revolution.

   C. the concept of the meridians of longitude.

   D. the concept of the parallels of latitude.

Use the photograph below to answer question 6.

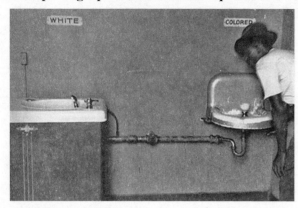

6. In which of the following rulings did the U.S. Supreme Court decide that the conditions of segregation illustrated in the photograph above violated the Fourteenth Amendment?

    A. *Plessy v. Ferguson*

    B. *Marbury v. Madison*

    C. *Brown v. Board of Education of Topeka*

    D. *Dred Scott v. Sandford*

Use the information below to answer question 7 that follows.

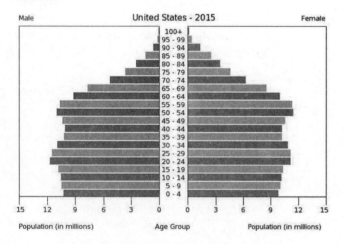

Source: United States Census Bureau

7. A population pyramid as shown in the figure is a complex example of what type of chart, diagram, or graph listed below?

    A. Bar graph

    B. Pie graph

    C. Pedigree chart

    D. Dot plot

8. The first 10 amendments to the U.S. Constitution are known as the

    A. doctrine of the separation of church and state.

    B. Bill of Rights.

    C. Right to Privacy.

    D. Right to Due Process.

9. The United States has 50 states and at least four territories. Based on these figures, what is the maximum number of senators who can serve in the U.S. Senate?

    A. 50

    B. 100

    C. 54

    D. 435

10. In what way did the Gutenberg printing press, invented in 1454, impact the world?

    A. Favorite stories were reprinted on demand.

    B. Affordable books could be illustrated in color.

    C. The spread and democratization of knowledge occurred rapidly throughout society.

    D. Governments embraced the technology to inform the people and to calm rebellions.

Revere, Paul, engraver. "The BLOODY MAS-SACRE perpetrated in King Street BOSTON on March 5th 1770 by a party of the 29th REGT." 1770. Courtesy of Prints and Photographs Division, Library of Congress.

11. The Paul Revere engraving of the Boston Massacre (1770), pictured above, is taught at what grade level?

   A.   6th grade

   B.   5th grade

   C.   4th grade

   D.   3rd grade

12. Cinco de Mayo is a holiday commemorating the victory of the Mexican army over the French forces of Napoleon III on May 5, 1862. This event is important to Mexican Americans because

   A.   the Mexicans defeated a ragtag army.

   B.   it led to Mexican Independence Day.

   C.   the general who led the Mexican forces was born in present-day Texas.

   D.   President Benito Juarez joined forces with the United States to defeat France.

13. Determining globes for a first grade classroom should be based on which of the following characteristics? Select *all* that apply.

   A.   Three or fewer colors to represent land.

   B.   At least seven colors to represent land.

   C.   Two or fewer colors to represent water.

   D.   Three or more colors to represent water.

   E.   A 12-inch globe.

14. Probably as a response to the war in Iraq and Afghanistan, the Organization of Petroleum Exporting Countries (OPEC) cut the production of oil. As a result of this action, the cost of gasoline increased to almost $3.00 per gallon in 2005. What is the economic principle or statement that best represents this scenario?

   A.   During war, the prices of fossil fuels increase.

   B.   The American economy is dependent on foreign oil.

   C.   The law of supply and demand determines the prices of goods and services.

   D.   OPEC was boycotting the United States.

15. Identify the statement that best describes the country of Iraq.

   A.   It is a linguistically and ethnically homogeneous Muslim nation.

   B.   It is a Muslim nation with multiple ethnic groups within its borders.

   C.   It is located in Southeast Asia.

   D.   It is a province of Pakistan.

Use the information below to answer question 16.

Texas GDP Ranking Among Nations
Gross Domestic Product, 2015
(in billions of U.S. dollars)

Rank	Nation	Billion $
1	United States*	$17,418
2	China	$10,380
3	Japan	$4,616
4	Germany	$3,859
5	United Kingdom	$2,945
6	France	$2,846
7	Brazil	$2,353
8	Italy	$2,147
9	India	$2,049
10	Russia	$1,871
11	Canada	$1,788
12	TEXAS**	$1,648
13	Australia	$1,444
14	Korea	$1,416
15	Spain	$1,406
16	Mexico	$1,282
17	Indonesia	$888
18	The Netherlands	$866
19	Turkey	$806
20	Saudi Arabia	$752

*Includes Texas
**If Texas were a nation

Sources: International Monetary Fund and the U.S. Bureau of Economic Analysis. Based on data provided by the Texas Comptroller of Public Accounts staff. Published June 2015.

16. Based on the table given, if Texas were an independent nation, its annual economic output would be which of the following? Select *all* that apply.

    A. Ahead of Canada by approximately US$140 billion

    B. More than double the GDP of Saudi Arabia

    C. More than half the GDP of the United Kingdom

    D. One notch above Australia

17. In Texas, the course that focuses on human or cultural geography is introduced in which of the following grades?

    A. Third

    B. Fourth

    C. Fifth

    D. Sixth

18. The English colonies were established in three regions: the New England Colonies, the Middle Colonies, and the Southern Colonies. The economy of the Southern Colonies was based on

    A. farming, shipping, fishing, and trading.

    B. farming and very small industries such as fishing, lumber, and crafts.

    C. trading and the mining of minerals and other natural resources.

    D. crops of tobacco, rice, indigo, and cotton.

Use the following passage to answer question 19.

We hold these truths to be self-evident. That all men are created equal; that they are endowed by their Creator with certain unalienable rights; that among these are life, liberty and the pursuit of happiness. That, to secure these rights, governments are instituted among men, deriving their just powers from the consent of the governed that, whenever any form of government becomes destructive of these ends, it is the right of the people to alter or to abolish it, and to institute a new government.

19. The excerpt is from which of the following?

    A. Articles of Confederation

    B. U.S. Constitution

    C. Declaration of Independence

    D. Missouri Compromise

20. How do topographic maps differ from other maps?

    A. Topographic maps use census data to show population density.

    B. Topographic maps use contour lines to show elevation change on the surface of Earth.

    C. Topographic maps use latitude and longitude to show relative location.

    D. Topographic maps use latitude and longitude to show absolute location.

21. Assessments that provide the teacher with information about student understanding as they are learning content are called

    A. direct assessments.

    B. informal assessments.

    C. summative assessments.

    D. formative assessments.

22. Which of the following best describes the way in which the Farm Security Administration labor camp in Robstown, Texas, relates to the beginning teacher's knowledge of geography? The beginning teacher

    A. understands the basic concepts of culture and the processes of cultural adaptation, diffusion, and exchange.

    B. understands the characteristics, distribution, and migration of populations in Texas and the United States.

    C. understands how people use oral tradition, stories, real and mythical heroes, music, paintings, and sculpture to create and represent culture in communities in Texas, the United States, and the world.

    D. understands the physical environments of Texas.

23. What is the only branch of government included in the Articles of Confederation?

    A. Judicial

    B. Legislative

    C. Executive

    D. Federal

24. What type of redress did the Civil Liberties Act of 1988, H.R. 442, offer to qualified Japanese Americans who were relocated and interned by the government of the United States?

    A. Payment of $20,000

    B. Guarantees of non-repetition

    C. Restoration of victims to their original situation before the violations occurred

    D. New housing for all detainees

25. On February 1, 1861, the Texas legislature voted to

    A. secede from the Union and join the Confederacy.

    B. relinquish all claims to New Mexico.

    C. annex Texas to the United States.

    D. adopt the Texas Declaration of Independence.

26. Which of the following best describes the way in which the U.S. Constitution assigns governmental power?

   A. It assigns it entirely to the states.

   B. It assigns it entirely to the national government.

   C. It divides it between the states and the national government.

   D. It does not divide power.

27. Which concept is NOT embodied as a right in the First Amendment to the U.S. Constitution?

   A. Peaceable assembly

   B. Freedom of speech

   C. Petition for redress of grievances

   D. Protection against unreasonable search and seizure

28. Which of the following best describes the historical diet of Atakapans and Karankawas American Indians who inhabited the coastal regions of present-day Texas?

   A. Atakapans and Karankawas consumed bear and deer from the land as well as alligators, oysters, clams, ducks, and turtles.

   B. Atakapans and Karankawas grew and consumed beans, squash, and sunflowers, along with eating bear, deer, and occasionally buffalo.

   C. Atakapans and Karankawas ate bison, fish, turtles, crawfish, snails, pecans, acorns, wild fruits, rattlesnakes, and rabbits.

   D. Atakapans and Karankawas gathered wild berries, plants, and other locally grown items.

29. Mr. Whitfield has his seventh-grade students regularly engage in small group discussions following a social studies lesson in which they discuss a shared text. Using small group roles, the students take turns reading the text, pausing to discuss the text according to each student's assigned role. One student is a question generator, one is a summarizer, one is a predictor, and the fourth student is a clarifier of tricky concepts in the text. What is the name for this strategy?

   A. Thinking aloud

   B. Role play

   C. Literature circles

   D. Reciprocal teaching

30. Which of the following played a significant role in the Chicano civil rights movement by fighting for better working conditions and fair compensation for farm workers?

   A. Rosa Parks

   B. Martha Cotera

   C. Dolores Huerta

   D. Ida B. Wells

31. Economics is best described as the study of

   A. how different political systems establish systems for production and consumption.

   B. how individuals and groups with limited resources make decisions to best satisfy their needs and wants.

   C. how currency is used in different societies.

   D. how trade has developed through a historic and systematic process.

32. Which of the following was the original motto of the United States and remains on the Great Seal of the United States?

   A. One nation under God

   B. *Carpe diem*

   C. *E pluribus unum*

   D. Freedom and justice for all

33. One activity used before and after introducing a new time period in history is the KWL chart by which students discuss and list what they know, what they want to know, and what they learned about the topic. A rationale for conducting this activity would be to

    A. help students compare and contrast main ideas in a chapter or reading.

    B. provide a structured assessment tool to grade understanding of the new information.

    C. help students better understand the historical time period.

    D. activate background knowledge and generate interest in the historical period.

34. In social studies, students are expected to make evidence-based claims to support larger arguments about a given event, situation, cultural group, and so on. How can primary and secondary sources provide the standards-based content needed for students to support a claim, or statement, made in a social studies class? Select *all* that apply.

    A. Standards-based content comes from textbooks aligned to the Texas Essential Knowledge and Skills with images, diagrams, and text, which should be used to support student claims.

    B. Standards-based content is gathered through a combination of sources, provided by teachers, which deepen and broaden student knowledge, which can be used to support student claims.

    C. Evidence-based reasoning is best if it comes from primary sources that provide first-hand accounts that require students to critically assess situations and events from new perspectives.

    D. Evidence for arguments can be found in related or disparate content-rich information sources of firsthand accounts and high-level synopses of events to support student reasoning.

35. A major conflict between colonial Americans and the British occurred over a series of British Acts of Parliament dealing with

    A. taxes.

    B. slavery.

    C. farming.

    D. Native Americans.

36. Which of the following movements was most influential in the crafting of the U.S. Declaration of Independence and the U.S. Constitution?

    A. Scientific revolution

    B. Industrialism

    C. Enlightenment

    D. Renaissance

Use the image below to answer the question that follows.

Source: National Museum of American History, Smithsonian Institution

37. Which of the following was the purpose of the poster?

    A. To encourage young women to go back to school

    B. To encourage women to stand up for themselves

    C. To encourage women to take factory jobs during World War II

    D. To encourage men to recognize the rights of women

38. The term *manifest destiny* connotes a culture of

    A. ancestral harmony.

    B. territorial expansion.

    C. geographic isolationism.

    D. economic capitalism.

39. Which branch of government is responsible for creating the nation's laws?

    A. Executive

    B. Legislative

    C. Judicial

    D. Fiscal

Use the photograph below to answer the question that follows.

Source: National Archives and Records Administration

40. In reference to the photograph, Eleanor Roosevelt said, "The destiny of human rights is in the hands of all our citizens in all our communities." From a social studies teacher's perspective, this quote applies

    A. only to U.S. citizens in the 20th century.

    B. only to U.S. citizens from early civilizations through today

    C. only to any human living after the 20th century.

    D. to any human from early civilizations through today.

41. Which of the following is an example of an activity that students could do to conduct *primary research* for a social studies project?

    A. Create a poster report using Internet resources

    B. Conduct a survey to gather information

    C. Synthesize facts from multiple informational texts

    D. Evaluate websites for accuracy of information

42. Article 55 of which of the following documents calls for "universal respect for, and observance of, human rights and fundamental freedoms"?

    A. The U.S. Constitution

    B. The Declaration of Independence

    C. The United Nations Charter

    D. The Texas Constitution

Social Studies Practice Test 1: Answer Key

Test Item	Answer	Competency 808-
1.	A	005
2.	B	002
3.	A	002
4.	B	001
5.	C	002
6.	C	001
7.	A	006
8.	B	004
9.	B	004
10.	C	005
11.	B	007
12.	C	001
13.	A, C, E	007
14.	C	003
15.	B	002
16.	B, C, D	002
17	D	007
18.	D	003
19.	C	001
20.	B	002
21.	D	007

Test Item	Answer	Competency 808-
22.	B	001
23.	B	004
24.	A	003
25.	A	001
26.	C	004
27.	D	004
28.	A	001
29.	D	007
30.	C	001
31.	B	003
32.	C	004
33.	D	007
34.	B, D	006
35.	A	001
36.	C	004
37.	C	001
38.	B	001
39.	B	004
40.	D	001
41.	B	006
42.	C	004

Social Studies Practice Test 1: Detailed Answers

1. A.

The correct answer is (A). Spindletop marked the change in the Texas economy from agrarian based to one that was also based on oil, technology, and innovation. As competition increased, so did innovative uses of technology. Money from the oil business was used to expand the research and development parts of oil companies as well as universities. Companies such as Texas Instruments soon formed and have been a strong representation of oil, innovation, and technology. Companies developed or moved to Texas that supported the oil industries. Jobs in Texas increased and universities were established and/or supported. Option (B) is incorrect. Spindletop was not a natural disaster. Option (C) and (D) are incorrect. Spindletop was the discovery of a large oil formation on a salt dome southeast of Beaumont, Texas. It was not an amusement attraction nor did it impact the Hispanic population. Instead, it marked the birth of the modern petroleum industry. **(Competency 808-005: Culture, Science, Technology and Society)**

2. B.

The correct answer is (B). A globe is a scale model of the Earth shaped like a sphere. Because a globe is the same shape as the Earth, it shows sizes and shapes more accurately than a map (a flat representation of the Earth). Option (A) is incorrect because a compass rose is printed on a map to show the relative position of the cardinal points (north, south, west, and east) and not a representation of the Earth. Some also include the intermediate directions (northeast, southeast, southwest, and northwest). Option (C) is incorrect because a map scale is used to show the distance between two places in the world. Option (D) is incorrect because a grid system provides lines to help determine absolute location. Typically, though not always, these lines are latitude and longitude. **(Competency 808-002 Geography)**

3. A.

The correct answer is (A). A compass rose is a design printed on a chart or map for reference. It shows the orientation of a map on Earth and shows the four cardinal directions (north, south, east, and west). A compass rose may also show intermediate directions (northeast, southeast, southwest, and northwest). Option (B) is incorrect because a map scale shows the distance between two places in the world. Option (C) is incorrect because features such as elevations and divisions are represented by different colors. Option (D) is incorrect because the ratio of the distance between two points on the Earth and the distance between the two corresponding points on the map is represented by a scale and not by a compass rose. **(Competency 808-002 Geography)**

4. B.

The correct answer is (B). The New England Colonies consisted of Massachusetts, Connecticut, Rhode Island, and New Hampshire. Option (A) is incorrect because Virginia, North Carolina, South Carolina, and Georgia formed the Southern Colonies. Option (C) is incorrect because New York, New Jersey, Delaware, Maryland, and Pennsylvania formed the Middle Colonies. Option (D) is incorrect because this answer represents a combination of some of the Southern Colonies and some of the Middle Colonies. **(Competency 808-001 History)**

5. C.

The correct answer is (C). The Earth is divided into 24 zones based on the meridians of longitude, which are determined using the rotation of the Earth and its exposure to sunlight. This rotation creates day and night, and consequently the concept of time. Option (A) is incorrect because the International Date Line is only one of 24 meridians of the Earth. Option (B) is incorrect because the term *revolution* describes the movement of the Earth around the Sun, which affects the seasons but not necessarily the time zones. Option (D) is incorrect because the parallels of latitude do not affect the time zones. (**Competency 808-002 Geography**)

6. C.

The correct answer is (C). The conditions represented in the photograph, which shows separate drinking fountains for whites and for African Americans, were ruled unconstitutional by the U.S. Supreme Court in *Brown v. Board of Education of Topeka* in May 1954. The case struck down *Plessy v. Ferguson* (A), the 1896 case in which the Court had established the "separate but equal" doctrine for determining the constitutionality of racial segregation laws. The Court's ruling in *Marbury v. Madison* (B) in 1803 established the doctrine of judicial review, but did not touch on issues of racial segregation. In contrast, race was central to the thesis put forth in the Supreme Court's *Dred Scott* decision (D) in 1857: that African Americans, regardless of whether they had been slaves or been granted their freedom, were not protected by the U.S. Constitution and could never become U.S. citizens. (**Competency 808-001 History**)

7. A.

Option (A) is correct. A population pyramid uses a series of bar graphs to represent the population of males and females at different ages. A population pyramid is a critical resource in social studies education. Elementary teachers should use them often to help students stay in practice with reading and interpreting the data on these graphs as they apply to different cultures and/or time periods in history. Middle school teachers should use population pyramids to understand current and historical societies and to analyze the graphs for patterns and irregularities to draw conclusions or make predictions. Option (B) refers to a circle divided into parts to represent data. Option (C) is a diagram that looks like a flow chart and is used to show lineage, or a family tree. Option (D) is a type of graph that is often seen in mathematics. It is like a bar graph except that it uses a dot to identify data. For example, if the bar graph extends a bar, or thick line, to the number 9, the dot plot uses a dot at the number 9 to represent the same information. Elementary teachers should use this commonality to help students transfer skills for reading and analyzing data in

multiple forms. (**Competency 808-006 Social Science Foundation and Skills**)

8. B.

The correct answer is (B). Civil rights are the legal and political rights of the people who live in a particular country. In the United States, the Constitution and the Bill of Rights guarantee civil rights to American citizens and residents. The first 10 amendments to the U.S. Constitution are known as the Bill of Rights. Choices (A), (C), and (D) are incorrect because these name certain rights included in the Bill of Rights, but fail to address the question. (**Competency 808-004 Government and Citizenship**)

9. B.

The correct answer is (B). The U.S. Constitution provides for two senators to represent each of the 50 states, for a total of 100. Territories are not represented in the U.S. Senate. Choice (D) is incorrect because it represents the current number of members of the U.S. House of Representatives. (**Competency 808-004 Government and Citizenship**)

10. C.

Option (C) is correct because for the first time books and other written materials could be produced cheaply and in mass quantities, thus making them available to all classes in society. As the greater masses became more literate they could read others' ideas and share their own. Ideas for people to have a voice in the government and choice in their daily lives began to spread. Knowledge was spread to all of society, not just the elite few. Option (A) is incorrect. Although it was possible for stories to be reprinted, it was not the lasting impact of the Gutenberg printing press. Option (B) is incorrect because the Gutenberg printing press was about the use of moveable type, not about providing colored illustrations. Option (D) is incorrect. At the time, many governments did not embrace democracy and, thus, did not set about using the Gutenberg printing press to inform the public. (**Competency 808-005: Culture, Science, Technology and Society**)

11. B.

Option (B) is the correct answer. Students are taught U.S. History in grade 5. The Boston Massacre was an important part of the Revolutionary War. Option (A) refers to World Cultures. Option (C) refers to Texas History. Option (D) refers to the social studies topic, "How Individuals Change their Communities and their World." **(Competency 808-007 Social Science Instruction and Assessment)**

12. C.

The correct answer is (C). General Ignacio de Zaragoza was one of the leaders of the Mexican Army. He was born south of the city of Goliad when this region was part of Mexico. Because the region is now part of Texas, Mexican Americans celebrate the accomplishment of this "Mexican American" hero. In the Battle of Puebla, the Mexican forces faced anything but a ragtag army (A); Napoleon III's French troops represented one of the world's best fighting forces, so the victory took on symbolic significance. Cinco de Mayo has nothing to do with Mexican Independence Day (B), which was established in 1810, a full half-century before the Battle of Puebla. Option (D) is incorrect because the United States did not participate in this war. The U.S. was fighting its own war—the American Civil War (1860–1865). **(Competency 808-001 History)**

13. A., C., E.

Options (A), (C), and (E) are correct because lower elementary grades (PreK–3) should use a smaller, simpler globe than upper elementary grades (4–6). Options (B) and (D) are characteristics of a globe for older elementary students. **(Competency 808-007 Social Science Instruction and Assessment)**

14. C.

The correct answer is (C). Reducing the production of oil while keeping the same demand for the product creates an imbalance between supply and demand. This imbalance results in a price increase. Options (A) and (B), while potentially and flatly true, respectively, do not articulate an economic principle, as the question requires. Option (D) presents an opinion that fails to address the true question. **(Competency 808-003 Economics)**

15. B.

The correct answer is (B). Iraq is a Muslim nation with multiple ethnic groups within its borders. The largest groups are the Arabs, consisting of Shiite and Sunni Muslims, who do not always get along. The Kurds are the largest minority group. (A) is incorrect. The multiple groups living in Iraq speak Arabic, Kurdish, Turkish, Assyrian, and other languages. (C) is incorrect because Iraq is located in the Middle Eastern part of Asia. (D) is incorrect because Pakistan is a Muslim country from the region, but there is no political association between the two nations. **(Competency 808-002 Geography)**

16. B., C., D.

Options (B), (C), and (D) are correct. Option (B) is correct because Texas's US$1.65 trillion GDP in 2014 was more than double Saudi Arabia's US$752 billion. Option (C) is correct because the United Kingdom chalked up approximately US$2.95 trillion in GDP in 2014, half of which would be US$1.48 trillion. Option (D) is correct because Texas ranks 12th while Australia ranks 13th, according to the table. Option (A) is incorrect because the statement is actually the inverse of the reality: the figures show Canada in 11th place in terms of GDP, a notch above Texas. **(Competency 808-002 Geography)**

17. D.

The correct answer is (D). The course designed to introduce students to cultural or human geography is introduced in sixth grade. Unfortunately, some teachers teach this from a world history perspective, not from a geographic perspective. A geographic perspective includes history as well as other information such as culture, geopolitics, demographic, and human-environment interaction. Geographic concepts and skills are taught at each grade level. However, the World Cultures course is designed to teach basic understanding of cultural geography in preparation for World Geography at the high school level. **(Competency 808-007 Social Science Instruction and Assessment)**

18. D.

The correct answer is (D). The economy of the Southern Colonies was based on the crops of tobacco, rice, indigo, and cotton. Plantations produced agricultural crops in large scale and exploited workers as well as the environment. Choice (A) is incorrect because it was the economy of the Middle Colonies that was based on farming, shipping, fishing, and trading. Choice (B) is incorrect because it was the economy of the New England colonies that was based on farming and very small industries such as fishing, lumber, and crafts. Choice (C) is incorrect because trading and mining for natural resources were not a part of the Southern Colonies' economy. **(Competency 808-003 Economics)**

19. C.

The quotation is from the Declaration of Independence (C), written in 1776 by Thomas Jefferson. The document specifically highlights the reasons the American colonies wanted to seek independence from British rule. The Articles of Confederation (A), adopted in 1781, was an agreement among the 13 founding states that legally established the United States of America as a confederation of sovereign states and served as its first constitution. The U.S. Constitution (B), adopted in 1787, established the governmental structure we still have today. The Missouri Compromise of 1820 (D) dealt primarily with how slave and free states would be admitted to the Union. **(Competency 808-001 History)**

20. B.

Answer (B) is correct, because it reveals the purpose behind why cartographers opt to use topographic maps. Topographic maps use contour lines to show elevation change on the surface of Earth. Even though both relative and absolute location provide information about where we are in the world, they are not what makes a topographic map special. Thus, choices (C) and (D) are incorrect. We use latitude and longitude to determine global location. Population maps show the density of humans in a given location, which means (A) is also incorrect. **(Competency 808-002 Geography)**

21. D.

Formative assessments (D) are ongoing and occur while students are learning information. These types of assessments help teachers make decisions about how the subject is taught, and they can make adjustments as needed. Summative assessments show what students know at a particular time, such as through a unit-based or comprehensive end-of-term exam. **(Competency 808-007 Social Studies Instruction and Assessment)**

22. B.

Response (B), the beginning teacher understands the characteristics, distribution, and migration of populations in Texas and the United States, best describes the way in which the Farm Security Administration labor camp in Robstown, Texas, relates to the beginning teacher's knowledge of geography. There is no explicit detailing of culture exchange or stories. Thus, choices (B) and (C) are incorrect. Choice (D) is an incorrect response because it relates primarily to physical geography and not migration patterns. **(Competency 808-001 History)**

23. B.

The Articles of Confederation mention only the legislative branch (B) in the form of Congress. The judicial (A) and executive branches (C) were later outlined in the U.S. Constitution, but were not mentioned in the Articles of Confederation. The federal branch (D) is not a branch of government, and is thus incorrect. **(Competency 808-004 Government and Citizenship)**

24. A.

Although the *United Nations* draft of Basic Principles and Guidelines on the Right to a Remedy and Reparation for Victims of Gross Violations of International Human Rights Law suggested five forms of redress, including (1) restitution, (2) compensation, (3) rehabilitation, and (4) satisfaction, and (5) guarantees of non-repetition, the United States' Civil Liberties Act of 1988, H.R. 442, offers only an apology and restitution. Thus, responses (B), (C), and (D) are incorrect. Only choice (A), indicating a payment of $20,000, is correct. **(Competency 808-003 Economics)**

25. A.

After the election of Abraham Lincoln, the Texas legislature held a special convention and voted to secede from the Union and join the Confederacy; thus, option (A) is the correct response. Response (B) is incorrect because Texas relinquished all claims to New Mexico in 1850 in line with the terms of the Compromise of 1850. The annexation of Texas by the United States occurred two decades earlier in 1845, making response (C) incorrect. A delegation at Washington-on-the-Brazos adopted the Texas Declaration of Independence on March 2, 1836, creating the Republic of Texas. Thus, response (D) is also incorrect. **(Competency 808-001 History)**

26. C.

The U.S. Constitution divides power between the state and national government (C) in what is referred to as federalism. There are powers that are specifically reserved for the federal government, powers specifically reserved for the state governments, and powers that are shared between the two. Thus, choices (A), (B), and (D) are incorrect. **(Competency 808-004 Government and Citizenship)**

27. D.

The First Amendment to the Constitution reads, "Congress shall make no law respecting an establishment of religion, or prohibiting the free exercise thereof; or abridging the freedom of speech (B), or of the press; or of the right of the people to assemble peaceably (A), and to petition the government for a redress of grievances" (C). Protection against unreasonable search and seizure is a constitutional right found in the Fourth Amendment, and thus option (D) is the only correct choice. **(Competency 808-004 Government and Citizenship)**

28. A.

The Atakapans and Karankawas lived in the coastal areas of present-day Texas. They consumed bear and deer from the land as well as alligators, oysters, clams, ducks, and turtles (A). It was the Caddo, in present-day eastern Texas, who grew and consumed beans, squash, and sunflowers along with eating bear, deer, and occasionally buffalo, so (B) is an incorrect response. Choice (C) is also incorrect. The Tonkawas inhabited the central regions of present-day Texas and typically ate bison, fish, turtles, crawfish, snails, pecans, acorns, wild fruits, rattlesnakes, and rabbits, so (D) is also incorrect. **(Competency 808-001 History)**

29. D.

Option (D) is correct because students who practice reciprocal teaching engage in the four "jobs," or roles, described in this question. Option (A) is incorrect because thinking aloud is primarily an individual, cognitive task. Option (B), role play, is incorrect because students are not enacting a scene or scenario from the text; rather, they are discussing the content using the four roles. Option (C) is incorrect because literature circles, while promoting group discussion about a text, are done in a wider variety of ways than described in this scenario. Literature circles also typically focus on the more open-ended responses of the reader. **(Competency 808-007 Social Studies Instruction and Assessment)**

30. C

Dolores Huerta (C) is a noted labor union activist who played a significant role in the Chicano civil rights movement of the 1960s by fighting for better working conditions and fair compensation for farm workers. Rosa Parks (A) was a civil rights activist primarily known for starting the Montgomery bus boycott for refusing to give up her seat to a white man. Martha Cotera (B) is also a Chicana civil rights activist and writer, but her efforts focused primarily around organizing the 1969 Crystal City walkouts that protested the exclusion of Mexican Americans in political representation. Ida B. Wells (D), who was born into slavery, became a fierce antilynching and women's suffrage activist and established several nineteenth century women's organizations. **(Competency 808-001 History)**

31. B.

Economics is *best* described as the study of how individuals and groups with limited resources make decisions to best satisfy their needs and wants. Choice (A) is incorrect because examining how political systems establish systems for production and consumption is only one part of economic study. Choice (C), how currency is used in different societies, might be of interest to anthropologists or sociologists, but is not the primary responsibility of economists. Choice (D), how trade has developed through a historic and systematic process, would be of interest to historians, but not the primary interest of economic study. Thus, option (B) is the best general description of economic study. **(Competency 808-003 Economics)**

32. C.

E pluribus unum is a Latin phrase that means "from many, one." The United States used it as an unofficial motto from 1782 to 1955. This motto appears in the official Great Seal of United States (adopted in 1782) on the banner in the bald eagle's beak. While both "one nation under God" (A) and "freedom and justice for all" (D) are phrases found in the U.S. Pledge of Allegiance, neither has been a motto of the United States. *Carpe diem* (B), Latin for "seize the day," is incorrect because it has never been recognized as a motto of the United States. "In God We Trust" was adopted as the national motto in 1956 and reaffirmed by Congress in 2011. **(Competency 808-004 Government and Citizenship)**

33. D.

KWL stands for "Know," "Want to know," and "Learned," and relates to the types of discussion and questioning that would take place before, during, and after discussing and learning about the topic at hand, which, for this question, is a time period in history. In the "Know" part, the teacher guides students to consider what background knowledge they have that relates to the time period. After these are shared, students pose questions about what they hope to know and learn about the time period. After the lesson or at different parts of the lesson, the teacher can discuss with students what they are learning or have learned as a result of the activities, visuals, and readings within the lesson. These activities help students anticipate what they will be learning prior to various activities to engage them by such things as discussing, visualizing, and reading. This will serve to activate their schema or background knowledge. Choice (D) is the correct answer because it best fits this purpose of building and activating background knowledge while helping students to anticipate the key ideas in the text, visuals, or other resources within the lesson. The other choices don't directly relate to this purpose.

(Competency 808-007 Social Science Instruction and Assessment)

34. B., D.

Options (B) and (D) are the correct responses. Primary and secondary sources are content-rich resources for students, who must be taught how to identify the type of sources as well as the key information provided. Social studies courses should be designed so that students must take a stand on an issue and then support their reasoning. They do this by making a claim stating their position. Teachers should model and expect students to use both primary and secondary resources to construct pieces of the content that will eventually be used to support their reasoning. Therefore, choice (A) is incorrect because it relies solely on a textbook, a secondary resource. The question asks about using both secondary and primary resources together. Choice (C) is also incorrect because it relies solely on primary resources. Choices (B) and (D) illustrate reasons for using both types of resources together, thus answering the question. **(Competency 808-006 Social Studies Instruction and Assessment)**

35. A.

The British imposition of taxes on colonial Americans (A) provoked major conflicts between these two groups. The colonists were upset with the British for implementing taxes when they felt they did not have any direct representation in the British Parliament. For choice (B), even though slavery continued in the colonies after it was abolished in England (1833), it was not a huge source of contention between the colonists and the British because the American Revolution had already occurred and the United States was free from British control. For choice (C), colonial farming was an industry, which received little interference from the British. Choice (D) is incorrect because no British Acts of Parliament were passed that dealt with Native Americans. **(Competency 808-001 History)**

36. C.

Of the four movements listed, the Enlightenment was the greatest influence on the writing of the U.S. Declaration of Independence and the U.S. Constitution, particularly the notion of the social contract. The scientific revolution (A) was an important movement in the sixteenth and seventeenth centuries that had a fundamental impact on Europeans view of the natural world, but did not directly influence the crafting of these documents. Industrialism (B) is incorrect because this revolution occurred in the nineteenth century after the crafting of the Declaration of Independence and U.S. Constitution. The Renaissance (D), which began in Italy and lasted from the fourteenth to seventeenth centuries, was a period of rebirth for literature, language, art, and culture, but had little impact on the crafting of these documents. **(Competency 808-004 Government and Citizenship)**

37. C.

Option (C) is correct. The purpose of the Rosie the Riveter poster produced in the early 1940s was to encourage women to take factory jobs during World War II. As men were deployed to fight in the war abroad, and war efforts demanded the production of more military machinery, women were encouraged to fill the increased demand for factory workers. Using critical and historical thinking skills, we can examine the image by analyzing the clothing and appearance of the woman represented, the choice of words used, and the agency that produced the poster. In examining the image, we can conclude that the poster was not designed to encourage young women to go back to school (A), encourage women to stand up for themselves (B), or encourage men to recognize the rights of women (D). **(Competency 808-001 History)**

38. B.

Manifest destiny is defined as a nineteenth century doctrine that the United States had not only the right, but also the duty, to expand throughout North America. This brought about core American cultural attributes of geographic expansion, so option (B) is the correct response. In many cases, manifest destiny worked against cultural practices of ancestral harmony, as its enactment broke families apart and moved many native peoples from their cultural connections to ancestral lands; thus, option (A) is incorrect. Option (C) is wrong because manifest destiny resulted in geographic expansion and engagement, which are the antithesis of geographic isolationism. Economic capitalism (D) had a relationship to manifest destiny as an economic influence and often a result, but

it does not connote any cultural aspects of manifest destiny. **(Competency 808-001 History)**

39. B.

Option (B) is correct. The legislative branch of government, comprising the two houses of Congress, is responsible for creating the nation's laws. The executive branch of government (A) is primarily concerned with carrying out the laws of the country. The judicial branch of government (C) is responsible for interpreting and enforcing the nation's laws. The fiscal branch (D) is incorrect because this is not one of the three branches of government. **(Competency 808-004 Government and Citizenship)**

40. D.

Option (D) is correct. When Eleanor Roosevelt said, "The destiny of human rights is in the hands of all our citizens in all our communities," we understand that she was referencing any human from early civilizations through today. The photograph gives us clues to the answer in that we have a United Nations logo and a headline about human rights. Human rights extend beyond the borders of the United States, which eliminates options (A) and (B). This is affirmed in Texas 4–8 social studies teachers' familiarity with the preamble to the declaration of human rights, which begins, "Whereas recognition of the inherent dignity and of the equal and inalienable rights of all members of the human family is the foundation of freedom, justice and peace in the world." Although the United Nations General Assembly adopted the universal declaration of human rights on December 10, 1948, three years after the end of World War II, it pulls from deep and ancient histories of human rights dating before that era, making option (C) incorrect. The Hindu Vedas, the Babylonian Code of Hammurabi, the Bible, the Quran (Koran), and the Analects of Confucius all address people's duties, rights, and responsibilities. Native Americans also addressed human rights via documents, including the Inca Aztec codes of conduct and justice and an Iroquois constitution. **(Competency 808-001 History)**

41. B.

In doing primary research, the student should gather original information from either a primary source document or from a person or group of people. In this case, a survey would be primary research and a way of gathering information that was not collected by someone else. The remaining choices, (A), (C), and (D), are examples of secondary research, or using documents of information that has already been collected. **(Competency 808-006 Social Science Foundations and Skills)**

42. C.

Article 55 of the United Nations Charter calls for "universal respect for, and observance of, human rights and fundamental freedoms" (C). Responses (A), the U.S. Constitution; (B), the Declaration of Independence; and (D), the Texas Constitution, although seemingly plausible, are incorrect answers to this fact-based question. **(Competency 808-004 Government and Citizenship)**

TExES Core Subjects 4–8 Practice Test 1: Science (809)

This pratice test plus an additional test are available at the online REA Study Center (www.rea.com/studycenter).

The TExES Core Subjects Science (809) test is computer-based, so we strongly recommend that you take our online practice tests to simulate test-day conditions and to receive these added benefits:

- **Timed testing conditions**—Gauge how much time you can spend on each question.

- **Automatic scoring**—Find out how you did on the test, instantly.

- **On-screen detailed explanations of answers**—Learn not just the correct answer, but also why the other answers are incorrect.

- **Diagnostic score reports**—Pinpoint where you're strongest and where you need to focus your study.

Science Practice Test 1: Answer Sheet

1. Ⓐ Ⓑ Ⓒ Ⓓ
2. Ⓐ Ⓑ Ⓒ Ⓓ
3. Ⓐ Ⓑ Ⓒ Ⓓ
4. Ⓐ Ⓑ Ⓒ Ⓓ
5. Ⓐ Ⓑ Ⓒ Ⓓ
6. Ⓐ Ⓑ Ⓒ Ⓓ
7. Ⓐ Ⓑ Ⓒ Ⓓ
8. Ⓐ Ⓑ Ⓒ Ⓓ
9. Ⓐ Ⓑ Ⓒ Ⓓ
10. Ⓐ Ⓑ Ⓒ Ⓓ
11. Ⓐ Ⓑ Ⓒ Ⓓ
12. Ⓐ Ⓑ Ⓒ Ⓓ
13. Ⓐ Ⓑ Ⓒ Ⓓ
14. Ⓐ Ⓑ Ⓒ Ⓓ
15. Ⓐ Ⓑ Ⓒ Ⓓ
16. Ⓐ Ⓑ Ⓒ Ⓓ

17. Ⓐ Ⓑ Ⓒ Ⓓ Ⓔ
18. Ⓐ Ⓑ Ⓒ Ⓓ
19. Ⓐ Ⓑ Ⓒ Ⓓ
20. Ⓐ Ⓑ Ⓒ Ⓓ
21. Ⓐ Ⓑ Ⓒ Ⓓ
22. Ⓐ Ⓑ Ⓒ Ⓓ
23. Ⓐ Ⓑ Ⓒ Ⓓ
24. Ⓐ Ⓑ Ⓒ Ⓓ
25. Ⓐ Ⓑ Ⓒ Ⓓ
26. Ⓐ Ⓑ Ⓒ Ⓓ
27. Ⓐ Ⓑ Ⓒ Ⓓ
28. Ⓐ Ⓑ Ⓒ Ⓓ
29. Ⓐ Ⓑ Ⓒ Ⓓ
30. Ⓐ Ⓑ Ⓒ Ⓓ
31. Ⓐ Ⓑ Ⓒ Ⓓ
32. Ⓐ Ⓑ Ⓒ Ⓓ

33. Ⓐ Ⓑ Ⓒ Ⓓ
34. Ⓐ Ⓑ Ⓒ Ⓓ
35. Ⓐ Ⓑ Ⓒ Ⓓ
36. Ⓐ Ⓑ Ⓒ Ⓓ
37. Ⓐ Ⓑ Ⓒ Ⓓ
38. Ⓐ Ⓑ Ⓒ Ⓓ
39. Ⓐ Ⓑ Ⓒ Ⓓ
40. Ⓐ Ⓑ Ⓒ Ⓓ
41. Ⓐ Ⓑ Ⓒ Ⓓ
42. Ⓐ Ⓑ Ⓒ Ⓓ
43. Ⓐ Ⓑ Ⓒ Ⓓ
44. Ⓐ Ⓑ Ⓒ Ⓓ
45. Ⓐ Ⓑ Ⓒ Ⓓ
46. Ⓐ Ⓑ Ⓒ Ⓓ

Practice Test 1: Science*

TIME: 55 minutes
46 questions

> **Directions:** Read each item and select the best answer. Most items on this test require you to provide the one best answer. However, some questions require you to select all the options that apply.

1. The students in Mr. Lawson's class are going to engage in an inquiry-based laboratory investigation during which they will be placing a glass thermometer in a beaker of ice and heating it on a hot plate to graph the heating curve of water. What is the first and most important thing Mr. Lawson should do before students begin this investigation?

    A. Provide students with the materials needed to conduct the investigation and let them begin.

    B. Give students a review sheet that explains and shows a completed graph of the heating curve of water before they begin the investigation.

    C. Read aloud and discuss all safety precautions of the investigation including wearing safety goggles and the use of glassware and heating surfaces.

    D. Instruct students on the clean-up procedures to follow after the investigation including where to store the glassware.

2. A student in Ms. Longfellow's class decided she needed some sodium hydroxide (NaOH) for an experiment she wanted to try at home. She saw a bottle of NaOH behind the glass of the chemical cabinet in the storeroom of her classroom. If Ms. Longfellow were following safety practices in her classroom, what should the student find to be true?

    A. The storeroom and cabinet where the NaOH is located would be open and available for student use because it is not a dangerous chemical.

    B. The storeroom and cabinet where the NaOH is located would be locked and the key not accessible to students, as with all laboratory chemicals.

    C. The NaOH would be stored near the sink and eyewash station in case the chemical spills.

    D. The NaOH would be stored near the fire extinguisher in the classroom in case the chemical catches fire.

3. What is the proper instrument to use in measuring the mass of an object?

    A. Meter stick

    B. Graduated cylinder

    C. Triple beam balance

    D. Sling psychrometer

---

* This REA Science practice test for the TExES Core Subjects 4–8 exam features slightly more items, and allows proportionately more time, than the actual exam. We do this to more thoroughly expose candidates to the unusually large number of competencies (23) assessed on the Science subject test. Candidates should bear in mind that the actual test is 50 minutes and features 42 questions.

4. The United States is the only industrialized country in the world that uses the English system of measurement in daily life. What is the rationale for using the metric system in scientific research and engineering?

   A. The metric system is widely used in the world.

   B. The English system is an archaic and outdated system used mostly in business.

   C. The metric system is more precise than the English system.

   D. The English system allows for the easy computation of measurements.

5. The parts of any scientific investigation (observations, question, procedure, etc.) are collectively referred to as which of the following?

   A. An experiment

   B. The scientific method

   C. Scientific inquiry

   D. A six-step approach

6. The most meaningful way to teach students about potential sources of error is to

   A. ask the students to conduct an investigation that follows one procedure and leads to only one conclusion.

   B. provide a lecture of sources of error in famous investigations from the history of science.

   C. perform a demonstration and identify sources of error for students.

   D. ask the students to conduct an investigation that is likely to result in findings of instrument error, random results, and/or unsupported personal opinion.

7. In which of the following ways does deforestation (cutting down) of the rainforests in South America impact residents of the United States?

   A. Deforestation does not impact the U.S. population.

   B. Deforestation results in a decrease in the amount of carbon dioxide in the atmosphere, which decreases the threat of global warming.

   C. Deforestation results in contaminated food crops that may be consumed by U.S. residents.

   D. Deforestation results in an increase in the amount of carbon dioxide in the atmosphere, which contributes to the threat of global warming.

8. Which of the following factors could lead to a decrease in the overall size of the human population?

   A. The number of births being higher than the number of deaths.

   B. An outbreak of a fatal virus with no known cure or vaccine.

   C. The number of births being equal to the number of deaths.

   D. The implementation of a new vaccine that will increase the life span of humans.

9. What is true about using models in teaching to represent the natural world in science?

   A. Models are exact in their representation of the actual phenomena.

   B. Models only work as a representation of actual phenomena if computer generated.

   C. Models will always have differences with the actual phenomena.

   D. Models of natural phenomena will always lead students to form misconceptions.

10. _____ and _____ are two related key concepts that are seen across the science disciplines.

    A. Empirical…supernatural

    B. Constancy…change

    C. Form…function

    D. Both (B) and (C)

11. A rocket burns fuel in bursts out of a nozzle allowing it to maneuver and turn in the vacuum of space. Which of Newton's Laws of Motion explains how this maneuvering is able to occur?

    A. An object in motion stays in motion unless an outside force acts on it.

    B. For every action, there is an equal and opposite reaction.

    C. Fast-moving air has low pressure.

    D. An object at rest stays at rest unless an outside force acts on it.

12. What does using two pulleys in a single system (movable pulley) to lift an object do to the force required compared to lifting the object without the movable pulley?

    A. The use of the movable pulley reduces the amount of force required by one-half.

    B. The use of the movable pulley increases the amount of force required by one-half.

    C. The use of the movable pulley changes the amount of force required to 5 Newtons.

    D. The use of the movable pulley does not change the amount of force required.

13. Which of the following is NOT a physical change?

    A. Mixing an acid and base to form a salt and water

    B. Pouring salt (NaCl) in a glass of water to form a mixture

    C. Cars forming rust from salt and ice on roads in winter

    D. Burning sugar in a crucible in the laboratory

14. In an exploration activity, the students measure 50 ml of water and pour it into one cup, and 50 ml of isopropyl alcohol and pour it into a second cup. They then drop one ice cube in the cup of water and one ice cube in the alcohol. The students observe that the ice cube floats in the water, but sinks in the isopropyl alcohol. Why?

    A. The ice cube is less dense than the water and more dense than the alcohol.

    B. The ice cube is more dense than the water and less dense than the alcohol.

    C. The ice cube has equal density as the water and is more dense than the alcohol.

    D. The ice cube has equal density of both the water and the alcohol.

15. Which of the following causes sound waves?

    A. Vibration of air molecules

    B. Vibration of objects such as strings on a piano

    C. Light waves colliding into sound waves

    D. Force equaling mass times acceleration

16. The chemical formula for water is H_2O. Water is which of the following?

    A. Element

    B. Compound

    C. Atom

    D. Ion

17. Which of the following variables need to be known about an object to calculate its density? Select *all* that apply.

    A.   Volume

    B.   Color

    C.   Mass

    D.   Texture

    E.   Odor

18. What do green plant leaves do with green wavelengths of visible light in the electromagnetic spectrum, and what is the evidence?

    A.   Green plants absorb green wavelengths and the evidence is that the leaves are green in color.

    B.   Green plants refract green wavelengths and the evidence is that the leaves may be green or yellow in color.

    C.   Green plants absorb green wavelengths and the evidence is that the leaves turn red and yellow in the fall.

    D.   Green plants reflect green wavelengths and the evidence is that the leaves are green in color.

19. What is the energy source for each of the following nonrenewable and renewable energy types used to generate electricity for human use, listed in the same order as the energy type?

    Nonrenewable and Renewable Energy Types:

    **Hydroelectric—Nuclear—Fossil Fuel—
    Geothermal—Solar**

    A.   Heat From Beneath Earth's Surface—Coal—Moving Water—Soil—Sun

    B.   Soil—Uranium—Wind—Volcanoes—Heat From Beneath Earth's Surface

    C.   Moving Water—Uranium—Coal—Heat From Beneath Earth's Surface—Sun

    D.   Moving Water—Sun—Heat From Beneath Earth's Surface—Sun—Uranium

20. Which of the following is an example of an exothermic reaction?

    A.   Melting ice cubes

    B.   Combining baking soda and vinegar

    C.   Using a cold pack

    D.   Burning firewood

21. Which item below is true of arteries?

    A.   They carry blood away from the heart.

    B.   They carry blood toward the heart.

    C.   They contain valves to prevent backflow of blood.

    D.   They always transport oxygenated blood.

22. Which of the following is the molecular building block of proteins?

    A.   Monosaccharide

    B.   Glycerol

    C.   Fatty acid

    D.   Amino acid

23. A scientist crosses a male and female guinea pig, both having a brown coat. Brown coat color is dominant over white coat color. Among the offspring, 75% have brown coats and 25% have white coats. The scientist can conclude that the genotypes of the parent guinea pigs were most likely:

    A.   BB × BB

    B.   BB × Bb

    C.   Bb × Bb

    D.   bb × bb

24. Which of the following is true regarding asexual reproduction?

    A. Asexual reproduction is the splitting of one cell, after replicating all of its genetic material, into two daughter cells, with each having genetic material identical to the parent cell.

    B. Asexual reproduction involves the joining of two cells, each consisting of half the number of chromosomes as the parent cells, with their union forming a new cell containing a mixture of genetic materials from each parent cell.

    C. Asexual reproduction involves the exchange of genetic material between two organisms of the same species to produce two identical daughter cells.

    D. Asexual reproduction is a process that occurs only in specialized cells of the organism to produce four daughter cells with half the number of chromosomes as the parent cell.

25. What does the ability of a lizard to lose its tail when pulled represent?

    A. An adaptation for survival when attacked by predators.

    B. A mechanism of reproduction of a new lizard from the tail.

    C. A form of molting as the lizard grows in size.

    D. An indication of environmental stress such as drought.

26. In evolution, the fossil record refers to which of the following?

    A. A large collection of fossils maintained by scientists for use in museums and scientific exhibitions to show the variety of species that lived on Earth long ago.

    B. Evidence that layers of rock are found on Earth in sequence according to age, allowing scientists to trace fossils of organisms buried in these layers during each time period to observe how characteristics of the same species have gradually changed over time.

    C. The finding that appendages of organisms may be homologous, meaning similar in structure, between two different present-day species, such as the bones of the wing of a bat and the arm of a human.

    D. The observation that some species have analogous structures, which are structures with the same function but different evolutionary origin, such as the wing of a bird and wing of a mosquito.

27. Bean seeds are planted in a cup inside a shoebox standing upright on its side with a 3-inch diameter circle cut out of the center of the shoebox close to the bottom of the box, as shown below.

The box is placed in a sunlit room, and the plant is watered regularly without exposing it to sunlight for any length of time. Over time, what will the researcher most likely observe has happened to the bean seeds, and why?

    A. The bean seeds will not have germinated and will die due to lack of sunlight.

    B. The bean seeds will germinate and grow straight up to the top of the box but the plant will be brown, shriveled and soon die due to lack of sunlight.

    C. The bean seeds will germinate and the plant will be observed to bend and grow out of the cutout circle due to a phototropism reaction.

    D. The bean seeds will germinate and the plant will be observed to bend and grow out of the cutout circle due to a geotropism reaction.

28. When a human is exposed to cold temperatures, the blood vessels constrict, and the person experiences shivering and numbness in extremities. When exposed to warmth, the blood vessels expand or dilate, perspiration occurs, and extremities may swell. Responses to cold and warm temperatures occur

    A. because the body is attempting to cause imbalance in the stable condition, or disrupt homeostasis.

    B. to promote the digestion of proteins for a needed supply of energy or impede the digestion of proteins to slow metabolism.

    C. as feedback mechanisms in response to stimuli in the body's effort to maintain homeostasis, or an internal stable condition.

    D. because changes in temperature and light exposure create a blood cell imbalance in the body that may interfere with feedback mechanisms and homeostatic responses.

29. Which of the following represents a symbiotic relationship known as mutualism?

    A. Mistletoe growing on a tree and using the food and nutrients from the tree for its own growth.

    B. A clown fish living among a type of sea anemone, whereby the fish aggressively protects the anemone from predators and the anemone's poison protects the fish from predators.

    C. Poison ivy producing a toxin that irritates the skin of many animal species, thereby protecting the plant from predation.

    D. Spiders building their web on plants to capture insects for food and to have a protective shelter.

30. In the flow of energy from one organism to the next in a food chain, energy is

    A. gained by each organism in the food chain as one organism gains energy from the organism ingested.

    B. lost by each organism in the food chain as one organism loses energy from the organism ingested.

    C. maintained along the food chain with each organism gaining an equal amount of energy from the organism ingested.

    D. not transferred along the food chain from one organism to the next; only inorganic nutrients are transferred.

31. Which of the following is the order of the layers of the Earth if one were to travel from the surface to its center?

    A. Crust, outer core, mantle, inner core

    B. Mantle, crust, inner core, outer core

    C. Outer core, inner core, crust, mantle

    D. Crust, mantle, outer core, inner core

32. What is the main function of Earth's atmosphere?

    A. To protect and preserve life

    B. To prevent the contamination of Earth

    C. To create a vacuum between Earth's crust and its mantle

    D. To recycle water and gases

33. Which type of rock is formed from the other types of rock after it has been subjected to extreme pressure and temperature over time?

    A. Igneous rock

    B. Metamorphic rock

    C. Sedimentary rock

    D. Conglomerate rock

34. Of the following, which best defines transpiration in the water cycle?

    A. The evaporation of water from the surface of lakes

    B. The condensation of water on the leaves of green plants

    C. The evaporation of water from the leaves of green plants

    D. The precipitation of water on the leaves of green plants

35. Which of the following best describes relative humidity and the instrument used to measure it?

    A. Relative humidity is a measure of the wind speed in a specific region and time, and is measured by an anemometer.

    B. Relative humidity is a measure of the amount of moisture in the air in a specific region and time, and is measured by an anemometer.

    C. Relative humidity is a measure of the moisture in the air in a specific region and time, and is measured by a psychrometer.

    D. Relative humidity is a measure of the air pressure in a specific region and time, and is measured by a barometer.

36. Which of the following regions of the U.S. experiences lake-effect snow in the winter?

    A. The Northeast states next to the Atlantic Coast

    B. The Northeast states just east of the Great Lakes

    C. The Midwestern states located in the Great Plains

    D. The Western states just east of the Rocky Mountains

37. What day in the Earth's Northern Hemisphere has the longest daylight hours of the year and why?

    A. The summer solstice because the Northern Hemisphere of the Earth is tilted toward the sun.

    B. The summer solstice because the Earth is closest to the sun at this time of year.

    C. The winter solstice because the Northern Hemisphere of the Earth is tilted toward the sun.

    D. The vernal equinox because the Earth is closest to the sun at this time of year.

38. Which of the following are objects in our solar system?

    A. Asteroids, planets, moons, and comets

    B. Planets, asteroids, moons, and black holes

    C. Planets, meteoroids, asteroids, and black holes

    D. Asteroids, Milky Way, quasars, and comets

39. Fossils of clam-like shells have been found deep in the sedimentary rock in Texas. These fossils indicate

    A. the state of Texas was once covered with small streams.

    B. the state of Texas was once covered by a sea or ocean.

    C. the state of Texas was once seismically active.

    D. there once were mountain ranges across the state of Texas.

40. In radiometric dating, scientists use which of the following information to determine the age of a fossil or rock?

    A. The appearance of the fossil or rock

    B. The location of the fossil or rock

    C. The presence of parent versus daughter isotopes in a fossil or rock

    D. The number of fossils within a rock

41. In Ms. Hernandez's class, the students are studying what plants need to survive. The students generate ideas to share. One need they identify for survival is food. When Ms. Hernandez asks the students where they think plants get their food, she notices that several students respond, "Plants get food from [eating] the soil." Which of the following is the best way to help students change this misconception that plants "eat the soil" to the scientifically accepted conception that plants make their own food from carbon dioxide and water through photosynthesis?

A. Have students conduct an experiment in which they plant seeds in two different containers, one in the dark and one in the light, and make observations over time.

B. Conduct a lecture/discussion session with students, explaining the process of photosynthesis by using pictures and diagrams.

C. Have students conduct an experiment in which they measure the mass of two pots of dry soil before planting seeds in the two pots; Then, after the plants have grown, measure the mass of the pots of dry soil again to see whether there has been a change.

D. Ask students to consult their textbook and search the Internet for information on how plants get food.

42. After students concluded their inquiry lab experiments about respiration, Mr. Davis provided real-life examples of anaerobic respiration. He used the example of intensely exercising muscle cells breaking the bonds of sugar molecules to release energy without the use of oxygen (anaerobically). This energy, which is in the form of ATP energy, will be added to the ATP energy made available to the body when sugar is metabolized through aerobic respiration (with the use of oxygen). Mr. Davis described playing football, wrestling, and boxing in his examples. Which of the following is a primary concern with Mr. Davis's approach to teaching?

A. The content of cell respiration is abstract, thus the teacher should not have used inquiry in teaching students this topic.

B. The teacher used only male-dominated sports examples, whereas he should have given a variety of examples that would appeal to a wider range of his students' interests.

C. The content the teacher is presenting to students is not accurate because it is not possible to carry on respiration in the absence of oxygen.

D. The teacher should have described anaerobic respiration and provided real-life examples before the students carried out their inquiry activities.

43. Mr. Freeman conducted an inquiry lesson in which his class of 30 students worked in groups of three and first read and recorded the room temperature with two thermometers. Then each student group taped one thermometer on a wall of the classroom near the floor, and the second thermometer on a wall of the classroom near the ceiling. After an hour, the students collected their thermometers and again read and recorded the temperature on each. What would be the best strategy to use next to help students reach the desired conclusion that the air near the ceiling is warmer than the air near the floor (demonstrating that warm air rises and cold air sinks, or the concept of convection)?

A. After students have collected their starting and ending temperatures on their thermometers, show a well-designed PowerPoint presentation with diagrams describing and showing convection. Follow the PowerPoint with discussion about other examples of convection, such as hot air balloons and a film about tornadoes.

B. After students have collected their starting and ending temperatures on their thermometers, ask each student group to review their starting and ending temperatures. Then ask each group to make a graph of their findings and develop a conclusion based on their group's measurement and results.

C. After students have collected their starting and ending temperatures on their thermometers, ask one student from each group to enter their starting and ending temperatures for their floor and ceiling thermometers on a class spreadsheet. Using all class data, ask students to make a line graph with one line showing starting and ending floor temperatures and another line showing the same for ceiling temperatures. Ask students to calculate the average starting and ending temperatures for ceiling and floor thermometers using class data.

D. After students have collected their starting and ending temperatures on their thermometers, have students conduct an experiment using a beaker filled with ice. Students measure the temperature of the ice and then place the beaker on a hot plate. After turning on the hot plate, the students measure and record the temperature of the ice every 30 seconds as it changes state from solid to liquid and then reaches the boiling point. The student groups record, share, and analyze findings in class discussion.

44. Which of the following are the best instruments to use in measuring the density of a relatively small, irregularly shaped rock?

A. A beaker of water and a metric tape measure.

B. A graduated cylinder of water and a metric tape measure.

C. A beaker of water and a triple beam or electronic balance.

D. A graduated cylinder of water and a triple beam or electronic balance.

45. Mr. Thomas, a seventh-grade science teacher, wants to use formative assessments to evaluate his students' authentic understanding of the process of scientific inquiry during their lab time. Which of the following would best be suited to this?

A. Do an item analysis of scores on the most recent science standardized test, and chart where students are making progress.

B. Evaluate the content of what students are writing in a scientific notebook by using a teacher-designed rubric.

C. Give a true/false quiz covering content in the most recent science unit, and go over the answers in class.

D. Test students on their knowledge of the vocabulary terms associated with the science unit by using a fill-in-the-blank format.

46. Which of the following best describes the primary role of science notebooks in the science classroom?

A. An opportunity for students to reflect on the day's activities, similar to a diary.

B. An opportunity for students to act like scientists by recording and exploring ideas related to investigative inquiries.

C. An opportunity for the teacher to assess grammar skills.

D. An opportunity for students to act like scientists by writing to inform, explain, persuade, and explore.

Science Practice Test 1: Answer Key

Test Item	Answer	Competency 809-
1.	C	001
2.	B	001
3.	C	002
4.	C	002
5.	C	003
6.	D	003
7.	D	004
8.	B	004
9.	C	005
10.	D	005
11.	B	006
12.	A	006
13.	B	007
14.	A	007
15.	A	009
16.	B	008
17.	A, C	008
18.	D	009
19.	C	010
20.	D	010
21.	A	011
22.	D	011
23.	C	012

Test Item	Answer	Competency 809-
24.	A	012
25.	A	013
26.	B	013
27.	C	014
28.	C	014
29.	B	015
30.	B	015
31.	D	016
32.	A	016
33.	B	017
34.	C	017
35.	C	018
36.	B	018
37.	A	019
38.	A	019
39.	B	020
40.	C	020
41.	C	021
42.	B	021
43.	C	022
44.	D	022
45.	B	023
46.	D	023

Science Practice Test 1: Detailed Answers

1. C.

Option (C) is correct because presenting the safety precautions is the first step in any laboratory investigation. The safety procedures should be printed on the students' laboratory sheets, posted on the walls of the classroom, and read aloud to students before beginning any investigation. Option (A) is incorrect because giving students the materials should not be done prior to a thorough explanation and discussion of both the safety precautions and the laboratory procedures. Failure to do so before allowing students to begin could have disastrous results and cause harm to students. Option (B) is incorrect because providing the "answers" and giving away the concepts to students should not be done before an inquiry investigation—students are to discover the concepts based on their own experiences and data. Option (D) is incorrect because although cleanup instructions are important, these instructions are not to precede a discussion on safety. Safety precautions must be implemented throughout the investigation, including during cleanup activities. **(809-001 Managing Learning Activities)**

2. B.

Option (B) is the correct answer. It is an important safety measure to keep all chemicals in a locked cabinet and ensure the key is not accessible to students. The door to the laboratory storeroom should also be locked. Students should never have access to chemicals without close supervision. The teacher is liable for any accidents due to negligence, such as leaving dangerous chemicals in an unlocked cabinet; therefore, option (A) is incorrect. The eyewash station (C) and fire extinguisher (D) are best placed near areas where chemicals or fire are used, but do not specifically pertain to students' access to chemicals. **(809-001 Managing Learning Activities)**

3. C.

Option (C) is correct because in science the triple beam balance is the instrument or piece of equipment used to measure mass. Option (A), the meter stick, measures length. Option (B), the graduated cylinder, measures liquid amount or volume. Option (D), the sling psychrometer, measures relative humidity. **(809-002 Use of Tools, Materials, Equipment, and Technologies)**

4. C.

Option (C) is the correct answer. The metric system is a very precise system that allows for the measurement of very small amounts of matter. For example, the metric system uses measurements divided into thousands (millimeters or milligrams), while the English system uses larger units of measurement, such as inches and ounces. Options (A) and (B) contain possible true statements and opinions, but they fail to address the question. Option (D) is incorrect; the English system does *not* have a simple way to compute measures. On the other hand, the metric system is a base-10 system, and the computations are typically easier. **(809-002 Use of Tools, Materials, Equipment, and Technologies)**

5. C.

Option (C) is the correct answer. Option (A) is not correct because not all scientific investigations use an experimental method. Option (B) is not correct because there is no single scientific method. Option (D) is not correct because there is no specific number of steps or sequence that makes an approach a scientific investigation. This leaves scientific inquiry, option (C), as the correct answer because it is general enough to describe all scientific investigations. **(809-003 Process of Scientific Inquiry and the History and Nature of Science)**

6. D.

The best way to teach students about potential sources of error is to have the students experience it themselves. This is what makes Options (B) and (C) incorrect. Option (A) is incorrect because types of error will likely be limited to those associated with the procedure or techniques. Allowing students to do more open inquiry will likely lead to more error personally experienced by nearly every student. **(809-003 Process of Scientific Inquiry and the History and Nature of Science)**

7. D.

Option (D) is correct because the high quantity of trees and massive foliage in South America carry on photosynthesis, which utilizes carbon dioxide gas to produce glucose, thus decreasing the amount of carbon dioxide in the atmosphere. Carbon dioxide gas in excess has been shown to absorb heat and increase warming of the atmosphere. If the foliage is removed, there will be fewer plants to take carbon dioxide out of the atmosphere, and it will accumulate in ever-increasing amounts. Global warming impacts the growth of food plants elsewhere across the globe, including the U.S., and these food plants have optimal growth within particular temperature and climatic ranges, which could be detrimental to their growth if conditions change. Option (A) is incorrect because there are interactions and interrelationships between what happens in one part of the globe and another. Option (B) is incorrect because the carbon dioxide in the atmosphere will increase rather than decrease. Option (C) is incorrect in that deforestation is not related to crop contamination. **(809-004 Science's Impact on Students' Daily Lives and Its Influence on Personal and Societal Decisions)**

8. B.

When a population is exposed to a new virus, with no means of fighting it, the virus is able to spread throughout the population. If the virus is deadly, the population is quickly impacted and can decrease in overall number, making Option (B) the correct answer. Answer (A) is incorrect because when the number of births is higher than the number of deaths in a population, the overall population will increase. Option (C) is incorrect because when the number of births is the same as the number of deaths in a population, the population

size is stable with neither an increase nor a decrease. Option (D) is incorrect because when individuals live longer, the overall population size will increase because more individuals are remaining in the population. **(809-004 Science's Impact on Students' Daily Lives and Its Influence on Personal and Societal Decisions)**

9. C.

Option (C) is correct because it is not possible to create a model that is exactly the same as the actual scientific phenomena or object being represented. A ball-and-stick model of molecules is only a representation of an atom; the ionic or covalent bonding is due to the charges in the atoms, particularly electrons, which cannot be adequately represented by a stick. Option (A) is incorrect because no model is exact in its representation; it is impossible to represent every detail of a phenomenon with a model—it will simply be the real phenomenon instead. For example, you can make a marsh ecosystem in the classroom in an aquarium to represent an actual marsh, but it could not possibly have all of the elements of the actual marsh ecosystem in nature. Option (B) is incorrect because although computer-generated models are often useful, many physical models are equally or more useful than those that are computer-generated. Making and flying an actual paper airplane to represent real airplane flight gives learners a different experience than making virtual paper airplanes on the computer. Option (D) is incorrect because, although sometimes students may develop misconceptions through the use of models, if implemented correctly, the models will actually help students build sound understandings of natural phenomena. In using models, teachers should ask the students to point out differences between the actual phenomena and the model. Students should understand that the model is simply a tool to help us visualize the natural phenomena but that they have limitations in their applicability. **(809-005 Unifying Concepts and Processes)**

10. D.

Option (D) is the correct answer because the concepts of constancy, change, form, and function are seen across the science disciplines. Constancy and change are seen in the geologic process, as well as biological processes. Form and function explain the structure of matter, the Earth, and living organisms. Option (A) is incorrect because the science disciplines do not address supernatural concepts. Science only addresses concepts for which observations and data and can be collected and evaluated. **(809-005 Unifying Concepts and Processes)**

11. B.

Option (B) is the correct answer because burning the fuel causes the gases released to be expelled at a very high speed out of a nozzle, which is computer-controlled in the desired direction to push the rocket in the opposite direction. This is Newton's third law, that for every action there is an equal and opposite reaction. Options (A) and (D) are incorrect because the force is not from outside of the rocket in this case. Option (C) is incorrect as it is a simplified version of Bernoulli's principle of lift. **(809-006 Forces and Motion and Their Relationships)**

12. A.

Option (A) is correct. A single pulley and movable pulleys are classified as simple machines. The amount of force required to lift an object with 2 pulleys in a single system reduces the force required to lift the object by one-half. Option (B) is incorrect because the movable pulley will not increase, but rather decrease the amount of force required. Option (C) is incorrect because the force will not be changed to a definite value of force; the reduction of force to be applied depends on the weight of the object to be lifted and the number of pulleys in the system. Option (D) is incorrect because the use of a movable pulley does reduce the amount of force required to lift the object. For more information, see: *http://www.ehow.com/how-does_5231254_much-weight-pulley-off.html.* **(809-006 Forces and Motion and Their Relationships)**

13. B.

Option (B) is correct because mixing salt (NaCl) in water does not change the substance in any way and it is reversible. The substance in the water is still salt, and if the water is evaporated, salt crystals will again be restored. Option (A) is incorrect because mixing an acid and base is a neutralization reaction—a chemical reaction that forms new substances, namely a salt and water. For example, mixing hydrochloric acid (HCl) with the base sodium hydroxide (NaOH) produces NaCl and H_2O. Option (C)

is incorrect because rust is the chemical reaction between oxygen in the atmosphere and iron (FeO). The salt and ice on roads in the winter are electrolytes that wear away the protective finish on automobiles and expose the metal to oxygen where rust can form (FeO). Option (D) is incorrect because burning is a chemical reaction in which oxygen combines with the substance to form a new substance. Burning sugar, a hydrocarbon-based substance, will form carbon dioxide and water. **(809-007 Physical Properties of and Changes in Matter)**

14. A.

Option (A) is correct because for something to float, it must be less dense than the liquid it is in, and for an object to sink, it must be more dense than the liquid it is in. Density is a measure of how tightly packed the matter is (mass) within a given amount of space (volume) or (D) = M/V. Water is unique with respect to its density because it is the only substance on Earth that is less dense in solid form (ice) than in liquid form (water); therefore the solid form floats in its own liquid. Alcohol is less dense (molecules are less tightly packed) than water, so the ice cube sinks. Option (B) is incorrect because if the ice cube was more dense than liquid water, it would sink in the water, and if less dense than the alcohol, it would float in this liquid. Option (C) is incorrect because if a substance has equal density to the liquid it is in, it would be suspended in the middle of the liquid. This statement is incorrect even though the second part of it—that the ice is more dense than the alcohol—is correct. Option (D) is incorrect because again, equal density means the ice cube would be suspended in the water (neither sink nor float) and in the alcohol. **(809-007 Physical Properties of and Changes in Matter)**

15. A.

Option (A) is correct because although sound initiates with vibration of an object, the sound waves are caused by the vibration of the air around the object, not the object itself. The vibrating air reaches the human eardrum, causing it to vibrate, which is sensed by the auditory nerve and carried to the brain for interpretation as sound. Option (B) is incorrect, as previously explained, in that it is not the object itself vibrating that causes sound, it is the movement or vibration of the air molecules in the vicinity of the object. Option (C) is incorrect because light colliding with sound waves is not the cause of sound, and in fact, light waves travel much faster than sound waves. Option (D) is incorrect because this is the formula for Newton's Second Law of Motion. **(809-009 Energy and Interactions between Matter and Energy)**

16. B.

Option (B) is correct because water is made up of two or more different kinds of atoms, hydrogen (H) and oxygen (O), which is a compound. Choice (A) is incorrect because elements are made of only one kind of atom. Option (C) is incorrect because water is made up of more than a single atom. Option (D) is incorrect because ions are positively or negatively charged atoms or molecules and water is a stable molecule. **(809-008 Chemical Properties of and Changes in Matter)**

17. A., C.

This item asks you to select all that apply. Choices (A) and (C) are correct. Mass and volume are the two variables necessary to calculate the density of an object using the formula D = M/V. Color, Texture, and Odor—choices (B), (D), and (E)—are physical characteristics of an object, but are not needed or relevant in calculating its density. **(Competency 809-008 Chemical Properties of and Changes in Matter)**

18. D.

Option (D) is correct because the colors we see around us are the wavelengths of light reflected by that object or substance. Green plants therefore do not absorb green light waves, but this color of visible light of the electromagnetic spectrum reflects off its surface and our eyes see the color green. Option (A) is incorrect because if the plant had absorbed green wavelengths, the color green would not be seen by our eyes because it would be absorbed into the substance of the leaves. Option (B) is incorrect because refraction is the bending of light rather than reflection, so the color would be bent rather than reflected to our eyes. Option (C) is incorrect because green plants in the growing season reflect and do not absorb green wavelengths of light, so the color we see is green. However, in the fall, deciduous trees, which are plants in which the leaves change color and fall off in the

winter, stop producing chlorophyll (the green pigment in plants), and instead produce other pigments, including red and yellow, as they become dormant. The red and yellow colors to which these leaves change indicate a shift in the wavelengths of light reflected. If our eyes see the color red, then the leaves are reflecting light in the red wavelength band of the electromagnetic spectrum. **(809-009 Energy and Interactions between Matter and Energy)**

19. C.

Option (C) is correct in that hydroelectric energy produces electricity through fast-moving water (e.g., the generators that tap the power of Niagara Falls). Nuclear energy utilizes the radioactivity of uranium. Fossil fuel energy produces electricity through the burning of coal, oil, and/or natural gas. Geothermal energy produces electricity by harnessing the energy beneath the Earth's surface to produce electricity. Solar energy captures the energy of the sun to produce electricity. Options (A), (B), and (D) are listed in the incorrect order and/or are incorrect sources of energy. **(809-010 Energy Transformations and the Conservation of Matter and Energy)**

20. D.

Option (D) is the correct answer. Exothermic reactions give off heat during the reaction. Endothermic reactions do the opposite: absorb heat during the reaction. Option (A) is incorrect because melting ice cubes is a physical change and is not a reaction. Options (B) and (C) are incorrect because although these are examples of chemical reactions, heat is not given off during the reaction. **(809-010 Energy Transformations and the Conservation of Matter and Energy)**

21. A.

Arteries always carry blood away from the heart. Veins always carry blood to the heart. There is one artery—the pulmonary artery—that carries blood away from the right side of the heart directly to the lungs and thus does not carry oxygenated blood, making option (D) incorrect. Options (B) and (C) are incorrect because only veins contain valves to prevent backflow of blood as the blood is returning to the heart from all parts of the body. **(809-011 The Structure and Function of Living Things)**

22. D.

Proteins are made up of a chain of amino acid molecules that are arranged in a particular order for that specific protein (for example, hormones, enzymes, hair, fingernails), making option (D) the correct option. There are 20 amino acids, arranged in a vast variety of sequences, with each sequence and shape that results being unique for that particular protein. Option (A) is incorrect because a monosaccharide is the building block of carbohydrates. Options (B) and (C) are incorrect because these molecules are the components of lipids (fats). **(809-011 The Structure and Function of Living Things)**

23. C.

In using the Punnett square diagram, the parental genotypes can be determined as follows:

Parent 1

	B	b
B	BB	Bb
b	Bb	b

Parent 2

As shown in the Punnett square, the result of the cross of Bb for one parent and Bb for the other parent is 75% with BB and Bb and 25% bb. The "B" allele for *brown* coat is dominant over the "b" allele for *white* coat, so the physical appearance or *phenotype* of 3 out of 4 or 75% of the offspring will be a brown coat. The recessive gene will appear in 1 out of 4, or 25% of the offspring, which is represented in the Punnett square diagram as "bb." Any other cross will not produce these percentages of brown and white coats in the offspring. Options (A) and (B) result in 100% of the offspring with the phenotype of brown coats. Option (D) results in 100% of the offspring with the phenotype of white coats. **(809-012 Reproduction and the Mechanisms of Heredity)**

24. A.

Asexual reproduction is accomplished through a process of binary fission, or mitosis, in which the DNA (genetic material) is first replicated, and, after a series of events, the parent cell divides into two daughter cells with genetic material that is identical to the one parent cell and to each other. Options (B), (C), and (D) all describe sexual reproduction, where parent cells divide into four daughter cells containing half the genetic material (DNA) as the original parent. The daughter cell may be a sperm or egg cell, for example. The daughter cell of one organism joins with the daughter cell of another organism of the same species to form a new cell that has a combination of genetic material from both parent cells. **(809-012 Reproduction and the Mechanisms of Heredity)**

25. A.

Lizards' tails easily drop off when touched or pulled as a form of adaptation that allows the lizard to survive by escaping from predators. The tail will grow back in time. However, a new lizard will not grow from the detached tail, making option (B) the incorrect choice. Lizards do not undergo molting, making option (C) incorrect. Molting is a characteristic of some insects and crustaceans. The lizard also does not lose its tail due to environmental stresses, making option (D) incorrect. **(809-013 Adaptations of Organisms and the Theory of Evolution)**

26. B.

The fossil record is one line of evidence for evolution, which refers to the layers of rocks that indicate periods of time throughout Earth's history, making option (B) the correct answer. These layers contain fossils that show clear patterns of change in species over time. Scientists now know that these changes were due to DNA mutations that provided the organism, and subsequently the offspring, with more favorable traits for survival in that environment. Option (A) is incorrect because it does not refer to the fossil record found in rock layers and sequencing according to geologic age. Options (C) and (D) are incorrect in terms of the fossil record, but do represent other lines of evidence for evolution in the area of morphology, namely homologous and analogous structures, respectively. **(809-013 Adaptations of Organisms and the Theory of Evolution)**

27. C.

The plant will grow and bend toward the light due to chemicals called auxins that create specific responses to stimuli in the plant from the environment. The environmental stimulus that produces a chemical response directing plant stems and leaves to grow toward light is called phototropism, so option (C) is correct. Option (A) is incorrect because seeds do not need sunlight to germinate, only the proper temperature for that particular plant species, as well as water and air (oxygen). Option (B) is incorrect because there will be some light entering the box through the circle cutout opening at the bottom, so although it may not be the healthiest of plants, it will not be entirely shriveled and will likely survive. Option (D) is incorrect because a geotropism is a plant's response to gravity, typically presented by the roots growing downward due to gravity. **(809-014 Regulatory Mechanisms and Behavior)**

28. C.

The body undergoes a series of feedback mechanisms in response to cold and warm temperatures in an effort to maintain a constant internal temperature. This is critical in maintaining an internal stable condition, or homeostasis, making option (C) the correct option. These responses conserve energy when exposed to prolonged cold temperatures and release energy when exposed to prolonged warm temperatures. The mechanisms described in blood vessels constricting or dilating, the body shivering or perspiring, and numbness (indicating lack of blood flow to extremities to maintain warmth and blood flow to critical internal organs) or swelling of extremities (indicating blood going to extremities to cool critical internal organs) are responses to the body's efforts to maintain homeostasis. Option (A) is incorrect because it describes processes that would be in opposition to maintaining homeostasis. Option (B) is incorrect because it describes digestive processes that are not part of the scenario described in this item to maintain homeostasis. Option (D) is incorrect because a blood cell imbalance will not cause the conditions described in the scenario. **(809-014 Regulatory Mechanisms and Behavior)**

29. B.

Mutualism is a form of symbiosis in which both organisms benefit from the relationship, making option (B) the correct option. Option (A) is an example of another form of symbiosis called parasitism, in which one organism benefits from the relationship at the expense of the other. Option (C) is not a form of symbiosis. Option (D) is a form of symbiosis called commensalism, in which one organism benefits and the other organism

neither benefits nor is harmed. **(809-015 The Relationships between Organisms and the Environment)**

30. B.

Energy is lost from one organism to the next along the food chain, making option (B) the correct option. The energy originates from the sun and is transferred to green plants in photosynthesis, where it is locked within the chemical bonds of simple sugars (glucose). Thus, green plants contain the most energy from the sun in the chemical bonds of the glucose molecules it forms. As each organism in the chain ingests an organism (sun → grass → rabbit → coyotes → decomposers), some of the original sun energy has already been lost to support the life functions of that organism, so energy content reduces as you progress along the food chain, with the most energy being supplied to the plants, followed by primary consumers, secondary consumers, and so on with the lowest levels of energy being available for decomposers. Option (A) is incorrect because energy is lost and not gained through the food chain. Option (C) is incorrect because energy is not maintained at the same levels since some energy is always used by the organism to carry on its own life functions. Option (D) is incorrect because energy along with inorganic nutrients is transferred from one organism to the next in a food chain. **(809-015 The Relationships between Organisms and the Environment)**

31. D.

Option (D) shows the correct order of the layers of the Earth from surface to center: crust, mantle, outer core, inner core. Options (A), (B), and (C) show an incorrect sequence of the layers of the Earth. For more information see *http://www.factmonster.com* (search "earth structure") **(809-016 The Structure and Function of Earth Systems)**

32. A.

Option (A) is the correct answer. The main function of the atmosphere is to serve as a buffer between space and the Earth's crust. This buffer provides the ideal conditions to protect and preserve life on Earth. Options (B) and (D) present two functions that can be linked to the atmosphere: recycling water and gases; however, they fail to highlight the real function of the atmosphere.

Option (C) is completely incorrect: the atmosphere is above the crust, not beneath it. **(809-016 The Structure and Function of Earth Systems)**

33. B.

Option (B), metamorphic rock, is correct because this type of rock is formed from igneous or sedimentary rock that is deep in the Earth and has been subjected to extreme pressure and temperature. Metamorphic rock may also exhibit signs of the Earth's folding due to plates colliding, which may also bend and twist the rock. Option (A), igneous rock, is the rock produced from hot lava or magma prior to exposure to pressure and/or folding. Option (C), sedimentary rock, is rock formed from eroded rock carried in bodies of water as sediments such as clays and sand. The sediments settle out of the water and form rock such as sandstone and shale. Option (D), conglomerate rock, is coarse-grained sedimentary rock. In conglomerates, rocks of different shapes and sizes are cemented together. See *http://flexiblelearning.auckland.ac.nz/rocks_minerals/rocks/index.html*. **(809-017 Cycles in Earth Systems)**

34. C.

Option (C) is correct. Transpiration is the evaporation of water from the stomata located on the underside of leaves on plants. Liquid water is absorbed through the roots and is carried through the plant in small vessels called the xylem. Water that is not needed or excreted evaporates, changing from liquid to gas (water vapor) as it leaves the stomata. This moisture in the air from transpiration contributes to humidity and to cloud formation, along with water evaporated from lakes, rivers, and oceans, which is eventually precipitated to Earth again in the water cycle. Option (A) is incorrect because evaporation from lakes and other bodies of water is simply evaporation—molecules of liquid water on the surface leave the surface in the form of water vapor. Option (B) is incorrect because condensation is water changing from water vapor (gas) to liquid water. Option (D) is incorrect because precipitation is water falling to Earth from clouds in the form of rain, snow, sleet, or hail. **(809-017 Cycles in Earth Systems)**

35. C.

Option (C) is correct because relative humidity is the percentage of water in the air and is measured by a psychrometer. Options (A) and (B) are incorrect because an anemometer measures wind speed. Option (D) is incorrect because humidity is not a measure of air pressure. See *http://www.space.com/17683-earth-atmosphere.html* **(809-018 The Role of Energy in Weather and Climate)**

36. B.

Option (B) is correct because those states just east of the Great Lakes, such as New York and Pennsylvania experience the most lake-effect snows. The air contains water evaporated over the Great Lakes (e.g., Lake Erie and Lake Ontario). As the air mass moves east it cools, which causes precipitation in the form of snow if the air is below the freezing temperature of water. Option (A) is incorrect because large bodies of water tend to keep the areas near the coast warmer than land. This is because water has high specific heat, meaning it cools off and warms up more slowly than any other substance on Earth. This is why coastal areas have comparatively warmer winters and cooler summers compared to inland regions at the same latitude. In addition, storms in the U.S. tend to travel from west to east. Options (C) and (D) are incorrect because these regions are not located near significant bodies of water. **(809-018 The Role of Energy in Weather and Climate)**

37. A.

Option (A) is correct because at the location in the Earth's orbit that is the summer solstice, the tilt of the Earth in the Northern Hemisphere is facing toward the sun, making the daylight hours longer than at other times of the year. On the date of the summer solstice, typically June 20 or 21, or the first day of summer, the Northern Hemisphere has approximately 15 hours of sunlight and 9 hours of darkness. Option (B) is incorrect because first, the Earth's distance does not impact daylight hours, and second, the Earth is actually farther away from the sun at the summer solstice than it is at the winter solstice (on or around December 21). Option (C) is incorrect because the Northern Hemisphere is tilted away from the sun at the winter solstice, with 9 hours of daylight, and 15 hours of darkness. So the winter solstice has the shortest number of daylight hours than any other day of the year. The Vernal Equinox occurs in the spring in the Northern Hemisphere, typically around March 20 or the first day of spring, and has an equal number of daylight hours and darkness hours (12 hours each). **(809-019 The Characteristics of the Solar System and the Universe)**

38. A.

Asteroids, planets, moons, and comets are all objects in the solar system. Black holes and quasars are theorized objects in distant galaxies, and the Milky Way is the name of our own cluster of stars or galaxy in which the solar system (sun, planets, dwarf planets, comets, asteroids, and meteoroids) reside. **(809-019 The Characteristics of the Solar System and the Universe)**

39. B.

Option (B) is the correct answer. Modern-day clams are found in both fresh and saltwater habitats, such as seas and oceans. Based on current understandings of clams, it is assumed that clam-like fossils would have inhabited the same environments. When fossils of fresh and/or saltwater organisms are found on currently dry locations, it is assumed that at some point in Earth's history, the location was once covered in water. Option (A) is incorrect because Texas currently has small streams. Option (C) is incorrect because fossils would not be the only indicator of seismic activity. There would also need to be evidence in the rock layers. Option (D) is incorrect because clams are not found on mountain ranges and would not indicate the presence of mountain ranges in Texas's history. **(809-020 The History of the Earth System)**

40. C.

Option (C) is the correct answer. Radioactive parent isotopes decay at particular rates in daughter isotopes. When scientists examine fossils and/or rocks, they can measure the amount of parent and daughter isotopes. With these amounts known, the scientists can then determine the age of the fossil and/or rock. Options (A), (B), and (D) are incorrect because none of these characteristics are used to determine the age of a fossil or rock. **(809-020 The History of the Earth System)**

41. C.

Option (C) is the correct answer. This investigation provides a concrete experience for students to observe that there is no change in the mass of the soil from the beginning to the end of the experiment. They observe that the plant must not be "eating" the soil, but the source of food must be something else. This experiment should be followed by a series of investigations designed to help students discover the source of food as a combination of carbon dioxide and water in the presence of light, thereby constructing the concept of photosynthesis. Option (A) is incorrect because, although student-centered, the concept discovered would be that "plants need light to grow." The seeds planted and placed in the dark will germinate but later die due to lack of sunlight, whereas those placed in the light will germinate, grow, and thrive. This experiment would help students discover the role of light in photosynthesis. Option (B) is incorrect because students do not learn best through lecture/discussion, which is often abstract and meaningless to them. Further, students do not tend to alter their misconceptions when they are simply "told"—they need to discover for themselves. Option (D) is incorrect because students will not know what to focus on in their readings and online searches and will likely be inundated with too much information, making a change from misconception to a more scientifically accepted conception unlikely. **(809-021 Teaching Science and How Students Learn Science)**

42. B.

Option (B) is the correct answer. The examples teachers provide in class should tap into the prior knowledge of students to help promote learning. In the examples given by Mr. Davis, only the prior knowledge of males in his class who have had these types of experiences was activated. Teachers must be careful not to use examples that appeal to only certain groups (e.g., based on gender, ethnicity), which marginalizes the rest of the students. Teachers must develop a wide range of examples that will address the interests of all students in the classroom, making option (B) the best response. Options (A) and (D) address the issue of students needing hands-on, concrete, and inquiry-based experiences (rather than lecture explanations) to best learn science, so Mr. Davis is correct in using inquiry to introduce the topic. Option (C) is incorrect because it is possible for cells to carry on certain types of respiration without the use of oxygen (e.g., anaerobic respiration and fermentation). **(809-021 Teaching Science and How Students Learn Science)**

43. C.

Option (C) is the correct answer. In this scenario, the students use the data collected to make sense of their findings. They are using a larger set of data because they are sharing with all groups. Science requires many trials of the same experiment before conclusions can be drawn. Collecting data in several repeated experiments helps the researcher discover patterns and also errors and outliers. The data in this scenario are represented graphically and mathematically, which also promotes sound interpretations. Option (A) is incorrect because students did not use their own collected data to draw conclusions and gain understanding of the concepts—their work was not *used*, so it became an irrelevant activity. Option (B) is incorrect because sound scientific conclusions cannot be drawn based on one set of data but are accomplished by repeating the experiment several times or days in a row using the whole class's set of data. Option (D) is incorrect because interpretations of the first experiment were not made, and no conclusions were drawn. In addition, the second experiment is not related to the first experiment—the first leads to the concept of convection, whereas the second leads to concept of phase changes in water. **(809-022 The Process of Scientific Inquiry and Its Role in Science Instruction)**

44. D.

Option (D) is the correct answer. Density is the amount of matter (mass) packed into a given amount of space (volume), and is measured by determining the mass of a substance divided by its volume, or density = mass/volume ($D = m/v$). To measure the density of an irregularly shaped object such as a rock, the proper instruments are a balance, to measure mass, and a graduated cylinder with water, to measure volume. The triple beam or electronic balance will provide the mass of the rock in grams. The volume of the irregularly shaped rock is obtained by filling a graduated cylinder one-half to two-thirds with water. The level of water in the graduated cylinder in milliliters is recorded. The rock is carefully dropped into the graduated cylinder, and

the change in the level of water (or the amount of water that was "displaced" by the rock) in milliliters is measured. One milliliter (liquid volume measure) is equal to one cubic centimeter (solid volume measure); thus, the change in water level after adding the rock is the volume of the rock. These values are then used in the formula ($D = m/v$) to determine the rock's density. Options (A), (B), and (C) are not the proper instruments to use in determining an irregularly shaped object's density. A beaker does not provide a precise enough measure of the amount of water displaced, or the volume of the rock. A measuring tape is not accurate for determining the volume of an irregularly shaped object. The proper determination of density requires the use of instruments that will measure the volume and the mass of the object. **(809-022 The Process of Scientific Inquiry and Its Role in Science Instruction)**

45. B.

Option (B) is correct because it focuses on the curriculum-based content the students are performing on a regular basis. Because the science notebook contains understandings about related science content, and a rubric is used (informal assessment), it is best suited to assessing students' knowledge about scientific inquiry. For instance, students can describe what the lab process was like and what they did during the process, they can make predictions, and so forth. Options (A), (C), and (D) are less authentic forms of assessment because they are based more on measuring student recall of knowledge rather than deeper understanding. **(809-023 Assessments and Assessment Practices)**

46. D.

The best answer is Option (D) because it describes the major outcomes desired of students in their writing and is also consistent with how scientists use their science notebooks. Option (A) is not correct because scientists do not use science notebooks as a diary but rather as a reflection focused on the ongoing investigation. Option (B) is reasonable, but it leaves students only with the act of recording their observations and "exploring their ideas." Option (D) includes the range of purposes seen in scientists' notebooks. **(Competency 809-023 Assessments and Assessment Practices)**

TExES Core Subjects 4–8
Appendix

Definitions and Formulas for the TExES Math 4–8

Calculus

First Derivative: $f'(x) = \dfrac{dy}{dx}$

Second Derivative: $f''(x) = \dfrac{d^2y}{dx^2}$

Probability

$P(A \text{ or } B) = P(A) + P(B) - P(A \text{ and } B)$

$P(A \text{ and } B) = P(A)P(B|A) = P(B)P(A|B)$

Algebra

i $\qquad\qquad i^2 = -1$

A^{-1} $\qquad\qquad$ inverse of matrix A

$A = P\left(1 = \dfrac{r}{n}\right)^{nt}$ $\quad$ Compound interest, where A is the final value

$\qquad\qquad\qquad\qquad\qquad$ P is the principal

$\qquad\qquad\qquad\qquad\qquad$ r is the interest rate

$\qquad\qquad\qquad\qquad\qquad$ t is the term

$\qquad\qquad\qquad\qquad\qquad$ n is the number of divisions within the term

$[x] = n$ $\qquad\qquad$ Greatest integer function, where n is the integer such that $n \leq x < n + 1$

Geometry

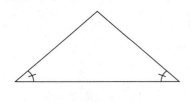

Congruent Angles

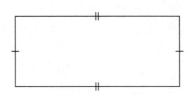

Congruent Sides

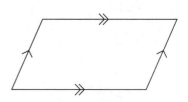

Parallel Sides

Circumference of a Circle: $\quad C = 2\pi r$

Volume

Cylinder: (area of base) $\times$ height

Cone: $\dfrac{1}{3}$ (area of base) $\times$ height

Sphere: $\dfrac{4}{3}\pi r^3$

Prism: (area of base) $\times$ height

Area

Triangle: $\dfrac{1}{2}$ (base $\times$ height)

Rhombus: $\dfrac{1}{2}$ (diagonal$_1$ $\times$ diagonal$_2$)

Trapezoid: $\dfrac{1}{2}$ height (base$_1$ $\times$ base$_2$)

Sphere: $4\pi r^2$

Circle: πr^2

Lateral surface area of cylinder: $2\pi rh$

Trigonometry

Law of Sines: $\dfrac{\sin A}{a} = \dfrac{\sin B}{b} = \dfrac{\sin C}{c}$

Law of Cosines: $c^2 = a^2 + b^2 - 2ab\cos C$

$b^2 = a^2 + c^2 - 2ac\cos B$

$a^2 = b^2 + c^2 - 2bc\cos A$

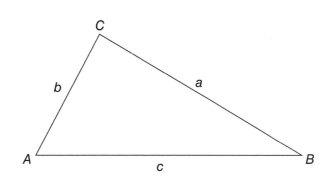

PERIODIC TABLE
Atomic Properties of the Elements

NIST
National Institute of
Standards and Technology
U.S. Department of Commerce

Physics Laboratory
physics.nist.gov

Standard Reference Data
www.nist.gov/srd

Frequently used fundamental physical constants

For the most accurate values of these and other constants, visit physics.nist.gov/constants
1 second = 9 192 631 770 periods of radiation corresponding to the transition between the two hyperfine levels of the ground state of ^{133}Cs

speed of light in vacuum	c	299 792 458 m s^{-1} (exact)
Planck constant	h	6.6261 × 10^{-34} J s ($\hbar = h/2\pi$)
elementary charge	e	1.6022 × 10^{-19} C
electron mass	m_e	9.1094 × 10^{-31} kg
	$m_e c^2$	0.5110 MeV
proton mass	m_p	1.6726 × 10^{-27} kg
fine-structure constant	α	1/137.036
Rydberg constant	R_∞	10 973 732 m^{-1}
	$R_\infty c$	3.289 842 × 10^{15} Hz
	$R_\infty hc$	13.6057 eV
Boltzmann constant	k	1.3807 × 10^{-23} J K^{-1}

Legend: Solids, Liquids, Gases, Artificially Prepared

Key:
Atomic Number — 58
Symbol — Ce
Name — Cerium
Atomic Weight† — 140.116
Ground-state Level — $^1G_4^\circ$
Ground-state Configuration — [Xe]4f5d6s^2
Ionization Energy (eV) — 5.5387

For a description of the data, visit physics.nist.gov/data

NIST SP 966 (September 2010)

†Based upon ^{12}C. ( ) indicates the mass number of the longest-lived isotope.

Group 1 / IA

1 H — Hydrogen — 1.00794 — $^2S_{1/2}$ — 1s — 13.5984

Group 2 / IIA

4 Be — Beryllium — 9.012182 — $^1S_0$ — 1s^{2}2s^2 — 9.3227
3 Li — Lithium — 6.941 — $^2S_{1/2}$ — 1s^{2}2s — 5.3917
11 Na — Sodium — 22.98976928 — $^2S_{1/2}$ — [Ne]3s — 5.1391
12 Mg — Magnesium — 24.3050 — $^1S_0$ — [Ne]3s^2 — 7.6462
19 K — Potassium — 39.0983 — $^2S_{1/2}$ — [Ar]4s — 4.3407
20 Ca — Calcium — 40.078 — $^1S_0$ — [Ar]4s^2 — 6.1132
37 Rb — Rubidium — 85.4678 — $^2S_{1/2}$ — [Kr]5s — 4.1771
38 Sr — Strontium — 87.62 — $^1S_0$ — [Kr]5s^2 — 5.6949
55 Cs — Cesium — 132.9054519 — $^2S_{1/2}$ — [Xe]6s — 3.8939
56 Ba — Barium — 137.327 — $^1S_0$ — [Xe]6s^2 — 5.2117
87 Fr — Francium — (223) — $^2S_{1/2}$ — [Rn]7s — 4.0727
88 Ra — Radium — (226) — $^1S_0$ — [Rn]7s^2 — 5.2784

Group 3 / IIIB

21 Sc — Scandium — 44.955912 — $^2D_{3/2}$ — [Ar]3d4s^2 — 6.5615
39 Y — Yttrium — 88.90585 — $^2D_{3/2}$ — [Kr]4d5s^2 — 6.2173
71 Lu — Lutetium — 174.9668 — $^2D_{3/2}$ — [Xe]4f^{14}5d6s^2 — 5.4259
103 Lr — Lawrencium — (262) — $^2P_{1/2}^\circ$? — [Rn]5f^{14}7s^{2}7p? — 4.9?

Group 4 / IVB

22 Ti — Titanium — 47.867 — $^3F_2$ — [Ar]3d^{2}4s^2 — 6.8281
40 Zr — Zirconium — 91.224 — $^3F_2$ — [Kr]4d^{2}5s^2 — 6.6339
72 Hf — Hafnium — 178.49 — $^3F_2$ — [Xe]4f^{14}5d^{2}6s^2 — 6.8251
104 Rf — Rutherfordium — (265) — $^3F_2$? — [Rn]5f^{14}6d^{2}7s^2? — 6.0?

Group 5 / VB

23 V — Vanadium — 50.9415 — $^4F_{3/2}$ — [Ar]3d^{3}4s^2 — 6.7462
41 Nb — Niobium — 92.90638 — $^6D_{1/2}$ — [Kr]4d^{4}5s — 6.7589
73 Ta — Tantalum — 180.94788 — $^4F_{3/2}$ — [Xe]4f^{14}5d^{3}6s^2 — 7.5496
105 Db — Dubnium — (268)

Group 6 / VIB

24 Cr — Chromium — 51.9961 — $^7S_3$ — [Ar]3d^{5}4s — 6.7665
42 Mo — Molybdenum — 95.96 — $^7S_3$ — [Kr]4d^{5}5s — 7.0924
74 W — Tungsten — 183.84 — $^5D_0$ — [Xe]4f^{14}5d^{4}6s^2 — 7.8640
106 Sg — Seaborgium — (271)

Group 7 / VIIB

25 Mn — Manganese — 54.938045 — $^6S_{5/2}$ — [Ar]3d^{5}4s^2 — 7.4340
43 Tc — Technetium — (98) — $^6S_{5/2}$ — [Kr]4d^{5}5s^2 — 7.28
75 Re — Rhenium — 186.207 — $^6S_{5/2}$ — [Xe]4f^{14}5d^{5}6s^2 — 7.8335
107 Bh — Bohrium — (272)

Group 8 / VIII

26 Fe — Iron — 55.845 — $^5D_4$ — [Ar]3d^{6}4s^2 — 7.9024
44 Ru — Ruthenium — 101.07 — $^5F_5$ — [Kr]4d^{7}5s — 7.3605
76 Os — Osmium — 190.23 — $^5D_4$ — [Xe]4f^{14}5d^{6}6s^2 — 8.4382
108 Hs — Hassium — (270)

Group 9 / VIII

27 Co — Cobalt — 58.933195 — $^4F_{9/2}$ — [Ar]3d^{7}4s^2 — 7.8810
45 Rh — Rhodium — 102.90550 — $^4F_{9/2}$ — [Kr]4d^{8}5s — 7.4589
77 Ir — Iridium — 192.217 — $^4F_{9/2}$ — [Xe]4f^{14}5d^{7}6s^2 — 8.9670
109 Mt — Meitnerium — (276)

Group 10 / VIII

28 Ni — Nickel — 58.6934 — $^3F_4$ — [Ar]3d^{8}4s^2 — 7.6399
46 Pd — Palladium — 106.42 — $^1S_0$ — [Kr]4d^{10} — 8.3369
78 Pt — Platinum — 195.084 — $^3D_3$ — [Xe]4f^{14}5d^{9}6s — 8.9588
110 Ds — Darmstadtium — (281)

Group 11 / IB

29 Cu — Copper — 63.546 — $^2S_{1/2}$ — [Ar]3d^{10}4s — 7.7264
47 Ag — Silver — 107.8682 — $^2S_{1/2}$ — [Kr]4d^{10}5s — 7.5762
79 Au — Gold — 196.966569 — $^2S_{1/2}$ — [Xe]4f^{14}5d^{10}6s — 9.2255
111 Rg — Roentgenium — (280)

Group 12 / IIB

30 Zn — Zinc — 65.38 — $^1S_0$ — [Ar]3d^{10}4s^2 — 9.3942
48 Cd — Cadmium — 112.411 — $^1S_0$ — [Kr]4d^{10}5s^2 — 8.9938
80 Hg — Mercury — 200.59 — $^1S_0$ — [Xe]4f^{14}5d^{10}6s^2 — 10.4375
112 Cn — Copernicium — (285)

Group 13 / IIIA

5 B — Boron — 10.811 — $^2P_{1/2}^\circ$ — 1s^{2}2s^{2}2p — 8.2980
13 Al — Aluminum — 26.9815386 — $^2P_{1/2}^\circ$ — [Ne]3s^{2}3p — 5.9858
31 Ga — Gallium — 69.723 — $^2P_{1/2}^\circ$ — [Ar]3d^{10}4s^{2}4p — 5.9993
49 In — Indium — 114.818 — $^2P_{1/2}^\circ$ — [Kr]4d^{10}5s^{2}5p — 5.7864
81 Tl — Thallium — 204.3833 — $^2P_{1/2}^\circ$ — [Hg]6p — 6.1082
113 Uut — Ununtrium — (284)

Group 14 / IVA

6 C — Carbon — 12.0107 — $^3P_0$ — 1s^{2}2s^{2}2p^2 — 11.2603
14 Si — Silicon — 28.0855 — $^3P_0$ — [Ne]3s^{2}3p^2 — 8.1517
32 Ge — Germanium — 72.64 — $^3P_0$ — [Ar]3d^{10}4s^{2}4p^2 — 7.8994
50 Sn — Tin — 118.710 — $^3P_0$ — [Kr]4d^{10}5s^{2}5p^2 — 7.3439
82 Pb — Lead — 207.2 — $^3P_0$ — [Hg]6p^2 — 7.4167
114 Uuq — Ununquadium — (289)

Group 15 / VA

7 N — Nitrogen — 14.0067 — $^4S_{3/2}^\circ$ — 1s^{2}2s^{2}2p^3 — 14.5341
15 P — Phosphorus — 30.973762 — $^4S_{3/2}^\circ$ — [Ne]3s^{2}3p^3 — 10.4867
33 As — Arsenic — 74.92160 — $^4S_{3/2}^\circ$ — [Ar]3d^{10}4s^{2}4p^3 — 9.7886
51 Sb — Antimony — 121.760 — $^4S_{3/2}^\circ$ — [Kr]4d^{10}5s^{2}5p^3 — 8.6084
83 Bi — Bismuth — 208.98040 — $^4S_{3/2}^\circ$ — [Hg]6p^3 — 7.2855
115 Uup — Ununpentium — (288)

Group 16 / VIA

8 O — Oxygen — 15.9994 — $^3P_2$ — 1s^{2}2s^{2}2p^4 — 13.6181
16 S — Sulfur — 32.065 — $^3P_2$ — [Ne]3s^{2}3p^4 — 10.3600
34 Se — Selenium — 78.96 — $^3P_2$ — [Ar]3d^{10}4s^{2}4p^4 — 9.7524
52 Te — Tellurium — 127.60 — $^3P_2$ — [Kr]4d^{10}5s^{2}5p^4 — 9.0096
84 Po — Polonium — (209) — $^3P_2$ — [Hg]6p^4 — 8.414
116 Uuh — Ununhexium — (293)

Group 17 / VIIA

9 F — Fluorine — 18.9984032 — $^2P_{3/2}^\circ$ — 1s^{2}2s^{2}2p^5 — 17.4228
17 Cl — Chlorine — 35.453 — $^2P_{3/2}^\circ$ — [Ne]3s^{2}3p^5 — 12.9676
35 Br — Bromine — 79.904 — $^2P_{3/2}^\circ$ — [Ar]3d^{10}4s^{2}4p^5 — 11.8138
53 I — Iodine — 126.90447 — $^2P_{3/2}^\circ$ — [Kr]4d^{10}5s^{2}5p^5 — 10.4513
85 At — Astatine — (210) — — [Hg]6p^5 —
117 Uus — Ununseptium — (294)

Group 18 / VIIIA

2 He — Helium — 4.002602 — $^1S_0$ — 1s^2 — 24.5874
10 Ne — Neon — 20.1797 — $^1S_0$ — 1s^{2}2s^{2}2p^6 — 21.5645
18 Ar — Argon — 39.948 — $^1S_0$ — [Ne]3s^{2}3p^6 — 15.7596
36 Kr — Krypton — 83.798 — $^1S_0$ — [Ar]3d^{10}4s^{2}4p^6 — 13.9996
54 Xe — Xenon — 131.293 — $^1S_0$ — [Kr]4d^{10}5s^{2}5p^6 — 12.1298
86 Rn — Radon — (222) — $^1S_0$ — [Hg]6p^6 — 10.7485
118 Uuo — Ununoctium — (294)

Lanthanides

57 La — Lanthanum — 138.90547 — $^2D_{3/2}$ — [Xe]5d6s^2 — 5.5769
58 Ce — Cerium — 140.116 — $^1G_4^\circ$ — [Xe]4f5d6s^2 — 5.5387
59 Pr — Praseodymium — 140.90765 — $^4I_{9/2}^\circ$ — [Xe]4f^{3}6s^2 — 5.473
60 Nd — Neodymium — 144.242 — $^5I_4$ — [Xe]4f^{4}6s^2 — 5.5250
61 Pm — Promethium — (145) — $^6H_{5/2}^\circ$ — [Xe]4f^{5}6s^2 — 5.582
62 Sm — Samarium — 150.36 — $^7F_0$ — [Xe]4f^{6}6s^2 — 5.6437
63 Eu — Europium — 151.964 — $^8S_{7/2}^\circ$ — [Xe]4f^{7}6s^2 — 5.6704
64 Gd — Gadolinium — 157.25 — $^9D_2^\circ$ — [Xe]4f^{7}5d6s^2 — 6.1498
65 Tb — Terbium — 158.92535 — $^6H_{15/2}^\circ$ — [Xe]4f^{9}6s^2 — 5.8638
66 Dy — Dysprosium — 162.500 — $^5I_8$ — [Xe]4f^{10}6s^2 — 5.9389
67 Ho — Holmium — 164.93032 — $^4I_{15/2}^\circ$ — [Xe]4f^{11}6s^2 — 6.0215
68 Er — Erbium — 167.259 — $^3H_6$ — [Xe]4f^{12}6s^2 — 6.1077
69 Tm — Thulium — 168.93421 — $^2F_{7/2}^\circ$ — [Xe]4f^{13}6s^2 — 6.1843
70 Yb — Ytterbium — 173.054 — $^1S_0$ — [Xe]4f^{14}6s^2 — 6.2542

Actinides

89 Ac — Actinium — (227) — $^2D_{3/2}$ — [Rn]6d7s^2 — 5.3807
90 Th — Thorium — 232.03806 — $^3F_2$ — [Rn]6d^{2}7s^2 — 6.3067
91 Pa — Protactinium — 231.03588 — $^4K_{11/2}$ — [Rn]5f^{2}6d7s^2 — 5.89
92 U — Uranium — 238.02891 — $^5L_6^\circ$ — [Rn]5f^{3}6d7s^2 — 6.1939
93 Np — Neptunium — (237) — $^6L_{11/2}$ — [Rn]5f^{4}6d7s^2 — 6.2657
94 Pu — Plutonium — (244) — $^7F_0$ — [Rn]5f^{6}7s^2 — 6.0260
95 Am — Americium — (243) — $^8S_{7/2}^\circ$ — [Rn]5f^{7}7s^2 — 5.9738
96 Cm — Curium — (247) — $^9D_2^\circ$ — [Rn]5f^{7}6d7s^2 — 5.9914
97 Bk — Berkelium — (247) — $^6H_{15/2}^\circ$ — [Rn]5f^{9}7s^2 — 6.1979
98 Cf — Californium — (251) — $^5I_8$ — [Rn]5f^{10}7s^2 — 6.2817
99 Es — Einsteinium — (252) — $^4I_{15/2}^\circ$ — [Rn]5f^{11}7s^2 — 6.3676
100 Fm — Fermium — (257) — $^3H_6$ — [Rn]5f^{12}7s^2 — 6.50
101 Md — Mendelevium — (258) — $^2F_{7/2}^\circ$ — [Rn]5f^{13}7s^2 — 6.58
102 No — Nobelium — (259) — $^1S_0$ — [Rn]5f^{14}7s^2 — 6.65

TExES Core Subjects 4–8
Index

INDEX

A

Abiotic components, 396
Absolute location, 270
Absolute value, 111
    function, 142
Academic honesty, 92
Accommodation, 420–421
Activation energy, 375
Acute angle, 156
Adams, John, 322
Adaptation, 392–394
Addition
    associative property, 112
    closure property, 112
    commutative property, 112
    decimals, 117
    fractions, 116
    identity property, 112
    operations of, 112
Adenine, 386
Aerobic respiration, 381
Aesthetic stance, 74
Affixes, 340–341
Afghanistan War, 256
African Americans, civil rights
        movement, 249–250
Age of Discovery, 218–220
Age of Reason, 223–224, 235
Agricultural revolution, 298
Alamo, 263
Algebra tiles, 206–207
Algonquians, 228
Alleles, 389
Allies, 253, 254
Alliteration, 30
Alphabetic principle, 32–33
    stages of learning, 32
    teaching grapheme-phoneme
        correspondence, 33

Alphabetic writing system, 33–34
Alternate exterior angles, 157
Alternate interior angles, 157
Amendment process, 311
American history, 229–258
    American Revolution, 235–237
    ancient civilization of, 226–229
    Articles of Confederation, 237
    Civil Rights movement, 249–251
    Civil War, 243–245
    Cold War, 256
    colonies, 229–235
    Constitution, 237–238
    Continental Congress, 236
    Declaration of Independence, 236
    Great Depression, 253
    indentured servants, 234–235
    Ku Klux Klan, 246, 247
    Manifest Destiny, 239
    Monroe Doctrine, 238
    Reconstruction era, 245–247
    representative government in
        colonies, 233–234
    slavery, 241–243
    Spanish-American War, 252
    Temperance movement and
        Prohibition, 248–249
    Truman Doctrine, 255
    urbanization, 247
    war in Syria, 256–257
    war on terrorism, 256
    westward expansion, 238–241
    women's rights movement, 252
    World War I, 253
    World War II, 253–254
American National Flag, 317
American Recovery and Reinvestment
        Act, 300
American Revolution, 235–237
American Transcendentalism, 282

Anaerobic respiration, 385
Analogous structures, 380
Anasazi, 228
Ancient World, 217
Anecdotal records, 60
Angle bisector, 159
Angles
    constructing angle bisector, 159
    formed by parallel lines cut by
        transversal, 157
    types of, 156
Animal cells, 381
    respiration, 384–385
    sexual reproduction, 387–389
Animals
    guidelines for using in classroom,
        354–355
    as taxonomic group, 380, 392
Animal tales, 68
Apache, 229, 240, 259–260
Appalachian highlands, 273
Applied questions, 58
Arab Liberation Army (ALA), 255
Arab Spring, 257
Archimedes, 323
Area
    area under parabola curve, 144–147
    formulas for, 162–163
Aristocracy, 305
Articles of Confederation, 237
Asexual reproduction, 387
Asking questions, for reading
        comprehension, 66
Assad, Bashar al-, 256–257
Assessment
    authentic assessment, 40, 429
    criterion-referenced tests (CRTs),
        38–39
    of English Language Learners, 40
    essay tests, 40

formal assessment, 38–41
formative and summative evaluation, 38
informal, 38
of literacy development, 37–42
mathematics, 208–209
norm-referenced test (NRT), 39
ongoing assessment, 41
performance-based assessment, 39
reading comprehension, 58–62
reading fluency, 51
rubrics for, 41
science, 430–432
word identification skills, 48–49
writing composition, 90–92
writing conventions, 79
Assimilation, 420
Associative property, 112–113
Atlantic-Gulf coastal plains, 273
Atmosphere, 402–403
Atomic bomb, 254
Atoms, 372
Audience, for writing, 87
Austin, Stephen F., 262
Australasia, 278
Authentic assessment, 40
Authentic literature-based texts, 29
Authentic multicultural literature, 68–69
Autocracy, 304
Automaticity, 49
Average, 176–177
Axis powers, 254
Aztecs, 227

B

Balanced reading program, 28–29
Banking, 295
Bar graph, 172, 337
Base-10 blocks, 124–125
Bell curve, 180–182
Bernanke, Ben, 295
Bias, 190
Bibliographies, 100
Big Bang, 411
Bill of Rights, 249, 311
bin Laden, Osama, 256
Binomial experiments, 186–188
Biogeochemical cycles, 406–407
Biography, 69

Biotic components, 396
Bivariate data, 174–175
Black Codes, 246
Bleeding Kansas, 243
Bloom's taxonomy, 58, 102, 415–417
Bolshevik revolution, 253
Boston dialect, 22
Boston Massacre, 236
Boston Tea Party, 236
Bowie, James, 263
Box-and-whisker plot, 178
Boyle, Robert, 324
Breckinridge, John C., 244
Brexit, 257
Brown, John, 243
Brown v. Board of Education of Topeka, 250, 251, 314
Bunker Hill, 237
Bureau of Refugees, Freedmen, and Abandoned Lands, 246
Burnet, David G., 263

C

Caddo, 259–260
Cambrian, 411
Capacity, units of, 150–151
Capital, 292
Capitalism, 293
Capone, Al, 248
Carbohydrates, 384, 385
Carbon cycle, 406
Cardiac muscle, 383
Cartilage, 382
Cascade Mountains, 274
Catholic missions in Texas, 261
Cattle industry, 265, 301
Cells
    animal and plant cells, 380–382
    reproduction, 387–389
Cell theory, 362
Celsius, 151
Census, 190
Central America, 275
Central Eurasia, 276
Centrally planned economy, 294–295
Central Powers, 253
Characterization, 72
Charts, 337–339
Chávez, Cesar, 251

Checklists, for assessment, 91
Checks and balances, 310
Chemical bonds, 372–373
Chemical change, 373–374
Chemical energy, 375
Cherokee, 229
Chicano movement, 250–251
Children's literature, 67–71
China, command economy of, 294–295
Chomsky, Noam, 18
Choral reading, 50, 51
Chromosomes, 389
Churchill, Winston, 254
Circle, area and perimeter of, 163
Circle graph, 172
Circulatory system, 382, 383
Citizenship in U.S., 315–316
Civil rights
    African American civil rights movement, 249–250
    desegregation, 314
    Dred Scott case, 313
    for freed slaves, 249
    Mexican American movement, 250–251
    separate but equal, 314
    in Texas, 251
Civil Rights Act, 250, 252
Civil Rights Movement, 249–250
Civil War, 243–245
    end of, 245
    Gettysburg, 245
    political, economic and social difference, 243–244
    Reconstruction Era, 245–247
    secession and, 244–245
    slavery and sectionalism, 244
    in Texas, 245
Clay, Mary, 51
Classification, 201, 338
Climate, 408
Closed circuit, 375
Closure property, 112
Cloze test, 58
Cluttering, 24
Coahuiltecan, 259–260
Cognates, 340–341
Cold War, 256
Colonial America, 229–235
Comanche, 240, 259–260

Combinations, number of, 127–128
Command economy, 294–295
Commerce, federal regulation of, 312–313
Common denominator, 116
Common multiple, 123
Communication disorders, 23–24
Communism, 293
Commutative property, 112
Comparative investigations, 358–359
Comparatives, 46
Compass rose, 270–271
Compatible numbers, 125
Compean, Mario, 251
Complementary angle, 156
Complementary event, 184–185
Complex numbers, 119–121
Composite numbers, 122
Compounds, 373
Compound words, 47
Comprehensive questions, for reading comprehension assessment, 60
Compromise of 1850, 242
Concord, 237
Concrete Operational stage, 200
Conditional probability, 185–188
Conduction, 403, 404
Cone
    net, 166
    volume and surface area formulas, 164
Confederate States of America, 244–245, 265
Confidence interval, 191
Congruent corresponding angles, 157
Connecticut colony, 230, 232, 233
Connotation, 20
Conservation, 200–201
Consolidated alphabetic stage, 32
Constitutional democracy, 305
Constitution of United States
    amendment process, 311–312
    fundamental principles of, 307–308
    writing, 237–238
Constructive processes, 399
Consumers, 397, 398
Context clues, 44
Contextual mathematics, 203–204
Continental Congress, 236, 237
Continental Divide, 273

Continental drift, 399, 412
Convection, 403–404
Convenience sample, 190
Conventional spelling stage, 77
Convergence, 380
Convergent questions, 58
Convergent sequence, 147
Cooperative learning, 343
Coordinate plane
    reflections in, 169
    translation in, 168
Copernicus, 323
Core, of Earth, 399
Coronado, Francisco Vázquez de, 261
Correlation coefficient, 175
Cosine, 152
Cotton, 239, 241
Cotton gin, 241
Counting principle, 125
Covalent bonds, 372–373
Criterion-referenced tests (CRTs)
    overview, 38–39
    reading, 61
    writing, 92
Critical-thinking skills, 101–102
Crockett, Davy, 263
Crust, of Earth, 399
Cuba, 252
Cuban Missile Crisis, 255
Cube
    Euler's formula, 166
    net, 164
Cubic function, 141
Cuisenaire rods, 206
Cultural context, 72
Cultural diffusion, 226, 283–284
Cultural diversity, 321
Cultural exchange, 226
Culture
    American Transcendentalism, 282
    cultural diffusion, 226, 283–284
    defined, 226
    diversity and, 321–322
    race and ethnicity, 282–283
    Renaissance and, 282
    role of family in customs and traditions, 320–321
    stories, art and music to express, 321
Cumulative tales, 68
Cunningham, Patricia, 47

Curie, Marie, 324
Curve, area under, 144–147
Cylinder
    net, 166
    volume and surface area formulas, 164
Cytosine, 386

D

Data retrieval charts, 337
da Vinci, Leonardo, 282
Davis, Jefferson, 244
D-Day, 254
Decentering, 201
Decimal numbers
    adding and subtracting, 117
    money as manipulatives for, 124
    multiplying and dividing, 117–118
    representation with base-10 blocks, 124–125
Declaration of Independence, 236
Decoding clues, 44
Decomposers, 396, 397
Deductive reasoning, 194–195
Deflation, 296
Deforestation, 280
Delaware colony, 230, 232, 233
de Leon, Alonso, 261
Demand, 291
Democracy, 303, 305, 306
Denali, 279
Denominator
    common, 116
    rationalizing, 120–121
Denotation, 20
Deoxyribonucleic acids (DNA), 386
Dependent clause, 79
Dependent variables, 359
Deposition, 280, 402
Derivational morphemes, 45
Descriptive statistics, 189
Descriptive studies, 358
Descriptive writing, 86
Desegregation, 314
Destructive processes, 399
de Vaca, Álvar Núñez Cabeza, 260
Dialogue, 70
Dialogue journals, 88
Dictatorship, 304

Differentiated instruction, 208
Digestive system, 382, 383
Dilation, 169
Direct experience, 414
Discriminant, 139–140
Distributive property, 113
Divergent questions, 58
Divergent sequence, 147
Diversity within unity, 322
Divisibility rules, 123
Division
  decimals, 117–118
  fractions, 116
Dolch, Edward W., 44
Dolch words, 44
Dominant chromosome, 389–390
Dot plot, 172
Double-sided geoboard, 207
Douglas, Stephen, 243
Drama, 69
Dred Scott v. Sandford, 243, 313
DRTA (Directed Reading/Thinking
  Activity), 100–101
Du Bois, W.E.B., 322
Dust Bowl, 247
Dutrochet, Henri, 362

E

Early literacy development, 27–42
Early readers, 35
Early writers, 83–84
Earthquakes, 401
Earth systems
  atmosphere, 402
  biogeochemical cycles, 406–407
  continental drift, 399
  deposition, 280, 401
  earthquakes and geologic faults, 401
  Earth-Sun-Moon system, 410–411
  energy transfer, 403–404
  erosion, 400–401
  gravity, 401–402
  history of, 411–412
  layers of Earth, 399
  minerals, 405–406
  natural and human influences on,
    402–403
  rocks, 405–406
  surface water and groundwater, 402

tectonic plates, 401
  tides, 406
  volcanoes, 401
  water cycle, 406
  weather and climate, 408–409
  weathering, 400
East Asia, 278
Easy combinations, for estimates, 125
Ebonics, 22
Echo reading, 51
Ecology, 396
Economic interdependence, 294
Economics, 288–301
  basic principles of, 289–290
  categories of economic activity, 291
  centrally planned or command
    economy, 294–295
  communism, 293
  economic indicators, 296–297
  economic interdependence, 294
  economic systems, 293–295
  factors of production, 291–292
  federal income tax system, 298
  free enterprise, 293–294
  globalization, 294
  goods and services, 291
  government regulation and taxation,
    298
  Gross Domestic Product (GDP),
    292–293, 296–297
  history of U.S., 299–300
  inflation and deflation, 296
  mixed economies, 295
  money and banking, 295
  in new millennium, 300–301
  savings, interest rates and
    investment, 295–296
  scarcity and surplus, 290
  socialism, 295
  supply and demand, 291
  Texas economy, 301
Edge, geometric body, 166
Edison, Thomas, 324
Efferent stance, 74
Egocentrism, elimination of, 201
Eighteenth Amendment, 248
Eighth Amendment, 311
Einstein, Albert, 324
Eisenhower, Dwight D., 254
Electricity, 375, 378

Electronic media, 94
Elements, 372
El Paso, 261
Emancipation Proclamation, 241
Emergent readers, 35
Emerging writers, 83
Endothermic reaction, 374
Energy, 369, 374–378
  forms of, 375–376
  heat transfer, 403–404
  transformation and conservation of,
    377–378
England. *See* Great Britain
English language arts, 15–105
  alphabetic principle, 32–33
  assessment of developing literacy,
    37–42
  literacy development, 27–42
  oral language, 16–27
  phonological and phonemic
    awareness, 29–32
  reading applications, 62–74
  reading comprehension and
    assessment, 52–62
  reading fluency, 49–52
  references, 102–105
  social studies integrations with, 336
  study and inquiry skills, 97–102
  viewing and representing, 92–96
  word identification skills, 42–49
  writing compositions, 80–92
  writing conventions, 74–80
  written communication, 80–83
English Language Learners
  assessing reading comprehension, 61
  assessment of, 40
  linguistic accommodation testing for,
    102
  social studies instruction and,
    340–342
  thematic instruction, 336
Enlightenment, 223–224, 235
Entrepreneurship, 292, 293
Environmental factors, 391
Eon, 411
Epochs, 411
Equal Pay Act, 252
Equilateral triangle, area and perimeter
  of, 163
Equivalent fractions, 114–115

Eras, 411
Eratosthenes, 323
Erosion, 400–401
Error of measurement, 151–152
Essay tests, 40
Estimation, 125
Eukaryotic cells, 381
Euler's formula, 166
Euro, 294
Europe, 276
European Union (EU), 294
Evolution
    behavior and, 395–396
    concept of, 393
Executive branch, 309–310
Exothermic reaction, 374
Expanded form, 109
Experimental evidence, 360
Experiments, 359–360
Exponential function, 141
Exponents, laws of, 118
Exposition, 70
Expository writing, 86

F

Fables, 68
Face, geometric body, 166
Factors
    factoring quadratic equations, 140
    prime factorization, 122
Factors of production, 291–292
Factor tree, 122
Fahrenheit, 151
Family, role of, 320
Farming, 247
Federal government, powers of, 308–309
Federal income tax system, 298
Federalism, 307, 308–309
Federal Republic, 305, 306
Federal Reserve System, 295
Feedback mechanisms, 396
Feminine Mystique, The (Friedan), 252
Fiction, 67
Fifteenth Amendment, 241, 246, 249, 312
Fifth Amendment, 311
Figurative language, 72
First Amendment, 311
5-E model, 419–425

5-up rule, 125
Flowchart, 339, 341
Fluency, reading, 49–52
Fluency disorders, 24
Fluent writers, 85
FOIL, 120
Food and Drug Administration, 294
Food web, 397–398
Force, 368–370
Formal assessment
    literacy, 38–41
    mathematics, 208–209
Formal Operational stage, 200
Formative evaluation, 38
Fourteenth Amendment, 241, 246, 249, 312
Fourth Amendment, 311
Fractional exponents, 118
Fraction bar, 204–205
Fraction circle, 205
Fractions, 114–116
    addition and subtraction, 116
    common denominator, 116
    converting improper fractions to mixed numbers, 115
    equivalent, 114–115
    greatest common factor, 115
    least common multiple, 116
    multiplication and division, 116
    reciprocal, 116
    simplifying, 114–115
France, American Revolution and, 237
Franklin, Benjamin, 238, 322
Freedman's Bureau, 246
Free enterprise, 293–294
French and Indian War, 235
Friedan, Betty, 252
Frustration level, as reading level, 59
Fugitive Slave Act, 242
Full alphabetic stage, 32
Fulton, Robert, 324
Functional writing, 88
Functions
    absolute value, 142
    cubic, 141
    exponential, 141
    linear functions, 130–135
    logarithmic, 141
    quadratic, 136–140
    transformations, 137

Fungi, 379, 396

G

Galaxies, 410, 411
Galileo, 323
Gametes, 388
Garvey, Marcus, 322
Gay, Geneva, 320
Genetics, 389–391
Genre, 67
Geographical tools, 284
Geography, 268–288
    adaptation and modification of physical environment, 280–281
    characteristics, distribution and migration of populations, 281
    concepts of, 269–270
    cultural and physical geography, 269
    cultural diffusion, 283–284
    deposition, 280
    geographical symbols, 270–271
    geographical tools, 284
    grid system, 270
    latitude and longitude, 335
    locations affect on people, 281
    map and globe concepts, 333–335
    physical geography influences settlement locations, 269
    rivers in United States, 274
    Texas regions and economic activity of, 272–273
    time zones, 271
    United States regions, 273–274
    world mountains, 279
    world regions, 274–278
Geologic faults, 401
Geometric probability, 188–189
Geometry, 154–170
    angles and measurement, 156–157
    area formulas, 162–163
    Euler's formula, 166
    lines of symmetry, 170
    nets, 164–166
    perimeter formulas, 162–163
    points, lines and planes, 154–161
    surface area formulas, 163–164
    tessellations, 170
    three-dimensional figures, 163–167

translations, reflections, rotations and dilations, 168–169

volume formulas, 163–164

Georgia colony, 230, 232, 233

Geospatial technologies, 335–336

Germany

    Hitler and, 254

    World War I, 253

    World War II, 253–254

Gettysburg, Battle of, 245

Ghost stories, 68

Gibbons v. Ogden, 312–313

Glide reflections, 169

Globalization, 294

Global warming, 403

Goliad, 263

Gonzales, 262

Gonzales, Rodolfo "Corky," 251

Goods, 291

Gorbachev, Mikhail, 256

Government and citizenship, 302–318

    amendment process, 311

    American government, 306

    American symbols, 317–318

    Bill of Rights, 311

    checks and balances, 310

    citizenship, 315–316

    Constitution of United States, 307–308

    executive, judicial and legislative branch, 309–310

    federalism, 307, 308–309

    forms of government, 303–305

    judicial review, 310, 312

    landmark Supreme Court cases, 312–314

    local and state government, 314

    power sharing between state and federal governments, 308–309

    representative government in colonies, 233–234

    separation of powers, 309–310

Government regulation, 298

Grammar

    identifying common problems, 78

    internal, 18

Granger, Gordon, 321

Grant, Ulysses S., 245, 265

Graphemes, 19

grapheme-phoneme correspondence, 33, 34–35

Graphic organizers, 98, 341–342

Graphs

    of historical information, 336–339

    types of, 171–173

Graves, Donald, 82

Gravity, 362, 401–402

Great Britain

    American Revolution, 235–237

    English colonies in America, 230–233

Great Depression, 253

    economic history of U.S. and, 300

Greatest common divisor (GCD), 115, 123–124

Greatest common factor (GCF), 115, 123–124

Great plains, 273

Great Seal of the United States, 318

Greenhouse gas, 404

Greenspan, Alan, 295

Grid system, 270

Gross domestic product (GDP), 292–293, 296–297

Gross national product (GNP), 296–297

Groundwater, 403

Guadalupe Hidalgo Treaty, 251, 264

Guam, 252

Guanine, 386

Guided oral repeated reading, 50

Guided practice reading, 54–55

Gutiérrez, José Ángel, 251

H

Hamilton, Alexander, 238

Harlem Renaissance, 322

Heat

    heat transfer, 375

    light and, 375

    transfer of, 403–404

Heredity, 389–391

Heterogeneous mixtures, 373

Hidden bias, 190

Hiroshima, 255

Histogram, 173

Historical context, 72

Historical fiction, 69

History, 215–267

    Age of Discovery, 219–220

    American history, 229–258

    ancient civilizations of Americas, 226–229

    Ancient World, 217

    culture and, 226

    Enlightenment, 223–224

    graphic representations of historical information, 336–339

    Industrial Revolution and modern technology, 224–225

    Middle Ages, 218

    Modern World, 220–223

    Revolution and Industry period, 220

    settlements and building community, 225–226

    Texas history, 258–267

    world history, 217

Hitler, Adolf, 254, 283

Hohokam, 228

Holocaust, 255

Homeostasis, 394–395

Homogeneous mixtures, 373

Homographs, 47

Homologous structures, 380

Homonyms, 46

Homophones, 47

Hooke, Robert, 362

Hooker, Thomas, 232

Hormones, 396

House of Burgesses, 230

Houston, Sam, 263

Huerta, Dolores, 251

Hutchinson, Anne, 231

Hypotenuse, 153–154

I

Ideas, determining important for reading comprehension, 66

Identity property, 112–113

Idioms, 47

Igneous rocks, 404–405

Imagery, 71

Imitation, in language acquisition, 18

Immune system, 383

Incas, 227

Income tax, 298

Indentured servants, 234–235

Independent clause, 79
Independent reading
    part of balanced literacy program, 51
    practice, 54–55
    as reading level, 59
    reading workshop to foster, 73
Independent variables, 359
Indian Removal Act, 240, 313
Inductive reasoning, 195
Industrial Revolution, 291
    economic history of U.S. and, 299
    modern technology and, 224–225
Inferences, drawing
    for reading comprehension, 66
Inferential questions, 58
Inferential statistics, 189–193
Inferring, for reading comprehension, 57
Infinite series, 147–148
Inflation, 296, 297
Inflectional morphemes, 45–46
Informal assessment
    literacy, 38
    mathematics, 208–209
    reading, 60–61
    writing composition, 90–91
Informed consent, 363
Inner core, 400
Inquiry, 344–345. *See also* Scientific inquiry; Study and inquiry skills
Instructional level, as reading level, 59
Integers, 109
Intelligibility, 21–22
Interactive journals, 89
Interactive reading programs, 50
Interest rates, 295–296
Interior highlands, 273
Interior plains, 273
Intermontane plateaus, 274
Internal grammar, 18
International Standard Book Number (ISBN), 70
Interquartile range, 178
Intonation patterns, 31
Invented spelling, 76–77
Investments, 296
Ionic bond, 372–373
Iran War, 256
Iroquois, 228

Irrational numbers, 110
Islamic State of Iraq and Syria (ISIS), 256–257
Israel, 255
Italy, World War II, 254–255

J

Jackson, Andrew, 240, 313
Jamestown, Virginia, 230
Japan, World War II, 254–255
Jefferson, Thomas, 236, 312, 322
Jim Crow laws, 247, 249, 250, 251
Johnson, Andrew, 246
Johnson, Lyndon B., 250
Journals
    interactive, 89
    journal writing, 88
Judicial branch, 310
Judicial review, 310, 312
Jumano, 259–260
Juneteenth, 265, 321

K

K2, 279
Kansas-Nebraska Act, 243
Kant, 282
Karankawas, 259–260
Kennedy, John F., 250, 256
Khrushchev, Nikita, 256
Kinetic energy, 375
King, Martin Luther, Jr., 250
Ku Klux Klan, 247, 251, 265
KWL chart, 66

L

Labor, 292
Land grant movement, 251
Language
    assessing speaking ability, 21–22
    components of, 19–20
    language acquisition, 18
    oral language, 16–27
    stages of development, 21
Language acquisition, 18
Language Acquisition Device (LAD), 18

Language arts. *See* English language arts
Language Experience Approach, 83
Language play, 25
La Salle, Robert de, 261
Latitude, 335
Laurentian highlands, 273
Laws of exponents, 118
Learning cycle, 420–427
Learning logs, 88
Learning styles, 38
Least common multiple, 116
Lee, Robert E., 245, 265
Legal constraints, 363
Legislative branch, 310
Lenin, Vladimir, 253
Lexicon, 20
Lexington, 237
Liberty Bell, 317
Life science, 379–398
    adaptation and evolution, 392–393
    organisms and environment, 396–398
    regulatory mechanisms and behavior, 393–396
    reproduction and heredity, 387–391
    response to stimuli, 395
    structure and functions of living things, 379–387, 391–393
Ligaments, 382
Light
    heat and, 375
    light energy, 376
Lightning, 376
Lincoln, Abraham, 241
    election of, 244
    Gettysburg Address, 245
Linear functions, 130–135
Line of symmetry, 136–138, 170
Line plot, 172
Lines
    parallel, 155
    perpendicular, 155
Line segment, 155
Lipids, 386
Lisping, 24
Literacy assessment
    assessing English Language Learners, 40
    authentic assessment, 40

constructing classroom-based tests, 40

criterion-referenced tests (CRTs), 38

essay tests, 40

formal assessment, 38–41

informal assessment, 38

monitoring with story retellings, 41–42

norm-referenced test (NRT), 39

ongoing assessment, 41

performance-based assessment, 39

rubrics for, 41

Literacy development, 27–42

alphabetic principle, 32–33

assessment of, 37–42

balanced reading program, 28–29

foundations for, 27–28

grapheme-phoneme correspondence, 33, 34–35

phonological and phonemic awareness, 29–32

stages of reading development, 35–37

technology to foster, 37

types of writing systems, 33–34

Literal questions, 58

Literary analysis, 72

Literary devices, 72

Literary style, 70–71

Logarithmic function, 141

Logical reasoning, 194

Logical thinking, 428–429

London Company, 230

Longitude, 335

Longitudinal waves, 377

Louisiana Purchase, 240

M

Macroeconomics, 289

Madison, James, 238

Manifest Destiny, 239

Manipulatives, in mathematics, 204–207

Mantle, of Earth, 399

Maps

grid system, 270

locating places and regions on, 269–270

relative and absolute location, 270

skills by grade, scope and sequence, 284–288

teaching map concepts, 333–335

types of, 269–270

Marbury v. Madison, 310, 312

Market economy, 293–294

Marshall Plan, 255

Maryland colony, 230, 231, 233

Mason, John, 231

Mass, 356, 370–371, 372

units of, 150

Massachusetts Bay Company, 230

Massachusetts colony, 230–231, 233

Mass production, 291

Mathematical literacy, 201–203

Mathematics, 107–211

assessment, 208–209

bivariate data, 174–175

cognitive development and, 200–201

combinations, 127–128

communicating mathematical ideas and concepts, 195–196

complex numbers, 119–121

curriculum requirements, 199–200, 207–208

decimal representation with base-10 blocks, 124–125

decimals, 117–118

differentiated instruction, 208

FOIL, 120

fractions, 114–116

geometry, 154–170

graphs and charts, 171–173

greatest common factor, 115, 123–124

infinite series, 147–148

laws of exponents, 118

learning environment for, 197–198

least common multiple, 116

linear functions, 130–135

major discoveries in throughout history, 323–324

manipulatives in, 204–207

mathematical literacy, 201–203

measurement, 147–148

mental math and estimation, 125

NCTM standards, 197–198

number concepts, 108–111

number theory, 121–128

operations and algorithm, 111–114

order of operations, 113–114

patterns, 129–130

permutations, 125–128

precalculus concepts, 142–148

prime factorization, 122

principles of, 198

probability, 182–189

properties, 112–113

quadratic functions, 136–140

in real-life situations, 203–204

reasoning and problem solving, 193–195

references, 210–211

statistics, 174–182, 189–193

TEKS standards, 199–200, 207–208

terminology and meanings, 202–203

three-dimensional figures, 163–167

variables, 130

Matter, 370–371

chemical properties, 371–374

physical properties, 370–371

Maximum, of parabola, 136

Mayans, 226–227

Mayflower, 230

Mayflower Compact, 230–231, 234

McCulloch v. Maryland, 312

Mean, 176–177

Measurement

concept of, 148–149

error of, 151–152

metric system, 357

standard system of, 357

temperature, 151

triangles, 152–154

units of, 149–151

Measures of central tendency, 176–177

Measures of variability, 179–180

Media

interpreting and evaluating visual images, 95–96

representing messages and meanings through, 95

types and characteristics of, 94

visual literacy, 96

Median, 176–177

Meiosis, 387–389

Memoir, 69

Mental functioning model, 421

Mental math, 125

Mentor text lessons, 90

Mercantilism system, 235–236
Meridians, 335
Metamorphic rocks, 405
Metric system of measurement, 357
Mexican Americans, civil rights
        movement and, 250–251
Mexican American Youth Organization
        (MAYO), 251
Mexican-American War, 264
Mexican War of Independence, 262
Microeconomics, 289
Microscope, 357
Middle Ages, 218
Middle Colonies, 230
Middle East, 277
Migration, 396
Military government, 305
Minerals, 405–406
Minimum, of parabola, 136
Miscue analysis, 48
Mississippian peoples, 227–228
Missouri Compromise, 242
Mitochondria, 380–381
Mitosis, 387
Mixed numbers, converting improper
        fractions to, 115
Mixtures, 373
Mnemonic devices, 99
Modern fantasy, 69, 176–177
Modern World, 220–223
Molecules, 372–373
Monarchy, 303–304
Monera, 379, 391
Money, 295
Monroe, James, 238
Monroe Doctrine, 238
Montgomery bus boycott, 250
Moon
        Earth-Sun-Moon system, 410–411
        phases of, 412
Morphemes, 19
        derivational morphemes, 45
        inflectional morphemes, 45–46
Morphology, 19
Motion
        force and, 368–370
        laws of, 362
Mound Builders, 227–228
Mountains
        tallest in the world, 279

        in United States, 279
Multicultural literature, 68
Multiplication
        associative property, 113
        closure property, 112
        commutative property, 112
        decimals, 117
        distributive property, 113
        fractions, 116
        identity property, 113
        operations of, 112–113
        zero property, 113
Muscles, 382
Muscogee Creeks, 228
Musculoskeletal system, 382
Mussolini, Benito, 253–254
Mutation, 393
Mutually exclusive event, 184–185

N

Nagasaki, 255
Narrative chart, 338
Narrative writing, 86
National Association for the
        Advancement of Colored
        People (NAACP), 249
National Council of Teachers of
        Mathematics (NCTM),
        197–198
National Organization for Women
        (NOW), 252
National Science Teachers Association
        (NSTA) Standards, 350–351,
        354–355
National supremacy, 312
Native Americans
        ancient civilizations in Americas,
        226–229
        Indian Removal Act, 240
        in Texas before European
        colonization, 259–260
        Trail of Tears, 240
        westward expansion and, 240
Natural numbers, 109
Natural resources, 291–292
Navajo, 229
Negative association, 174–175
Negative exponents, 118
Nervous system, 382

Nets, 164–166
New Deal, 253, 300
New England Colonies, 230
New Hampshire colony, 230, 231, 233
New Jersey colony, 230, 231, 233
Newly fluent readers, 37
Newly fluent writers, 84
Newton, Isaac, 324, 362
New York colony, 230, 231, 233
9/11 attacks, 256
Nineteenth Amendment, 252, 312
Ninth Amendment, 311
Nitrogen cycle, 407
Nocturnality, 395–396
Nonfiction, 67, 69
Non-homologous structures, 380
Non-mutually exclusive events, 185
Nonrenewable energy, 378
Noodlehead tales, 68
Normal distribution, 180–182
Norm-referenced test (NRT), 39
North Africa, 277
North America, 275
North American Free Trade Agreement
        (NAFTA), 294, 298, 301
North Carolina colony, 230, 232, 233
Northwest Regional Educational
        Laboratory (NREL), 85–86
Note-taking, 98
Nucleic acids, 385–387
Number concepts, 108–111
Numbered heads together, 344
Numbers
        compatible numbers, 125
        complex, 119–121
        composite, 122
        easy combinations, 125
        mixed, 115
        natural, 109
        prime, 122
        rational and irrational, 110
        real, 110
        rounding, 125
        whole, 109
Number theory, 121–128

O

Obama, Barack, 300–301
Obtuse angle, 156

Occasion, for writing, 87
Oil industry, 266, 298, 301
Oligarchy, 305
Olmecs, 227
Oñate, Juán de, 261
Ongoing assessment, 41
    writing composition, 90–91
Open circuit, 375
Operations
    basic, 111–113
    order of, 113–114
Opportunity costs, 290, 296
Opposite angle, 157
Oral language, 16–27
    activities to promote, 24–25
    assessing speaking ability, 21–22
    communication disorders, 23–24
    connecting to reading instruction, 26
    explicit, systematic instruction,
        26–27
    imitation, 18
    internal grammar, 18
    language components, 19–20
    learned in social settings, 19
    Speaking Checklist, 22–23
    spoken English connection to written
        English, 26–27
    stages of development, 21
    technology to develop, 27
    transition to written communication,
        75
Oral tradition, 321
Order of operations, 113–114
Organs, 381
Organ systems, 382–384
Outer core, 400
Outliers, 179–180
Oxygen cycle, 406–407

P

Pacific mountain system, 274
Paired reading, 50
Pair interview, 25
Palestine, 255
Parabola, 136–140
    area under curve, 144–147
    elements of, 136
Parallelism, 392
Parallel lines, 155

constructing, 157–158
Parallelogram
    area of, 162
    perimeter of, 162
Paraphrasing, for reading
        comprehension, 57
Paris, Treaty of, 237
Parks, Rosa, 250
Parliamentarian monarchy, 305
Partial alphabetic phase, 32
Pasteur, Louis, 324
Patriotic symbols, 318
Pattern blocks, 205–206
Patterns, 129–130
Pearl Harbor, 254
PEMDAS, 114
Penn, William, 232
Pennsylvania colony, 230, 232, 233
Performance-based assessment, 39
Perimeter formulas, 162–163
Permutations, 125–128
    defined, 126
    with like objects, 127
    with and without replacement, 126
Perpendicular bisector, constructing, 161
Perpendicular lines, 155
    constructing, 160
Personal journals, 88
Persuasive writing, 86
Philippines, 252
Phonation disorder, 23
Phonemes, 19
    grapheme-phoneme correspondence,
        33, 34–35
Phonemic stress, 30
Phonetic spelling stage, 77
Phonics, 43–44
Phonological and phonemic awareness,
        29–32
    alliteration, 30
    defined, 29–30
    importance for reading and writing,
        29
    intonation patterns, 31
    phonemic stress, 30
    strategies for teaching, 31–32
    syllabication, 30
    word stress, 30
Phonology, 19
Photosynthesis, 375, 380, 384

Physical science
    chemical properties, 371–374
    energy and interactions, 374–377
    forces and motion, 368–370
    matter properties and physical
        changes, 370–371
Piaget, Jean, 200–201
Pictographic writing system, 33
Pictographs, 171
Pictorial graph, 337
Picture books, 67
Pie chart, 172
Pie graph, 337
Pilgrims, 230
Pistil, 389
Place value, 109
Plagiarism, 92–93
Plane, 155
Planets, 411
Plant, as taxonomic group, 379
Plant cells
    photosynthesis and respiration, 384
    sexual reproduction, 387–389
Plate tectonics, 362, 401
Pledge of Allegiance, 317
Plessy v. Ferguson, 249, 314
Plot, 70
Plymouth, 230
Plymouth colony, 231
Plymouth Company, 230
Pocahontas, 230
Poetry, 67, 69
Points, 155
Point-slope formula, 132
Polk, James K., 239
Polya, George, 194
Polyhedron, 166
Popular sovereignty, 242, 306
Population (statistics), 190
Populations
    characteristics, distribution and
        migration of, 281
Portfolio, for assessment, 91
Positive association, 174–175
Potential energy, 375
Pottawatomie Massacre, 243
Pourquoi Tales, 68
Powell, Jerome, 295
Power of a power, 118
Power of a quotient, 118

Pragmatics, 20
Pre-alphabetic phase, 32
Precambrian, 411
Predators, 398–399
Predicting, for reading comprehension
    confirming, 67
    making, 66
Prefixes, 45
Preoperational stage, 200
Pre-reading activities, 55
Presentations, 25
Previewing, for reading comprehension,
    57
Price index, 297
Prime factorization, 122
Prime numbers, 122
Print media, 94
Prior knowledge
    activating, 66
    linking to new knowledge, 55–56
    reading comprehension and, 54
Probability, 182–189
    binomial experiments, 186–188
    concept of, 183–184
    conditional probability, 185–188
    geometric probability, 188–189
    mutually exclusive and
        complementary events,
        184–185
    non-mutually exclusive events, 185
    sample spaces and counting, 182
Problem-solving process, 326–327
Process writing, 82
Producers, 396–397, 398
Prohibition, 248–249
Project Based Learning, 365
Prokaryotic cells, 381
Proteins, 385–386
Protista, 379
Pseudo-letter spelling stage, 76
Pueblo Indians, 229
Puerto Rico, 252
Punnett square, 390
Puritans, 230
Purpose, in writing, 87
Pyramid, volume and surface area
        formulas, 164
Pythagoras, 324
Pythagorean Theorem, 153–154

Q

Quadratic formula, 139
Quadratic functions, 136–140
Quakers, 232
Questions
    levels of, for assessing reading
        comprehension, 58–59

R

Radiation, 404
Radiometric dating, 411
Railroads, 240, 247, 266, 298, 301
Range, 179–180
Rational numbers, 110
Ray, 155
Raza Unida Party, 251
Readers' Theatre, 50–51
Reading
    balanced reading program, 28–29
    children's literature, 67–71
    choral reading, 50, 51
    connecting oral language to
        instruction in, 26
    early readers, 35
    echo reading, 51
    emergent readers, 35
    foundations for, 27–28
    guided oral repeated reading, 50
    independent, 51
    interactive reading programs, 50
    literacy assessment, 37–42
    mentor text lessons, 90
    newly fluent readers, 37
    pairing students, 50
    phonological and phonemic
        awareness, 29
    Readers' Theatre, 50–51
    silent sustained reading (SSR), 50
    speed expectation, 49
    stages of development, 35–37
    strategies for, 65–67
Reading applications, 62–74
    activating prior knowledge, 66
    authors as mentors, 73
    children's literature, 67–71
    confirming predictions, 67
    content area literacy, 65
    determining important ideas, 66

    drawing inferences, 66
    fluent and efficient readers, 65
    literary analysis, 72
    overview, 62–63
    predicting and asking questions, 66
    reader response, 74
    reading workshop to foster
        independent reading, 73
    reflecting, 67
    reflecting reading on bias in
        traditional stories, 72
    skimming, 67
    story grammar, 71–72
    structure of text, 64
    synthesizing, 66
    technology and, 73
    transition from learning to read to
        reading to learn, 64
    visualizing, 66
Reading comprehension and
        assessment, 52–62
    anecdotal records, 60
    assessing comprehension, 58–62
    background knowledge, 54–55
    comprehensive questions, 60
    in content areas, 101
    continuum of, 54
    criterion-referenced test, 61
    fluency and, 49
    guided and independent practice,
        54–55
    inferring, 57
    informal reading inventories, 60–61
    interventions for students with
        challenges, 62
    linking prior knowledge to new
        knowledge, 55–56
    monitoring comprehension, 57–58
    observation and checklist, 60
    overview of, 52–54
    paraphrasing, 57
    pre-reading activities, 55
    previewing, 57
    prior knowledge, 54
    questions for assessment, 58–59
    reading level assessment, 59–62
    self-monitoring, 57
    setting purpose for reading, 55–56
    speed and, 58
    story retelling, 60

strategy instruction, 57
summarizing, 57
text structure identification, 57
visualizing, 57
writing journals for, 61
Reading fluency, 49–52
assessing, 51
comprehension and, 49
defined, 49
developing, 51–52
importance of, 42–43
speed expectations, 49
teaching, 50–51
timed reading, 51–52
Real numbers, 110
Recessive chromosome, 389–390
Reciprocal fraction, 116
Reciprocal teaching, 56
Reconstruction Era, 245–247, 265
Rectangle, area and perimeter of, 162
Rectangular prism
Euler's formula, 166
net, 165
Rectangular solid, volume and surface
area formulas, 163
Reflection
geometry, 169
light, 376
reading comprehension, 67
Reflective journals, 88
Reflex angle, 156
Refraction, 376
Regulation, 298
Relative location, 270
Renaissance, culture and, 282
Renewable energy, 378
Reproduction
asexual, 387
cell, 387–389
hereditary material, 389–391
plant, 387
sexual, 387–389
Reproductive system, 384
Republic, 305
Resonance disorder, 23
Respiration, plant and animal cells,
384–385
Respiratory system, 383
Revere, Paul, 237
Reversibility, 201

Revolution and Industry period, 220
Rhode Island colony, 230, 231, 233
Ribonucleic acids (RNA), 386
Richter scale, 401
Right angle, 156
Right triangles
angles and sides of, 152
area of, 163
perimeter of, 163
Pythagorean Theorem, 153–154
Rio Bravo, 264
Rivers, in United States, 274
Roanoke, 229
Roaring Twenties, economic history of
U.S. and, 300
Robinson, Jackie, 250
Rocks
rock cycle, 405
types of, 405
Rocky Mountains, 274
Role-play, 24
Rolfe, John, 230
Roosevelt, Franklin D., 253, 254–255
Roosevelt, Theodore, 294
Roots, 138
Rosenblatt, Louise, 74
Rotations, 169
Rounding, 125
Running record, 38
Russia
Bolshevik revolution, 253
Cold War, 256
World War II, 254–255

S

Safety guidelines for science
instruction, 352–355
Sample, statistical, 190
San Antonio, 261
San Jacinto, Battle of, 263
Santa Anna, Antonio López de, 262,
263
Savings, 295–296
Scaffolding tools, 48
Scarcity, 290
Scatter plot, 174–175
Science, 349–434
adaptation and evolution, 392–394
assessment, 430–432

cells, 380–382
chemical compounds of life, 385–
386
circulatory system, 382–383
developmentally appropriate
teaching practices, 414–419
digestive and excretory system, 383
Earth system cycles, 405–408
Earth system structure and function,
398–404
energy, 374–378
ethical considerations, 361, 363
force and motion, 368–370
heredity, 389–391
history and nature of, 362–364
history of Earth system, 411–412
immune system, 383
impact on daily lives, 364–367
life functions and cells, 380–382
logical thinking and scientific
reasoning, 428–429
major discoveries in throughout
history, 323–324
matter, 370–371
musculoskeletal system, 382
nervous system, 382–383
organisms and environment, 396–
398
organ structure and functions,
382–384
photosynthesis and respiration,
384–385
physical science, 368–378
references, 432–434
regulatory mechanisms and behavior,
394–397
reproduction, 387–389
reproductive system, 384
respiratory system, 383
response to stimuli, 395
safety guidelines for classroom,
352–355
science thinking skills, 419
scientific inquiry, 419–427
scientific inquiry process, 358–361
similarities and differences in
taxonomical groups, 391–392
solar system and universe, 410–412
taxonomic groups of living things,
379–380

teaching standards overview, 349–352

tools and equipment for teaching, 355–357, 427–428

unifying concepts of, 367–368

weather and climate, 408–409

Science thinking skills, 420

Scientific inquiry, 419–428

  interpreting findings, 426–427

  learning cycle and 5-E model, 419–425

  planning and implementing, 419–425

Scientific notation, 110

Scientific reasoning, 427

Scott, Dred, 243

Scribbling stage, 76

Secant line, slope of, 143–144

Second Amendment, 311

Sedimentary rocks, 405

Segregation, 249

Self-assessment, of writing, 91

Self-monitoring, for reading comprehension, 57

Semantic cues, 44

Semantic mapping, 59

Semantics, 20

Semantic web, 341

Seminoles, 228

Sensorimotor stage, 200

Sentence builders, 78

Sentences

  basic pattern, 19

  kernel, 19

Separate but equal, 314

Separation of powers, 307, 309–310

Sequence, 147

Serialization, 201

Series, 147–148

Services, 291

Setting, 72

Seventh Amendment, 311

Seven Years' War, 235, 237

Sexual reproduction, 387–389

Shantytown, 247

Shia Alawite, 256

Sight words, 44

Silent sustained reading (SSR), 50

Simple random sample (SRS), 190

Sine, 152

6+1 Trait Writing, 85–86

Sixteenth Amendment, 298, 312

Sixth Amendment, 311

Size transformation, 169

Skeletal muscle, 382–383

Skeletal system, 382–383

Skimming, 67

Slavery, 241–243

  beginning of, in U.S., 241

  civil rights for freed slaves, 249–250

  Civil War, 243–245

  compromises, 241–243

  cotton and, 241

  Dred Scott case, 313

  Emancipation Proclamation, 241

  sectionalism and, 244

Slope

  of line, 132

  point-slope formula, 132

  of secant line, 143–144

  of tangent line, 143–144

Smith, John, 230

Smith, Susan Sperry, 200–201

Smooth muscle, 383

Socialism, 293, 295

Social studies, 213–347

  academic vocabulary in, 342–343

  culture, 226

  culture, science, technology and society, 318–324

  curriculum, 330–335

  economics, 288–301

  English Language Learner support, 340–342

  foundations and skills for, 324–329

  geography, 268–288

  government and citizenship, 302–318

  graphic representations of historical information, 336–339

  history, 215–267

  information sources for, 328, 335–336

  instruction and assessment, 329–345

  interconnection of disciplines, 327

  issues and trends in, 328

  language arts integration with, 336

  map and globe concepts, 333–335

  problem-solving process, 326–327

  professionally modeled thinking, 327

  references for, 345–347

  research in, 326

  spatial thinking, 329

  TEKS standards, 330–335

Solar system, 410–411

Solutions, 373

Sound energy, 377

South America, 276

South Asia, 278

South Carolina colony, 230, 232, 233

Southern Christian Leadership Conference (SCLC), 250

Southern Colonies, 230

Spanish American War, 252

Spatial thinking, 329

Speaking Checklist, 22–23

Speaking skills

  articulation problems, 24

  assessing speaking ability, 21–22

  fluency disorders, 24

  Speaking Checklist, 22–23

  spoken English connection to written English, 26–27

  voice disorders, 23

Spelling, stages of, 76–77

Sphere, volume and surface area formulas, 164

Spindletop Oil Field, 266

SQ4R, 100, 342

Square, area and perimeter of, 162

Square-based pyramid

  Euler's formula, 166

  net, 165

Stalin, Joseph, 253–254

Stamen, 389

Standard deviation, 179–180

Standard form, of linear equations, 133

Standard system of measurement, 357

Stars, 411

Star-Spangled Banner, 238, 317

State governments, powers of, 308–309

State of Texas Assessments of Academic Readiness (STAAR)

  criterion-referenced test, 61

  linguistic accommodation testing for ELLs and special education students, 102

  science, 431–432

  writing expectations, 77

  writing prompts from, 84

Statistics
  bivariate data and scatter plots, 174–175
  box-and-whisker plot, 178
  correlation coefficient, 175
  descriptive, 189
  inferential, 189–193
  mean, median and mode, 176–177
  measures of central tendency, 176–177
  measures of variability, 179–180
  negative and positive association, 174–175
  normal distribution, 180–182
  population and sampling, 190
  range, standard deviation, outliers, 179–180
Statue of Liberty, 317
Stem and leaf plot, 173
Stimuli, response to, 395
Story analysis, 71
Story grammar, 71–72
Story retellings, 60
  monitoring comprehension with, 41–42
Stowe, Harriet Beecher, 244
Straight angle, 156
Stratified sampling, 190
Structural clues, 45–46
Student Teams Achievement Division (STAD), 343–344
Study and inquiry skills, 97–102
  bibliographies, 99
  critical-thinking skills, 101–102
  DRTA, 100–101
  graphic organizers, 98
  note-taking, 98
  overview, 97–98
  reading comprehension in content areas, 101
  SQ4R, 100
  study plans, 99–102
  summarizing and organizing content, 99
  think-alouds, 98–99
Study plans, 99–102
Stuttering, 24
Sub-Saharan, 278
Subtraction
  closure property, 112

  decimals, 117
  fractions, 116
  identity property, 112
  operations of, 112
Summarizing, for reading comprehension, 57
Summative evaluation, 38
Sunni muslims, 256
Superlatives, 46
Supplementary angle, 156, 157
Supply, 291
Surface area formulas, 163–164
Surface water, 403
Surplus, 291
Syllabication, 30
Syllabic writing system, 33
Symmetry, line of, 136–138, 170
Syntactic clues, 44–45
Syntax, 19
Synthesizing, for reading comprehension, 66
Syria, war in, 256–257
Systematic sampling, 190

T

Tabulation, 338
Taliban, 256
Tall tales, 68
Tangent, 152
Tangent line, slope of, 143–144
Taxes, 298
Technology
  to develop oral language, 27
  to foster early literacy, 37
  geospatial technology, 335–336
  Industrial Revolution and modern technology, 224–225
  major discoveries in throughout history, 323–324
  for producing communications, 96
  reading applications and, 73
  Texas and innovations in, 323
  for writing process, 89–90
Tectonic plates, 401
Tectonics, 362
Temperance movement, 248
Temperature, 151, 375
Tenth Amendment, 311
Teotihuacán, 227

Territoriality, 396
Terrorism, war on, 256
Tessellations, 170
Test-taking strategies, 11–14
Tetrahedron
  Euler's formula, 166
  net, 165
Texas
  cultural traditions in, 321
  economy of, 298
  regions of, and economic activity, 272–273
  scientific discoveries and technological innovations and, 323
  Texas patriotic symbols, 318
Texas Education Agency, 39
  social studies standards, 330
Texas English Language Proficiency Assessment System (TELPAS), 61
Texas Essential Knowledge and Skills (TEKS)
  map skills by grade, scope and sequence, 284–288
  mathematics curriculum, 199–200, 207–208
  science, 431–432
  social studies, 330–335
Texas history, 258–267
  battle of San Jacinto, 263
  battles of Alamo and Goliad, 263
  boom or bust economic cycles in, 265–266
  Catholic missions in, 261–262
  civil rights in, 251
  Civil War, 245
  Confederacy period, 265
  Dust Bowl, 247
  economic development after Reconstruction, 265
  European colonization, 260–262
  before European colonization, 259–260
  facts and symbols of Texas, 267
  French influence in, 261
  joins United States, 264
  Mexican American civil rights movement, 251
  Mexican-American War, 264

Mexican War of Independence, 262
military and wartime industry, 266
Reconstruction period, 246–247, 265
Republic period, 264
San Antonio, 261
six flags over Texas, 266
Stephen F. Austin and Anglo
    presence in, 262
Temperance movement and
    Prohibition, 248–249
Texas Declaration of Independence,
    263
Texas War for independence,
    262–263
timeline of, 258–259, 264
urbanization, 247
Woman Suffrage movement, 252
Texas Rangers, 251
TExES Core Subjects 4-8 test
breaks during test, 8
format of, 3
multiple-choice questions, 4
overview of material covered, 2–3
passing score for, 6
practice tests for, 2
receiving score report, 7
registration for, 6
retaking subtests, 7
study schedule and tips, 7–8
test day tips, 9
unfamiliar question types, 4–5
when to take, 5–6
Text structure identification, for reading
    comprehension, 57, 64
Theme, 70, 72
Theocracy, 304
Think-alouds, 98–99
Think-pair-share, 344
Third Amendment, 311
Thirteenth Amendment, 241, 246, 249,
    312
Three-dimensional figures, 163–167
Three-fifths compromise, 241–242
Thymine, 386
Tides, 407
Tijerina, Reies López, 251
Time, units of, 151
Timed reading, 51–52
Timeline, 338, 341

Timelines
Ancient World, 217
Discovery, Age of, 219–220
Industrial Revolution and modern
    technology, 224–225
Middle Ages, 218
Modern World, 220–223
Revolution and Industry, Age of, 220
Texas history, 258–259, 264
Time zones, 271
Tissue, 381
Toltecs, 227
Tone, 71
Totalitarian, 304
Traditional literature, 68
Trail of Tears, 240
Transcontinental Railroad, 240
Transformations, of functions, 137
Transitional spelling stage, 77
Translation, 168
Transverse wave, 377
Trapezoid, area and perimeter of, 162
Travis, William, 263
Tree diagram, 341
Triangles
area of, 163
perimeter of, 163
Pythagorean Theorem, 153–154
right triangles, 152
similar, 153
Triangular prism
Euler's formula, 166
net, 165
volume and surface area formulas,
    163
Truman, Harry, 250, 255
Truman Doctrine, 255
Tunisia, 257
Twenty-fifth Amendment, 312
Twenty-first Amendment, 248
Twenty-sixth Amendment, 312
Two-color counters, 204

U

Undercoverage, 190
Unemployment rate, 297
Union of Soviet Socialist Republics
    (USSR), 253

United Farm Workers, 251
United States
regions of, 273–274
United States history. *See* American
    history
United States Supreme Court
landmark cases of, 312–314
Units of measurement, 149–151
Urbanization, 247

V

Variability, measures of, 179–180
Variables, 130
Velasco, Treaty of, 263
Venn diagram, 342
Vernal sentences, 19
Versailles, Treaty of, 253
Vertex, 136–138
Vertical angle, 156, 157
Vertices, 166
Virginia colony, 230, 233
Virginia House of Burgesses, 234
Visible light, 376
Visual images
interpreting and evaluating, 95–96
representing messages and meanings
    through, 95
viewing and representing, 92–96
visual literacy, 96
Visualizing, for reading comprehension,
    57, 66
Visual media, 94
Vocabulary, 70
Voice disorders, 23
Volcanoes, 401
Volume, 356, 370–371
Volume formulas, 163–164
Voting
black men, 249, 251
women, 252

W

War of 1812, 238
Washington, George, 236, 238
Water
surface and ground, 402
water cycle, 407

Watt, James, 324
Weapons of mass destruction (WMD), 256
Weather, 407–409
Weathering, 400
Wegener, Alfred, 362, 399
Weight, 372
Westward expansion, 238–241
Wheelwright, John, 231
White Caps, 251
White House, 317–318
Whitney, Eli, 239, 241, 291
Whole numbers, 109
Williams, Roger, 231
Wilson, Woodrow, 238, 253, 295
Winthrop, John, Jr., 232
Woman Suffrage movement, 252
Women's rights movement, 252
Wonder tales, 68
Woodland peoples, 227
Worcester v. Georgia, 313
Word identification skills, 42–49
    assessing, 48–49
    contextual clues, 44
    decoding clues, 44
    derivational morphemes, 45
    Dolch words, 44
    homonyms, homophones, and compound words, 46–47
    importance of, 42–43
    inflectional morphemes, 45–46
    phonics, 43–44
    semantic cues, 44
    sequence of word analysis instruction, 43–47
    sight words, 44
    structural clues, 45–46
    syntactic clues, 44–45
    words that create comprehension problems, 46–47
Word-processor software, 96
Word stress, 30
Work, 369

World history, 217
    Age of Discovery, 218–220
    Ancient World, 217
    Middle Ages, 218
    Modern World, 220–223
    Revolution and Industry period, 220
World Trade Center, 256
World War I, 253
World War II, 253–254
    D-Day, 254
    economic history of U.S. and, 300
    Hiroshima and Nagasaki, 255
    Holocaust and creation of Israel, 255
    Marshall Plan, 255
    Pearl Harbor, 254
    Yalta Conference, 254–255
Writing
    alphabetic writing system, 33–34
    assessment, 79, 90–92
    audience, 87
    connecting discourse, 78
    conventions, 74–80
    dependent and independent clauses, 79
    descriptive writing, 86
    early writers, 83–84
    emerging writers, 83
    expectations for, 77–78
    expository writing, 86
    fluent writers, 85
    functional writing, 88
    identifying common grammar problems, 78
    interactive journals, 89
    interventions for below grade level, 80
    journal writing, 88
    mentor text lessons, 90
    modeling, 77–78
    modes of, 86–87
    narrative, 86
    newly fluent writers, 84

    occasion for, 87
    persuasive, 86
    phonological and phonemic awareness, 29
    pictographic writing system, 33
    plagiarism and academic honesty, 92
    process writing, 82
    punctuation exercises, 78
    purpose, 87
    sentence builders, 78
    sentence connectors, 78
    6+1 Trait Writing, 85–86
    spelling stages, 76–77
    spoken English connection to written English, 26–27
    STAAR expectations for, 77
    stages of, 83–85
    strategies to promote, 89
    syllabic writing system, 33
    technology for, 89–90
    technology for producing communications, 96
    transition from oral language to, 75
    trends in, 85–86
    types of writing system, 33–34
    written communication, 80–83
    written compositions, 80–92

Y

Yalta Conference, 254–255
Yeamans, John, 232
Yellen, Janet, 295
Yellow journalism, 252

Z

Zapotecs, 227
Zavala, Lorenzo de, 263
Zero multiplication property, 113
Zeros, 138

NOTES

NOTES

NOTES

NOTES

NOTES

NOTES

NOTES

NOTES

NOTES